The Muvipix.com Guide to
Photoshop Elements &
Premiere Elements 9

Steve Grisetti

The tools in Adobe's amazing suite of programs, and how to use them together to create professional-looking movies and great-looking photos on your personal computer.

Dedication

I continually look to my friends and colleagues at Muvipix.com for inspiration, challenge and, more often than not, help. To you, dear friends, I dedicate this book.

Thank you, Jeanne, for once again giving me the time, support and occasional neck massages that enabled me to complete this major project

Thank you, dear daughter Sarah, for blessing my heart by finding the inspiration in my work to take your own video work to the next level.

And thank you, Danielle, for jumping on board and helping me refine my text and chase down those stubborn typos.

And a special thanks to my Muvipix.com co-founders, Ron and Chuck, whose friendship and support for over half a decade have meant more to me than they can know.

About Muvipix.com

Muvipix.com was created to offer support and community to amateur and semi-professional videomakers. Registration is free, and that gets you access to the world's friendliest, most helpful forum and lots of ad-free space for displaying your work. On the products page, you'll find dozens of free tips, tutorials, motion backgrounds, DVD templates, sound effects, royalty-free music and stock video clips. For a small annual subscription fee that we use to keep the site running, you'll have unlimited downloads from the ever-growing library of support materials and media.

We invite you to drop by and visit our thriving community. It costs absolutely nothing – and we'd love to have you join the neighborhood!

http://Muvipix.com

About the author

Steve Grisetti holds a master's degree in Telecommunications from Ohio University and spent several years working in the motion picture and television industry in Los Angeles. A veteran user of several video editing programs and systems, Steve is the co-founder of Muvipix.com, a help and support site for amateur and semi-professional videomakers. A professional graphic designer and video freelancer, he has taught classes in Photoshop and lectured on design. He lives in suburban Milwaukee.

Other books by Steve Grisetti

Adobe Premiere Elements 2.0 In a Snap (with Chuck Engels)
The Muvipix.com Guide to Adobe Premiere Elements 7
The Muvipix.com Guide to Adobe Premiere Elements 8
The Muvipix.com Guide to Adobe Premiere Elements 9
The Muvipix.com Guide to Photoshop Elements & Premiere Elements 7
The Muvipix.com Guide to Photoshop Elements & Premiere Elements 8
The Muvipix.com Guide to DVD Architect Studio 4.5
Cool Tricks & Hot Tips for Adobe Premiere Elements

An Introduction

Adobe has made a real effort to improve the performance of all of the programs in version 9 of the Elements bundle. And, for the most part, it looks as though they've succeeded!

Premiere Elements is back to its old responsive self (after the challenges of version 8). Photoshop Elements is tight and stable. And even the Elements Organizer seems to have benefited from the tune-up.

Beyond that, the programs look terrific! Gone are the candy-colored tabs and challenging-to-read text. In their place is a dark, high-contrast interface with big, bold, bright text – with a look much more in line with Adobe's professional Creative Suite of programs. (Unfortunately, this can make reproducing some of the screens as illustrations in this book challenging at times. My apologies in advance if some screen caps are a bit murky.)

You won't find a lot of new bells and whistles in version 9. There are some very nice, subtle, new features. But rather than burdening the programs with lots of new toys, the real focus has been on improving how the existing features work – and that's something we can all appreciate.

Additionally, this is the first Elements bundle that has been released in its entirety in both a Windows and a MacIntosh version. The two versions look almost identical and behave virtually the same way. (Mac users will find a few minor features unavailable – and we've to noted them in this book.) In fact, the challenge of building good, stable versions of these programs for the Mac platform seems have forced Adobe to up its game on the Windows versions also. And, while Windows versions of any intensive program do have certain inherent challenges (namely that, unlike designing for the Mac OS, writing programs for Windows means trying to build something that will work on any of an infinite number of hardware and software configurations), users should find version 9 of any of the Elements programs much more reliable and easier to get up and running.

You'll find a complete list of the new features at the beginnings of each section of this book. (We've included the Organizer's new features listed among those for Photoshop Elements.) But a couple are well worth noting:

- Photoshop Elements includes new tools for its Photomerge feature as well as some new "Fun" Guided Edits (like adding a reflection below your photo or making a picture into an Andy Warhol-style photo collage).

- Photo Elements also includes some new features borrowed from its professional big brother – namely Layer Masks and the very cool Content Aware Fill option for its Healing Brushes.

- The Elements Organizer's People Recognition tool has undergone a major overhaul. It will even help you identify people in your photos so that you can include their names as Keyword Tags!

- The Timeline in Premiere Elements includes an option for viewing each track either closed or open, making much better use of the program's vertical workspace.

- Premiere Elements now includes support for Flip pocket camcorders – both the standard and hi-def versions.

- Premiere Elements will even *warn* you if your project isn't set up properly for the first clip you try to add to it! How cool is that?!

Muvipix.com was created in 2006 as a community and a learning center for videomakers at a variety of levels. Our community includes everyone from amateurs and hobbyists to semi-pros, professionals and even people with broadcast experience. You won't find more knowledgeable, helpful people anywhere else on the Web. I very much encourage you to drop by our forums and say hello. At the very least, you'll make some new friends. And it's rare that there's a question posted there that isn't quickly, and enthusiastically, answered.

Our goal has always been to help people get up to speed making great videos and, once they're there, provide them with the inspiration and means to get better and better at doing so.

Why? Because we know shooting pictures and making movies is a heck of a lot of fun – and we want to share that fun with everyone!

Our books, then – like the tips, tutorials and media available on our site – are a manifestation of that goal. And my hope for you is that this book helps *you* get up to speed. I think you'll find, once you get over the surprisingly small learning curve, making movies on your home computer is a lot more fun than you ever imagined! And you may even amaze yourself with the results in the process.

Thanks for supporting the Muvipix.com mission, and happy moviemaking!

Steve
http://Muvipix.com

What do you want to do?

Table of Contents

Chapter 5
Select and Isolate Areas in Your Photos 59
Working with selections

Table of Contents

Table of Contents

Chapter 13

Learn About Your Photoshop Elements File 149
Important information on your Photoshop Elements file window

Part 2: Premiere Elements 9

Chapter 14

Get to Know Premiere Elements 9 159
What's what and what it does

Chapter 15

Chapter 16

Table of Contents

Table of Contents

Chapter 30

A Premiere Elements Appendix 347

More things worth knowing

Part 3: The Elements Suite

Chapter 31

The Elements Organizer 365

Managing your media files

Chapter 32

Create Fun Photo Pieces 377

Make something of your photos

Chapter 33

Share Your Photos and Videos 389

Output and upload your files

Table of Contents

Chapter 34

Photoshop.com 397

Your online connection

Chapter 35

Use the Elements Programs Together 409

How the programs complement each other

Part 1
Adobe
Photoshop Elements 9

Pixels & Resolution

Raster vs. Vector Graphics

Image Size vs. Canvas Size

Selection

Layers & Alpha

RGB Colors

The Option Bar

Native PSD files

Chapter 1

Things You Need to Know
Principles of photo and graphic editing

Photoshop Elements is a surprisingly powerful photo and graphics editor that borrows a large number of tools from its big brother, Photoshop, the industry standard for photo and graphics work. In fact, both programs can even open and edit the same types of files.

The few limitations Elements does have, in fact, might well be things you'll never even miss (unless you're preparing files that will ultimately go on to a printing press).

But before we go too deeply into the tool set of this fine program, there are a couple of basic principles you'll need to understand.

Pixels

The building blocks of all digital photos are rectangular (usually square) blocks of color known as pixels.

Pixels are the building blocks of all digital graphics and photos. Whether you can see them or not, all photos and graphics created in Photoshop Elements are made up of these little squares of color. Even a tremendously rich, detailed digital photograph, if you blew it up large enough, would reveal itself to be little more than thousands (or millions) of little squares of solid color, each one some mixture of red, green and blue.

This is easier to see on a low resolution image, such as a graphic created for a web site. Zoom in as far as Photoshop Elements will let you go and you'll soon see that even in the apparently smoothest gradation of color there are actually little blocks of solid color.

An understanding of pixels is vital to developing a deeper understanding of how Photoshop Elements works. In order to fully comprehend how virtually any tool does what it does or how any setting affects your image – or how to measure the relative size of your images – you must learn to see your images not merely as pictures of people, animals and places but also as compositions of thousands and thousands of little blocks of color.

Non-square pixels – and more than you probably want to know

Like all digital devices, video camcorders paint their on-screen images with pixels. But, unlike in a typical photograph, a video's pixels aren't square blocks of color – they're rectangular.

Even more confusing, the shapes of these rectangular pixels varies, depending on the nature of the medium.

Standard NTSC, the television and video format used in North America and Japan, uses pixels that are only 90% as wide as they are tall.

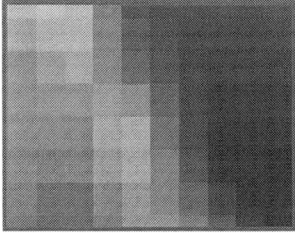

Square (photograph) pixels   NTSC non-square 4:3 pixels   NTSC non-square 16:9 pixels

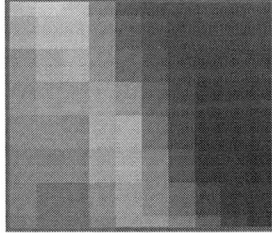

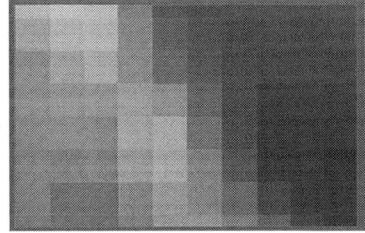

PAL, the TV format used in most of Europe, uses pixels that are 107% as wide as they are tall. Because of this, a 720x480 pixel NTSC image and a 720x576 pixel PAL image both produce a video frame that is in the same proportion – a 4:3 ratio!

Widescreen TV uses the same number of pixels to create a video frame as standard TV. The pixels are just proportioned differently. (The pixels are 120% as wide as they are tall in NTSC and 142% as wide as they are tall in PAL.) In other words, there are exactly the same number of pixels in a 4:3 video frame as there are in a 16:9 video image, as illustrated above.

Even high-definition TV uses non-square pixels. In hi-def TV, the pixels are 133% as wide as they are tall, so that 1440x1080 pixel image produces a 16:9 image.

All of this is related to technology dating back to the origins of television. And, unless you're creating graphics for video, it pretty much falls into the "nice to know" rather than "need to know" category. But it is nice to know – in case anyone ever asks you why a 720x480 video file becomes a 640x480 web video.

But, in most cases, as you're designing artwork for your videos, you won't need to concern yourself with non-square pixels. This is because Premiere Elements will automatically adapt your square pixel images to the non-square pixel video environment. Just use these **square pixel** equivalents for creating full-screen graphics:

Standard NTSC video	640x480 pixels
Widescreen NTSC video	855x480 pixels
Standard PAL video	768x576 pixels
Widescreen PAL video	1024x576 pixels
High definition video	1920x1080 pixels

Resolution

Resolution means, basically, how many pixels are crammed into how much space. Video, like images created for the Internet, doesn't require a particularly high resolution image. Print, on the other hand, can require a pixel density of two to four times that of an on-screen image.

High resolution photo

Same size photo, at much lower resolution (fewer pixels per inch)

Just as digital photos are made up of pixels, printed images are made up of little dots of color or ink. A good, press-worthy image may need 300 dots of color per inch (or more) in order to appear to the eye as a smooth color image. Home printed pieces, like the kind you'd print off your desktop printer, can have as few as 150 dots or pixels per inch. Graphics that will be used on-screen (for the Web or in a video) are about 72 pixels per inch. This is why, if you download a graphic from a web site and print it out, you'll often find that the picture prints fuzzy, jagged or "pixelated."

This means that in order to get a good, high-resolution print-out of a 4" x 3" photo, you'd need a photo that measured as much as 1200 pixels wide and 900 pixels tall. That's a lot of pixels when you consider that a standard TV frame measures only 640 x 480 square pixels. In other words, that 1200 x 900 photo you used for your print-out has four times as many pixels as an equivalent full-screen image on your TV set!

And that's why we say video is a relatively low resolution medium. High-definition video needs a bit more image data – but only a fraction of what print artwork requires (and less than half of the resolution produced by a 5 megapixel digital still camera).

The measurements of any graphics and photos you prepare for video, by the way, are *never* expressed in inches or centimeters. Even the resolution of your images, in terms of pixels per inch, isn't really relevant.

A video frame is measured only in pixels. So, as you're working on images for your videos, their dimensions, in pixels, are the only relevant measurement.

Why doesn't linear measurement matter in the world of video graphics? Well, basically, it's because the size of a video frame, in inches, is determined by the size of the TV you're watching it on!

TVs and computer monitors come in a variety of sizes and screen settings. A graphic may appear to be 2 inches across on a 17" computer monitor, 4 inches across on a 22" TV set and 30" across on a big screen TV! The graphic is always the same number of *pixels* in size – but those pixels are as large or as small as the screen you're viewing them on.

So, when you're creating your graphics for video (or for the web), always think in terms of measurements in pixels. That's the only constant in on-screen graphics.

Just for convenience sake, most people still do use 72 ppi (pixels per inch) as their resolution setting when creating their on-screen graphics. But ultimately the resolution setting makes no difference in this case. In a video or on the Web, a 640x480 pixel image is exactly the same size whether it's 72 ppi or 600 ppi.

Raster vs. vector graphics

All computer-created graphics fit into one of two categories – raster art or vector art – each behaving in its own unique way.

Raster graphics are graphics or photos that are created with pixels. Digital photos that you work with are built from pixels. The graphics files you'll be working with and importing into Premiere Elements will be made up of pixels. And, as we've discussed, all raster art requires a certain density of pixels – or resolution – in order for those pixels to be perceived as a smooth blend of colors. If you stretch or enlarge a photograph so much that its pixels show, it will appear jagged and blurry.

Vector graphics, on the other hand, are defined not by pixels but by a series of end points that define their outline, and by fill colors. Programs like Adobe Illustrator, for instance, create graphics in vector. They can be as simple as a square or a circle or nearly as complicated as a photograph.

But vector graphics, because they are defined by *outlines and fill colors*, don't have any resolution. They can be resized indefinitely – even scaled to many times their original size – without breaking up into pixels. They remain simply outlines and fills. If you've used a simple drawing tool, such as the one in Microsoft Word, to draw a circle or square, you've worked with vector art.

Photoshop Elements is predominantly a raster art program. It is generally concerned with pixels of color. However, there are a few features in the program that behave like vector art:

Shapes. The **Shape Tools** in Photoshop Elements can draw a variety of useful shapes – from circles and squares to lines and arrows and splashes. The shapes it creates, however, have some unique characteristics, as you'll see once you start using them.

Like vector art, these shapes can be easily resized and stretched without concern for resolution. And, if you'll look at a shape layer in the **Layers** panel (as illustrated on the previous page), you'll notice that they don't even look like most Photoshop art. They also won't share their layer with any other graphics. These shapes, then, are *pseudo vector graphics*. They have all of the editing advantages of vector graphics, and they remain as such until you output your Photoshop Elements file as a graphics file or you select the option to manually render or simplify the shape layer.

Fonts. We usually don't think of text as vector art, but it essentially behaves the same way. You can stretch or resize text as needed in your Photoshop Elements document without concern for resolution. The text will also remain editable until you output your Photoshop Elements document as a graphics file or you select the option to manually render or simplify the text layer.

Text and shapes in Photoshop Elements, like vector art, can be resized without regard for the layer's resolution.

Once you output your Photoshop Elements file as a graphics file other than a PSD (a JPEG, TIF or GIF, for instance) or you import the file into Premiere Elements, all of the elements in your graphics file become raster art. It all becomes pixels. And, because of that, the resolution and size of the images (measured in pixels) of your file will determine how large the graphic or photo will be.

Image Size vs. Canvas Size

As you resize your photos or graphics files (under the **Resize** tab, as we'll discuss in **Chapter 6**), it's important to understand the difference between resizing the **Image Size** and the **Canvas Size**.

The distinction is an important one: If you resize the **Image Size**, the entire image gets bigger or smaller; if you resize the **Canvas Size**, the image remains the same size but you either add more space around it or, if you size your canvas smaller, trim the sides of the image off, as illustrated on the previous page.

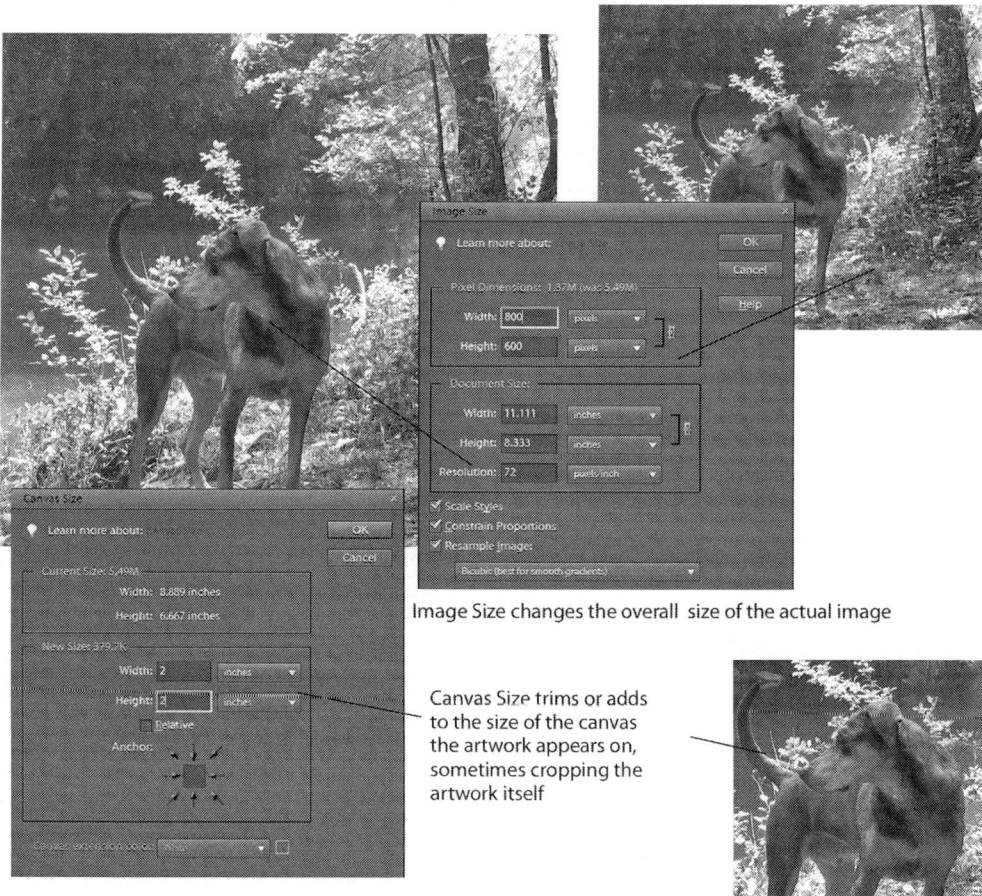

Image Size changes the overall size of the actual image

Canvas Size trims or adds to the size of the canvas the artwork appears on, sometimes cropping the artwork itself

Selections

Selection is a key concept in both Photoshop and Photoshop Elements. A number of the tools in this program are designed to enable you to select – or isolate – areas of your photo or image file and then either remove, add to or add an effect to that area only, without affecting the rest of the image.

Because your photo or graphics work will often involve precise adjustments, understanding how to select areas of your image and then add to, remove from or refine that selection is one of the keys to accessing the program's power.

We'll spend considerable time discussing how to select areas and then use those selections in **Chapter 5, Select and Isolate Areas in Your Photos.**

Many of the tools in Photoshop Elements are designed to allow you to select and isolate areas of your photos so that effects are applied only to your selection.

Layers

The biggest difference between a native Photoshop PSD file and virtually all other photo or raster graphic formats is that PSD files can include layers and layers of artwork. These layers can include additional images, text, shapes or effects, and it's important to understand how they are stacked and how their order affects how they interact with each other.

Think of your layers as a stack of images and other elements. The topmost layers will be entirely seen, while the layers below will be seen "behind" the upper layers or quite possibly obscured completely by them.

Layers can be rearranged. They can also be hidden or made partially transparent or even made to react to certain qualities of the layers below them. When the background layer is removed, you can even produce non-rectangular graphics that include transparent areas.

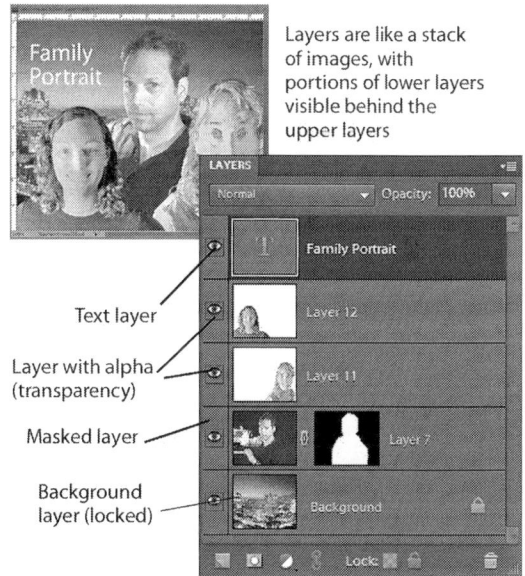

Layers are like a stack of images, with portions of lower layers visible behind the upper layers

Text layer

Layer with alpha (transparency)

Masked layer

Background layer (locked)

Editable text is always on its own layer. Likewise, shapes, until rasterized, are always on their own layers. Layers also give you the advantage of working on your image files in portions, which you can combine and position in a variety of ways.

In addition, layers and layer groups play a vital role in creating and customizing DVD menu templates for Premiere Elements, as we'll discuss in **Chapter 8, Work with Photoshop Elements Layers**.

Alpha

Alpha means, essentially, transparency. However, in order for your graphic file to communicate from one program to another that an area of your image file is transparent, it needs to do so through an "alpha channel." An alpha channel is sort of like a color channel except that, in this case, the color is transparent.

Transparent GIFs (see **Chapter 8**) use an alpha channel so that, unlike JPEGs, when used on a web site, the graphics can be other-than-a-square shape, allowing the background of the site to display through them.

Transparency, represented by default as a checkerboard background in Photoshop Elements, can be carried with the PSD file to Premiere Elements as an "alpha" channel.

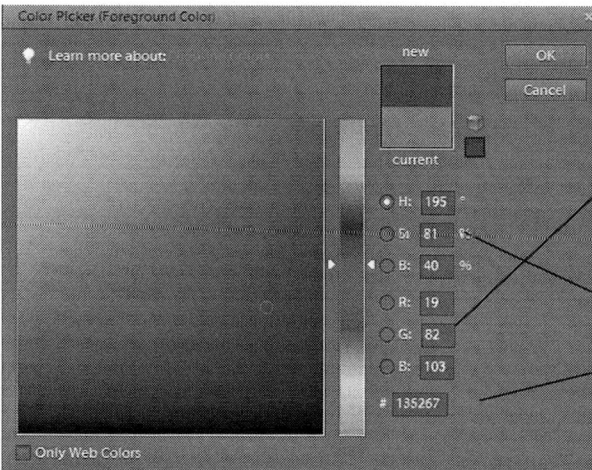

Likewise, alpha allows you to create graphics for your videos that have non-rectangular shapes or are text only, with no background.

Some graphics formats can carry alpha channels and some can not. We'll show you how to use alpha channels and which graphics file formats to use to convey it in **Create non-square graphics** in **Chapter 8, Work with Photoshop Elements Layers**.

RGB

Virtually every graphic or photo you work with in Photoshop Elements will use the **RGB** color mode, meaning that every pixel in that image is a mixture of levels of red, green and blue, the three primary colors in video.

The red, green and blue in each of those pixels is one of 256 levels of intensity, for a grand total of 16,777,216 possible color combinations. As we work with colors (**Foreground/Background Colors** in **Chapter 4, The Toolbox**), you'll see the R, the G and the B and those 256 levels of each at work.

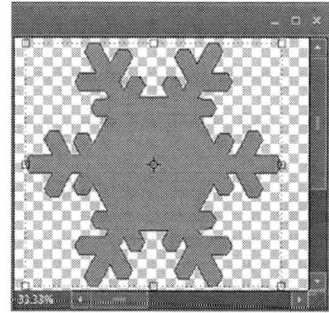

No matter how "real" a digital photo looks, it is merely composed of pixels, each pixel a mix of one of 256 levels of red, green and blue.

Colors can also be designated with hue, saturation and brightness or with a six-digit, alpha-numeric "hex" code.

The **Color Picker**, which launches when you select the option to create a color, builds colors by mixing based on **red** (R), **green** (G) and **blue** (B) values; by setting its **hue** (H), **saturation** (S) and **brightness** (B); or designating the color's **Hex** value – a color format most often employed when with working with HTML and Web site design.

The Tool Option Bar

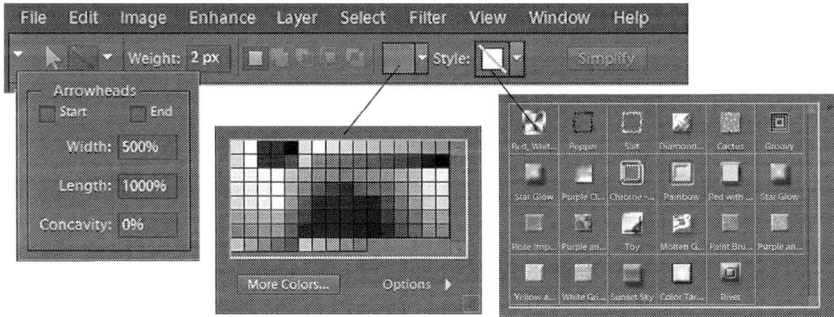

Every tool, even something as basic as a line, includes a number of features on its Option Bar.

Virtually every tool you will use in Photoshop Elements is customizable. Select any tool in the tool panel and its settings and options appear along the top of the program's interface, in the tool's **Option Bar**.

Even something as simple as a line drawing tool can include a myriad of options. The line drawing tool, for instance, includes settings for the width of the line, options for arrowheads on either or both ends as well as its size settings for the arrowheads

Drop-down menus along this bar allow you to select colors and even unusual textures, like glass, plastic and chrome for your shape.

The **Option Bar**, then, greatly extends the function and versatility of every tool. And, as we discuss the **Toolbox** in **Chapter 4**, we'll often refer to the options available on this bar for each of the individual tools.

What is a native PSD file?

The basic working file for both Photoshop and Photoshop Elements is the **PSD file** (so named, of course, because that's the suffix the file is assigned on your computer), the project file that these programs natively produce.

There are unique characteristics to PSD files – namely that they can include layers, editable text and pseudo vector shapes. The word "native" simply means that it's in a native state, the format that all Photoshop files originate in.

Photoshop and Photoshop Elements can export or save in a number of graphics formats, from TIFs to JPEGs to GIFs to PNGs (and a dozen others), though these formats generally don't allow for re-opening layers and text for further editing, as PSDs do.

In the ancient days of technology (like, 10 years ago), Photoshop users had to export their image files to one of these graphics formats in order to import it into another program. But, as Adobe has become the leader in pretty much all facets of print and video production, it's become possible to move graphics files from program to program in their native Photoshop (PSD) state.

In other words, you can import native PSD files directly from Photoshop Elements into your Premiere Elements project. All of the artwork becomes flattened and the shapes and text become rasterized once the file is rendered as video – although any transparent areas in the PSD will remain transparent in your video.

Just as importantly, the native PSD file – including the text and layers – remains editable in Photoshop Elements. And any updates you make to the file will automatically update in Premiere Elements.

Chapter 2

Get to Know Photoshop Elements 9
What's what and what it does

Welcome to Photoshop Elements – a terrific, affordable photo retouching application and graphics editor that just seems to get better and more feature-packed with every generation!

This is a program that seems to offer more wonderful surprises the deeper you dig into it. It provides not only the obvious tools for cleaning, stylizing and creating images, but also lots of not-so-obvious tools for managing your image files, outputting a variety of print projects and even sharing your work online.

Bypass the Welcome Screen

You can't turn off the Welcome Screen completely, but you can configure the Premiere Elements and Photoshop Elements 9 programs to launch simultaneously with it.

To select this option, click on the launch configuration button in the upper right of the Welcome Screen and, in the panel that opens, select the option to **Always Launch Photoshop Elements Editor behind the Welcome Screen.**

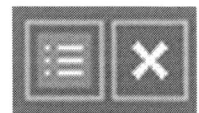

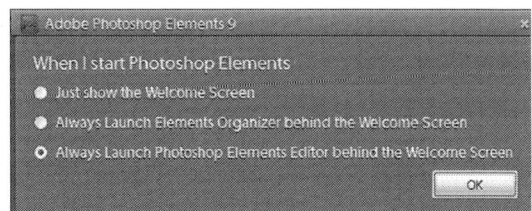

Adobe Photoshop Elements 9

When I start Photoshop Elements

- Just show the Welcome Screen
- Always Launch Elements Organizer behind the Welcome Screen
- Always Launch Photoshop Elements Editor behind the Welcome Screen

OK

The Photoshop Elements 9 Welcome Screen

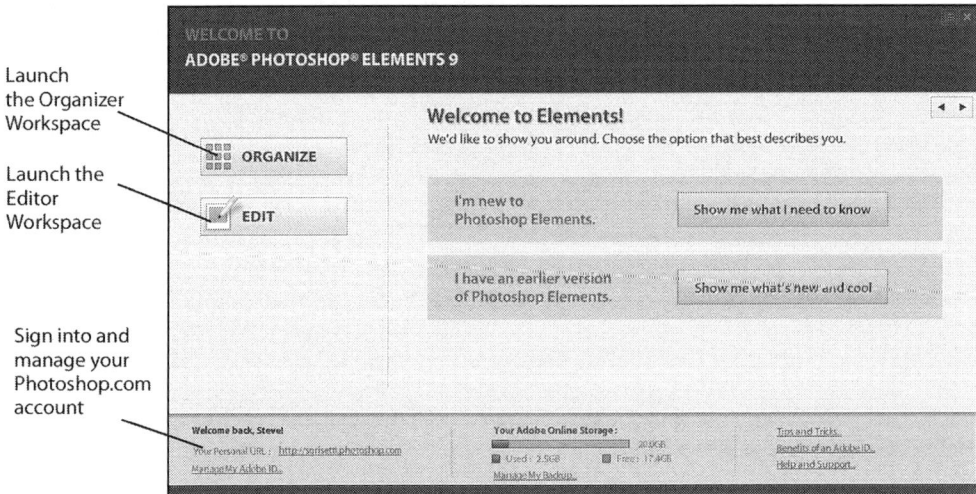

Launch
the Organizer
Workspace

Launch the
Editor
Workspace

Sign into and
manage your
Photoshop.com
account

In this chapter, we'll look at the various workspaces in Photoshop Elements –
and then we'll dig deeper, looking at the dozens of cool tools Adobe has
added to make the program even more fun to use.

The Welcome Screen

The **Welcome Screen** is the option panel that greets you whenever you launch
the program. (There's a similar **Welcome Screen** for Premiere Elements.)

From this screen, you have access to the Elements Organizer or the Edit
workspace as well as a link-up to **Photoshop.com**, Adobe's new online
support service for Photoshop and Premiere Elements.

We discuss **Photoshop.com** and its many workspaces and tools in detail in
Chapter 34.

If you don't have an account with **Photoshop.com**, it's well worth signing up.
A basic account costs nothing – and creating an account gets you access to
a gallery where you can share your photos and enjoy the pictures posted by
others, as well as free online storage space.

The site also includes the **Inspiration Browser,** a library of tutorials and
tips created by Adobe and a number of other content providers (including
Muvipix.com).

You can access the **Inspiration Browser** from the link under the **Help** buttons
on both the Photoshop Elements Editor and Organizer workspaces. If you're
relatively new to Photoshop Elements or Premiere Elements, or if you just
want to improve your skills, these tutorials are well worth checking out.

Additionally, your basic **Photoshop.com** membership includes 2 gigabytes
of online storage space, which you can use to automatically back up your
computer's media files.

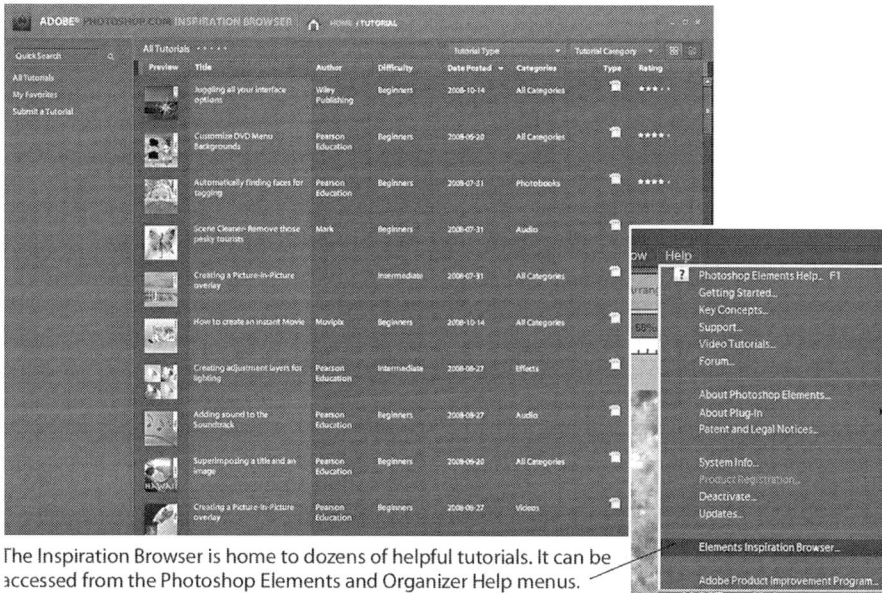

The Inspiration Browser is home to dozens of helpful tutorials. It can be accessed from the Photoshop Elements and Organizer Help menus.

With a **Plus membership**, you have the option of purchasing 20, 40 or 100 gigabytes of backup space. A **Plus membership** also gets you access to additional content for both Photoshop Elements and Premiere Elements as well as even more tutorials.

Once you've created an account with **Photoshop.com**, you can log into your account by clicking on the link along the bottom of the **Welcome Screen** (or on the similar **Welcome Screen** in Premiere Elements). And, once you've done this, you will automatically be linked to Photoshop.com whenever you launch either program or the Organizer, allowing Photoshop Elements, Premiere Elements and the Organizer to interact seamlessly with the site as you work.

By the way, you can re-launch this **Welcome Screen** from any of the Photoshop Elements workspaces at any point by clicking on the little house icon in the upper right of both the **Editor** and **Elements Organizer** interfaces.

Launch a Photoshop Elements workspace

There are two photo editing workspaces which can be launched from the Photoshop Elements **Welcome Screen**.

- **The Edit button launches the main Editor workspace**, where you'll likely do most of your photo and image file editing.

- **The Organize button launches the Elements Organizer,** a media file management program that also includes tools for cleaning up photos, creating photo projects and sharing your photo and video projects. We discuss the Elements Organizer and its many powerful tools in **Chapter 31.**

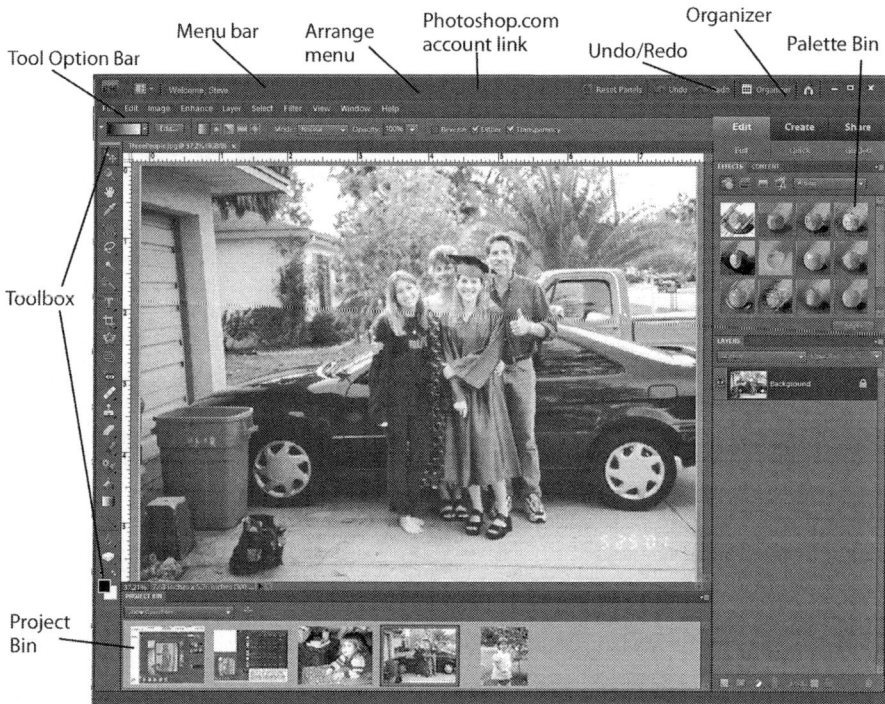

The callout labels around the screenshot:
Tool Option Bar · Menu bar · Arrange menu · Photoshop.com account link · Organizer · Undo/Redo · Palette Bin · Toolbox · Project Bin

The Editor workspace

The Editor workspace in Photoshop Elements 9 is actually *several* photo editing workspaces, each with its own set of tools and features.

- The main workspace, which dominates the screen, is the **Full Edit** workspace, which includes a comprehensive photo editing and graphics creation **Toolbox**. This is likely where you'll do most of your editing.

- If you click on the down arrow to the right of the orange **Full Edit** tab at the top of the **Palette Bin**, you'll see that the program also offers tools for **Quick** and **Guided Edits**. We discuss these workspaces in more details in **Chapter 3, Apply Quick Fixes and Guided Edits**.

- Additionally, the Editor workspace includes a great number of tools under the **Create** and **Share** tabs for doing quick fixes and automatic adjustments as well as options for creating photo pieces and outputting to a variety of media and devices. We discuss the tools in these workspaces and how to use them in **Chapter 14, Create Fun Photo Pieces** and **Chapter 15, Share Your Photos in Cool Ways**.

The Full Edit Workspace

The **Full Edit** workspace is modeled after the interface in the professional version of Photoshop CS5. Like the current version of Photoshop, Photoshop Elements 9 has a cleaner, more readable look without any drastic changes to the basic interface.

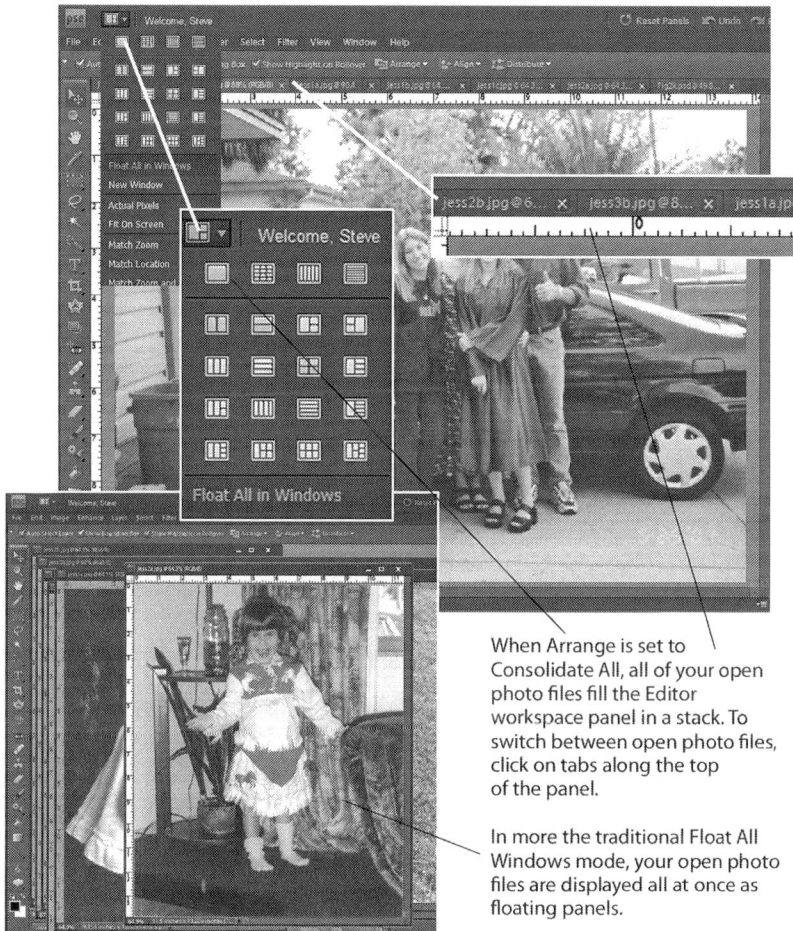

When Arrange is set to Consolidate All, all of your open photo files fill the Editor workspace panel in a stack. To switch between open photo files, click on tabs along the top of the panel.

In more the traditional Float All Windows mode, your open photo files are displayed all at once as floating panels.

In Photoshop Elements, you can have the option of displaying your open photo and image files as floating windows – a stack of open files that you can position around the workspace as you need to – or a single tabbed set, each photo filling the Editor workspace panel and each open file represented by a a tab at the top of the workspace.

The option to display your files like in either mode – as well as a number of optional tabbed arrangements – is found under the new **Arrange** menu.

The **Arrange** menu button appears either to the right of the menu bar or directly to the right of the blue "**pse**" logo (depending on whether or not you have the program window maximized). .

As many veteran Photoshop users know, there are advantages to displaying your photos as floating windows rather than a tabbed set. When your files are displayed as floating windows, you can copy images, portions of images and even entire layers from one image file to another simply by dragging these elements from one open file to another. (This function comes in handy when you're creating or modifying Premiere Elements DVD and BluRay menu templates, as we discuss in **Chapter 35, Use the Elements Programs Together**.)

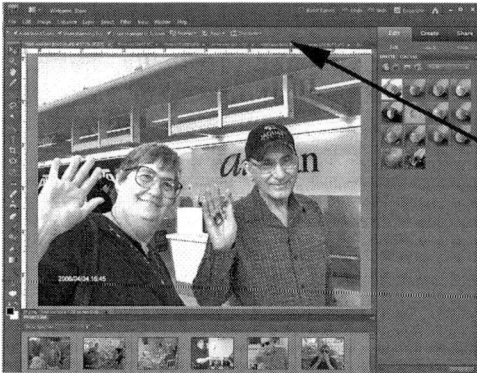

By default, in Consolidate All mode, all open photos display maximized in the work panel. You can switch between your photos by clicking on the tabs along the top of the panel.

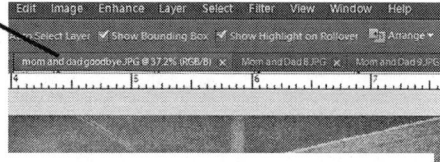

By dragging its tab, you can undock a photo from the tabbed set and make it a floating window.

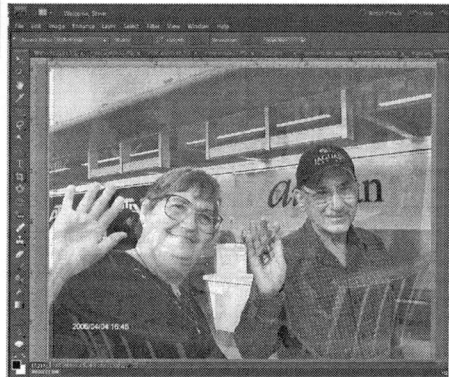

To dock or re-dock a floating window back into a tabbed set, drag it over the tabbed set by its docking header (the top of the frame) until it becomes semi-transparent and a bright blue line displays around the photo. When you release your mouse button, the photo will dock with the rest tabbed set.

There are two ways to switch between displaying your photos as a docked, tabbed set and displaying them as floating windows:

- **Set the Arrange menu to Float All Windows.** When you set the **Arrange** drop-down menu to **Float All Windows**, all of your photo files will display as more traditional floating windows.

- **Undock a photo from the tabbed set by dragging on its tab.** When you pull the photo file by its tab from the others in a tabbed set, it becomes a floating window.

The one disadvantage to creating a floating window this way is that floating windows *always float over your tabbed photo files*. This means that, in order to get to the other photos in your docked set, you will have to either minimize your floating window or move it out of the way!

To dock or re-dock a photo into a tabbed set, simply drag the floating window by its docking header (the top of the window) onto another open photo or tabbed set. When the photo file becomes semi-transparent (as illustrated on the previous page) release your mouse button and the photo will dock to the set.

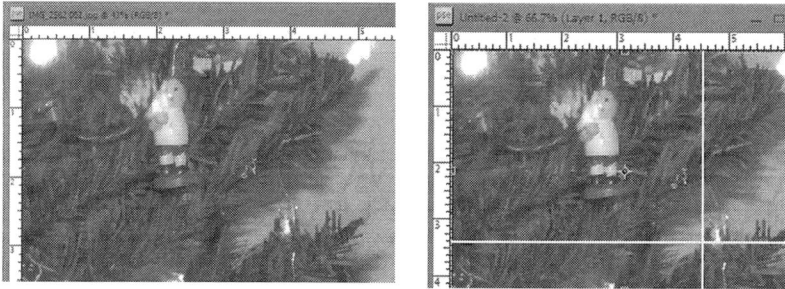

Photoshop Elements can optionally display Rulers and Guides over your image files to help you with placement and measurement of your imagery. To create a guide line, drag onto your photo from one of the rulers.

Guides and Rulers

A welcome feature that Photoshop Elements borrows from its big brother, Photoshop CS4, is the ability to display **Guides** over your image files. These horizontal and vertical lines don't show up on your final piece, of course. But they can be a great help for placing elements and text and ensuring that they are properly lined up.

The program will also display **Rulers** which, like **Guides**, can be very helpful in measuring and placing your imagery.

To display **Rulers**, select the option from the **View** drop-down on the Photoshop Elements Menu Bar.

To create a new **Guide**, click and drag onto your photo from one of the **Rulers** running along the tops and sides of your image files. (Drag from the **Ruler** along the top of your photo to create a horizontal guide or from the **Ruler** along the left of your photo to create a vertical guide.)

To toggle between displaying and hiding your guides on your image files, press **Ctrl+;** on a PC or ⌘**+;** on a Mac.

The Toolbox

Along the left side of this workspace is the program's **Toolbox**. The tools in this panel serve a number of functions, from selecting areas in your image file to creating graphics and text to patching and cloning areas of your images. As each tool is selected, that tool's individual settings are displayed in the **Options Bar** that runs along the top of the editing workspace.

We'll spend considerable time getting to know these powerful tools and how to use their settings and options in **Chapter 4, Get to Know the Photoshop Elements Toolbox**.

The Menu Bar

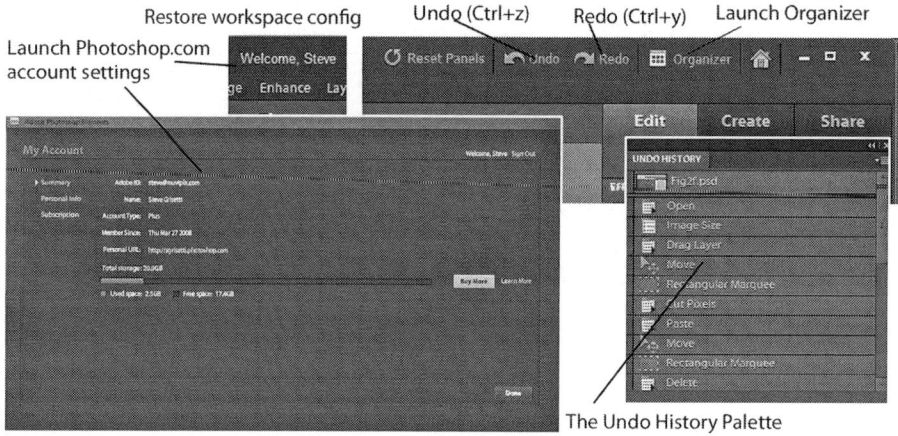

Restore workspace config — Undo (Ctrl+z) — Redo (Ctrl+y) — Launch Organizer

Launch Photoshop.com account settings

The Undo History Palette

Along the top of the interface is the **Menu Bar**, which gives you access to both basic program functions (**Save, Edit, Paste**, etc.) and advanced image manipulation and selection functions – all of which we discuss in greater detail in subsequent chapters.

To the top right of this Menu Bar you'll find a number of other buttons, as illustrated above:

- **The Photoshop.com link.** If you've signed up for and logged in to **Photoshop.com**, you'll find a quick link here to your online account. (This will be displayed as the words "**Welcome**" and your name.) Clicking this button (you'll be prompted for your password) brings up your account profile and information on your online storage space. In **Chapter 32, Photoshop.com**, we'll show you how to set up your account to automatically back up your media files online.

- **Undo/Redo and Undo History.** To the right of this quick link, you'll find the **Undo** and **Redo** buttons. Photoshop Elements, like Premiere Elements, includes a virtually unlimited number of **Undos**. (By default, the program will save 50 undo's, although you can optionally set your **Preferences** to save as many as 1,000.) By clicking this button (or pressing **Ctrl+z** on a PC keyboard, ⌘**+z** on a Mac) you can undo anything you've done, one step at a time, all the way back to the point at which you opened your image file. To step forward again and redo your undo, click the **Redo** button or press **Ctrl+y** on a PC or ⌘**+y** on a Mac. (You can change it to the more traditional **Ctrl+Shift+z** (or ⌘**+Shift+z**) in the program's **Edit/Preferences**, by the way.)

  For quick access to any **Undo** point in your work, go to the **Window** drop-down on the Menu Bar and open the **Undo History** palette. This palette lists every action you've taken on your image file since opening it, and when you click to select any point listed, your image file will instantly revert to that point in your work.

- **The Organizer launch button.** Finally, in the upper right of the Editor workspace is a quick-launch button that opens the **Elements Organizer.**

The many faces of the Palette Bin

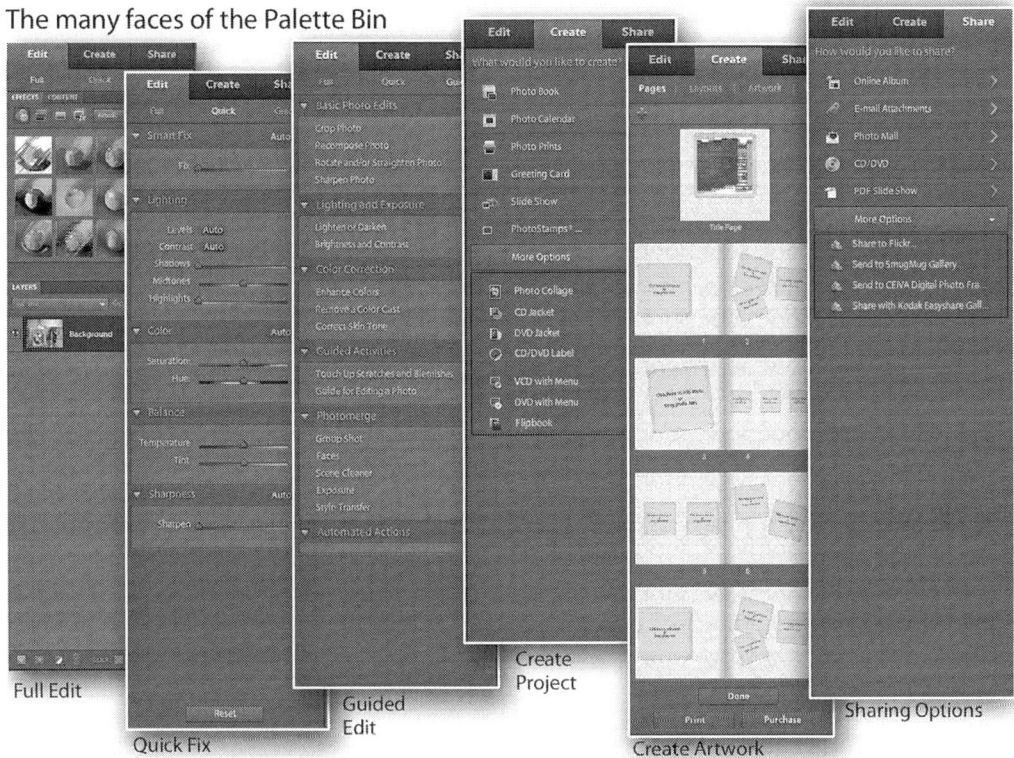

Full Edit

Quick Fix

Guided Edit

Create Project

Create Artwork

Sharing Options

The Palette Bin

To the right of the editing workspace is the **Palette Bin**, which includes a number of tools and palettes that vary, depending on whether you've selected the **Full Edit, Quick Fix, Guided Edit, Create** or **Share** tab, as illustrated above. (You'll see similar tabs both in the Organizer and in Premiere Elements.)

In **Full Edit** mode, this bin includes, by default, the **Layers** and the **Effects** palettes. However, if you click on the **Window** drop-down in the menu bar at the top of the interface, you'll find options to open (or close) nearly a dozen palettes, all of which can either "float" over the interface or be dragged into and "docked" in the **Palette Bin**.

We discuss in detail how to use the various tools under each of these tabs in **Chapter 3, Apply Quick Fixes and Guided Edits, Chapter 32, Create Fun Photo Pieces** and **Chapter 33, Share Your Photos and Videos.**

The Project Bin

Running along the bottom of the Editor workspace is a small but powerful panel known as the **Project Bin**.

By default, all photos and image files you have open in your Editor workspace appear as thumbnails in this bin.

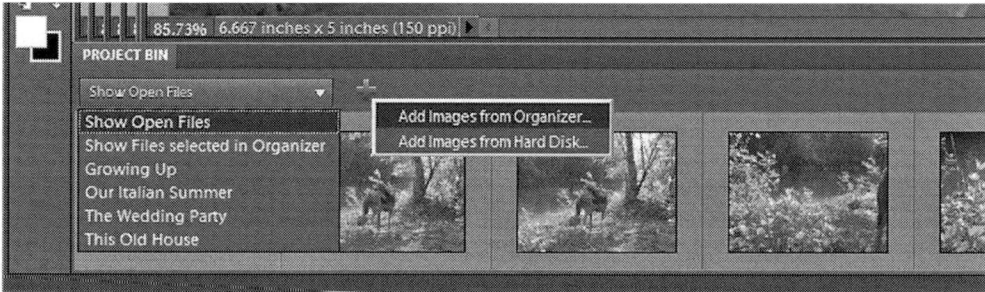

Show and Open options in the Project Bin.

To bring an open file to the front of your **Full Edit** workspace, double-click on its thumbnail in the **Project Bin**.

However, although this is the default and most common way to use the **Project Bin**, it is certainly not its only function. The **Project Bin** also interfaces with a number of other workspaces.

To access and change the **Project Bin's** display options, click on the bin's drop-down menu, which reads **Show Open Files** by default, as in the illustration above.

Show Open Files. Displays, as thumbnails, all of the image files you currently have open in your **Editor** workspace.

Show Files from the Organizer. If you have both the Elements Organizer open and files selected in its **Photo Browser** area, selecting this option displays those files in the **Project Bin**. These photos or image files can then be launched in the Editor workspace by double-clicking on them.

Albums. If you have **Albums** created for your image files in the Organizer, these **Albums** will also be listed on this drop-down menu (as in the illustration above), and their images can be accessed as a group simply by clicking on the **Album's** name. To learn more about creating **Albums**, see **Chapter 31, The Elements Organizer**.

A second drop-down menu in the **Project Bin** (opened by clicking on the green **+** sign) opens one of two browsers for locating and opening photo files on your computer.

Selecting **Add Images from the Organizer** opens a condensed version of the Elements Organizer (as illustrated at the top of the facing page). This screen gives you the option of locating a file by browsing your entire catalog, isolating your search to files in a designated *Album* or locating a file by **Keyword Tag** or **Rating**. Once you've narrowed your search, you can then designate specific photo files for opening in your Editor workspace. For more information on creating and using **Albums, Keyword Tags** and **Ratings**, see **Chapter 31, The Elements Organizer**.

Selecting **Add Images from Hard Disk** opens your Windows Explorer or Finder browser screens so that you can locate a file on your computer.

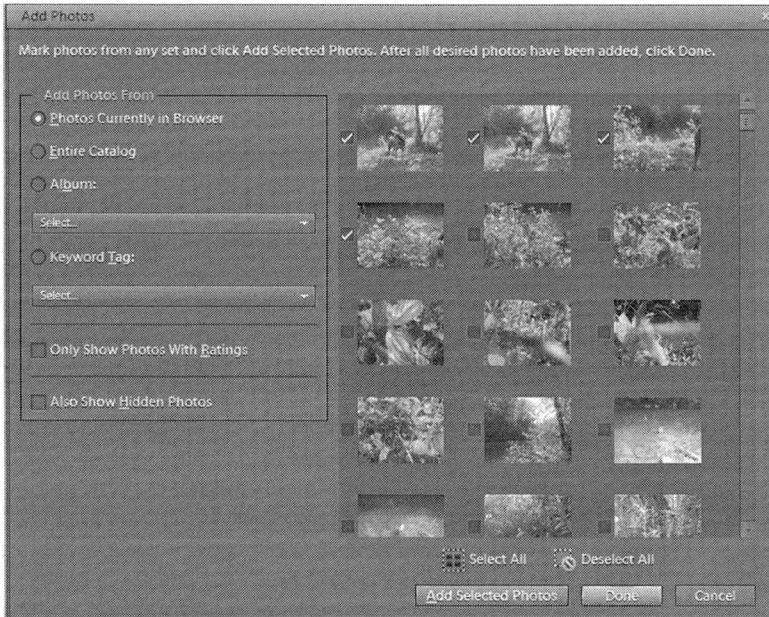

Selecting the option to Add Images from the Organizer from the + drop-down menu in the Project Bin opens a condensed version of the Elements Organizer in which you can isolate, search and select photos to open in your Editor workspace.

Need some Basic Training?

Need more help learning the basics of Photoshop Elements?

Check out my free tutorial series **Basic Training for Photoshop Elements** at Muvipix.com.

This simple, eight-part series will teach you the basics of photo resolution and show you how to adjust lighting and correct color in your photos, work with layers, add effects, scan your pictures and even share your photos and videos online.

And, yes, it's absolutely free!

To see the series, just go to http://Muvipix.com and type "Basic Training for Photoshop Elements" in the product search box. (We also offer Basic Training tutorials for other products, include Premiere Elements.)

And while you're there, why not drop by the Community forum and say hi! We'd love to have you become a part of our growing city.

Hope to see you there!

Steve, Chuck, Ron and the whole Muvipix team

What's new in Photoshop Elements 9?

Adobe continues to refine and improve this already terrific product. Version 9's new features may not be as immediately apparent as in previous version of the program, but a couple are definitely worth noting.

A cleaner interface

As with the entire Elements suite, Photoshop Elements has been given a major facelift, giving it a new, cleaner interface. Gone are the brightly-colored **Palette Bin** tabs of the previous versions. In its place is a sleak, cool, black and gray look.

Effort has also been made to improve the interface's readability. The text on the tabs and in the various menus is whiter and bolder, often backed by a drop-shadow, making it much clearer, cleaner and easier to read.

Greater Mac support

For the first time ever, Premiere Elements as well as Photoshop Elements will be released in a Mac as well as a Windows version. (We've made an effort, throughout this book, to address the Mac as well as the Windows interface and keyboard shortcuts.)

Even the Elements Organizer – previously a Windows-only feature – will be included with the Mac version of the Elements suite. This new Mac Organizer includes a tool for migrating your photo files catalog from iPhoto. For more information, see **Chapter 31, The Elements Organizer**.

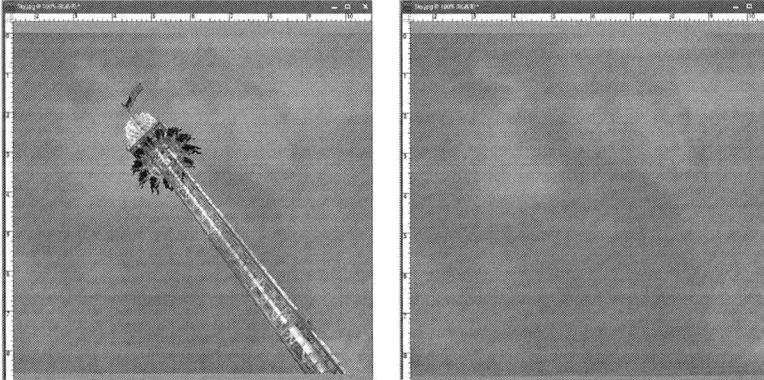

Content Aware Fill seamlessly removes elements from your photos by replacing the removed area with imagery similar to that of the rest of the photo.

Content Aware Fill

In previous versions of the program, the **Healing Brushes** created a fill for any designated area by averaging the pixels around this area.

Photoshop Elements' new **Content Aware Fill** tool now considers the entire *context* of the area designated, so that the replaced area matches not only the nearby pixels but the actual *content* of the photo.

In other words, when the **Healing Brush** is used to, say, remove telephone lines from a photo of a sunset, the **Content Aware Fill** feature will not just patch the area by averaging the colors but will actually *fill* the area where the telephone lines were with very natural-looking sky!

To see how this new tool works, see the **Healing Brush Tool** in **Chapter 4, Get to Know the Photoshop Elements Toolbox**.

Layer Masks

Layer Masks can be used to "hide" areas of your photos, making these areas essentially invisible or transparent without actually removing any pixels from your photo. A **Layer Mask** can be used, for instance, to create a soft or feathered edge for a photo without actually removing any of the photo data from around the edges of your photo.

We'll show you how to use this amazing feature – previously available in only a limited form in Photoshop Elements – in **Chapter 8, Work with Photoshop Elements Layers**.

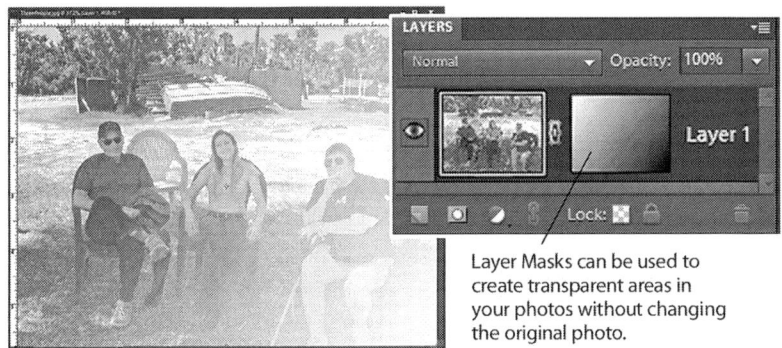

Layer Masks can be used to create transparent areas in your photos without changing the original photo.

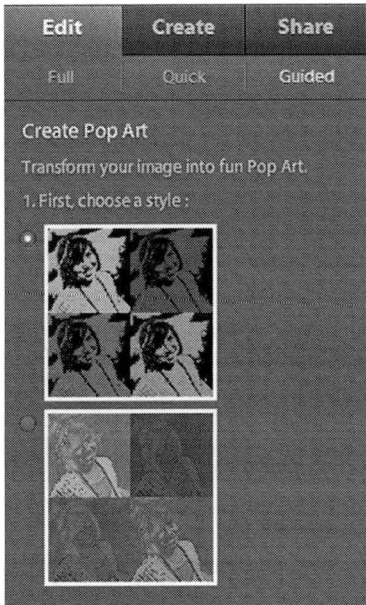

Guided Fun Edits include options for stylizing your photos.

Guided "Fun" Edits

Added to the **Guided Edits** library of effects are step-by-step tools for creating interesting, funny or stylized pictures from your photos.

Among the options are effects for making your picture look like it was taken with a Lomo camera, tools for making designated elements in your photos (an arm or a head, for instance) pop out beyond boundaries of the photo's frame, a Pop Art tool for turning your photo into one of those Andy Warhol's Marilyn Monroe-style collages and a tool for making your photo appear along with one of several possible reflection textures (a mirror, semi-opaque glass or water).

We'll show you how to use this tool in **Guided Edits** in **Chapter 3, Apply Quick Fixes and Guided Edits**.

Photomerge Styles

A sixth tool has been added to Photoshop Elements's already amazing **Photomerge** toolkit – a cool feature which lets you combine elements from several photos into one.

The **Photomerge Styles** tool will apply one photo's look and style (its lighting, color and sharpness) to another photo.

We'll show you how to use it in the **Photomerge** section of **Chapter 12, Utilize Advanced Photoshop Elements Tools**.

People Recognition

Adobe has completely revamped the Elements Organizer's **People Recognition** tool, making it easier to use and much "smarter" than in previous versions. We'll show you how it works – and how to teach it how to recognize faces – in **Chapter 31, The Elements Organizer**.

Multi-touch Support

Finally, Photoshop Elements 9 also includes the ability to interface with computers that use touch screen technology.

By dragging your fingers over your computer's touch screen, you can use tools or position files in the Editor workspace. And, by opening or closing your fingers across the screen, you can even zoom in and out on your photo file's image!

Chapter 3

Quick Fixes and Guided Edits
Easy ways to touch up photos

In addition to its more professional photo touch-up and graphic design tools, Photoshop Elements includes a number of simplified and semi-automatic tools for fixing, enhancing and adjusting your image files.

A number of these are Quick Fixes, with simplified controls and automatic functions.

Others are incorporated into Guided Edits, adjustments made as you work through a series of questions.

The Editor workspace is a full-featured toolkit for fixing your photos, correcting color and creating graphic and photographic effects.

However, if you just need a simple fix – or you're intimidated by the multitude of tools and options in the Photoshop Elements Editor, the program also offers some simpler **Quick Fix** tools for editing your photos and graphic files. If you'd prefer, you can even work through a **Guided Edit**, the program taking you step-by-step through the process.

Apply a Quick Fix

The **Quick Fix** work area for any open image file can be launched by clicking either the **Edit Quick** option under the **Edit** tab in the Editor workspace or the **Quick Photo Edit** option under the **Fix** tab on the Organizer.

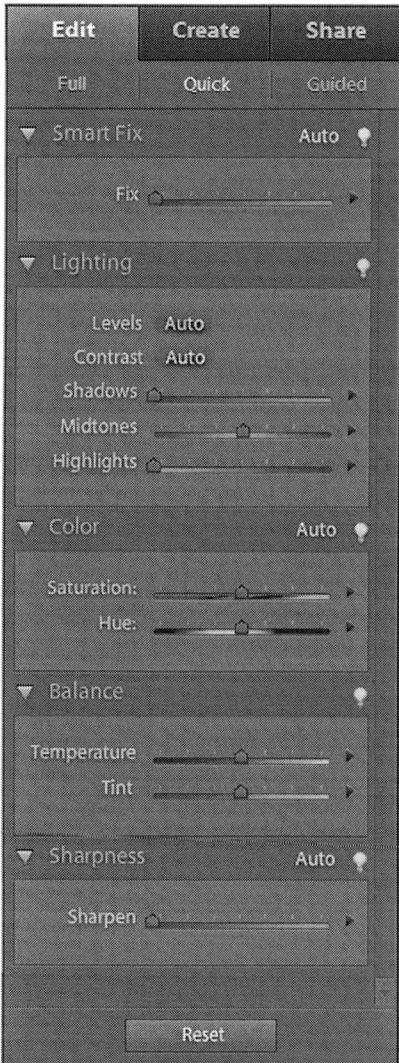

However, regardless of which workspace it is launched from, when the **Quick Fix** option is selected, the Editor workspace is launched (if it is not already opened) and the actual photo editing is done there.

To leave the **Quick Fix** work area once you have finished applying any fixes to your image file, click the **Full Edit** button under the **Edit** tab.

You may then choose to save the changes you've made to the image file or close it, discarding any changes.

Understand the Quick Fix work area

The **Quick Fix** work area includes a number of tools for viewing and manipulating your image file. The four tools on the **Toolbox** to the left of the before-and-after view panels work similarly to their counterparts in the Editor workspace Toolbox. (For more information, see **Chapter 4, Get to Know the Photoshop Elements Toolbox.**)

The **Zoom Tool** (magnifying glass) controls your view.

The **Hand Tool** allows you to move your image around in your viewing area.

The **Quick Selection Tool** allows you to select areas on your image file for manipulation, by "painting" to define the selected area.

The **Crop Tool** can be used to crop and trim your image.

Touch-Up Tools. The three **Touch-Up Tools** can be used to remove red-eyes, whiten teeth, make skies bluer and add high contrast to black & white images. For more information on how these tools work, see **Smart Brush Tools** in **Chapter 4, Get to Know the Photoshop Elements Toolbox.**)

The Quick Fix Work Area

Before & After View

Additionally, the **Quick Fix** work area includes two other view controls.

The View pop-up menu, to the lower left of the image file display, allows you to set your view to display either an **After Only** look at how your fix has affected your image file, a **Before Only** look or a **Before & After** comparison.

The **Reset** button to the upper right of the display area causes your image file to revert back to its settings before any **Quick Fixes** were applied.

Apply Quick Color, Lighting and Sharpen fixes

There are five categories of **Quick Fixes**. Each includes both an **Auto** button and simplified manual controls for adjusting your image file's quality.

Smart Fix combines both a color and lighting fix.

Lighting combines controls for brightening and darkening and for increasing and decreasing contrast.

Color combines controls for saturation (how much color) and hue (tint of color).

Balance controls allow you to change the color temperature (more blue vs. more red) or tint.

Detail increases or decreases the sharpness of your image.

Edit	Create	Share
Full	Quick	Guided

▼ Basic Photo Edits

Crop Photo >
Recompose Photo >
Rotate and/or Straighten Photo >
Sharpen Photo >

▼ Lighting and Exposure

Lighten or Darken >
Brightness and Contrast >
Adjust Levels >

▼ Color Correction

Enhance Colors >
Remove a Color Cast >
Correct Skin Tone >

▼ Guided Activities

Touch Up Scratches and Blemishes >
Guide for Editing a Photo >
Fix Keystone Distortion >

▼ Photomerge

Group Shot >
Faces >
Scene Cleaner >
Exposure >
Style Transfer >

▼ Automated Actions

Action Player >

▼ Photographic Effects

Line Drawing >
Old Fashioned Photo >
Saturated Slide Film Effect >

▼ Fun Edits

Lomo Effect >
Out Of Bounds >
Perfect Portrait >
Pop Art >
Reflection >

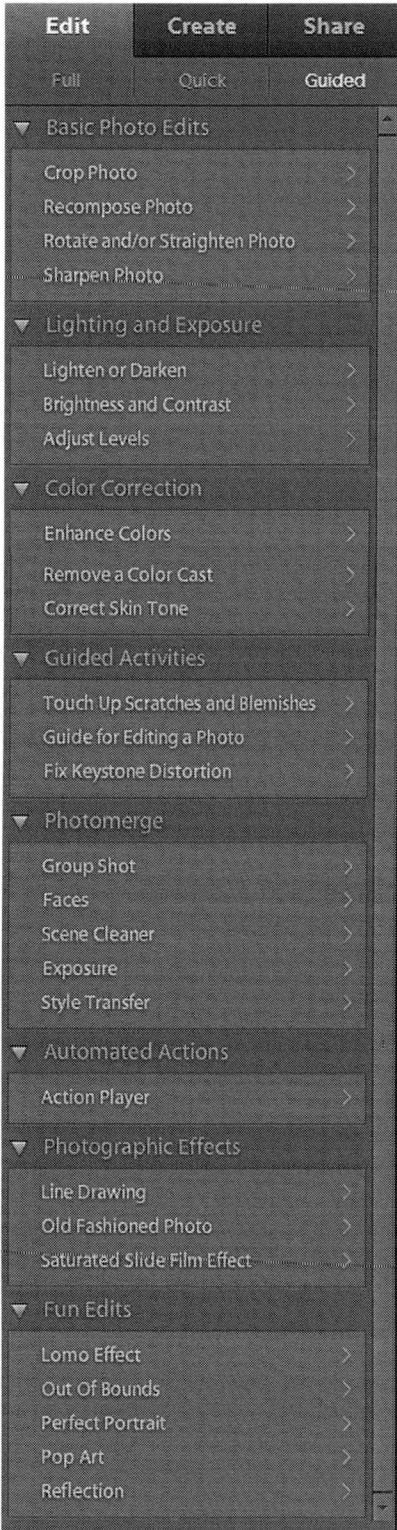

Use Guided Edits

As with **Quick Fixes**, **Guided Edits** can be launched from either the Editor workspace (from under the **Edit** tab) or from the Organizer workspace (from under the **Fix** tab) – although the actual **Guided Edits** are ultimately done in the Editor.

A **Guided Edit**, as the name implies, is a simplified and very intuitive means of working your image file through a series of adjustments. Using a **Guided Edit** is as easy as answering the question "What would you like to do?"

Whatever fix you select, Photoshop Elements guides you along the way – explaining how each tool works, offering an automatic fix if available and then giving you the option of either keeping the change (clicking **Done**) or rejecting the change and returning to the main menu (**Cancel**).

If you're at all intimidated by the **Full Edit** workspace, a **Guided Edit** may be the way to go.

However, by its very nature it's likely a work area you'll quickly outgrow as you become more proficient with using the Editor's more complete **Toolbox,** as we discuss in **Chapter 4**.

Launch a Fix from the Elements Organizer

	Organize	Fix	▾	Create	Share

her ▾ 📝 Full Photo Edit...
📝 Quick Photo Edit...
📝 Guided Photo Edit...
📝 Edit Videos...
🔳 Growing Up

Like Photoshop Elements and Premiere Elements, the Elements Organizer includes a tabbed tasks panel with access to a number of tools and workspaces.

When a photo or video file is selected in the Photo Browser area of the Organizer and a **Fix** option is selected, the Organizer will automatically open the file in Premiere Elements, the Photoshop Elements Full Editor or one of the Photoshop Elements **Fix** workspaces.

Guided "Fun" Edits

New to Photoshop Elements 9, the Guided Fix area includes five "fun" edits for creating highly-stylized photographic effects. Because these are Guided Edits, of course, the program really does walk you through the process of creating them, step-by-step:

The **Lomo Effect** makes your photos look as if they were shot with a LOMO, a primitive, Soviet-made camera whose bizarre results have given it something of a cult following.

The **Out of Bounds Effect** lets you crop your photo, excluding certain elements, so that, say, a person's head, hand or foot extends beyond the borders of the picture. Instructions for using this tool are described in the section below.

Perfect Portrait guides you through using tools for cleaning up your photo's color, healing blemishes, removing red-eyes and even whitening teeth.

Pop Art creates a colorful photo collage, a la Andy Warhol's famous Marilyn Monroe portrait.

Reflection creates a reflection of your picture, which you can customize so that it appears to be shining off a floor below your photo, a sheet of glass or even rippling water.

A guided "Out of Bounds" edit effect

Creating an **Out of Bounds Effect** involves basically two steps. The first is redefining the frame of your photo, which will be cropped down from its current size. The second is designating which elements in the photo will be effected by this new cropping.

For my example I've chosen an action shot of a young girl doing a tae kwon do high kick. To make this shot more interesting, we'll crop the photo's frame around the girl so that her kick seems to be popping right out of the picture!

1. With the photo open in the Editor workspace, click the **Edit** tab and select **Guided** from the sub-tab.

    The **Guided Edit** option screen will open in the **Palette Bin** and the photo will appear in the **Guided Edits** workspace.

2. Click to select the **Out of Bounds** effect. You may need to scroll down the list of **Guided Edits**, since there are quite a few listed!

    The **Palette Bin** will switch to the **Out of Bounds Effect Guided Edits** option panel.

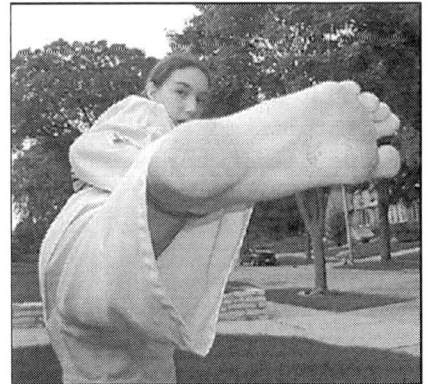

Edit	Create	Share
Full	Quick	Guided

Create an Out Of Bounds Effect

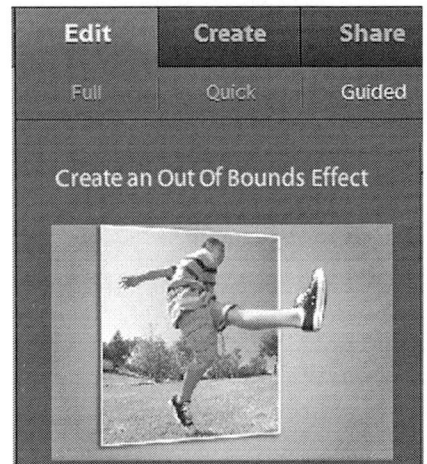

Add a Frame

Quick Selection Tool

Create Out of Bounds

At the top of this panel is a photos showing an example of the finished effect. If you roll your mouse over it, you'll see the "before" picture that your **Out of Bounds** effect was created from.

3. Click the **Add a Frame** button.

 A box will appear over your photo. Drag the corner handles of this box to define what will be your photo's newly cropped frame.

 When this cropping box is in position, lock it in place by clicking the green check mark or by pressing the **Enter** key on your keyboard.

The photo will now appear with its new cropping displayed as a semi-opaque overlay.

4. Click the **Quick Selection Tool** button on the **Guided Edits** palette. (You may need to scroll down the palette to see this button.)

As we show you in **Chapter 4, Get to Know the Photoshop Elements Toolbox**, the **Quick Selection Tool** works like a paintbrush. Click and drag the tool over the elements in your photo you'd like to extend beyond the photo's newly cropped frame. In my case, this will be the girl and her foot. As you drag the tool over your photo, your selected area will be displayed with a moving dotted line around it (commonly called "marching ants").

The **Quick Selection Tool** will automatically add areas of similar color to your selection – whether you want it to or not. But don't worry. If it adds more than you'd like to your selection, you can always un-select these areas later.

At the top left of the **Guided Edits** workspace, you'll see an **Option Bar** with some basic settings for the **Quick Selection Tool**. The **Brush** drop-down menu on this bar allows you to set the size of the tool's selection brush. (You can also quickly widen or narrow your brush's size by pressing the [and] keys on your keyboard.)

To add to your selection, select the **+** tool from the **Option Bar** or hold down your **Shift** key as you continue to paint with the **Quick Selection Tool**.

To de-select a selected area, select the **-** tool from the **Option Bar** or hold down the **Alt/Option** key on your keyboard as you paint with the **Quick Selection Tool**.

5. When you're satisfied with your selection, click the **Create Out of Bounds** button on the palette.

The program will crop your photo per your settings, except for the area you've selected.

As you can see, there are some additional effects which can be added to your photo effect in this workspace, including a **Drop Shadow** and a **Gradient background**.

And, if after you've clicked **Done** your results still seem a bit rough, you can return to the **Full Edit** worskpace and use some of the other tools (the **Eraser**, for instance) to clean up and refine the edges of the effect.

If you look at the **Layers** palette, you'll see that this simple trick actually involves a number of high-end tools and effects, including **Layer Masks** and multiple copies of your photo on separate layers.

In fact, if you look at one of the bottom-most layers, you'll see that your **Original Image** is still there.

Just in case you want to throw out the whole effect and start from scratch!

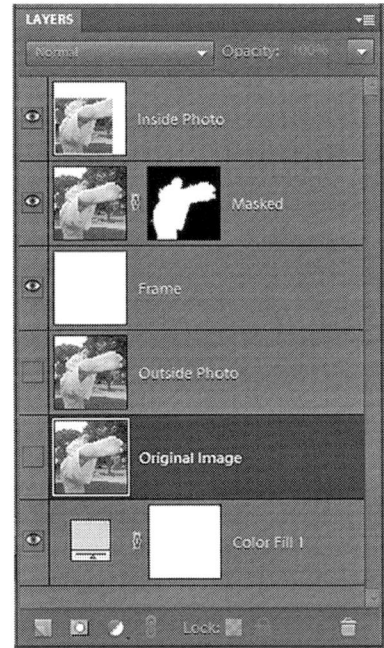

Chapter 4

Get to Know the Photoshop Elements Toolbox
Your main photo editing tool kit

The most visible tools in the Photoshop Elements Editor workspace are those gathered into the Toolbox, displayed as a column of colorful little icons running along the left side of the interface.

Understanding these tools, how they work and how to customize them for your particular needs will take you a long way toward mastering this program.

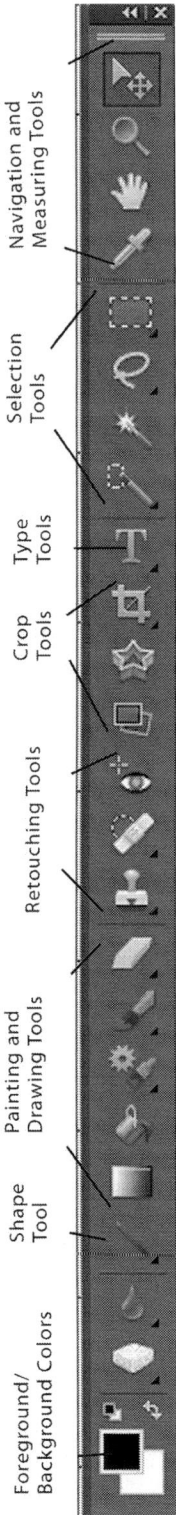

Navigation and
Measuring Tools

Selection
Tools

Type
Tools

Crop
Tools

Retouching Tools

Painting and
Drawing Tools

Shape
Tool

Foreground/
Background Colors

The Toolbox

The **Toolbox** runs along the left side of the Editor workspace. The tools in the **Toolbox** can be divided into nine general categories:

Navigation and Measuring Tools. Tools for positioning your image file in the workspace, zooming and sampling color.

Selection Tools. Tools for selecting and isolating areas in your image file.

Type tools. Tools for creating, editing and shaping text. Because working with text is a category all its own, we'll discuss these tools in depth in **Chapter 9, Create and Edit Text**.

Crop Tools. Tools for cropping, shaping and straightening your image file.

Retouching Tools. Tools for cleaning up and changing your image file. This category includes the tools for blurring, sharpening, dodging and burning, based on techniques long used by professional photographers.

Painting and Drawing Tools. Tools for drawing, painting, coloring and erasing.

Shape Tools. Tools for creating lines and vector-based shapes.

Foreground/Background Color. Not so much tools, I guess, as much as tool settings – but having them in the **Toolbox** gives you much-appreciated easy access to them.

Access many tools under one button

A few of the buttons in the **Toolbox** include more than one tool under a single button. These tools are indicated by a small, black triangle in the lower right corner of that button. To activate one of the "hidden" tools for a button, click and hold on the tool button until the "hidden" tools display.

The Option Bar

When you select any tool, the often unique, custom settings for that tool will appear in the **Option Bar,** which runs along the top of the Editor workspace, just below the Menu Bar (as illustrated below). Some of these custom settings are so deep that one tool can actually work as several tools. And a few tools even allow you to *add* custom settings of your own!

Many **Option Bars** include drop-down menus that list patterns, brushes or effects. We discuss the options on this bar, as well as its drop-down menus, as we discuss each individual tool.

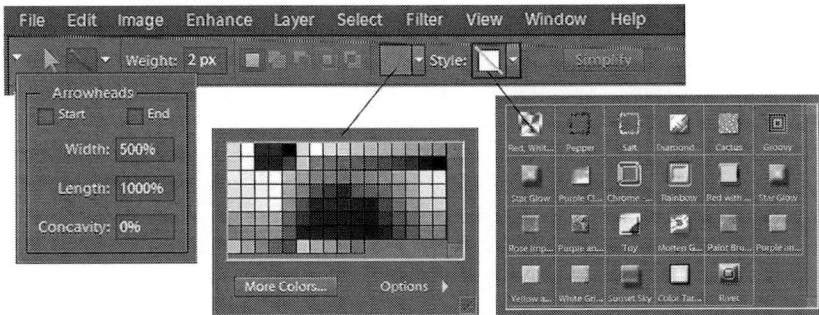

Foreground/Background Colors

You'll likely refer often to this swatch icon, displayed at the very bottom of the **Toolbox**. The colors that are set here play a role in how a number of your tools function.

Foreground Color

Background Color

Generally, the **Foreground Color** will be the default color in which new items you create will appear.

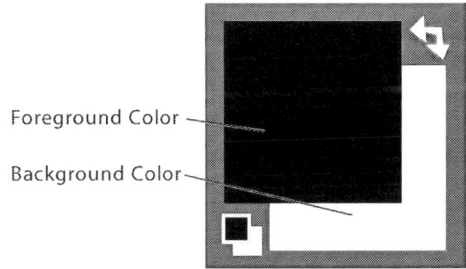

- When a painting or drawing tool is selected, for instance, the brush will paint with or the shape will appear in the **Foreground Color** by default.

- When you use the **Typing Tool,** your text will also appear, by default, in the **Foreground Color.**

- When you use the **Eraser Tool**, the area you erase will be replaced by the **Background Color**. (At least when you're erasing from a background layer or flattened image file. When working on a layer, erasing makes that area on the layer transparent.)

- When you use **Fill** or **Stroke**, you will have the option of doing so with the **Foreground** or **Background Color**.

- When you use the **Gradient Tool**, the gradation of color you create will be painted, by default, from the **Foreground Color** to the **Background Color**.

There are a number of ways to set the colors that appear as **Foreground** and **Background Colors**. The easiest is to simply click on either the **Foreground** or **Background Color** swatch on the **Toolbox**. This will launch the **Color Picker**.

The Color Picker

The **Color Picker** displays a color sampling screen and a slider bar, representing **hue, saturation** and **brightness**. (Hue is your color's shade or tint; saturation is the amount of that hue in your color; brightness is the amount of lightness in your color.)

Your current color is displayed in the lower half of the box, located in the upper center of the **Color Picker**, as illustrated to the right.

Your new color will appear in the upper half of this box.

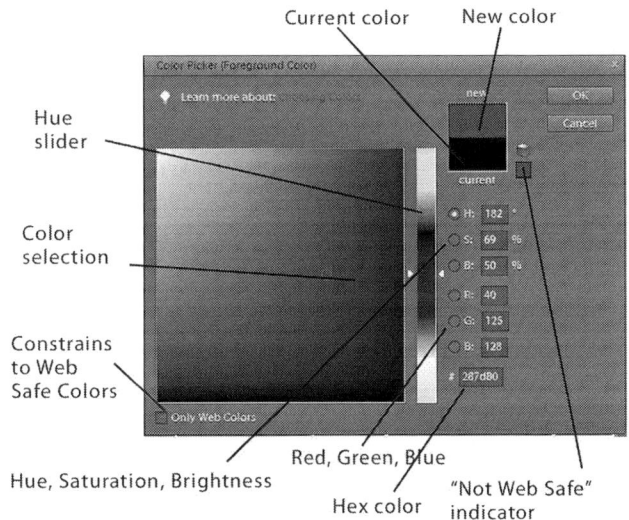

Current color   New color

Hue slider

Color selection

Constrains to Web Safe Colors

Hue, Saturation, Brightness

Red, Green, Blue

Hex color

"Not Web Safe" indicator

To adjust the hue for your color, move the white triangles up or down on the **Hue slider** that runs down the center of the **Color Picker**. Then to select a color, click in the big gradient box, representing the saturation and brightness of that hue.

By checking the **Only Web Colors** box in the lower left corner of the **Color Picker**, you can restrict the available colors in the picker to only those colors that display consistently on Web pages.

Colors can also be set digitally in the **Color Picker** by typing in numbers for **Hue**, **Saturation** and **Brightness** or for the 256 levels of **Red**, **Green** and **Blue** in the color mix. The alpha-numeric **Hex** numbers for the color, in the lower right, can also be manually designated.

Once you've selected your color, click **OK**. Your selected color will become your new **Background** or **Foreground Color**.

The Eyedropper/Sampler Tool

Another way to set the **Foreground Color** is by sampling a color from an open photo or image with the **Eyedropper/Sampler**.

To sample a color using this tool, click on an area in an open image file.

The Color Swatch palette

The **Color Swatch** palette is opened by selecting it from the **Window** drop-down on the Menu Bar.

When you click on a swatch in the **Color Swatch** palette, it will become your **Foreground** Color.

The **Color Swatch** palette includes hundreds of color options, categorized in several swatch sets. These various swatch sets can be accessed from the drop-down menu at the top of the palette.

You can even create additional colors for your swatch library.

To do so, select a **Foreground Color** from the **Color Picker**, then click the **New Swatch** icon in the lower right of the **Color Swatches** palette. The color will be permanently added to your swatch library.

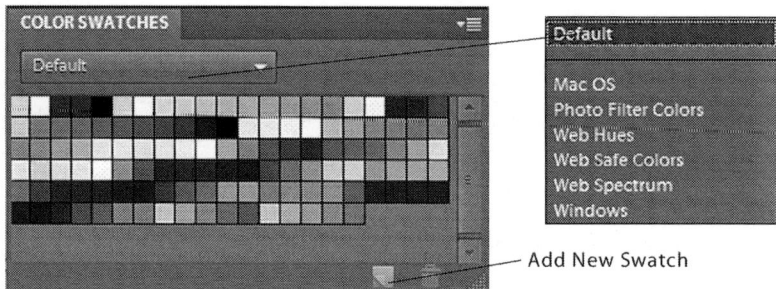

The Foreground and Background Colors can also be set by selecting a chip from the Color Swatches palette. The drop-down menu at the top of this panel offers options for displaying a number of additional color libraries.

Additional Foreground/Background Color options

Swap Foreground and Background Colors. You can quickly switch the **Foreground** and **Background Colors** by clicking on the double-headed arrow to the upper right of the **Foreground/Background Color** swatch icons, or by pressing the **X** key on your keyboard.

Swap Foreground and Background colors

Reset colors to black and white

Quickly set Foreground/Background Colors to black and white. You can quickly reset the **Foreground** and **Background Colors** to black and white, respectively, by clicking on the black/white icon to the lower left of the **Foreground/ Background Color** swatch icon on the **Toolbox**. A keyboard shortcut for quickly setting the colors back to black and white is to simply press the **D** key.

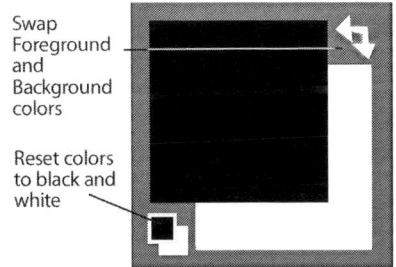

The Move, Zoom and Hand Tools

The top three tools in the **Toolbox** are tools for viewing and positioning your image file.

The Move Tool

More or less the default tool in Photoshop Elements, this tool is used to move or drag the elements, selections, text or layers in your image files to new positions.

The settings in the **Option Bar** for this tool are useful for arranging the positions and order of objects in your image. But they'll be of particular interest as we edit Premiere Elements DVD and BluRay Disc menu templates in **Chapter 35, Use the Elements Programs Together**.

The Zoom Tool

Represented by a magnifying glass, this tool is used, naturally, to zoom in and out of your image.

Select this tool and click on your image and you will zoom in. (Or you can use the keyboard shortcut **Ctrl+✛** on a PC or ⌘+✛ on a Mac.)

Hold down the **Alt** key and click on your image and you will zoom out. (Or you can use the keyboard shortcut **Ctrl+─** on a PC or ⌘+─ on a Mac.)

The buttons and checkboxes on the tool's **Option Bar** can be used to 'jump' your view to specific zoom levels.

The Hand Tool

Represented by a hand icon, this tool is useful if you're zoomed in so closely to an image that sections of your image are outside the file's window. When the **Hand Tool** is selected, you can click and drag the image's view around within the viewable area.

A keyboard shortcut for the **Hand Tool** is the **Spacebar** on your keyboard. No matter what tool you're working with, you can always reposition your view by holding down the **Spacebar** and dragging your image around the viewing area.

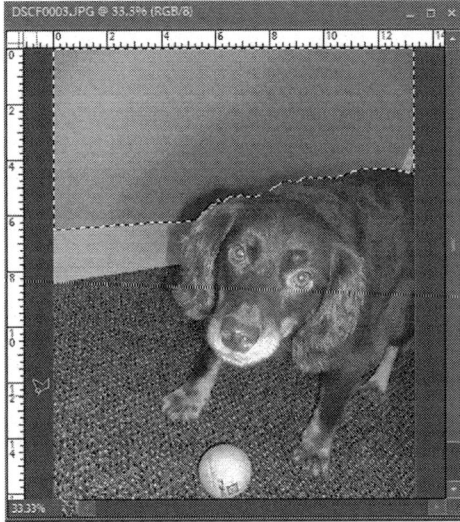

The selected area of your image file will appear surrounded by a moving dotted line, commonly called "marching ants."

The Option Bar for each Selection Tool includes settings for adding to or subtracting from the selection.

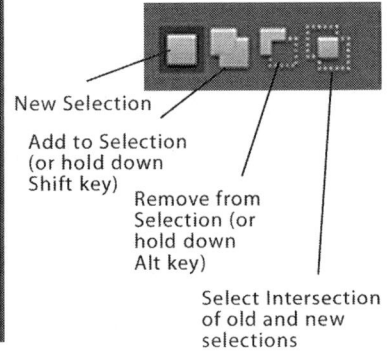

New Selection

Add to Selection (or hold down Shift key)

Remove from Selection (or hold down Alt key)

Select Intersection of old and new selections

Selection Tools

A number of tools in the Toolbox are designed so that you can select areas of your images.

A selected area can be cut, copied or pasted. But, more so, a selected area is *isolated*, so that you can cut, paste, color or apply effects to that isolated area without affecting the rest of the image. Selecting and isolating is a very powerful function of Photoshop Elements, which is why we spend an entire chapter (**Chapter 5, Select and Isolate Areas in Your Photos**) discussing it in depth.

Your selected areas will be surrounded by little, moving dotted lines – which are traditionally referred to as "marching ants."

Add to and subtract from a selection

When selecting an area in a photo or image file, you don't have to get the selection exactly right the first time:

- Once you've selected an area, you can add to it by clicking **Add to Selection** on the **Option Bar** (as illustrated above) or by holding down the **Shift** key as you continue to draw your selection.

- To remove from your selected area, click **Subtract from Selection** on the **Option Bar** or hold down the **Alt/Option** key as you drag over the area you want to deselect.

- To select only the area overlapped by your current and your new selection, click **Intersect with Selection** on the **Option Bar.**

Using these tools to add to or subtract from your selection, you can hone your selection until it is precisely the area you want to work with.

- To turn off, or **deselect**, all of the selected areas for your image file, press **Ctrl+d** on a PC or ⌘**+d** on a Mac.

The Marquee Tool can be set to make either a Rectangular or Elliptical selection.

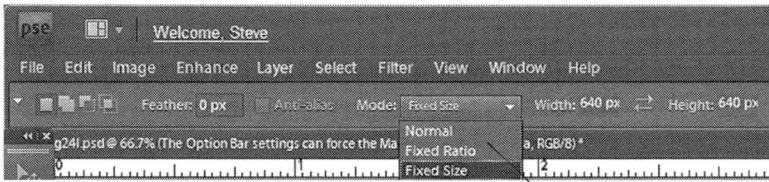

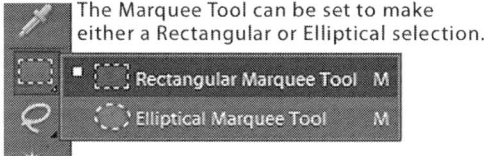

The Option Bar settings can force the Marquee to constrain to a specific size or aspect ratio.

The Marquee Selection Tools

The **Rectangular Marquee Tool** and the **Elliptical Marquee Tool** are both available under the same **Toolbox** button. (To switch between them, click and hold on the tool button.)

To select an area on your image with either of these tools, click and drag across your image file. As long as that tool remains selected in the **Toolbox**, you can reposition the selected area by dragging it. To deselect the area press **Ctrl+d** on a PC or ⌘**+d** on a Mac.

Beyond the **Feathering** (discussed above), the **Option Bar** for this tool includes a few functions which can also be activated with keyboard shortcuts.

To constrain the tool to select a perfectly circular or square area, select the **Fixed Aspect Ratio** option from the **Mode** drop-down on the **Option Bar** – or hold down the **Shift** key as you drag to make your selection.

When the **Mode** is set to **Fixed Size**, you can designate the exact size for your selected area.

Feathering

An additional selection option is **Feathering** – which is available on the **Option Bar** for the **Marquee Selection Tools** and as a refinement option under the **Select** drop-down on the Menu Bar.

Feathering means softening the edge of a selected area so that, rather than a sharp division between the selected and unselected areas, there is a soft gradation of selection.

A "feathered" selection has a softer edge so that, when the selection is removed or an effect is added to it, the distinction between the selected and unselected area of your image is a gradation rather than a solid line.

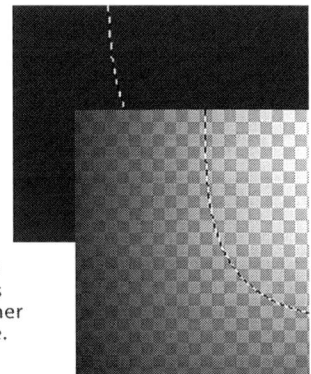

We'll look at how it works and how to set it in **Understand Feathering and Refine Edge** in **Chapter 5, Select and Isolate Areas in Your Photos**.

The Lasso Tool selects as you draw freehand.

The Polygonal Lasso Tool draws a selection from point to point as you click.

The Magnetic Lasso Tool follows the edge of a color break as you drag or click to create points.

The Lasso, Magnetic Lasso and Polygonal Lasso Tools

These three tools, which share the same **Toolbox** button, include an **Option Bar** similar to that of the **Marquee Selection Tools**.

Click and hold the button on the **Toolbox** to view and toggle between these three buttons.

Lasso Tools are about defining a selected area by drawing a line around it (as if wrapping it in a lasso). There are three **Lasso Tools**, each functioning slightly differently.

- **The Lasso Tool** is a freehand tool for selecting an area. To select an area with the **Lasso**, you just drag and draw. When you release your mouse button, the defined area will be selected.

- **The Polygon Lasso Tool** works similarly to the **Lasso Tool** except that, to designate an area to be selected, you click and release to create a series of dots, which will be connected by straight lines.

- **The Magnetic Lasso Tool** will follow the path you draw freehand – however, it will do so while following a line between the different colors of pixels.

  In other words, if you were drawing a selection around someone to separate him or her from a background, the **Magnetic Lasso** would try to follow the shape of the person, based on the difference in color between that person and the background.

  An important option setting for this tool is **Edge Contrast**. This setting defines the tool's tolerance for color contrast between the areas it does and does not select.

  In other words, if the person you were drawing a selection around is a very different color than the background, you could use a high **Edge Contrast** percentage to ensure that the tool found the edges.

  If the person is not so clearly distinguished from the background, you'll need a much lower **Edge Contrast** percentage, and you'll likely need to be more careful guiding the tool around the selection, or you may need to refine (add to or subtract from) the select later.

To close a **Lasso Tool** selection, finish the selection by clicking onto your selection's starting point or by double-clicking.

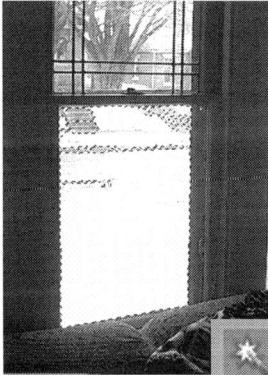

The Magic Wand Tool selects everything within a color range, based on the Tolerance level you've set.

The Selection Brush Tool draws a selection as you "paint" an area with its brush.

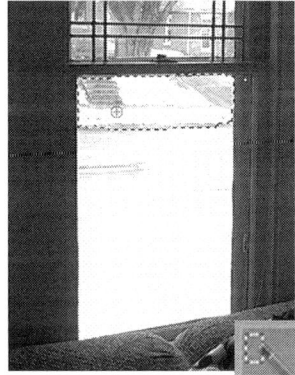

The Quick Selection Tool combines the the behaviors of both tools, selecting a similar color range as you "paint" across your image file.

The Magic Wand Tool

One of the most useful tools in the **Toolbox**, the **Magic Wand Tool**, automatically selects an area on your image based on color similarities. (We put it to good use in **Chapter 11, Learn Basic Photoshop Elements Tricks**.)

When you click with this tool, adjacent pixels of a similar color are automatically selected. By holding down the **Shift** key to add and the **Alt** key to subtract, you can continue to select or de-select areas of your image file to build your desired selection.

The most important setting on the **Option Bar** for this tool is **Tolerance**. The lower the number, the narrower the range of colors the **Magic Wand** will select. A higher **Tolerance** number widens the range of colors the **Magic Wand** will consider similar.

The Quick Selection and Selection Brush Tools

These two selection tools share the same button. To switch between them, click and hold on the tool button.

- **The Selection Brush Tool** works just like it sounds like it would – as you "paint" with it, you create a selected area. The **Option Bar** includes settings for defining the size and hardness of the brush. You'll find more information on brush options in our discussion of **Brush settings and options**, later in this chapter.

- **The Quick Selection Tool** works like a combination of the **Magic Wand** and the **Selection Brush Tool**. As you drag it across your image, it "paints" a selection area, grabbing nearby areas of similar color along the way. This is a great tool for quickly paint-selecting a flat-colored background that you'd like to remove or replace. Its **Option Bar** includes setting for the size, shape and hardness of the brush.

The Typing Tools

Because working with text is a subject unto itself, we've dedicated a chapter to working with text and the **Typing Tools**. For more information, see **Chapter 9, Create and Edit Text**.

Crop Tools

There are four tools in Photoshop Elements that are classified as **Crop Tools** – although, technically, only one actually *crops*, or changes the canvas size of, the actual image file.

The Crop Tool

The **Crop Tool** is the tool used for cutting both the image and canvas. To use it, click to select the tool, then drag to create a box on your image file. (The **Crop Tool** and the new **Recompose Tool** share the same button. To switch between them, click and hold on the button.)

Once you've dragged to create the cropping area, it can be reshaped and even moved, by dragging on its corner handles, until you've isolated the area of the image file you want to keep.

To finalize and crop your photo, click on the green checkmark or press **Enter** on your keyboard.

The **Crop Tool's Option Bar** gives you options for constraining the area that you've cropped. The **Aspect Ratio** drop-down can be used to constrain your cropping to a perfect square.

Additionally, if you fill in specifics for **Width**, **Height** and **Resolution**, you can prefigure the tool to cut your image down to a precise size and resolution!

The Crop Tool resizes your canvas based on your selected area. Once selected, the area can be resized, repositioned or canceled. To finalize your crop, click the green check mark or press Enter on your keyboard.

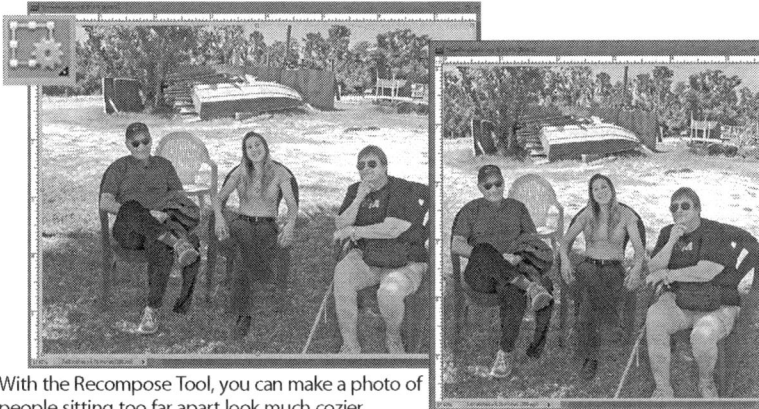

With the Recompose Tool, you can make a photo of people sitting too far apart look much cozier.

The Recompose Tool

The cool and powerful **Recompose Tool** allows you to reshape a photo – re-positioning people or other elements in it nearer together – without distorting these elements in any way. What's most amazing about this tool is that it does most of what it does automatically (although there are also manual ways to "protect" certain elements in the photo).

When you **Recompose** a photo, you squeeze it, either from top to bottom or from side to side, compressing the elements of the photo so that they become closer together – but without changing the shapes of any of the key elements in the picture.

In many cases, when you're using this tool, the **Recompose Tool** will automatically recognize people in your photo and it will protect them, as much as possible from distorting as you resize your photo. It will also try to keep certain major elements in the background of the photo – trees or cars – from distorting. It merely makes these key elements look closer together.

In our experience, however, the program can often use a little help identifying which elements in the photo you want to preserve. Fortunately, that's very simple to do.

What is Anti-Aliasing?

Anti-Aliasing is a method of smoothing or slightly feathering the edges of an object or text so that it looks more natural. When **Anti-Aliasing** is turned off, the object or text will have very sharp edges, usually resulting in a very blocky, unnatural look.

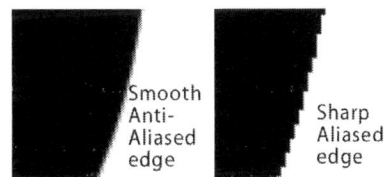

Smooth Anti-Aliased edge

Sharp Aliased edge

The **Recompose Tool** shares the same button on the **Toolbox** as the **Crop Tool**. To toggle between these two tools, click and hold on the tool's button until the "hidden" button appears.

1. With your photo file open, click to select the **Recompose Tool**. (The tool will launch a help screen that explains how to use the tool. You can elect not to see this screen again by checking the box in its lower left corner.)

   In **Recompose** mode, you'll see handles on each corner and in the middle of each side of your photo file. Dragging on these corner handles will resize your photo.

2. Drag one side of your photo in to squeeze your photo. In most cases, people and other major elements in the photo will move closer together – though may very soon begin to distort.

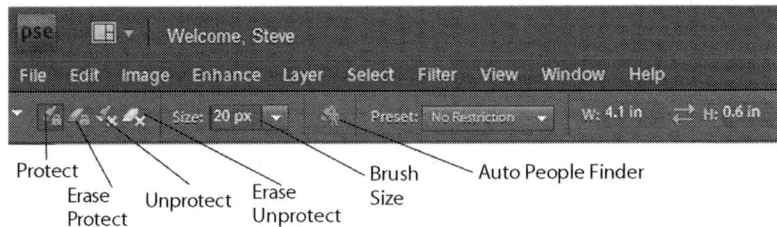

3. To "protect" the elements you don't want to distort, select the green paint brush from the **Recompose Option Bar** at the top of the interface and paint over the elements you want to preserve. As with any brush-based tool, you can enlarge or reduce the size of the brush by setting its size on the **Option Bar** or pressing the [or] buttons on your keyboard.

   In my illustration, on the facing page, I've painted "protection" over the three people and their chairs.

   To remove protection from an area, paint with the green eraser tool.

   To designate an object or person as something you want to see distorted or removed, paint it with the red "unprotect" brush. To remove this indicator, use the red erase brush.

   There is also a green "people finder" tool that can often automatically find and protect the people in your photo. It tends to work best when the photo was shot in ideal lighting conditions.

4. With your designated elements protected, drag the handle on the side of your photo in to compress the photo. As you do, the elements and people you've protected will move closer to each other and yet will not change shape.

   (There is, of course, a saturation point at which even protected elements will distort.)

   You can also change the dimensions of the photo numerically by typing a width or height on the **Option Bar**.

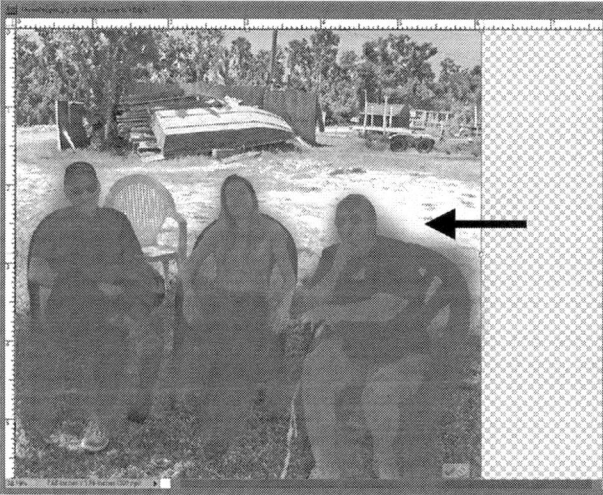

With key elements in your photo designated as protected, these elements move closer together, undistorted, as you resize the photo by dragging on its side handle.

When you are happy with your new composition, click the green check mark or simply press **Enter**. Photoshop Elements will process and re-render your photo.

Note that, because of the way this tool works, your new photo will be layered. So, in order to save it as something other than a PSD or layered TIF, you will need to flatten the layers by selecting **Flatten Image** under the **Layer** drop-down on the Menu Bar.

The Cookie Cutter Tool

The **Cookie Cutter Tool** is technically more of a mask than a true crop tool – except that, when the mask is applied, it permanently trims your image to the shape you've designated.

(The shaped image will have alpha, or transparency, around it so that, if you save your image file as a PSD, the shaped image will appear with no square background when the file is used in Premiere Elements.)

To use the tool, select a shape from the **Shape** drop-down menu on the **Option Bar** and then drag to draw the shape on your image file. Once you click on the green checkmark or press **Enter** on your keyboard, your image file will be cut to that shape.

There are many pages of options for shapes, by the way. And you can access them by clicking on the fly-out menu (**>>**) button in the upper right corner of the option panel that appears when you click on the **Option Bar's Shape's** drop-down menu.

The Cookie Cutter Tool cuts your image into any of over 550 shapes

With the Straighten Tool selected, drag a line to define an object you would like to appear perfectly horizontal. The tool will automatically rotate and straighten your photo accordingly.

Straighten Tool

I love this tool! It's great for straightening a crooked image. To use it, just select the tool and then drag to draw a line along an element in your image (a rooftop, a mantle, somebody's shoulders) that you would like to appear perfectly horizontal. When you release your mouse button, the image will instantly rotate and straighten!

Retouching Tools

Retouching Tools are used to change your image file – whether to clean up a photo or to change it or add a special effect. Some of these tools are simple and almost automatic. Others can do some pretty complex effects!

The Red Eye Removal Tool

You know what this tool is for. It's for when you've taken a flash picture in dim lighting and you find that, in the final photo, your best friend or dog has eyes that glow like some evil robot's!

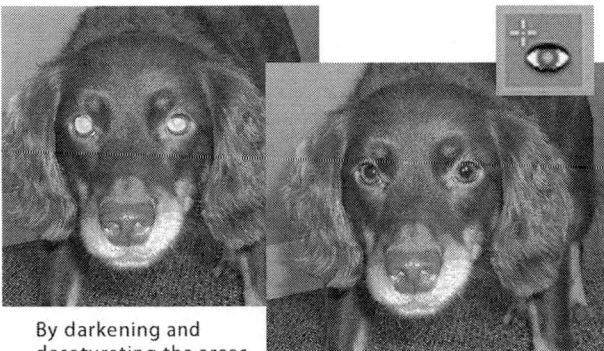

To use it, select the tool and then click on subject's bright, red pupils. The tool essentially strips the color out of the pupil area and darkens it.

The **Option Bar** for this tool allows you to set the **Pupil Size** and **Darken Amount**.

By darkening and desaturating the areas you click on, the Red Eye Removal Tool instantly tames demonic-looking subjects.

The Healing Brush uses a Content Aware Fill system to replace blemishes, telephone lines and other unwanted elements in your photos with imagery from the surrounding area!

Using a Content Aware Fill system, the Spot Healing Brush uses nearby imagery to replace blemishes and other flaws in your photos virtually invisibly!

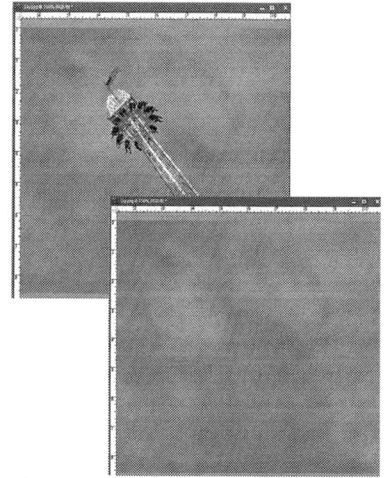

The Content Aware Fill feature in the Healing Brush Tools makes it easy to remove even large objects from many scenes.

The Spot Healing Brush Tool

This tool is great for getting rid of unwanted moles, blemishes or other such flaws in your photos.

When you click an area or "paint" with it, the tool blends the selected area with color information from the surrounding pixels. The **Option Bar** includes settings for the brush's size and hardness. (For more information on brushes, see **Brush settings and options**.)

The Healing Brush Tool

Similar to the **Clone Stamp Tool** (discussed on the next page), this tool borrows color and texture information from one area of your photo (which you've defined by **Alt-clicking** on it) and uses it to paint over another area.

The difference between this tool and the **Clone Stamp** is that the **Healing Brush Tool** then blends this borrowed imagery with the colors of the existing pixels to form a natural "healing patch" over the area.

As with the **Spot Healing Brush Tool**, the **Option Bar** includes settings for the brush's size and hardness.

Content Aware Fill

A new and very exciting enhancement to the **Healing Brush** and **Spot Healing Brush Tools** in Photoshop Elements 9 is something Adobe calls **Content Aware Fill**.

In past versions of the **Healing Brushes**, the tool filled areas that you designated by averaging the colors of the surrounding pixels to create a smooth patch. This was very effective for removing blemishes and small marks in a photo – but it was less so at patching larger areas.

Content Aware Fill essentially looks at the entire area around what you're trying to hide or remove, and it smoothly fills the area you designate with very natural-looking imagery.

This makes it especially effective at removing telephone wires from an otherwise perfect picture of a sunset – or even painting former friends completely out of a scene!

A favorite tool for "stunt photo work," the Clone Tool lets you paint over portions of your image file – removing objects or even people – with imagery from another area of your image file (defined by Alt+clicking).

The Clone Stamp Tool

This amazing tool takes imagery from one area of your photo file (which you define with an **Alt-click**) and paints it onto another.

The tool is popular for doing special effects, like "erasing" somebody or something from a scene (see **Chapter 11**).

In addition to settings for the brush size and hardness, the **Option Bar** includes an **Opacity** setting. Opacity, or transparency, controls whether the area you paint over is replaced entirely with the new image or is blended with the old to some degree.

The Pattern Stamp Tool

Rather than painting an area in your photo with imagery from another area in your image, the **Pattern Stamp Tool** paints over your image with a pattern, as selected from the drop-down menu on the **Option Bar**.

There are many pages of patterns available for this effect, by the way. And you can see the other categories of patterns by clicking on the flyout menu (>>) button in the upper right corner of the option box that appears when you click on the "pattern" drop-down.

An **Impressionist** option turns the pattern into a liquid swirl of paint that intensifies as you hold down on your mouse button.

The Pattern Stamp tool paints over your image with any of dozens of patterns.

The Eraser Tool removes what you drag across, replacing it with your Background Color or, if a layer, transparency.

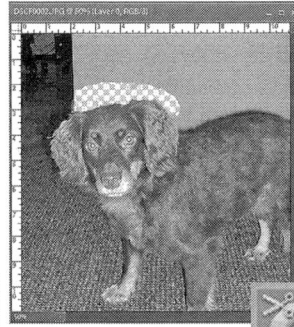

The Background Eraser erases up to color breaks, based on the Tolerance level you've set on the Option Bar.

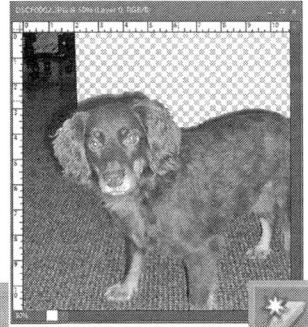

The Magic Eraser instantly removes an area you click on, based on its color range and the Tolerance level you've set.

The Eraser Tool

Simply put, the **Eraser Tool** removes the image from your file as you "paint" with it.

- If you're erasing from a flattened image or a background layer, what you erase will be replaced with your **Background Color** (see page 37).
- Erasing from a layer creates transparency in that layer.

Option Bar settings for this tool include brush size, hardness and opacity (transparency level).

The Background Eraser Tool

The **Background Eraser** erases one color or color range and ignores dissimilarly colored areas in your image file.

In other words, this tool can be used to erase the background from a photo of a person and yet not erase the person!

The tool determines the color you want erased based on the pixels that are in the tool's crosshairs as you "paint" with it. So, as you erase, if you keep the crosshairs off of what you don't want removed, the tool will erase along the edge of the color break, as in the illustration above, in which it erased the wall but not the dog.

The **Option Bar** includes settings for the brush size and hardness as well as **Tolerance** – how much distinction must exist between the area you're erasing and the area you're not in order for the tool to recognize the difference.

The Magic Eraser Tool

Like the **Magic Wand Tool,** this tool selects, and then erases, areas in your image file that fall within a range of colors, based on the pixel you click on or the pixels you drag across.

In other words, using this tool, you could easily remove a consistently green background from an image in a single click or simple click and drag.

The **Tolerance** setting, on the **Option Bar**, designates how wide of a range of colors is considered similar to your selected pixels, and thus are erased. (The higher the number, the more pixel colors are removed.) The **Opacity** level determines if the image is erased completely or simply softened.

51

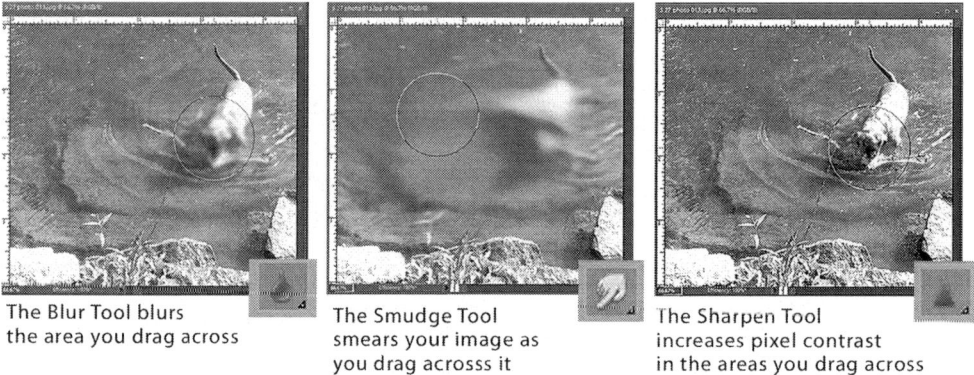

The Blur Tool blurs the area you drag across

The Smudge Tool smears your image as you drag acrosss it

The Sharpen Tool increases pixel contrast in the areas you drag across

Blur, Smudge and Sharpen

These three tools, which share the same button in the **Toolbox**, treat your image file a bit like liquid, allowing you to blur, smear or sharpen it.

To access the various tools and reveal the "hidden" buttons, click and hold on the visible button on the **Toolbox**.

The three tools share similar settings on the **Option Bar** – Brush size, hardness and **Strength** (amount) of the blur, smudge or sharpening. (For information on brush settings, see **Brush settings and options**, later in this chapter.)

The Blur Tool

Dragging this tool across your image softens the pixel edges of the area you drag across, blurring them.

The Smudge Tool

This tool treats your image as if it were wet paint. When you drag across it, you smear it!

The Sharpen Tool

The Sharpen Tool increases the contrast between pixels, giving your image a crisper look as you drag across it.

Unlike the **Unsharp Mask** (discussed in **Chapter 7, Correct Color and Lighting**), the **Sharpen Tool** is directed toward specific areas of your image.

The Sponge, Dodge and Burn Tools

These three tools are sometimes referred to as the "darkroom tools" because they're based on techniques photographers sometimes use in the darkroom to enhance their prints. The three tools share similar settings on the **Option Bar** for brush hardness and size.

The Sponge Tool

The Sponge Tool desaturates, or removes color from, an area of your image as you drag over it. (The **Option Bar** includes an option for reversing the process, or increasing color saturation.)

The **Flow** setting on the **Option Bar** determines how much color is removed.

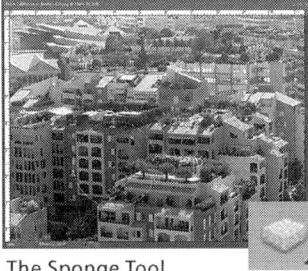

The Sponge Tool desaturates, or removes color from, an area

The Dodge Tool lightens the area you drag across

The Burn Tool darkens the area you drag across

The Dodge Tool

The Dodge Tool lightens the area you drag over, as if it were a photographic print which received less exposure in the darkroom.

The **Option Bar's Exposure** setting designates how intensely the area is dodged.

The Burn Tool

The Burn Tool darkens the area you drag over, as if it were a photographic print which received more exposure in the darkroom.

The **Option Bar's Exposure** setting designates how intensely the area is darkened.

The Brush Tools

The four **Brush Tools** share the same button. To access the four, click and hold on the button in the **Toolbox**.

The Pencil Tool

As the name implies, this is a freehand, hard-edged line drawing tool.

The **Option Bar** for this tool offers settings for the size of the pencil and the opacity of the line. The **Auto-Erase** option allows you to toggle the **Pencil Tool** (with a click of the mouse) between working as a drawing tool and working as an erasing tool.

The Brush Tool

This tool is your basic paintbrush – similar to the **Pencil Tool** as a line drawing tool, except that the **Brush Tool** includes options for painting soft-edged or even textured lines.

The **Option Bar** for this tool includes settings not only for the size and hardness of the brush and the opacity of the paint but also for switching the brush to **Airbrush** mode – which, as you'd expect, paints a stroke that grows more intense the longer you hold it on one spot.

In addition, if you click on the **paintbrush icon** on the **Option Bar**, you'll find an option panel for creating your own brush. See the sidebar on page 55 for more information on brushes and brush settings.

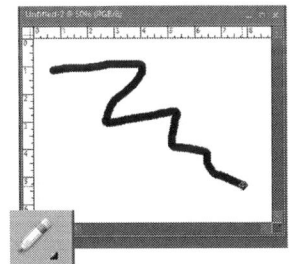

The Pencil Tool draws a hard freehand line.

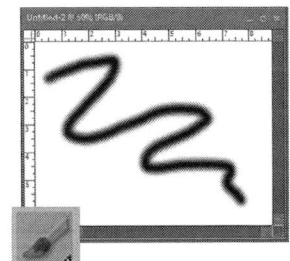

The Brush Tool paints a soft or textured freehand line.

53

The Impressionist Brush swirls your image.

The Color Replacement Brush overlays color, but only over the range of colors you designate.

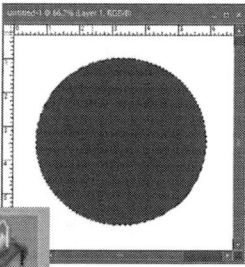

The Paint Bucket fills your canvas or your selected area.

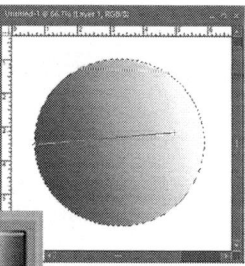

The Gradient Tool

The Impressionist Brush

The **Impressionist Brush** is a pretty cool special effects tool.

When you click and hold or paint with this brush, it "liquefies" and swirls the colors in your image so that it resembles an impressionist painting.

The Color Replacement Brush

The **Color Replacement Brush** replaces the color of an area you "paint" over in your image file with the **Foreground Color** (although, in the **Option Bar**, you can also set it to replace only hue, saturation or luminosity).

Because of the way this brush senses the differences in color ranges within your image, it can, amazingly enough, paint the leaves on a tree but leave the sky alone or even, as illustrated on the left, tint the darker leaves of a tree in the background while leaving the brighter leaves of the tree in the foreground alone!

The **Tolerance** level you have set in the **Option Bar** determines how much distinction there must be between the areas to be re-colored and those left intact.

The Paint Bucket (Fill) Tool

When you drag the **Paint Bucket** to your canvas, it paints your image file with the current **Foreground Color**. It does this in one big, even flow of paint.

If you have a **Selected** area on your canvas or on your image file, the **Paint Bucket Tool** will fill only the selection.

There are two keyboard shortcuts that also fill with color, by the way:

Alt+Backspace will fill a selected area with your **Foreground Color**.

Ctrl+Backspace will fill a selected area with your **Background Color**.

On the **Option Bar** for the **Paint Bucket**, the tool can be set to fill an area with a pattern rather than a color.

The Gradient Tool

The **Gradient Tool** paints your image or selected area with a gradation of one color to another. By default, this gradation will begin with your **Foreground Color** and blend to your **Background Color**.

The **Option Bar** includes presets for color blends other than the default. You can access them from the drop-down menu on this bar.

The **Option Bar** also includes a number of patterns for your gradients, from linear gradients to radial gradients to pattern gradients.

Additionally, the **Option Bar** also includes a setting for **Opacity**, so that you can set whether the gradient covers your image file completely or blends to some degree with the existing image.

Brush settings and options

Many tools behave like brushes. The tool's effects or colors are essentially painted on.

In fact, the size and softness settings on the **Options Bar** for many tools are nearly identical to those of the **Paint Brush Tool**.

There are two basic brush settings: the **Size** of the brush (measured in pixels) and its **Hardness**.

Brush sub-categories, textures and sizes available under the Option Bar.

Hardness determines sharpness of the edge of the stroke that the brush paints. The softer the edge, the more feathered the area between the brushed area and the unbrushed area. When using the **Clone Tool**, for instance, a softer edged brush may show a more natural, less abrupt line between your old and newly-added image areas.

Some brushes, called **Scatter** brushes, create an effect like painting with steel wool. Their effect is scratchy and hard.

Brushes can also have shapes. These oblong shapes (included among the **Calligraphy** presets) will paint a wider line when you are painting one direction than they will another, as when you are writing with a calligraphy pen.

Brushes can even be set to paint **patterns**. When a pattern is selected for a brush, the pattern's image will appear again and again as you paint. This can be used, for instance, to paint several stars across a sky in a single brush stroke or to paint a trail of footprints.

In addition to the over 300 preset brushes you'll find in Photoshop Elements, you can also save your own personal brush settings. To do this, once you've set your brush to the shape and size you want, click on the **>>** menu on the upper right of the brush preset drop-down menu and select the option to **Save Brush**.

You'll be prompted to name your brush. It will then be available in the preset menu for future projects.

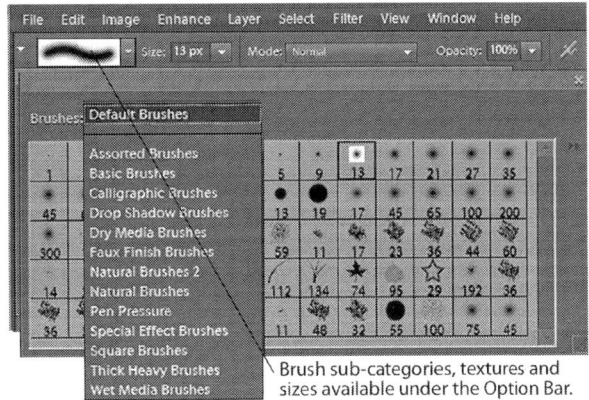

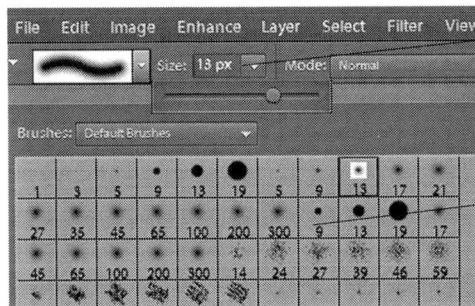

Brush sizes are measured in pixels and can be selected from the presets or set using the slider

Brushes can have soft or hard edges or can even be set to paint patterns

The Smart Brush Tools

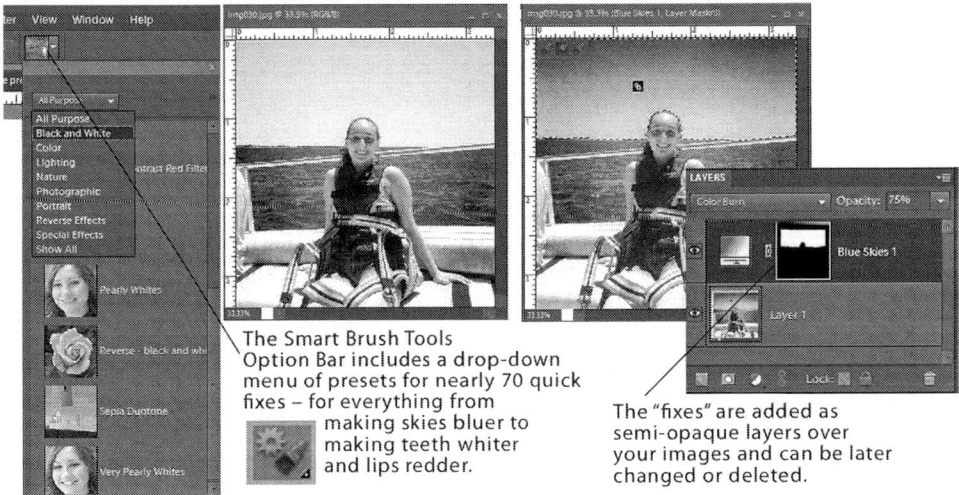

The Smart Brush Tools Option Bar includes a drop-down menu of presets for nearly 70 quick fixes – for everything from making skies bluer to making teeth whiter and lips redder.

The "fixes" are added as semi-opaque layers over your images and can be later changed or deleted.

The **Smart Brush Tool** and the **Details Smart Brush Tool** are part of a great **Quick Fix** tool set built into Photoshop Elements. (Click and hold on the button on the **Toolbox** to toggle between these two tools.)

Both tools work similarly, the main distinction being that the **Details Smart Brush Tool** affects only the area you "paint" with the brush (like the **Selection Brush**), while the **Smart Brush Tool** expands the selected areas of your picture, based on their similarities to the areas you paint (like the **Quick Selection Tool**).

The **Smart Brush Tools** enhance your photos automatically, using presets available under the drop-down menu on the **Option Bar**. These presets will make grass greener, skies bluer, teeth whiter, lipstick redder, etc.

To apply a **Smart** fix, select the appropriate preset from the option bar's drop-down menu, illustrated above, and then paint over the area in your image file that you'd like to add effects to.

When you release your mouse button, the program will automatically make the adjustments to your picture, as in the illustration above.

Using the **+** and **–** brush icons that appear on your image as you work, you can paint to add to or remove from the selected area (or hold down the **Shift** key to add and the **Alt** key to subtract). The program will update the effect automatically.

The true beauty of these adjustments is that they don't permanently change the image itself! If you look at the **Layers** palette, you'll see that these adjustments are actually just masks added as what are called **Adjustment Layers**, as illustrated on above right. By clicking on these **Adjustment Layers**, you can reactivate the **Smart Brush Tools** and make further adjustments, or even delete the **Adjustment Layers** completely. The original image remains unmolested! That is, at least until you flatten the layers or save the file as something other than a PSD file.

The Shape Tools

The **Shape Tools** draw shapes as you drag across your image file. These shapes appear as a new layer on your file, and remain editable until you simplify the layer or flatten your image. (See **Simplify and flatten layers** in **Chapter 8, Work with Photoshop Elements Layers**.)

There are about half a dozen common shapes available under the **Shape Tool** button. You can access and alternate between them by clicking and holding on the button on the **Toolbox**.

If you select the **Custom Shape Tool** option under this button, you will have access to hundreds of more shapes. These custom shapes are available under the drop-down menu on the tool's **Option Bar**, and include everything from basic snowflakes and arrows to cartoon talk bubbles, animals, flowers, faces and ornaments. (To access more than the default shapes on this drop-down menu, click on the flyout menu (>>) button in the upper right corner of the option box.)

When **Add to Shape Area** is selected on the **Option Bar**, you can even combine several shapes to create just about any shape!

Shapes possess some unique characteristics. As you can see, if you look at your **Layers** palette after you've added a shape to your image file, shapes aren't simple raster objects, but are, rather, "masks" with color added to them.

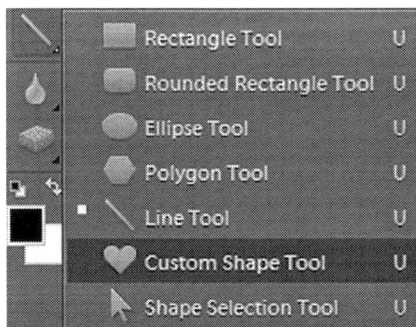

The Shape Tool includes several common shapes, from lines to polygons. The Custom Shape Tool option drop-down menu offers over 550 more, including faces, flowers, plants, animals and funny hairstyles! Each are vector art and can be resized until their shape layer is simplified.

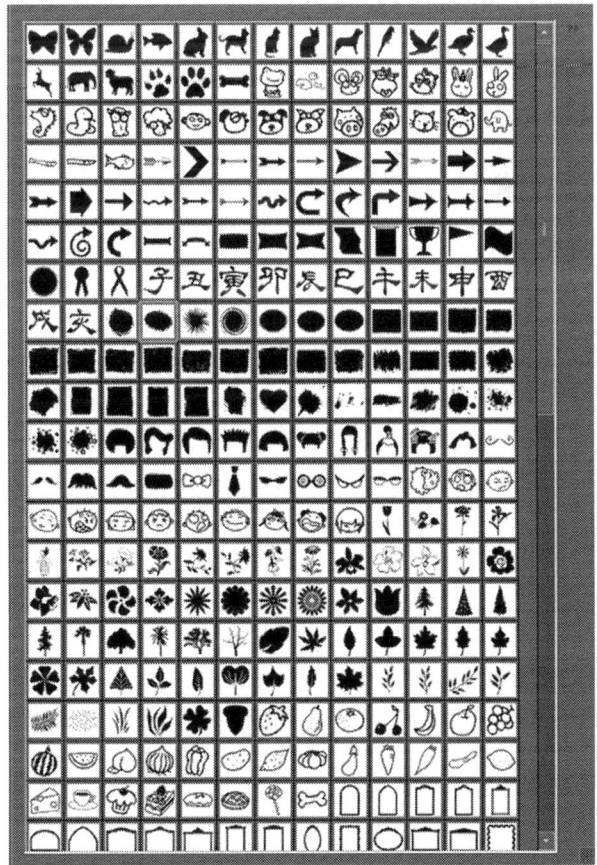

The designers at Adobe have decided to treat shapes this way so that they behave like vector art. In other words, once you've added a shape to your image file, you can resize it and reposition it without any concern for its resolution or pixel depth. You can also re-color it just by double-clicking on the shape in the **Layers** palette and changing its color property.

Some of the common **Shape Tools** have interesting customization settings available on their **Option Bars**:

The Rectangle Tool, Ellipse Tool and Rounded Rectangle Tool

These tools include options for constraining the shape to a perfect square or a circle. Additionally, the **Rounded Rectangle Tool** has an option for setting how round its corners are.

The Polygon Tool

The Polygon Tool has options for setting the number of sides, how round its corners are and if the sides make it a flat-sided polygon or a star.

The Line Tool

The Line Tool includes options for setting its width and if it includes arrowheads on its start and/or end points.

Chapter 5
Select and Isolate Areas in Your Photos
Working with selections

A key function of Photoshop Elements – and one which a number of tools support – is selecting.

Selecting means isolating areas of your image file so that effects can be applied to that area only, without affecting the rest of the image.

Selections can have hard edges or soft. They can be changed and refined and even saved.

Selecting and isolating are true keys to this program's power.

When an area of your image file is selected (surrounded by a moving dotted line), effects and tools applied will only affect the selected area, leaving the rest of your image unchanged.

Why select and isolate?

There are three main reasons for selecting an area of your image file:

1. To **apply an effect** or adjust the color or lighting of one section of your image file without affecting the rest of the image;

2. To **protect areas** of your image file so that, for instance, you can paint or erase a background without touching another area of your image;

3. To **cut an area** of your image file – cutting a person from a photo, for instance – so that you can either paste him or her in another image file or to remove him or her completely.

In **Chapter 4, Get to Know the Photoshop Elements Toolbox**, we discuss a number of tools that can be used to select and isolate areas of your image file.

The **Marquee Tools**, which include the **Rectangular Marquee** and **Elliptical Marquee Tools,** allow you to select a circular or rectangular area of your image file.

The **Lasso Tools**, which include the **Magnetic Lasso, Polygonal Lasso** and freehand **Lasso Tool,** allow you to draw any shape as a selected area.

The **Magic Wand Tool** automatically selects an area of your image that shares a similar color range, based on the tolerance level you've set.

The **Quick Selection Tool** allows you to select an area by "painting" across it, selecting adjacent pixels of similar color as you paint.

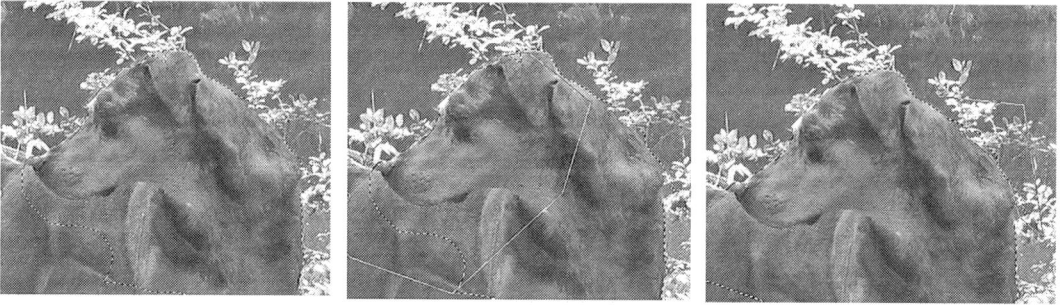

A complicated selection may require several passes with several tools to get it exactly right – using the Add to Selection and Subtract from Selection controls to refine the selected area.

As you select an area, it will appear with a moving, dotted line surrounding it – commonly referred to as "marching ants." As we discuss in the individual descriptions of each tool in **Chapter 4**, the selection tools can be used in combination with each other – while selecting the **Add to Selection** and **Subtract from Selection** options – to create or refine any shape of selection.

Feathering

Selection tools usually include an option to **"feather"** your selection. **Feathering** means softening the edges of the selection.

For instance, if you were to use the **Elliptical Marquee Tool** to select an area of your image file, this selection would be, by default, a perfect oval or circle, with a clearly defined, hard edge.

But in a number of situations, you'd like that edge softer.

A "feathered" selection has a softer edge so that, when the selection is removed or an effect is added to it, the distinction between the selected and unselected area of your image is a gradation rather than a solid line.

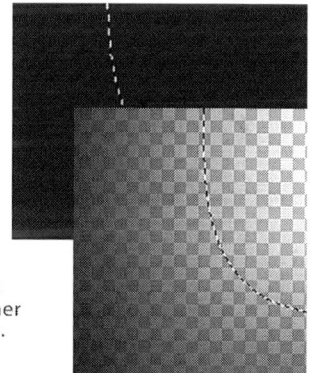

If you're applying an effect to a selected area in a photograph, for instance, you might like the boundary between the affected area and the non-affected area to be softly defined. This can make the effect seem more natural than a hard, abrupt edge might.

Also, when you're cutting a subject from one photo in order to paste him or her into another, a slight feathering around the edge can help blend the pasted image so that it fits more naturally into the new background.

Feathering is measured in pixels. This means that, when working with a low-resolution image, you'll need fewer pixels in your feathering than you will in a higher-resolution image to achieve a similar softened edge effect.

Feathering also plays a role in the **Refine Edge** function, as we discuss later in this chapter.

The Option Bar for each Selection Tool includes settings for adding to or subtracting from your selected areas.

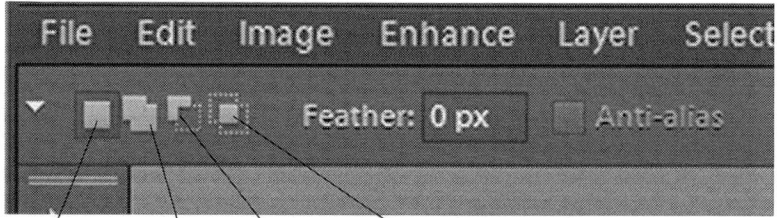

File Edit Image Enhance Layer Select

Feather: 0 px Anti-alias

New Selection
(Default)

Add to Selection
(or hold down
Shift key)

Remove from
Selection (or
hold down
Alt key)

Select Intersection
of old and new
selections

You can add to an already selected area by clicking on the **Add to Selection** button on the **Option Bar,** or by holding down the **Shift** key as you continue to select.

You can remove an area from your selection by clicking the **Subtract from Selection** button on the **Option Bar** or by holding down the **Alt/ Option** key as you select.

You can refine your selection so that it includes only the area overlapped by your current and new selections by clicking the **Intersect with Selection** button on the **Option Bar.**

As you build your selected area, two other keyboard shortcuts are worth noting:

To go back a step at any point in the program – even deselecting the most recent area you've selected or removed from your selection – press **Ctrl+z** (⌘+z on a Mac) or click the **Undo** button in the upper right of the interface.

To deselect an area completely, press **Ctrl+d** on a PC or ⌘+d on a Mac.

The Select drop-down menu

The **Select** drop-down on the Menu Bar offers a number of solutions for refining and changing your selected area.

Select Filter View W
All   Ctrl+A
Deselect   Ctrl+D
Reselect   Shift+Ctrl+D
Inverse   Shift+Ctrl+I

All Layers
Deselect Layers
Similar Layers

Feather...   Alt+Ctrl+D
Refine Edge...
Modify

Grow
Similar

Transform Selection

Load Selection...
Save Selection...
Delete Selection...

Select All (**Ctrl+a** on a PC or ⌘+a on a Mac) selects your entire displayed image. If you are working on a layered file, you will select only the image that appears on the active layer. (For more information, see **Chapter 8, Working with Layers.**)

Deselect (**Ctrl+d** or ⌘+d) deselects all of your selections.

Reselect (**Ctrl+Shift+d** or ⌘+Shift+d) re-selects all that you've just deselected – in case you suddenly change your mind.

Inverse (**Ctrl+Shift+i** or ⌘+Shift+i) switches your selection so that the areas you currently have unselected become your selected areas and vice versa.

Feather (**Ctrl+Alt+d** or ⌘+Option+d) allows you to apply feathering, after the fact, to the currently selected area.

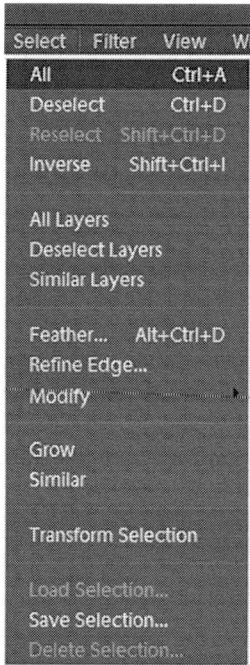

All Layers and **Selected Layers** expand your current selection to other layers in your image file, if you are working on a layered file.

Grow expands your selected area to similarly colored adjacent pixels in your image file, based on your current selection.

Similar selects all similarly colored pixels throughout your image file, whether they are adjacent to your current selection or not.

Refine the edge of your selection

Once you've selected an area in your image file, you can refine the edge of the selection by selecting **Refine Edge** under **Select** on the Menu Bar. This is a great tool for softening the hard edges of your selection to make them seem more natural and less abrupt. The three settings are:

Smooth. This determines how detailed your selection is. The higher you set **Smooth**, the more the fine details in the edge of your selected area will be rounded out.

Feather. As discussed above, feathering softens the boundary between the selected and unselected areas, giving sometimes a more natural, less abrupt edge to your selection.

Contract/Expand adds or removes a few extra pixels from around the edge of your selection. This can be helpful if, for instance, you're cutting a person from a background and, in your current selection, some of the background is still showing around the edges. **Contract/Expand** and **Feather** are often used in combination to refine a very clean, natural edge.

If you have **Preview** checked in the option box, your selection will be updated live as you adjust the settings.

The **Overlay Preview** option displays your photo with a temporary red mask over it, giving you a preview, of sorts, of what your selected area will look like when isolated or removed from the rest of the image. The overlay, of course, is for preview only, and will not appear once you've **OK**ed your **Refine Edge** settings.

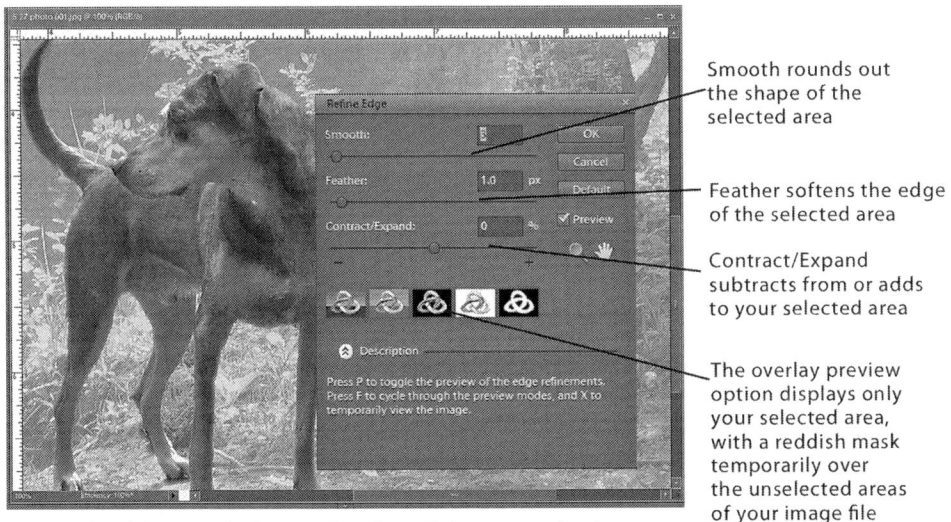

Smooth rounds out the shape of the selected area

Feather softens the edge of the selected area

Contract/Expand subtracts from or adds to your selected area

The overlay preview option displays only your selected area, with a reddish mask temporarily over the unselected areas of your image file

The Refine Edge panel offers options for refining your selection.

By drawing a selection around the dog, I can isolate him – applying, for instance, color correction to him only, not affecting the background

When I reverse the selection (by selecting Inverse from the Select menu) – my selection becomes everything in the image file *except* the dog. I am now able to apply effects or use brushes – I can even paint a new background with the Clone Tool – affecting everything in the photo *except* the unselected dog!

Work with selected areas

A key reason to select an area of a photo is so that an effect can be applied to the area you've isolated without affecting the rest of your image file.

In the example above, for instance, the dog in the original picture is too green. However, we'd prefer that any color corrections we make affect the dog only, and leave the rest of the picture as is.

Using a combination of tools – adding to and subtracting from my selection and then refining the edges – I isolated the dog. I was then able to make color changes to the dog only, without affecting any other part of my image file.

I then inversed the selection (choosing **Inverse** from the **Select** menu) so that the background was selected and the dog was not. Using the **Clone Tool**, I painted in more foliage behind the dog. Because the background was selected and the dog was not, the **Clone Tool** added these trees and leaves right around the dog, as if he was not even there!

Cut and paste a selection into another photo

As you work with Photoshop Elements, you will likely be doing a lot of cutting and pasting. This is, for instance, a simple way to take a person photographed in front of one background and place him or her in front of another.

To cut your subject from a background, draw a selection around him or her by using a combinations of tools – adding to and subtracting from your selection as needed. (If your subject is well defined from the background, you may be able to do most of this with the **Magic Wand Tool**, using the other selection tools and the **Add to Selection** or **Subtract from Selection** options.)

Then, to ensure your selection has a slightly softened, natural edge, use **Refine Edge** to **Contract/Expand** and **Feather** it.

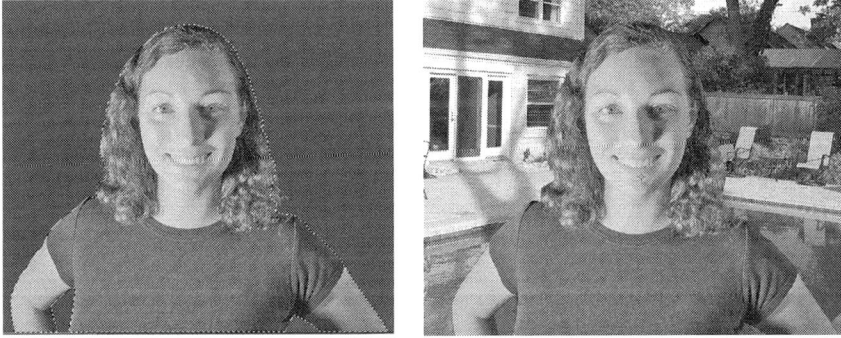

Because she was shot against a green screen, the young woman is easily selected by selecting the background with the Magic Wand Tool and then inversing the selection. She is then pasted over the pool background.

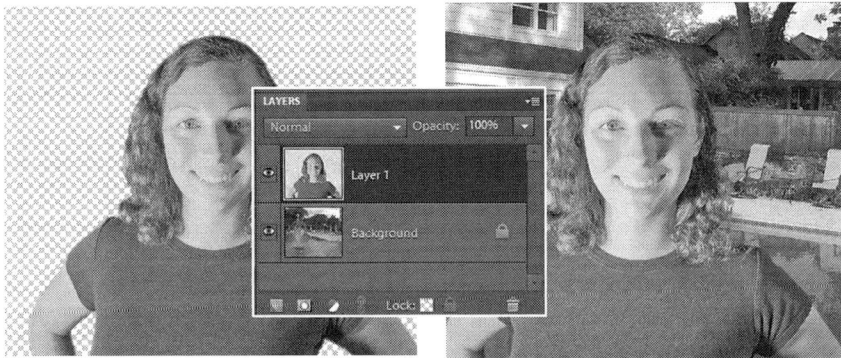

Because pasting places her on a layer, her image can be refined separately – the edges can be softened and she can be tinted to match the background more naturally.

To cut your subject from his or her current background, press **Ctrl+c** on a PC or ⌘+**c** on a Mac.

Open a photo file that you'd like to use as your subject's new background. To paste your subject into this new background press **Ctrl+v** on a PC or ⌘+**v** on a Mac.

Whenever you paste an image into another image file, it will appear as a new layer in that file, as seen in the illustration on the previous page. (In fact, even if you paste the image into the *same* image file you cut it from it will become a new layer.)

This is to your advantage for a number of reasons:

1. If you need to, you can continue to refine the edge of your pasted-in image so that it fits more naturally with its new background (even using the **Eraser Tool**, if you'd like, to remove more of the image). A very effective feature for adding a more natural edge to your pasted image is the **Defringe Layer** tool, which we discuss in **Chapter 7, Correct Color and Lighting**;

2. While it remains a layer, you can resize the pasted-in image separate from the rest of the image file.

Resizing a layer is very easy in Photoshop Elements.

When a layer is selected (by clicking on it to activate it in the **Layers** palette), it appears in your image file outlined in a dotted line, defined on each side and on the corners with a "corner handle." (If your layer image is larger than your current image file, these corner handles may appear outside of the image file, and you may need to **Ctrl+⁻** on a PC or ⌘+⁻ on a Mac to see these handles.)

To resize the image on your selected layer, click and drag on these corner handles.

As you drag the corner handles, you may notice that the **Option Bar**, along the top of the interface, displays a number of **Transform** options. Using these transform options, you can resize or rotate your layer's image precisely by typing numbers into the spaces on the **Option Bar**.

If **Constrain Proportions** is checked, your image will resize its height and width proportionately – which is usually what you'll prefer. If you turn off **Constrain Proportions**, you will resize the layer's height and width separately, resulting in a squeezed or disportionate picture.

To finish the resizing, click the green checkmark on your image file or press the **Enter** key.

(While you're in resizing image mode, no other functions in Photoshop Elements will work. So, if you find after resizing your image that no other tool will activate, press **Enter** or click on the green checkmark to complete the resizing.)

If you're enlarging your layer's image by dragging the corner handles, keep in mind the golden rule of raster art: *You can't add pixels where they don't exist.*

You can expand the size of your image only so far before the pixels will begin to break up and your image will appear fuzzy or pixelated. For this reason, it's best to cut and paste between image files that are of similar size and resolution.

Your layer will remain a layer until you flatten your layers or save your file as a file format other than a Photoshop (**PSD**) file. (For information on flattening a layered image see **Chapter 8, Work with Photoshop Elements Layers**.)

Fill or stroke a selection

Any area that's selected can also be filled or stroked. In fact, even a selected area on an otherwise blank layer can be filled or stroked.

Filling means painting the selected area with color or a pattern

A selected area can be filled in any one of a number of ways:

1. Dragging the **Paint Bucket Tool** onto the selected area. The selection will then be filled with the **Foreground Color**.

2. Selecting the **Gradient Tool** and dragging a line across the selection. The selection will be filled with a gradation of the **Foreground** to **Background Color** (or however you've defined your gradient), colored from the beginning to the end of the line you've drawn.

The option to stroke a selection is under the Edit drop-down menu.

Even when a blank layer is selected on your canvas, a stroke can be added to your selected area, outlining it with your Foreground Color or any custom color.

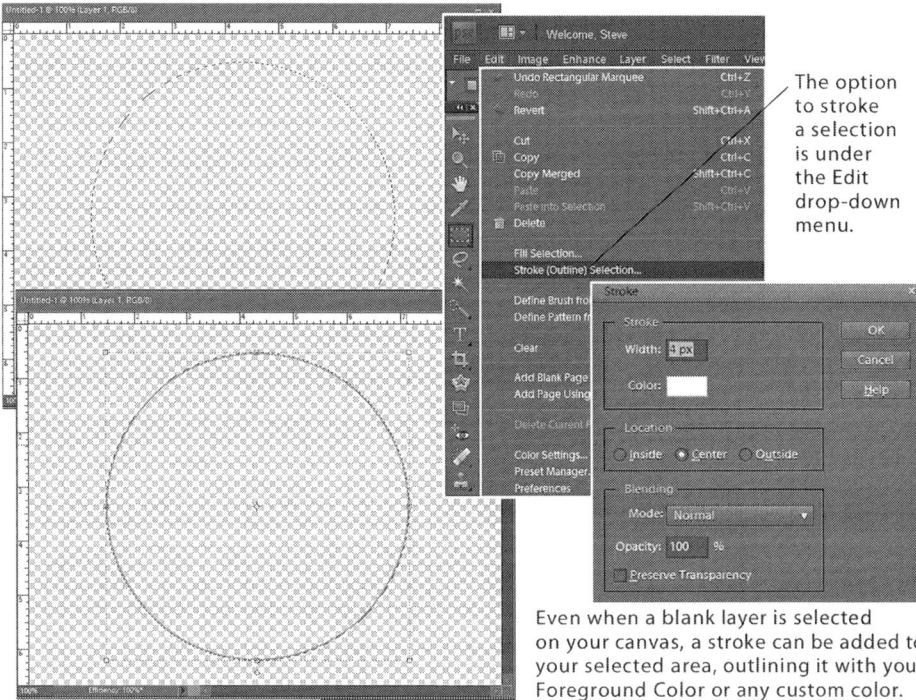

3. Pressing **Alt/Option+Backspace**. The selection will be filled with the **Foreground Color**.

4. Pressing **Ctrl+Backspace** (or ⌘+**Backspace** on a Mac). The selection will be filled with the **Background Color**.

5. Selecting the **Fill Selection** option from the **Edit** drop-down on the Menu Bar.

   The **Fill** option panel offers a number of possible ways for filling your selection, including: with the **Foreground Color, Background Color** or a custom color; black, white or gray; or a **Custom Pattern** from the dozens of patterns available in the pattern library.

The Paint Bucket fills your canvas or your selected area.

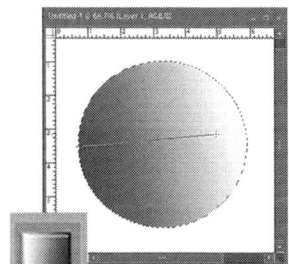

Stroking means outlining a selected area.

A selected area can be stroked by selecting **Stroke (Outline) Selection** from the **Edit** drop-down on the Menu Bar.

By default, the stroke color will be the current **Foreground Color**. However, by clicking on the color swatch square on the **Stroke** option panel, you can launch the **Color Picker** (See **Chapter 4**), from which you can select any color for your stroke.

The width of the stroke is measured in pixels, by default. And you may set the stroke to appear just outside your selected area (**Outside**), on your selection line (**Center**) or just inside the selection line (**Inside**).

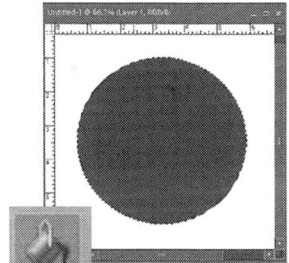

The Gradient Tool fills your canvas or selected area with (by default) a gradation from the Foreground to the Background Colors.

Chapter 6

Resize Your Images
Image and canvas sizes

Resizing can mean a number of different things in Photoshop Elements.

- You may want to enlarge or reduce the overall size of your image file.

- You may want to enlarge or reduce the canvas your image appears on.

- You may want to trim the edges off your image by cropping.

Each of these functions has methods and challenges for getting the best results.

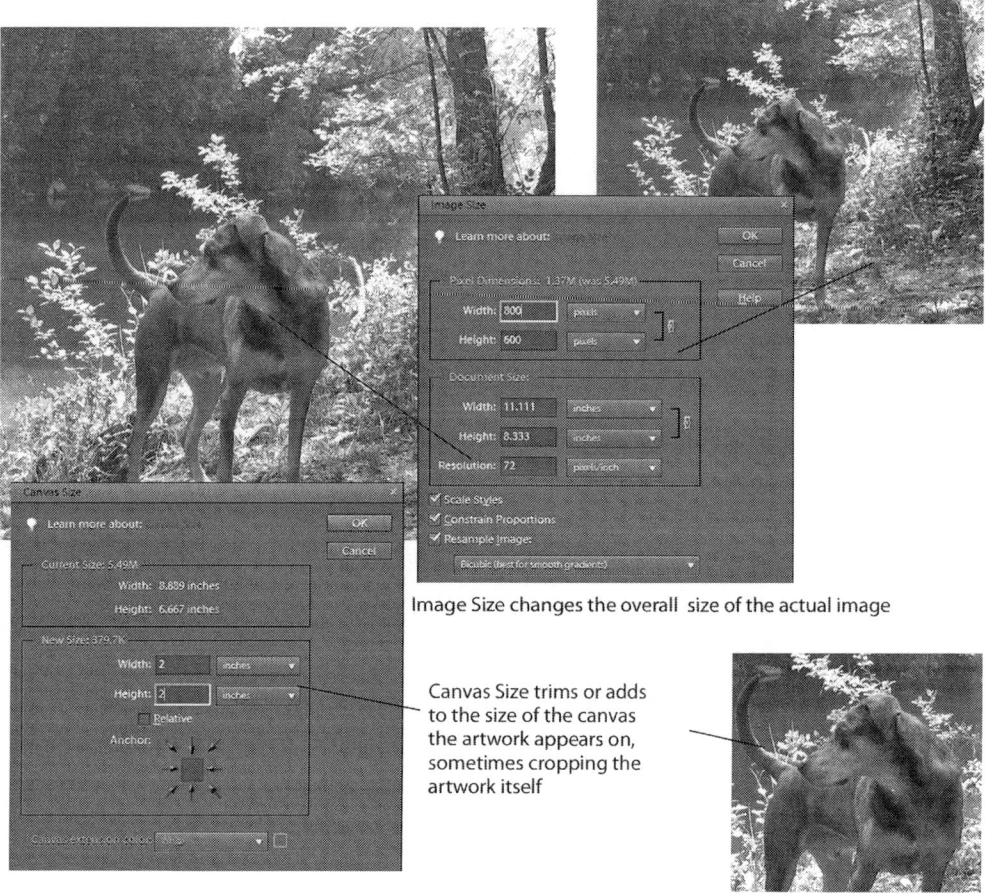

Image Size changes the overall size of the actual image

Canvas Size trims or adds
to the size of the canvas
the artwork appears on,
sometimes cropping the
artwork itself

Image Size vs. Canvas Size

As we discussed in **Chapter 1, Learn the Basics**, there is a key difference
between **Image Size** and **Canvas Size**.

Image Size is the overall size of your image file. Changing the
Image Size changes the size of the entire image file without
removing or adding to its basic content. In other words, in
changing the **Image Size** of your photograph of a city skyline, the
content of the picture will remain essentially the same. The entire
skyline image will remain. Only the size and/or resolution of the
image file will change.

Canvas Size refers to the size of the *canvas*, or background,
your image appears on. Changing the **Canvas Size** changes
the *content* of the image file, adding to or subtracting from
(essentially either cropping or adding to) the image itself.
Reducing the **Canvas Size** of the photograph of the city skyline,
for instance, will *chop off* the edges of the image itself without
changing the size or resolution of the imagery.

Cropping is a form of changing the **Canvas Size**. When you crop an image, you don't change the size or resolution of the content. You merely trim the canvas. (For more information on cropping, see **Crop Tools** in **Chapter 4, The Photoshop Elements Toolbox**.)

Both **Image Size** and **Canvas Size** are available under the **Image** drop-down on the Menu Bar, listed under the **Resize** options.

You can't create pixels!

This is a principle we repeat several times in this book.

Your image file is made up of pixels – thousands or even millions of little boxes of color. You can't create pixels where none exist. You can't add more resolution to a low resolution image.

Well, *sometimes* you can. But mostly you can't. And it's never a good idea to try.

See, when you add to the **Image Size** of a file – increasing a 640x480 pixel image to 800x600 pixels, for instance – you're essentially telling the program to create more pixels for that image. Photoshop Elements will do its best to oblige – but it can't work miracles. So what the program does is create new pixels by duplicating existing pixels.

This works to a certain extent. (A rule of thumb is that it will work somewhat effectively for up to about a 10% increase in size.) But, since the result will simply be made of *duplicated* pixels, your image will be larger – but you won't get any more detail.

In fact, if you increase your image's size too much, your image will eventually just look fuzzy and pixelated. (Officially, "over-rezzed.")

Remember that those little blocks of color can only get so big before they start to show. And, if you've ever downloaded a photo or a logo from a web site and then tried to enlarge it and print it, you know exactly what I mean. There's no magic way to increase detail where none exists.

However, there may well be times when you need to *cheat* your image resolution just a bit. Force it up in size – maybe 10%. Going from 640x480 to 700x525 pixels, for instance. And when you do, Photoshop Elements allows you to set *how* it creates these new pixels for the best possible results. This process is called **Resample Image**, and we discuss it in **Image Resizing**, on the following page.

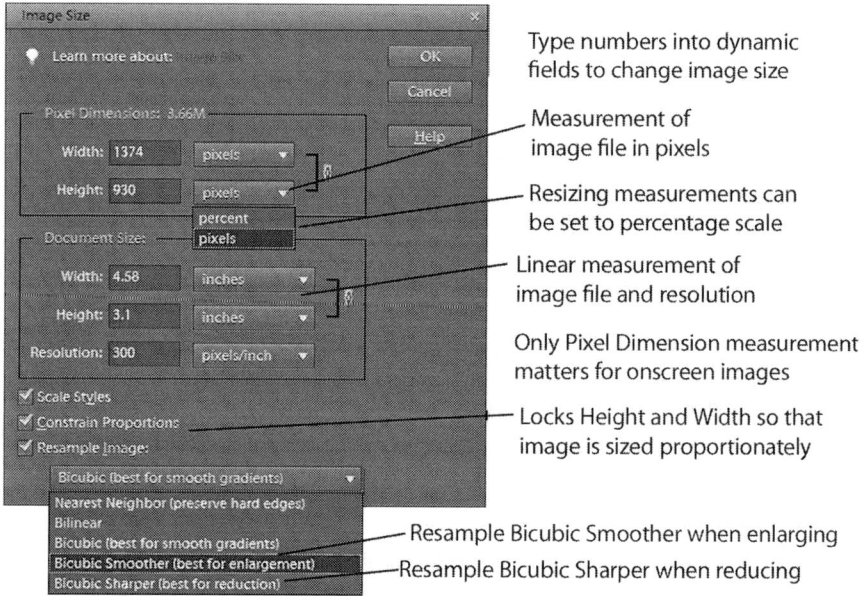

Type numbers into dynamic fields to change image size

Measurement of image file in pixels

Resizing measurements can be set to percentage scale

Linear measurement of image file and resolution

Only Pixel Dimension measurement matters for onscreen images

Locks Height and Width so that image is sized proportionately

Resample Bicubic Smoother when enlarging

Resample Bicubic Sharper when reducing

Image Resizing

The option panel for resizing an image is launched by selecting **Image Size** under **Image** on the Menu Bar, under the **Resize** sub-menu.

Resizing an image means increasing or reducing the size or resolution of the image file itself, usually without substantially changing the photographic content of that image.

In other words, resizing a photograph of a scene from 2048x1536 pixels (the size of an image from a 3 megapixel camera) to 640x480 pixels (the size, in square pixels, of a video frame) reduces the file size, details and resolution of the photo, but it does not change the essential scene in the photograph itself.

The **Image Size** option screen displays the size of your image file in pixels as well as in linear measurements (inches, centimeters, etc.). It also includes a resolution setting, listed in **Pixels per Inch** (or centimeters, etc.). (For more information on picture resolution, see **Resolution** in **Chapter 1, Learn the Basics**.)

The information listed on the **Image Size** option panel is:

Pixel Dimensions is a measurement of your image file's size, an actual count of the number of pixels (**Width** and **Height**) that make up your image file.

As we discussed in **Chapter 1, Learn the Basics**, if you're working on photos or graphics for video or for the Web, these **Pixel Dimensions** are the *only* measurements that you really need to be concerned with. Linear measurements, including resolution, are meaningless in the onscreen image world.

Document Size is a measurement of your image file in inches, centimeters, points, picas, etc. (the drop-down menu next to each number allows you to change the measurement method), as well as resolution.

If you are producing photos and graphics for print, these three measurements are very important, since stretching, or "over-rezzing," an image beyond its actual size can produce a poor quality or fuzzy picture. All three numbers are important in the print world because, to produce a relatively clean print image, your photo or graphic will need at least 150-200 pixels per inch and 300 or more p.p.i. for a very high-quality print.

Changing the Image Size changes the size of the photo itself without affecting content.

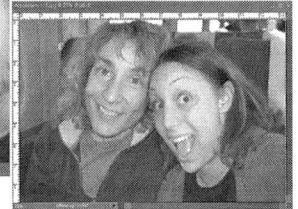

These measurements are all dynamic fields, and you can change the size of your image by typing new numbers into the boxes. (The **Pixel Dimensions** fields, in fact, can be changed from **pixel** measurements to **percentages** so that you can accurately re-scale your image.)

The **Image Size** option panel also includes a number of checkboxes that play important roles in your image resizing.

Scale Styles. This checkbox applies to any styles or effects you've added to your image file. (**Drop Shadows**, for instance.) When this box is checked, the size of the **effect** is changed, proportionately, as your image file is resized. I recommend leaving it checked.

Constrain Proportions. When checked, this feature automatically calculates the **Width** to match whatever **Height** you type in (or vice versa) in order to keep your image file proportionate. This is another box I recommend you keep checked.

Resample Image. Resampling is a vital function of resizing. Resampling is how Photoshop Elements creates new pixels when you enlarge an image, and how it averages pixel information when you reduce an image 's size.

If this box is unchecked, with the **Nearest Neighbor** option set, you will not be able to dynamically change your **Pixel Dimensions**. I very much recommend you leave this box checked when you are resizing your images.

The **Resample Image** drop-down menu offers a number of options for resampling your image's pixels when you resize a file. Only two are really of value for the vast majority of your work.

Bicubic Sharper. When you are **reducing** an image file's size, select this resampling method. This creates the cleanest-looking reduced image.

Bicubic Smoother. When **enlarging** an image file, select this resampling method. As we've said, there are limits to how much you can increase the size of any image file – but the **Bicubic Smoother** will create the smoothest and most natural blends of color among the new pixels it creates.

Photoshop Elements also includes a function for batch-resizing a number of photos or image files at once. For more information on batching processes, see **Process Multiple Files** in **Chapter 12, Utilize Advanced Photoshop Elements Tools**.

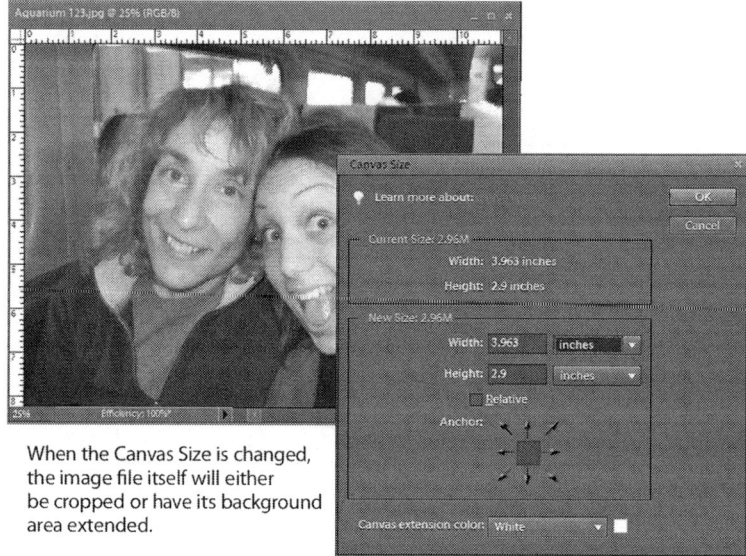

When the Canvas Size is changed, the image file itself will either be cropped or have its background area extended.

Canvas Resizing

The option panel for resizing your image's canvas is launched by selecting **Canvas Size** under **Image** on the Menu Bar, under the **Resize** sub-menu.

The "canvas" is the image file itself, the canvas on which your imagery exists. When you reduce or enlarge the canvas for a photo, you are adding more to the sides or cropping from the size of the image file.

This tool is particularly effective for changing the shape (aspect ratio) of your image file.

The **Canvas Size** option panel displays the dimensions of your image file.

The **New Size** area of this panel contains two dynamic measurement listings, which you can write over. Using the drop-downs, you can set the measurements for these dimensions to any of the standards available in Photoshop Elements. For video, web or other onscreen graphic or photo, you will want to set these measurement standards to **Pixels**.

Though the most common way to resize your canvas is to designate what you want its new **Height** or **Width** to be, you can also simply designate how much you want removed instead. Checking the **Relative** option allows you to designate precisely the amount of your canvas that will be added or removed when it is resized. In other words, if you check **Relative** and set the **Width** to -20 pixels, 20 pixels will be cropped from the width of your canvas.

The **Anchor** area of this panel displays a square with arrows that point up, down, right, left and from each corner of the square. This **Anchor** setting represents how and from where your image canvas will be added to or subtracted from when you resize it – as indicated by the directions its arrows point.

In other words, if you were to set the **Anchor** so that the arrows point down and to the right, increasing the size of the canvas would add space *below and to the right* of your current image.

Likewise, if you were to set the **Anchor** so that the arrows point down and to the right and then *decrease* the size of your canvas, your image would be resized by cropping from the *bottom right* of your image file.

Because the Anchor is set to the lower right corner, the reduced Canvas Size crops from the upper left of the image file.

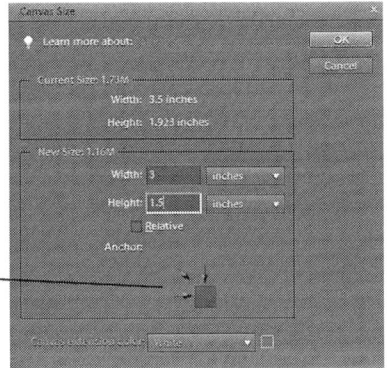

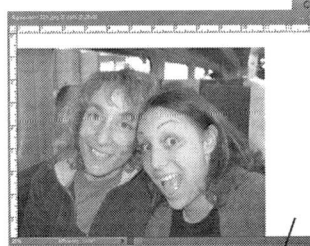

Each of these arrows determines which area of your canvas will be affected by the changes to the **Height** or **Width**.

If no arrow is selected, the tool will crop from or add to your canvas equally, around all sides.

By default, any canvas added to your image file will appear in the **Background Color**. However, the **Canvas Extension Color** drop-down menu at the bottom of this option panel allows you to set the added canvas to appear in the **Foreground Color**, black, white, gray or any other custom color.

Because the Anchor is set at the lower left corner of the image, increasing the Canvas Size adds "canvas" to the upper and right side of the file.

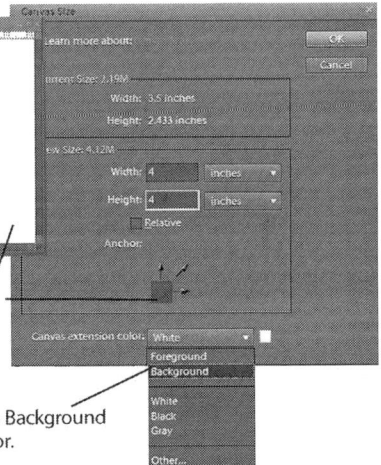

Added canvas is, by default, the Background Color, but can be set to any color.

Auto Fixing Your Photos

Adjusting Brightness & Contrast

Adjusting Color

Adjusting Sharpness

Adjustment Layers

Chapter 7

Correct Color and Lighting
Adjust and clean up your images

Under the Enhance drop-down menu, Photoshop Elements includes a number of tools for cleaning up, correcting color and adjusting the lighting of your image files.

Many of these tools are based on advanced tools in the professional version of Photoshop. Others are more simplified "quick fixes."

Whether your goal is to clean up your photos or to change the colors in your image files to produce a special effect, there's likely an adjustment tool for your general or specific need.

Auto Fixes

Under the **Enhance** drop-down on the Menu Bar, there are six automatic fixes for your image files. In many cases, an automatic fix may be the easiest way to correct your photo's lighting and color.

But remember that automatic fixes are just math, not magic. Automatic fixes merely look at the lightest spot in your image file and assume it should be pure white, then look at the darkest spot in your image file and assume it should be pure black – and then they calculate the rest of the image's color and light values as a range between them.

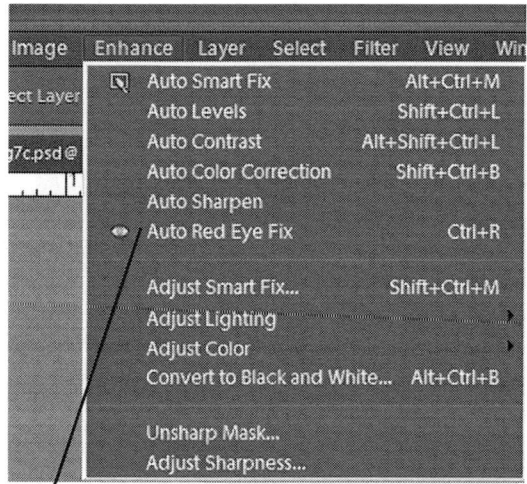

Photoshop Elements includes a number of "auto" fixes under the Enhance drop-down for correcting color and lighting.

So, although in many cases, auto fixes can be very effective – they're still just a best guess. And, depending on the results, you may want to move on to manual adjustments from there or even **Ctrl+z** to undo the fix and do it entirely manually.

Virtually every auto fix has a manual adjustment alternative.

The six automatic fixes are:

Auto Smart Fix. A good, general automatic fix, correcting for poor exposure, contrast problems, color balance and color saturation in a single sweep.

Auto Levels considers the luminance values of red, green and blue in calculating its best color and lighting adjustments.

Auto Contrast considers only the brightness and contrast levels in calculating its best guess settings, without regard to the image file's colors.

Auto Color Correction focuses on the mid-tones in the image, correcting the image file's color by presuming the middle range of colors as gray and balancing the other colors based on that. Unlike **Auto Levels**, **Auto Color Correction** does not look at the individual color channels but judges the colors of the image file as an overall mix.

Auto Sharpen increases the contrast between pixels, which can make a photo appear clearer, sharper or more focused.

Auto Red Eye Fix uses its best guess to locate "red eyes" on the people in your photos and then darken and desaturate them.

Control what gets changed

When an area of your image file is selected (defined by "marching ants"), any changes made to color or lightness will affect *only* the area within the selection.

The color and lighting adjustments you make to your image files may be applied to the entire file or to isolated areas of your file. You may, for instance, want to brighten or adjust the color of a person in the foreground of a photo but not change the color or lighting for the background. Or you may want to make the sky bluer in a picture but keep the grass a rich green.

There are three ways to control how and where your effects are applied in your image files:

1. **Selection**. As we discuss in **Chapter 5, Select and Isolate Areas in Your Photos**, when you select an area in your image file, only that area will be changed by any added effects or adjustments. This is far and away the most common way to control what areas of your image files are affected.

2. **Brushes**. As we discuss in **Chapter 4, The Photoshop Elements Toolbox**, a number of tools are designed for applying effects only to certain areas of your image file. These tools are in the form of brushes. With brushes you "paint" the effect onto only certain, specific areas of your image file.

    An example of this is the **Red Eye Removal Tool,** which darkens and desaturates only the area you brush – removing the bright red reflections from your subject's eyes.

    Other examples would be the **Dodge** and **Burn Tools**, which allow you to lighten or darken specific spots of your image file. Brushes, as we explained in **Chapter 4,** can be large and wide or very small and fine, and may have hard edges or soft, feathered edges.

3. **Layers**. As we discuss in **Chapter 8, Work With Photoshop Elements Layers**, unless you specifically direct Photoshop Elements to affect several layers at once, any changes you make to an active layer in a layered image file will apply *only* to that layer. As we demonstrate in **Cutting, pasting and layers** in **Chapter 5, Select and Isolate Areas in Your Photos**, this is a very useful function as you work to match a person who has been cut and pasted from another document onto a new background.

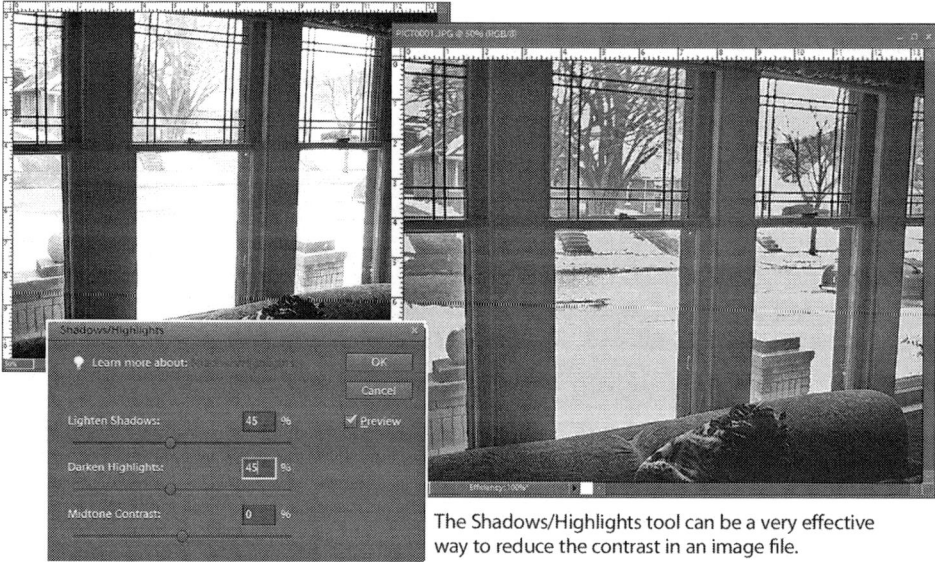

The Shadows/Highlights tool can be a very effective way to reduce the contrast in an image file.

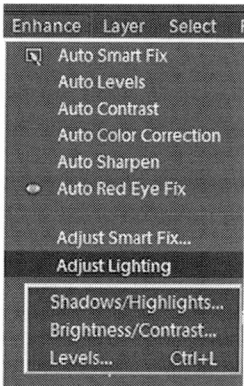

Adjust Lighting

Certainly the most basic adjustments you'll make to your photos will be to adjust their brightness and contrast. As with all adjustments you can make in Photoshop Elements, there are simplified and complex tools for making these adjustments. The more complicated the adjustment, the more control you will have over the results.

These functions are located under **Enhance** on the menu bar, in the **Adjust Lighting** sub-menu.

Brightness/Contrast

As basic an adjustment as you'll find in Photoshop Elements, **Brightness** lightens or darkens your photo while **Contrast** determines the difference between the blackest blacks and whitest whites in your image file.

Shadows/Highlights

A personal favorite, this great tool has saved many photos for me. Basically, it decreases the contrast in your image file by enhancing the midtones, as illustrated above. This would be helpful if, for instance, you have a photo of a bird in flight, which appears as just a dark silhouette against the bright sky. The tool reduces the contrast between bird and sky and brings out details in the bird that would otherwise be indiscernible. It's great for bringing out details in an image shot on a very sunny or snowy day, a photo with such high contrasts that its lights are too light and its darks are too dark.

Levels

In my opinion, **Levels** really is more of a *color* adjustment than a lighting adjustment. In fact, it's my favorite go-to tool for color correcting an image file.

The Levels histogram displays a count of all of the pixels in your image file, graphed by level. It can be set to display the color mix or only the red, green or blue channel.

Darkest point

Midtone center

Whitest point

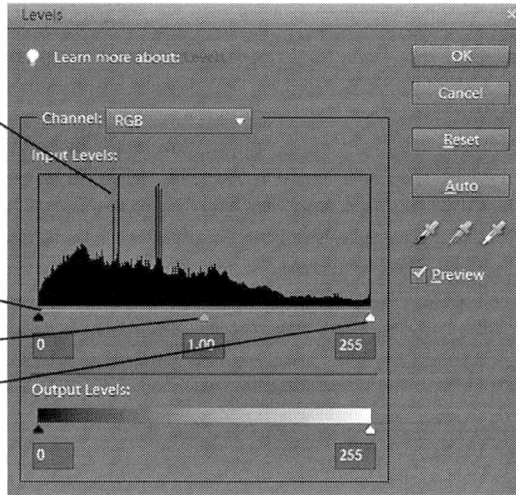

The histogram on the **Levels** option screen (as seen to the left) maps the pixels in your image from darkest to lightest.

By moving the arrows on either end of the histogram in or out, you define the darkest dark and lightest light points in your image file. The middle arrow defines the center midtone. The **Output Levels** widen the distance between dark and light. In essence, then, this is a more precise way to set your brightness and contrast.

But you can go even deeper in your adjustments on this Levels screen. If you drop down the **Channel** menu at the top of the panel, you'll see that you can set these levels for each individual color also. This makes this tool one way to, say, lower the amount of red in a photo or increase the amount of blue.

The **Levels** tool also makes a great color correction tool, as we discuss in the sidebar on page 83.

Smart Fixes and Guided Fixes

Smart Fixes are semi-automatic fixes to color and lighting that Photoshop Elements applies to your image file. These include "red eye" fixes, fixes for enriching the color of the sky or whitening teeth and many simplified and automatic fixes for correcting color and light.

Guided Fixes, as the name implies, are adjustments that are automatically applied to your image file as you work through a list of options.

These fixes are available in both the Editor and Organizer workspaces.

We discuss them and how to use them in greater detail in **Chapter 3, Apply Quick Fixes and Guided Fixes**.

Preview changes

When Preview is checked on any adjustment panel, you will see a preview of any adjustments to your image file.

When you launch an option screen for any adjustment or effect, you may notice a checkbox labeled **Preview** on the screen. **Previewing** allows you to see, in real time, how your adjustments will affect your final image.

When this function is enabled, your image file will temporarily display any changes or adjustments you make.

Additionally, by checking and unchecking the **Preview** option as you make your adjustments, you can do a before-and-after comparison of your changes.

If you click **OK**, these changes will be permanently applied to your image file. If you click **Cancel**, your changes will not be applied.

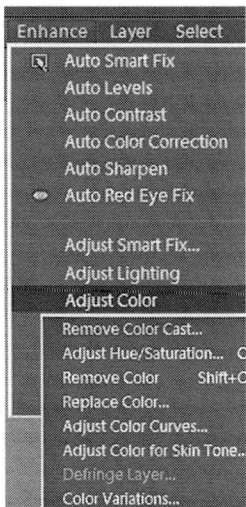

Adjust Color

As every photographer knows, there's almost no such thing as perfect lighting. Natural sunlight tends toward blue while indoor lighting tends toward yellow, and even the best cameras can have a problem adjusting their white balance for every situation. Fortunately, Photoshop Elements offers a number of tools for adjusting and correcting color.

These tools are available under **Enhance** on the Menu Bar, under the **Adjust Color** sub-menu.

Remove Color Cast

This tool is a smart fix that bases its color correction calculations on a single point that you define. To use it, click on the eyedropper on the panel and then click on a spot on your image file that you'd like to appear as either pure white, pure black or pure gray. The tool will then automatically adjust all the other colors in the image based on that definition.

Adjust Hue/Saturation

Hue is the tint of a color, its levels based on the 360 degrees of a color wheel.

Saturation is the amount of color. (The opposite of saturation is no color, or black & white.)

Lightness is how dark or light the color is.

Adjust Hue/Saturation is probably less effective as a color correction tool than it is as a color *changing* tool. But it does serve as an alternative to adjusting your image's colors based on red, green and blue values.

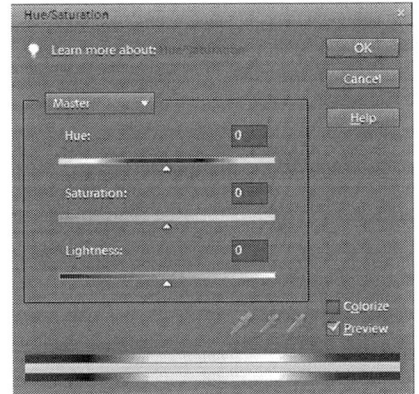

Use Levels to color correct a photo

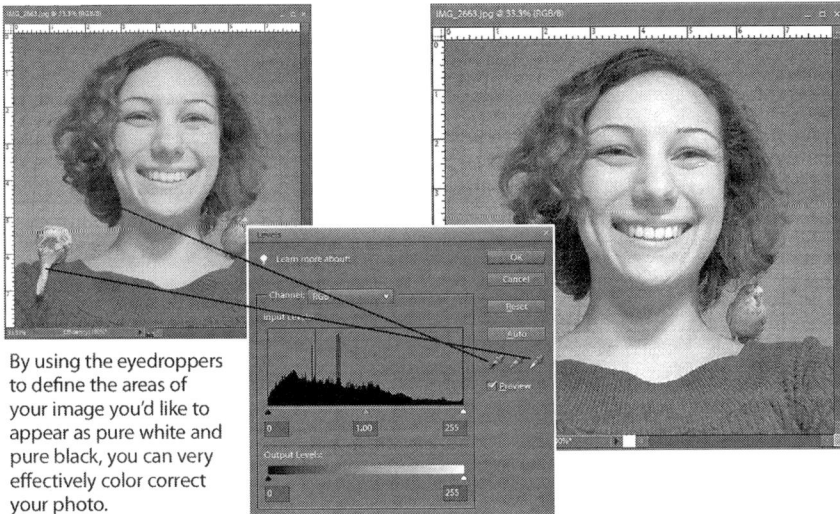

By using the eyedroppers to define the areas of your image you'd like to appear as pure white and pure black, you can very effectively color correct your photo.

Here's a professional trick that I often use to correct color in a photo using this **Levels** panel.

The three eyedroppers to the right of the histogram can be used to define the black, white and midtone points in your image file.

To correct the colors in a photo, click on the first (**Black Point**) eyedropper, and then use that eyedropper to click on the blackest spot in your photo (as seen in the illustration at the top of the next page).

Then click on the third eyedropper (**White Point**) and click on the whitest spot in your photo.

If you want to further correct color, you can use the center eyedropper (**Gray Point**) to define a spot on your image file you'd like to appear as central gray.

By defining the blackest and whitest areas of your photo, you can usually neutralize any color hues and set a clear contrast level.

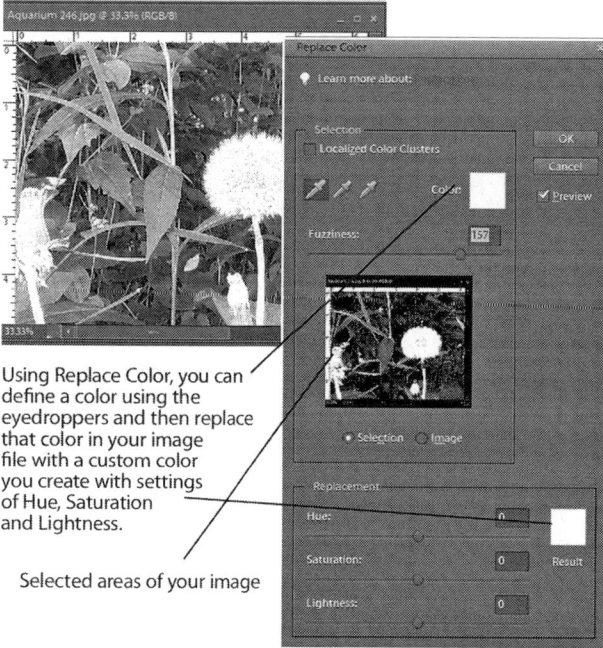

Using Replace Color, you can define a color using the eyedroppers and then replace that color in your image file with a custom color you create with settings of Hue, Saturation and Lightness.

Selected areas of your image

Remove Color

Desaturates your image file, leaving it as pure grayscale (black & white). But it's probably not the best way to get a quality grayscale image from a color photo.

A better, more powerful alternative for creating a grayscale image from a color photo is **Convert to Black and White**, discussed on the facing page.

Replace Color

Replace Color uses the same color adjustment tools as **Adjust Hue/ Saturation**, but it applies these changes to a defined area of your image file only.

To define the area of your photo to be changed, create a **Selection** using the eyedropper in the option panel (as well as the add to/subtract from eyedroppers). Your selected areas will appear as levels of white in the preview window. Once you've defined your selection, the mixture of **Hue, Saturation** and **Lightness** you create in this panel will replace the colors in your selected areas.

Adjust Color Curves

Adjust Color Curves is a very high-level correction tool that allows you to not only adjust the levels of the darkest and lightest areas in your image file but also, by adjusting the points in the curve or by moving the sliders, you can adjust the intensity for several color level points in your image, as illustrated below.

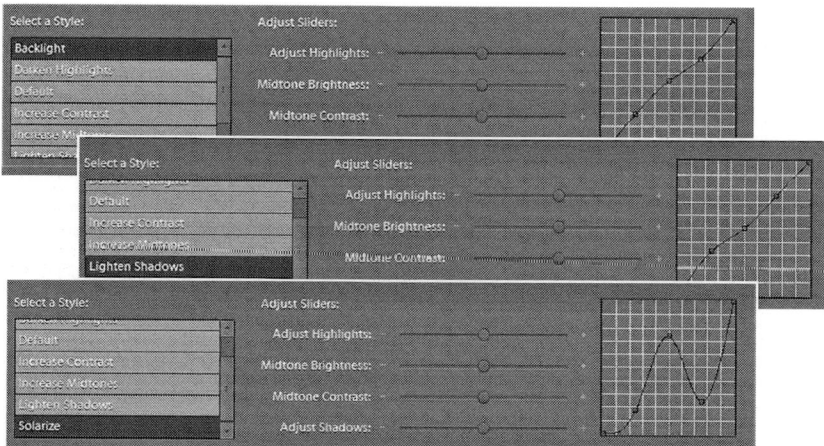

Curves adjusts the color for your image files from five separate levels of brightness. The styles listed under Select a Style offer preset curves for making some general adjustments.

The **Select a Style** window allows you to select some color curve presets – although, once selected, these can be further tweaked by moving the sliders.

Adjust Color for Skin Tone

Skin tones are often the single most challenging element in a photo to color correct. With this tool, you focus on skin tones only, assuming the rest of your photo will follow suit. To use it, click to select a sample of skin tone in your photo, then adjust the **Tan**, **Blush** and color **Temperature** sliders until the skin colors look right.

Defringe Layer

Defringe Layer is designed to work with layered image files. It's particularly effective when you're pasting a person or other subject from one image file into another (which automatically places the pasted image on a new layer, as we demonstrated in **Cutting, pasting and layers in Chapter 5, Select and Isolate Areas in Your Photos**). Based on the number of pixels you designate, **Defringe Layer** blends the outline of the pasted layer so that it fits more naturally with its new background.

Convert to Black and White

As the name implies, this tool desaturates – or removes the color from – your image file, rendering it as grayscale. But, unlike the simplified **Remove Color** tool discussed earlier in this chapter, **Convert to Black and White** includes options for enhancing the grayscale in your image so that your final black & white image is as vivid as the original color image.

Under **Select a Style**, you'll find half a dozen presets for improving your image. In most cases, one of these presets alone will give you a strong, vivid grayscale. But if you'd prefer, by adjusting the sliders, you can further tweak the image to give you the strongest possible results.

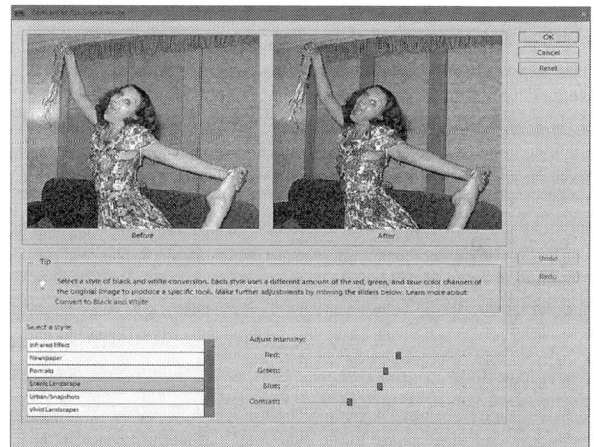

With the proper adjustments (or preset adjustments) a black & white photo can look as vivid as the original color photo.

Adjust Sharpness

A somewhat simplified version of the **Unsharp Mask**, **Adjust Sharpness** uses pixel contrast levels to correct for a certain amount of fuzziness in your photos.

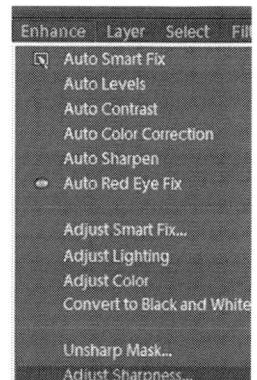

It can't make an out-of-focus picture suddenly look crisp and focused, of course. But, when a photo is just a bit soft or blurred, **Adjust Sharpness** can make it appear crisper and clearer.

As with the **Unsharp Mask**, you can only add so much sharpness to an image before it becomes counter-productive. Too much sharpness can make your photo appear grainy and overly-sharp, its individual pixels too highly contrasted. So remember, the goal with either of these tools is sharpness, not crystal clarity.

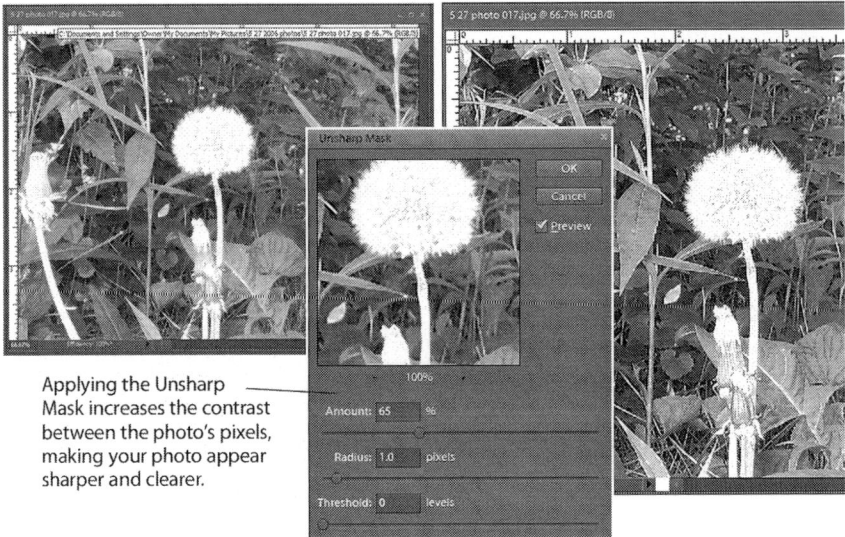

Applying the Unsharp Mask increases the contrast between the photo's pixels, making your photo appear sharper and clearer.

Unsharp Mask

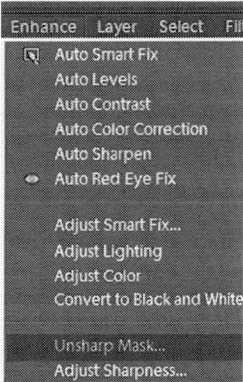

Traditionally, the last adjustment made to any photo is to apply the **Unsharp Mask**. Although the results for **Unsharp Mask** and **Adjust Sharpness** are similar, **Unsharp Mask** is traditionally considered the more "professional" of the two.

The **Unsharp Mask** increases the contrast in your pixels (dark pixels become darker, light pixels become lighter), the result being a cleaner, sharper image.

As a general rule, **Amount** should not be set to more than 100%, **Radius** is usually set to 1.0 pixels and **Threshold** is set to 0 levels. Although the best settings will vary depending on the needs and resolution of your photo, too much **Unsharp Mask** can result in an overly sharpened, grainy image.

Work with Adjustment Layers

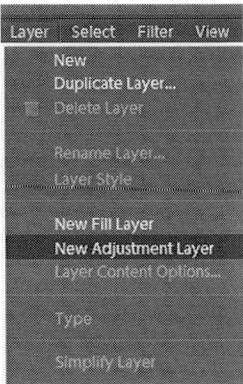

When working with most adjustment tools in Photoshop Elements, any changes you make to your image file are permanent. The image itself is changed – the pixels are lightened or darkened or colors are shifted. The only way to remove an adjustment is to undo it (by pressing **Ctrl+z** on a PC or ⌘+z on a Mac or using the **Undo** button or the **Undo History** palette) – and then you're also undoing whatever other work you've done since that adjustment.

However, Photoshop Elements also provides a way to keep these changes separate from the original image file. The effect is the same – your adjustments show change in the edited image file. But the changes are not permanent until you save the file as something other than a Photoshop (**PSD**) file or you flatten the image.

To launch an **Adjustment Layer** for your image file, go to the **Layer** drop-down on the Menu Bar and select **New Adjustment Layer** and then, from the sub-menu, whatever adjustment (**Levels**, **Brightness/ Contrast**, **Hue/Saturation**, etc.) you'd like to make.

The option screens for an **Adjustment Layer** (as illustrated on page 88) are identical to the option screens for any adjustment selections available under the **Enhance** drop-down. And, as when you make direct adjustments to your image file, your changes will be displayed in the image file if the **Preview** option is checked.

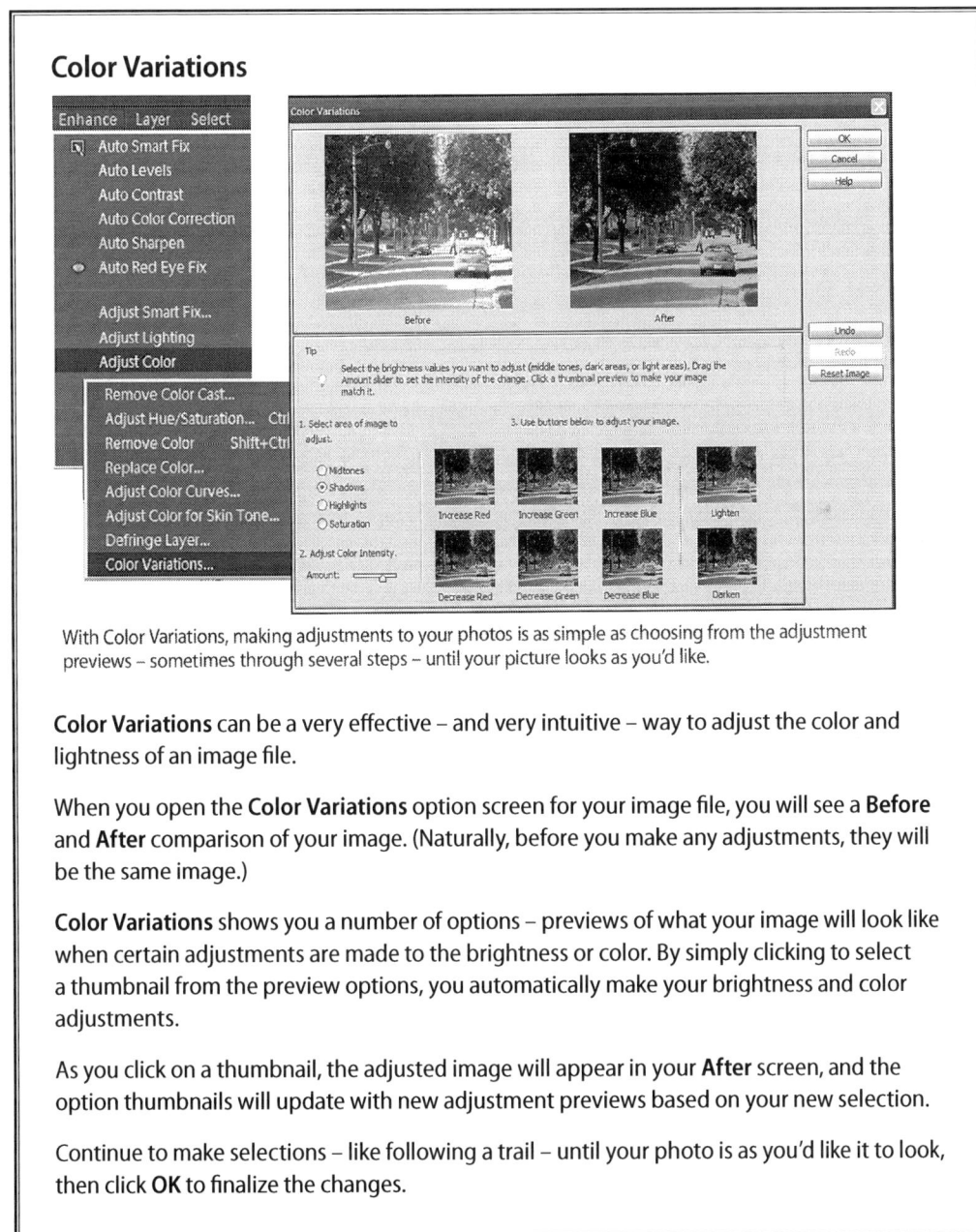

Color Variations

With Color Variations, making adjustments to your photos is as simple as choosing from the adjustment previews – sometimes through several steps – until your picture looks as you'd like.

Color Variations can be a very effective – and very intuitive – way to adjust the color and lightness of an image file.

When you open the **Color Variations** option screen for your image file, you will see a **Before** and **After** comparison of your image. (Naturally, before you make any adjustments, they will be the same image.)

Color Variations shows you a number of options – previews of what your image will look like when certain adjustments are made to the brightness or color. By simply clicking to select a thumbnail from the preview options, you automatically make your brightness and color adjustments.

As you click on a thumbnail, the adjusted image will appear in your **After** screen, and the option thumbnails will update with new adjustment previews based on your new selection.

Continue to make selections – like following a trail – until your photo is as you'd like it to look, then click **OK** to finalize the changes.

When using an Adjustment Layer, changes to lightness or color appear in your image – but these changes are actually a separate layer and your original image remains unchanged.

The difference is that, when you **OK** your changes, the changes are not applied to the original image. Rather, your adjustments show up as a separate layer – an **Adjustment Layer** – in the **Layers** palette.

There are a number of advantages to using **Adjustment Layers** rather than changing the actual image file:

1. **Your changes do not affect the original file.** Remember, once you change your native file and save it, there's no going back. Once you've closed and re-opened your image file, you can't even undo your changes. Using **Adjustment Layers**, your original, native file remains in its original, native form.

By turning Adjustment Layers on and off (by clicking the eyeball icon), you can do a before-and-after comparision for your adjustments or even compare several adjustments on several Adjustment Layers!

2. **Adjustment Layers can be turned off and on.** By clicking on the eyeball icon to the left of each layer in the **Layers** palette, you can turn that layer on or off. This is also true of **Adjustment Layers**. By turning your **Adjustment Layers** off and on, you can do a before-and-after comparison of your adjustments.

3. **You can create several alternative versions.** There's no limit to the number of **Adjustment Layers** you can add to an image file and, by turning these layers off and on, you can try to compare several different adjustments (**Levels** vs. **Brightness/Contrast** for instance) to see which gives you the best results.

4. **Adjustment Layers can be re-adjusted.** By double-clicking on the "gears" icon on any **Adjustment Layer** on the **Layers** palette, you can re-launch your adjustment screen for that layer, allowing you to further tweak your settings.

When none of your changes are permanent, you're more free to experiment, to try a variety of changes and even make a few easily-undoable mistakes. And, with **Adjustments Layers**, you're also able to compare your options.

Whenever possible – particularly if you're creating proofs for a client – I recommend your using **Adjustment Layers** to create your variations. The ability to turn any changes off or on, or remove them completely, helps prevent you from making changes that are impossible to undo.

The Layers Palette

Simplify Vector Layers

The Layer Mask

Copy Layers from One File Another

Create Non-Square Graphics

Chapter 8
Work With Photoshop Elements Layers
Stacks of image data

If you're new to Photoshop Elements, layers may seem a bit intimidating – and maybe even a bit superfluous. But, as you work with them, you'll begin to see how powerful a feature they are in the program.

It's not uncommon for an advanced Photoshop user to have a dozen or more layers stacked up in his or her image file at once.

Layers also play an important role in the creation and editing of DVD templates for Premiere Elements.

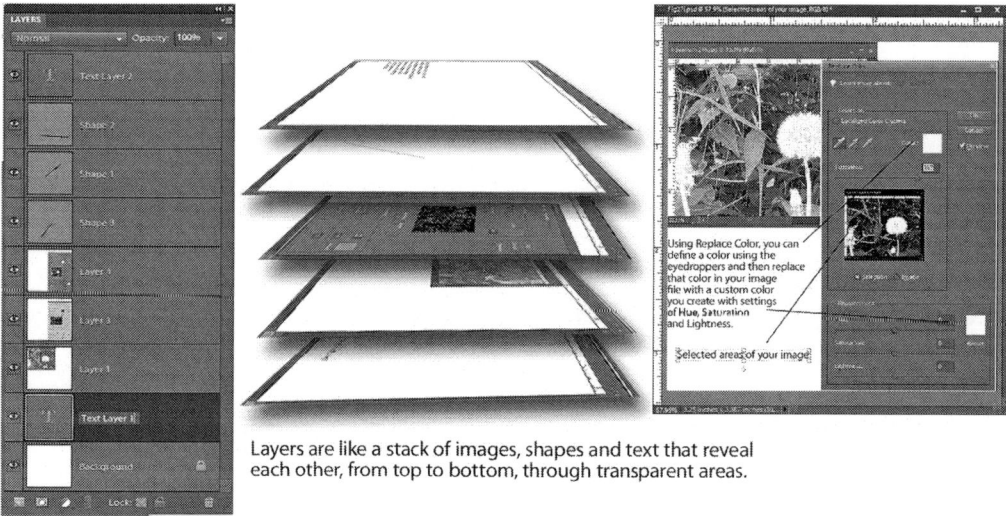

Layers are like a stack of images, shapes and text that reveal each other, from top to bottom, through transparent areas.

How layers work

The simplest way to understand how layers work is to imagine them as a stack. The top layer in the stack is completely visible. And, if the top layer does not cover the entire canvas or if there are transparent areas in it, the layers below show around or through it.

One advantage of having some elements of your image file on a separate layer rather than merged into a single layer is that each layer remains editable, separate from the rest of the image file.

Some other functions of layers include:

- As discussed in **Cutting, pasting and layers** in **Chapter 5, Select and Isolate Areas in Your Photos**, when you cut and paste elements from one image file to another (or even cut from and paste into the same image file) the pasted elements will appear as a new layer. This function allows you to further manipulate and adjust the pasted layer so that it better blends with the background.

- When you add text to an image file (as we discuss in **Chapter 9, Create and Edit Text**) it will appear as a separate layer. The text on this layer remains editable until the layer is simplified or flattened.

- When you create a shape for your image file, it also appears as its own layer (as we discuss in **Chapter 4, Get to Know the Photoshop Elements Toolbox**). Like text, shapes remain editable until you simplify or flatten the layer. (See **Simplify and flatten layers**, later in this chapter.)

- As we discuss in **Chapter 7, Correct Color and Lighting**, an **Adjustment Layer** allows you to make adjustments to the lighting and color of your image file without actually changing your image file. (The adjustments appear as a separate layer.)

The **Smart Brush Tool** (discussed in **Chapter 4, Get to Know the Photoshop Elements Toolbox**) works similarly. The **Smart Brush Tool's** color and lighting adjustments remain separate from the image itself. These adjustments can then be further tweaked – or even removed altogether – without making any permanent changes to your original image file or photo.

Additionally, there are a couple other functions of layers worth mentioning.

- **You can duplicate your layers**, making several versions of the same layer, each with unique effects or adjustments applied to it. In this way, you can create several versions of your image, comparing them to each other by simply turning the layers on and off.

  The easiest way to duplicate a layer is to drag it, in the **Layers** palette, down onto the **Create a New Layer** icon at the bottom left of the palette (as illustrated on the following page).

- **Layers are the key to creating non-square graphics!** Non-square graphics include logos, shapes and text-only graphics files.

  By removing the background, using layers and saving your files to the proper format, you can create and export graphics in any shape you want, without the constraints of that pesky rectangular background (as we'll demonstrate in **Create non-square graphics**, later in this chapter).

Select a layer to edit

To select the layer you want to work on, click on it in the **Layers** palette. The selected layer will then be highlighted.

In Photoshop Elements, you can also select a layer simply by clicking on the graphic or text in your image file in the **Editor** workspace. (The layer that the graphic is on will automatically be selected in the **Layers** palette.)

This makes repositioning the layered elements in your image file fairly intuitive.

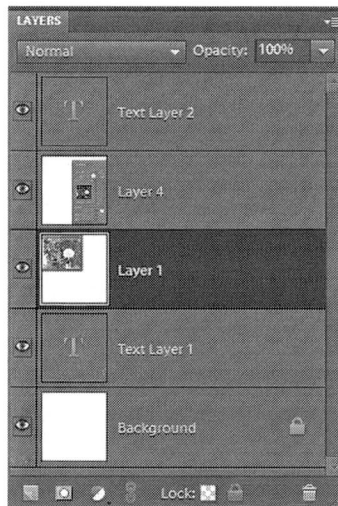

Layer blending options

Currently selected layer (highlighted)

Shape layer

Text layer

Image layer

Disable/enable Layer (eyeball icon)

Background layer

Make New Layer

Add Layer Mask

Create Adjustment Layer   Link layers

Lock Layer

Delete Layer

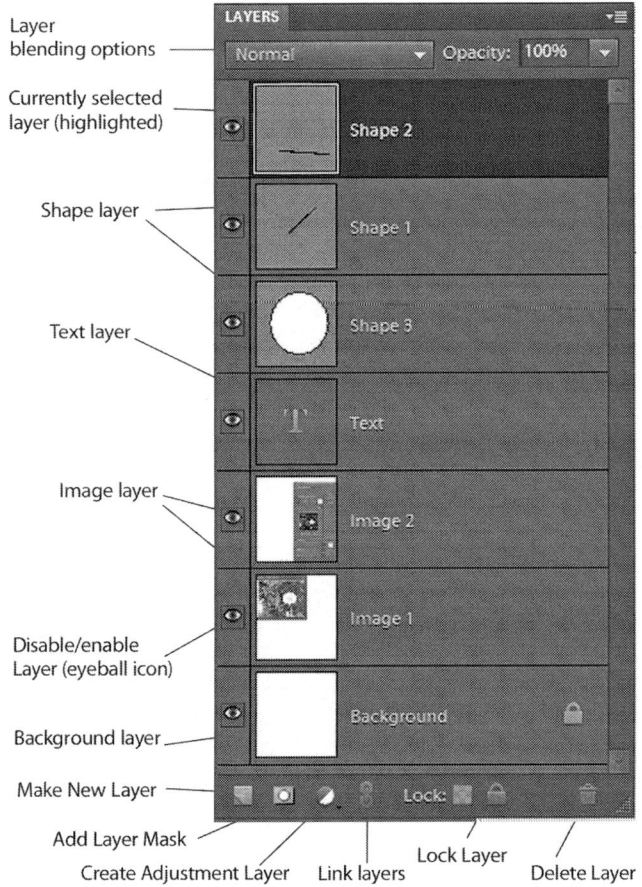

The Layers palette

The layers of your image file will appear stacked in the **Layers** palette. Your image file will usually include, at the bottom of this stack, a **Background** layer (unless you've manually removed it).

With the exception of Photoshop (PSD) files (and some rare TIFs), graphic formats (JPEGs, GIFs, PNGs) are flat. When you open them in Photoshop Elements, the only layer that will appear in the **Layers** palette will be the **Background** layer. (This layer is locked by default, indicated by a padlock icon on it. However, it can be unlocked and turned into a layer simply by double-clicking on it.)

As can be seen in the illustration above, the **Layers** palette includes a number of tools for working with and managing your layers:

> **New layers can be created** by clicking on the **Make New Layer** or **Create Adjustment Layer** buttons at the bottom of the palette, as illustrated above. As mentioned earlier, some functions – such as cutting and pasting, creating shapes and adding text – automatically create new layers.

Layers can be re-ordered or re-stacked by dragging them around in the palette. For instance, if you'd like a shape on one layer to appear *over* rather than *under* the image in another, you can just drag it into that new position on the **Layers** palette.

Layers can be deleted – singularly or several at once – by selecting them (or Shift-clicking to select several) and dragging them to the trash can or clicking on the trash can icon.

Layers can be linked. When you select two or more layers at once (by **Ctrl- or ⌘-clicking** or **Shift-clicking** to select), any transformation or positioning changes applied to one will apply to *all selected layers*. You can lock the link between two or more layers by selecting them and clicking on the **Link Layers (the chain)** button at the bottom of the **Layers** palette.

Layers can be locked. Locking a layer (the padlock) prevents it from being accidentally edited or moved.

Layers can be temporarily disabled (made invisible) by clicking on the eyeball icon to the left of each layer. Clicking on the eyeball icon again re-enables the layer.

There are two advanced tools on the **Layers** palette – the first of which is worth knowing well and the other of which is worth merely knowing about:

- The **Blending** options are in the form of a pop-up menu that appears at the top of the palette. By default it reads **Normal** – and it is not available for use with the **Background** layer.

  Blending affects how the selected layer reacts with the layers below it. It's a pretty high-level tool, but it can also create some pretty interesting effects. When the **Overlay** blend option is selected, for instance, you can paint on one layer and it will "colorize" the image on the layer below it!

  More advanced uses for this feature are beyond the scope of this book, but are worth experimenting with.

- **Layer Sets** are essentially folders on the **Layers** palette that contain groups of layers. They can be turned on or off, moved or manipulated as a group or as individual layers.

  Layer Sets can't be created in Photoshop Elements. They're a function of the professional version of Photoshop.

  However, depending on how large the file is you're working on, you can often open and edit a **Layer Set** in Photoshop Elements – a key process when using **Edit DVD and BluRay disc templates in Photoshop Elements** (as discussed in **Chapter 35, Use Photoshop Elements and Premiere Elements Together**).

A shape remains a vector-like graphic until it is simplified or flattened.

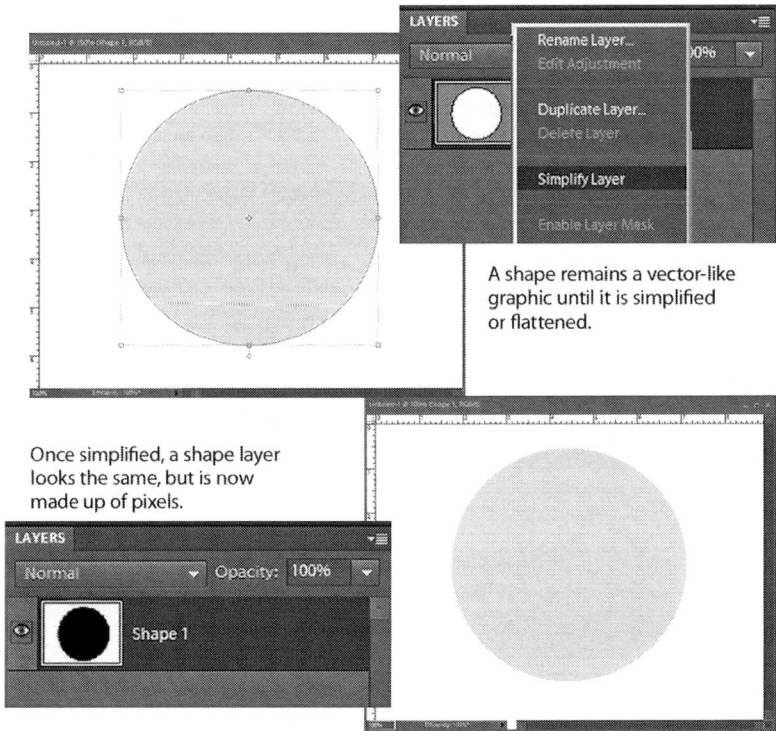

Once simplified, a shape layer looks the same, but is now made up of pixels.

Simplify or Flatten a Layer

The image layers you'll be working on in Photoshop Elements are raster art. They're made up of pixels and, on some layers, may include transparent areas.

Two types of layers, however, are more vector than pixel-based, and include some unique abilities and liabilities.

Shape Layers (as discussed in **Chapter 4, Get to Know the Photoshop Elements Toolbox**) are in reality something called "masks." In other words, although a shape may look like a circle, it is actually a colored layer with all the area around the circle made transparent. (You can see this if you look at their representation in the **Layers** palette, as in the illustration above.) This gives shapes some unique characteristics – namely that you can manipulate them like vector art, resizing and reshaping them without regard for resolution.

Text, likewise, is not pixel-based art. It is a font, which behaves like vector art. In fact, if you click on a block of text with the **Selection Tool**, you can even resize the text block by dragging on its corner handles, just as if it were a shape! Text also remains editable as long as it remains a separate text layer.

These two types of Photoshop Elements objects float as layers over your image until one of two things happens:

- **The layer is simplified.** To simplify a text or shape layer, right-click on it in the **Layers** palette and select the **Simplify Layer** option. Although the shape or text may not appear different, it has now become raster art. It is now made up of pixels and can no longer be edited as vector art.

- **The file is flattened.** You can flatten all of the layers in your image file onto your background or you can just merge two layers together. The result is the same: The separate layers become one single collection of pixels.

Layers can be merged onto one another or flattened completely.

- To merge one layer onto the layer below it, right-click on the layer in the **Layers** palette and select **Merge Down** (or press **Ctrl+e** on a PC or ⌘**+e** on a Mac).

- To flatten all of the layers in your image file, right-click on the **Layers** palette or select from the **Layers** drop-down on the Menu Bar the option to **Flatten Image**. All of your layers will flatten into a single, rasterized **Background** layer.

Although TIFs can also be forced to maintain layers, only PSDs maintain all of your layers in an editable format. All other formats are flat. That's why, as you work on an image file, it's best to maintain a native, working PSD of your work file in addition to the JPEGs, TIFs or whatever else you are using for your output.

Although other file formats don't maintain layers, certain graphics formats can save transparency information in the form of something called an "alpha channel." That's an important function we'll explain in **Creating non-square graphics**, later in this chapter.

Copy layers from one image file to another

Layers can be easily copied from one image file to another.

Although you could certainly use **Copy and Paste** to move elements from one image file to another, you can more easily copy layers, layer sets, shapes and text by simply *dragging* the layers from the **Layers** palette of one image file onto another open image file.

By **Shift-clicking** to select several layers at once, you can copy a whole group of them from one image file to another!

This function becomes very useful when **Editing DVD and BluRay disc templates in Photoshop Elements**, as discussed in **Chapter 35, Use the Elements Programs Together**.

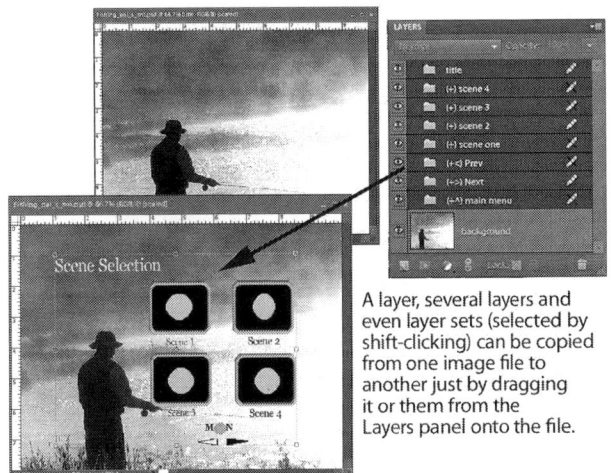

A layer, several layers and even layer sets (selected by shift-clicking) can be copied from one image file to another just by dragging it or them from the Layers panel onto the file.

Add transparency with Layer Masks

An exciting new feature in Photoshop Elements 9 is the ability to add **Layer Masks** to your image file layers – a feature previously available only in the professional version of the software.

Layer Masks create transparent and semi-transparent areas in your image layers. But, because they do so by masking rather than actually removing pixels, they don't actually change or remove any image data from the image itself. The areas are merely *masked*.

Add a mask to a layer by clicking the Add Layer Mask button. The Layer Mask appears as a white box, linked to the side of the layer in the palette.

1. To create a **Layer Mask**, select a layer in one of your graphics files.

   (If you are working with a flat graphic or photo, you can make the *Background* a layer by double-clicking on it in the **Layers** palette.)

2. Click the **Add Layer Mask** button at the bottom left of the Layers palette.

   A white box will be added to your selected image's layer.

   This white box is your **Layer Mask**.

   A **Layer Mask** reads any white you paint onto it as opaque and any black you paint onto it as transparent. Shades of gray are read as levels of opacity.

3. Click to select this white box on the **Layers** palette, then select a brush from the Photoshop Elements **Toolbox**, set the **Foreground Color** to black (by pressing **D** on your keyboard) and paint right across your image in the **Editor** workspace. (You are actually painting on the **Layer Mask**.) For more information on working with brushes and colors, see **Chapter 4, Get to Know the Photoshop Elements Toolbox**.

The areas of your image that you paint black will become transparent. If you are using a soft-edged brush, the feathered edges of your brush strokes will appear semi-opaque.

In my example, I took a 640x480 pixel photo and, using a 104 px, rough-edged brush from the **Thick Heavy** brush collection, I painted a ragged black frame around the sides of my **Layer Mask**. The result, as you can see, is a photo with a ragged, grungy edge. (Although, since this is only a mask, it can be easily revised or removed completely without affecting the original photo.)

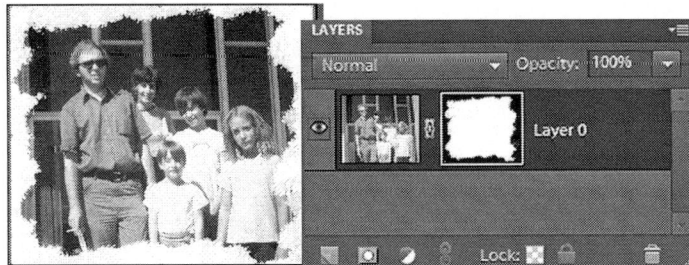

Create non-square graphics

Most commonly-used graphics formats (JPEGs and TIFs, for instance) are rectangular. They are a certain number of pixels wide and a certain number of pixels tall, and they have four sides and four corners.

However, your graphics (logos, titles, etc.) are often not. And when you have non-square graphics, you'll want to bring them into Premiere Elements in the shape of the graphic itself. Not square, not rectangular. And with the area around it – and sometimes even some areas through it – transparent.

Using layers, you can create graphics for Premiere Elements in shapes other than rectangular.

This is accomplished by utilizing something called an **alpha channel**.

Because of the way graphic files carry their visual data, transparency has to be communicated from program to program with a separate channel of visual information – the same way that the colors red, green and blue are communicated as individual channels. Transparency, then, is essentially a fourth color – commonly referred to as "alpha." Only a few graphics formats have the ability to carry transparency as an alpha channel.

Use graphics which include alpha channels

Not all graphics formats can carry alpha data. JPEGs and BMP files can not. TIFs and PDFs can, but they aren't typically used for partially transparent graphics. There are five commonly-used graphic formats that can include transparency, and all five will work in Premiere Elements.

Graphic formats that include alpha channel information are transparent around the layered graphic or text.

PSDs. This is the native Photoshop and Photoshop Elements format. It's far and away the most common way to deliver a non-square graphic to Premiere Elements. This is because, not only do PSDs communicate alpha information between the programs, but the original files also remain easily re-editable (even the text) in Photoshop Elements.

GIFs and PNGs. GIFs (pronounced "jiffs", according to their inventors) are the graphics you see all over the Internet. They're the ones that include animation (like those annoying, flashing Web banner ads). PNGs (pronounced "pings") were designed to replace GIFs, and they do display color much better. Outputting either of them with their alpha channels intact involves a similar process, which we demonstrate below.

EPSs and AIs. These are vector-based file formats created by programs like Adobe Illustrator. Though they technically don't carry alpha as a separate color channel, vector art is created by connecting corner points rather than assembling pixels. Because of this, they have no background layers.

Create a backgroundless graphic in Photoshop Elements

To create a partially transparent graphic in Photoshop Elements, you need to remove the background layer from the **Layers** palette.

When you first open a PSD or other graphics or photo file in Photoshop Elements, it will likely consist of one layer, labeled "**Background**" on the **Layers** palette. Even if the file does include layers, there may be a **Background** layer at the bottom of the layers stack.

Double-click on the **Background** layer in the **Layers** palette. The **Background** layer will become a floating layer.

Layered files behave very differently once they have no **Background**. Layers with no background have transparency behind them.

For instance, if you erase or cut an area on a **Background** layer, that area would be replaced by your **Background Color.** However, if you erase or cut an area from a layer, you cut *through* the layer.

If you have converted your **Background** into a layer by double-clicking on it, you can remove areas of it by using the **Eraser Tool** or by selecting non-essential areas of the graphic (selecting the white around it using the **Magic Wand** or the **Quick Selection Tool**, for instance) and pressing your **Delete** key.

That gray checkerboard you see around your graphic represents alpha. That means there is nothing there. No background. No canvas. Just transparency.

Double-clicking on a Background layer converts it to a floating layer.

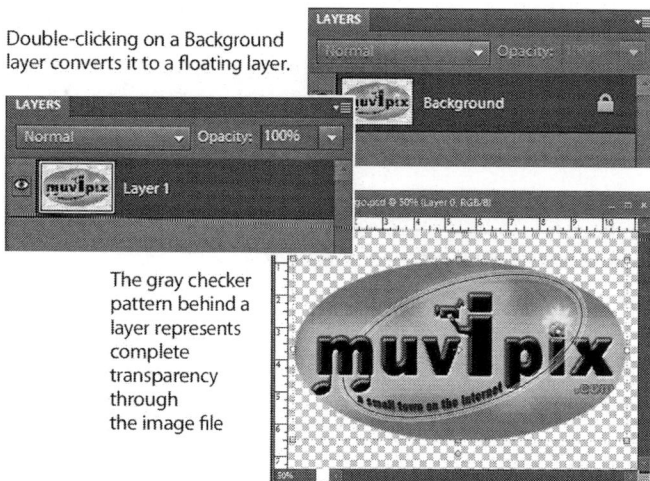

The gray checker pattern behind a layer represents complete transparency through the image file

If you'd like to start with a clean slate, you can even remove everything on the layer (press **Ctrl+a** on a PC or ⌘+**a** on a Mac to select all and then press the **Delete** key).

Once you've removed the background, whatever you draw, write or place on a layer – a graphic, a shape, text, a photo of a person with the background cut from behind him – if it does not cover your entire canvas, has transparency around it.

If the area around the graphic, text, shape or image you've added to a layer reveals that checkerboard pattern around or through it, your graphic will include areas of transparency.

And, if you were to save this file without flattening it in a format that supports alpha (ideally a **PSD**), the unused area will remain transparent when you import the file into another program – such as Premiere Elements.

If you place a graphics file containing transparency on the upper track of a Premiere Elements project, those transparent areas will also be transparent in your video. Only the graphic itself will show – your video on a lower track will be visible behind and around it.

File formats that support alpha

Although **PSDs** are the ideal (and easiest) format for sending non-square graphics to a Premiere Elements project, there are two other file formats you can export from Photoshop Elements that will include alpha. These are the formats you will use if you are creating non-square graphics for the Web or for a program that doesn't support PSD files.

GIFs were invented by Compuserve (remember them?) in the early days of the Internet, and they remain, along with JPEGs, the main file format for the web.

But GIFs don't handle color very efficiently. So **PNGs** were invented to unite the color qualities of a JPEG with the alpha channel abilities of a GIF.

To export a graphic as a GIF or PNG and maintain transparency around the graphic, go to the **File** drop-down on the Photoshop Elements Menu Bar and select **Save for Web**.

This will open a workspace for resizing, compressing and optimizing your graphics for export as a JPEG, GIF or PNG (as in the illustration on the left).

Select **GIF** or **PNG-24** from the **Preset** drop-down menu.

Once you've done that, a checkbox will appear offering the option of **Transparency**.

Check this option and your graphic will be exported as a flat graphic, but with the same transparency as your original **PSD** file.

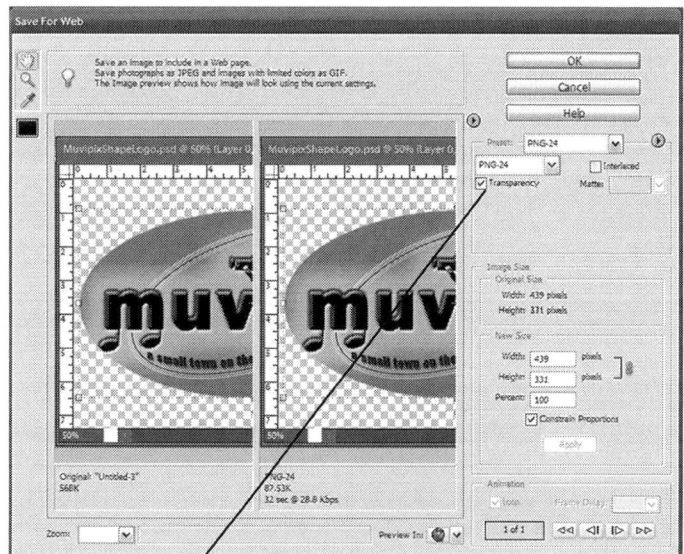

The option to preserve transparency on the Save for Web screen.

Chapter 9

Create and Edit Text
Typing, sizing, coloring and shaping

The text tools in Photoshop Elements run surprisingly deep.

Not only does the program allow you to work with such basic text attributes as font, style and color, but it also includes a variety of tools for shaping and warping text.

Text sizes and shapes can be edited using the text editor, or a block of text can be sized and shaped as if it were an object – all while remaining editable text.

Four Type Tools share the same button on the Toolbox bar.

The Horizontal and Vertical Type Tools type text across or down the page.

The Horizontal Type Tool

T o o o l

T y p e

V e r t

T h e

T Horizontal Type Tool   T
T Vertical Type Tool   T
T Horizontal Type Mask Tool   T
T Vertical Type Mask Tool   T

T o o l

M a s

V e r

T h e

The Horizontal Mask Tool

Type Mask tools create a selection in the shape of the typed text.

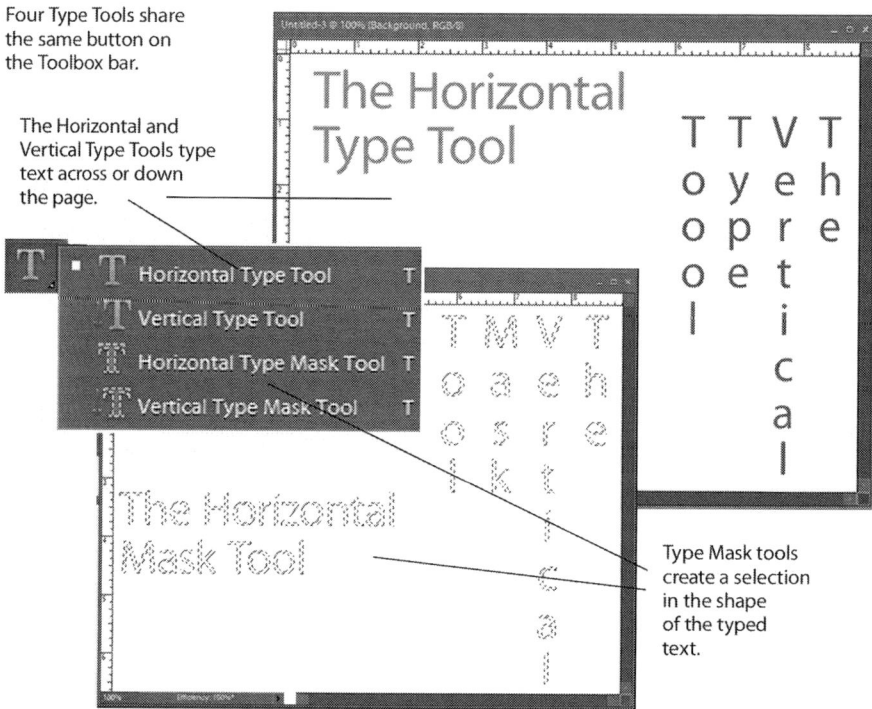

The Type Tools

The **Type Tools** in the **Toolbox,** along the left side of the **Editor** workspace, include four different tools for adding text to your image file. To select among these four tools, click and hold on the **Type Tools** button until the "hidden" tools display.

Two of these tools add text to your image file as you type.

The Horizontal Type Tool, as the name implies, types your text from left to right, by default in the **Foreground Color.**

The Vertical Type Tool types your text from top to bottom, by default in the **Foreground Color.** When you press **Enter** as you type, a new column of text is created *to the left* of the first.

Horizontal text can be turned into vertical text, and vice versa, by clicking on the **Change the Text Orientation** button on the **Option Bar** when the **Type Tool** is selected.

The two other **Type Tools** create a "mask" or selection.

The Horizontal Type Mask Tool creates a text-shaped selection mask from left to right as you type.

The Vertical Type Mask Tool creates a text-shaped selection mask from top to bottom as you type.

Though called **Masks**, these type tools actually create **selections**. (**Layer Masks,** discussed on page 88, are very different and have a very different function in the program.)

As you type with a **Type Mask Tool**, your image file will be temporarily covered by a semi-opaque, red mask. Your text will appear to be cut out of this mask. When you click off of your text or select another tool, your typed text area will become a **selection** (surrounded by "marching ants"). (For more information on making and working with selections, see **Chapter 5, Select and Isolate Areas in Your Photos**.)

The selection created by your **Type Mask Tools** can be manipulated in a number of ways:

- **A selection can be deleted** by pressing the **Delete** key, removing the area you've selected from the layer you've selected it on. Or you can select **Inverse** from the **Select** drop-down on the Menu Bar and, by pressing the **Delete** key, remove all *except* the text-shaped area.

- **A selection can be cut and pasted** into another image file or onto a new layer in the current file.

- If you switch to the **Move Tool, your selection can be resized or reshaped** by dragging its corner handles.

- **A selection can be colored** using **Stroke** or **Fill**.

- **A selection's lighting and color can be adjusted**, and your adjustments will affect only the selected area.

For the most part, **selections** made using the **Type Mask Tools** are no different than any other **selections** – except that their shape is defined by the shape of the text you type.

Re-edit a text layer

Your text will remain editable as long as it remains a separate text layer in a PSD file. You'll easily recognize a text layer in the Layers palette because the layer will appear as a big, gray "**T**", followed by the layer's name (which, by default, will be the text you typed).

Double-clicking the "T" on a text layer makes the text re-editable.

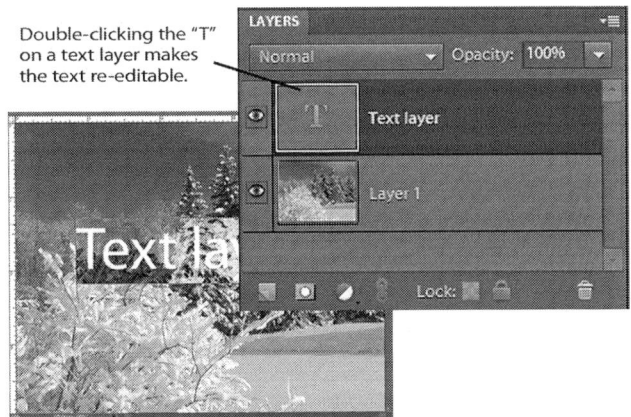

As long as it remains a text layer, you can re-edit your text. To re-edit a text layer, double-click on the big, gray "**T**" representing the layer on the **Layers** palette. The text layer will be activated and the **Type Tool** will automatically be selected.

Font Style Anti-Aliasing Alignment Warped Text
Text Orientation
Font Font Size Faux Styles Leading

Myriad Pro   Regular   8 pt   Style:

Text color

Text Layer Styles

List View
Thumbnail View
Remove Style

Bevels
Drop Shadows
Inner Glows
Inner Shadows
Outer Glows
Visibility

Complex
Glass Buttons
Image Effects
Patterns
Photographic Effects
Wow Chrome
Wow Neon
Wow Plastic

More Colors...   Options

Additional
Layer Styles

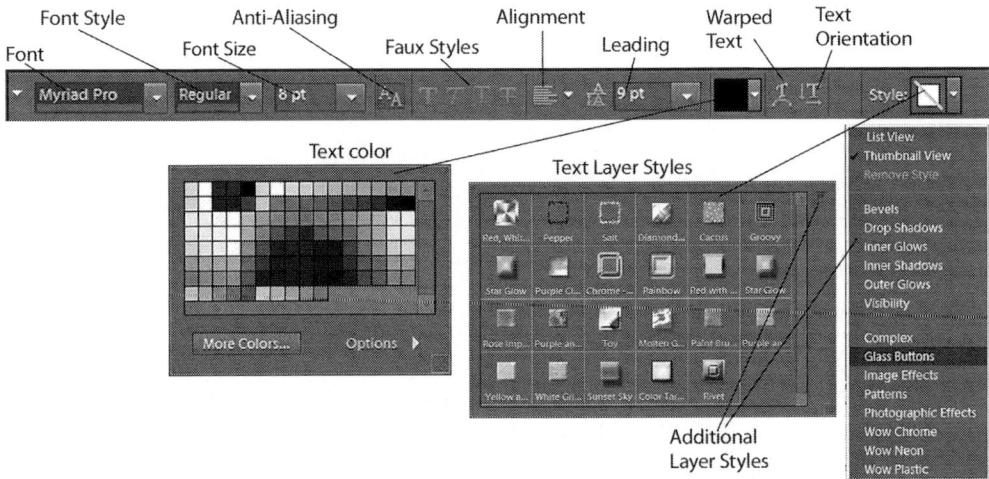

The Type Tools Option Bar

All of the **Type Tools**, whether text tools or mask tools, use a similar **Option Bar** set, as illustrated on the following page.

The **Type Tools Option Bar** is primarily used for setting basic text styles, colors and sizes.

In most cases, the default settings for the **Type Tools** options will be the *last settings used*. In other words, if you used 8 pt. Myriad Pro Regular to type text onto your image file, the next time you select a **Type Tool**, it will be set to 8 pt. Myriad Pro Regular.

Font. The **Font** drop-down menu lists pretty much every font available on your system. These fonts will vary from computer to computer. Windows includes around 20 basic fonts. Other programs you've installed, including Premiere Elements and Photoshop Elements, may have added a few more.

The symbol to the left of each font indicates if it is a True Type (**TT**) or an Open Type (**O**) font. Without getting into too deep a discussion of font systems, True Type is the most basic font system. Open Type is the more advanced font system, sometimes including dozens of styles and options within the font. (An Open Type font, for instance, may include the option to use *ligatures* to make an adjacent "f" and "i" into one, combined character with no dot over the "i", as in the word "find.")

A quick way to "call" a font is to type its name into the **Font** box on the **Option Bar** (without opening the drop-down menu). As you type the name of the font, Photoshop Elements will automatically search and load the font for your **Type Tool**.

Font Style. Most fonts include specific text styles such as Bold and Italic. Because these styles are designed as part of the font family, setting them in this drop-down menu is preferred to applying the **Faux Styles** to the right.

Font Size. Measured in "points", font sizes are relative to the pixel density in your image files. In other words, a 14 point font on a low-resolution image will appear much larger than a 14 point font will on a high-resolution image. In addition to setting font sizes numerically, you can size your text as a block, as described in **Shape and Size Your Text**, later in this chapter.

Anti-Aliasing. Aliasing has to do with how sharp the edges of a font are. With **Anti-Aliasing** turned off, text can look unnaturally sharp and jagged. You'll probably want to keep your **Anti-Aliasing** turned on. (For an illustration, see **What is Anti-Aliasing?** in **Chapter 4, Get to Know the Photoshop Elements Toolbox**.)

Faux Styles are ways to add styling (Bold, Italic, etc.) to fonts. They're called "faux styles" because they aren't part of the font's original design, but rather the program's *simulation* of the style. In other words, Faux Bold merely thickens the font; Faux Italic slants it to one side, etc.

Paragraph Alignment aligns your text to the left, right or center. **Paragraph Alignment** is important if you plan to create Premiere Elements DVD templates (see **Chapter 35, Use Photoshop Elements and Premiere Elements Together**) because it will determine the direction your custom text will flow when you type in the names of your scenes or chapters.

Leading is the space between lines of text. In most cases, the **Auto** setting will give you the best results. However, for aesthetic reasons, you can manually set your leading tighter or looser. The numerical settings correspond to the font's size.

Text Color. By default, your text will be the **Foreground Color** that was set when you selected the **Type Tool**. You can manually change the **Text Color** by selecting it from this drop-down menu or by clicking a swatch displayed in the **Color Swatches** palette (available under the **Window** drop-down on the Menu Bar).

Style. There is a wealth of styles which can be applied to your text layer, from bevels to drop-shadows to glows to patterns. To open the **Styles** palette, click on the **Style** drop-down menu. To see the various pages of available styles, click on the pop-up **>>** button on the upper right of the **Styles** palette.

Warped Text. You can choose a **Warp** style before, after or while you are typing your text. The various warps include arcs, bulges, fish-eyes, waves and twists. And, as you select each, your text will preview the warp for you. Also, once you've selected a warp, you can customize it by adjusting the **Bend, Horizontal Distortion** and **Vertical Distortion** to create pretty much any look you want.

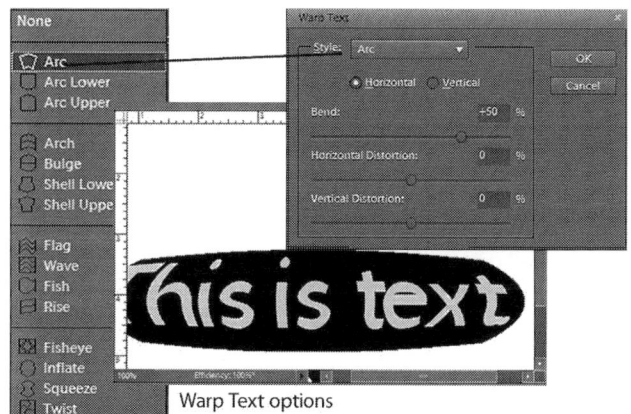

Warp Text options

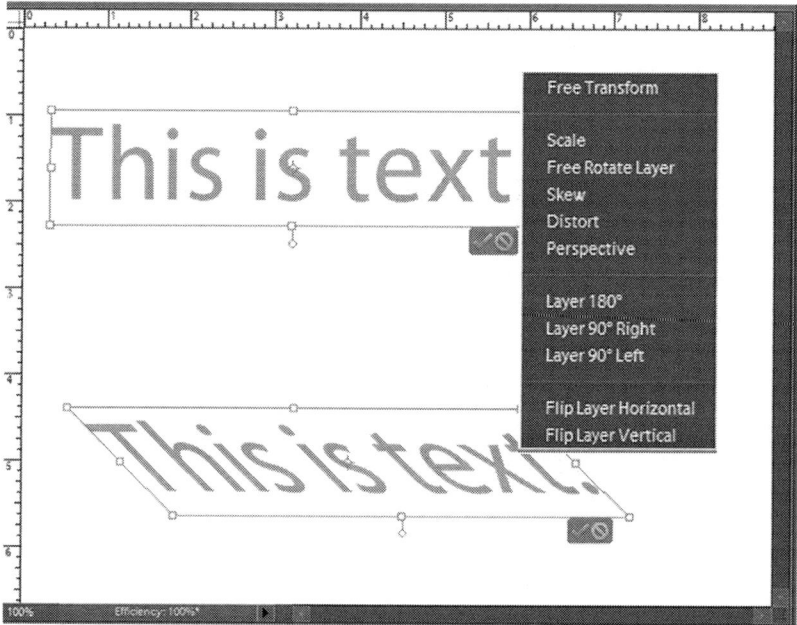

When the Move Tool is selected, text can be resized as if it were vector art by dragging on the corner handles. The right-click (Ctrl-click) option to Skew allows you to angle your text block.

Shape and resize your text

You can resize and reshape a text layer just as you can any other image or shape layer. Because it behaves like vector art, you can enlarge or stretch your text layer without regard to resolution.

To resize a text layer, select the **Move Tool** and then select the text layer by either clicking directly on it in your image file or clicking on the layer in the **Layers** palette.

Press **Ctrl+t** on a PC or ⌘**+t** on a Mac to put the Editor into **Transform** mode.

The text block will appear with handles on each corner and on the sides. Drag on these corner handles to resize and reposition your text. As long as the **Constrain Proportions** option is selected on the **Option Bar**, the text block will resize proportionately.

Other reshaping options are available by **right-clicking** on the text block (**Ctrl-clicking** on a Mac). These options are:

Free Transform (default). This option allows for both resizing and rotating of the text block.

Scale. You have the option of resizing the block, but rotation is locked out.

Free Rotate Layer. You will be able to rotate the block, but scaling is locked out.

Skew. By dragging the corner handles, you will slant the text block, as in the illustration on the facing page.

Lock in any changes by clicking the green checkmark or by pressing **Enter**.

Cancel any changes by clicking the red cancel icon or pressing **ESC**.

Other transform options

The **Distort** and **Perspective** transform options are grayed-out of the text block's **right-click** menu. These options are only available for raster art, but can be applied to text if the text layer has been simplified (converted to pixels).

To simplify a text or shape layer, **right-click** on the text layer in the **Layers** palette (**Ctrl-click** on a Mac) and select the **Simplify Layer** option. (Simplifying text turns it into pixels, so it will no longer be editable text.)

Distort. By dragging the corner handles of your layer, you will be able to shape it into any four-sided shape you'd like.

Perspective. Dragging the corner handles stretches two sides at once – allowing you to stretch and shape your layer so that it appears to have perspective.

For more information on simplifying layers, see **Simplify and flatten your layers** in **Chapter 8, Work with Photoshop Elements Layers**.

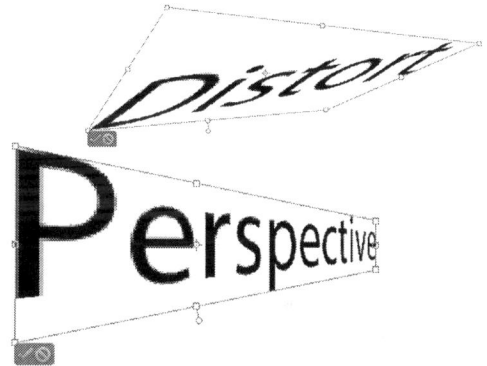

Chapter 10

Add Photo Effects and Filters
Use Photoshop Elements' special effects

Photoshop Elements includes hundreds of customizable effects and filters that can be applied your image files.

Filters can add new elements to your image file or they can make your photo look like an artist's sketch or painting.

Effects can be used to add drop shadows and glows around your layers.

Additional effects can make your new photographs look like they were taken a hundred years ago!

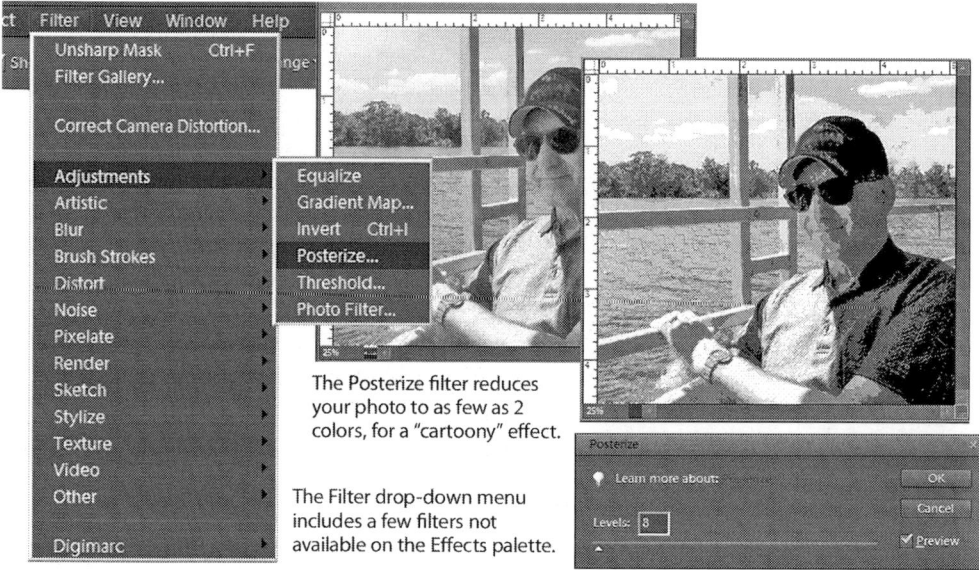

The Posterize filter reduces your photo to as few as 2 colors, for a "cartoony" effect.

The Filter drop-down menu includes a few filters not available on the Effects palette.

Effects and filters can be used to stylize or create interesting, new looks for your photographs and other image files. You can also just use them to have fun – to make your photo look like a watercolor painting, for instance, or to make a modern photo look like a withered, old snapshot.

Many of Photoshop Elements' filters can be found under the **Filter** drop-down on the Menu Bar. But virtually all of these filters can also be found, displayed as intuitive thumbnails, in the **Effects** palette, located by default in the **Palette Bin** to the right of the **Editor** workspace. (If, for some reason, the **Effects** palette has been closed, you can re-open it in the **Palette Bin** by selecting it under the **Window** drop-down on the Menu Bar.)

The Filter drop-down menu

The are six filters under the **Filter** drop-down on the Menu bar that are *not* included in the **Effects** palette set. These are the **Adjustment** filters, and they include:

Equalize. This filter interprets the darkest area of your image file as black and your lightest area as white and then it evenly distributes the levels of colors between. The process often softens the contrast in a photo.

Gradient Map. This filter turns your photo into a grayscale image and then it replaces that grayscale with any set of colors, based on the selections you make by clicking on the pop-up menu (as displayed when you click the grayscale area on the option screen).

Invert. Creates a negative of your image file.

Posterize. This filter reduces the number of colors displayed in your image file, based on your settings.

Threshold. Converts your image file into a high-contrast, black & white image, based on the level you set.

Photo Filter. This filter applies one of 20 **photographic filters** to your image file, as if the camera shooting the photo used a tinted lens. It can also be used to "warm" or "cool" the colors in a photograph.

Additionally, the **Filter** drop-down includes an amazing filter for correcting some distortions caused by certain lenses (or, if you're of the mind to, creating some).

Correct Camera Distortion is a filter which reshapes your photo to compensate for rounding or keystoning – unnatural distortion to a photo which can occur because of the use of a wide-angle lens or because it was shot from an unusual angle. Launching the **Correct Camera Distortion** filter opens a workspace in which you can "un-round" or "round" your photo or even reshape it so that it widens at the top, bottom or side, as in the illustration above. This filter works automatically when you combine several shots in a **Photomerge**, as discussed in **Chapter 12, Utilize Advanced Photoshop Elements Tools**.

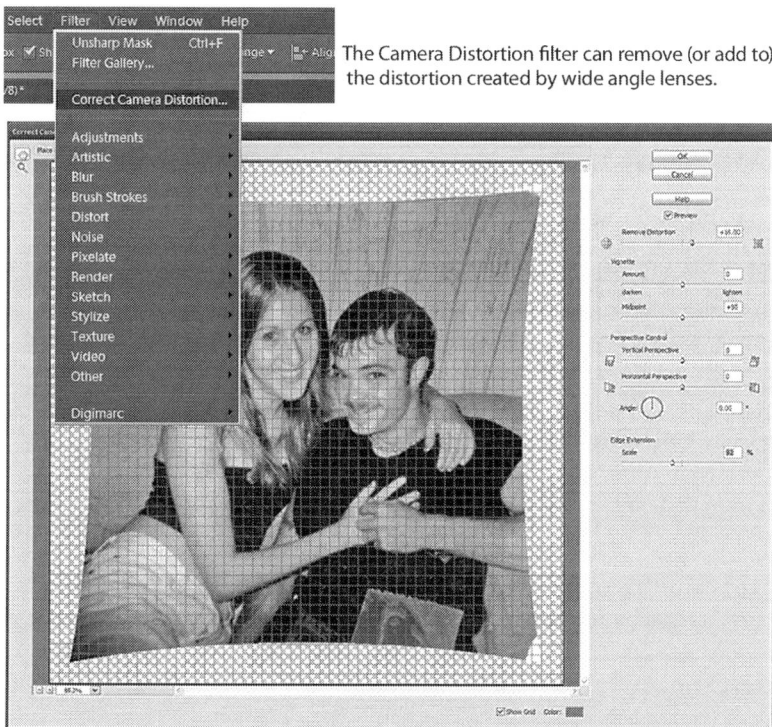

The Camera Distortion filter can remove (or add to) the distortion created by wide angle lenses.

The Filter Gallery is a workspace for test-driving and multiplying filters applied to an image file.

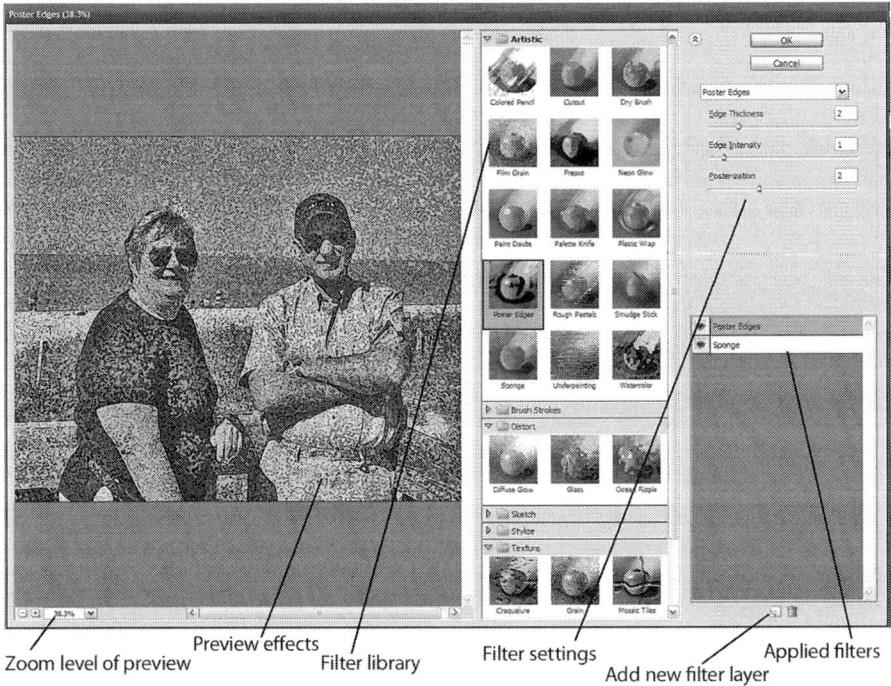

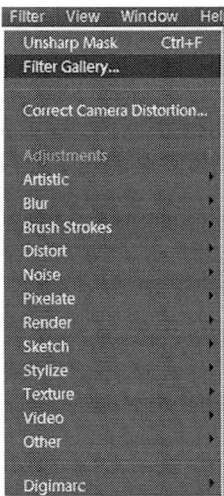

Zoom level of preview — Preview effects — Filter library — Filter settings — Add new filter layer — Applied filters

The Filter Gallery

The **Filter Gallery** is a workspace for setting the levels for a filter and previewing the results. It is also a means of quickly accessing a large portion of the **Filter** library, displayed as thumbnails down the center of the panel. In this workspace, you can test drive a number of the filters as well as apply one or more filters to your image file.

To launch the **Filter Gallery,** select the option from the **Filter** drop-down on the Menu Bar.

The **Filter Gallery** displays as four work areas.

To the left is the **Preview** window. This window displays your image file as it will appear when the selected filter is applied to it. To the lower left of this display you will find controls for zooming in or out of your image.

The center area of the of the **Filter Gallery** contains a large portion of Photoshop Elements' **library of filters,** each displayed as a thumbnail representing its effect. These filters are arranged in six categories, which you can open and close by clicking on the little triangles to left of each category's name.

As you click on each filter, a preview of its effect on your image file will be displayed in the **Preview** window. When you select a new filter, the old will automatically be removed when the new is applied.

The **levels** for each filter are set in the upper right of the **Filter Gallery.** (The drop-down menu above these settings is yet another way to switch from filter to filter.)

In the lower right of the **Filter Gallery** is a **properties** panel, which displays a listing of the filters you have applied to your image.

- You can combine and apply as many filters as you'd like to your image file. To add an additional filter, click on the **New Effect Layer** button at the bottom of this properties listing space.

- Your filters can be turned off and on in this area by clicking the eyeball icon to the left of each effect listing. And filters can be removed completely from this listing by selecting the filter from the list and clicking on the trashcan icon.

The Effects palette

There are nearly 300 effects available on the **Effects** palette , which resides, by default in the **Palette Bin** to the right of the Photoshop Elements Editor workspace. Some of the tools on this palette are filters (also available under the **Filter** drop-down on the program's Menu Bar). Many more are effects (such as **Drop Shadows** and **Glows**) that can be applied to layers, text or shapes in layered image files or to create a photographic special effect.

These effects and filters are available in different categories, which can be accessed by clicking on one of the three category buttons at the top of the palette (**Filter, Layer Styles, Photo Effects**) or by selecting from the drop-down list of categories to the right of these buttons. Alternatively, each of these filters and effects can be accessed by selecting the fourth button, **Show All**.

You can get a general idea of how the filters or effects will change your image file by looking at the thumbnails displayed in the **Effects** palette.

The size of these thumbnails can be adjusted by selecting one of the **Thumbnail Views** available under the **>>** pop-out menu in the upper right of the palette, as illustrated.

The Effects palette

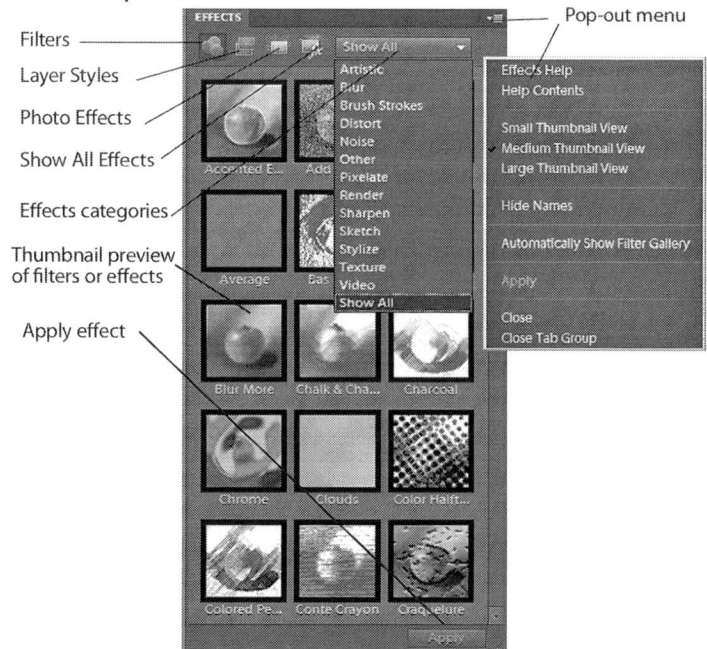

Filters — Layer Styles — Photo Effects — Show All Effects — Effects categories — Thumbnail preview of filters or effects — Apply effect — Pop-out menu

The **Effects** palette, like all of the palettes in the **Palette Bin**, can be undocked, if you'd prefer, and placed anywhere on your computer's desktop. To undock a palette, drag on the docking header at the top of the palette (where the word "**Effects**" is displayed).

Once you remove it from the bin, it becomes a "floating" palette and you can position it wherever you'd like in your workspace.

To re-dock the panel, just drag it by its docking header back into the **Palette Bin** and release your mouse button. The palette will pop back into the bin.

To return the **Palette Bin** to its original array of palettes, go to the **Window** drop-down on the Photoshop Elements Menu Bar and select **Reset Panels**.

The Filters

Photoshop Elements divides the **Filters** on the **Effects** panel into 13 general categories. I've highlighted a few personal favorites.

Artistic. These filters give your photo a "painterly" look, as if they were created by an artist's brush or sketch pencil. It includes **Plastic Wrap**, an effect which makes the elements in your photo look as if they were sealed in Saran Wrap!

Blur. These filters soften or blur an image file or selected area. Among the blurs are a **Radial Blur**, which gives your photo a spinning effect, and a **Motion Blur**, which can make your image file or selected area appear to be zipping by your camera.

Brush Strokes. These filters make your photo look as if it were painted with fine arts brushes or drawn with ink.

Distort. This category includes 3D filters for distorting and reshaping your image files. The **Liquify** filter makes your image file behave as if it were made of smearable paint.

Noise. Filters for softening scratches or flaws in a photo – or creating noise as an effect!

Other. A miscellaneous category of filters, like **High-Pass** and **Offset**, for creating customizable image effects.

Pixelate. Filters which clump pixels, creating mosaic-like versions of your images.

Render. We discuss this unique category of effects in detail in the sidebar on page 118.

Sharpen. The **Unsharp Mask** in this category increases the contrast between pixels to sharpen the look of a photo.

Sketch. Gives your photos a hand-drawn look, with some filters even simulating the look of various drawing papers. **Photocopy** makes your photo look as if it were run through a Xerox machine. **Chrome** makes it look as if it were formed out of metal.

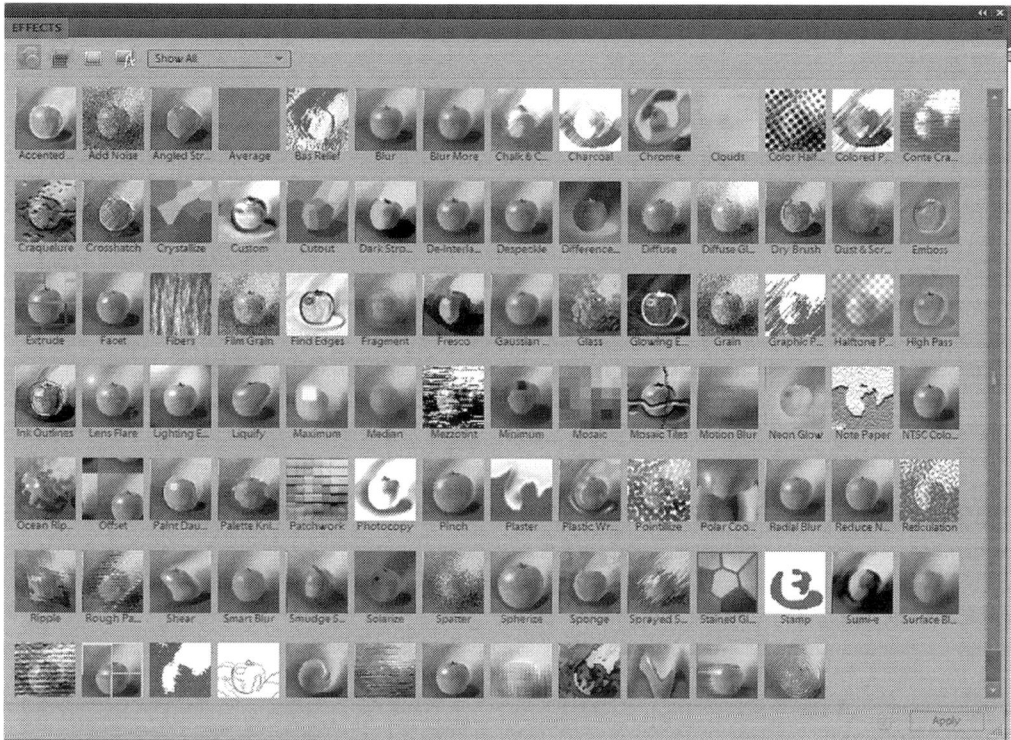

Filters available on the Effects palette

Stylize. These filters create an impressionistic effect or they create very unnatural special effects. **Emboss** makes your image file look as it if were pressed into a piece of paper. **Wind** makes the color look as if it was smeared by a blast of air.

Texture. Add a 3D texture to the image, as if it was printed onto a texturized paper. The **Stained Glass** filter adds a mosaic look, which makes your photo look like a stained glass window!

Video. The **De-Interlace** filter in this category can soften some of the horizontal lines that often appear in a **Freeze Frame** from a video in Premiere Elements. (See **Chapter 20, The Monitor Panel**.)

Layer Styles

The **Layer Styles** effects are made available by clicking the **Layer Styles** button on the **Effects** palette. The styles are displayed as thumbnails representing their effect. Photoshop Elements includes over 175 **Layer Styles** effects in 15 categories.

Layer Styles are, as you might suppose, effects applied to layers in an image file.

In fact, if you try to apply these effects to a flat image file or a **Background** layer, a message will pop up warning you that these effects will only work on layers.

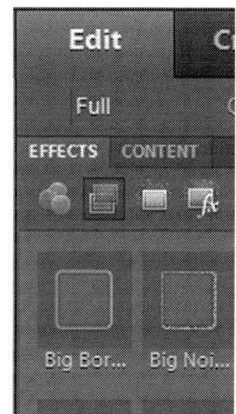

Render Filters, a close-up

The **Render** set of **Filters** deserves a more detailed discussion, because these filters often don't so much change your image file as add new elements to it. They include:

3D Transform. This filter takes your image file and wraps it around a 3D object (like a cube, a sphere or a cylinder), which you can then manipulate in space.

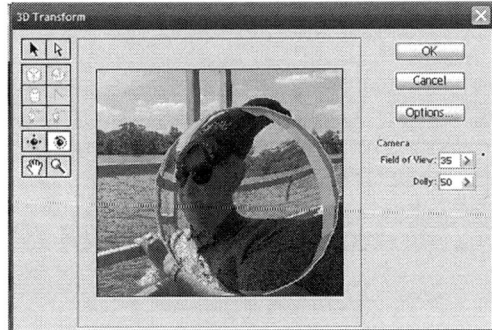

The 3D Transform effect wraps your image files around a 3D shape

To use this effect, select one of the shapes in the **3D Transform** option screen, then position and size it over the preview image.

Then, selecting the **Trackball** tool, drag across the preview image to rotate the shape and create the 3D effect.

Clouds. When applied to an image file, layer or selection, this filter draws clouds. These clouds will be a combination of the **Foreground Color** and **Background Color** you currently have set.

Difference Clouds. This filter draws clouds over your image file or selected area, producing colors that are complementary to the image file's existing colors.

Fibers. This filter draws a fibrous pattern, based on the settings you provide and the **Foreground Color** and **Background Color** you currently have selected.

Lens Flare. A popular effect, this filter creates the effect of a bright light shining back into the camera.

On the option screen, you can set both the brightness and type of light and, by dragging the crosshairs, set where in the photo you'd like the flare to appear.

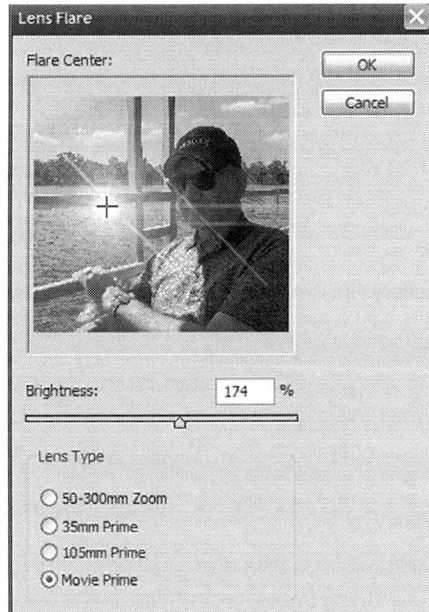

The Lens Flare filter adds a bright sparkle

Lighting Effects. This filter lets you create the effect of bright light and shadow across your photo, based on a variety of settings.

The circular control allows you to set the angle and intensity of the light, while the various style and slider settings allow you to create dozens of different lighting effects.

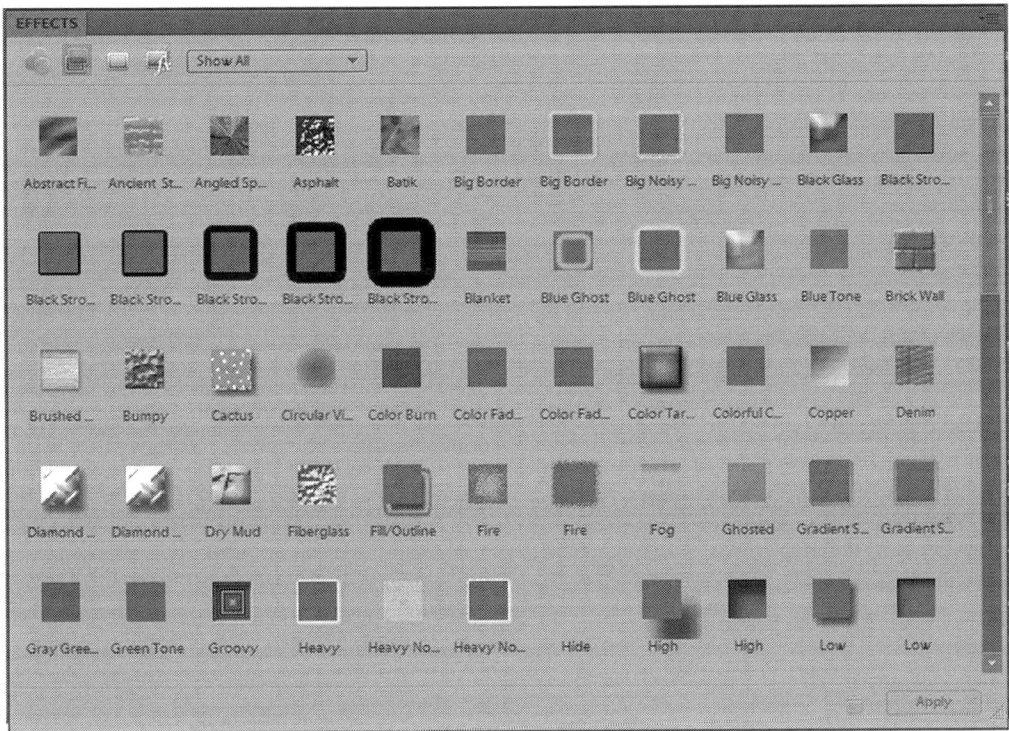

Some of the more than 175 Layer Styles available on the Effects palette

Many of these effects take advantage of the unique nature of layers. The **Drop-Shadows** and **Outer Glows**, for instance, clearly wouldn't show any effect if they were applied to a **Background** layer. Likewise, the **Visibility** effects, which make your layer semi-transparent, by nature deal with the way layers interact.

Layer Styles can be applied to text layers and shape layers as well as image layers. They can even be applied to layered image files with no **Background** layer.

A **Layer Style** is applied by selecting a layer in the **Layers** palette and then either selecting a style and clicking the **Apply** button or double-clicking on the effect.

Many **Layer Styles** can be customized on the **Style Settings** screen. To open **Style Settings**, double-click on the "*fx*" button on a layer to which **Layer Styles** have been applied, as in the illustration on the following page.

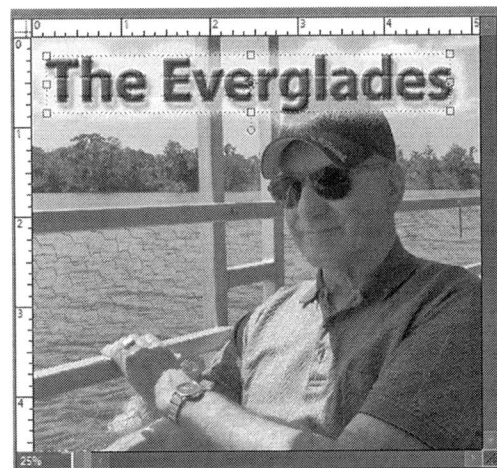

Layer Styles can be added to text layers as well as shape and image layers – and more than one style may be applied to a single layer.

Double-clicking the "fx" button on a layer to which Layer Styles have been added launches the Style Settings screen, where the layer effects can be customized or turned off or on.

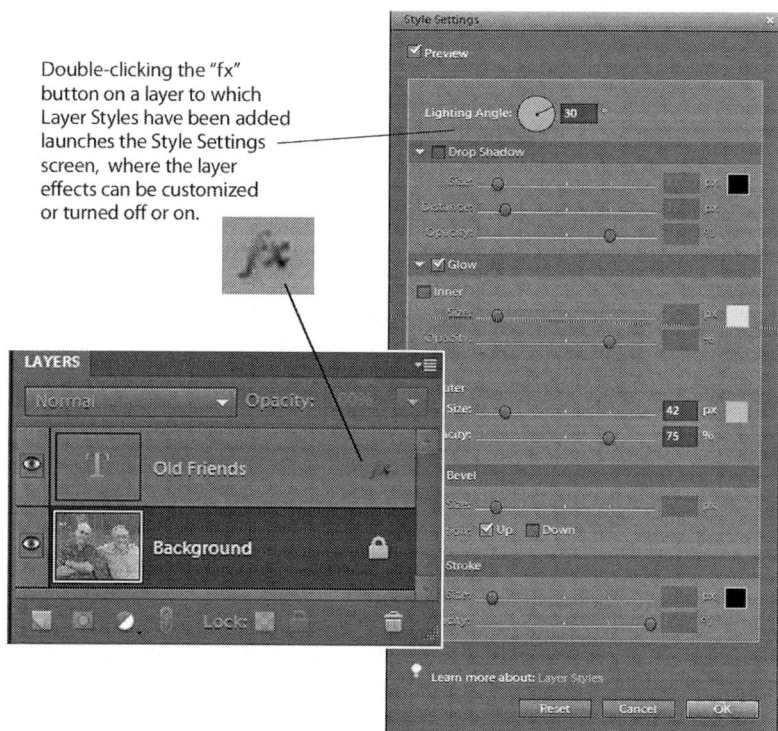

Style Settings for the **Bevel** effect, for instance, include settings for the depth of the bevel and a toggle for setting whether a selected layer bevels up or down. **Glow** settings affect the size and opacity of the glow.

Additionally, by checking or unchecking the styles listed on the **Style Settings** screen, you can toggle your **Layer Styles** off and on.

To undo the effect, either click the **Undo** button or press **Ctrl+z** on a PC or ⌘+z on a Mac. To remove all effects from a layer, **right-click** on the *"fx"* indicator on the layer in the Layers palette (**Ctrl-click** on a Mac) and select the option to **Clear Layer Style**.

The 15 categories of **Layer Styles** are:

Bevels. Bevels create a 3D effect by making your layer look as if it or its frame bulges out of your image file or is impressed into it.

Complex styles combine **Bevel**, **Pattern**, **Texture** and/or **Drop-Shadow** effects to your selected layer.

Drop-Shadow styles cast a shadow from the layer onto lower layers or the **Background**. To change the angle or other characteristics of a **Drop Shadow** once it has been applied, open **Style Settings** by double-clicking on the *"fx"* button on the layer in the **Layers** palette, as discussed earlier.

Glass Buttons styles turn your selected layer into a beveled, glass-like button.

Image Effects add effects like snow, rain, a jigsaw puzzle texture or a night vision look to your layer.

Inner Glows add a glow color inward from the edge of the layer.

Inner Shadows add a drop shadow inward from the edge of the layer, as if the layer were sunken into the image file.

Outer Glows add a glow outward from the edges of your layer.

Patterns replace your layer with a texture like a brick wall, blanket, stone, etc.

Photographic Effects add a tint to your layer or give it a sepia tone.

Strokes create a frame for your layer in a number of line weights and colors.

Visibility makes your layer semi-opaque, showing the other layers or the **Background** through it.

Wow Chrome replaces your layer with a 3D chrome texture.

Wow Neon replaces your layer with a bright, 3D glowing texture.

Wow Plastic replaces your layer with a shiny, 3D plastic texture.

Photo Effects

Photo Effects are special effects which can be applied to make your photographs look aged or have a 3D effect.

All but a few of these **Photo Effects** work by creating a duplicate of the **Background** layer and then applying color or texture effects to it. Because of this, the effects it applies don't change the original artwork. The original photo remains in its unaffected state, hidden behind the layer to which effects have been applied.

The original and the layers to which effects have been applied remain separate as long as you save your file as a layered PSD (Photoshop) file and you do not flatten the layers or save your image file as a format that does not support layers (such as a JPEG or a non-layered TIF).

Photo Effects can make bright, new photos look old and worn.

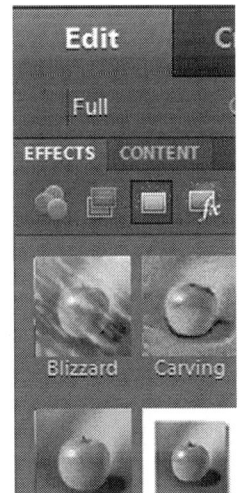

The layer to which the effect has been applied can then be accepted and kept or deleted (by selecting the layer and clicking on the trashcan icon on the **Layers** palette).

The **Photo Effects** include:

Faded Photo creates an old photo effect by fading areas of your photo from color to black & white.

Frame creates a frame or drop-shadow effect by shrinking your image file so that it is smaller than the canvas.

The **Text Panel** effect adds a resizable layer of white to your photo so that you have a semi-opaque area on which to add text.

Misc. Effects apply any of a number of texture or special effects to your photo.

Monotone Color reduces your color photo to tints of monochrome or a single color.

Old Photo adds aging and distressed effects to your photo, as illustrated above.

Vintage Photo is another "old photo" effect, this one making it appear that the paper your photo is printed on is cracked and withered.

Chapter 11

Photoshop Elements Tricks
Have fun with your photos

Stunt photography – or trick photography – is the fun side of Photoshop Elements.

It's about swapping out elements in your photos – or adding new things or removing things you don't want.

It's about creating situations that didn't really exist.

But there's a "legitimate side" to Photoshop Elements tricks too. They can be very helpful for cleaning up little messes on your photos.

Stunt photography can be a lot of fun. Swapping a friend's face for the Mona Lisa's, for instance. Or making your child look like she's walking on the Moon. It's fun – and surprisingly easy, using just a few basic tools.

But, of course, these tricks can also be functional. Occasionally you've shot a perfect photo – except for a stray wire hanging in the background or an untimely blemish. And sometimes, for a variety of reasons, you just want to place someone in a location other than where he or she was actually photographed.

It's all good. And it's all based on a couple of simple tricks and the basic Photoshop tools described earlier in this book.

Swap out a face

It's about more than just swapping faces, of course. It can be about placing someone into a scene – or even creating a composite of elements from a couple of photos.

I was challenged once with touching up the photo of a person who had a muscle weakness in one eye that caused his left eye to drift. In the photo I had of him, his eyes seemed to be looking in two different directions. By copying a clip of his left eye from another photo, I was able to seamlessly replace the drifting eye with one more in line with the right, creating a much more flattering picture of the poor guy.

The process of swapping in an element from one photo to another is best accomplished when you use two key principles:

- Ensuring that the two photo sources have similar resolution, lighting and color; and
- Blending the edges as smoothly as possible between the two photos

In my illustration on the previous page, I've gathered two classic Grisetti photos. The first is of me, at age 8, all fully equipped for a day of playing army with my friends. The second, from about 10 years later, is a real-life photo of me from my army days.

So what would happen if I grafted my somewhat adult face onto my childhood picture?

Well, the resolutions and textures aren't quite the same, and I'm facing a slightly different direction in each photo – but this is just for fun, so let's see how it goes.

1. Dragging the **Elliptical Marquee Selection Tool** over my Basic Training picture, I select my head (and a little beyond).

2. Then, using the **Move Tool**, I (literally) drag the selected area from the Basic Training photo onto my childhood picture, as illustrated above.

   Although I also could have done this with a cut-and-paste command, dragging from one file to another is the easiest way to copy elements (and even layers) between image files. Because my childhood picture is a black & white photo and my army photo is in color, the area I've copied from one photo to another automatically converts to grayscale.

   Also note that the area I've moved from one photo to the other has become a new layer on the childhood picture.

3. Ensuring that Layer 1 (my face) is selected on the childhood picture, I slide the **Opacity** level on the Layers palette to about 60%, as illustrated on page 126. This allows me to see both the background and layer (as sort of a double-exposure) so that I can scale and position my new face over my old.

4. Dragging the corner handles around my face, I size and position my older face over the younger in the childhood picture.

   Because I was facing to the right in one picture and a bit more to the left in the other, I will flip the "face" layer horizontally by dragging the side handle for my face completely across and over the to other side, turning it into a mirror image.

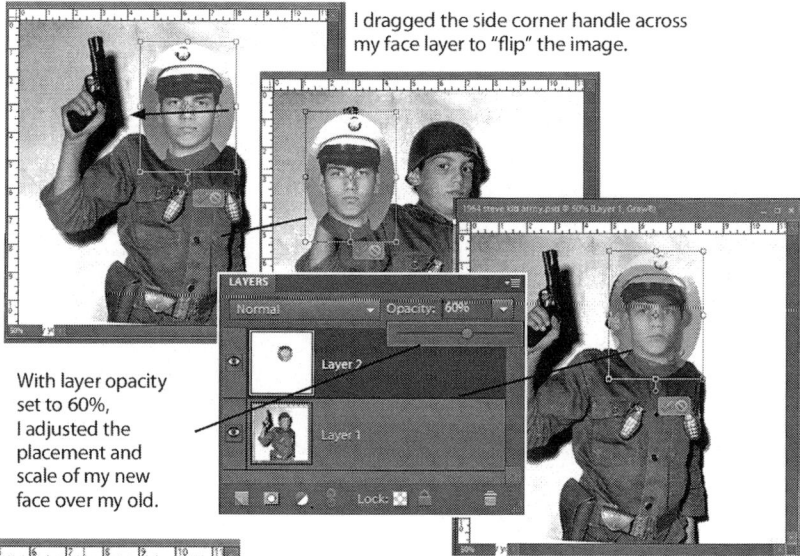

I dragged the side corner handle across my face layer to "flip" the image.

With layer opacity set to 60%, I adjusted the placement and scale of my new face over my old.

With opacity back at 100%, I used the Eraser Tool to remove all but my face from the layer.

The final, rather creepy, result

(I could also do this, by the way, by going to the **Image** drop-down on the Menu Bar and selecting **Flip Horizontal** from the **Rotate** sub-menu.)

I knew the two faces weren't going to match up perfectly but, by stretching, scaling and rotating, I am able to line up the eyes and the mouths.

Once the layer was in position, I press **Enter** to lock in the scaling. Then I set the **Opacity** for the layer back to 100%.

5. Selecting the **Eraser Tool** and, setting it to a soft-edged 45 px brush on the **Option Bar**, I erase all the unwanted imagery around my "face" layer.

    Because the **Eraser Tool** brush has a soft edge, there is a feathering or soft line between the erased and unerased areas on the layer.

    Because my face had changed shape over the years, I can't completely replace my young head with my older head – but, when I erase around the sides of my face, my older face blends in pretty well with my younger head.

The result, at left, is just a bit creepy – but it works!

The first step in pasting Sarah into the Monaco scene was using the Magic Wand Tool to select the green background in her photo.

Swap out a background

Swapping in a background uses essentially the same principles as swapping in a head, except that you're trying to create an entire scene from a composite of images.

In the illustration above, I've decided to take Sarah, who was conveniently shot in front of a green screen, and place her in front of the castle wall, overlooking downtown Monaco.

Green screens and blue screens are, of course, great photographic backgrounds for doing this kind of work – as well as for doing Chroma Key and Videomerge, similar background-swapping tricks performed in video.

This is because not only do green and blue screens give you a nice, even color that's easy to select and delete, but these bright shades of green and blue don't show up in human skin tones. This makes it easier to separate the human from the background.

1. Using the **Magic Wand Tool**, as illustrated above, I select the green background, behind Sarah.

    How much gets selected on a single click of this tool depends on how high the **Tolerance** is set on the **Option Bar**. In order to select the entire green area, I set the **Tolerance** to 25 – and even then will need to hold down the **Shift** key and click on a couple of areas to build the selection until I had the entire green screen selected. (At this point, I won't worry about the green showing between her curls.)

2. From the **Select** drop-down on the Menu Bar, I select **Inverse**. This swaps the selection area so that now *Sarah* is selected rather than the green screen background.

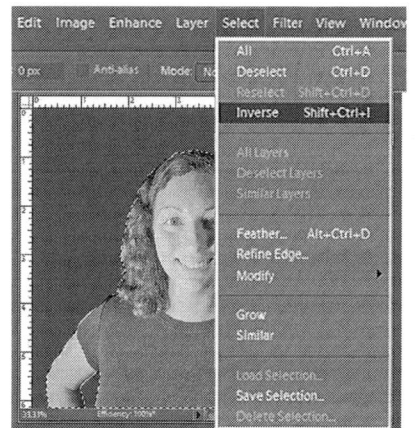

Inverse swaps the selection so that Sarah is now selected rather than the background.

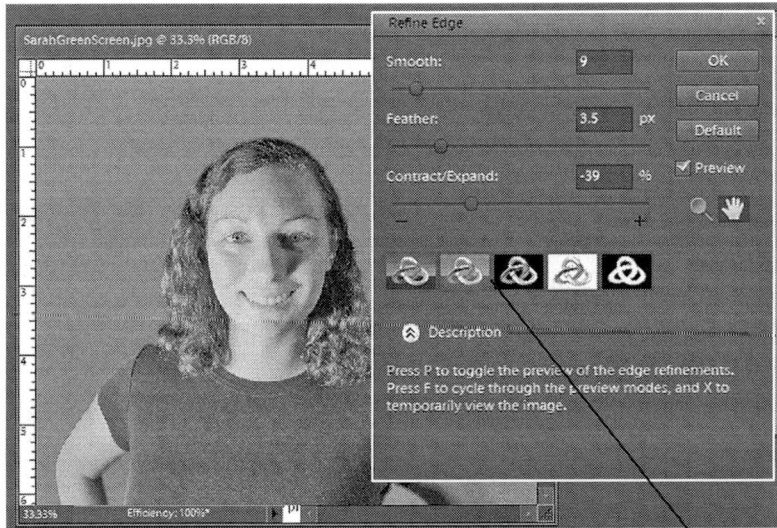

The Refine Edge tool tightens the edge around the selection and adds some feathering so that the selection blends with its new background. The Overlay Mode shows unselected areas as overlayed with a red mask.

3. From the **Select** drop-down, I select the **Refine Edge** tool. This tool allows me to tweak the edges of my selected area a bit.

By adjusting the **Contract/Expand** slider, I ensure that my selection does not include any of the green screen. I also adjust the **Feather** slider to 3 px so that the selection edge will be softer and more natural.

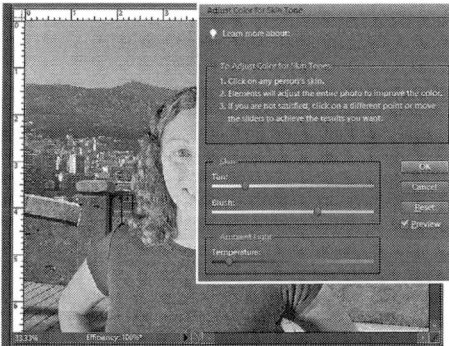

Finally, using the Adjust Color for Skin Tone tool, Sarah's color temperature is adjusted to more closely match her new background.

4. I then drag the selected area, Sarah, onto the Monaco photo. Because I ensured that the photos had similar resolution, Sarah fits nicely onto her new background.

5. Using the 45 px soft-edged brush setting, I use the **Eraser Tool** to clean up any stray green left around Sarah. Remember, when you are working with a layer, erasing *cuts through* the layer – revealing the background or layers below.

Using different sized **Eraser Tool** brushes, I remove what I could from between the curls in her hair. Depending on how much detail you're trying to clean up, this part of the process can be the most challenging and time consuming.

Stray green spots, particularly around the hair, are removed with a soft-edge Eraser Tool brush.

6. Finally, with **Layer 1** (Sarah) selected, I go to the **Enhance** drop-down on the Menu Bar, select the **Adjust Color** sub-menu and then **Adjust Color for Skin Tone**. Using the eye-dropper, I sample a mid-tone of skin on Sarah's face. Then moving the **Ambient Light** slider (and, to a lesser degree, the **Tan** and **Blush** sliders), I fine-tune Sarah so that she matches the color tones of someone standing under the Mediterranean sun.

Removing blemishes, spots and other embarassments is easy with the Spot Healing Brush.

Remove warts and blemishes

Nobody's perfect. And neither is any scene. Fortunately, Photoshop Elements makes it easy to dab away the occasional blemish.

In the illustration above, we see Sarah posing with her pet budgies. Unfortunately, Sally, the bird on the left, has left an ugly deposit on Sarah's sweater, marring an otherwise very cute picture.

The **Healing Brush Tool** and **Spot Healing Brush** are both very effective for removing these little flaws and spots.

1. With the photo open in the **Editor**, I selected the **Spot Healing Brush** from the **Toolbox** and, on the Option Bar, I set the brush size to 34 px (which is just about the size of the spot I wanted to remove).

2. Dragging the mouse over the area, I "paint" the spot with the **Healing Brush**.

    When I release the mouse button, Photoshop Elements automatically fills in the area with color and texture information borrowed from surrounding pixels.

And we're done! The **Spot Healing Brush** is a terrific, virtually automatic tool that I find all but indispensable.

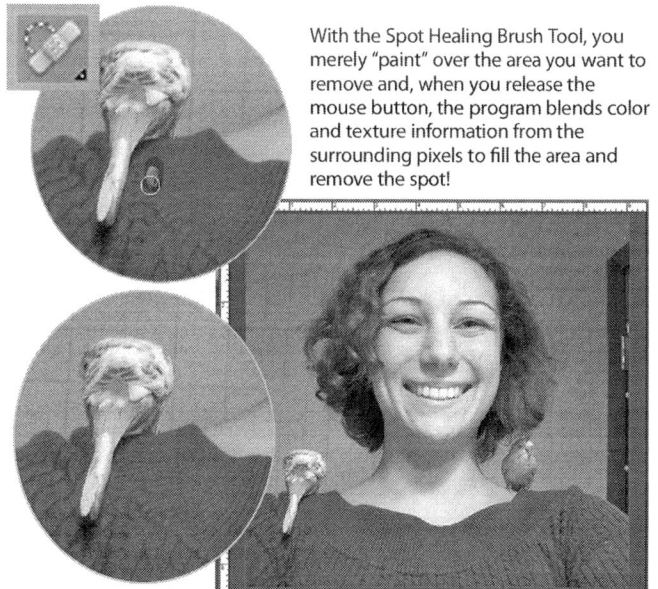

With the Spot Healing Brush Tool, you merely "paint" over the area you want to remove and, when you release the mouse button, the program blends color and texture information from the surrounding pixels to fill the area and remove the spot!

The Magnetic Selection Tool makes it easy to follow the color break along Buddy's fur and hat and create a selection isolating the arm area.

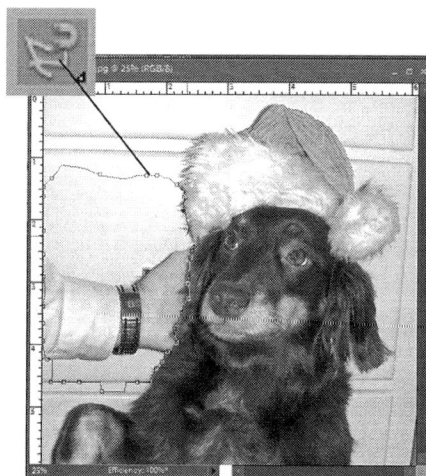

Remove big things from your photos

Sometimes you want to remove something larger than a blemish or spot from your photo. Sometimes you may even want to remove an entire person! This is most easily accomplished by "painting" over the object or person with imagery "cloned" from of another area of your photo – using one of the most powerful and popular Photoshop tools in the program's tool kit.

As illustrated above, my friend Ron dressed up and posed his dog, Buddy, for a photo he plans to use for the cover of his Christmas card. Ron, however, prefers that the final photo not include his arm in the shot so that it looks more like Buddy is standing up on his own.

1. Using the **Magnetic Lasso Selection Tool**, I draw a selection lasso along the edge of Buddy's fur and around the area where Ron's arm appears.

Selecting an area isolates it so that any changes I make will affect only the selected area, and won't affect Buddy).

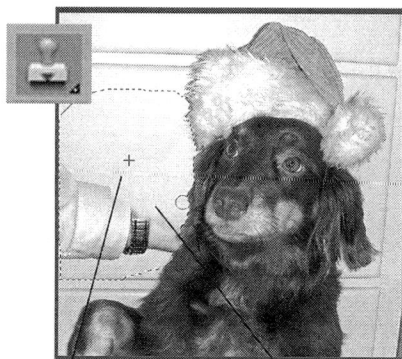

The Clone Tool uses imagery from the designated area to paint over the brushed area, while the selection restricts changes to the selected area.

The **Magnetic Selection Tool** makes it easy to draw my selection because, as I drag it along Buddy's outline, it follows the color break between Buddy's fur and the much lighter background.

2. Switching to the **Clone Stamp Tool, I Alt+clicked** to designate the source area of my photo – the area of the photo from which I will to "borrow" picture information to paint over Ron's arm.

Since I want to replace Ron's arm with the color and texture of the painted wall behind it, I hold down the **Alt** key and click to select a spot on the white wall, above Ron's arm. This "source" area is designated with crosshairs, as seen in the illustration on the left.

Once my source spot is selected, I release the **Alt** key.

3. With the **Clone Tool** set to a fairly large brush (200 px in this case) with soft edges (to blend the imagery I'll be adding to the background), I "paint" over Ron's arm, replacing it with the area I'd designated as my clone source.

   Because I have created a **selection area**, there is no danger of my accidentally painting the background over Buddy – since he was outside my selection. My painted area was restricted to the area within the "marching ants" dotted lines.

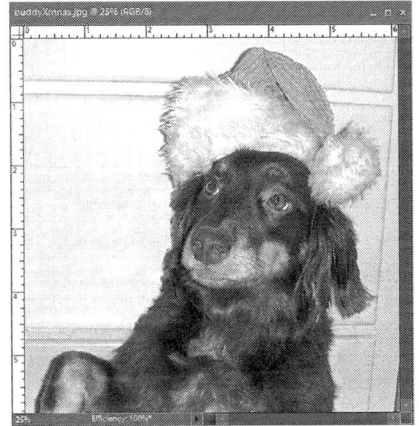

Add things to your photos

Just as the **Clone Tool** can be used paint over and remove images from your photos, it can also be used to paint new imagery onto a photo – even imagery borrowed from another photo!

For instance, the world may never wonder how I'd look with Jeanne's hair – but it can still be fun to find out.

1. With both photos open (I also ensured both photos were of similar resolution and that our heads were in a similar position), I select the **Clone Stamp Tool**. I then **Alt+click** on Jeanne's photo to select her hair, at approximately the top center of her scalp. This defines the area of the image I'm going to use as my cloning source.

2. I then click on the Steve photo (to activate it) and, dragging the **Clone Tool** across it, I paint Jeanne's hair over mine, starting at approximately the same spot on my head I'd designated as my source on hers.

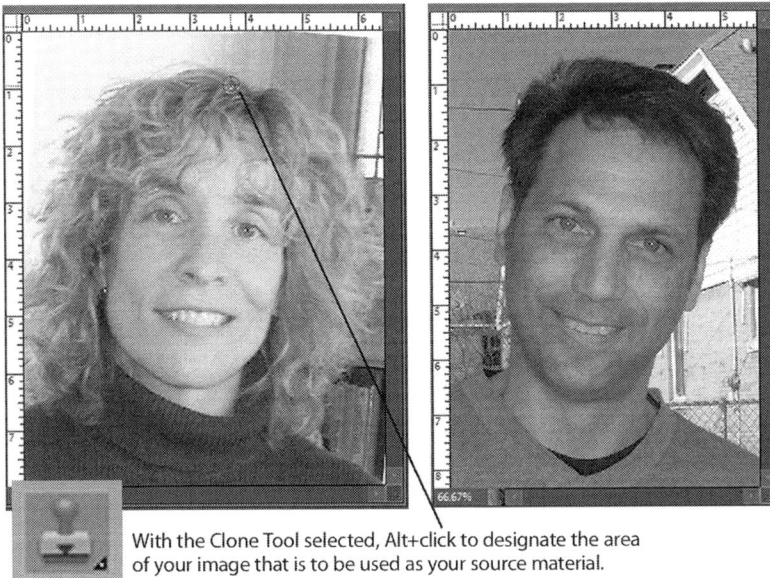

With the Clone Tool selected, Alt+click to designate the area of your image that is to be used as your source material.

131

Because I'm using such a soft, large brush (100 px, in this case) and because Jeanne has such curly hair, I'm getting the background from her picture along with the hair.

I could also have created a new layer on the Steve picture and painted the hair onto it – and then used the **Eraser Tool** to clean up the layer, removing the background or other unwanted elements that slipped over from Jeanne's picture.

And, okay. I guess I wouldn't make such an attractive blonde.

Though, if I were, I might have a career as an aging rock star!

As you drag the Clone Tool over your destination image file, the destination is "painted" with imagery from your source.

Photomerge: A powerful Photoshop Elements tool

A great, multi-faceted tool that many people don't even realize is in the Photoshop Elements toolset is **Photomerge**, a tool for combining elements from several photos into one great picture!

- **Photomerge** can be used to create panoramic photos, combining several photos of a scene into one, big one.

- Or it can be used to build great photos out of the best bits and pieces of several slightly-flawed ones.

- You can even use it to add a person from one group shot to another!

We discuss a couple of its key features and how to use them in the next chapter.

Chapter 12

Advanced Photo Editing Tools
Photoshop Elements extras

Have you ever scanned in several photos at once and then found yourself cropping and straightening each one individually?

Or have you ever taken several photos of a scene and wondered if there was an easy way to stitch them all together into one big picture?

Photoshop Elements includes tools for doing these things – plus a few more tools worth knowing about, including the ability to interface with a camera or scanner.

In addition to tools for creating and editing graphics and photos, Photoshop Elements includes a number of tools that don't fit into any neat category. These include tools for interfacing with a scanner or camera and tools for processing photo files before you actually bring them into the program. There are also a couple of the program's preferences that are worth knowing about.

Scan your photos

Built into Photoshop Elements is a tool for interfacing with your scanner.

The scanning itself is done by your scanner's software – and that software does vary just a bit, from device to device and brand to brand. But the basic principles are the same. Through a system called TWAIN, the scanner's software becomes a "plug-in" for Photoshop Elements. You seamlessly launch the scanner from within the program.

You can, in fact, launch your scanner's software in one of two ways, from either Photoshop Elements or the Organizer:

- From the **File** drop-down menu in Photoshop Elements , select **Import**, then the name of your scanner; or
- From the **File** drop-down menu in the Organizer, select **Get Photos and Videos**, then **From Scanner**.

Whichever you choose, the same scanner software is launched.

As I've said, this software can vary from model to model and from brand to brand of scanner. But the principles are still the same:

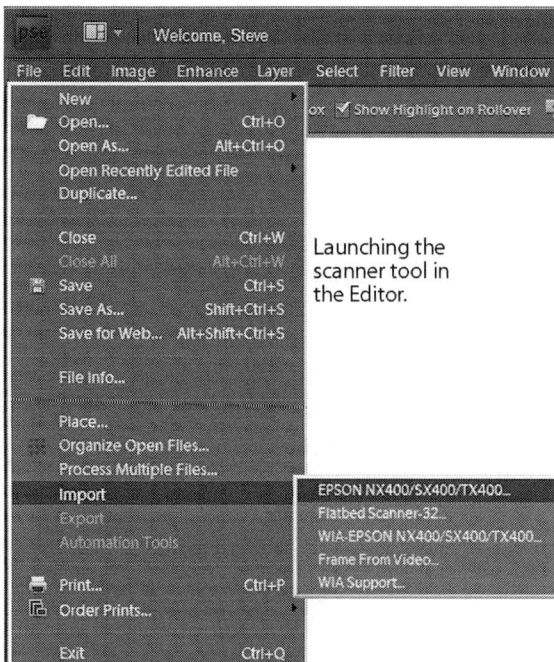

Launching the scanner tool in the Editor.

Many consumer scanners include an **automatic mode**, which configures the scanner for you and scans your photos at a preset resolution and color setting but which you can customize to some degree. This is the simplest solution – but also produces, of course, the most generic results.

The **professional mode** usually includes options for a number of settings:

Reflective vs. Film (or Transparency). If your scanner includes the ability to scan slides and films, this setting controls whether your scanner scans a reflection of the photo or shines light through it.

Photo vs. OCR. Some scanners include the ability to scan documents with **Optical Character Recognition**. This **OCR** function scans your document in as text, which you can later edit in a word processing program. It's not a flawless system, but it *can* save you a lot of retyping.

Resolution. Remember that the size of the document you will get from your scan is a combination of its size and its resolution. In other words, you may only need a 72 dpi image – but if the photo you're scanning is only the size of a postage stamp, you will need to scan it at a much higher resolution to get enough image data to work with.

My scanner software includes a setting for **Target Size**. If I set this, the software automatically configures the scan to the necessary scan resolution. (Remember, you're always better off having too much resolution and having to rez down than not having enough resolution and needing to force your image larger later.)

Your scanner is controlled by the software that came bundled with it. However, most scanners use similar settings.

Scan reflective (photo) or transparent (slide)

Color mode

Size/resolution

Unsharp Mask

Reduce "dotty" look while scanning from newspapers and magazines

Enrich color on old photos

Auto light correction

Soften image to hide dust and scratches

Preview scan

Final scan

Color Mode. There are three main color modes:

24-bit Color is standard **RGB color** – 8-bits per color channel.

Grayscale is monochrome, often called black & white.

But don't confuse it with **Black & White** (also known as **Bitmap**), which reduces all your colors to either 100% black or 100% white. **Black & White** is a color mode that is generally reserved for things like scanning signatures, which generally doesn't include shades of gray.

Some scanners also include on-the-fly picture adjustments or scan settings. Here are a couple of valuable adjustments.

Unsharp Mask. This will automatically sharpen your scanned images. It's usually best to have it turned on.

Descreening. When scanning photos from newspapers, magazines and low-end print pieces (like high school yearbooks), you may notice your scanned images have a lot of "dotty-ness." Descreening can help soften those low-quality printing artifacts.

Color Restoration. This feature will automatically enrich the color as you scan a faded, old photo.

Dust Removal. This feature adds a slight blur to your scan, sometimes hiding dust or scratches on a photo.

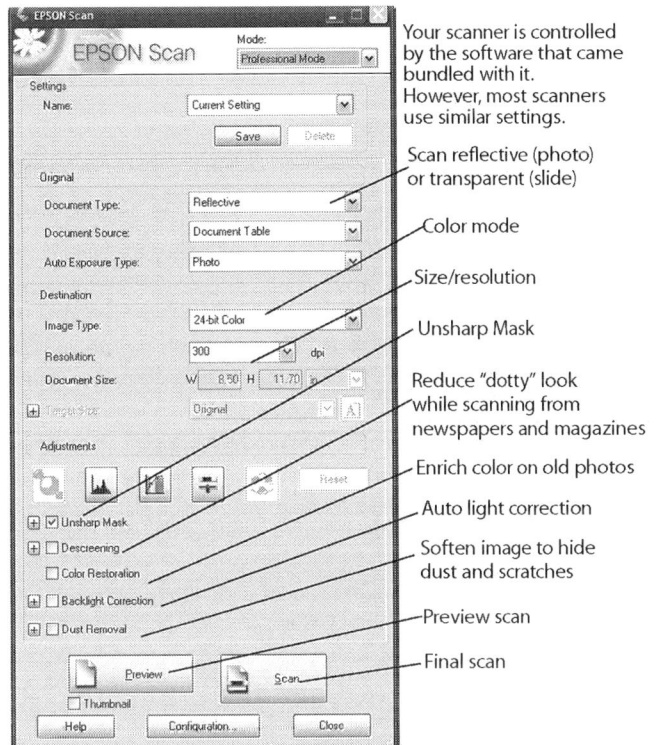

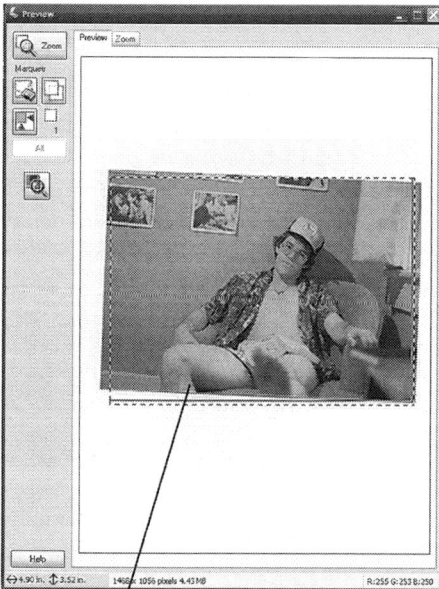

After a Preview Scan, you will have the option of designating the area of the Final Scan (indicated by a "marching ants" dotted line marquee outline).

Scanning is usually done in two steps:

1. **Preview Scan.** A **Preview Scan** gives you a low-resolution preview of everything that's on your scanning table. Your **Preview Scan** will usually include an option for you to define the final scan area by dragging or resizing a marquee, displayed as a moving dotted line outline (the "marching ants").

   The area you designate with this outline will be the only area actually included in your final scan.

2. **Full Scan.** This final scan will be a scan of your *defined area only*, using the color, resolution and adjustment settings you've configured. It will produce an image file that will open in your Photoshop Elements **Editor** for further editing.

A Photoshop Elements feature that is a great supplement to your scanning tools is **Divide Scanned Photos,** discussed later in this chapter.

Download photos from your digital camera

As with the scanner, the software that interfaces with your camera can vary from model to model and brand to brand. And your computer probably includes a number of ways for you to get photos from your camera – all of which will produce editable photo files for Photoshop Elements.

The chief advantage to using Photoshop Elements to interface with your camera and download your photos is that your photos will also be automatically added to your Organizer catalog.

There are two ways to launch the Photoshop Elements Photo Downloader for your digital camera:

- Unless you've selected the **Always Do This** option, when you plug your camera into your computer and turn the camera on, **Windows will launch a pop-up screen** offering a number of optional functions. One of these will be to use Photoshop Elements to download your photos; or
- From the **File** drop-down in the Organizer, select **Get Photos and Videos,** then **From Camera or Card Reader.**

Both methods launch the same **Adobe Photoshop Elements Photo Downloader.** This option screen allows you to designate where the photos are downloading from, what to name the files and where to save them on your computer.

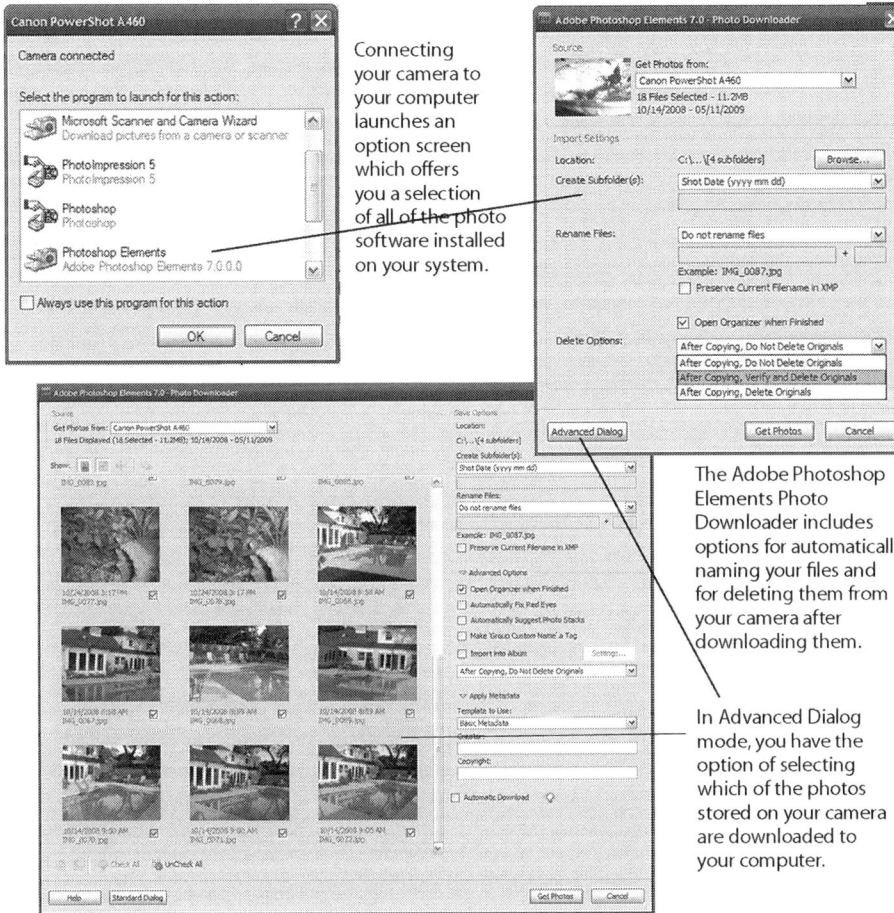

Connecting your camera to your computer launches an option screen which offers you a selection of all of the photo software installed on your system.

The Adobe Photoshop Elements Photo Downloader includes options for automatically naming your files and for deleting them from your camera after downloading them.

In Advanced Dialog mode, you have the option of selecting which of the photos stored on your camera are downloaded to your computer.

Get Photos From. From this drop-down menu, select your digital camera.

Import Settings/Location. Click the **Browse** button to browse to a location on your hard drive into which you'd like to save your photos.

Create Subfolder. Automatically creates a new photo storage folder on your hard drive for the photo download, according to the specifications you set in the drop-down menu.

Rename Files. Names your downloaded photos according to the specifications you set in the drop-down menu.

Delete Options. Offers the option of deleting your photos from your camera once you've downloaded them to your computer – an easy way to clean up your camera's photo storage.

Advanced Dialog. Clicking this button opens up an option screen which displays all of the photos in your camera's memory. By checking and unchecking the checkboxes, you can select which photos are included in your download and which will remain on your camera.

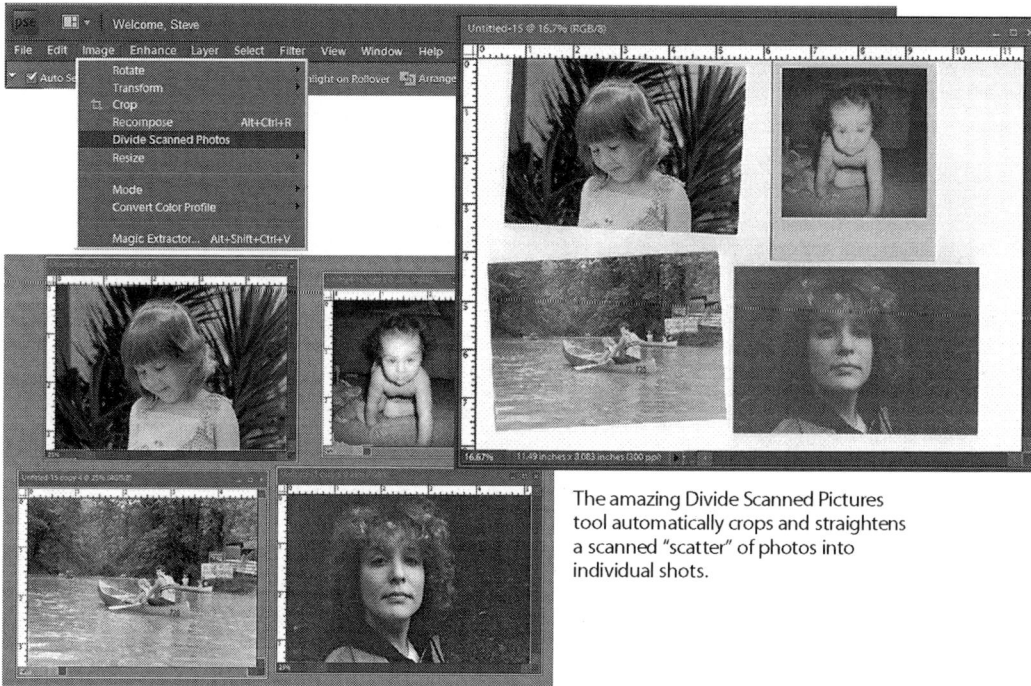

The amazing Divide Scanned Pictures tool automatically crops and straightens a scanned "scatter" of photos into individual shots.

Divide Scanned Photos

If you've ever needed to scan a number of photos in one sitting, you've probably tried to save a little time by scanning several pictures at once. This leaves you with a "scatter" of pictures.

Often, however, it's a such a chore to crop, straighten and save each photo that the time you save scanning several photos at once is traded off in the time it takes to separate and straighten the results!

Thankfully, Photoshop Elements now includes a tool for automatically doing this latter chore for you. To use it:

1. **Scan a group of photos** at once, as described earlier in this chapter. Although the photos don't need to be straight and aligned, they do need to be far enough from each other that Photoshop Elements sees them as separate image files (as illustrated).

2. In Photoshop Elements, go to the **Image** drop-down on the Menu Bar and select **Divide Scanned Photos**.

The program will automatically separate each photo into a separate image file, cropping and straightening each as needed.

Photomerge

Photomerge is not just one but an entire package of great, little tools for combining elements from more than one photo in order to either create an enhanced picture or to create a brand new photo composition. These tools are available under Photoshop Elements' **File/New** menu.

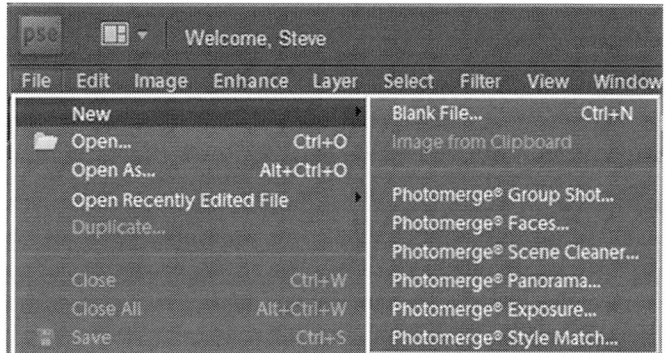

> **Photomerge Group Shot** is a tool for creating a composite shot in which a person or people who appear in one photo can be painted into another.

> **Photomerge Faces** is a tool for creating a perfect portrait by combining the best elements from several photos of the same face.

> With **Photomerge Scene Cleaner** you can combine elements from two photos of the same scene, borrowing the best elements from each shot, so that you can remove unwanted elements – or even unwanted *people* – from an otherwise perfect shot!

We'll show you step-by-step how to use **Photomerge Panorama, Photomerge Exposure** and **Photomerge Style Match** (a new tool in Photoshop Elements 9.)

Screen captures

In addition to scanning and downloading photos, you can add images to Photoshop Elements by, essentially, "taking a snapshot" of your computer screen. This can be a very helpful function if you're trying to show someone some strange behavior on your computer or if you, like me, are creating software illustrations for a book. This snapshot is called a **Screen Capture**.

Screen Captures are very easy to do on PCs. To do so, you simply press the **Prt Scr** (short for Print Screen) button on your keyboard. (Holding down the **Alt** key as you press this button captures only the current, active window.) On a Mac, press ⌘+**Shift+4**.

The image will be copied to your operating system's Clipboard. You can then paste this image into virtually any program (including Microsoft Word) by using the **Edit/Paste** option or by pressing **Ctrl+v**.

You can also open the entire captured image as an image file for editing in Photoshop Elements. To do this, go to the **File** drop-down on the Photoshop Elements Menu Bar and select **New**, then **Image from Clipboard**.

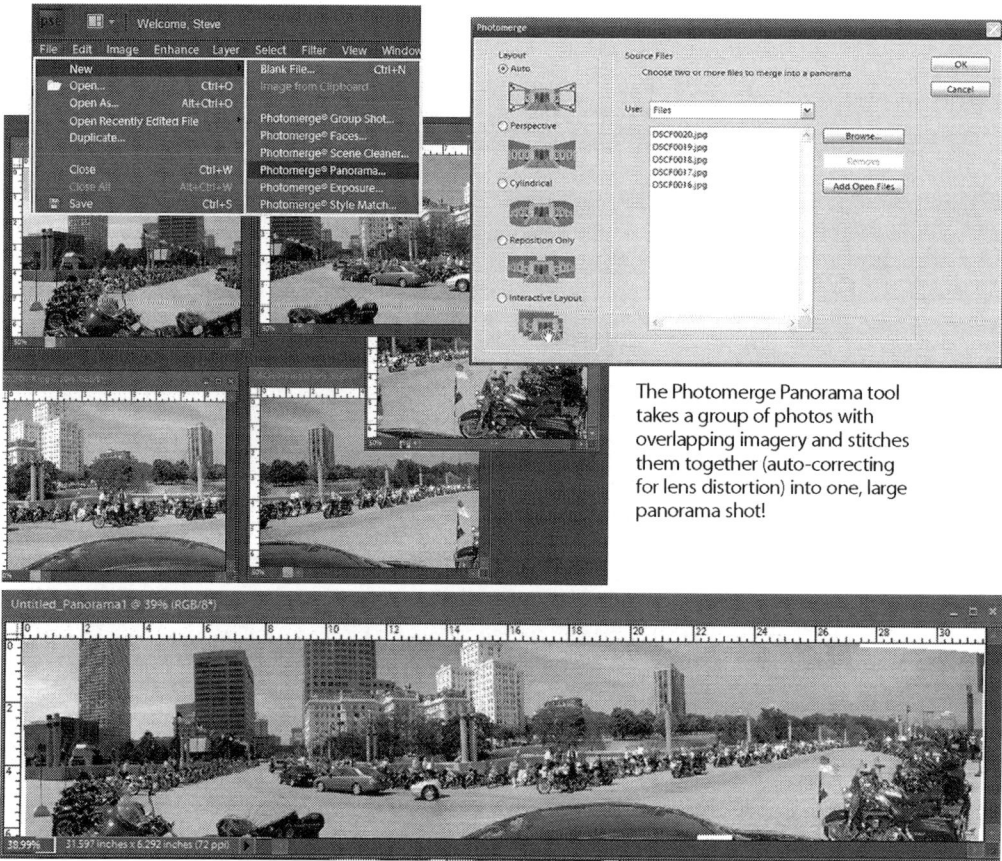

The Photomerge Panorama tool takes a group of photos with overlapping imagery and stitches them together (auto-correcting for lens distortion) into one, large panorama shot!

Combine photos with Photomerge Panorama

Sometimes a single photo doesn't capture the entirety of a scene or landscape. The Grand Canyon, the Golden Gate Bridge, Vatican Square – a single snapshot just can't tell the whole story.

Photoshop Elements' **Photomerge Panorama** tool combines several photos of a scene into one complete photo – producing, for instance, a panoramic image of a wide scene from three or four photos taken of adjacent areas of that scene.

The tool works amazingly well in most cases – even compensating for lens distortion and slight color differences between shots. About the only requirement is that there be a little bit of overlap in the photos' contents so that the program can interpret the scene composition and calculate where to combine the images.

In my illustration above, I gathered a number of photos I'd shot while watching a Harley-Davidson "birthday" parade in downtown Milwaukee.

1. With your photos open, launch **Photomerge** by going to the **File** drop-down on the Editor's Menu Bar and selecting **New**, then **Photomerge Panorama**.

Why you should clear your camera's memory regularly

Sometimes, when your camera's storage gets full, you may be tempted to delete just a few photos to make room for a few new ones. There are serious liabilities to doing this.

Your photos are stored in your camera or on your camera's storage card as JPEGs. These JPEGs vary slightly in size. Removing a photo or two leaves a "hole" of a certain size. When you take a new picture, if it is of a slightly larger size, your camera's storage may corrupt and you could lose several pictures!

For this reason alone, it's good, safe housekeeping to regularly clear off your digital camera's storage completely to "clean" or reformat the memory card.

---

2. In the option screen that appears, browse to select the photo files or photo folder you'd like included in your **Panorama**. (You can also indicate for the tool to use the photos that are currently open in the Editor workspace.)

3. In most cases the **Auto Layout** setting produces very good results. However, should you need to tweak the composition, the **Interactive Layout** option opens a dialog box for manually repositioning your **Photomerge** elements.

As you can see in my example on the previous page, there is a small flaw. In the center of the picture you can see the front end of a car that appeared in one photo but not the photo adjacent to it. But, otherwise, the results are nearly perfect.

And, at 32 inches long, it might make a very nice poster!

Mix elements from two photos with Photomerge Exposure

Another **Photomerge** tool is **Photomerge Exposure**, a tool for taking the best elements of two or more photos and combining them into one great-looking picture.

This is terrific tool for combining the best parts of several shots taken with a flash at night or in which the subject is standing in front of a window or other brightly-lit background.

It works similarly to **Photomerge Faces** and **Photomerge Scene Cleaner** in that you select acceptable elements in each photo and the program combines them into a best-of composite photo.

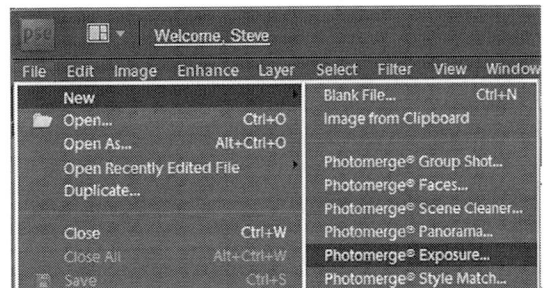

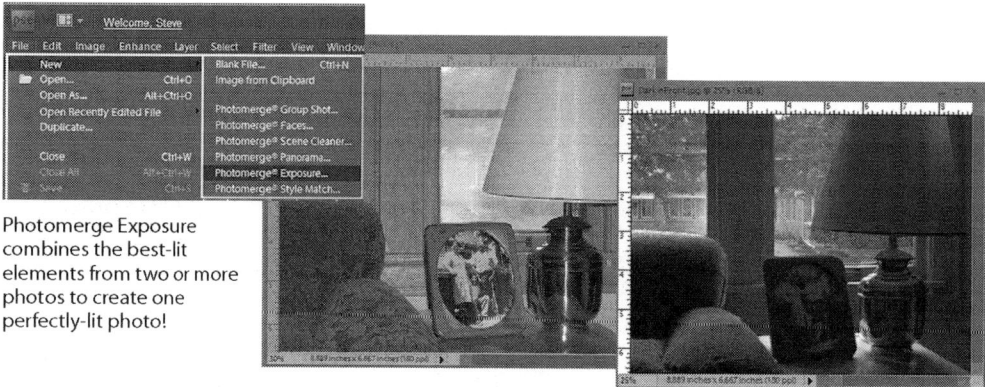

Photomerge Exposure combines the best-lit elements from two or more photos to create one perfectly-lit photo!

Above are two photos. The first was shot with a flash – lighting the foreground but leaving the view through the windows in the background washed out. The second photo was shot with natural lighting, the result being that the background (the view through the windows) is perfectly exposed but the furniture in the foreground is too dark.

1. I open both of my photos in the Editor workspace. You can combine elements from any number of photos.

2. From the **File** drop-down on the Menu Bar, I select **New**, then **Photomerge Exposure**.

    The program will analyze my open photos and, by default, the first photo in my **Project Bin** will be displayed as my master **Foreground**. (To use a different photo for your **Foreground**, double-click on its thumbnail in your **Project Bin**.)

3. I then drag another photo from my **Project Bin** into the **Background** panel, as on the illustration on the next page.

    The program will adjust and even skew the photos a bit so that their elements line up. This alignment may mean that your photos don't go all the way to the edges of their frames, as seen on the facing page. This is a necessary part of the alignment process, and you can crop away these blank areas once your **Photomerge** is complete.

Manually align your photos for Photomerging

If the program does not automatically align your **Foreground** and **Background** photos, you can manually align them by selecting the **Alignment Tool** under the **Advanced Option** arrow on the **Photomerge** palette.

When the **Alignment Tool** is selected, three alignment points will appear on your **Background** photo. Place those three alignment points on key reference points in the photo. Then click to select the **Foreground** photo. When three similar alignment points appear on it, move them to the exact same reference points as you did on the **Background** photo and click **Align**.

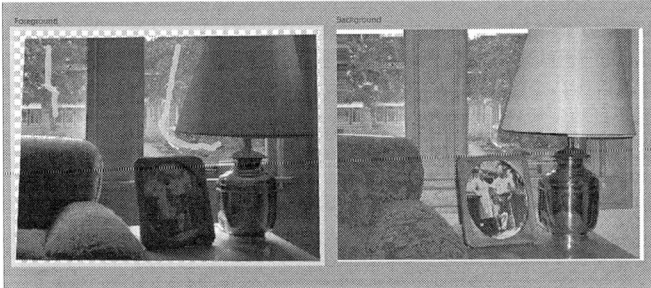

It only took a couple of scribbles drawn through the window area to select these elements for Photomerging onto my Background photo. The second photo shows the results of the Photomerging of elements.

4. In some cases, clicking on the **Automatic** tab on the **Photomerge** palette will automatically create your composite photo – although it will likely benefit from some tweaking by moving the sliders in either **Simple Blending** or **Smart Blending Mode**.

   In most cases – as in my example, the under-exposed and over-exposed areas aren't black or white enough – you'll be best designating manually which elements should be cloned from the **Foreground** to the **Background** photo.

5. To manually designate the elements to be **Photomerged**, I clicked on the **Photomerge** palette's **Manual** tab. Then, using the **Selection Tool** (pencil), I painted the elements to be cloned.

   Like the **Pencil Tool** on the main **Toolbox**, you can set the tool's "brush" to different sizes using the slider on the **Option Bar** at the top of the panel.

   As illustrated above, you don't need to completely cover the selected elements. Painting over part of an area tells the program to grabbed all similarly-colored elements.

   Use the **Eraser Tool** to un-designate selected elements.

To make the combination of elements look more natural, you can select the option to **Blend** (soften) **Edges** or use the slider to make your added elements semi-transparent.

The biggest challenge with the tool is that, because the **Selection Tool** selects elements in your photos based on pixel color similarity, you sometimes end up cloning more from your **Foreground** photo to your **Background** photo than you'd like. In my example, for instance, when I used the photo with the over-exposed background as my **Foreground**, every time I selected the lampshade, I also got the whited-out windows!

The solution for me was to swap the photos I was using as my **Foreground** and **Background**. Remember, just because you plan to use elements which are in the *background* of your photo doesn't necessarily mean that the photo with these elements won't make a better **Foreground** source image!

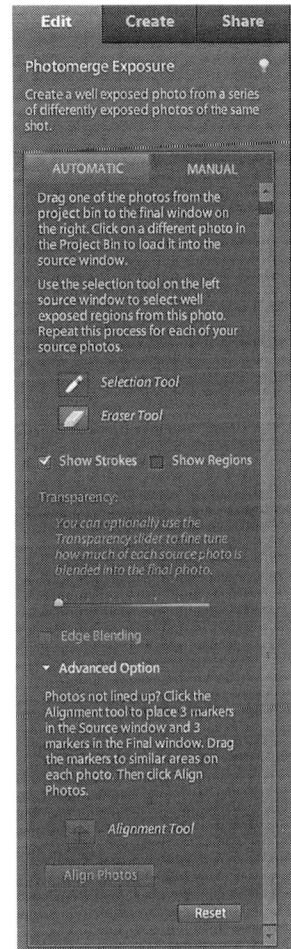

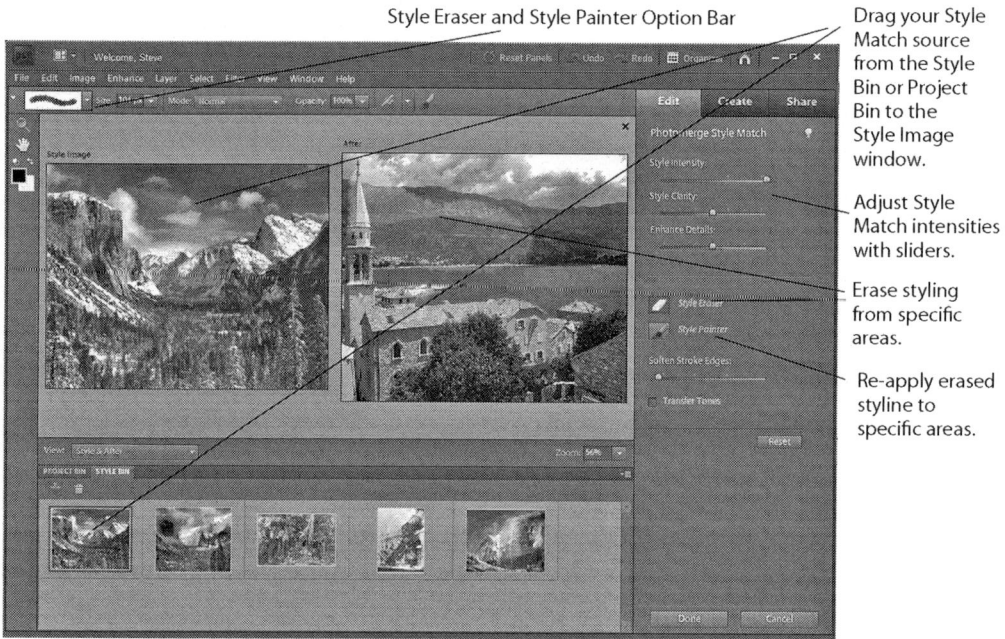

Style Eraser and Style Painter Option Bar

Drag your Style Match source from the Style Bin or Project Bin to the Style Image window.

Adjust Style Match intensities with sliders.

Erase styling from specific areas.

Re-apply erased styline to specific areas.

Stylize your photos with Photomerge Style Match

New to Photoshop Elements 9 is **Photomerge Style Match**, a tool for applying the lighting and tone of one photo onto another.

Photoshop Elements comes included some stylish photos that you can use for your style source – but you can use your own photos as templates as well.

1. With the photo you want to stylize open in the Photoshop Elements Editor space, launch the **Photomerge** tool by going to the **File** drop-down on the Menu Bar and selecting **New**, then **Photomerge Style Match**.

   If you'd like to use a style from one of your own photos rather than from one of the Photoshop Elements templates, make sure that this photo is also open in the Editor so that it appears in your **Project Bin,** along the bottom of the interface. .

2. Drag the photo that you are going to use as your style source from the **Style Bin,** along the bottom of the interface, into the **Style Image** box (the box labeled 'Drag Style Image Here').

   If you are using one of your own photos as your style source, select the **Project Bin** tab at the bottom of the interface, then drag your photo from the **Project Bin** into the **Style Image** box.

   Once you've provided a style source, your working photo (which appears in the **After** box in the **Style Match** workspace) will show some change.

If you'd like to replace the photo you are using as your style source, just drag a new photo from the **Style Bin** or **Project Bin** into the **Style Image** box.

3. Using the sliders in the **Photomerge Style Match** control panel, on the right, adjust **Style Intensity, Style Clarity** and **Enhance Details** to your satisfaction.

4. If you'd like to remove applied styles from specific areas of your photo, select the **Style Eraser** and drag it across your photo in the **After** window. By adjusting the **Soften Stroke Edges** slider, you can control how subtle the effect of the **Style Eraser** is.

   You can also select different brush textures and sizes for this (as well as for the **Style Painter** tool) from the **Option Bar** at the top of the interface.

5. To re-apply styles to an area you've erased them from, select the **Style Painter** tool and repaint the style back onto your photo. As with the **Style Eraser**, you can control the subtlety of the re-applied style by adjusting the **Soften Stroke Edges** slider.

6. When you are satisfied with your results, click **Done**.

Photoshop Elements Preferences

The Photoshop Elements **Preferences** are opened under the **Edit** drop-down on the **Editor's** Menu Bar. Many of these settings are pretty self-explanatory. But here are a few that I think are worth noting:

- **Saving Files**. By default, the program is set to **Always Ask** whenever you try to save or overwrite a file. This drives me crazy! When I want to save my work, I want to save my work!

   Unless you want to save versions of your photos as you work, I recommend setting **On First Save** to **Save Over Current File**.

- **File Extensions**. For most of your work, it won't matter if your **File Extensions** (.jpg, .gif, .psd) are saved in upper case or lower case. However, in some environments – particularly if you're creating images for the Internet, it can make a big difference. HTML sees upper case letters as different names than lower case. There is no right or wrong setting here, but you do want to be aware of how the program is naming your files so that you can maintain some consistency and control.

- **File Compatibility**. I recommend checking the option to **Prefer Adobe Camera Raw for Supported Raw Files**. RAW is a function of higher-end digital cameras that stores its images unprocessed, giving you more control over how the imagery is interpreted and adjusted. If your camera supports it, you'll probably want access to it.

Process Multiple Files

The **Process Multiple Files** feature is a tool for editing or revising a whole batch of photo files in one action. This means that, for instance, you can apply a **Quick Fix** – like **Auto Levels**, **Auto Contrast**, **Auto Color** or **Sharpen** – to an entire folder full of photos with just a few clicks! You can also rename an entire batch at once or convert an entire batch to a new file format.

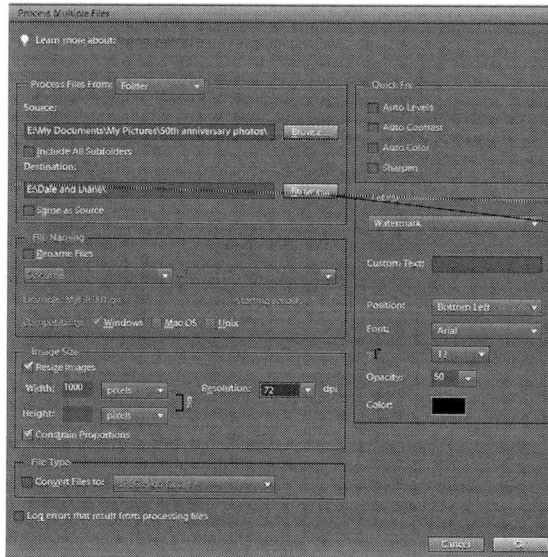

The Process Multiple Files tool (located under the File menu) will process, rename or resize a batch of files in one action.

Creating a separate Destination folder preserves your original files in their original state and size.

A common use of **Process Multiple Files** is to **resize** an entire batch of photos in one action. By properly configuring this tool, you can also send the resized images to another location, preserving your original photos in their original sizes.

1. To launch **Process Multiple Files**, select the option from the **File** drop-down on the **Editor's** Menu Bar.

   Process Multiple Files can be applied to a folder or to all of the photo files you have open at the time the tool is launched.

2. Select the appropriate option from the drop-down menu at **Process Files From** and, if appropriate, browse to the photo folder at **Source**.

3. Set the **Destination** if you'd like your changed photo files saved to a new location.

4. If you'd like to rename your photo batch, check the **Rename Files** option and set your desired naming conventions. Generally, a batch of photos uses a similar front name followed by a sequence of alphabetic or numeric suffixes.

5. If you'd like to change the **Image Size** for your batch of photo files, check the **Resize Images** option and then set the **Width** or **Height** and **Resolution**.

As long as **Constrain Proportions** is checked, there's no need to set *both* the **Width** and **Height** for your photos. The tool will resize your photos proportionately, based on the single dimension you define.

For instance, if you are resizing your photos for video, you need only to set the **Width** to 1000 pixels. As long as **Constrain Proportions** is ticked, each photo will be resized to the 1000 pixels wide and whatever height is necessary to keep the photo in its correct proportions.

- **Transparency**. Transparency in an image file is usually represented in Photoshop and Photoshop Elements by a gray and white checkerboard pattern (as seen in **Create non-square graphics** in **Chapter 8, Work With Photoshop Elements Layers**). This preference screen allows you to customize the pattern or turn it off completely.

- **Units & Rulers**. This preference screen sets the default measurements that are displayed on your image files in the Editor workspace. For most online work or for editing graphics and photos for video, you may want to set your **Rulers** to **Pixels**, a more relevant measurement than inches or centimeters.

- **Type**. This one is just a personal preference, a peeve left over from my years as a layout artist. If you're planning to work with type in your image files, select the option to use **Smart Quotes**. **Smart Quotes** are the difference between quotation marks and plain old tick marks. The difference, for instance, between " (which are tick marks, used for measurements) and the slightly curved " (true quotation marks). Using true quotation marks can mean the subtle difference between a layout looking "typewritery" and one looking truly designed.

The Organizer has its own set of **Preferences**, also located under the **Edit** drop-down on its Menu Bar. Among them are settings for configuring how the program interfaces with the scanner and camera.

Also, the Organizer's **Backup/Synchronization** preferences define how the program automatically backs up your media files online. For more information on using online file backup, see **Chapter 34, Photoshop.com**.

Chapter 13

Learn About Your Photoshop Elements File
Important information on your
Photoshop Elements file window

There is a lot more to a PSD, or an
image file, than meets the eye!

In this chapter, we'll take a close look
at an image file, what Photoshop
Elements has to tell us about it and,
ultimately, what it all means.

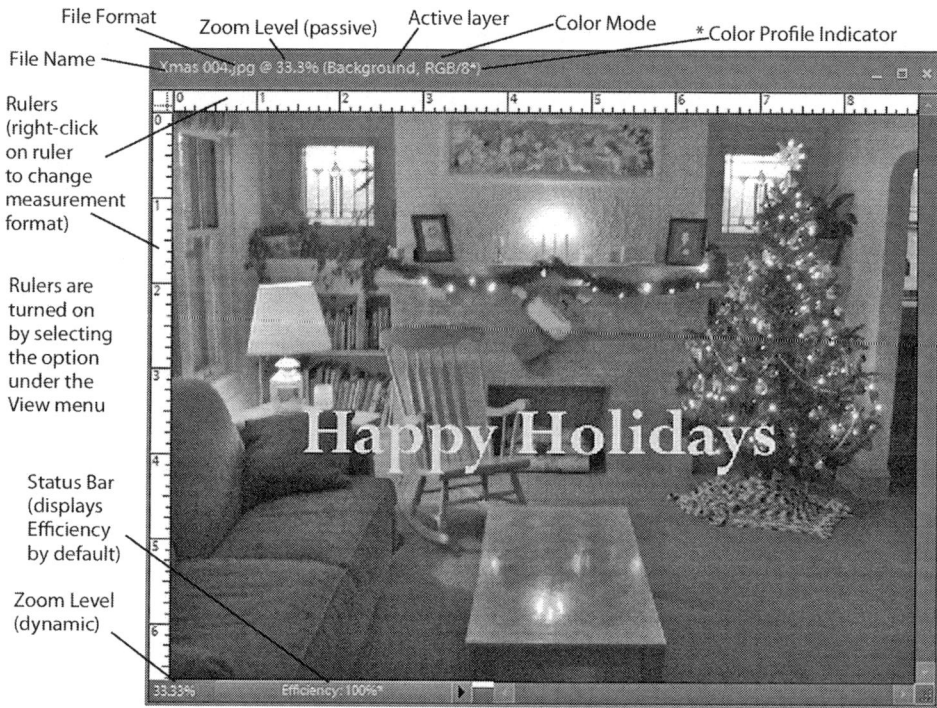

File Format   Zoom Level (passive)   Active layer   Color Mode   *Color Profile Indicator

File Name

Xmas 004.jpg @ 33.3% (Background, RGB/8*)

Rulers (right-click on ruler to change measurement format)

Rulers are turned on by selecting the option under the View menu

Status Bar (displays Efficiency by default)

Zoom Level (dynamic)

33.33%   Efficiency: 100%*

The Info Bar

Whenever you open a photo or an image file in Photoshop Elements' Editor workspace, it appears with a frame around it. This frame includes a lot of useful information about the file.

> **File Name**. This is the name of the file, of course – including the suffix, which defines the file's format (PSD, TIF, JPG, etc.).

> **Zoom Level**. Displayed both after the **File Name**, at the top of the image frame, and in the lower left corner of the image frame, this number, a percentage, tells the scale of the image, as currently displayed in your Editor workspace. You can zoom in or out by pressing **Ctrl++** (the Ctrl and plus key) or **Ctrl+‒** (the Ctrl and minus key) on your keyboard.

This **Zoom Level** number can be a bit misleading, however. This is because it is measuring the scale of the picture's size in *pixels* rather than in linear numbers, such as inches or centimeters.

That means that if you're looking at an image file with a resolution of 300 ppi at 100% zoom, the picture is going to look about *four times larger* on your computer monitor than it will when it is printed.

But, for most of the images you're working on for video or for the web, at 100% zoom your image should appear at just about its actual size.

> **Layer**. If you have a layered PSD file open in your **Editor** workspace, the layer that is currently selected will appear in parentheses, following the **Zoom Level**.

Color Mode. Following the **Layer** notation, or alone in the parenthesis, is the **Color Mode** of your image file. In most cases, this mode will be **RGB/8**. However, if you are editing a monochrome (black & white) photo, this mode will read **Gray/8**.

The **RGB** mode means that the pixels in your image are composed of combinations of red, green and blue. Each of these colors can be set to any of 256 levels (0-255).

Why 256? Well, this seemingly arbitrary number is actually a very *real* number, with its origins in binary code, the base 2 numbering system that is at the heart of all computer programming. Every instruction written into every computer program is based on some base 2 number.

256 is 2^8 (2 to the 8th power, or 2x2x2x2x2x2x2x2). Hence, the red, green and blue color levels are each 8-bit settings (with 256 possibilities) – which is why the number 8 appears after the RGB listing.

There are other, by the way, even deeper RGB modes. 16-bit color, for instance. However, 8-bit color is the standard for video and online graphics, and it is the only color mode that Premiere Elements can work with. Besides, the 256 levels of red, green and blue yields 16,777,216 possible combinations of these colors, which is more than enough colors for our purposes.

Color modes can be selected for your image files under the **Image** drop-down on the Menu Bar.

Grayscale, as we've mentioned earlier, is monochrome or black and white (256 levels of the single color, black).

Indexed Color is a system for reducing the number of colors in an image. If you've worked on graphics for the Web, you likely understand how reducing colors on a GIF can also reduce the file size (although this format is generally not appropriate for photographs, which require a full color range).

Bitmap color mode converts all of your pixels to either pure black or pure white.

Why does a "full-screen" video fill only part of my computer screen?

Remember, a standard NTSC video frame is only the equivalent of a 640x480 pixel image. Most likely your computer monitor is set to a resolution of between 1024x768 pixels and 1280x1024 pixels. That means that a full-screen video image at 100% zoom may take up only one-fourth of your computer screen!

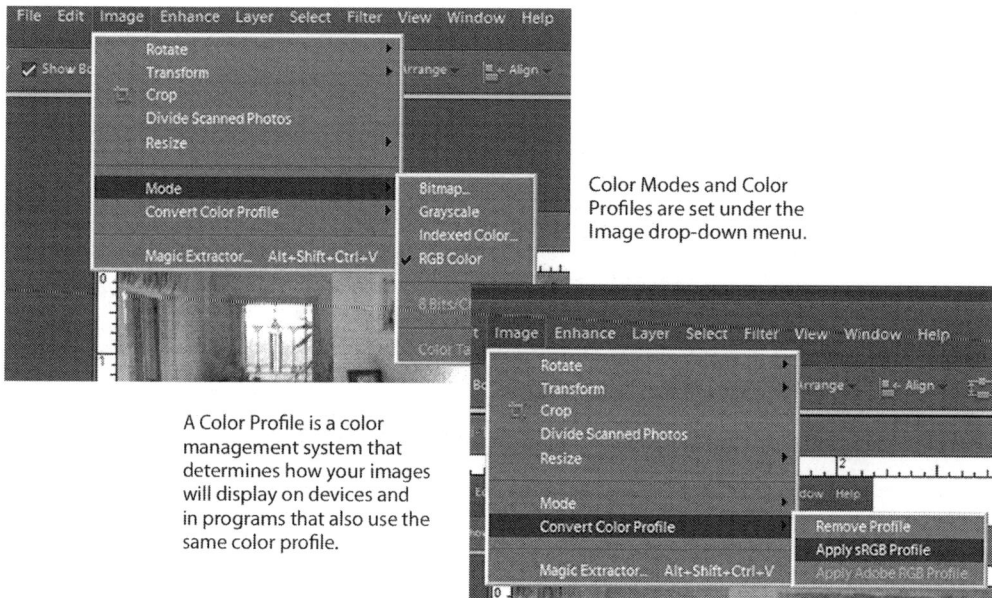

Color Modes and Color Profiles are set under the Image drop-down menu.

A Color Profile is a color management system that determines how your images will display on devices and in programs that also use the same color profile.

The professional version of Photoshop includes additional color modes, which are useful for preparing files for production on an offset press. However, for our purposes – and particularly as you produce graphics and imagery for use in Premiere Elements or for the Web – you'll usually be working with **RGB** or **Grayscale** mode only.

* (Color Profile). An asterisk appearing after the Color Mode listing is an indication that a **Color Profile** has been assigned to the image.

A **Color Profile** is a standardization system for color that can be applied across several programs and hardware devices. This ensures that the image's colors appear the same on every device, and in every application, that's using that same profile. The only profile available in Photoshop Elements is **Adobe sRGB**, which is probably the most standardized color profile in the world.

Many graphics cards and monitors will allow you to set a color profile for them. If it is available on your computer, you'll usually find it listed under **Color Management**, under **Settings/Advanced** for your display. (On a PC you can access these settings by right-clicking on your computer's desktop and selecting **Properties**. On a Mac, open your **System Preferences** and click on **Display**.)

Using the same color profile for all of your programs and hardware is the best way to ensure that what you see on your computer is ultimately what you get, image-wise.

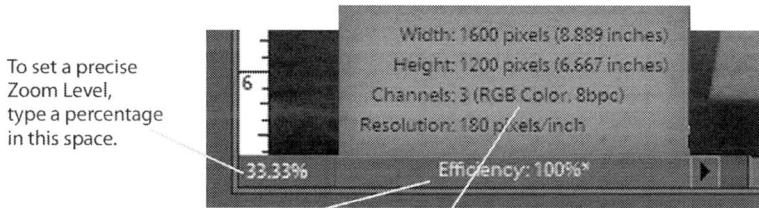

To set a precise Zoom Level, type a percentage in this space.

Width: 1600 pixels (8.889 inches)
Height: 1200 pixels (6.667 inches)
Channels: 3 (RGB Color, 8bpc)
Resolution: 180 pixels/inch

33.33%   Efficiency: 100%*

Efficiency displays how much of your work is being stored in your RAM.

Clicking and holding on the Status Bar displays a pop-up info panel.

The Status Bar

There's even more information about your file on the **Status Bar** which runs along the bottom of the image frame.

Zoom Level. Although this number, a percentage, is the same as the information displayed at the top of the panel, the **Zoom Level** displayed at the bottom left of an image frame is *dynamic*. In other words, you can type any number in this space and, when you press **Enter,** Photoshop Elements will zoom the view of your image file to that precise scale.

Efficiency. Along the bottom of your image panel, in an area known as the **Status Bar,** you'll see a listing for **Efficiency**. This number is a helpful indicator of how your computer is functioning with your image files.

In most cases, on an adequate computer with adequate RAM, particularly while working on smaller images, this number will read 100%. Lower numbers indicate that, due to the size of the image file, Photoshop Elements is being forced to use **scratch disk space**, utilizing a portion of your hard drive as temporary RAM. When this **Efficiency** number is lower, you'll find Photoshop Elements running a bit slower.

This isn't a reason to panic. When working with larger photos, it is probably inevitable. (Although if you're always seeing less than 100% listed here, you may want to invest in some more RAM.) It's simply a way to for you to monitor your scratch disk use, in the event your Photoshop Elements performance seems a bit sluggish and you wonder why.

More Information. If you click on the **Status Bar** (where **Efficiency** is listed by default) at the bottom of your image frame, a pop-up panel will appear, displaying even more information about your image, including its resolution and dimensions, as illustrated above.

Additionally, the arrow button to the right of the **Status Bar** allows you to set this area to display a number of other facts about your image, including the name of the tool that you currently have selected, the size of your image file and even how long it would take your image file to download from a Web site!

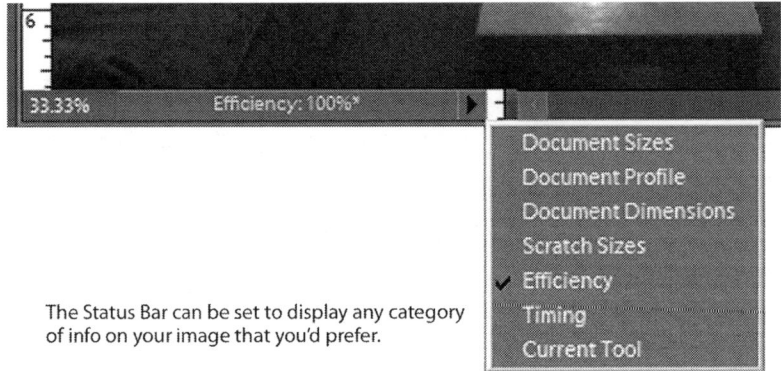

The Status Bar can be set to display any category of info on your image that you'd prefer.

The Info Palette

Another tool for getting information about your image file is the **Info** palette – which is launched from the **Window** drop-down on the Menu Bar. This panel displays color and location information about specific pixels you have selected in your image as well as measurements of selected areas.

- **Color Info**. As you hover your mouse over your image, you'll see numbers appearing next to the R, G and B listings in the upper left panel of this palette. These are the color level settings for the individual pixels your cursor is currently over.

  The R, G and B listings on the upper right panel on the palette display as an alpha-numeric combination.

  The six number and letter combinations from these three colors are called the pixel color's **Hex** code, a common system for identifying colors on Web files.

  In Hex code, for instance:

  Black is 000000
  White is ffffff
  A medium gray is 808080

  If you click on the eyedroppers in either panel on this palette, you can set that panel to display this information using other color definitions, including **HSB** (hue, saturation and brightness).

- **Vector Position**. The current position of your mouse cursor over your image file is listed in the lower left panel of this palette, as measured in pixels from the top left corner of your photo or image file.

  By clicking on the **+** sign on this palette, you can set this information panel – as well as the information panel on the **Dimensions** panel, to the right – to display these measurements as pixels, inches, metric measurements, percentages or even picas.

- **Dimensions**. If you are working with one of the **Marquee Selection Tools** or one of the **Shape** drawing tools (see **Chapter 4, Get to Know the Photoshop Elements Toolbox**), the lower right panel of this palette will display the dimensions of the area you are selecting or drawing. (Professional designers sometimes use this **Info** palette, along with the **Rectangular Marquee** tool, to select and measure areas of their image files.)

Color of selected pixel, listed as RGB.

Color of selected pixel, listed as Hex.

Dimensions of selected area or shape.

Vector postion of pixel, measured from top left corner of image file.

Size of layered image file.

Size of flattened image file.

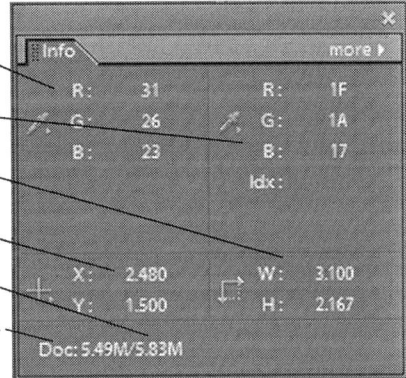

The Info palette provides a variety of information about your image file.

- **Doc Size**. The size of the image file you're currently editing is displayed along the bottom of the Info palette.

  If you're working on a layered image file, you'll see two numbers listed. The first is the size of the image file once all of the layers in your image file have been flattened; the second is the size of the image file if saved as a layered PSD file.

Part 2

Adobe
Premiere Elements 9

Get to Know the Workspace

Basic Editing Moves

What's New in Version 9?

Chapter 14

Get to Know Premiere Elements 9
What's what and what it does

The interface for Premiere Elements has been designed by Adobe to be as simple and as intuitive as possible. It is also remarkably customizable, with a wealth of powerful tools in obvious and, once in a while, not so obvious places.

There are few major changes to the interface since the last edition of the program. But you'll quickly find that Premiere Elements has been designed to be as simple and as intuitive as possible to use – and yet easily customizable.

The Monitor Panel

Docking Headers

The multi-purpose Tasks panel

The Sceneline

The Timeline

Panels and tabs

There are three major panels that are visible by default when you open your Premiere Elements project. They are the **Monitor** panel, the **My Project** panel (aka the **Timeline/Sceneline**) and the **Tasks** panel.

We'll discuss each of these in greater detail as we explore the program's tools in upcoming chapters – and we'll recommend a few other panels (many available under the **Window** drop-down menu and some launched from buttons on other panels).

The Monitor panel

The **Monitor** panel displays the video that you've assembled on your timeline or sceneline. The buttons along the bottom of the **Monitor** control your timeline's playback, while the tools in the lower right can be used for splitting clips, creating titles and grabbing a **Freeze Frame** from your video. We discuss the **Monitor** panel and these tools in detail in **Chapter 21, Edit with Monitor Panel Tools**.

The Multi-Function Tasks Panel

The Premiere Elements **Tasks** panel is your multi-function access point for the vast majority of Premiere Elements' workspaces and tools.

The Monitor panel includes a toolbar for the playback of your video on the timeline and sceneline, access to the Titles workspace and some valuable editing functions.

Adobe has tried to make getting to each of the **Tasks** panel's workspaces and tools as intuitive as possible by making the paths to them task-oriented.

To gather your media, for instance, you click on the **Organize** tab and select **Get Media**. Your video editing tools are accessible under the **Edit** tab. You select and customize your DVD and BluRay disc menus under the **Disc Menus** tab, and you output to various media or devices by way of the **Share** tab.

Workspaces in the multi-purpose Tasks panel are accessed by following intuitive, task-oriented tabs and buttons.

Timeline editing mode

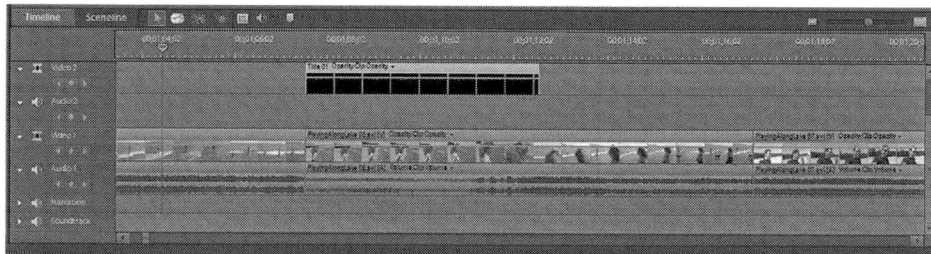

Sceneline editing mode

The 'My Project Panel' (or, as we call it, the Timeline/Sceneline Panel)

The Timeline/Sceneline "My Project" Panel

The **My Project** panel (which, most of the time, we'll refer to as the **Timeline** or the **Sceneline** panel) is where the actual assembly of your movies will take place.

In **Sceneline** mode, you can quickly and easily assemble your movie's clips and add audio, effects and transitions to them. The focus here is on content more than how the elements in your video interact. Most veteran editors consider **Sceneline** the more elementary workspace for creating videos.

In **Timeline** mode, the emphasis is on time – not just what elements are included in your movie, but how and when they interact with each other. This mode is the much more traditional video editing workspace, giving you much greater access to Premiere Elements' true power.

In **Timeline** mode, you have a virtually unlimited number of audio and video tracks (officially up to 99 of each) as well as the ability to control effects, audio volume and the positions of your clips (such as titles) that may appear on top of or share screen space with your main video clips.

In short, if you have any interest at all in doing any *really cool* video editing, **Timeline** mode is where you'll likely spend most of your time.

In **Chapter 18**, we'll show you how to work in **Sceneline** mode. In **Chapter 19**, we'll show you how to assemble your movie in **Timeline** mode. And, in **Chapter 20**, we'll show you how to work with your timeline's audio tracks.

Show Docking Headers

At Muvipix.com, we recommend that, as soon as you start up the program, you select the option to **Show Docking Headers**. This option is available under the **Window** drop-down on the Menu Bar.

These **Docking Headers** (gray bars along the tops of each panel that display the panel's name) serve a couple important functions.

The primary function of these headers is to allow you to "undock" the various panels in the interface. In other words, if you want to spread out your workspace or change their arrangement in the interface, you can do so by dragging a panel around your desktop by its **Docking Header**. This separates the panel from the rest of the interface so that you can place it anywhere you'd like on your computer's desktop.

The >> menus offer quick access to tools and features

This is particularly useful if you're using a very large monitor or even a two-monitor computer system. Spreading these panels out makes it much easier to see and to get to all of the tools on each.

But there's another reason for revealing the **Docking Headers**.

Do you see the black **>>** buttons in the upper right of many of the panels (as illustrated above)? These buttons open pop-up menus that allow you to turn off or on a number of very important features and functions for that particular work panel. In some cases, they also give you easy access to some great tools!

But, unless you **Show Docking Headers,** you won't even *see* these buttons on many of the panels! (In fact, until you reveal the **Docking Headers**, you won't even be able to see the *names* of the panels!)

So, whether you intend to undock your panels from the rest of the interface or not, activate the **Show Docking Headers** feature. You might well need access to what's otherwise hidden with them.

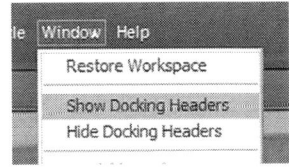

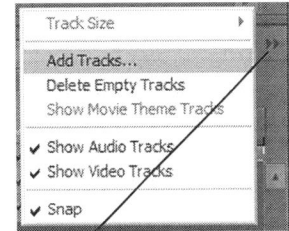

Customize your workspace

The sizes and the arrangements of the various panels in the interface are easily customizable. Panels can be resized by dragging on the seams between them. They can also be "undocked" from the interface and moved to more convenient or efficient areas on your desktop.

To resize your panels, hover your mouse over the seams between the panels until you see the double arrows – then click and drag.

Feel free to experiment and resize the panels by dragging on the borders between them. Or, if you've got a large computer monitor or, even better, a dual-monitor set-up, and you've activated **Show Docking Headers** (above) undock the panels by dragging them by their headers and position them to best take advantage of your computer's desktop.

As you move your panels around, you'll note that there is one panel you can not undock from the program's interface. The **Tasks** panel (the multi-purpose panel that houses most of the program's functions) is locked to the interface.

But, other than that, particularly if you've got lots of computer desktop space, you'll likely very much appreciate how much more accessible all of the program's tools are if you spread things out as much as possible.

And, if you ever do find the program misbehaving or if you just feel like you've lost control of your workspace, you can easily get back to the default look by simply going to the **Window** drop-down menu and selecting **Restore Workspace**.

Minimum screen resolution

Because of the size of the panels and the number of tools that Adobe fits into some rather tight spaces, we recommend that this program not be used on a computer with a monitor with less than 1280x1024 resolution.

There's simply no room for it all to fit otherwise! And you'll waste far too much time scrolling panels around, trying to get to all the tools. (The **Monitor** panel alone, for instance, demands at least 665 pixels across in order to display its entire playback and tool set – and even on a 1024x768 monitor, that doesn't leave much horizontal space for the all-important **Tasks** panel!)

What's a CTI?

The CTI
(Current Time
Indicator)
in Timeline mode

Vital vocabulary alert! That thin, vertical, red line that moves along the Timeline as you play your video? It's called a **CTI**, which stands for "Current Time Indicator."

That's an all-important vocabulary term that you'll definitely want to know as we continue to work

Trust us on this. Especially since there's no other word that comes close to describing this thing – and we're going to use the term often throughout this book.

Basic editing moves

No matter what you plan to do with your video and no matter how creatively you plan to do it, the video editing process itself will still fit the same basic structure.

Here's a brief review of the steps you'll take for creating any video project in Premiere Elements.

Starting a new project in Premiere Elements 9

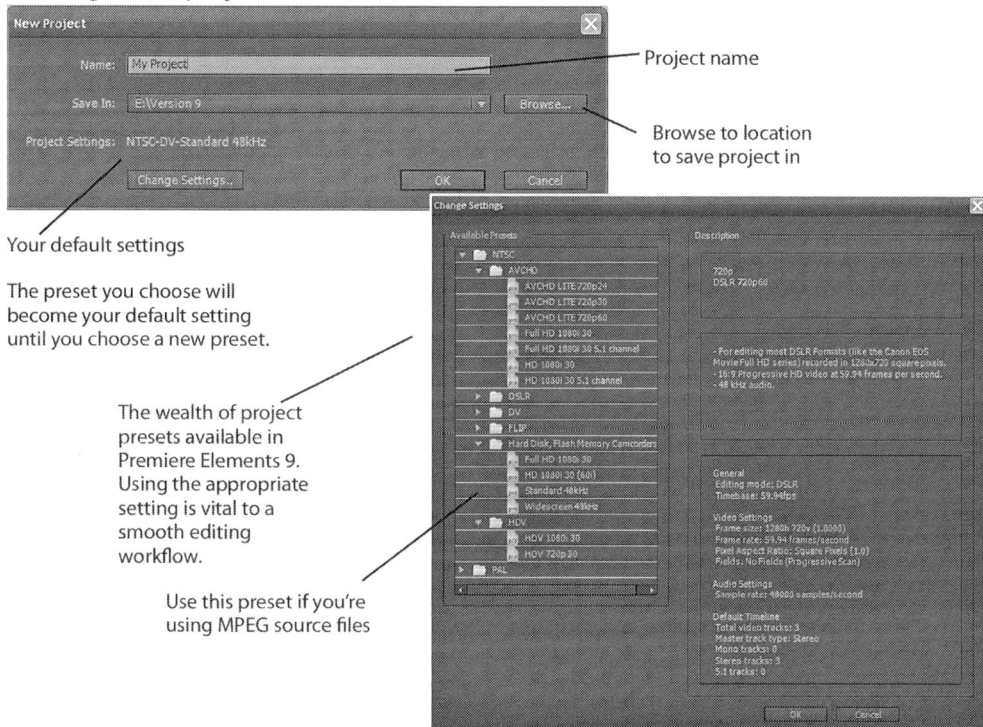

Project name

Browse to location to save project in

Your default settings

The preset you choose will become your default setting until you choose a new preset.

The wealth of project presets available in Premiere Elements 9. Using the appropriate setting is vital to a smooth editing workflow.

Use this preset if you're using MPEG source files

1 Start a project

When you select the option to begin a new project, the current project settings will be listed on the lower left of the **New Project** panel. If you'd like to change them, click on **Change Settings** and select the appropriate settings from the list of presets.

Unlike a Word document, a Premiere Elements project must be *defined* as well as created. And the option to select the settings for your project is only available when you *first begin your project*. You can't change your project's settings midway through.

Which settings you choose should be based on what format of video you're going to be building your project from – and you may well use the same settings for all of your video projects.

But selecting the correct project settings now can very likely save you a lot of frustration later in your project.

In **Chapter 15, Start a New Project**, we'll show you how to ensure your project is using the right project preset.

Get Media options, under the Organize tab

The DV, HDV and Webcam or WDM (Webcam) Device options launch the Capture workspace.

The DVD/DVD Camcorder, and the Flip, AVHCD Cameras and Phones options launch the Video Importer, while the Digital Still Camera & Phones option launches the Photo Downloader.

The PC Files and Folders option allows you to browse to files on your computer.

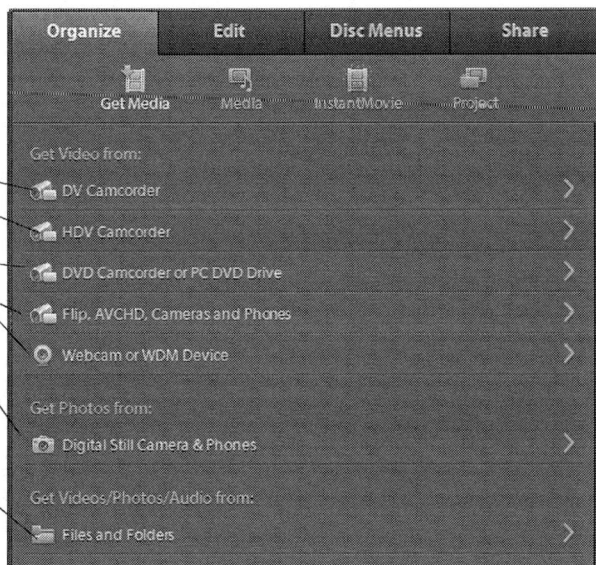

2 Gather your media

The assets, or media, you gather to create your movie can come from a variety of sources. It can be video, audio, music, photos or graphics. And, as you gather, or import, your assets into your project, they will appear in the media panel. This panel is accessed by clicking the **Project** button under the **Organize** tab.

To import your media into your project, click on the **Get Media** button under the **Organize** tab and then click the button representing your video's source device or location.

There are three ways to get your media into your project, all accessed by one of the seven buttons on the **Get Media** panel (illustrated above). We show you how and when to use each in **Chapter 16, Get Media Into Your Project**.

- **Stream, or capture, your video into your project.**

  The capture function works with tape-based camcorders, like miniDV (the **DV Camcorder** button) or HDV (the **HDV Camcorder** button), which are connected to your computer by a FireWire cable (aka IEEE-1394 or iLink). Video can also be streamed into the program using a DV bridge, like the ADS Pyro AV Link or Canopus ADVC units – although you will not be able to control the playback of these units from the capture screen.

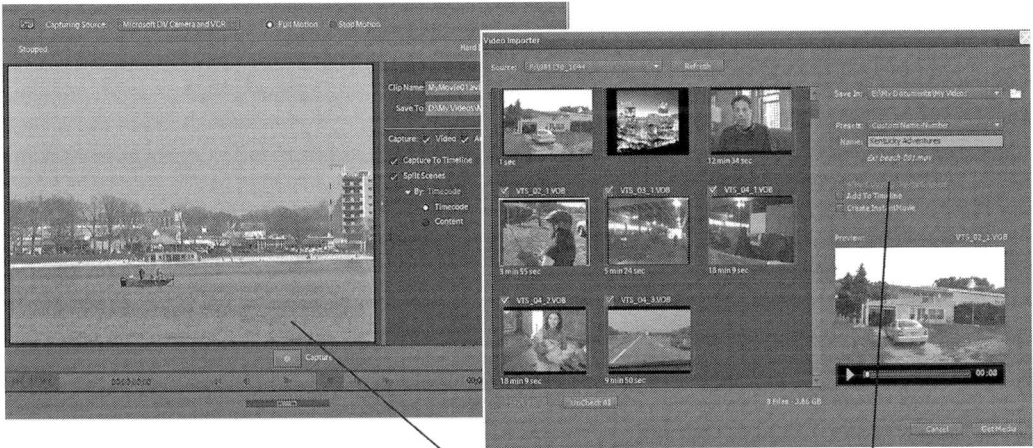

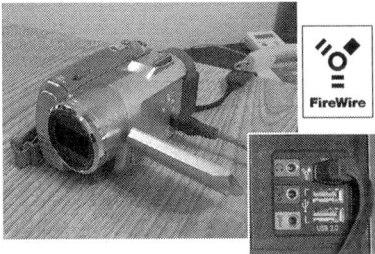

Video captured from tape-based camcorders is streamed into your Premiere Elements project over a FireWire connection. The camcorder's playback is controlled by the software and you can select which segments to capture.

Video from non-taped-based sources – including hard drive camcorders, Flip and AVCHD camcorders and DVDs – is imported into your Premiere Elements project by the Video Importer, while still photos are downloaded from your digital camera or phone with the Photo Downloader.

Tape-based video, captured over FireWire, by the way, is by far the format which Premiere Elements works with most efficiently. Premiere Elements includes an option for streaming in and capturing video from a **Webcam or WDM Device**.

- **Download your video from a hard drive camcorder or other device.**

Hard drive camcorders, including high-definition AVCHD and Flip cam units (the **Flip, AVCHD, Cameras and Phones** button), download their video as files rather than stream it into the program. Media can also be downloaded from other sources, including DVDs (the **DVD Camcorder or PC DVD Drive** button) and **Digital Still Cameras & Phones**, although these files may need additional preparation or even conversion before they can be used effectively in Premiere Elements.

- **Browse to gather media files which are located on your computer's hard drive(s).**

When you select the **PC Files and Folders** button under **Get Media**, Windows Explorer or the Mac OSX Finder opens, allowing you to browse to video, stills, graphics or music files already on your computer's hard drive.

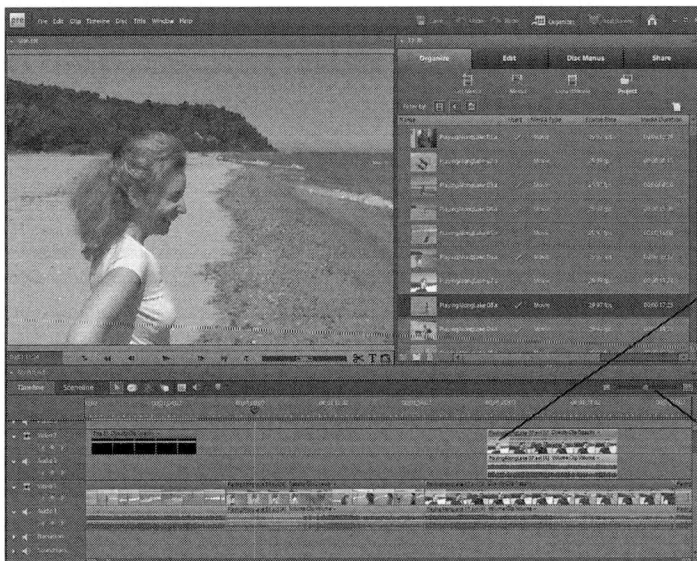

To add a clip to your timeline or sceneline, simply drag it from the Project media panel.

In Timeline mode, the other clips will "ripple", moving aside if you add the clip in the middle of a project.

To override the ripple effect (as when you're adding music or a video clip to a parallel track) hold down the Ctrl key (the ⌘ key on a Mac) as you add the clip.

Zoom in or out on the timeline by pressing + or - or using the Zoom slider.

3 Assemble the clips on your timeline or sceneline

Once you've imported your media clips into a project, they will appear listed in the **Project** media panel and you can begin the process of assembling your movie. This process is as simple, and as intuitive, as dragging the clips from the media panel to your timeline or sceneline and then arranging them in the order you'd like them to appear!

Once you add your files to your timeline or sceneline, you'll have a number of options:

- **Trim your clips.** Trimming means removing footage from either the beginning or the end of a clip. To trim a clip, click to select the clip on your timeline and then drag in either the beginning or end to shorten it, as in the illustration on the following page.

Timeline mode is the more powerful editing workspace

Although there are some advantages to editing in **Sceneline** mode, the **Timeline** mode is by far the more powerful editing workspace, allowing you much more control over how your clips behave and, more so, how they interact with each other at specific points in your movie. We encourage you to make it your default editing workspace.

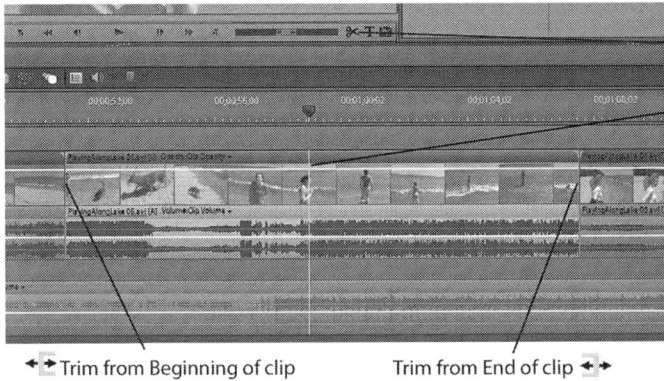

To slice a clip in two, click the Split (scissors) tool on the Monitor panel.

If a clip is selected on the timeline, only that clip will be split at the position of the CTI; If no clips are selected, all clips on every track on the timeline will be split at the position of the CTI.

Trim from Beginning of clip   Trim from End of clip

To trim a clip on the timeline, hover your mouse over the beginning or end of a clip until the Trim from Beginning or Trim from End icon appears, then click and drag in or out.

- **Split your clips.** Splitting means slicing through your clips so that you can remove footage from the middle or delete one sliced-off segment completely. To split a clip, position the **CTI** (playhead) over your clip at the point at which you'd like the slice to occur and then click on the scissors icon at the lower right of the **Monitor** panel.

- **Place your clip on upper video or audio track.** An important feature of editing in **Timeline** mode is the ability to place your video or audio on tracks other than **Video 1** and **Audio 1**.

  The use of multiple tracks of video is, in fact, key to the creation of many of the more advanced video effects, including **Chroma Key** and **Videomerge.**

  We'll discuss how to assemble your movie on both the **Sceneline** and **Timeline** in **Chapter 18** and **Chapter 19**, respectively. We'll also show you how to use multi-track editing in order to create a a variety of effects and take advantage of a number of key storytelling techniques.

  In **Chapter 20,** we'll show you how to use both automatic and manual tools to work with your audio clips.

4 Add and adjust effects

Premiere Elements comes loaded with over a hundred video and audio effects as well as hundreds of preset effects for working magic on your movie. Most video and preset effects show you a thumbnail preview of the effect in action on the **Effects** panel.

Adding an effect in Premiere Elements is very easy, as we show you in **Chapter 24, Add Video and Audio Effects**.

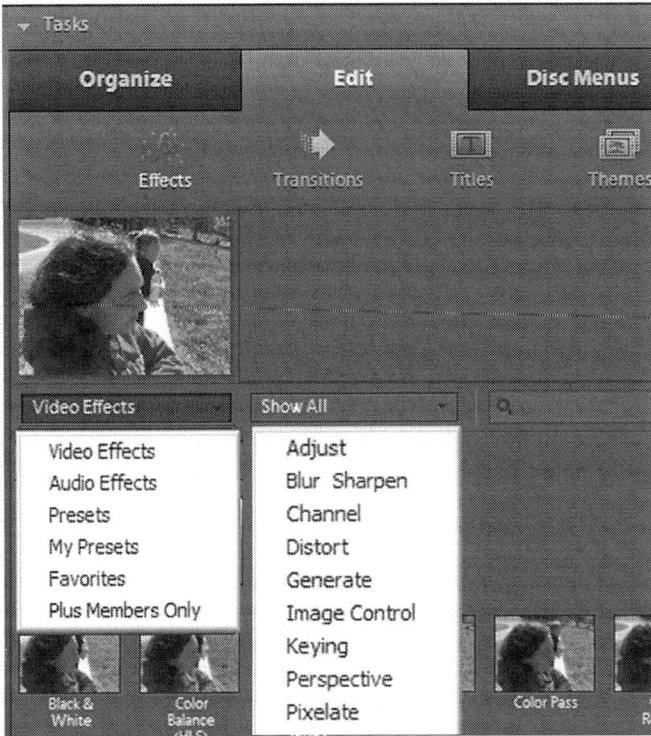

There are several sets and categories of effects in Premiere Elements.

1. Click on the **Edit** tab and then click the **Effects** button.

   This will open the **Effects** screen in the **My Tasks** panel.

2. Select an **Effects** set.

   The **Effects** panel displays **Video Effects** by default. But, by selecting the drop-down menu on the upper left of the panel, you can set it to display **Audio Effects, Presets, Favorites** or even your custom-created **Presets**. If you've got a Plus account with Photoshop.com, there will be additional effects displayed under that option.

3. Select an effect.

   You can browse through the list of effects on the panel, select a category of effects from the second drop-down menu or quickly call up an effect by typing its name in the Quick Search box on the upper right of the panel.

4. Apply the effect.

   To apply the effect, either drag it from the **Effects** panel onto a clip on your timeline – or select the clip on the timeline, select the effect in the panel and click the **Apply** button.

5. Open the **Properties** panel.

   Although you may see an immediate change in your clip once you apply an effect to it, virtually all effects can benefit from some custom tuning in the **Properties** panel.

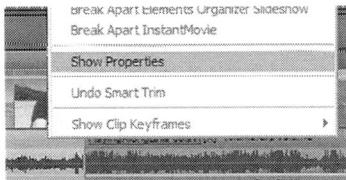

A clip's effects are adjusted and fine tuned in the Properties panel. The quickest way to access this panel is to right-click on the clip whose effects you want to adjust and select Show Properties.

There are four ways to open the **Properties** panel in Premiere Elements 9. And, because you may want to refer to them often, we've placed them in the box at the top of the facing page.

Throughout the book, I usually refer to the most efficient method for opening this panel: **right-clicking** on a clip (**Ctrl-clicking** on a Mac) on your timeline and selecting **Show Properties**.

Once the **Properties** panel is open, scroll down the list to locate the effect you've just added. Open up the effect's properties by clicking on the little triangle to the left of the effect's listing.

Four ways to open the Properties panel

1 Click on the **Edit Effect** button on the **Effects** panel;

2 **Right-click** on the clip (**Ctrl-click** on a Mac) and select **Show Properties**;

3 Click on the **Properties** button on the top left of the **Timeline** or **Sceneline**; or

4 Select **Properties** from the **Window** drop-down on the program's Menu Bar

---

6. Adjust the effect's settings.

Settings for various effects can be changed numerically, by (depending on the effect) moving sliders, sampling colors or selecting presets from down menus. You should be able to see the change your new settings are making to your clip in the **Monitor** panel.

The **Properties** panel is a tremendously powerful workspace. Not only can you use it to change the settings for individual effects, but it is the main workspace for creating and adjusting **keyframes**, Premiere Elements' tool for creating animations, motion paths and effects that change over the course of the clip's playback.

This panel is probably second only to the **Timeline** itself as the most important workspace in the program.

In **Chapter 24**, we'll show you how to do basic effects adjustments in the **Properties** panel.

Then, in **Chapter 26**, we'll show you how to use the **Properties** panel to create effects and motion paths with keyframing.

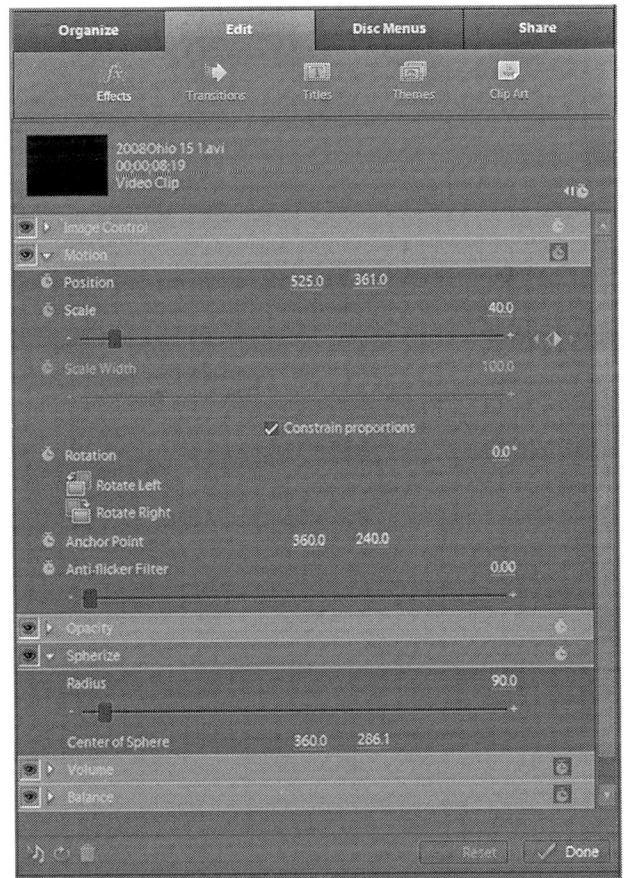

Effects that have been added to a clip appear in that clip's Properties panel, where they can be adusted and customized.

171

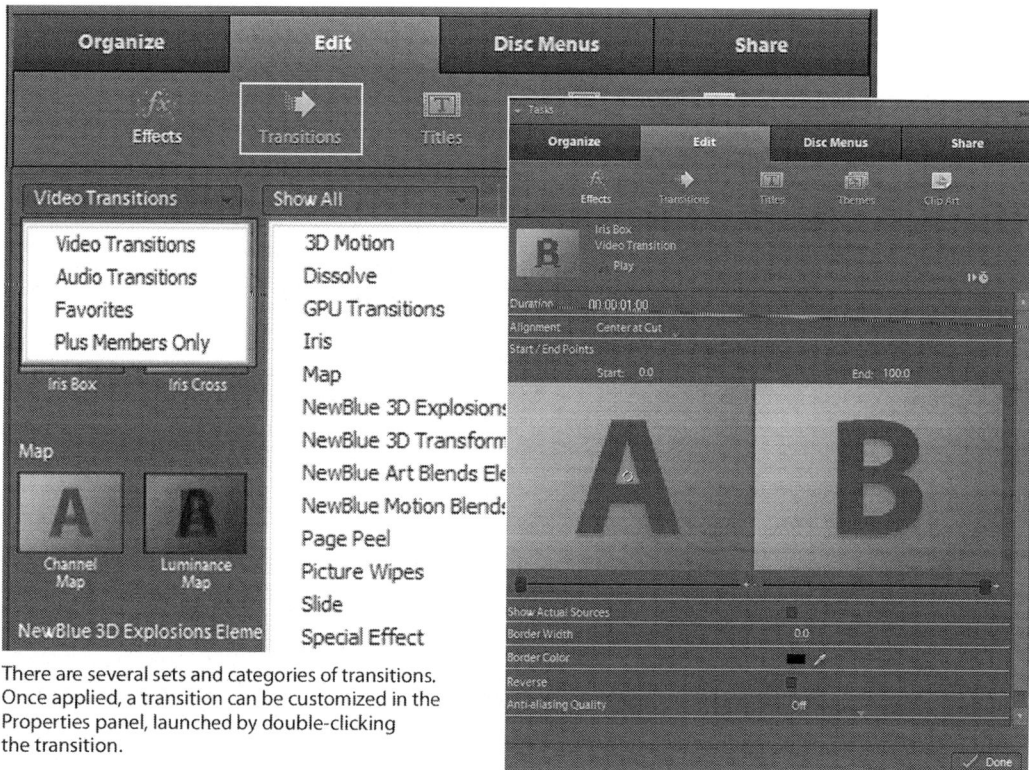

There are several sets and categories of transitions. Once applied, a transition can be customized in the Properties panel, launched by double-clicking the transition.

5   Add and adjust transitions

Transitions are the effects that take us from one clip to another. Some are gentle and nearly invisible – others are showy and draw attention to themselves. Most transitions are added to your timeline and adjusted similarly to effects:

1. Click on the **Edit** tab and then click the **Transitions** button.

   This will open the **Transitions** screen in the **My Tasks** panel.

2. Select a **Transitions** set.

   The **Transitions** panel displays **Video Transitions** by default. But, by selecting the drop-down menu on the upper left of the panel, you can set it to display **Audio Transitions**. If you've got a Plus account with Photoshop.com, there will be additional effects displayed under that option.

3. Select a transition.

   You can browse through the list of transitions on the panel, select category of transition from the second drop-down menu or quickly call an effect by typing its name in the **Quick Search** box on the upper right of the panel.

4. Apply the transition.

    Apply a transition by dragging it from the **Transitions** panel onto
    the intersection of two clips on your timeline or sceneline.

5. Open the **Transition Properties** panel.

    Transitions are customized in the **Transitions Properties** panel,
    illustrated on the facing page. To open this panel, double-click on a
    transition on your timeline or sceneline.

6. Customize your transition.

    Nearly all transitions include a number of properties that can be
    customized, depending on the nature of the transition. Virtually all
    include options for designating where the transition centers and
    the duration of the transition as well as an option for setting the
    transition to reverse its movement (i.e., wiping from right to left
    rather than left to right).

    We'll show you just about everything there is to know about adding
    and customizing transitions – including why they sometimes seem
    to behave in very strange ways – in **Chapter 25**. As a bonus, we'll
    even show you how to use the **Gradient Wipe**, a tool for creating
    your own custom transition effects!

6   Add titles

Titles are text, and sometimes graphics, placed over your clips
to provide additional visual information for your video story. In
most cases, you'll create your titles in Premiere Elements' **Titles**
workspace – a process that automatically places the title on an
available video track on your timeline at the position of the **CTI**
(playhead). To create a title:

1. Open the **Titles** workspace.

    The **Titles** workspace can be launched either by clicking the "**T**" icon
    on the lower right of the **Monitor** panel (which takes you directly to
    the main **Titles** workspace) or by clicking on the **Titles** button under
    the **Edit** tab (which takes you to the same **Titles** workspace, but by
    way of panel offering optional title templates).

2. Type your title over the placeholder "**Add text**."

    Additional text blocks can be created on the same title by clicking,
    with the text tool, on other locations on the **Titles Monitor** panel.

3. Customize the text.

    With your text selected, you can apply text attributes – including
    setting the font, size, style and alignment. You can also apply a style
    to your selected text by clicking on one of the **Text Styles** listed on
    the panel.

The Premiere Elements Titles workspace is launched by clicking on the "T" on the Monitor panel. It includes a number of tools for customizing your text and animating your titles.

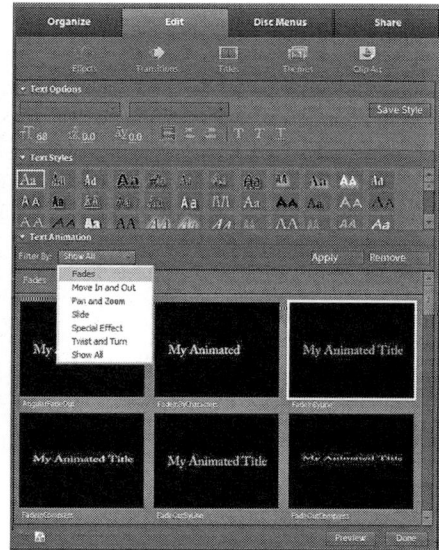

4. Apply a **Text Animation.**

   By clicking on a **Text Animation** and then clicking the **Apply** button, you can apply an animation to your text. (Note that this feature only works on titles that are one line long. If your text runs more than one line, its **Text Animation** will not function.)

5. Position the text and other elements.

   By switching from the **Text Tool** to the **Move Tool** (by clicking on the arrow icon on the **Titles Toolbar**), your cursor will become an "arrow" tool for positioning text and other graphic elements you add to your title. Objects and text blocks on your title can be centered, both horizontally and vertically, by selecting these elements and then clicking on one of the two centering tools at the bottom of the **Titles Toolbar.**

6. Exit the **Titles** workspace.

   Once your title is finished, click on the **Done** button in the lower right corner of the **Titles** panel. The **Titles** workspace will close and you'll return to regular **Edit** mode. Your new title will appear as a clip on an upper video track at the position of your **CTI**, where it can be repositioned and customized like any other clip.

   We'll show you how to create and customize your titles in **Chapter 23**.

7 Share your movie

When you're happy with the video project you've created, you'll find a number of options for outputting, or sharing it, as we discuss in **Chapter 29**.

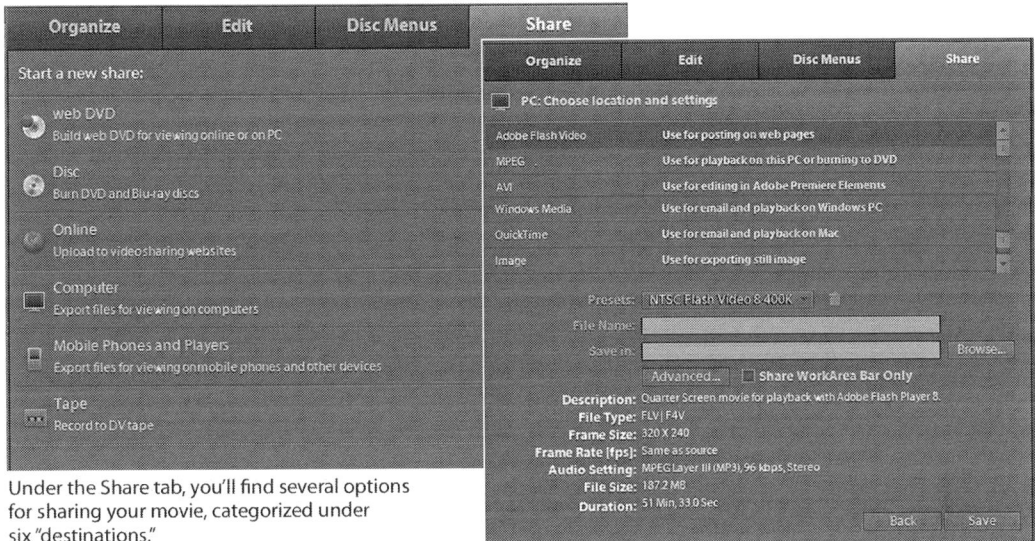

Under the Share tab, you'll find several options for sharing your movie, categorized under six "destinations."

- **To Web DVD.** New to version 9, this option allows you to save your DVD files as Web site files that function just like a an interactive DVD – complete with menus and scene link buttons!

- **To Disc.** Built into Premiere Elements are tools for creating menus and scene markers for creating DVD and BluRay disc projects.

- **Online.** The program comes complete with facilities for loading your finished video to your own personal Web site, YouTube, Photoshop.com or podcast hosting site PodBean.

- **To Your Computer.** The program will save your finished project as an AVI file, MPEG, Quicktime (MOV) file, Windows Media (WMV) file and a Flash (FLV) file on your computer's hard drive. Once the output is complete, you can then share these files any number of ways, including posting them online or using them as segments in a larger video project.

- **To a Mobile Phone or Player.** You can output your movie to an iPod, iPhone, Zune or virtually any other portable video player.

- **To Tape.** Though this is rarely used anymore except as a means of archiving completed projects, the program will port your HDV or miniDV project back to your camcorder for storage on tape.

And that's basically it!

You gather your assets; you assemble them on your timeline or sceneline; you add effects, transitions and titles; you share it with the world.

But between the lines of this simplicity are the countless variations that can elevate your movie project from the realm of a basic structure to something truly amazing!

What's new in version 9?

In version 9 of Premiere Elements, Adobe has put the bulk of their efforts into improving performance rather than adding lots of new bells and whistles. And, for the most part, they have succeeded. Version 9, at least in our preliminary tests, is a much more stable and dynamic product than version 8, and it's support for a wider range of video sources is most welcome.

Adobe also claims to have greatly improved the program's performance with high-definition HDV and AVCHD video. With more of the consumer market moving up to these higher-resolution camcorders, a more efficient workflow in this area is also very much welcome.

Here are some of the program's other highlights.

Mac support

For the first time, Premiere Elements will be rolled out in both Mac and PC versions. For the most part, the two versions look and perform identically – with the exception of some better support for Quicktime video on the Mac version and the inclusion of a few keyboard shortcuts that are only available on the PC.

Throughout this book, we'll reference both the Mac and PC keyboard shortcuts. Mac's shortcuts more often use the **Command** (⌘) key in combination with other keys while PCs use the **Ctrl** key. Also, a number of **right-click** functions on a PC are available with a **Ctrl-click** on a Mac.

But chances are , if you're comfortable with the PC interface for this program, you'll also feel right at home on the Mac version.

Cleaner interface

Adobe has redesigned the interface in Premiere Elements 9 to look cleaner and more like their professional Creative Suite software.

The brightly-colored tabs in the **Tasks** panel have been replaced by much more readable gray and white tabs with sharper, brighter text.

The **Timeline**, likewise, has a much cleaner look – closer in style to the look to that of Adobe's Premiere Pro and After Effects. Its clips display in bright colors with more readable text.

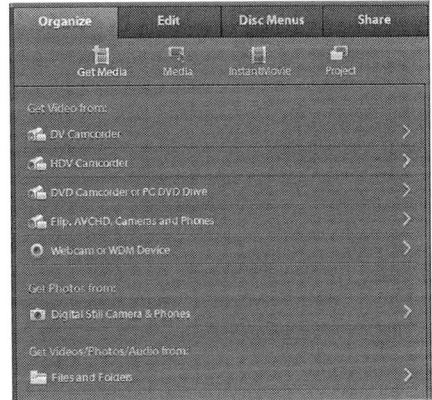

Even the drop-down and right-click menus that appear throughout the program have been redesigned with black or dark gray text on a white background, further improving their readability.

Support for Flip camcorders and DSLR video

A very welcome addition to Premiere Elements 9 is support for the popular, new pocket camcorders – most notably the Flip line of standard and high-definition cams. Flip camcorders download their video into the program over a USB connection, just as AVCHD and other hard drive camcorders. And, as we indicate in **Chapter 15, Start a New Project**, Premiere Elements 9 now includes project presets specifically designed to work with the Flip's unique codecs and format.

Timeline enhancements

The **Timeline** panel in Premiere Elements 9 is much cleaner and more streamlined than in previous versions of the program.

Audio adjustment and timeline marker tools are hidden under icon-based drop-down menus to reduce clutter.

To make more efficient use of the panel's vertical space, individual tracks on the Timeline can be toggled between a compressed and an open view.

And, even more interestingly, the video and audio tracks can be toggled individually to display in either a compressed or wide view, making it available to work with a greater number of tracks on your timeline without increasing the height of the Timeline panel unmanageably.

These new features are discussed in much greater detail in **Chapter 19, Edit Your Video in Timeline Mode.**

Web DVD output

Premiere Elements 9 includes a new **Share** option for saving your video as an interactive Web site that functions like a DVD – complete with menus and links! For more information on this new feature, see **Chapter 29, Share Your Movie**.

Automatically fix mismatched project settings

A very cool feature in version 9 of Premiere Elements is the new **Mismatched Project Settings Preset** notification and repair tool.

If you attempt to add to the timeline or sceneline of a new project a video clip that requires settings other those that you have set for your project, a notification window will pop up notifying you of the mismatch and offering to fix it for you.

This feature only works when this mismatched footage is the *first clip* you add to your timeline or sceneline in a project. And it doesn't correct issues that may arise from mixing more than one video format in the same project. However – considering the liabilities of using the wrong settings for a project – it can prove a real lifesaver.

More information on project settings can be found in **Chapter 15, Start a New Project**.

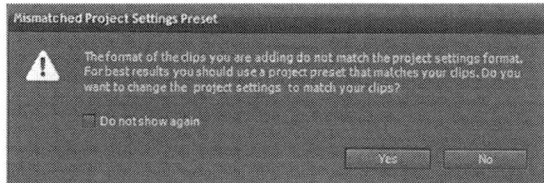

Need some Basic Training?

Want some help with the basics of Premiere Elements?

Want some free hands-on training?

Check out my free tutorial series **Basic Training with Premiere Elements** at Muvipix.com.

This simple, eight-part series will show you how to set up a project, how to import media into it, basic editing moves, adding transitions and effects, how to create titles, how to add and customize your DVD and BluRay disc menu navigation markers and how to export your finished video.

And did I mention that it's free?

To see the series, just go to http://Muvipix.com and type "Basic Training" in the product search box.

And while you're there, why not drop by the Community forum and say hi! We'd love to have you become a part of our growing city.

Happy moviemaking!

Steve, Chuck, Ron and the whole Muvipix team

Chapter 15

Start a New Project
Creating and opening your projects

When you first launch Premiere Elements, you'll be greeted by the "splash screen" – a Welcome Screen to the program that serves as your starting point for creating a new, or opening your existing, video projects.

Bypass the Welcome Screen

You can't turn off the Welcome Screen completely, but you can configure the Premiere Elements and Photoshop Elements 9 programs to launch simultaneously with it.

To select this option, click on the launch configuration button in the upper right of the Welcome Screen and, in the panel that opens, select the option to **Always Launch Premiere Elements Editor behind the Welcome Screen**.

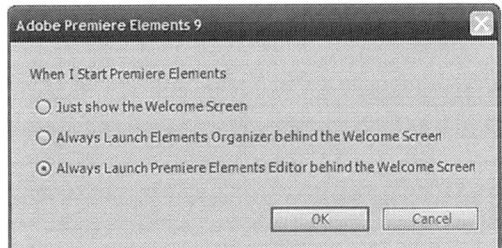

Launch the Organizer   Start a new project   Open a previous project

WELCOME TO
ADOBE® PREMIERE® ELEMENTS 9

Welcome to Elements!
We'd like to show you around. Choose the option that best describes you.

ORGANIZE

NEW PROJECT

OPEN PROJECT

I'm new to
Premiere Elements.   Show me what I need to know

I have an earlier version
of Premiere Elements.   Show me what's new and cool

Welcome back, Steve!
Your Personal URL : http://stevegrisetti.photoshop.com
Manage My Adobe ID...

Your Adobe Online Storage :   2.0GB
Used : 13.7MB   Free : 1.9GB
Manage My Backup...

Tips and Tricks...
Benefits of an Adobe ID...
Help and Support...

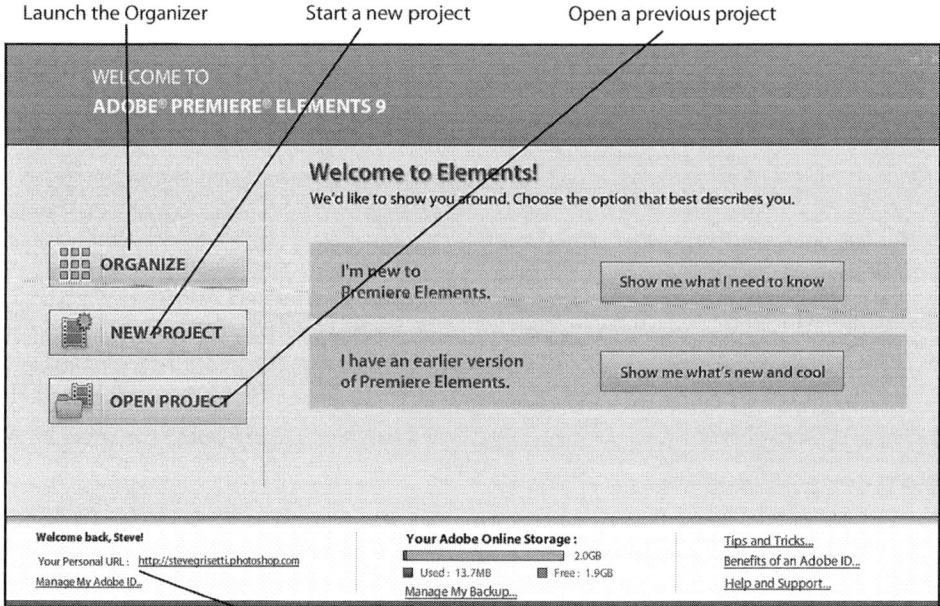

Registration and autologon to Photoshop.com, a site for displaying
photos and from which Premiere Elements 9 accesses additional content.

The Welcome Screen

When you first start up Premiere Elements, you'll be greeted by the
Welcome Screen. Very similar to the **Welcome Screen** in Photoshop
Elements, it is a launching point for the various workspaces for the
program.

From this **Welcome Screen** you can start a new Premiere Elements
project, open an old one or launch the Organizer.

Additionally, this screen offers you the option of logging into (or creating
an account with) **Photoshop.com**, Adobe's online portal for a variety of
services and content.

Once you select the option to launch Premiere Elements or the Elements
Organizer, the **Welcome Screen** will close. You can re-open the **Welcome
Screen** by clicking on the little house icon that appears along the top of the
Premiere Elements, Photoshop Elements or Organizer workspace.

Launch the Elements Organizer

The Elements Organizer is a powerful media file management program
that interfaces with both Premiere Elements and Photoshop Elements.

The Organizer allows you to catalog and search your media files based on
a wide variety of criteria. Additionally, the Organizer includes a number of
tools for creating and sharing your video and photo projects.

The Organizer reads the EXIF data off your digital photos, adds **Keyword Tags** (both manually and automatically) to your media clips, gives you the ability to sort your files into **Albums** and serves as a launching point for a number of Photoshop Elements and Premiere Elements functions.

We discuss its features and functions in more detail in **Chapter 31, The Elements Organizer.**

Open a new project

Clicking the **New Project** button takes you to an option screen for setting up your Premiere Elements project.

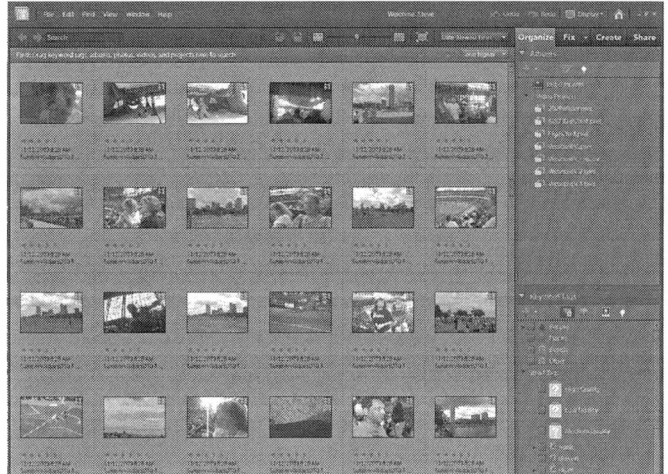

The Elements Organizer is a separate file management and project tool shared by both Premiere Elements and Photoshop Elements.

Part of creating a new project is selecting the project's settings. In most cases, these settings will be determined by the video format you are using as your movie's source.

Its' very important that you choose the correct settings for your project. Doing so can save you a lot of frustration and heartache later!

It's also very important to note that these settings can only be selected when you *first create your project*. You will not be able to change them later! So determining and selecting the correct project settings at this point is a very critical step.

Log on to Photoshop.com

Along the lower left of the Welcome Screen is a tool for logging on to **Photoshop.com**.

Photoshop.com is Adobe's free online photo-sharing and file back-up service. You can create an account right here, at this **Welcome Screen** or at the Web site.

Once you've signed on and created an account, you'll automatically be logged onto the site whenever you start one of the Elements programs.

Photoshop.com is a site on which you can share your photos and videos. Connecting to **Photoshop.com also** gives you access to the **Inspiration Browser**, a collection of tutorials and tips for Premiere Elements, Photoshop Elements and the Elements Organizer. You also get 2 megabytes of free space for backing up for your files. A **Plus membership** gets you additional storage space as well as access to additional movie themes and templates that are loaded automatically into your Premiere Elements program.

For more information on **Photoshop.com** and its services, see **Chapter 34, Photoshop.com.**

Starting a new project in Premiere Elements 9

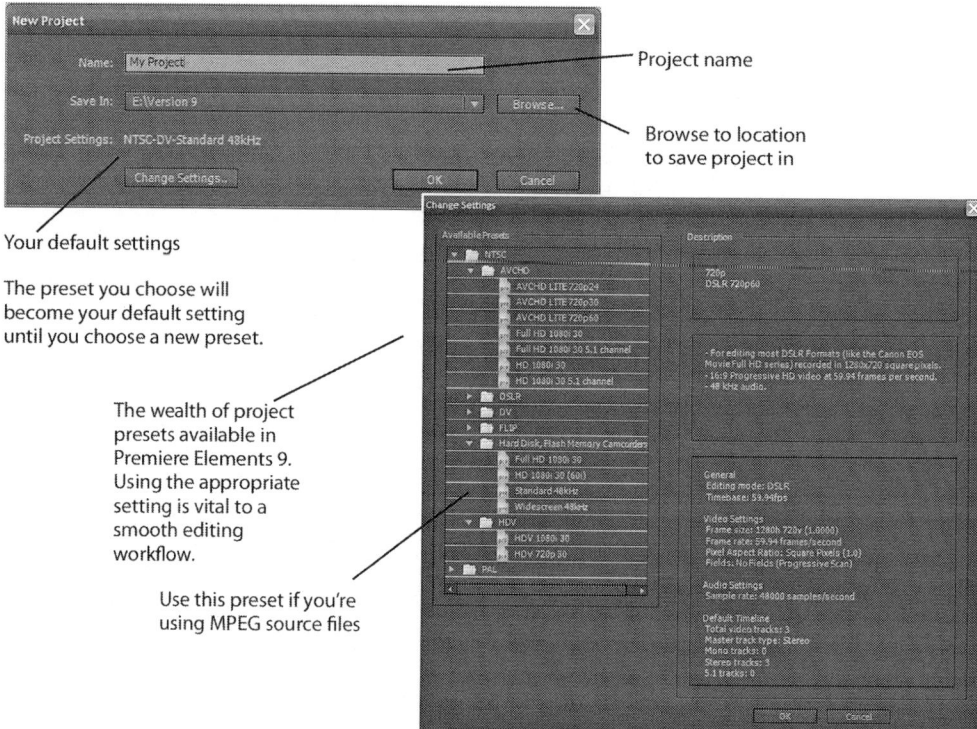

Project name

Browse to location
to save project in

Your default settings

The preset you choose will
become your default setting
until you choose a new preset.

The wealth of project
presets available in
Premiere Elements 9.
Using the appropriate
setting is vital to a
smooth editing
workflow.

Use this preset if you're
using MPEG source files

1. Click the **New Project** button.

   The **New Project** option screen will appear, as illustrated above.

   Type the title for your new project in the box displayed at **Name**.

2. Click the **Browse** button to choose a location to save your new
   project file.

   We at Muvipix recommend always selecting the **Browse** option
   and, wherever you choose to save your file, *creating a new folder* for
   every new project file.

   This little bit of housekeeping keeps all of your new project's files in
   one neat, little folder. And, when your project is done and you want
   to clear it from your computer, you can then remove not only the
   project file but all of the temp, render and scratch disk files Premiere
   Elements has created for that project, simply by deleting that single
   folder!

   This makes post-project clean-up a much easier and neater process.

3. Select your **Project Settings**.

   Project Settings, at the bottom left of the **New Project** panel, will
   display the last settings you used for a Premiere Elements project.

AVCHD Lite
camcorders

1920x1080 AVCHD

1440x1080 AVCHD

Digital SLR
camcorders
shooting 1080p

Digital SLR
camcorders
shooting 640x480

Digital SLR
camcorders
shooting 720p

MiniDV 4:3

MiniDV 16:9

Flip standard def
camcorders

Flip HD camcorders

Flash Memory
hi-def camcorders

DVD or Hard drive
standard DV 4:3

DVD or Hard drive
standard DV 16:9

HDV tape-based
video 1440x1080

HDV tape-based
video 1280x720

Change Settings

Available Presets

- NTSC
  - AVCHD
    - AVCHD LITE 720p24
    - AVCHD LITE 720p30
    - AVCHD LITE 720p60
    - Full HD 1080i 30
    - Full HD 1080i 30 5.1 channel
    - HD 1080i 30
    - HD 1080i 30 5.1 channel
  - DSLR
    - 1080p
      - DSLR 1080p24
      - DSLR 1080p30
      - DSLR 1080p30 @ 29.97
    - 480p
      - DSLR 640x480p60
    - 720p
      - DSLR 720p24
      - DSLR 720p24 @ 23.976
      - DSLR 720p60
  - DV
    - Standard 48kHz
    - Widescreen 48kHz
  - FLIP
    - Flip Mino and Ultra 29_97p
    - Flip Mino and Ultra 30p
    - Flip Mino HD and Ultra HD 29_
    - Flip Mino HD and Ultra HD 30p
  - Hard Disk, Flash Memory Camcord
    - Full HD 1080i 30
    - HD 1080i 30 (60i)
    - Standard 48kHz
    - Widescreen 48kHz
  - HDV
    - HDV 1080i 30
    - HDV 720p 30
- PAL

Description

AVCHD
HD 1080i 25

- For editing with 1440x1080i AVCHD camcorders.
- 16:9 interlaced HD video at 25 frames per second.
- 48kHz audio.
- Drop-Frame Timecode numbering.

General
Editing mode: HDV 1080i
Timebase: 25.00fps

Video Settings
Frame size: 1440h 1080v (1.3333)
Frame rate: 25.00 frames/second
Pixel Aspect Ratio: HD Anamorphic 1080 (1.333)
Fields: Upper Field First

Audio Settings
Sample rate: 48000 samples/second

Default Timeline
Total video tracks: 3
Master track type: Stereo
Mono tracks: 0
Stereo tracks: 3
5.1 tracks: 0

OK   Cancel

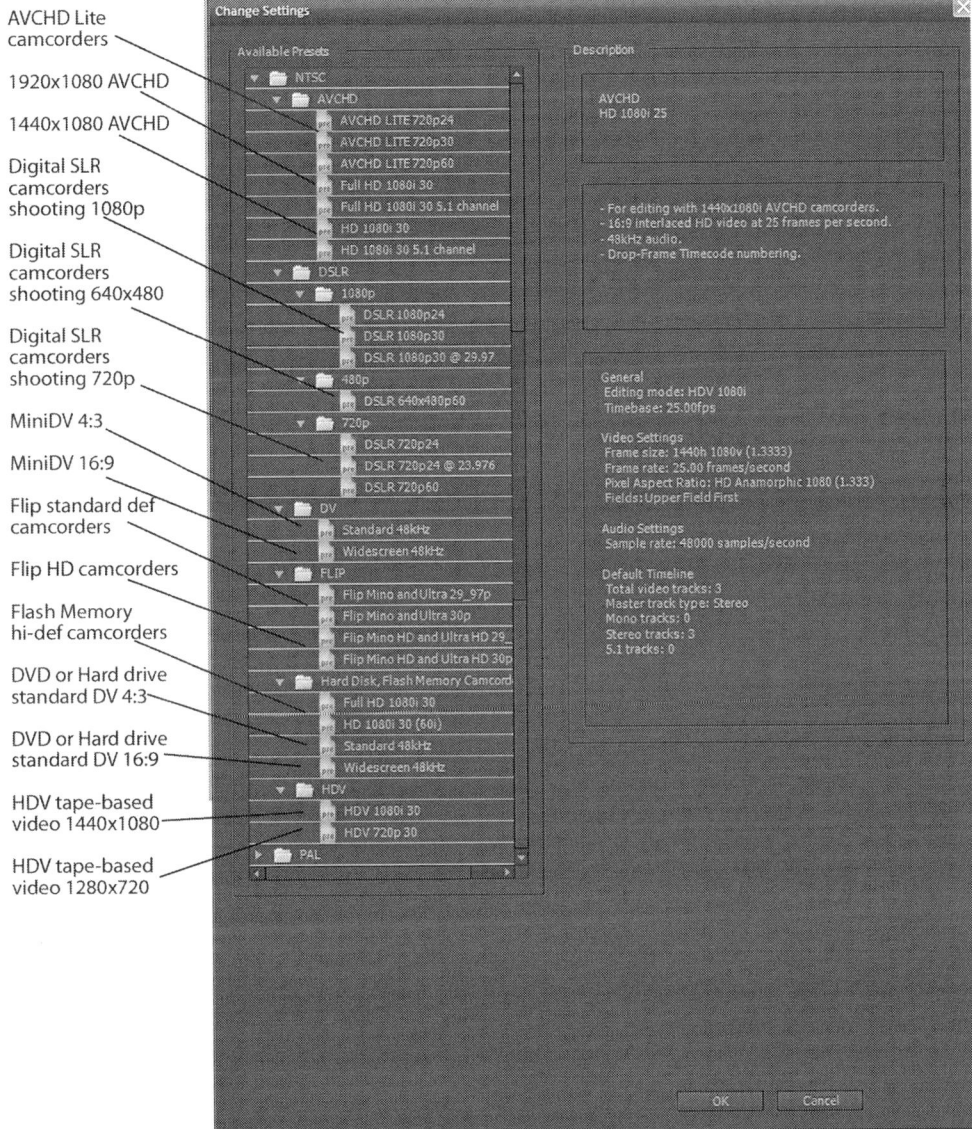

You'll most likely be working with the same settings for most of your projects. But, if not, clicking the **Change Settings** button will display a wealth of available project presets.

In addition to the option for switching from PAL to NTSC or vice versa, this screen offers presets for a number of resolutions and video formats. Each of these folders, in turn, can be opened to reveal even more options, including the options for a widescreen 16:9 or standard 4:3 video frame and, in the case of high-definition video settings, the HDV or AVCHD video format, vertical screen resolution and audio channel format.

Premiere Elements 9 project preset options

Below is an explanation of each of the presets available in Premiere Elements 9. The PAL and NTSC options are identical except that the frame rates for PAL presets are 25 fps rather than 30.

In addition to traditional video project settings, Premiere Elements now includes support for both AVCHD Lite and video from DSLRs (digital still cameras). Many of these project settings are pretty precisely defined by their frame rates. For best results, fully check out your camera's specs and match your project's settings as closely as possible to the video that your camera records.

For information on loading each of these formats into your Premiere Elements projects, see **Chapter 3, Get Media Into Your Project**.

AVCHD	AVCHD Lite 720p24	AVCHD Lite video (1280x720) shooting at 23.976 fps.
	AVCHD Lite 720p30	AVCHD Lite video (1280x720) shooting at 29.97 fps.
	AVCHD Lite 720p60	AVCHD Lite video (1280x720) shooting at 59.94 fps.
	Full HD 1080i 30	AVCHD video (1920x1080i square pixel, hard drive, high definition) from camcorders that shoot in stereo audio.
	Full HD 1080i 30 5.1 Channel	AVCHD video (1920x1080i square pixel, hard drive, high-definition) from camcorders that shoot in 5.1 channel audio. *This is the most common format for most newer hard drive, high-definition camcorders.*
	HD 1080 30	AVCHD video (1440x1080i non-square pixel, hard drive, high definition) from camcorders that shoot in stereo audio.
	HD 1080 30 5.1 Channel	AVCHD video (1440x1080i non-square pixel, hard drive, high-definition) from camcorders that shoot in 5.1 channel audio. This is the most common format for older hard drive, high-definition camcorders. *Note that, although this format uses less horizontal pixels, it produces the same high-quality, 16:9 image as 1920x1080 video. The pixels are just non-square, or wider than they are tall – as in the traditional television standard.*
DSLR Presets – Use these presets for working with high-quality video from digital still cameras (such as the Canon EOS Movie Full HD series).		
1080p	DSLR 1080p24	1920x1080 16:9 video shooting at 23.976 fps.
	DSLR 1080p30	1920x1080 16:9 video shooting at 30 fps.
	DSLR 1080p 30@29.97	1920x1080 16:9 video shooting at 29.97 fps.
480p	DSLR 640x480p 60	640x480 16:9 video shooting at 59.94 fps.
720p	DSLR 720p24	1280x720 16:9 video shooting at 24 fps.
	DSLR 720p24 @23.976	1280x720 16:9 video shooting at 23.976 fps.
	DSLR 720p60	1280x720 16:9 video shooting at 59.94 fps.
DV	Standard 48 kHz	720x480 4:3 video from a miniDV tape-based camcorders.
	Widescreen 48 kHz	720x480 16:9 video from miniDV tape-based camcorders.

continued on facing page

More Premiere Elements project presets

Flip	Flip Mino or Ultra Flip 29.97	Flip standard definition (640x480) video camcorders shooting at 29.97 fps.
	Flip Mino or Ultra Flip 30	Flip standard definition (640x480) video camcorders shooting at 30 fps.
	Flip Mino HD or Ultra HD 29.97	Flip high definition (1280x720) video camcorders shooting at 29.97 fps.
	Flip Mino HD or Ultra HD 30	Flip high definition (1280x720) video camcorders shooting at 30 fps.
Hard Disk, Flash Memory Camcorder	HD 1080i 30	High-definition video (1920x1080) from non-AVCHD hard drive or flash memory camcorders (such as the JVC GZ-HD7).
	HD 1080i 30 (60i)	High-definition video from (1440x1080) from non-AVCHD hard drive or flash memory camcorders that record in 60i format. (The PAL equivalent is, of course, 50i.)
	Standard 48kHz	Standard-definition (720x480) 4:3 video from hard drive camcorders as well as video from DVDs. *It is very important to use this or the following preset with standard-definition MPEG or VOB sources because it will automatically reverse the field dominance in your video, correcting an interlacing issue that can otherwise cause stuttering in your output videos.*
	Widescreen 48 kHz	Video from standard-definition (720x480) 16:9 hard drive camcorders and video from DVDs.
HDV Presets	HDV 1080i 30	Video from tape-based, high-definition HDV camcorders that shoot full HDV at 1440x1080 pixels.
	HDV 720p 30	Video from tape-based, high-definition HDV camcorders that shoot full HDV at 1280x720 pixels.

Setting your project up using the proper preset is essential to a smooth workflow and the highest quality output results, so consider carefully the nature of your source files as you choose your settings.

The illustration on page 183 and the charts on these pages detail each setting and which video source it is designed to work with.

Matching your project settings to your video source is vital to a successful video editing experience.

4. Once you've chosen the settings, name and location for your project, click **Okay** and the program will open to the project workspace.

Open an old project

Clicking the **Open Project** button on the **Welcome Screen** will get you access to any work-in-progress or old Premiere Elements project.

Your most recent projects will appear in the drop-down menu. Additional Premiere Elements projects on your computer can be accessed by selecting the **Browse** option.

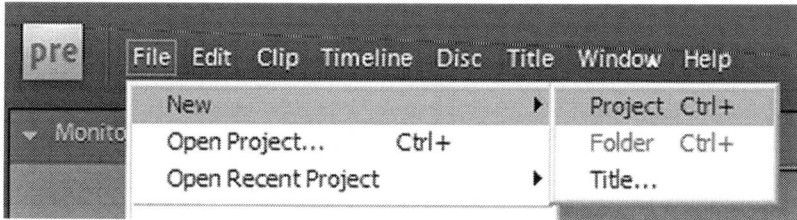

Open a project from within the program

Naturally, you don't have to go all the way out to the **Welcome Screen** to create a new project or to re-open an old one.

Both options are available from the **File** drop-down on the Menu Bar in the Premiere Elements workspace.

Selecting New **Project** from this menu gives you access to the very same **New Project** settings as are available from the **Welcome Screen**.

Open a project created by a previous version of the program?

Our advice: Don't do it.

It should work. And sometimes it does work. But, for the most part, Premiere Elements goes through such an overhaul from generation to generation, that it usually just leads to trouble. Only open version 9 projects with version 9, version 8 projects with version 8, etc.

Doing otherwise nearly always leads to buggy behavior – audio tracks that mysteriously disappear, clips that behave really strangely. A **Project** media panel that seems to have lost its mind.

Your best bet is to finish your Premiere Elements project in the same version of the program you began it in. Trust us on this.

Once it's far enough along that you consider it (or the segment you're working on) to be finished, you can export it – using **Share/Personal Computer/AVI** (as we discuss in **Chapter 29, Share Your Movie**). You should then be able to import that AVI segment into your version 9 project with no problems, no bugginess and virtually no loss of quality.

But we very much recommend against opening even a version 8 project in version 9.

Chapter 16

Get Media into Your Project
Capturing video and importing
video, audio and photos into your project

Before you can edit your video, you need to get it (along with your other source media) into your Premiere Elements project.

This is a relatively simple process, but unfortunately one that can occasionally present some challenges.

Before you can begin editing your video, photo or audio sources, you need to import – or **Get Media** – into your Premiere Elements project.

As the chart on the facing page indicates, there are three ways to bring your media files into your project: Capturing your video over a FireWire connection; downloading your media from a device over a USB connection or from your computer's DVD/CD drive; or browsing to media files already on your computer and importing them into your project.

Note that many of the formats you will be bringing into your Premiere Elements project must be uniquely processed by the program, and so it is very important to ensure that your project's settings match the format of the video you will be bringing into your project. (More information on selecting your correct project settings can be found in **Chapter 15, Start a New Project**.)

It is not possible to change your project's settings once you've begun your project, so it's very important that you set up your project correctly at the outset.

It can also be a challenging to combine formats that require different project settings in the same project. For this reason, it's not recommended, then, that you combine video from a miniDV camcorder and video from an AVCHD hard drive camcorder in the same project.

Once you've captured, downloaded or imported your media into your Premiere Elements project, it will appear listed in your **Project** media panel (as we discuss in **Chapter 16**). Once the media is in your **Project** media panel, you'll be able to begin assembling and editing it on your timeline or sceneline.

In this chapter, we'll look at each of the major media devices and sources and show you how to best gather your media from each.

We'll also show you how to work with photos, music and other media. And, as a bonus, we'll show you how to successfully capture video from analog camcorders and video players, as well as how and when to convert potentially troublesome formats.

We'll even include some troubleshooting steps for when things don't seem to go as they should.

Three ways to the Get Media options

1. Click **Get Media** under the **Organize** tab.
2. **Right-click** on a blank area in the **Project media** panel (**Ctrl- click** on a Mac) and select the **Get Media** option.
3. Select **Get Media From** from the **File** drop-down menu.

Getting Media

There are three basic ways to get media into your Premiere Elements project:

- **Capture your** tape-based video over a FireWire connection;
- **Download** your video or other media from a hard drive camcorder, camera or other device over a USB connection; or
- **Browse** to import media into your project from your computer's hard drive.

The chart below lists the methods of getting media from a number of devices.

MiniDV tape-based camcorder	Capture video over a FireWire connection using the Premiere Elements capture interface.
HDV tape-based hi-def camcorder	Capture video over a FireWire connection using the Premiere Elements capture interface.
Webcam	Capture video using the Premiere Elements capture interface.
AVCHD hard drive hi-def camcorder	Download video to computer using the **Video Importer** with a USB connection.
Flip Mino or Ultra camcorders	Download video to computer using the **Video Importer** with a USB connection.
Flash-based camcorders, such as the JVC-GZ series	Download video to computer using the **Video Importer** with a USB connection.
DVD camcorders or DVDs	With the finalized disc in your computer's DVD drive, rip the video files to your computer using the **Video Importer**.
Analog video	Capture through a DV bridge or pass-through set-up using the Premiere Elements capture interface, as discussed later in this chapter.
Digital still cameras	Download stills using the **Photo Downloader** or video using the **Video Importer** over a USB connection.
Music or audio from CDs	Rip music to your hard drive from CD and then browse to the file(s) using the **Get Media** option **PC Files or Folders**.
Video, music or still photos already on your computer's hard drive	Browse to the file(s) using the **Get Media** option **PC Files or Folders**.

Whatever video or audio source you use, it is very important to ensure that your project's settings match your media's format or source. Information on setting your project up for a variety of media sources can be found in **Chapter 15, Start a New Project**. (Note that your project's settings can only be selected when a project is initiated. They can not be changed once a project has been started.)

Also note that some commercial DVD and music formats (including iTunes) include digital rights management, copy protection software that will prohibit their use in a Premiere Elements. Information on working around some forms of digital rights management can be found in **Add music files to a Premiere Elements project**, later in this chapter.

FireWire is the common term for an IEEE-1394 connection, also known as iLink.

Get Media options,
under the Organize tab

The DV, HDV and Webcam
or WDM (Webcam) Device
options launch the
Capture workspace.

The DVD/DVD Camcorder,
and the Flip, AVHCD Cameras
and Phones options launch
the Video Importer, while the
Digital Still Camera & Phones
option launches the
Photo Downloader.

The PC Files and Folders
option allows you to browse
to files on your computer.

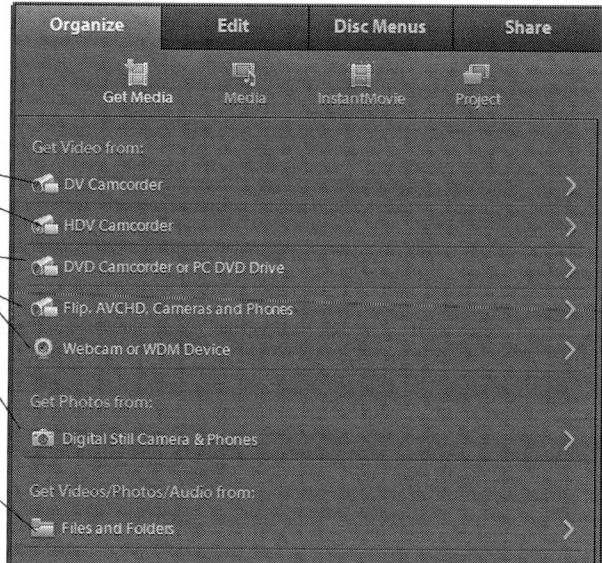

| Organize | Edit | Disc Menus | Share |

Get Media | Media | InstantMovie | Project

Get Video from:

DV Camcorder

HDV Camcorder

DVD Camcorder or PC DVD Drive

Flip, AVCHD, Cameras and Phones

Webcam or WDM Device

Get Photos from:

Digital Still Camera & Phones

Get Videos/Photos/Audio from:

Files and Folders

Get media with the "Get Media" tool

To bring media into your Premiere Elements project – whether from a
location on your hard drive or from a camcorder or other device – use the
Get Media tool.

The simplest way to launch this tool is to click the **Organize** tab in the
Tasks panel and select **Get Media**.

At the **Get Media** screen, Premiere Elements offers seven options for
bringing your media into your project (as illustrated above).

- The **DV Camcorder, HDV Camcorder** and **Webcam or WDM Device**
  options will launch the program's capture workspace.

  In the **Capture** workspace, the program interfaces with the video
  device. This usually gives you remote control of the device, allowing
  you to preview the video in real time and select only the segments
  you want imported into your project.

- The **DVD/DVD Camcorder or PC DVD Drive** and the **Flip, AVCHD,
  Cameras and Phones** options launch the **Video Importer**, Adobe's
  interface for downloading videos from DVDs, camcorders and other
  devices, while the **Digital Still Camera & Phones** option launches the
  Photo Downloader.

  Video or photo files are downloaded from the device to your
  computer using these interfaces. You will not have the option of
  capturing your video in real time with this software.

- The **PC Files and Folders** option will open Windows Explorer so that
  you can browse to your media files.

A MiniDV camcorder connected via FireWire.

Capture MiniDV, HDV Video or video from Webcams or WDM Devices

The process of capturing video to Premiere Elements is virtually the same, whether you're capturing from a miniDV camcorder, an HDV (hi-definition) camcorder or even from a DV bridge (see **Capture through DV bridges and pass-throughs**, below), as long as these devices are connected to your computer via FireWire (also known as IEEE-1394 and iLink).

You can also capture video from most Webcams.

1. With your camcorder in VTR mode, connect your camcorder to your computer's FireWire port (as illustrated above).

    When your camcorder is properly connected, powered on and set to play, Windows should register the connection (usually with a "bing-bong" sound effect) and a camcorder icon should appear on the right end of your Windows Task Bar.

Capture over a FireWire connection

All miniDV camcorders have FireWire connectors, even if they also offer a USB connection.

Our advice is to not bother with the USB connection, even if it means you have to buy your own FireWire cable. A few camcorders and some capture software will work with a USB connection, but with FireWire you'll know for sure you're properly connected.

Option to capture frames of
video for time lapse effect

Remaing space
on hard drive

Capture device

Device controls and
settings under >>

Clip name

Browse to select
capture to location

Capture video only
or audio only

Capture to timeline

Split clip options

Shortcut to beginning or end of scene

Camcorder
Playback controls

The scrubber

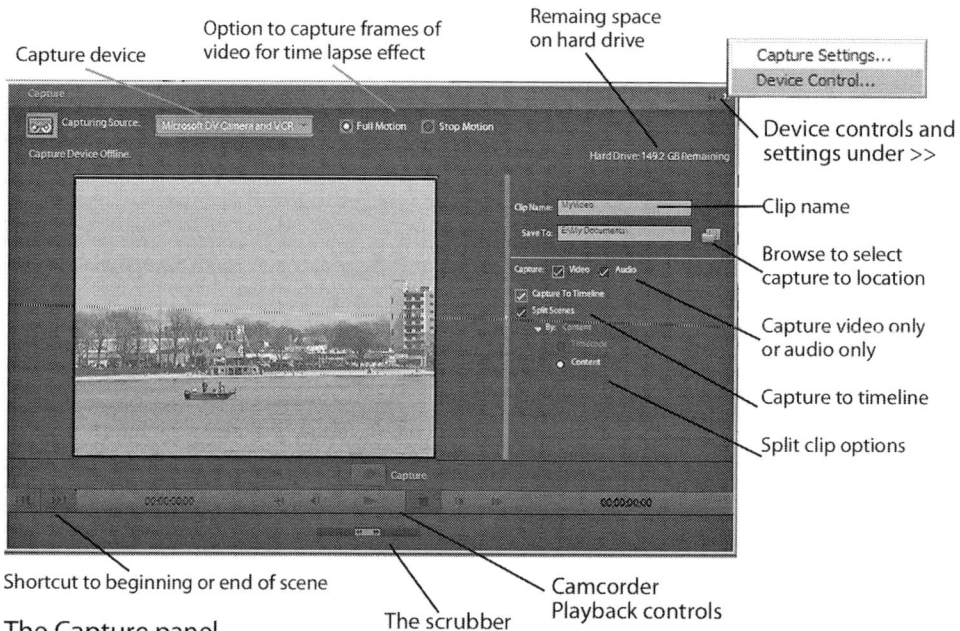

The Capture panel
Streaming capture from miniDV, HDV or Webcam

Windows should also launch an option screen offering you a handful of methods for capturing your video, among which Premiere Elements should be listed.

If this is not the case, something is wrong, possibly at a mechanical level, and you'll need to troubleshoot your FireWire connection and camcorder set-up before you proceed. (Troubleshooting steps are listed at the end of this chapter.)

If you have a good connection to your camcorder, cancel out of this Windows option screen and, if you're not already running Premiere Elements, launch the program.

2. In Premiere Elements, select the **Organize** tab and click **Get Media**, then select the **DV Camcorder, HDV Camcorder** or **Webcam or WDM Device** option.

The **Capture** workspace will open, as illustrated above.

If your camcorder (or DV bridge) is properly connected to your computer via FireWire, the panel will show **Capture Device Online** in the upper left corner of the panel and the **Capturing Source** drop-down should list the camcorder or DV bridge you are interfacing with. If not, you may want to try some of the capture troubleshooting steps at the end of this chapter.

With a proper camcorder connection, the playback buttons along the bottom of this panel will remotely control your camcorder. (If you're using a DV bridge or a pass-through, the source device or camcorder isn't connected directly to the computer, so these buttons will have no function.) **Play, Fast Forward, Stop** and **Rewind** you'll recognize immediately. Once you press **Play**, your camcorder's video should display in the panel and the **Play** button should become a **Pause** button.

The buttons to the right of **Rewind** and to the left of **Fast Forward** are incremental advance and rewind buttons. They allow you to advance or back up your camcorder's playback one frame at a time.

The slider under the playback buttons (called a **Scrubber**) allows you to advance or rewind your video at a variety of speeds, depending on how far you push it to the left or right.

At the lower left of the panel are two "shortcut" buttons. Clicking on these buttons will automatically advance or rewind your video to the previous or next scene (the last point at which your camcorder was stopped or paused).

Premiere Elements only reads these scenes when capturing from a miniDV camcorder, by the way, so these buttons will not function during HDV capture.

To the right of the screen are the capture options. Type the name you would like applied to your captured video in the **Clip Name** space.

(Premiere Elements will add numbers to the end of this name as it creates new clips during capture.)

You also have the option of designating a location for your captured video for this session. By default, the clips will be saved to the same folder as your project file.

- With the various checkboxes in the space below these options, you can designate that the program capture **Audio Only** or **Video Only**. If the **Capture to Timeline** option is selected, your video will be automatically added directly to your project's timeline or sceneline as it is captured.

- The **Split Scenes** option allows you to set whether the captured video is broken into clips based on **Timecode** (each time your camcorder was paused or stopped while shooting) or **Content** (when the video content changes significantly). Since, when you're capturing through a DV bridge or pass-through, timecode is not being streamed into your computer from the video device, you can not split scenes based on timecode while using a DV bridge or pass-through.

   If you elect the option to **Split Scenes** in your captured video based on **Content**, the Organizer's **Media Analyzer** will launch automatically once you've finished your capture. Your clips will automatically be **Smart Tagged** and will appear in your **Project** media panel as shorter, trimmed clips, based on the changing content of the video.

   For more information on the **Media Analyzer** and its **Smart Tags** function, see **Chapter 15, The Elements Organizer**.

To capture your tape-based or webcam video:

3. Use the playback controls to locate the segment you want to capture, pause your tape, then click the red **Capture** button.

4. When you want to stop your capture, click the **Stop Capture** button.

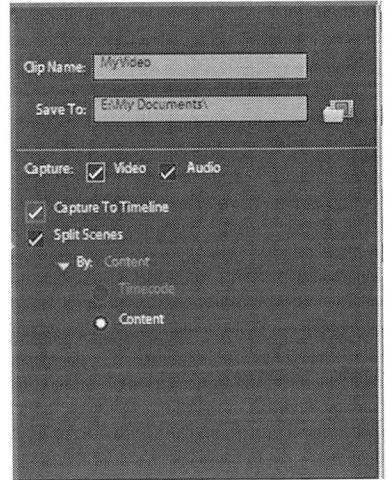

Why tape-based miniDV and HDV are still the standards

MiniDV camcorders hit the market over a decade ago. HDV, a high-definition tape-based video format, was introduced a few years later. Based on the professional DV compression system still used in broadcast video, miniDV and HDV camcorders record to a tape cassette not much bigger than a Zippo lighter, each cassette holding about an hour's worth of video at standard speed.

There have been many formats introduced since – hard disk camcorders, DVD camcorders, flash memory camcorders – but none matches miniDV or HDV for their ability to interface with computers and PC-based video editing systems. This is as true for Macs as it is for Windows-based computers. Most home computer-based video editing software was designed to interface ideally with miniDV and HDV camcorders.

The chief advantage of miniDV and HDV camcorders is that, when connected to a computer by a FireWire cable (also known as an IEEE-1394 or iLink), video data is not so much *captured* from these camcorders as it is *streamed* into your computer.

The digital video data remains exactly the same as it flows from the camcorder to your computer (or back to the camcorder). The only change is that the capture software encapsulates the data from miniDV camcorders into AVI files (known more accurately as DV-AVIs) or DV-MOV files on a Mac. HDV video data is encapsulated into MTS files.

Since the video data is not *converted* during capture – as it would be if digitized by a capture device – there is no change to the video data itself, and hence no loss whatsoever of the data's quality in the move from camcorder to computer!

This is an ideal data flow system: A computer in the camcorder sending video data to your editing computer and vice versa – both speaking the same digital language!

Virtually all Windows and Mac professional style, computer-based editing systems are built around this DV workflow. When DV video files are used in programs like Premiere Elements, they are *not even re-rendered* by the program (unless an effect has been added to them).

This is not true of other video formats, many of which need to be continually rendered as you work with it on your timeline.

This means that video from miniDV and HDV camcorders flows smoothly and efficiently through the editing process.

Capture from miniDV and HDV camcorders is also done in "real time". That means that the capture software controls the camcorder remotely as you capture only the segments of your video that you actually want. You play the tape; you watch it on the **Capture Monitor**. You need capture only what you want to use in your video project.

Could you ask for a better marriage between software and camcorder?

Capture				
	Capturing Source:	Microsoft DV Camera and VCR ▾	○ Full Motion	● Stop Motion

☑ Time Lapse   Set Time   ▮ Delete Frame

Set Time ✕

Frequency:

0 hrs 0 min **30** sec

Duration

0 hrs 0 min 0 sec

OK   Cancel

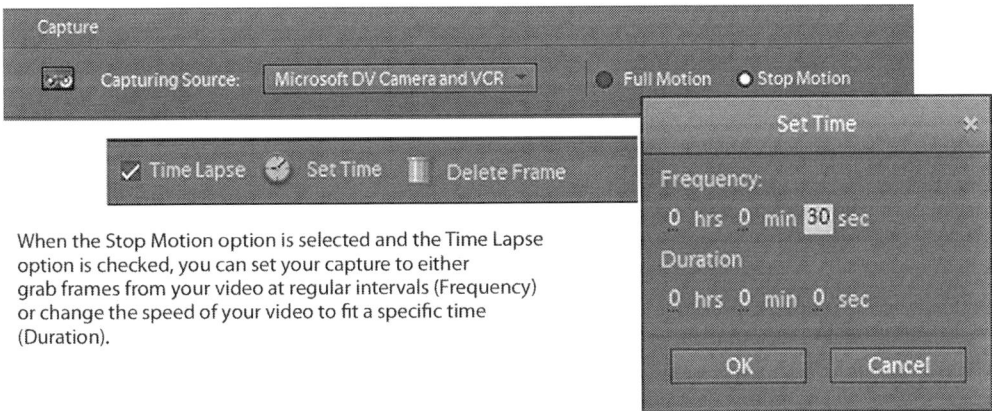

When the Stop Motion option is selected and the Time Lapse option is checked, you can set your capture to either grab frames from your video at regular intervals (Frequency) or change the speed of your video to fit a specific time (Duration).

Finally, at the top center of the **Capture** panel, you'll note that you have the option of capturing your video in **Full Motion** or **Stop Motion**.

The **Stop Motion** option will allow you to set up your capture so that it grabs frames from your video at regular intervals, rather than a continuous stream of video – the result being that the video will play very fast, as a "time lapse" sequence when placed on your timeline or sceneline.

Set your **Stop Motion**, for instance, to capture only one frame every 30 frames, and your captured video will seem to play at *30 times* normal speed.

This is great for showing clouds rolling through the sky or the sun quickly rising and setting, or a flower opening in mere seconds. Great visual effects, even if it does mean you go through a lot of tape to get a very short sequence!

Get standard DV from an HDV Camcorder

Just because you're shooting your video in high-definition, it does not necessarily mean you'll need to edit it in high-definition.

And, unless you're planning to output your video as a BluRay disc or other high-definition media file, you can achieve excellent results on a standard DVD by *downsampling* your HDV video to standard DV within your camcorder before you capture it into Premiere Elements.

To capture downsampled video from your camcorder, connect your HDV camcorder to your computer via FireWire and set your camcorder to **DV** (called **iLink Conversion** or **DV Lock** on some brands), then capture it into your Premiere Elements project (using standard DV project settings) as if from a miniDV camcorder. The video quality, although no longer in high-definition, will remain excellent, usually much better than you would get from a regular miniDV video.

The overall quality of the results – compared to video captured in HDV and downsampled by Premiere Elements on output – will not be significantly better. However, working with standard DV puts a lot less demand on your system's resources, so you're likely to find it a much faster and more efficient workflow.

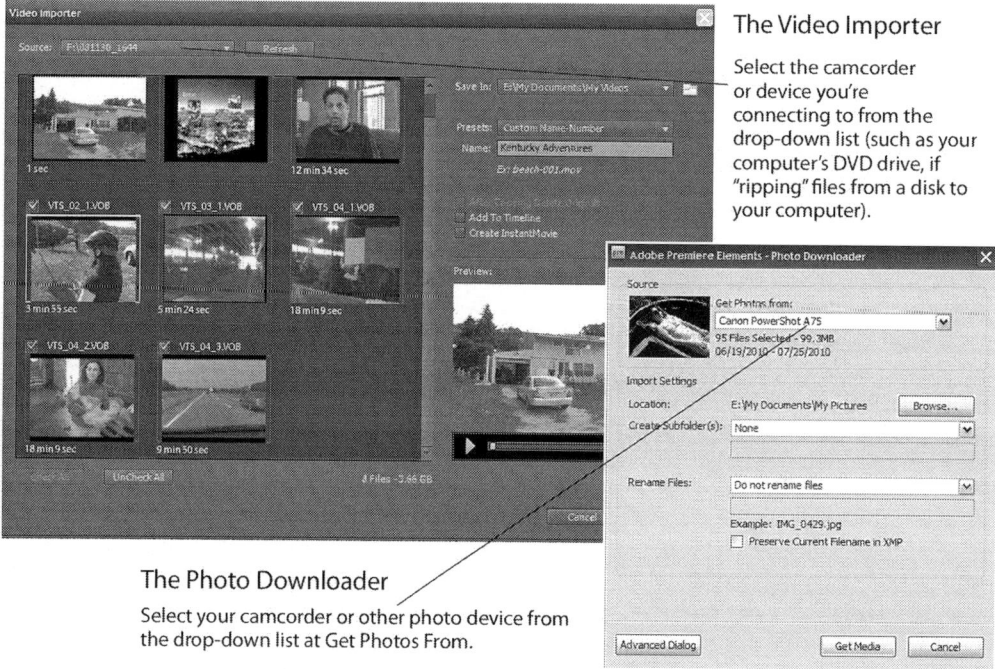

The Video Importer

Select the camcorder or device you're connecting to from the drop-down list (such as your computer's DVD drive, if "ripping" files from a disk to your computer).

The Photo Downloader

Select your camcorder or other photo device from the drop-down list at Get Photos From.

Get video from DVDs and DVD Camcorders

Video from sources other than miniDV and HDV camcorders – including video from DVD camcorders and hard drive camcorders – is not captured into Premiere Elements the way miniDV is. That is, it's not *streamed* in and captured in real time, as miniDV and HDV video are.

Rather, video from non-tape sources, is *downloaded* into your computer and your Premiere Elements project using Adobe's **Video Importer** or **Photo Downloader** software.

To get video from a DVD or DVD camcorder:

1. Place the DVD into your computer's DVD drive

   Note that discs from DVD camcorders must be *finalized* before Premiere Elements can rip the video from them.

2. Select the **DVD Camcorder or PC DVD Drive** option from the **Get Media** panel.

   This will launch the **Video Importer**, as illustrated above.

3. Select your computer's DVD drive from the **Source** drop-down menu at the top of the **Video Importer**.

4. Click the **Browse** button to indicate where on your computer you'd like to save the DVD's files, then click the **Get Media** button at the bottom of the panel to rip the video files to your hard drive.

If you're going to use video from a DVD in Premiere Elements, we recommend you ensure you are using it in a project set to the **Hard Drive, Flash Memory Camcorder** project preset, as discussed in **New Project** in **Chapter 15, Start a New Project**.

Get video from Hard Drive and Flash Drive Camcorders

As with video from DVDs and DVD camcorders, the video from hard drive and flash drive camcorders is *downloaded*, rather than captured, into Premiere Elements.

To get video from these types of camcorders

1. Connect your camcorder to your computer with a USB cable.

2. Select the **Flip, AVCHD, Cameras and Phones** option from the **Get Media** panel.

   This will launch the **Video Importer**, as illustrated on page 196.

3. Select your camcorder from the **Source** drop-down menu at the top of the **Video Importer**.

4. Click the **Browse** button to indicate where on your computer you'd like to save the captured files, then click the **Get Media** button at the bottom of the panel to download your video.

If you're going to use video from a hard drive or flash drive camcorder in Premiere Elements, we recommend you use it in a project using the proper **Hard Drive, Flash Memory Camcorder** project preset, as discussed in **Open a new project** in **Chapter 15, Start a New Project**.

Get video from Flip camcorders

Flip camcorders plug directly into your computer's USB port. As with hard drive camcorders, the video from Flip camcorders is *downloaded* rather than streamed or captured into Premiere Elements.

1. Connect your Flip camcorder to your computer's USB port.

2. Select the **Flip, AVCHD, Cameras and Phones** option from the **Get Media** panel.

   This will launch the **Video Importer**, as illustrated on page 196.

3. Select your Flip camcorder from the **Source** drop-down menu at the top of the **Video Importer**.

4. Click the **Browse** button to indicate where on your computer you'd like to save the captured files, then click the **Get Media** button at the bottom of the panel to download your video.

If you're going to use video from a Flip camcorder in Premiere Elements, we recommend you use it in a project using the appropriate **Flip Mino or Ultra** or **Flip Mino HD or Ultra HD** project preset, as discussed in **Open a new project** in **Chapter 15, Start a New Project**.

Get video from AVCHD camcorders

As with other hard drive camcorders, the video from AVCHD camcorders is *downloaded* rather than streamed or captured into Premiere Elements.

1. Connect your AVCHD camcorder to your computer's USB port.

2. Select the **Flip, AVCHD, Cameras and Phones** option from the **Get Media** panel.

    This will launch the **Video Importer**, as illustrated on page 196.

3. Select your camcorder from the **Source** drop-down menu at the top of the **Video Importer**.

4. Click the **Browse** button to indicate where on your computer you'd like to save the captured files, then click the **Get Media** button at the bottom of the panel to download your video.

If you're going to use video from an AVCHD camcorder in Premiere Elements, we recommend you use it in a project using the appropriate **AVCHD** project preset. There are four possible presets for AVCHD camcorders, and it is very important that you choose a preset that matches your audio (stereo or 5.1) as well as your video format. For more information on these presets see **Chapter 15, Start a New Project**.

HDV (High Definition Video) versus AVCHD

One of the most exciting video formats to become available to consumers in recent years is high-definition video.

When configured to work with **HDV**, Premiere Elements handles the MPEGs from an HDV camcorder as smoothly and as efficiently as it does video from a miniDV source.

Though do note that HDV is much more compressed and contains much more video data than miniDV (approximately twice the horizontal and twice the vertical data). And that can put a lot more strain on your computer's resources.

The process of capturing HDV in Premiere Elements is essentially the same as capturing standard DV.

The newest type of high-definition video is an even more highly compressed format called **AVCHD**, which stores the video data to the camcorder's internal hard drive as MPEG4s.

Although this format can be more convenient to use, the fact that it is so highly compressed means that it puts *even more* strain on your system's resources. So it's very important to make sure you've got a powerful enough computer to handle these files!

Our **Premiere Elements Appendix (Chapter 30)** offers our system recommendations for working with these more intensive formats and recommends Windows tweaks for ensuring you're getting every bit of power your computer can muster.

Get video from DSLR still cameras and other devices

Premiere Elements Media Downloader can also download media from other devices, including mobile phones.

1. Connect your device to your computer's USB port.

2. Select the **Flip, AVCHD, Cameras and Phones** option from the **Get Media** panel.

   This will launch the **Video Importer,** as illustrated on page 196.

3. Select your USB-connected device from the **Source** drop-down menu at the top of the **Video Importer**.

4. Click the **Browse** button to indicate where on your computer you'd like to save the captured files, then click the **Get Media** button at the bottom of the panel to download your video or photos.

As we discuss in the sidebar below, when working with video from still cameras, you'll get the best results if you use the right project settings.

Get stills from still cameras or cell phones

1. Connect your still camera to your computer's USB port.

2. Select the **Digital Still Camera & Phones** option from the **Get Media** panel.

   This will launch the **Photo Downloader** as illustrated on page 196.

3. From the **Get Media From** drop-down menu at the top of the **Photo Downloader**, select your camera or other device.

4. Click the **Browse** button to indicate where on your computer you'd like to save the captured files, then click the **Get Media** button at the bottom of the panel to download your video or photos.

As we indicate in **Use photos in your Premiere Elements project** on page 203, for best results your still photos should be resized to an optimal, video resolution size.

Video from still cameras

Adobe has added support for a wide variety of DSLR (digital still camera) video in Premiere Elements 9. But, as with any video source format, you'll get the best results – and the program will function must effectively – when you match your project settings as accurately as possible to your source video footage.

The charts on pages 184 and 185 detail the project settings available in Premiere Elements 9. We strongly recommend you study your camera's specs carefully and select the project setting that best represents the format your camera is recording to.

Convert your video to DV and DV-AVIs

MPEGs and VOBs are essentially the same thing. VOBs are MPEG2s on a DVD.

They are both highly compressed video formats that provide excellent quality playback. Like DV-AVIs, they form video frames through interlacing – creating every frame of video in two passes, drawing every other horizontal line of pixels in each pass. This they do about 30 times every second (25 times every second on PAL video), too fast for your eyes to see.

The challenge is that MPEGs and VOBs usually create their interlaced frames with the *upper field* of lines first, while DV-AVIs create their interlaced frames with the *lower field* first.

That's not a significant issue *until* you bring an MPEG into a DV-AVI workflow, such as Premiere Elements. You may not see the difference when playing back your video in your project but, when you output your video or create a DVD from these types of files in Premiere Elements, the MPEG-based segments will often look very jumpy and jittery.

The old solution was to right-click on every MPEG clip on your timeline or sceneline and select **Field Options**, then **Reverse Field Order**. Very inconvenient and time consuming if you've got a lot of MPEGs in your project.

But, in Premiere Elements, Adobe has provided project settings especially for working with MPEGs as source files – the **Hard Disk, Flash Memory Camcorder** project preset. (For more information on project settings, see the **Open a new project** discussion in **Chapter 15, Start a New Project**.)

Video imported into a project using these settings will automatically have its field order reversed, and your MPEGs will render and output perfectly from Premiere Elements.

If you use MPEGs or VOBs almost exclusively as your video source files, this is the project preset you want to use.

Remember, however, if you mix DV-AVIs and MPEGs in the same project, you will have to change the field order for one of these video formats manually, as described above. Otherwise you may end up with a DV-AVI getting its field order reversed and playing all jumpy and jittery on your DVD!

That said, although Premiere Elements can work with MPEGs, VOBs and other video formats, the best – *the absolute best* – way to use these types of video files efficiently in Premiere Elements is to convert them to DV-AVIs, as described on the facing page.

Get media from PC Files and Folders

To load video, audio or stills already on your computer into your Premiere Elements project:

1. Click on the **Organize** tab and select **Get Media**.

2. Select the **PC Files and Folders** option on the **Get Media** panel.

3. Browse to the file(s) you'd like to import on your hard drive.

You can also quickly open a browse screen for your project by double-clicking in a blank space (beyond the media listings) in your **Project** media panel.

Capture video through DV bridges and pass-throughs

There's a difference between a DV bridge and a plain old capture device or capture card. Capture devices merely digitize your video input to any of number of video formats. DV bridges, on the other hand, are specifically designed to **convert any video and audio input into DV-AVI files**, the preferred video format for PC-based video editors. (Macs also prefer DV video, although they are saved as DV Quicktime files rather than AVIs. The video data content, however, is identical.)

DV bridges range from relatively inexpensive to high-end professional devices with time base correction and other video optimizers. The best value on the market in DV bridges and a Muvipix recommended "best buy" is the **ADS Pyro AV Link**, a favorite of many videographers.

Convert non-DV-AVI files

For the cleanest results and smoothest operation in Premiere Elements, we recommend that, whenever possible, you use exclusively DV-AVIs as source files for your standard video projects.

If you're not shooting your video on a miniDV or an HDV camcorder, this may present a bit of a challenge. However, there are a number of very easy to use, very *free* programs available for converting almost any file to a DV-AVI, and we've listed a couple in **Chapter 30**.

A favorite program for converting MPEGs and VOB files to DV-AVIs is the free utility **Super Video Converter**, from eRight Software. Instructions for downloading and using this program appear in this books **Chapter 30**.

This process of converting may seem a bit inconvenient at first. But the trade-offs in terms of improved performance, trouble-free operation and higher quality outputs from Premiere Elements will very soon convince you that it's well worth the little extra effort.

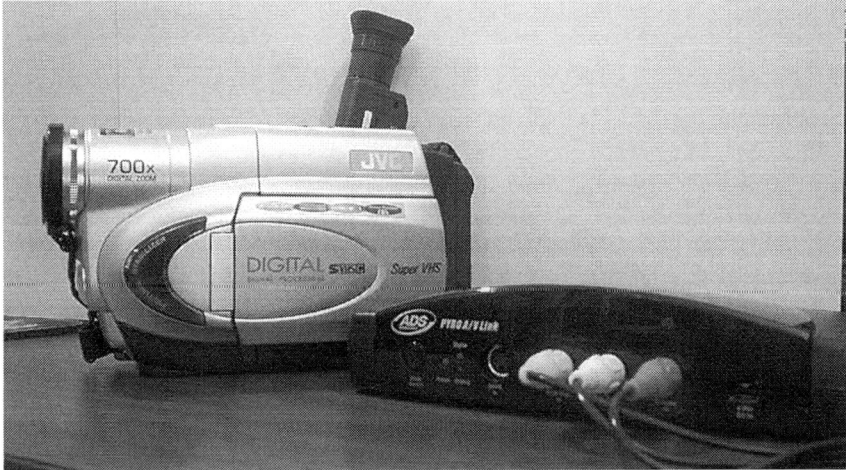

A camcorder connected through an ADS Pyro AV Link (a DV bridge)

The **Pyro AV Link** will take any AV input (a camcorder, a DVD player, a VCR or virtually any other video source, including live video) and port it into your computer as a high-quality DV-AVI file. This great device can be had for a street price of less than $150, a great value if you plan to edit a lot of video from non-DV sources.

Capturing video from a DV bridge is easy. Just plug your camcorder's, DVD player's or VCR's AV cables (RCA jacks) into the DV bridge's inputs and plug the bridge (connected by FireWire) into your computer.

Your computer will recognize the device just as it would a miniDV camcorder connection.

The capture process itself is essentially the same as capture from a miniDV camcorder. The only difference is, since there's no direct connection between your video source device and the computer, you won't be able to control the device with the **Capture Monitor's** playback controls or break scenes by timecode.

But, once you've got the device cued up to the segment you want to capture, you just click the **Capture** button and you're good to go!

By the way, the **ADS Pyro AV Link** can also be used with DVD camcorders and hard drive camcorders, so it's a great way to make any non-miniDV video 100% Premiere Elements compatible.

An alternative to a DV bridge is a set-up called a **pass-through**, which essentially uses a miniDV camcorder as a makeshift DV bridge.

To set up a pass-through connection, attach your non-DV camcorder to your miniDV camcorder via its AV input cables, then link the miniDV to your computer via FireWire.

With the miniDV camcorder in play mode (but without a tape inside) the non-DV camcorder's video flows through the miniDV and into the computer, where it's captured as DV-AVIs.

The biggest challenge to using this method is that fewer and fewer new miniDV camcorders support a pass-through connection. And it's very difficult to learn, from most spec sheets, which camcorders do.

But, if your miniDV camcorder is pass-through capable, this is a simple and effective method of digitizing almost any analog video input.

Use photos in Premiere Elements

Premiere Elements can work with virtually any of the major photo or graphics formats, including JPEGs, GIFs, TIFs, vector art (EPSs and AI files) and PSDs (native Photoshop and Photoshop Elements files).

The exceptions are images using the CMYK color mode or RGB photo files using other than standard 8-bit color. But, if you are creating your graphics or using photos from a consumer graphics program (such as Photoshop Elements) or from a digital camera, scanner or other device, then you don't need to worry about these exceptions. Virtually all photo and graphics files from these sources are compatible with the program.

Premiere Elements will also support transparency (alpha channels) so that file formats like GIF, PNG, EPS, AI and PSD files with transparent areas will display, when used in a video project, with these areas transparent.

This is particularly useful if you're using one of these graphics file types on an upper video track with a video layer behind it (see **Use L-cuts, J-cuts and multiple tracks** in **Chapter 19, Edit Your Movie in Timeline Mode**) or as a graphic added to a title (see **Add a graphic to your title** in **Chapter 23, Add Titles**).

Photos make great source files for a Premiere Elements project, but you'll find the highest quality results and the best performance from the program if the sizes of your photos are properly optimized before you bring them into your project.

Graphics and photo formats

For photos, the most size-efficient file format is the JPEG. As an alternative, PSD files and TIFs use less compression and, though larger, also produce excellent results.

Because JPEGs are highly compressed, they do not make the best format for graphics that include clean, distinct edges, such as logos or graphics that include text. In these cases, PSDs, TIFs, AIs, EPSs and even PNGs produce the crispest lines.

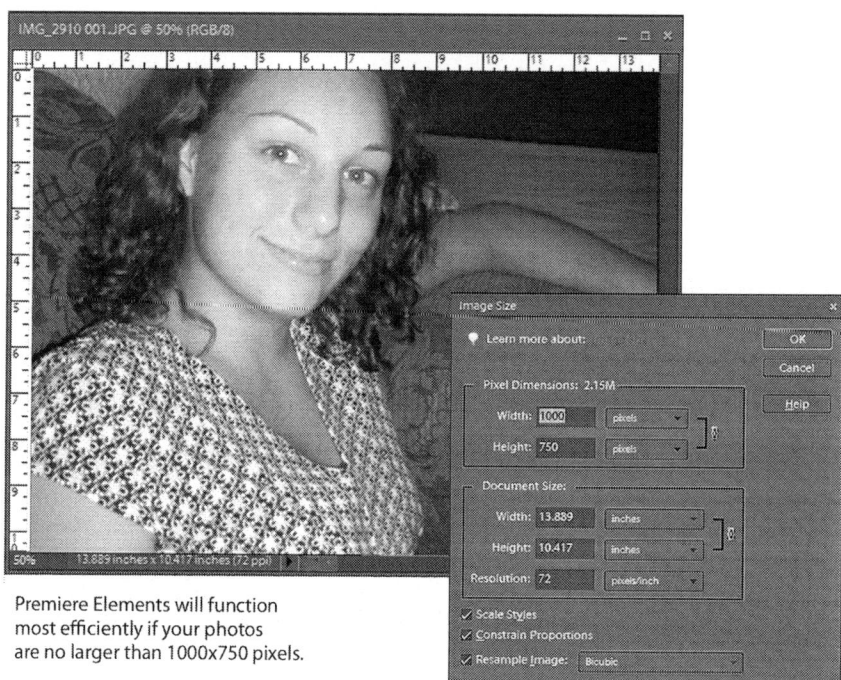

Premiere Elements will function most efficiently if your photos are no larger than 1000x750 pixels.

We urge you to make sure that any photo you use (especially if you use several in a slideshow) has been resized to no larger than 1000x750 pixels before you bring it into your Premiere Elements project to ensure the best quality and optimal program performance. (Photos taken directly from digital cameras can be 20 to 25 times that size!)

At first this may seem to go contrary to common wisdom.

Traditionally, the higher the resolution of your photo, the better the quality of the output. But remember that Premiere Elements is a *video* editing program, and video is a relatively low resolution medium (essentially the equivalent of 640x480 pixels). And, to a point, reducing the resolution of a photo or graphic to be used in a video actually *improves* the quality of the video output. (1000x750 pixels seems to be that point).

The reason for this has to do with a process called downsampling, the system a video program uses to bring high-resolution photos down

Optimize photos for high-resolution video projects

For high-definition video slideshows, the optimal size for a photo is 2200x1235 pixels (approximately, since photos are usually 4:3 rather than 16:9) – although note that photos at this size will put a bit more strain your system's resources.

to video size. Premiere Elements does a fair job of this – but, as any pro knows, nothing that happens automatically will be as clean or as efficient as what you do manually. "Down-rezzing" is definitely one of those things.

There's also a more pressing reason for downsampling your photos yourself. The process of "down-rezzing," like the process of assimilating non-DV-AVI files into a video project, is a very intensive process. So intensive, in fact, that it is *the single biggest reason Premiere Elements crashes*, particularly during the disc burning process.

It also takes a lot longer for the program to down-rez a, for instance, 4000x3000 pixel photo than it does a 1000x750 pixel photo.

Much, much longer. And would you rather wait an hour or two for the program to create your DVD or 10 hours for a process that might end up with the program choking and dying anyway?

Trust us on this. Optimize your photo sizes to 1000x750 pixels before you import them into Premiere Elements. It will save you hours of anguish and misery in the end.

Photoshop Elements, by the way, has a very nice batch resizing feature that can resize a whole folder full of photos in just a few clicks. This feature is called **Process Multiple Files**, and it is located under the Photoshop Elements **File** menu.

Add music files to a Premiere Elements project

Although Premiere Elements works with a variety of audio file formats, it's probably best to exclusively use **MP3s** and **WAVs** as your source files.

They seem to provide the most trouble-free operation.

One word of warning, though, in connection with using music files in your video projects: Many music download sites (iTunes, for instance) employ electronic **Digital Rights Management** (DRM) in their downloaded files.

This DRM system will throw up an error code if you try to load a copy-protected music file into your Premiere Elements project, blocking you from using the file.

There is software available on the Web for breaking this DRM. But probably the easiest way to get around this copy protection is to burn the music file to a CD and then use a program like Windows Media Player to rip the CD music file back to your computer as an MP3.

The resultant MP3 should load right into Premiere Elements.

This process, of course, doesn't exempt you from respecting the rights of the artist who created the music. So please don't abuse the privilege.

Also, *before* you do bring those photos into your video project, go to **Edit/Preferences/General** in Premiere Elements and uncheck **Default Scale to Frame Size**.

Left checked, **Scale to Frame Size** automatically sizes your photo to fill your video frame, giving a false representation of your photo in the video frame in addition to really getting in the way when you're trying to add motion paths to your photos.

In the event this option was checked when you imported your photos into your project, you can also turn it off for your photos individually by **right-clicking** on each photo on the timeline (**Ctrl-clicking** on the Mac) and unchecking the **Scale to Frame Size** option on the pop-up menu.

For more information on using photos and still graphics in your Premiere Elements project, see **Add still photos to your project** in **Chapter 19, Edit Video in the Timeline Mode**.

Troubleshoot Windows video capture in Premiere Elements

Video capture from a miniDV or HDV tape-based camcorder seems like it should be easy. And, since you can't do anything in Premiere Elements until you have your video captured into your computer, when capture fails it can be very frustrating!

I wish I could tell you that there was a magic bullet for making all the problems go away, but sometimes there just is no simple fix.

The following, though, can help you troubleshoot your problems. And, if they don't work, the third-party solutions we recommend below will get you through the day (and may ultimately become your preferred workflow!)

1. Before you blame the software, make sure your operating system and its components are optimized and up to date. Following the maintenance regimen in our **Chapter 30** – which includes ensuring that your operating system, its firmware and drivers are up to date – is essential to the smooth operation of a process as intensive as video editing!

   Remember, you're using a very intensive program on an operating system that's constantly changing, updating and evolving. Like a race car driver who knows that even a few pounds of pressure in one tire can mean the difference between a stable ride and one fraught with problems, you should always make sure your computer's operating system is in perfect working order.

   And always make sure you have the latest version of **Quicktime** and the newest **RealTek drivers** on your system! This may not seem like an obvious solutions to your problems, but more times than not, a simple update makes all the difference.

2. As mentioned earlier in the chapter, if your operating system isn't even registering your camcorder as connected, you're dealing with a more fundamental problem than a Premiere Elements issue.

Check your connections. Make sure your camcorder is set up right for capture (i.e., is in VTR/play mode). Possibly even check the camcorder on another computer to see whether it's the computer, the FireWire cable or even your particular camcorder that's failing.

3. Make sure you're using a FireWire/IEEE-1394/iLink connection for capture. Some miniDV camcorders also offer a USB connection – but, most of the time, they won't work with Premiere Elements. Trust us on this. You want a FireWire connection if it is at all possible.

4. If all connections are working and Windows recognizes your camcorder but Premiere Elements doesn't, note the auto-launch window that Windows opens when you plug your camcorder into your computer.

What software does it offer to launch to capture your video? Some software (such as Nero) is less willing to share capture devices with any other software. And sometimes that means, unfortunately, that capturing directly into Premiere Elements may simply not be possible – at least not without way more work than it's worth. In that case, you may want to consider our third-party solutions below.

5. If all seems to be in order and Premiere Elements still isn't recognizing your camcorder, click on the **>>** button on the upper right corner of your **Capture** panel. (If this button doesn't show, go to Premiere Elements **Window** drop-down menu and select **Show Docking Headers**.)

Select the **Device Control** option and, from the panel that opens, click on the **Options** button.

This button will open another panel in which you can set the program to the exact brand and model of camcorder or DV bridge you're connected to. (There are **Standard** settings also, in the event your camcorder model isn't listed.)

In all honesty, changing these settings rarely revives a dead camcorder connection. However, it can "refine" a connection in which the camcorder is recognized but capture doesn't seem to be going quite right.

Finally, if none of these solutions works, you can use a third-party capture solution. **Chapter 30** lists some great resources for free or low-cost **Capture Utilities** that can help.

Our personal favorite capture software utility for miniDV capture is **WinDV**. This free and fully-loaded capture utility will often work even when nothing else seems to (assuming Windows sees the camcorder connection).

Like Premiere Elements itself, WinDV captures miniDV video in small DV-AVI clips that are perfectly compatible with Premiere Elements and other editors.

Other options include the low-cost **Scenalyzer** and the absolutely free **Windows MovieMaker** (included with your Windows operating system). Both will capture your miniDV files in the DV-AVI format, which you can then import into your Premiere Elements project.

For high-definition video, **HDVSplit** is, like WinDV, free and yet very stable and nicely featured.

Because of the stability, reliability and sometimes extra features included with these free or low-cost utilities, many of our Premiere Elements users actually *prefer* to capture with these third-party applications and save Premiere Elements for what it does best.

Editing video!

Automatically fix mismatched project settings

A very cool new feature in version 9 of Premiere Elements is the **Mismatched Project Settings Preset** notification and repair tool.

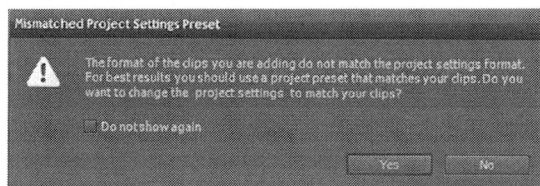

If you attempt to add to the timeline or sceneline of a new project a video clip that requires settings other than those that you have set for your project, a notification window will pop up notifying you of the mismatch and offering to fix it for you.

If you click **Yes**, the program will automatically update the project's settings to match those of this footage.

This feature only works when this mismatched footage is the *first clip* you add to your timeline or sceneline in a project. And it doesn't correct issues that may arise from mixing more than one video format in the same project. However – considering the liabilities of using the wrong settings for a project – it can prove a real lifesaver.

More information on project settings can be found in **Chapter 15, Start a New Project**.

The Media Panel
The Clip Monitor
The Create Slideshow Tool
Color Bars and Countdown Leaders

Chapter 17
Explore the Project Media Panel
The parts that will form your movie

The Project media panel is the catalog
from which you'll draw all of the video,
audio and still clips that you'll use to create
your movie.

If you select the Organize tab and click on
the Project button, the panel will display a
list of all of the sound, video and graphics
files that have been captured or imported
into your Premiere Elements project.

The Project panel

A catalog of the media files imported into your project

Filter to display only video, audio and/or stills

Clips are dragged from here onto the timeline or sceneline

Media clips can be more easily managed by moving them into folders

View as list or, by clicking here, as icons

Move up a folder level

Create folder

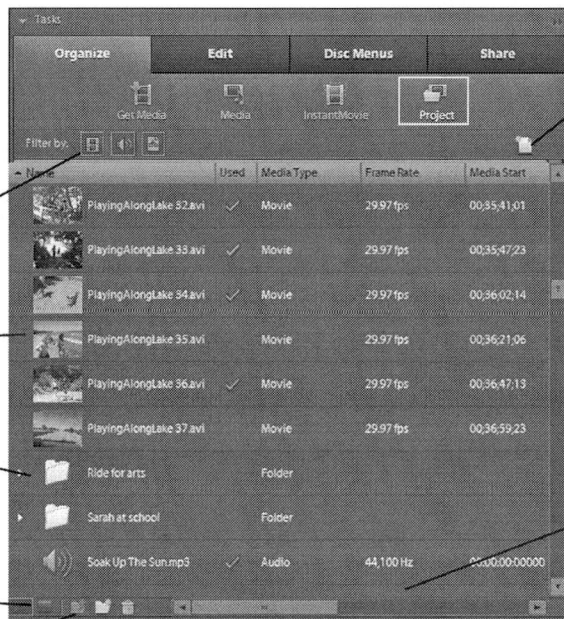

The New Item button and features:

Title

SmartSound

Bars & Tone

Black Video

Color Matte

Countdown Leader

Right-click beyond list for Get Media shortcut

The **Project** media panel (opened by clicking the **Project** button under the **Organize** tab) is the catalog from which you'll draw all of the video, audio and still clips that you'll use to create your movie. Whenever you **Get Media** for your Premiere Elements project (as discussed in **Chapter 3**), it will appear listed in this panel.

To bring a clip from this panel into your movie, simply drag it from the panel to your movie's sceneline or timeline (as we discuss in **Chapter 18, Assemble Your Video in Sceneline Mode,** and **Chapter 19, Edit Your Video in Timeline Mode**.) In fact, that's about 90% of what editing your video will consist of – simply dragging clips from here and placing them there.

But in addition to serving as a holding area for your video project's media, this panel includes a number of great tools for managing, ordering and preparing your clips for your movie's timeline or sceneline.

Different viewing modes and folders make managing and keeping track of a large number of media files relatively simple.

And the **Clip Monitor** is an invaluable tool for trimming your clips prior to adding them to your movie.

Organize your media files in folders

The two folder icons in the lower left corner of the panel are for creating and navigating folders for your media files in this panel.

This is one of my favorite Premiere Elements features, extremely valuable when you're trying to sort through a large number of media files.

Click on the **Create Folder** icon to create and name a new folder.

Once you have a folder created, you can drag your media files into it – sorting your clips so that all of your files for a particular sequence of your project are in the same folder, for instance.

You can even create sub-folders within your folders – so that it becomes very easy to manage and locate the files you need without having to scroll through the entire list of imported clips every time you need to locate a clip.

You can move your media clips in and out of these folders at any point in your project. I like to categorize all of my video clips in folders and sub-folders before I even begin editing. But you can drag a clip in or out of a folder at any point in your work without affecting its placement on your timeline.

Control how your media files are displayed

In the lower left corner of this panel, you'll see two blue icons. These are for switching the view of your media files from **List View** (the default) to **Icon View** (which has the chief advantage of allowing you to drag your clips into any order you'd like – a valuable feature if you use the **Create Slideshow** feature, as we discuss later in this chapter).

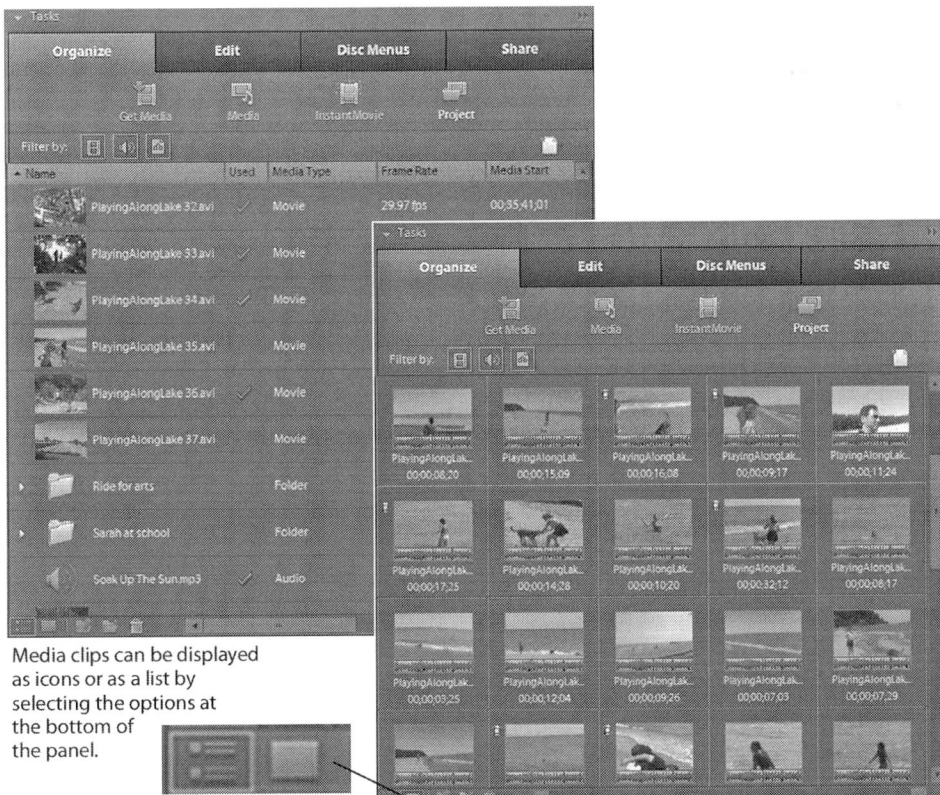

Media clips can be displayed as icons or as a list by selecting the options at the bottom of the panel.

So, what's the Media panel?

The **Media** panel is possibly the most confusing panel in the entire Premiere Elements interface – even more so since it's *called* the **Media** panel even though it may or may *not* display media clips that are actually *in* your Premiere Elements project!

The audio clips, video clips and still photos that are in your project *– and the only clips you really need to be concerned with –* **are located in the Project media panel**, opened by clicking on the **Project** button under the **Organize** tab.

The **Media** panel – which is opened by clicking on the **Media** button under the **Organize** tab – is more closely related to the **Elements Organizer** program (discussed in detail in **Chapter 31**).

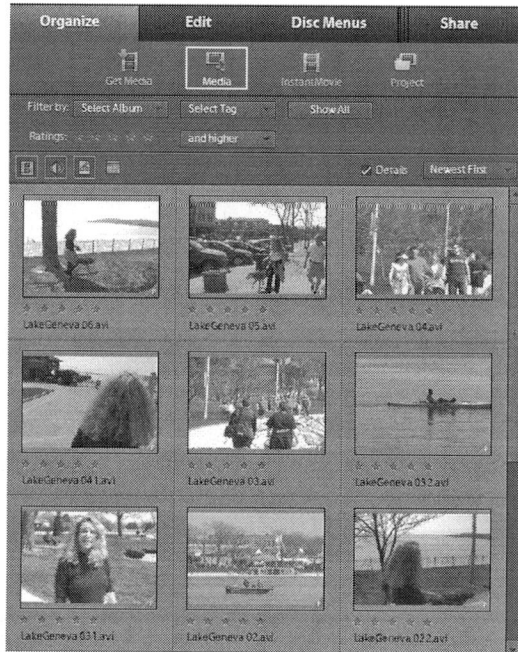

By default, the **Media** panel will display only the *last batch of video or audio clips you've added to your project*. And that's very confusing because that means, when you add newer clips to your project, the older clips in the **Media** panel seem to disappear! This is even more confusing because, whenever you add new clips to your project, the program will automatically *default* to displaying the **Media** panel again!

But don't be confused. The video, audio and stills that are a part of your project and can be used to build your movie are displayed in the **Project** media panel. *Not* in the **Media** panel.

The **Media** panel can be used to browse for additional audio and video clips on your computer. If you click on the **Select Album** and **Select Tag** drop-down menus, you can display in this panel media clips that have been assigned to various **Albums** or have had various **Keyword Tags** applied to them in the Elements Organizer (more on that in **Chapter 31**).

The **Media** panel can also be used to gather clips to create an **InstantMovie** (as we discuss in **Chapter 22**). And it can be used to add media to "**Drop Zones**" in **Disc Menu** templates (as we discuss in **Chapter 28**). But, beyond that, it's mostly just confusing.

In short, despite the fact that it seems to pop open regularly as you work with this program, try your best to ignore it. It will only confuse you.

For the most part, the only media clips you need to worry about as you assemble and edit your movie are those in the **Project** media panel.

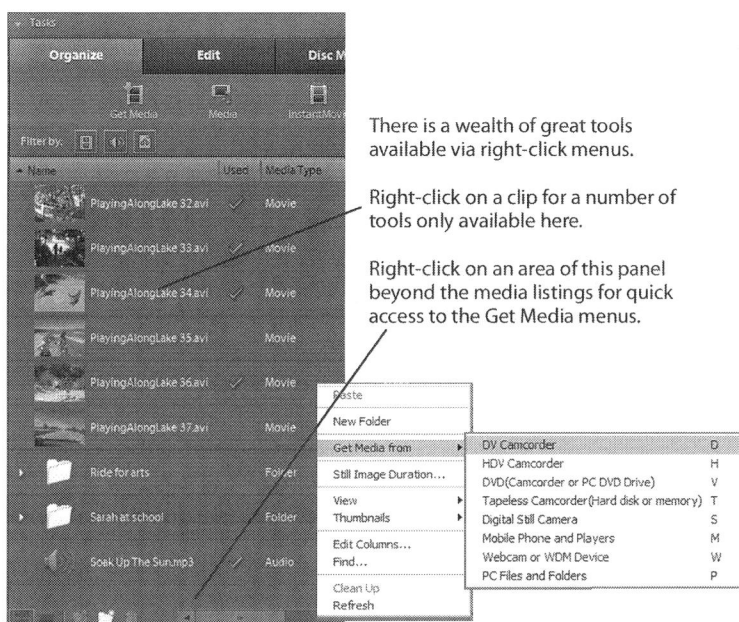

There is a wealth of great tools available via right-click menus.

Right-click on a clip for a number of tools only available here.

Right-click on an area of this panel beyond the media listings for quick access to the Get Media menus.

Valuable Project media panel right-click (and Ctrl-click) tools

There are a number of great tools available throughout Premiere Elements that can be (and sometimes can *only* be) accessed by **right-clicking** on clips or panels (or **Ctrl-clicking** on a Mac).

I do a thorough discussion of these tools in my *Steve's Tips* article "Powerful Tools in Premiere Elements' Right-Click Menus," available on the Muvipix.com product pages.

Here are a couple of my favorite right-click tools available exclusively in the **Project** media panel.

Interpret Footage – Believe it or not, standard 4:3 video and widescreen 16:9 video use exactly the same number of pixels to create a video frame. The difference is that the pixels (the tiny squares of color that combine to create every frame of video) are shaped differently. Widescreen 16:9 pixels are much wider than standard 4:3 video pixels.

Right-clicking on a clip (**Ctrl-clicking** on a Mac) and selecting **Interpret Footage** gives you access to options for conforming a widescreen clip to fit in a standard video or vice versa.

This tool is invaluable if, for some reason, you find yourself with a clip that looks strangely squished, stretched or distorted.

Duplicate – This selection makes a duplicate of the clip you've right-clicked on. This is very helpful, for instance, if you've created a title slide with a style you'd like to re-use. You merely **duplicate** it and then revise the duplicate as needed.

Rename – You can rename a clip by selecting this right-click option or by simply double-clicking slowly on the name of the file in the **Project** media panel listing so that the name becomes highlighted. Renaming a clip doesn't change the name of the file on your hard drive, by the way. Nor does it affect the clip's position or function on the timeline. But it can make it easier for you to identify the file later.

Pre-edit your clips in the Clip Monitor

The **Clip Monitor** is a pop-up screen for previewing playback of a clip. It's also a work area in which you can trim a clip prior to adding it to your project by setting **In** and/or **Out** markers.

The **Clip Monitor** is launched either by **right-clicking** on a clip (**Ctrl-clicking** on a Mac) and selecting the **Open in Clip Monitor** option – or by simply double-clicking on a clip.

You can launch the **Clip Monitor** by double-clicking a clip in the **Project** media panel or by double-clicking a clip on the **Timeline** or **Sceneline**.

As illustrated on the facing page, when you set **In** or **Out** markers in your **Clip Monitor**, only the segment of the clip between those markers will be displayed during the clip's playback in your movie.

In other words, if you have a 5-minute clip, you can set the **In** and **Out** markers so that only a 30-second segment of the clip is actually displayed in your movie – rendering the clip essentially a 30-second clip.

In the **Clip Monitor,** the "live" segment of the clip is indicated with a lighter, blue segment area on the **Clip Monitor's** mini-timeline. You can adjust this live area's length by either dragging the end points in or out, or by playing the clip using the playback controls at the bottom of the **Clip Monitor** and clicking on the **Set In** or **Set Out** buttons to isolate the segment you want to use.

The **In** and **Out** markers in the **Clip Monitor** can be used to isolate segments in audio clips as well as video.

You can not set **In** and **Out** markers on titles and still images, however, because they are stationary elements.

Take a shortcut to "Get Media"

If you want to import additional media from your computer into your Premiere Elements project, or if you want to launch a video capture without going all the way out to the **Organize** workspace, you can open the **Get Media** menu right from the **Project** panel.

As illustrated at the top of the previous page, **right-click** on a *blank* area of the **Project media** panel (**Ctrl-click** on a Mac), beyond your media listings, and select the **Get Media** option from the menu that displays.

This "shortcut" gets you access to all of the same **Get Media** options as clicking the **Get Media** button under the **Organize** tab.

To quickly open a browse screen so that you can import a media clip already on your computer, simply double-click on a blank area of your **Project** media panel's listings.

The Clip Monitor launches when you double-click on any clip on the timeline or sceneline or in the Project media panel.

Clips can be trimmed in the Clip Monitor either by dragging the in and out points on the mini-timeline or by playing the clip and clicking the Set In and Set Out buttons.

Although the original clip remains its original length, only the "trimmed" segment (the blue segment in Premiere Elements) displays on the timeline.

Once the **Clip Monitor** has been launched, it will stay open as long as you keep your project open or until you manually close it.

Because this panel tends to pop up in the middle of the workspace whenever it launches, I usually launch it as soon as I open a project, position it off to the side and out of the way and leave it open. That way, if I later need to open a clip in this panel for previewing or trimming, the **Clip Monitor** will play this clip where I've positioned it instead of in the middle of my work.

Create color mattes, bars & tone and countdown leaders

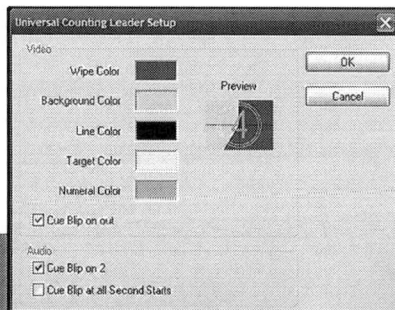

Among the custom clips available under the New Item button are Color Bars & Tone, a Countdown Leader and a color clip (Color Matte) of any color you want.

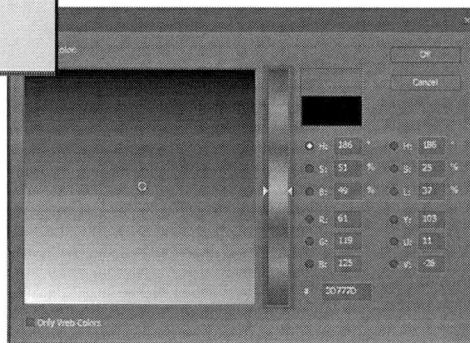

In the upper right of the panel you will find the **New Item** button (a white square). Clicking on this button launches options for creating a number of very valuable, short clips for your project.

Title launches the Premiere Elements **Title** workspace. We explore this area more in **Chapter 23, Add Titles.**

Color Bars & Tone creates a clip of bars and audio tone, which broadcasters often require at the beginning of every video in order to calibrate their equipment to your movie's sound levels and color profile.

Black Video and **Color Matte** create blank clips of whatever color you designate and which can be used behind titles or as blank spaces in your video.

Universal Countdown Leader creates a customizable countdown sequence (including an audio "blip" at two seconds) which can be placed at the beginning of your video – another feature broadcasters often require so that they can cue up the beginning of your movie.

You'll also find a link here for launching **SmartSound Quicktracks**, the amazing third-party tool for creating custom, professional-sounding music clips for your project.

For more information about **SmartSound QuickTracks**, see **Chapter 20, Edit Audio on the Timeline**.

Once you've selected the stills from the Project media panel, you can launch Create Slideshow by clicking on the >> menu in the upper right corner of the panel.

New Folder
Rename
Delete

Create SlideShow...
Still Image Duration...

Find...

View
Thumbnails

Clean Up
Refresh

Edit Columns...

Cut
Copy
Paste
Clear

Interpret Footage...

Open in Clip Monitor

Create Slideshow...

Or you can right-click on your selected stills and select Create Slideshow from the right-click menu.

Set the order of the slides according to the order they appear in the media panel or according to the order you've selected them.

Create Slideshow

Ordering: Sort Order — OK

Media: Take Video Only — Cancel

☑ Place Images/Clips at Unnumbered Markers

Image Duration: 150 — Frames

☑ Apply Default Transition (Cross Dissolve)

Transition Duration: 30 — Frames

To change the default transition, right-click a transition in the Effects window and choose 'Set Selected as Default Transition.'

If you've selected video clips for your "slideshow", you have the option of using the video only (no audio).

If you've created unnumbered markers with the Beat Detect feature, you can set the slides to change at these markers.

Apply a transition between the slides.

The Image and Transition Durations can be set by frames or by seconds.

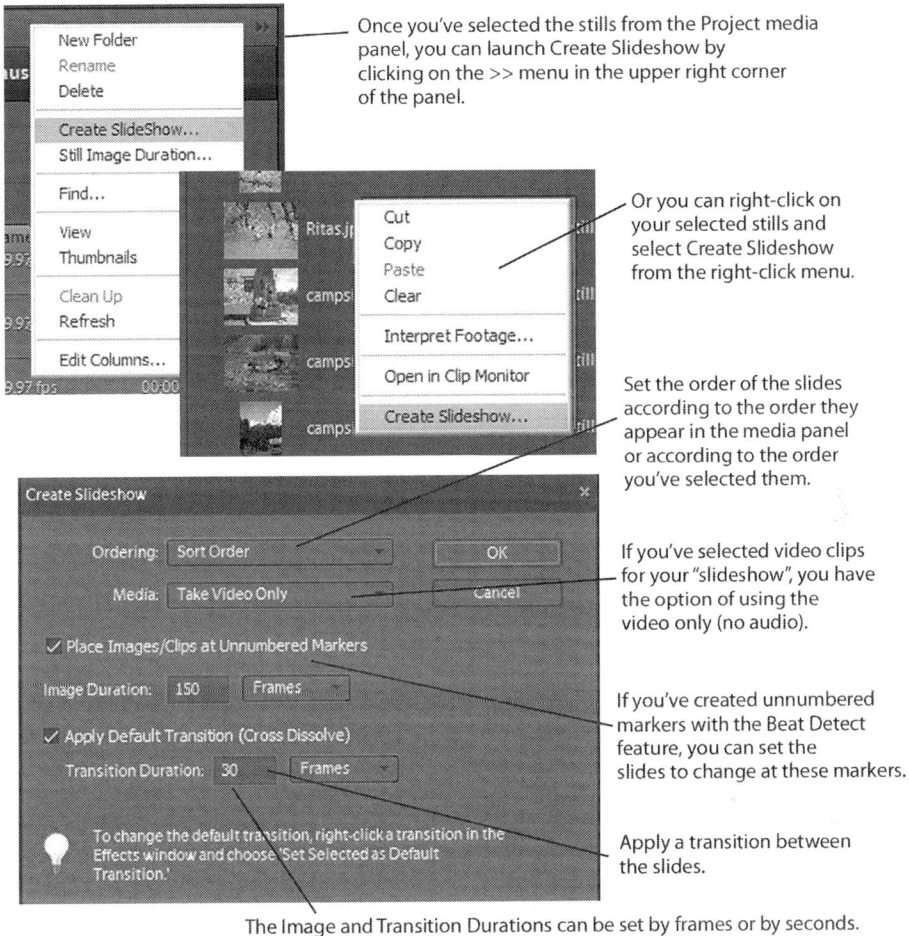

Create a slideshow

One of my favorite automatic tools in Premiere Elements is the **Create Slideshow** feature.

To create a slideshow automatically in Premiere Elements, you merely select a number of clips or stills from the **Project** media panel (by holding down the **Ctrl** or **Shift** key as you select) and then either **right-click** on the selected clips (**Ctrl-click** on a Mac) or click on the **>>** button in the upper right of the panel to access the **Create Slideshow** tool.

As you can see in the illustration of the **Create Slideshow** option screen, above, you can set the order of the slides in your show in a couple of ways.

You can simply have them appear in the same order as they appear in your **Project** media panel or you can have them appear in the order that you've selected them.

There are a couple of ways to set the order of your clips in the **Project** media panel prior to launching the **Create Slideshow** tool:

1. If you've set your **Project** media panel to display your media in **Icon View** (by clicking the blue button in the lower left corner), you can drag to arrange your clips into whatever order you'd like prior to launching the **Create Slideshow** tool.

2. Alternatively, with the **Project** media panel in **List View**, you can order your clips by renaming them alpha-numerically so that they are listed in the order you'd like them to appear in your slideshow.

In the **Create Slideshow** option window, as illustrated on the previous page, you can set the duration of your slides in a number of ways:

- You can set your slides to change after a designated interval of time.

- You can set them to change at **Unnumbered Markers** on the **Timeline** (For more information on **Unnumbered Markers**, see **Detect Beats** in **Chapter 20, Edit Audio on the Timeline**).

You can use either video or still clips in your slideshow – although only stills can be set to change at a given duration or at the unnumbered markers created by the **Detect Beats** tool.

If you use video clips in your slideshow, the **Create Slideshow** panel includes the option to remove the audio from the clips.

You can also select the option to apply a **Default Transition** between your slides. (For information on designating the **Default Transition**, see **Chapter 25, Add and Customize Transitions**.)

For information on how to optimize your stills for a slideshow, see **Use photos in Premiere Elements** in **Chapter 16, Get Media into Your Project**.

There are actually a number of different ways to create a slideshow in Premiere Elements, including a **Create Slideshow** tool built into the Elements Organizer and **InstantMovie** slideshow themes.

For more information on the tools and other methods of creating slideshows using features in both Premiere Elements, Photoshop Elements and the Elements Organizer – and the advantages of each – see my *Steve's Tips* article "Creating Slideshows with Photoshop Elements and Premiere Elements," available on the products page at Muvipix.com.

By the way, you can also create a slideshow using one of the **Slideshow InstantMovie** themes. For more information on creating **InstantMovies**, see **Chapter 22**.

Add Clips to Your Sceneline

Add Transitions

Add and Adjust Audio

Chapter 18

Assemble Your Video in Sceneline Mode
The drag-and-drop editing space

Premiere Elements offers two workspaces for assembling your video projects – the professional-style Timeline panel and the simple, drag-and-drop Sceneline.

There are advantages to each. But for quickly assembling your movie, it's hard to beat the Sceneline's simple drag-and-drop interface.

In Sceneline mode, assembling your movie is as simple as dragging your video clips and stills to the area labeled Drag Next Clip Here. Transitions are added in the smaller blocks between the clips. Audio, music and narration are added to the tracks below the sceneline.

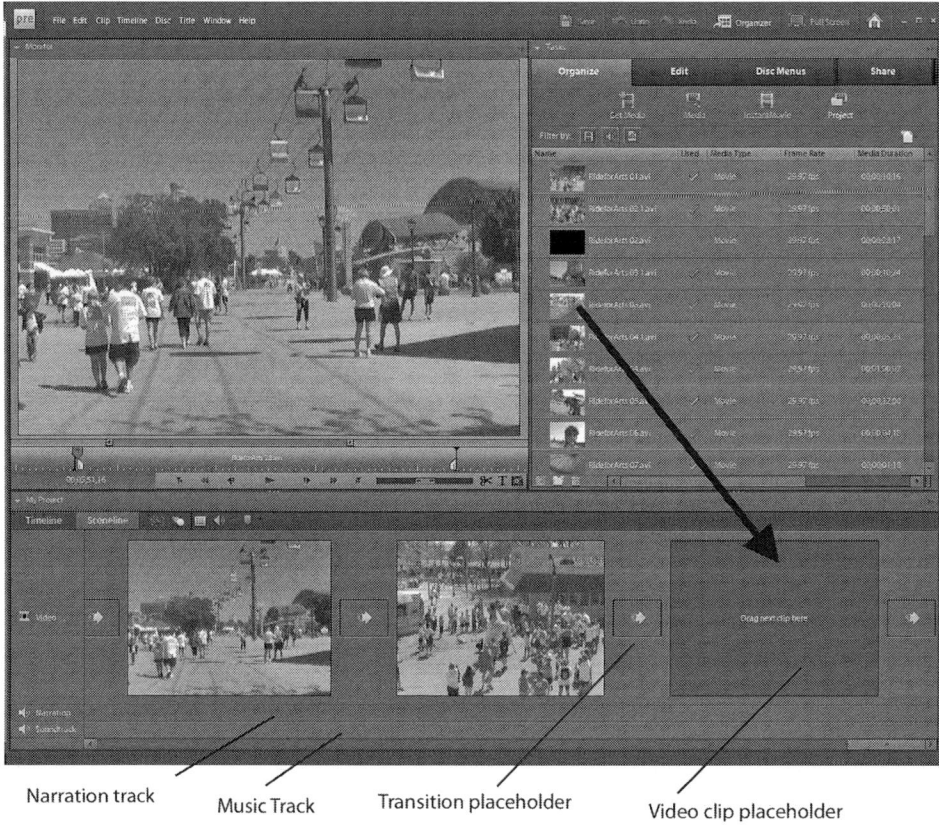

Narration track   Music Track   Transition placeholder   Video clip placeholder

The **Sceneline** is the simpler of the two workspaces for editing your Premiere Elements project. It's also, by nature of its simplicity, rather limited in its function and not always the easiest workspace for fine-tuning the elements of your movie. But, for the basic assembly of a single track of clips and three tracks of audio, it couldn't be easier to use.

While the **Timeline**, as the name implies, is about *time* – when things happen and how your clips interact with each other – the **Sceneline** is about *content*. It's about simply gathering your clips or slides together and creating a movie.

Add video to your sceneline

Adding video clips to the **Sceneline** is as simple as dragging them from your **Project** media panel (under the **Organize** tab), and into the "**Drag Next Clip Here**" placeholders. Clips are not overlapped. They simply line up, one after another, as you add them, each clip represented by a single thumbnail.

Once your clips have been placed on your sceneline, you can trim them, removing undesired footage or audio from the beginning or end of each clip.

The "timeline" for your audio or video clips is displayed, in **Sceneline** mode, along the bottom of the **Monitor** panel, as illustrated to the right. The "live area" of the clip (the only part that will actually be played in your movie project) is represented by the light blue strip, with the end points for the "live" segment represented by markers at either end of this strip. By adjusting the positions of these **In** and **Out Point** markers, you can trim or extend each clip, from either the beginning or end.

In Sceneline mode, each clip's timeline appears as a blue line along the bottom of the Monitor. A clip can be trimmed by adjusting the In and Out Points at either end of this blue timeline.

Add transitions

Between each clip on your sceneline is a placeholder for transitions. As with adding your video and audio clips, adding transitions is as simple as dragging them from the **Transitions** panel (under the **Edit** tab) to the placeholders between your sceneline clips.

Transitions can also be accessed by **right-clicking** on a transition placeholder on your sceneline (**Ctrl-clicking** on a Mac) and browsing through the transitions option menus.

Each transition offers a variety of customizable options. To access these options, open the **Transitions** panel (by clicking the **Transitions** button under the **Edit** tab) and, with the transition you want to customize selected on your sceneline, click the **Edit Transition** button.

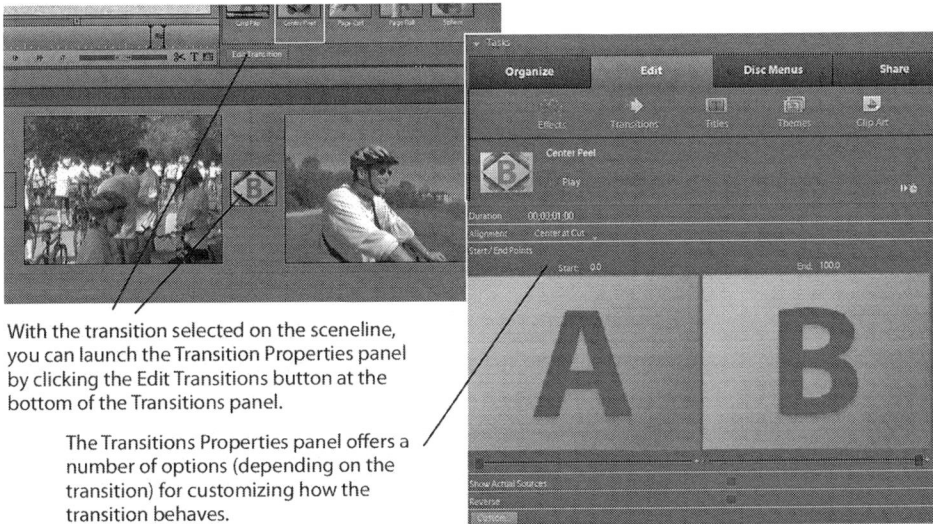

With the transition selected on the sceneline, you can launch the Transition Properties panel by clicking the Edit Transitions button at the bottom of the Transitions panel.

The Transitions Properties panel offers a number of options (depending on the transition) for customizing how the transition behaves.

221

Sceneline mode includes two audio tracks (in addition to the "invisible" track included with your video clips).

Although labeled Narration and Soundtrack, any audio can be loaded onto either track.

Add audio to your sceneline

As you add your video clips to your sceneline, the accompanying audio will be added automatically, as part of an unseen audio track.

In addition to the clip's audio, **Sceneline** mode offers two additional audio tracks. (Although the icons to the left of each track imply that they are for **Narration** and **Soundtrack**, any audio can be used on any track.) As with your video clips, adding audio clips is as simple as dragging them from your project media panel to one of these audio tracks. **Narration** can also be added to your movie using the Premiere Elements narration recorder (as we discuss in **Chapter 20, Edit Audio on the Timeline**) or by recording the narration separately and manually importing the audio clip into your project.

If you drag a clip that includes both audio and video onto one of the audio tracks, by the way, only the audio from that clip will be added to your sceneline.

Adjust your audio levels

There are a couple of ways to adjust the audio levels in **Sceneline** mode. The simplest method is to adjust the level for the entire track. This is useful if, for instance, you'd like to turn down your soundtrack music or the audio on your video clips so that your narration can be better heard.

To turn down the audio for an entire track, click on the speaker or musical note icon to the left of the track (as illustrated on the facing page). This will reveal a levels slider, which you can adjust to the audio level you prefer.

But more often you'll need more precise audio level control, as when you'd like your music to start at one level, then fade back when your narration comes in. This can be accomplished by using the **Audio Mixer** (launched by clicking the green speaker icon along the top of the **Sceneline** panel).

As you adjust the sliders in the **Audio Mixer** as your movie is playing, the mixer will create audio keyframes, raising or lowering the audio levels at precise points, based on your adjustments.

The audio level for a track can be adjusted by clicking on the icon to the left of the audio track and raising or lower the slider which then appears.

The speaker icon to the left of the video clips represents the video clips' audio

Audio can be adjusted more precisely by launching the Audio Mixer (by clicking the green speaker icon) and adjusting the sliders as your movie plays.

This can be a bit tricky though. And, if you don't like the way your audio has been adjusted, it can be challenging to reuse the **Audio Mixer** to undo your mistakes because the mixer merely adds more keyframes rather than replacing the old.

To adjust your audio levels with more precise control as well as the ability to re-adjust your settings, you'll be much better off if you use audio keyframes, as we discuss in **Adjust audio at specific points in your video** in **Chapter 20, Edit Audio on the Timeline**.

Add titles

As we discuss in greater detail in **Chapter 23, Add Titles**, the **Titles** workspace in Premiere Elements can be accessed in one of two ways.

- Clicking the "**T**" icon at the bottom right of the **Monitor** panel takes you directly to the Titles workspace.

When the Titles workspace is launched by clicking the "T" in the lower right of the Monitor panel, a title is automatically created in your movie at the position of the CTI playhead.

- Clicking the **Titles** button (under the **Edit** tab) also takes you to this workspace – but it does so by taking you through the titles templates workspace first.

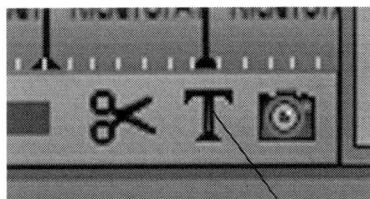

The presence of a title (or any video clip on an upper track) is represented in the upper right of a clip on your sceneline by a blue square.

The presence of narration or other audio on your audio track is represented in the upper right of a clip on your sceneline by a microphone icon.

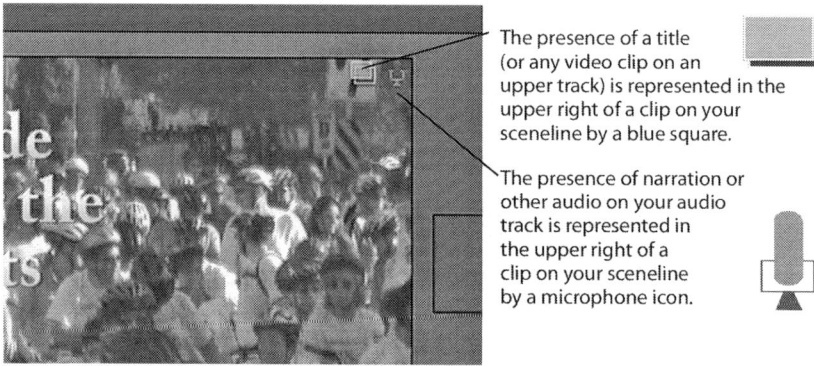

Once you've created a title, it is automatically added to your sceneline at the position of the **CTI** (Current Time Indicator). The presence of a title over your clip is indicated by an icon which will appear in the upper right corner of the clip or clips on your **Sceneline**.

Controlling the length of time the title displays and when in your movie it appears can be a bit challenging in **Sceneline** mode, however.

As we've said, **Sceneline** mode is mostly about assembling your clips into a movie. Switching to **Timeline** mode, you'll have much more control over when and how things happen. In **Timeline** mode, it is relatively simple to locate the title on an upper video track, position it precisely where you'd like it to appear and extend or reduce the time it is displayed.

The limitations of Sceneline mode

Although many of the features discussed in **Chapter 19, Edit Your Video in Timeline Mode**, and **Chapter 20, Edit Audio on the Timeline**, are also available in **Sceneline** mode, many of the program's more advanced functions are limited or can only be used in **Timeline** mode.

Features that function to a limited degree or not at all in **Sceneline** mode include:

Multi-track editing. The **Sceneline** is limited to one video track. J-Cuts, L-Cuts, split screen and picture-in-picture effects can not be created in **Sceneline** mode.

Chroma Key and Videomerge. Because **keying** effects, including **Videomerge**, require at least two tracks of video in order to create their composite effects, these effects can not be created in **Sceneline** mode.

Time Stretch. Because the **Time Stretch** effects are a function of time, fast motion, slow motion and reverse play effects can not be easily created in **Sceneline** mode.

Titles. Although titles can be created in **Sceneline** mode, they can not be precisely positioned, extended or trimmed to a specific length, or have effects or transitions – including fade ins and fade outs – applied to them.

Audio Keyframing. Audio can not be set to specific levels at specific points in a clip on the sceneline. Audio keyframes must be created and adjusted in the **Properties** panel.

Add Clips to Your Timeline

Auto Enhance Your Clips

Split and Trim Your Clips

Work with Multiple Tracks of Video

Smart Trim Your Movie

Motion Tracking

The Time Stretch Tool

Chapter 19
Edit Your Video in Timeline Mode
Where your movie comes together

Although every panel in Premiere Elements has its role in your editing workflow, the Timeline/Sceneline panel (or, as Adobe calls it, the My Project panel) is the arena where the real video editing action takes place.

It's where your clips are gathered, ordered, trimmed, sliced, rearranged, and where effects are applied. It's where your clips interact with one another.

In short, it's where your movie finally comes together.

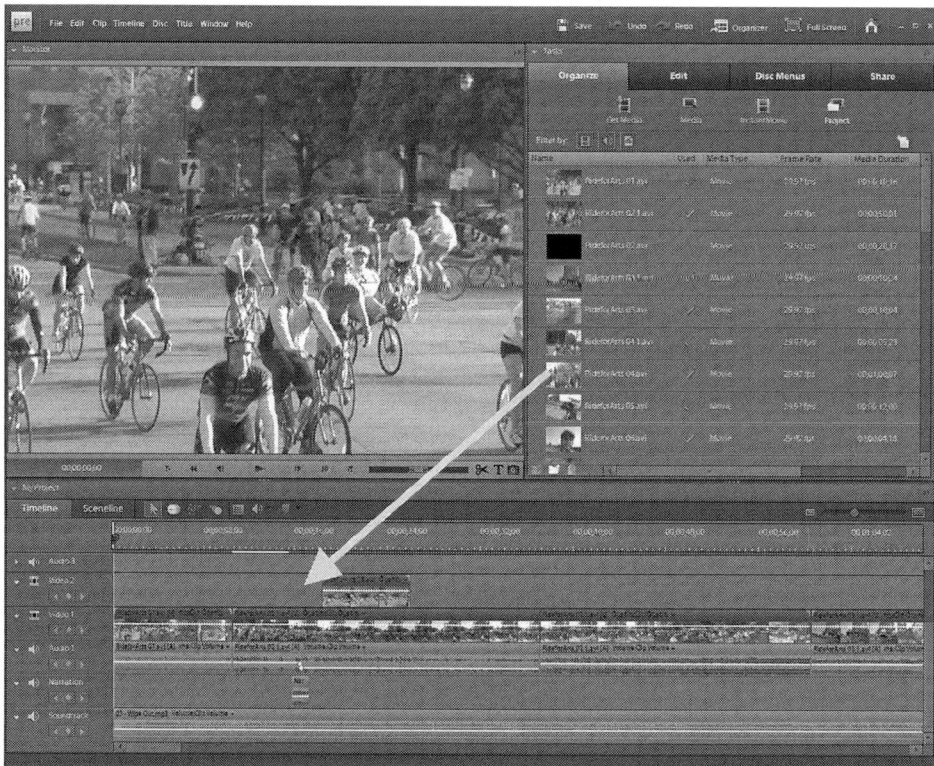

In Timeline mode, your clips are dragged from the Project media panel to any of up to 99 audio and/or video tracks. Transitions are added to points at which clips meet.

There are two workspaces in which you can build your movie in Premiere Elements. The **Sceneline**, as we discuss in **Chapter 18**, is the simpler of the two – a drag-and-drop workspace for quickly assembling your video project's parts.

The real power of the program, however, is in the **Timeline** workspace. In **Timeline** mode, you can not only arrange your clips into any order, but you can also control how and when they interact with each other. Further, you can control precisely how and when effects are applied or titles appear. And, with virtually an unlimited number of video and audio tracks at your disposal (officially 99 of each), you can create a variety of special effects – including transparent "keying" effects and **Picture-in-Picture** compositions – using techniques that otherwise are not be available in **Sceneline** mode.

In short, the **Timeline** is the more powerful, more professional-style video editing workspace.

(You can, of course, switch back and forth between the two modes, taking advantage of the best features of each as you work.)

In **Timeline** mode, as in **Sceneline** mode, the Video 1 track appears by default with three audio tracks. Additional video tracks and audio tracks can be added, as needed, stacked above this basic set.

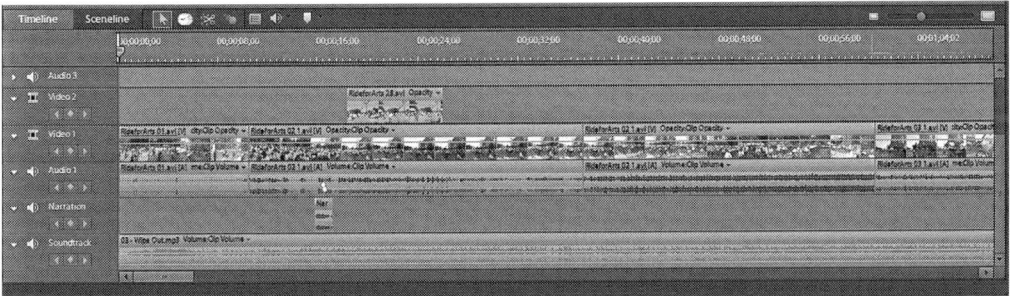

In Timeline mode, the emphasis is on time, and how the different clips interact with each other.

Overriding the timeline ripple function

The timeline in Premiere Elements is set, by default, to "**ripple**" as you add and remove clips from your project.

In other words, as you add and remove clips, the other clips on the timeline will move left or right to allow for inserted footage or to fill gaps.

- When you **Delete** a clip from your project, the clips to the right will slide to the left to fill in the gap (unless there is a clip filling this gap on a parallel track).

- When you **Insert** a clip into an assemblage of clips – even if on a parallel video or audio track – the clips to the right of that clip on the timeline will **split** and move to the right to accommodate the new clip.

In most cases, rippling will work to your advantage. If you've got an assemblage of audio and video clips in your movie and you decide to reorder it or add a clip to the middle of your project, you'll want the rest of the clips in your movie to stay in relative position, moving as a group to allow for the inserted clip.

But there may also be times when you'll want to override this ripple function – as when you've assembled a movie and you're trying to add background music to it or you want to add a video clip to the middle of your movie without changing the positions of any of its other clips.

Holding down the Ctrl key on a PC or the ⌘ key on a Mac as you add your new clip(s) to your timeline will override this ripple function.

When you override the ripple function, the rest of your clips will remain locked in their positions on your timeline as you add your new clip, and you'll be able to place your music on an audio track – or any clip on any other audio or video track – without disturbing the rest of your movie.

Particularly, if you're doing multi-track editing, holding down this **Ctrl** key on PC or the ⌘ key on a Mac is just about the only way to keep your movie clips in place as you continually add and remove clips on other tracks.

Smart Fix your clips

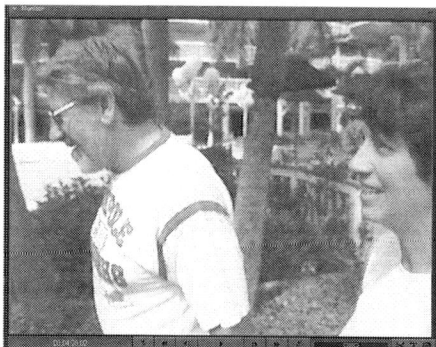

When your clips have been Media-Analyzed and Smart Tagged, the program will offer to apply a Smart Fix Auto Ehance when you place the clip on your timeline – correcting the contrast and brightness and, if necessary, stabilizing the camera movement.

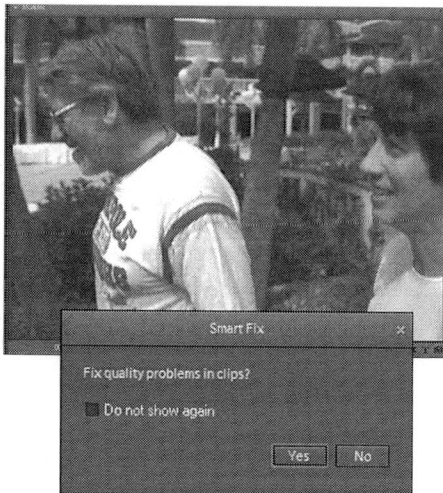

Premiere Elements 9 includes the option to have the program automatically apply a **Smart Fix** to your clips as you add them to your timeline or sceneline.

When this tool is enabled in the program's **Preferences** (under the **Edit** menu, as discussed below), an option panel will appear each time you add a new clip to your timeline or your sceneline, asking if you would like the program to "**Fix quality problems in your clips?**." (This option panel will only appear if your clips have been **Smart Tagged** prior to your adding them to your project, as discussed on the facing page.)

If you select **Yes**, Premiere Elements will automatically apply the necessary contrast levels to the clip and, if it judges the clip as too shaky, will apply automatic image stabilization!

If the clip is very long and has inconsistent quality issues, the program will even keyframe variations of contrast! (There is no way to set this feature to correct only contrast *or* only stabilization, by the way. Your options are only to have both applied or neither.)

In our experience, the results are usually very good (even if the applied effects mean that the program must then render the clips before they play back smoothly).

This feature can be turned off any time by checking the **Do Not Show Again** box in the **Smart Fix** pop-up panel, as illustrated above.

To re-activate this feature later, go to the **Edit** drop-down on the Menu Bar and select **Preferences**. On the preferences **General** page, check the box that says **Show All Do Not Show Again Messages**.

Smart Fix can also be applied manually to clips that are already on your timeline or sceneline. To apply this feature, **right-click** on a clip (**Ctrl-click** on a Mac) and select **Smart Fix** from the context menu.

As discussed in the sidebar on the facing page, the **Smart Fix** tool will only be available for clips that have been previously **Smart Tagged**.

Timeline views

Premiere Elements includes a number of features for viewing your timeline, depending on how closely you want to look at your movie.

Using the zoom tool, for instance, you can zoom out to view your entire movie at once – or you can zoom in close enough to see your video's individual frames.

To zoom in or out on your timeline, drag the slider, on the upper right of the **Timeline** panel left or right – or use the following keyboard shortcuts:

Pressing the – key on your keyboard zooms out.

Pressing the + key zooms in.

Pressing the \ key (above the **Enter/Return** key) automatically zooms out to display your entire movie.

Open or closed video and audio tracks

New to version 9, you can also toggle the views of the individual tracks on your timeline to display as either open – which allows you to view your video clips as thumbnails and your audio clips as waveforms – or closed, reducing the amount of vertical space the **Timeline** panel requires when you are using multiple tracks of video and audio, as illustrated on the right.

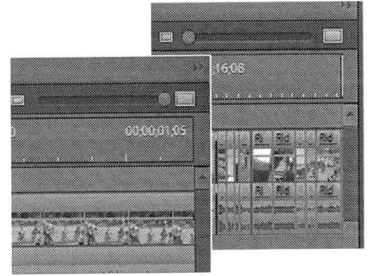

Using the Timeline zoom slider (or your +, – and \ keys) you can zoom out to see your whole project or or zoom in close enough to see individual frames.

To make more efficient use of the panel's vertical space, individual tracks on the Timeline can be toggled between a compressed and an open view.

Clips must be Smart Tagged in order to be Smart Fixed

The **Smart Fix** option panel, discussed on the facing page, will only appear as you add your clips to your timeline or sceneline *if* these clips have been previously **Media-Analyzed** prior to your adding them to your project. This is because the **Smart Fix** tool takes its cue from information gathered by **Media Analyzer,** an Elements Organizer feature that automatically analyzes and records metadata to your clips based on content and quality issues.

The **Media Analyzer** is set up in the Elements Organizer's **Preferences**, located under its **Edit** drop-down menu. (For more information, see **Enable or disable the Smart Tags Media Analyzer** in **Chapter 31, The Elements Organizer.**) In this preference panel, you have the option of setting the **Media Analyzer** to automatically **Smart Tag** every clip in your Organizer catalog, or to only analyze clips meeting specific criteria. On most faster computers, the **Media Analyzer** will work unobtrusively in the background, without interfering with your other editing work, running when you are not working on your computer.

You may, as an alternative to this automatic function, manually prep your clips for **Smart Fix** (or the other Premiere Elements tools that require **Smart Tagging**) by selecting these clips in the Elements Organizer **Photo Browser,** either one at a time or several at once, **right-clicking (Ctrl-clicking** on a Mac) and selecting the option to **Run Media Analyzer** from the context menu.

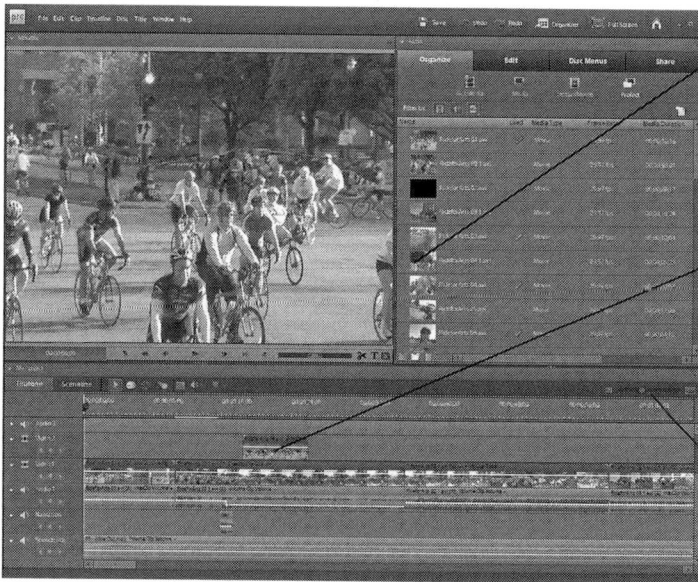

To add a clip to your timeline or sceneline, simply drag it from the Project media panel.

In Timeline mode, the other clips will "ripple", moving aside if you add the clip in the middle of a project.

To override the ripple effect (as when you're adding music or a video clip to a parallel track) hold down the Ctrl key as you add the clip.

Zoom in or out on the timeline by pressing + or - or using the Zoom slider.

Add clips to your timeline

Adding clips to your project's timeline is about as intuitive as it can be. You simply drag in the clips from the **Organizer** or your **Project** media panel (under the **Organize** tab) onto a video or audio track.

You can reorder the clips on the timeline by dragging them around. Placing a clip to the left of another clip will cause it to slide it aside ("ripple" it) to accommodate the move. (See page 235 for information on overriding this feature.)

To delete a clip from your timeline, click to select it and press the **Delete** button on your keyboard or **right-click** on it (**Ctrl-click** on a Mac) and select **Delete**. Unless there are clips on parallel video or audio tracks, the timeline will ripple to fill in the gap.

To remove a clip *without* causing the other clips to ripple or fill in the gap, **right-click** on the clip (**Ctrl-click** on a Mac) and select **Clear** instead.

Once your clips are assembled, you can apply transitions between them by dragging a transition between them from the **Transitions** panel. More information on this feature can be found in **Chapter 12, Add and Customize Transitions**.

Trim or split your clips

Once your clip is on your timeline, you can edit it to remove unwanted portions by **trimming** and/or **splitting** it.

Trimming removes footage from the beginning or end of a clip.

Splitting divides your clip into segments, which you can then remove or rearrange.

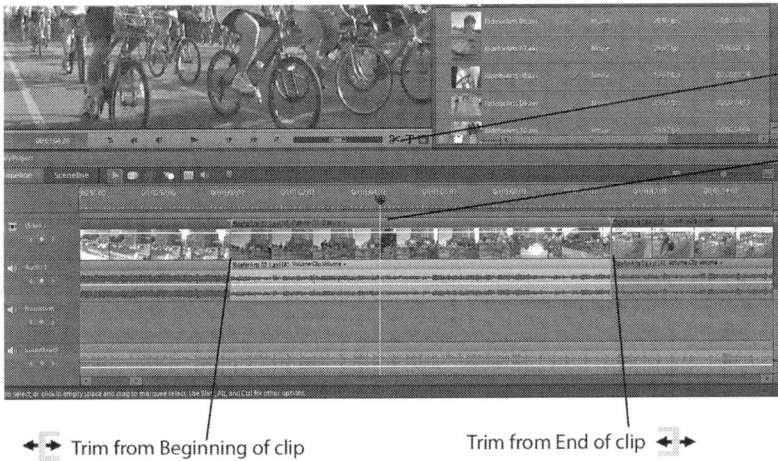

To slice a clip in two, click the Split Clip (scissors) tool on the Monitor panel.

If a clip is selected on the timeline, only that clip will be split at the position of the CTI; If no clips are selected, all clips on every track on the timeline will be split at the position of the CTI.

◄► Trim from Beginning of clip   Trim from End of clip ◄►

To trim a clip on the timeline, hover your mouse over the beginning or end of a clip until the Trim from Beginning or Trim from End icon appears, then click and drag in or out.

Trim a clip on your timeline

To **trim a clip**, click to select the clip on your timeline and hover your mouse over the clip's beginning or end.

As you hover your mouse over either end of a clip, it will switch to trim mode (becoming a ⇥ or a ⇤ cursor). Click and drag the end of the clip to trim it – removing footage from or adding footage to the clip's beginning or end.

The **Monitor** will preview the new in or out point as you drag. (For information on pre-trimming your clip before you drag it to the timeline or sceneline, see **Pre-edit your clips in the Clip Monitor** in **Chapter 16, Explore the Project Media Panel**.)

If you find, after removing a segment, that you've removed too much of a clip – or not enough – you can simply re-drag the end of the clip to replace or remove the extra frames. (In non-linear editing, nothing is ever permanently removed from a clip.)

Split a clip on your timeline

To **split a clip** – either to remove a portion of it or to isolate a segment so that you can move, or add an effect to, it – position the **CTI** (Current Time Indicator) at the point on your timeline you'd like to slice and then click the **Split Clip** (scissors icon) on the lower right of the **Monitor** panel.

If you have a clip selected on your timeline, this tool will slice only that clip; if you have no clips selected, the tool will slice through *all* of the clips on all tracks at the **CTI's** current position.

If you then want to delete the segment you've sliced (or sliced on either side of), click to select the segment, **right-click** (**Ctrl-click** on a Mac) and choose **Delete** or **Clear**, depending on whether or not you'd like the timeline to ripple to fill the gap.

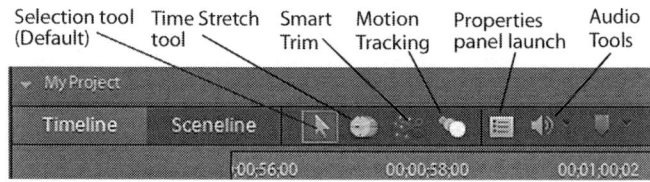

Tools on the Timeline panel

Several editing tools can be found along the top left of the **Timeline/ Sceneline** panel:

Smart Trim will trim a clip on your timeline, automatically indicating and offering to remove segments it sees as having quality issues. More information on the **Smart Trim** tool can be found below.

Time Stretch controls the playback speed of a clip. With **Time Stretch** you can set your clip to run in slow motion, fast motion or even reverse. We show you how to use this tool on page 247. (This **Time Stretch** tool is not available in **Sceneline** mode.)

Motion Tracking enables you to link a piece of clip art, title or even another clip to a person or object in your movie so that it follows it, him or her movement around your video frame. We show you how to use this tool on page 248.

Properties opens the **Properties** panel. We discuss this powerful workspace in detail in **Chapter 26**.

Audio Tools are discussed in detail in **Chapter 20, Edit Audio on the Timeline**.

Smart Trim your video

The **Smart Trim** tool analyzes clips you add to your movie's timeline and then recommends trims to remove segments from your clips (or automatically trims the segments for you) which do not meet your indicated quality standards.

1. **Smart Trim** mode is enabled by clicking on the "magic scissors" icon on your timeline or sceneline.

   Once this mode is enabled, a **Smart Trim Options** button will appear at the top of your **Monitor** panel, as illustrated on the facing page.

2. Click on the **Smart Trim Options** button to open the **Smart Trim Options** panel.

The **Smart Trim Options** panel allows you to set a **Quality Level** and an **Interest Level** for any new clips you add.

Quality automatically checks your clips for issues like blurriness, shakiness, brightness and contrast.

Interest searches through the segments that **Quality** recommends deleting and re-evaluates their content to see if they're actually worth saving, based on the level you've set.

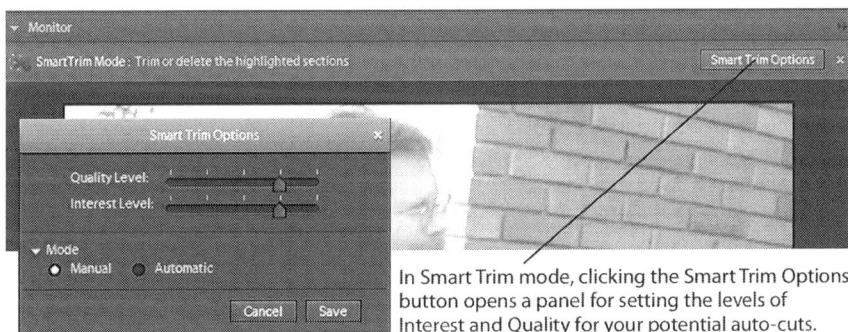

In Smart Trim mode, clicking the Smart Trim Options button opens a panel for setting the levels of Interest and Quality for your potential auto-cuts.

In other words, the **Interest Level** and **Quality Level** balance each other out, according to the levels you set.

When you add a new clip to your timeline or sceneline with this mode enabled, **Smart Trim** automatically **Media-Analyzes** all of the clips in your **Project** media panel – unless they have already been **Media-Analyzed** in the Elements Organizer – adding **Smart Tags** to the clips indicating whether they include areas that are out of focus, too dark, etc.

As these clips are added to your timeline or sceneline, a blue, diagonal line shading will be displayed over segments which are not up to the **Quality** and **Interest Levels** you've set, designating them as **Smart Trim regions** for potential deletion.

If you are in **Sceneline** mode, this shading will appear on the timeline that runs along the bottom of the **Monitor**, as illustrated on the right.

In **Timeline** mode, these **Smart Trim regions** will appear on the clip right on your timeline, as illustrated on the lower right.

In Sceneline mode, the Smart Trim regions appear along the bottom of the Monitor.

- If you've selected the **Automatic** radio button in the **Smart Trim Options** panel, the program will then offer to automatically delete these segments.

- If you've elected not to have the program automatically trim these segments, or if you have the **Smart Trim Options** set to **Manual**, the program will not delete these segments. Rather they will remain shaded until you indicate what you'd like done with them.

As you hover your mouse over each **Smart Trim** region, the program will indicate the criteria for recommending the segment be removed, such as the segment is too blurry, too shaky, includes poor contrast, etc.

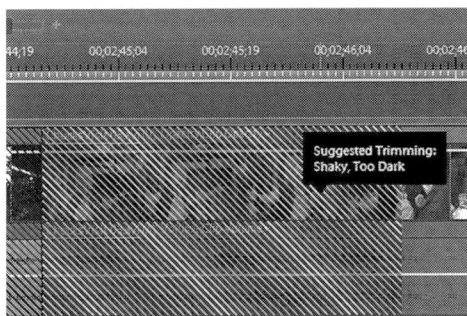

If you hover your mouse over a Smart Trim region, Premiere Elements will suggest why the region should be removed.

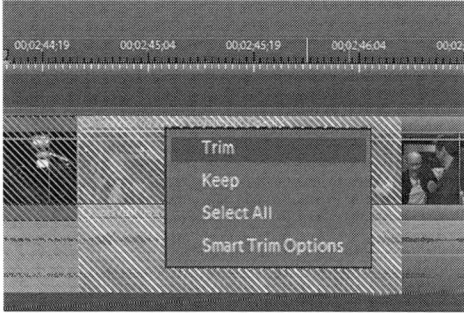

Right-click on the Smart Trim region to select whether to cut the region or to override the recommendation.

3. Click on one of these overlayed **Smart Trim regions** to select it.

   The diagonal shading will highlight in light blue.

   By dragging on either end of this blue overlay, you can trim or extend the length of this **Smart Trim region**.

4. Once you've tweaked your **Smart Trim regions**, these segments can be manually removed or the feature disabled in a number of ways:

   • Right-click on a **Smart Trim region** and select **Trim** to remove that segment from your clip.

   • Right-click on a **Smart Trim region** and select **Select All** to select all of the clip's **Smart Trim** regions for deletion.

   • Right-click on a **Smart Trim region** and select **Keep** to turn off the **Smart Trim** option for this particular region.

In addition to **Smart Trimming** these regions from your clips, Premiere Elements can be set to automatically add a transition when you remove a **Smart Trim region**.

To exit **Smart Trim** mode, click again on the "magic scissors" icon on the **Timeline** or **Sceneline** panel.

Add still photos to your project

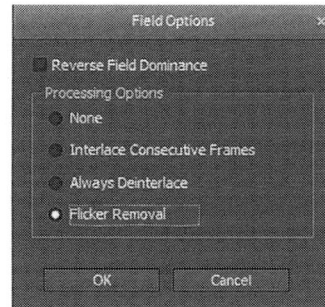

Still photos are dragged to the timeline or sceneline just as video clips are. By default, the duration of a still photo in a Premiere Elements project is **five seconds**. (This default can be changed under **Edit/Preferences** – although changing it will only affect photos brought into the program *after* the preference has been changed.)

You can increase or decrease how long the photo displays on the timeline by dragging to trim or extend it, just as you would to trim or extend any video clip, as described in **Trimming and Splitting**.

As explained in **Use Photos in Premiere Elements** in **Chapter 16, Get Media into Your Project**, you'll get the best performance from stills in a standard video project if they are sized to no larger than 1000x750 pixels.

Additionally, once you've placed a photo on your timeline, you can eliminate a somewhat common problem (related to interlacing) by **right-clicking** on the still on the timeline (**Ctrl-clicking** on a Mac) and selecting **Field Options** and then selecting the **Flicker Removal** option.

Applying this setting will preempt a fluttering problem that sometimes manifests itself in video outputs when highly detailed or high contrast photos are used in Premiere Elements projects.

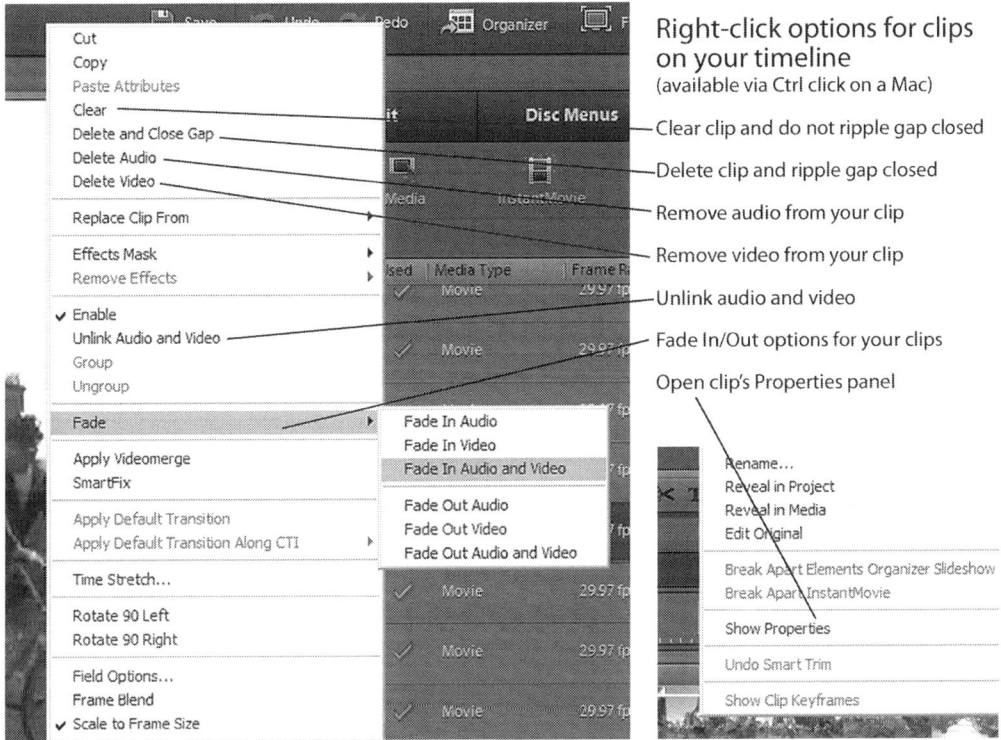

Right-click options for clips
on your timeline
(available via Ctrl click on a Mac)

— Clear clip and do not ripple gap closed

— Delete clip and ripple gap closed

— Remove audio from your clip

— Remove video from your clip

— Unlink audio and video

— Fade In/Out options for your clips

Open clip's Properties panel

Remove audio or video from your clip

There are times you want to use only the video of a clip without the audio. There are also times when you want the audio from a clip but not the video.

Deleting one or the other from a clip on the timeline is as simple as **right-clicking** on the clip (**Ctrl-clicking** on a Mac) and selecting either **Delete Audio** or **Delete Video** from the right-click menu, as illustrated above.

Fade in and out of your clip

The simplest way to fade into or out of a clip is to **right-click** on it and select **Fade In** or **Fade Out** from the right-click menu. (Separate options are offered for fading in or out of your video and your audio, if your clip includes both.)

By default, your fades will last one second. You can, however, adjust the keyframe positions to lengthen or shorten that time.

To do this, look for the white dots that Premiere Elements has placed to create the fade on the thin, horizontal, yellow line that runs through your clip.

These dots are called **keyframes**, and we discuss them in much greater detail in **Chapter 27, Keyframing**.

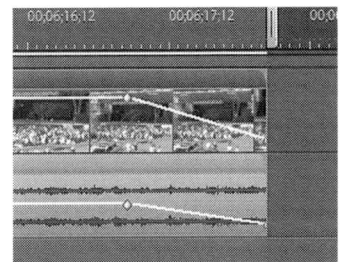

Fade ins and fade outs are really just keyframed Opacity and Volume properties. You can change the length of the fade by changing the positions of the keyframe points on the timeline.

By default, that yellow line represents **Opacity** on your video clips and it represents **Volume** on your audio clips.

See how the line slants down before or after that keyframe? That's your fade in or fade out of the clip's **Opacity** or **Volume** levels.

Adjusting that dot's position relative to the end of the clip by clicking on it and dragging it extends or shortens the duration of your fade in or fade out.

To find out more about adjusting your audio's volume and how to control it at specific points In your movie, see **Adjust audio levels at specific points on your timeline** in **Chapter 20, Edit Audio on the Timeline.**

Use L-cuts, J-cuts and multiple tracks

The ability to compose your video using several audio and video tracks greatly expands your ability to use interesting and professional-style editing techniques in your video projects.

Multiple tracks of audio, of course, merely mix into a single soundtrack for your movie. (See **Mix Audio** in **Chapter 20, Edit Audio on the Timeline**.)

But, with multiple tracks of video you can combine elements from several video clips at once using a variety of properties and effects.

Think of multiple tracks of video as a stack, like layers in a photo. In most cases, only the uppermost track in the stack will be visible.

However, if you change the scale and position of the clips on the uppermost track – or on several tracks – you can display several tracks at once. (This **Picture-in-Picture** effect can be achieved using **Presets**, as discussed in **Chapter 24, Add Video and Audio Effects**, or by adjusting their **Scale** and **Position**, as discussed in **Chapter 26, Customize Effects in the Properties Panel**.)

You can also reveal portions of clips on lower tracks by using effects such as **Chroma Key** (as discussed in **Chapter 24, Add Video and Audio Effects**), any of the **Matte** effects or even the **Crop** effect.

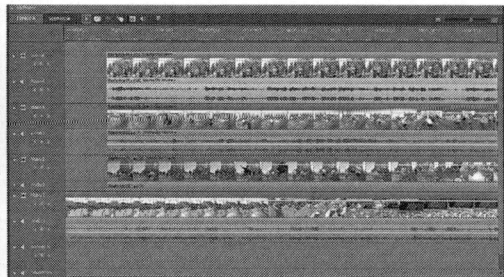

Using Scaling and Position settings with multiple tracks of video allows for Picture-in-Picture effects as well as the opportunity to do split screens, showing several video clips on screen at once

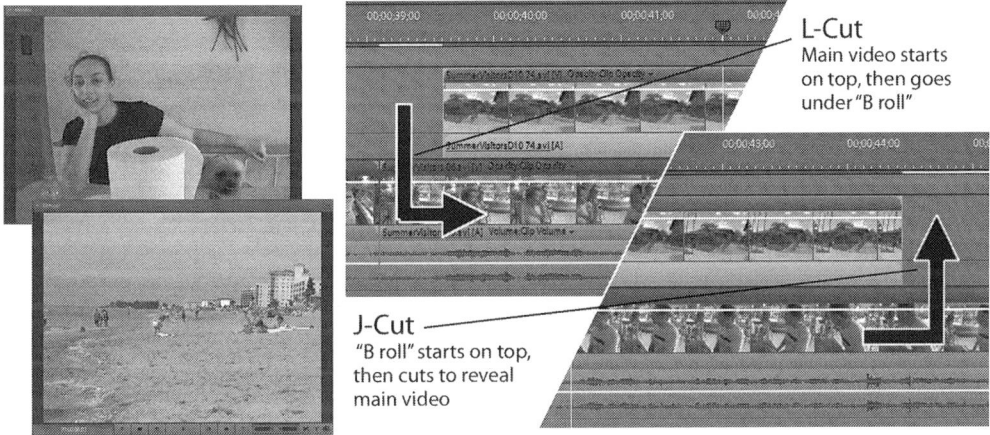

L-Cut
Main video starts on top, then goes under "B roll"

J-Cut
"B roll" starts on top, then cuts to reveal main video

As audio from main clip continues, video cuts to or from "B roll" footage.

By keyframing the effects in the **Properties** panel, you can also make these positions, sizings or other settings change over the duration of the clip. (For more information, see **Chapter 27, Keyframing**.)

Using multiple tracks of video and then scaling and positioning your clips on each, you can have any number of video images in your video frame at the same time. (Think of the grid of faces in the opening credits of *The Brady Bunch* – or see my multiple-panel illustration above.) The products page at Muvipix.com offers a wealth of tutorials describing techniques for achieving these effects using a number of video tracks and effects.

Additionally, two popular techniques that use multiple tracks of video are the **L-cut** and the **J-cut** – so named because, back in the days of single-track editing, when a segment of video had to be removed and the audio left in place to allow for the placement of alternate video, the primary video and audio clip resembled an "L" or a "J" (depending on which segment was removed).

Consider a TV news report that features video of a reporter shown standing in front of a burned-out building, describing the fire that destroyed it.

As he continues speaking, the video cuts away to footage shot earlier of the fire itself. That's an **L-cut**. (A **J-cut**, on the other hand, begins with the cut-away video and the reporter's voice heard on the soundtrack, then cuts to the reporter finishing his report.)

Creating an **L-cut** is easy with multi-track editing.

1. Put the main video, the clip of the reporter speaking to the camera (we'll call it **Clip A**), on Video track 1.

2. Holding the **Ctrl** key (to override the timeline's ripple function), place the second video – the footage of the fire (**Clip B**) – on Video track 2.

3. Overlap the latter part of **Clip A** with **Clip B**, as seen in the illustration on the previous page.

4. **Right-click** on **Clip B** (**Ctrl-click** on a Mac) and select **Delete Audio**, if you need to remove its audio track.

Voila! Tweak **Clip B**'s position for maximum effect and you're done! We begin with the reporter speaking to the camera and, as he continues to speak, we cut away to the footage of the fire.

L-cuts and **J-cuts** are very effective for news-style reports as well as for interviews, in which you cut away from the person speaking to separately shot footage of what he or she is describing. It's a great way to reinforce, with images, what's being presented verbally.

By the way, here's some professional vocabulary to impress your friends with. That secondary footage that plays as the main video's audio continues? It's commonly called **"B-roll footage"**, a relic from the days when this kind of editing actually did involve pasting in footage from a separate roll of film or video.

Output a segment of your video using the Work Area Bar

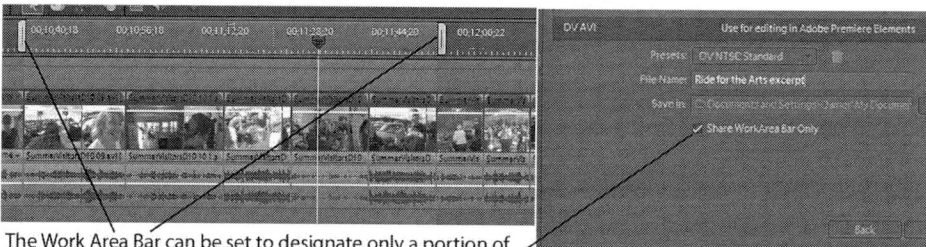

The Work Area Bar can be set to designate only a portion of your video project. Most Share options allow you to output the Work Area Bar segment only.

The **Work Area Bar** is the lighter gray area that runs along the ticker at the top of the timeline, defined by a silver marker on either end. Usually, this bar covers your entire video project and grows and shrinks with your project as you edit.

But, by dragging its beginning and end handles, you can manually set the **Work Area Bar** to cover only a portion of your video editing project, as illustrated above. In this way, you can designate only a portion of your project for output.

Nearly all of the output options under the **Share** tab include a checkbox option **Export Work Area Bar Only**, as in the illustration. Checking this option directs the program to output *only* the segment of your project you've defined with the **Work Area Bar**.

For more information on this function, see the discussions under each output option in **Chapter 29, Share Your Movie**.

Use Time Stretch to speed up or slow down your video

There are actually two **Time Stretch** tools – one operates numerically, based on the speed percentage you designate, and the other operates more intuitively, based on how long you stretch your clip.

These are essentially two sides of the same tool, however, and you can use one tool to fine tune the results of the other.

To Time Stretch numerically, right-click on a clip on your timeline (**Ctrl-click** on a Mac) and select **Time Stretch** from the context menu.

- In the **Time Stretch** option panel, type the percentage of speed you would like your clip to play at. (50% means that your clip plays at half its normal speed, e.g.). As an alternative, you can type in the time duration (hours;minutes;seconds; frames) you would like your clip to play and the playback speed will set automatically.

- The **Reverse Speed** checkbox allows you to reverse your clip's playback.

- **Maintain Audio Pitch** will apply a pitch shift tweak to your audio so that, for instance, if you speed the clip up, the voices won't sound quite so much like chipmunks.

Time Stretch for a clip can be set numerically by selecting the option from the right-click menu.

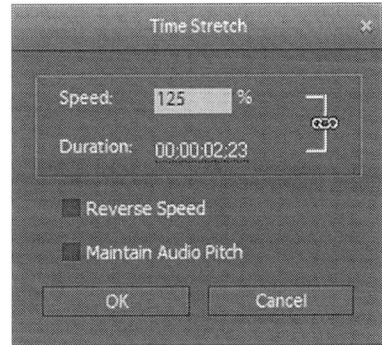

To Time Stretch using the Timeline tool, click on the **Time Stretch** button (the clock) on the top left of the **Timeline** panel. (Because of how this tool functions, it is not available in **Sceneline** mode.)

- Drag the endpoints on the clip on your timeline inward or outward, as if you are trimming the clip. The shorter you make the clip, the faster it will play; the longer you stretch the clip, the slower it will play.

- To turn off the **Time Stretch** tool and return to normal editing mode, click on the **Selection Tool** button (the arrow) on the top left of the Timeline panel.

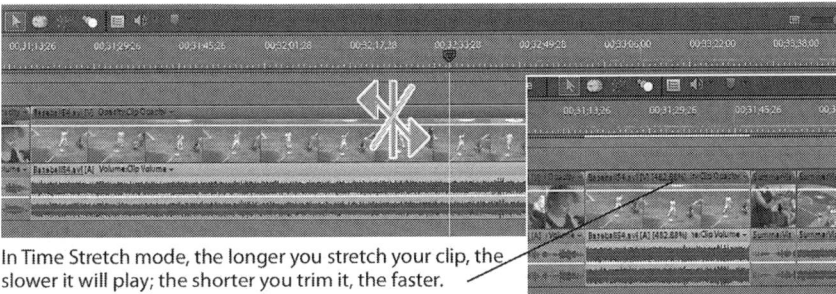

In Time Stretch mode, the longer you stretch your clip, the slower it will play; the shorter you trim it, the faster.

In Motion Tracking mode, click on Add Object to designate an object or person to be tracked.

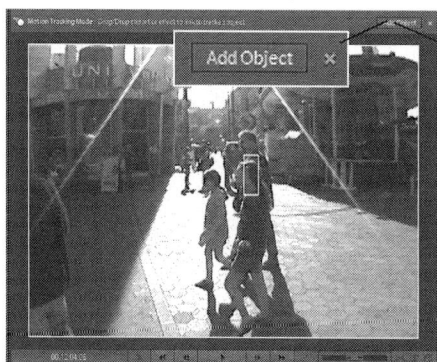

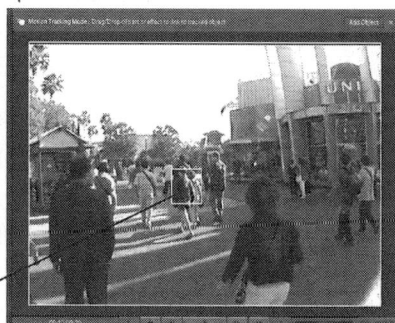

The program will follow the object across the video frame.

Follow an object with Motion Tracking

Premiere Elements' **Motion Tracking** tool will lock onto an object or person you indicate in a clip and follow it, him or her around your video frame.

You can then link a piece of artwork, another clip or a title to that object or person and the program will automatically create a motion path so that it moves around the video frame along with the tracked object!

You can, for instance, link someone running across your frame with clip art of a hat or a cartoon talk bubble, and that hat or bubble will stay with that person throughout the clip.

To use **Motion Tracking,** click to select a clip on your timeline or sceneline and then click the **Motion Tracking** mode button (the yellow ball icon) along the top of the **Timeline/Sceneline** panel.

1. The program will ask you if you want to **Media Analyze** the clip to track moving objects. **Media Analyzing** is related to the program's automatic metadata creation system and is not necessary for this tool to function.

2. Regardless of whether you elect to **Media Analyze** the clip, a box will appear over your clip in the center of the **Monitor** panel. This box will include four corner handles so that it can be reshaped and resized. Drag the corner handles and move the box to indicate the person or object in the frame you want to track.

3. Once you've framed the object or person to be tracked, click on the **Track Object** button at the top of the **Monitor** panel.

    The program will analyze the motion in the clip.

    When it has finished, if you play or scrub the clip (by dragging the **CTI** back and forth), The box should follow the indicated object or person around your video frame.

4. Once the **Motion Tracker** has completed its analysis, you can link an object to this motion track.

Under the **Edit** tab, Premiere Elements includes a collection of nearly 250 pieces of **Clip Art** that can be linked to a motion track. Titles and picture-in-picture clips can also be linked to a track.

To link artwork to motion track, drag your clip or **Clip Art** onto the **Motion Track** box on your **Monitor**.

The clip will be added to a video track above your current video. You can size or position this clip by dragging on the corner handles or dragging it around. As long as the object you are tracking in the main video has an active yellow box around it, the clip will follow the motion track once the program automatically creates the necessary keyframes.

In the same way, you can drag any clip from the **Project** media panel onto your motion track. As long as the yellow rectangle is displayed when you drag the clip to the **Monitor**, the clip should lock to the motion track. (An indication that your clip is locked to a motion track is that the added clip will be noticeably smaller than its actual size.)

You can link several objects and clips, on a number of video tracks, to the same **Motion Track**. Just ensure that the main background clip is selected on your timeline and that the **Motion Track** mode is enabled. (The yellow rectangle will indicate that your motion track is active.)

You can also link text or a title to a motion track, although it takes an extra step or two.

1. Click the "**T**" on the **Monitor** panel to create your title (as we discuss in **Chapter 23, Add Titles**). Once your title is created and you have returned to **Edit** mode, locate the title on its video track and delete it. (It will remain in the **Project** media panel.)

2. Select the clip that you've **Motion Tracked** and click on the **Motion Track** mode button so that the yellow rectangle is visible on the clip in the **Monitor**.

3. Drag the title you created earlier from the **Project** media panel (under the **Organize** tab) onto the yellow motion track rectangle. (As with any clip you add to a motion track, it will appear smaller than its actual size.)

When Clip Art, a title or a Picture-in-Picture clip is linked to the Motion Track object, the program creates keyframes so that the clip follows the object across the video frame.

Premiere Elements includes a set of animated clips that move or change shape as they follow your Motion Track across your video frame.

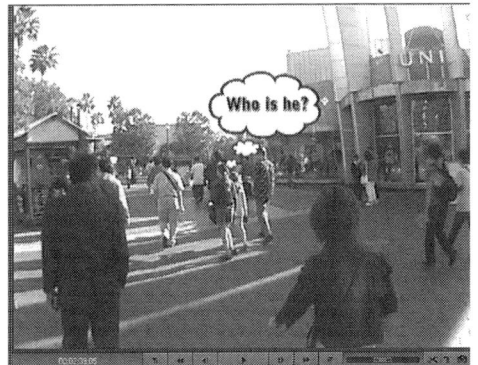

More than one clip can be linked to your Motion Track, combining, for instance, a cartoon thought bubble and a title.

Size and position your title as needed.

The title should lock to the motion track and follow the tracked object around the frame.

You can have several **Motion Tracks** on the same video clip and link different clips to each **Motion Track**.

To create a new motion track, click the **Add Object** button that appears at the top of the **Monitor** panel while you are in **Motion Tracking** mode, then size and position the rectangle that appears over the object or person you want to track.

When more than one motion track appears on a clip, the active motion track will be highlighted with a blue rectangle. The other motion tracks on the clip – those that are present but not currently activated – will appear as yellow rectangles.

(Click on the various motion track rectangles displayed in your **Monitor** to select or to deselect them.)

When you link your clip or clip art, it will follow the **Motion Track** that was indicated with a blue rectangle when the clip or clip art was added.

Render your timeline

Premiere Elements uses a DV-AVI workflow for its standard (non-high definition) video. That means that, whatever video or photos you put into it, Premiere Elements assimilates them and eventually renders them as DV-AVI video files before it outputs them as another video format.

And that's true even if you put an MPEG in and then output an MPEG from the project you've created with it. *Everything* goes through the process of becoming a DV-AVI before Premiere Elements encodes it as anything else.

This is why a project that is made up of non-DV-AVI files can take much longer to transcode to a DVD than one that is purely DV.

The Premiere Elements process of creating DV-AVI video from non-DV-AVI source files is called **rendering**.

A red line just below the ticker along the top of the timeline indicates a segment that requires rendering.

Once the sequence is rendered, the red line will turn green.

Photos, MPEGs, MOVs and VOBs must all be rendered by the program. Additionally, the program must re-render DV-AVIs to which effects, titles or transitions have been added.

When you use a non-DV-AVI video source, or apply an effect, title or transition to a DV-AVI source file, a **red line** will appear above the clip on your project timeline, as illustrated on the left. This line indicates that this particular video segment must be **rendered** in order to play at full resolution.

If you play back a video segment with a red line above it, the program will play back a lower resolution "soft render" of the clip.

And, depending on what the video clip is, how many effects have been applied and how fast your computer system is, this playback can look pretty bad. Fuzzy. Low resolution. It may even have problems playing evenly.

If you **Render** the clip, however, by pressing the **Enter** key (on a PC) or by selecting **Render Work Area** from the **Timeline** drop-down on the Menu Bar, the program will create a "hard render," a temp file of DV video that will show you a much better representation of what your video will actually look like when you do a final output.

Once your clip has been rendered, the red line above the clip will turn green and your playback will be much cleaner and smoother.

You can render your clips as you're working. Or you can wait until your playback performance starts to lag. It's up to you. But do be aware that, if you're having playback problems and your **Timeline** has a lot of red lines running across the top, a few seconds of rendering can usually make the program's performance much snappier again.

Enable or disable Background Rendering

Among the optional tools available in Premiere Elements is a feature called **Background Rendering**.

When your computer is idle, **Background Rendering** will locate segments on your timeline that require rendering and automatically create hard renders of these segments for you – freeing you from having to render these segments manually, as discussed above.

However, because this feature can often interrupt your regular editing work, particularly on slower computers, Adobe has this feature turned off by default.

To turn on **Background Rendering**, go to the **Edit** drop-down on the Menu Bar and select **Preferences**. On the **General** page, check the box to **Enable Background Rendering**.

Whether or not the benefits of this feature outweigh its liabilities is a matter of your personal workflow.

If you find your computer lugging while this process works, you can turn it off by unchecking **Enable Background Rendering** in the program's **Preferences**.

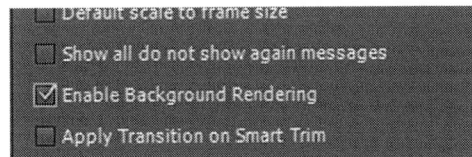

In Premiere Elements preferences (under the Edit drop-down menu) is the option to Enable Background Rendering.

Adjust Audio Levels with Keyframes

Monitor and Mix Your Audio Levels

Smart Mix Your Audio Levels

SmartSound QuickTracks

Detect Beats

Chapter 20

Edit Audio on the Timeline
Working with sounds and music

Great sound is as important as great visuals in your video project. And Premiere Elements includes a number of tools for adding and enhancing your audio and music files.

Premiere Elements 9 even includes SmartSound QuickTracks, an amazing tool for creating musical tracks – based on your custom specifications– for your movies!

Audio tools on the Timeline panel

A number of powerful audio tools can be accessed by clicking on the green speaker button on the top left of the **Timeline/Sceneline** panel:

Audio tools on the Timeline and Sceneline panels drop down from under the green speaker button.

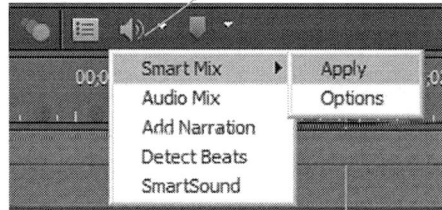

Smart Mix will automatically mix the audio levels for your movie, based on criteria you set. We show you how to use this tool on page 257.

Audio Mix launches the **Audio Mixer,** which we discuss on page 256.

Add Narration launches a tool for creating narration for your video. We show you how to use it on page 260.

Detect Beats will drop markers on your timeline based on the beat of a music track you've selected. These markers can be used as a cue to change slides when you use the **Create Slideshow** feature (discussed in **Chapter 17, Explore the Project Media Panel**). We show you how to use **Detect Beats** on page 261.

SmartSound Quicktracks is an amazing tool for creating custom music tracks of specific lengths based on your style and tempo specifications. We show you how to use it on page 258.

Adjust the audio levels at specific points in your video

The audio levels of the clips on your timeline is represented by thin, horizontal, yellow lines that run through your clips. You can easily raise or lower the volume level for a clip by dragging that line higher or lower. (See also **Monitor and mix your audio levels** on page 260.)

But what about if you want to raise and lower the audio levels for a clip at specific points?

Say you want to fade your music down for a few seconds so that your narration track can dominate? Or you have a conversation recorded in which one person speaks very quietly and you need to raise the audio level for his part of your clip, while leaving the audio level for the rest of the clip as is?

That's when you use audio keyframes. (For a more detailed discussion of keyframes, see **Chapter 27, Keyframing**.)

Audio **Volume** keyframes can be created and adjust in **Properties** panel (as discussed in **Chapter 26**) or, more conveniently, right on your timeline.

Audio keyframes adjust audio levels at specific points

When a clip is selected (clicked on), audio keyframes can be added with the timeline's Add/Remove Keyframe button.

Keyframes are added at the position of the CTI, but can be dragged to any position.

Dragging the keyframes higher raises the clip's audio level; dragging them lower reduces the audio level.

Dragging the yellow line with no keyframes applied raises or lowers audio level for the entire clip.

Setting audio volume keyframes

To create a **keyframe** on your audio clip:

1. Click to select an audio or audio/video clip on your timeline and position the **CTI** (Current Time Indicator) over the approximate spot where you want to add a keyframe.

   (A clip must be selected and the **CTI** positioned over it in order to create a keyframe on the timeline.)

2. Click on the little, diamond-shaped **Make Keyframe** button on the track header, left of the video or audio track, as illustrated above.

   This will create a keyframe point, which will appear as a white dot on your audio clip at the position of the **CTI**. You can drag this dot to any position on the clip, or change or delete it at any time.

3. Adjust the keyframe point's position to adjust audio levels.

   • Positioning the keyframe higher on the clip increases the audio volume level at that point.

   • Lowering it decreases the audio volume level.

In the illustration above, the audio for the video on the Video 1 track has been lowered so that the narration can be heard.

You can create as many keyframes as you need, using several to set the audio level higher for some segments, and lower for other segments, on your clips.

To delete an audio keyframe, **right-click** on the white diamond keyframe point (**Ctrl-click** on a Mac) and select **Delete** from the context menu.

Monitor and mix your audio levels

The **Audio Mixer** can be used to monitor your audio levels as well as adjust them.

The Audio Mixer will display separate controls for each audio track. If adjustments are made while playback is stopped, adjustments will affect the entire clip. If made during playback, audio keyframes will be created.

To open the **Audio Mixer**, click on the green speaker icon on the top-left of the **Timeline** or **Sceneline** panel and select **Audio Mix** from the drop-down menu.

The **Audio Mixer** displays the audio levels for each of your active audio tracks and offers controls for raising and lowering these audio levels.

The **Audio Mixer** is a great panel to keep open as much as possible so that you can monitor your movie's audio levels, particularly as you begin the final phases of editing your project. For best results, never let your audio levels peak in the red. Overmodulated audio can sound distorted and fuzzy.

The **Audio Mixer** can also be used to adjust the levels for your individual audio clips:

- When you're not playing your video project, click to select a clip on the timeline at the position of the **CTI** (Current Time Indicator). Raising or lowering the **Audio Mixer** sliders will raise and lower the volume level for that entire clip.

- If you adjust the sliders as your video is playing, keyframe points will be added to the clip so that the audio is raised or lowered only at the point at which you adjusted the slider.

As you play your project, watch the meters for each track, adjusting the sound levels as necessary to keep these levels as much as possible in the green, with the bulk of the audio peaking at zero or a little beyond.

An occasional peak in the red will probably not cause problems, but too much will cause your video output to sound distorted.

In our opinion, this tool serves much more effectively as an audio meter than an audio level adjustment tool.

If used to adjust audio levels while the video is playing, it simply places too many hard-to-adjust audio keyframes on the timeline. You'll get much neater and much more effective results if you use the technique we describe in **Adjust audio levels at specific points in your video** on page 254.

Smart Mix your audio

Premiere Elements' **Smart Mix** tool will automatically adjust the levels of several audio tracks, to allow one track to dominate over the others.

In other words, if you've got a sequence that includes music, narration and the original audio from a video clip, **Smart Mix** will automatically lower the music and clip levels wherever there is a narration clip (a feature sometimes called "auto ducking").

1. To set the criteria for your audio clip adjustments, click on the green speaker button on the upper left of the **Timeline** or **Sceneline** panel and, from the drop-down menu, select **Smart Mix**, then **Options**.

   The **Smart Mixer Options** panel displays each audio track in your Premiere Elements project and allows you to indicate, with drop-down menus, which tracks will serve as your audio **Foreground**, which will serve as **Background** and which will be **Disabled** completely.

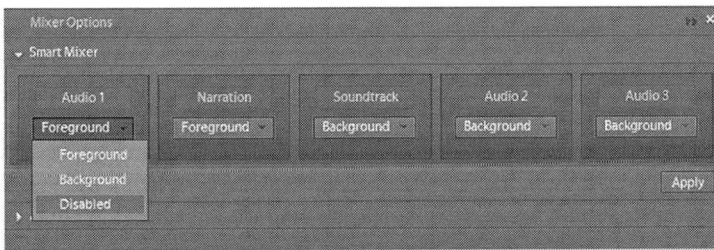

In Smart Mix Options, you designate which audio tracks will dominate and which will be lowered or eliminated completely.

2. Once you've set your preferences for the tool, activate the **Smart Mix** feature by clicking on the **Apply** button on the **Smart Mixer**.

   (You can also start the **Smart Mix** tool without opening this mixer by selecting **Apply** from the **Audio Tools/Smart Mix** button on the **Timeline** or **Sceneline** panel.)

When applied, Smart Trim automatically creates the necessary keyframes to lower the audio on the tracks you've designated as Background.

The **Smart Mixer** will create the necessary audio keyframes – which appear as little white diamonds on your audio clip(s) – to lower the volume of the audio clip(s) that you've designated as **Background** audio.

Further, if you move or change a clip you've indicated as your **Foreground** and re-apply **Smart Mix**, the **Smart Mixer** will automatically remove or revise the audio keyframes!

To set preferences for the **Smart Mixer** – including how much the **Background** audio is reduced in volume and if the **Foreground** audio is automatically **Normalized** – go the Premiere Elements **Preferences** under the **Edit** drop-down on the Menu Bar and select **Audio**.

Create custom music with SmartSound Quicktracks

SmartSound Quicktracks is a terrific, third-party music creation feature for Premiere Elements.

This amazing little program will create custom, professional-style music tracks, based on criteria you select, at whatever time duration you require.

1. To launch **SmartSound Quicktracks**, click the green speaker button on the upper-left of the **Timeline** or **Sceneline** panel and select **SmartSound**.

    Because this is a third-party program, you'll need to accept the licensing agreement and register the first time you use it.

2. At the **Quicktracks** splash screen that launches, click on the **Click Here to Select Music link** to open the **SmartSound Maestro** workspace.

Normalize: A great audio tool

One other audio tool that merits mentioning is the **Normalize** tool. Although it will override any other adjustments you've made to your clip's audio volume, it's a powerful and easy-to-use way to bring up or down the audio level for an entire clip with just a couple of clicks of the mouse.

To use it, **right-click** on your audio clip (**Ctrl-click** on a Mac), select **Audio Gain** from the right-click menu and then click the **Normalize** button on the option screen. The tool will automatically analyze your clip and optimize the audio level for that clip, raising it as much as necessary to create a full sound. (You can also set the **Gain** numbers manually).

Because it sets levels based on the loudest sound on the clip, and affects the entire clip equally, it's not the perfect solution in every case. But it is a great quick fix for improving a clip with a low but even audio level.

SmartSound Quicktracks for Premiere Elements

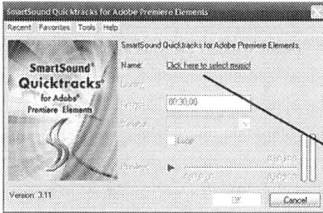

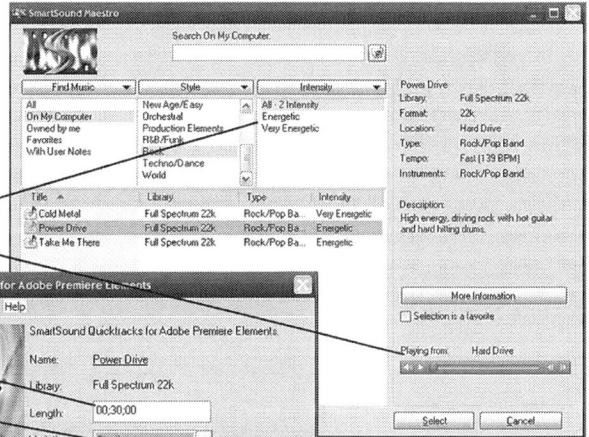

Click to launch SmartSound Maestro

Select music, based on Style and Intensity

Play samples from the Library, then Select

Set duration of clip

Select Variation

Play clip

Click OK to generate your custom music clip

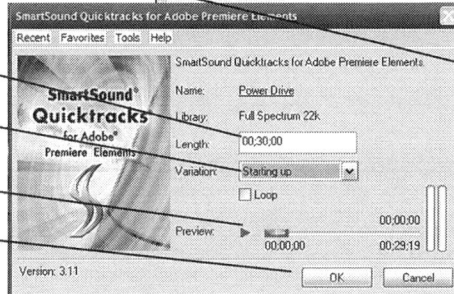

3. The **SmartSound Maestro** offers a number of free music tracks. You'll find several complimentary tracks under the **Find Music/On My Computer** and **Owned by Me** selections.

   Select a **Style** and **Intensity**, then click to select a music track from the **Library**, as illustrated on the previous page.

   You can play a sample of your selected track using the player that will appear in the lower right of the interface.

   Once you've selected your music, the real magic begins!

4. You'll be returned to the **SmartSound Quicktracks** screen, where you can select a variation of your musical selection and even set the *exact length* for the clip you want – which you can again preview.

   When you click **OK,** the program will custom-create a rich, professional-style music track, precisely to your specifications. And, best of all, the track is royalty-free, so you can use it in any of your productions without restriction.

SmartSound also offers hundreds of musical clips and styles for purchase. (These are the clips you'll find if you select **Find Music/All**.) These can be purchased individually (for typically around $14.95), or you can buy an entire package of similar music styles for $99. (Their Web site offers frequent discounts.)

If you drop down the **Find Music** menu, you'll see that **Smart-Sound** also offers a large number of sound effects for purchase.

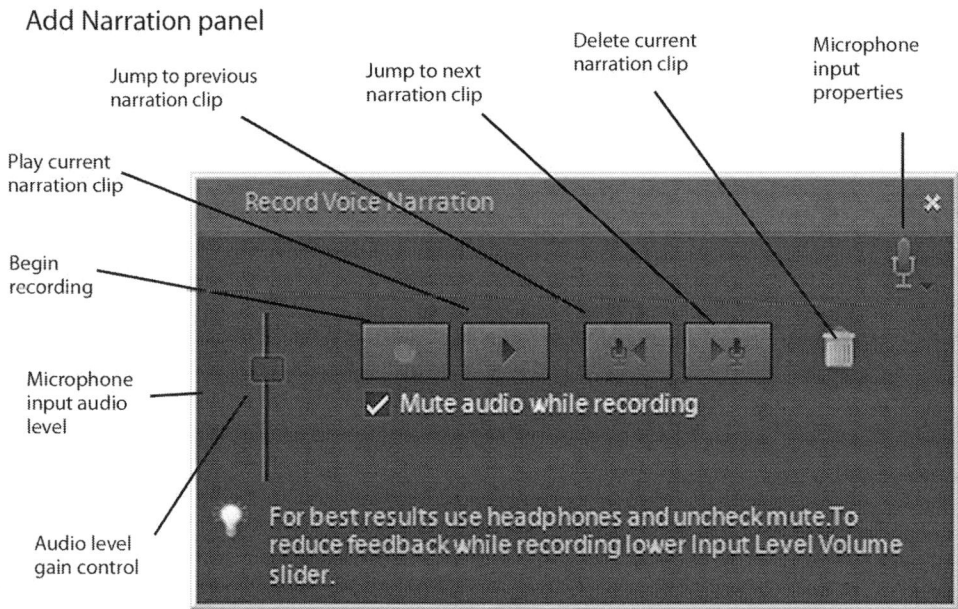

Add Narration panel

Jump to previous
narration clip

Jump to next
narration clip

Delete current
narration clip

Microphone
input
properties

Play current
narration clip

Begin
recording

Microphone
input audio
level

Audio level
gain control

Record Voice Narration

✓ Mute audio while recording

For best results use headphones and uncheck mute.To
reduce feedback while recording lower Input Level Volume
slider.

Add Narration

With this tool, you can add narration to your project – and even record it
as you watch your video playing.

1. To launch the **Record Voice Narration** tool, click on the green
   speaker button on the upper left of the **Timeline** or **Sceneline** panel
   and, from the drop-down menu, select **Add Narration**.

   The **Record Voice Narration** panel will open.

   The microphone recording level displays on the meter that runs
   along the left side of the panel. You'll want to keep it green and full,
   adjusting the slider as necessary for optimal sound.

   Turn down your computer's speakers or select the option to **Mute
   Audio While Recording** so that you don't get feedback from the
   speakers as you record.

2. To record your narration, click the red **Record** button. The panel will
   display a three-second countdown and then will begin recording as
   your movie plays. Click the same button again to stop the recording.

   The program will place the narration clip that you've recorded
   on the **Narration** audio track, at the current position of your **CTI**
   (Current Time Indicator), on the timeline or sceneline.

The two shortcut buttons on the panel will jump you back to the
beginning of the clip you've just recorded (or to the next or previous
narration clip). You can then click the play button to hear the results.

3. If you're unhappy with the results, you can click the shortcut button to jump back to the beginning of the clip and record new narration. (Your new narration will replace the old automatically.) Or, by clicking the trashcan icon, you can delete it completely.

A good microphone and sound card are essential to getting a good strong narration recording.

Premiere Elements seems to work best with microphones that are connected through you audio card. Microphones attached via USB can prove problematic.

If you're having problems getting this **Record Voice Narration** tool to work with a microphone connected through your sound card, check the Windows audio settings (under **Sounds and Audio Devices** in your Windows **Control Panel**) to ensure all is in order there. And ensure that your microphone isn't muted!

Also, clicking on the microphone icon in the upper right corner of the **Record Voice Narration** panel will display the **Mic Source**. Ensure that the microphone or audio jack listed here is the same one you've got your microphone plugged into. (Some computers have more than one microphone jack, so make sure you're plugged into the right one.)

If the microphone connection isn't properly configured in the program, go to Premiere Elements' **Edit** drop-down menu and select **Preferences/ Audio Hardware**. Click the **ASIO Settings** button, and adjust whatever settings are necessary there.

Finally, if you can't get the **Narration** feature to work at all in Premiere Elements, you can, as an alternative, record your narration into **Windows Audio Recorder** (usually under **Accessories/Entertainment** under your **Start** menu) or similar software and then import the audio clip into your project.

I've found I get the best quality for the narration for my videos by just recording myself with my camcorder and then capturing the video as **Audio Only** (as described in **Capture MiniDV, HDV Video or Video from Webcams or WDM Devices** in **Chapter 16, Get Media into Your Project**.)

Detect Beats in your music

This cool tool can be used as part of the process of creating a slideshow that changes in rhythm with a music clip.

To use the **Detect Beats** tool:

1. Click to select a music clip on your timeline or sceneline.

   When a clip is detected on your timeline, it will be highlighted.

2. Click on the green speaker button on the upper left of the **Timeline** or **Sceneline** panel and, from the drop-down menu, select **Detect Beats**.

The Detect Beats Tool

Adjust settings as needed for your music

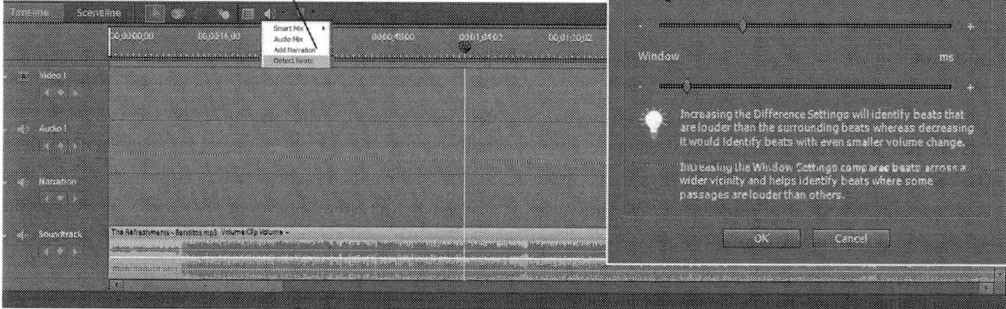

Click to select your musical clip on the timeline or sceneline, then select Detect Beats from the Audio Tools drop-down menu

The tool will place unnumbered markers (musical notes) on the timeline, which can be used to time slide changes in a slideshow

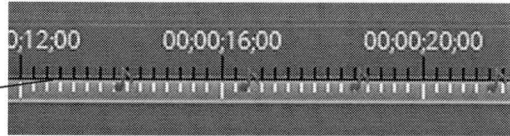

The **Beat Detect Settings** option screen will open.

3. Set the sensitivity and limitations of your beat detection.

4. Click **OK**.

The tool will then analyze your music clip and create unnumbered markers along the timeline to the beat of the song. (They'll look like little musical notes.)

Once these markers have been created, you can use them as indicators for the **Create Slideshow** tool in the **Project** media panel so that your slides change in rhythm with the music.

For information on this **Create Slideshow** tool, see **Chapter 17, Explore the Project Media Panel**.

Chapter 21

Edit with Monitor Panel Tools
Viewing, splitting, adding clips and adding titles

The Monitor panels displays the video you've assembled on your timeline or sceneline.

The majority of the controls available on this panel's toolbar, along the bottom of the panel, control playback. However, the Monitor panel also includes some valuable video editing tools.

The Monitor panel
Playback of Timeline and Sceneline, plus some editing tools

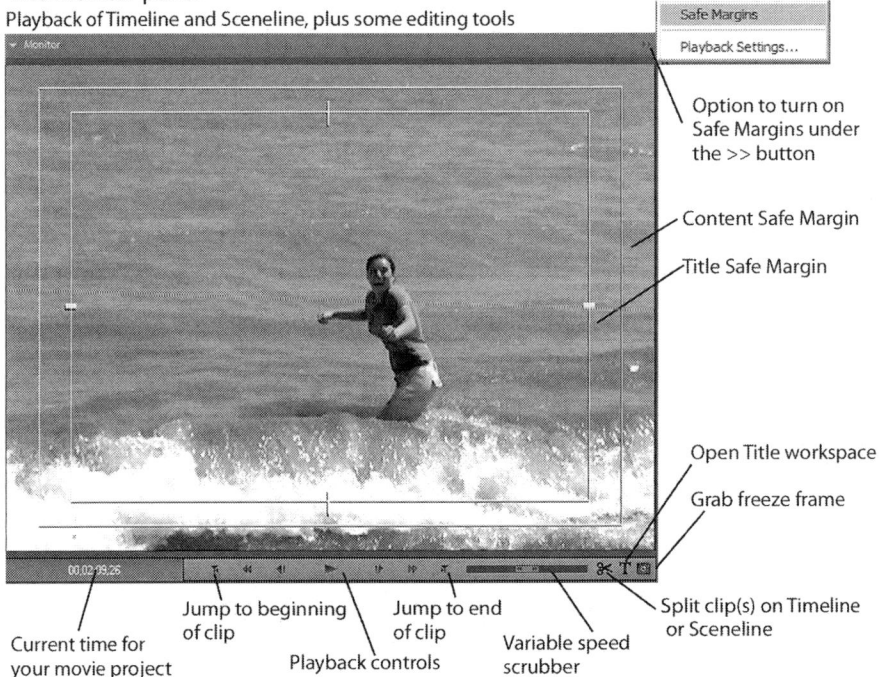

Option to turn on Safe Margins under the >> button

Content Safe Margin

Title Safe Margin

Open Title workspace

Grab freeze frame

Split clip(s) on Timeline or Sceneline

Jump to beginning of clip

Jump to end of clip

Current time for your movie project

Playback controls

Variable speed scrubber

Play and navigate your video

You'll probably recognize the **Playback Control** buttons for playing, rewinding and fast forwarding through your video.

Additionally, between **Play** and **Rewind**, and between **Play** and **Fast Forward**, are buttons which look like this: ◄▌ and this: ▐►.

These buttons will advance or rewind the playback incrementally – a single frame at a time – for precise navigation of your video.

On either end of the playback button set are the ⊺◄ and ◄⊺ buttons. These buttons will quickly jump you to the beginning or end of your current clip.

The numbers to the left of the playback buttons are **timecode**. This timecode represents the current time position of the playhead (**CTI**) in your project.

The numbers are displayed as 00;00;00;00, which represents hours; minutes; seconds; video frames. There are roughly 30 frames in each second of NTSC video and 25 frames in each second of PAL video. That's why that last set of numbers will only advance to 29 (or 24) before rolling over to zero again and advancing the seconds count.

To the right of the playback controls is a slider called the **Scrubber**. The **Scrubber** will advance or rewind your video at various speeds, depending on how far to the right or left you slide it.

Use Safe Margins

If you've selected **Show Docking Headers** from the **Window** drop-down menu, as we recommended in **Chapter 14**, you'll see the **>>** button in the upper right corner of the **Monitor** panel.

Click on it and you'll find the option to turn on your **Safe Margins**.

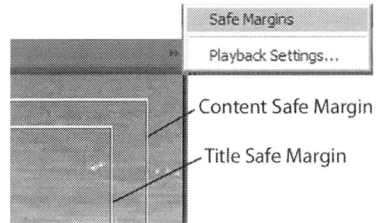

Safe Margins will display as a pair of rectangular guides over your video display, as illustrated in the **Monitor** panel illustration on the previous page. (These guides will not be on your final output. They're just for your information as you edit your video.)

Safe Margins are great helps for ensuring that what you want to have on screen during your video's play will *definitely* be on screen in your final video output.

The challenge is that televisions can vary in how much of a video they actually show onscreen. All TVs cut off a little of the video image from around the edges of your screen (technically called "overscan") – and some cut off more than others.

The purpose of these margins isn't so that you will resize your entire video so that it fits inside the inner margin, of course. But you should use them as guides to make sure that your *essential* video information falls within your "safe area", ensuring that it will appear on all TV displays.

The outer rectangular guide represents the **Video Safe Margin**. As you edit, you'll want to make sure all of the "must-see" video falls inside this rectangle.

Otherwise – well, you know that big group picture of everyone at your family reunion waving to the camera? Well, if you've not ensured everyone in the picture is inside the **Video Safe Margin**, some TVs may not show Cousin Bill, standing off to the side of the picture, outside the **Safe Margin**!

The inner rectangular guide is your **Text Safe Margin**. This is for your titles, subtitles and captions.

Never place any text or titles outside of the Text Safe Margin!

Otherwise, some TVs may display your "Gone With the Wind" title as simply "one With the Win"!

We recommend that, as much as possible, you work with both of these **Safe Margins** turned on.

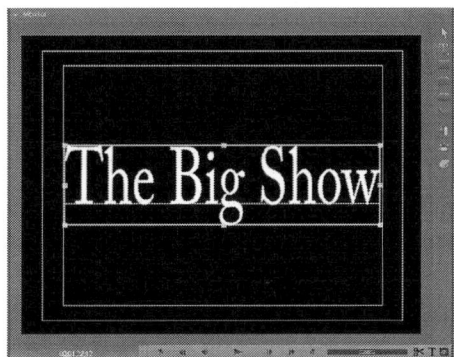

Add media options on the Monitor panel

In addition to dragging video clips to your timeline or sceneline from your **Project** panel, you have the option of adding your clips to your movie through the **Monitor** panel.

When a clip is dragged from the **Project** media **panel** onto the **Monitor,** it will automatically be added to the end of your timeline or sceneline.

This is true regardless of where the **CTI** (Current Time Indicator) is in your project timeline at the time.

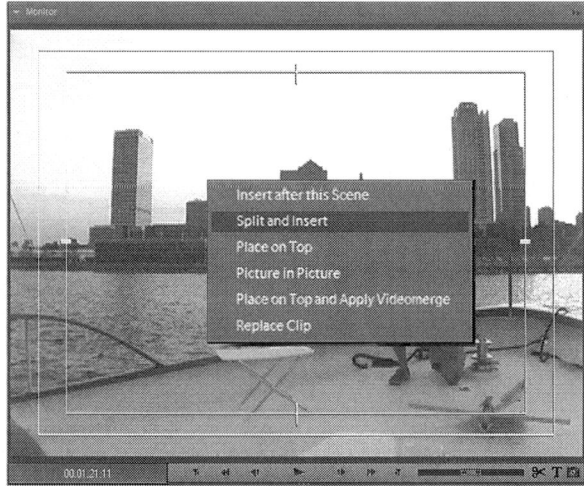

If you hold down the Shift key as you drag a clip from the Project media panel onto the Monitor, you'll be offered several options for loading the clip to your project's timeline.

Even more options are available if you hold down the **Shift** key as you drag your clip from the **Project** media panel onto the **Monitor:**

Insert After Scene – The new clip will be added immediately after the scene currently displayed in the **Monitor.** If there is already another scene following the current scene, the new clip will be inserted in between the two.

Split and Insert – The current clip displayed in the Monitor will split at the position of the **CTI** (Current Time Indicator) and the new clip will be inserted within the split in the clip.

Place on Top – The new clip will be placed on the video track above the currently-displayed clip.

Picture-In-Picture – The new clip will be placed on the video track above the currently-displayed clip and will be scaled to 50% of its actual size. Once this new clip appears in the **Monitor,** you can click on it and drag it, and/or resize it (by dragging the corner handles), to any position you'd prefer.

Place on Top and Apply Videomerge – The new clip will be placed on the video track directly above the currently-displayed clip and **Videomerge** will automatically make the background transparent. (More information on **Videomerge** can be found in **Chapter 24, Add Video and Audio Effects**.)

Replace Clip – The new clip will replace the currently-displayed clip on the timeline. If the new clip is a different length than the previous clip, the program will automatically trim it or add black so that it fills exactly the same space on the timeline.

Editing tools on the Monitor panel

Split a clip

The scissors icon in the lower right of the panel is the **Split Clip** tool.

Clicking this tool will slice through the clip(s) on your timeline or sceneline at the position of the **CTI** (Current Time Indicator), cutting the clip(s) in two.

How this tool functions with several layers of video or audio clips depends on whether or not you have a clip on your timeline selected.

If you have a clip selected on your **Timeline** (it will be highlighted if you have it selected), selecting the **Split Clip** tool on the **Monitor** panel will slice through *only that clip.*

If you have no clips selected, the **Split Clip** tool will slice through every clip on every Video/Audio track at the **CTI's** position. (This excludes clips on the **Narration** and **Soundtrack**, which will not be split unless specifically selected.)

Add Text (Title)

Clicking the "T" icon in the lower right of the **Monitor** panel launches **Add Text** (better known as the **Title** tool).

When you select this tool, you will be taken to the **Titles** workspace and default text ("**Add Text**") will appear on the **Monitor** screen. Typing over this text creates your new title.

We discuss this workspace in much greater detail in **Chapter 23, Add Titles**.

Jump to a position using timecode

You can jump your **CTI** to very precise positions on your timeline – positioning it, for instance, to exactly one second from the end of the clip – by using the timecode in the lower left of the **Monitor** panel.

When you click to select this timecode, the numbers become dynamic, and you can overwrite them with whatever minutes, seconds or even frame numbers that you'd like. When you press **Enter** after, the **CTI** playhead will jump to that precise position on your timeline!

Grab a Freeze Frame

The camera icon in the lower right of the **Monitor** panel is called the **Freeze Frame** tool. (Although it might more accurately be called a "frame grab" tool, since it doesn't so much *freeze* a frame of your movie as it *grabs* a frame from it.)

Clicking on this tool brings up an option screen which displays the grabbed frame from your video (based on the position of the **CTI** on your timeline) as well as a number of options for saving it, as illustrated below.

- You can choose to simply **insert** the still in your movie. The inserted still will display in your video project at whatever duration you've indicated in **Freeze Frame Duration**.

- Selecting the option to **Edit In Photoshop Elements After Inserting** loads the still into your movie and simultaneously launches it in the edit space of Photoshop Elements.

  Once you've made any adjustments to the photo in Photoshop Elements and saved the file, the updates will automatically appear in the photo in Premiere Elements.

- Whether or not your choose to insert the still into your movie, your **Freeze Frame** will be saved to your hard drive as a Bitmap (BMP) file and will appear in your current **Project** media panel.

If you'd like to save a **Freeze Frame** of your movie as a JPEG or TIF for use in either another video, Web or print project, use the **Share** output we discuss in **Output a still of your current video frame** in **Chapter 29, Share Your Movie**.

Freeze Frame options
Grabbing a still photo from your video

Clicking the camera icon on the Monitor panel launches the Freeze Frame option screen

Duration of still if added directly to timeline

Option to launch in Photoshop Elements editor

Option to export as a picture file

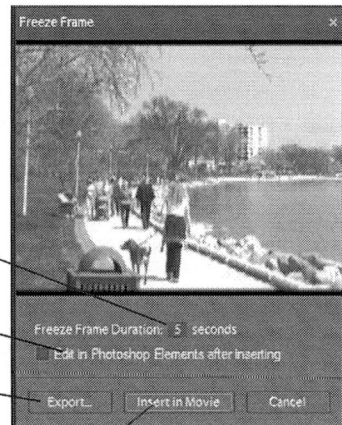

Option to insert still directly to movie's timeline or sceneline

Create an InstantMovie in the Media Panel

Use Themes to Create Movies on Your Timeline

Chapter 22

Use Movie Themes and InstantMovies
The easy way to create movies

Themes are a tool in Premiere Elements that can be used for creating automatic or InstantMovies.

Themes include a combination of titles, music and special effects that can be customized in a variety of ways and then applied to a set of clips you've gathered or selected.

In addition to their use in creating InstantMovies, Themes can also be applied to a sequence of clips already on your timeline or sceneline.

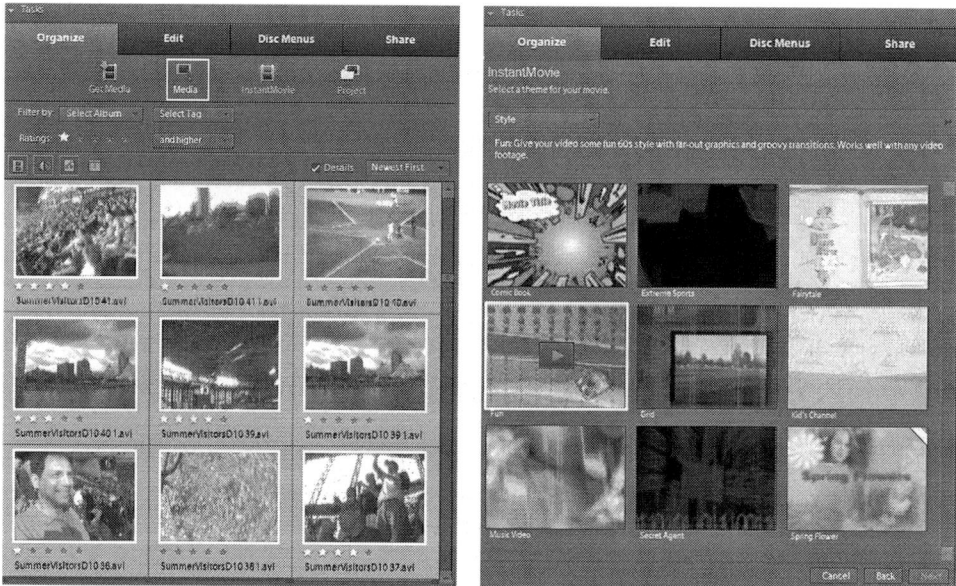

Creating an InstantMovie is as easy as grabbing video clips from the Premiere Elements Media panel, clicking the InstantMovie button and applying a Theme.

Create an InstantMovie in the Media panel

Themes can be used to create an **InstantMovie** from scratch, or they can be applied to clips already on your timeline.

To create an **InstantMovie** from scratch, using files gathered from the **Media** panel, click on the **Organize** tab.

1. The **Tasks** panel will display your video clips, audio clips and stills in the **Media** panel.

   Using the various buttons and drop-downs, you can filter this list to display only certain types of files or files, that include certain **Keyword Tags** or that have been gathered into an **Album**. (For more information on using filters, **Albums** and **Tags**, see **Chapter 31, The Elements Organizer.**)

   Select your movie's assets by either holding down the **Shift** or **Ctrl** key as you select, or by clicking and dragging your mouse to "lasso" the clips you'd like included in your **InstantMovie**.

2. Click the **InstantMovie** button.

   The panel will display a library of movie **Themes**.

   The drop-down menu at the top of the panel (set to **Show All** by default) will allow you to filter the **Themes** displayed in this panel by category or to access additional themes available from **Photoshop.com**.

   You can see an animated preview of any **Theme** by clicking on the thumbnail representing it.

3. Once you've selected a **Theme** for your **InstantMovie**, click the **Next** button in the lower right of the panel.

4. The panel will display a list of the optional elements that make up your **Theme's** template, as illustrated on the right.

   Type the titles you'd like included in the boxes provided, then select or deselect the elements you'd like applied to your movie.

   You can even swap out music by selecting the **My Music** option and browsing to a music file on your computer.

   (You may need to scroll down to see the entire list of optional elements, then click on the little white triangles to the left of the listed categories of options to see the entire options list.)

   Once you've selected and customized the elements you'd like included, click the **Apply** button in the lower right corner of the panel.

Premiere Elements will process all of the options and apply the elements you selected to the clips you selected.

After your automatically-generated movie appears on your timeline or in your sceneline, the program will offer to render it for you.

Once you've selected a Theme, you can customize it by including your own text and selecting which elements will be applied.

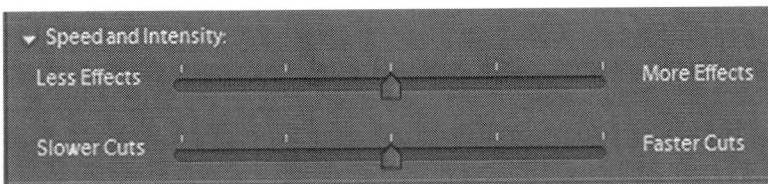

It's a good idea to accept this offer, as your movie will likely need to be rendered before it will play at full quality. The rendered video will provide you with a much cleaner representation of what your final video output will look like.

For more information on the rendering process, see **Render your timeline** in **Chapter 19, Edit Your Video in Timeline Mode**.

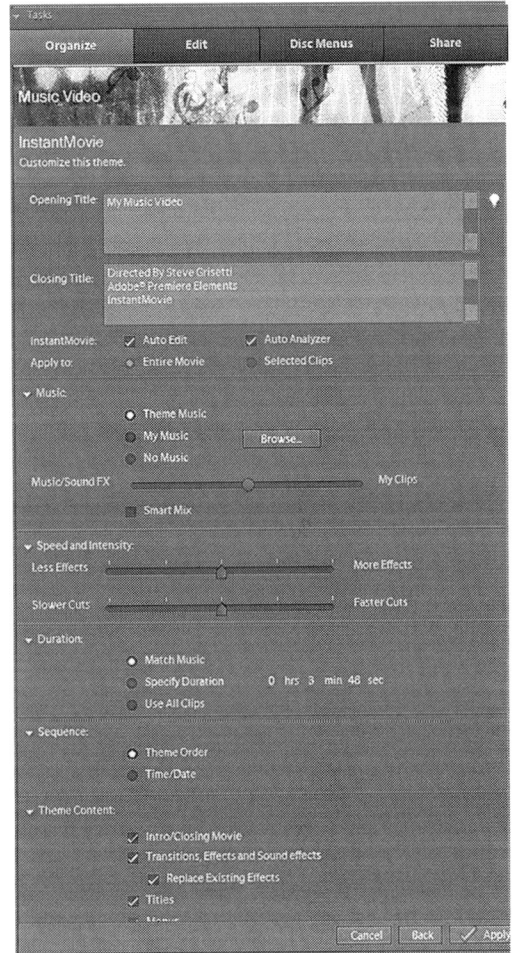

Instant Movie Themes include sliders for setting the speed of the cuts and the intensity of the effects.

To "lasso" (select) a sequence of clips on your timeline, click and drag from beyond
the end of your movie across the clips.

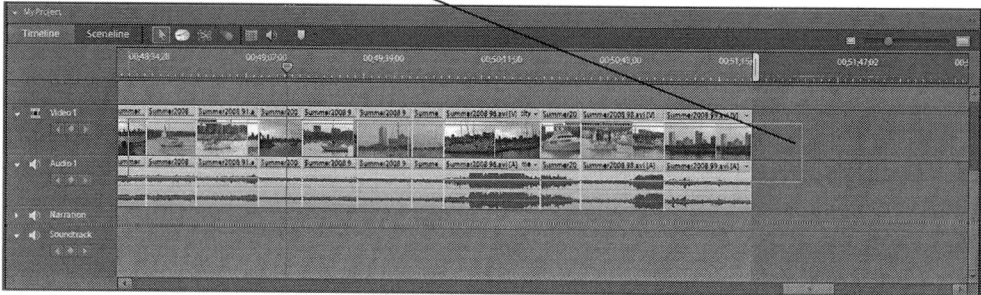

Apply a Theme to clips on the Timeline or Sceneline

Themes can also be applied to clips that you've already gathered on the
Timeline or **Sceneline**. (In **Timeline** mode, these clips must all be on the
Video 1 track.)

1. To apply a **Theme** to clips on your project's timeline or sceneline,
   select the clips on your timeline by "lassoing" the clips you'd like to
   include in your **InstantMovie**.

   To lasso clips on the **Timeline**, click on an area of the **Timeline** in
   which there are no clips, then drag your mouse across the clips
   you'd like to select, as illustrated above. (Or, to select all of the clips
   on your timeline, press **Ctrl+a** on a PC or ⌘**+a** on a Mac.)

   Once you've selected a group of clips, click the **Edit** tab in the Tasks
   panel and select **Themes**.

2. The **Tasks** panel will display available **Themes** for your
   InstantMovie.

   Select your **Theme**, then proceed as described in **Create an
   InstantMovie in the Media panel**, earlier in this chapter.

Chapter 23
Add Titles
Using title templates and text

With Titles, you can create opening or closing credits for your movie.

Or you can use them to add subtitles or captions to your videos.

The Titles workspace can be launched by clicking the "T" on the Monitor panel (which takes you directly to the Titles workspace) or by clicking the Titles button under the Edit tab (which takes you to the Titles Templates area first)

There are actually two different routes to the **Titles** panel and workspace.

One path gets you directly there; the other takes you to the same workspace by way of a colorful **Title Templates** panel.

Create a title

To go directly to the **Titles** workspace, click on the "T" icon on the toolbar that runs along the bottom of the **Monitor** panel.

To go to the **Titles** workspace by way of the **Title Templates** panel, click on the **Edit** tab and then click the **Titles** button on the Tasks panel. Once you've selected and **Applied** a template in this workspace, you'll be taken to the **Titles** workspace.

Whichever route you take, once you select a template or enter the **Titles** workspace by way of the button on the **Monitor** panel, a title clip will automatically be added to your project's timeline or sceneline.

In **Timeline** mode, you will be able to see the clip on an upper track of your project's timeline at the position of the **CTI** (Current Time Indicator). Premiere Elements will place the title on the lowest video track in your project that contains no other clips.

As with any clip, you can shorten or lengthen its duration by dragging on its ends, or you can slide it to any other position on the timeline. (See **Trim or split a clip** in **Chapter 19, Edit Your Video in Timeline Mode.**)

In **Sceneline** mode, you will only be able to see the title as a separate clip if it has been added to a movie in a space with no other video. Otherwise, it will be displayed in the **Monitor** and will be indicated in the sceneline by a small icon in the upper right corner of your clip's thumbnail, as illustrated on the facing page.

Use Title Templates

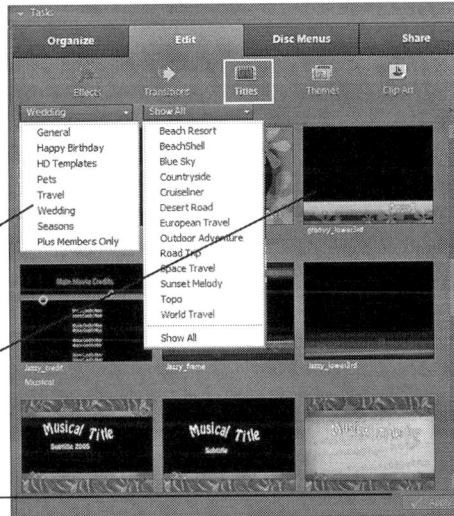

The Titles Templates drop-down gives you access to the various categories of title templates.

Title Templates can be searched by category or specific template, using drop-down menus

Many templates are animated, and you can preview the animation by hovering your mouse over the template's thumbnail.

To apply a template and proceed to the Titles workspace, click Apply.

Clicking the **Titles** button under the **Edit** tab in the Tasks panel displays a library of title templates, each shown as a thumbnail. (Black areas in the thumbnail usually represent transparency, through which your main or background video will be displayed.)

Using the drop-down menus, as in the illustration above, you can isolate your templates by category or select a specific template. You also have the option of downloading additional materials from **Photoshop.com**, if you have a **Plus** premium membership.

The templates usually include a graphic design and placeholders for adding your own custom text – and many are animated! Once you've clicked on a template to select it, click the **Apply** button in the lower right corner of the panel. The title template will be applied, the title will appear on your timeline or sceneline and you'll move into the **Titles** workspace.

When you create a title, it is automatically added to your movie project. In Timeline mode, the title will appear on the lowest available video track. Double-click it to launch the Titles workspace for re-editing.

In Sceneline mode, if overlayed on a video clip, the title will be indicated by an icon in the upper right corner of the thumbnail.

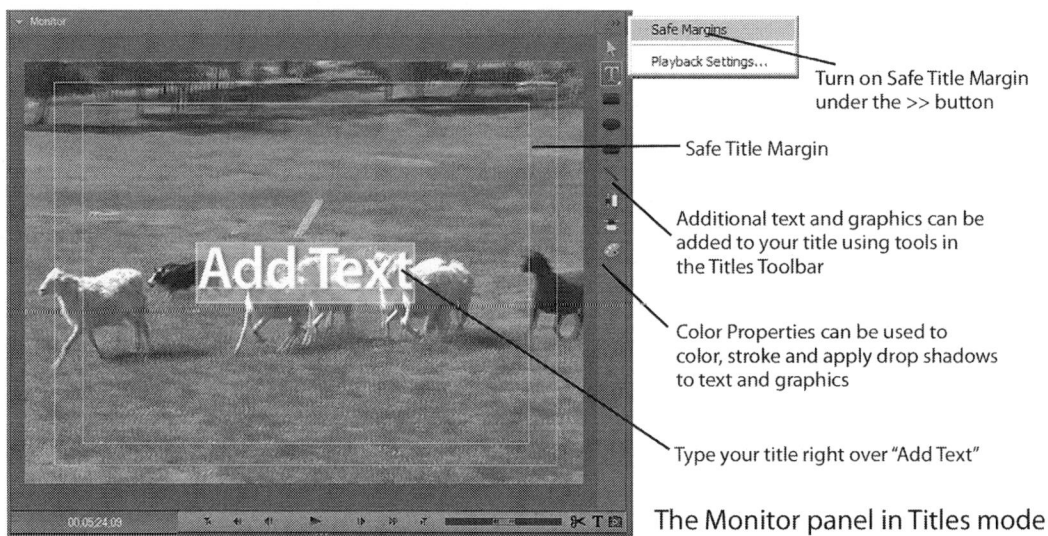

Turn on Safe Title Margin under the >> button

Safe Title Margin

Additional text and graphics can be added to your title using tools in the Titles Toolbar

Color Properties can be used to color, stroke and apply drop shadows to text and graphics

Type your title right over "Add Text"

The Monitor panel in Titles mode

Open the Titles workspace

The **Titles** workspace is loaded with tools for creating and customizing your project's titles.

If you've come to the **Titles** workspace directly, by clicking on the "**T**" icon on the toolbar along the bottom of the **Monitor** panel, the words "**Add Text**" will be displayed in the **Monitor**.

This placeholder text will already be selected when you launch this workspace and, when you start typing, your new text will replace it.

If you've come to this workspace by way of the **Title Templates** workspace, your title is already well underway, and you can click on any of the placeholder text boxes on your template to replace the text with your own.

You can also move or remove any of the text or graphics on your template by switching to the **Selection Tool** (the arrow) on the **Titles Toolbar** (see page 112), to select the element or text box. Once you've selected it, you can drag the text block or graphic to a new position or remove it completely by pressing the **Delete** key.

Show Title Safe Margins

If you haven't turned on the **Safe Margins** on the **Monitor**, make sure you do so before building your titles.

To turn on the **Safe Margins,** click on the **>>** button in the upper right corner of the **Monitor** panel and check the option for **Safe Title Margin**, as in the illustration above.

(If the **>>** button isn't visible, go to the **Window** drop-down and select **Show Docking Headers.**)

The **Safe Title Margin** (the inner rectangle of the two sets of rectangular guides that are displayed on your **Monitor**) won't show up on your final video output. It's purpose is to offer a guide to protect you from TV screens that cut off the edges of your video image (quite common).

Keeping all of your onscreen text within the bounds of the inner **Safe Title Margin** ensures that it will always be displayed completely, with no chance of any accidental cut-off. (See page 265 for more information.)

Set Text Options

While in the **Titles** workspace, the Tasks panel displays a number of options for stylizing your title's text. Drag over your text to select it or use the **Selection Tool** (the "arrow" icon in the **Toolbar**) to select a text box in order to apply these options to it.

The basic options for your title's text are **Font**, **Size**, **Baseline Shift** (raising or lowering the selected text relative to the unselected text), **Left Align/ Center/Right Align** and **Font Style**.

Once you've applied these settings to your selected text and colored it (using the **Color Properties** on the **Toolbar**, discussed on page 112), you can then save it as a permanent style in your **Text Styles** menu.

To save a custom style, select the text, click the **Save Style** button on the panel and then name your style. It will then appear as an **"Aa"** thumbnail among the other **Text Styles**.

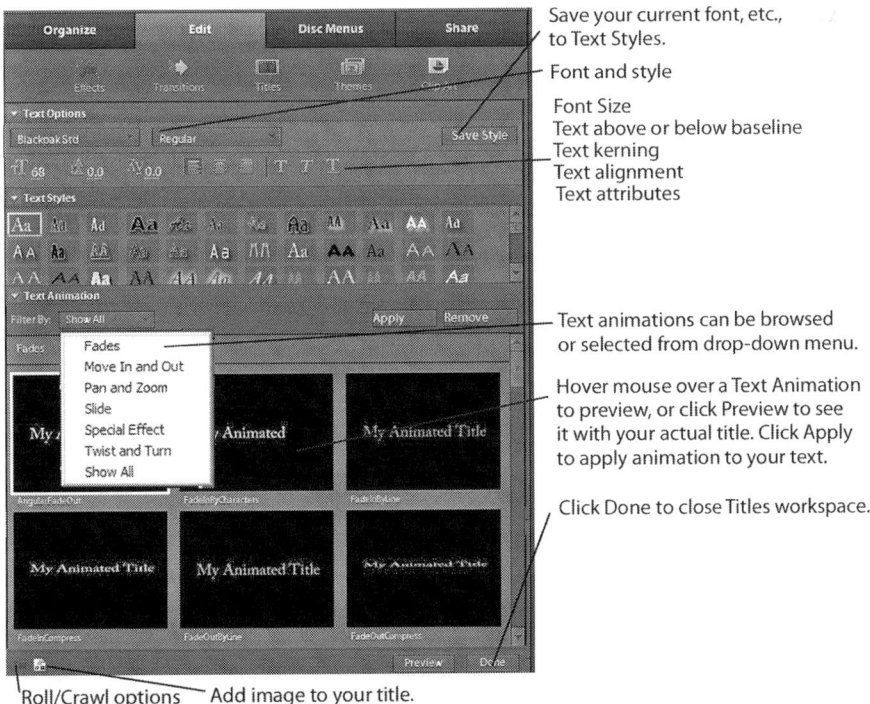

Save your current font, etc., to Text Styles.

Font and style

Font Size
Text above or below baseline
Text kerning
Text alignment
Text attributes

Text animations can be browsed or selected from drop-down menu.

Hover mouse over a Text Animation to preview, or click Preview to see it with your actual title. Click Apply to apply animation to your text.

Click Done to close Titles workspace.

Roll/Crawl options   Add image to your title.

Customize your title with the Titles Toolbar

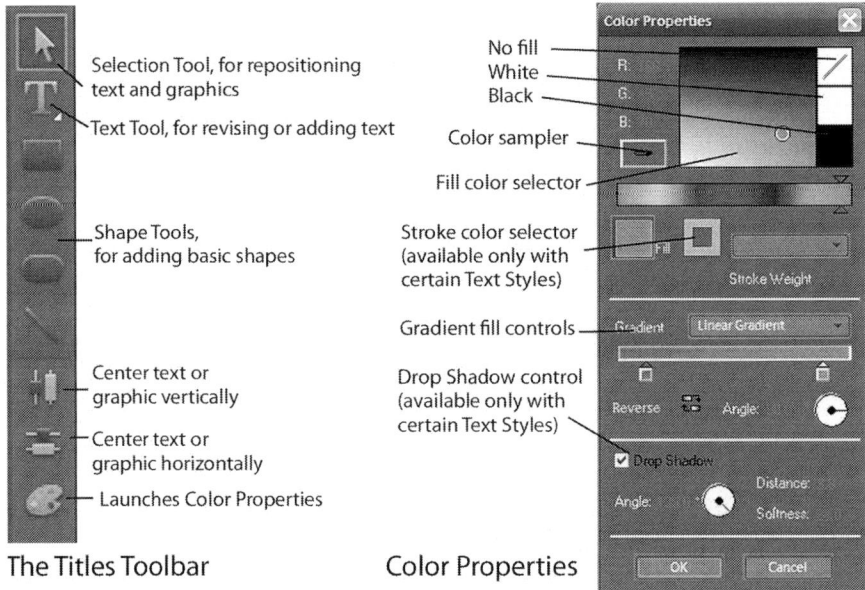

Selection Tool, for repositioning text and graphics

Text Tool, for revising or adding text

Shape Tools, for adding basic shapes

Center text or graphic vertically

Center text or graphic horizontally

Launches Color Properties

No fill
White
Black

Color sampler

Fill color selector

Stroke color selector (available only with certain Text Styles)

Gradient fill controls

Drop Shadow control (available only with certain Text Styles)

Color Properties

R.
G.
B.

Fill

Stroke Weight

Gradient | Linear Gradient

Reverse | Angle

Drop Shadow
Distance:
Angle: | Softness:

OK | Cancel

The Titles Toolbar   Color Properties

The **Titles Toolbar** is displayed along the right side of the **Monitor** in the **Titles** workspace. The tools include:

The Selection Tool (the arrow) – Clicking the **Selection Tool** allows you to use your mouse to drag the text blocks and graphic elements to new positions on your title.

The Text Tool (the "T") – The **Text Tool** changes the mode of your cursor to a text editor. If you click on an existing text box on your title, you will be able to edit the text; if you click any place else on your title space, you will create a new text box (in the same title) into which you can add more text.

The Shape Tools (the **Rectangle**, the **Oval**, the **Rounded Rectangle**, the **Line**) – Selecting a **Shape Tool** allows you to draw a basic geometric shape on your title by clicking and dragging.

You can recolor these shapes by clicking to select them and then using the **Color Properties** tool, as described below.

The Center Vertical and **Center Horizontal Tools** – If you've selected a text box or graphic element on your title using the **Selection Tool** (above), clicking on either of these tools centers it in your video frame.

Color Properties (the artist's palette) – After you've dragged over text to select it, or used the **Selection Tool** (above) to select a text box or shape, you can recolor it by clicking on this icon.

Continued on facing page

Use Text Styles

Text Styles are fonts, font styles and colors that can be applied to your selected text simply by clicking on the "**Aa**" thumbnail representing the style.

Some of the styles include outlined or "stroked" text. If you apply a **Text Style** that includes an outline, or "stroke," you will have the option to change the color and weight of the stroke in **Color Properties** (as discussed in the **Titles Toolbar** sidebar).

If you **right-click** on any of these **Text Styles** in the **Titles** panel (**Ctrl-click** on a Mac), you will find the option to set it as the **Default Style**. The **Default Style** is the font, color and font style that will appear whenever you create new text for a title, and will appear as your default font and color whenever you create a new Premiere Elements title.

Select a Text Animation

Text Animations, as the name implies, are ways of animating how your title text is introduced onto or removed from your video frame.

Premiere Elements' **Text Animations** are in several categories, and you can filter the animations displayed in the panel by selecting a category from the drop-down menu that displays **Show All** by default.

To see a preview of how the animation looks, hover your mouse over the animation thumbnail until a **Play** button appears, then click on this **Play** button.

The Titles Toolbar (continued)

On the **Color Properties** panel that opens, **Fill** is the color of the shape or text itself; **Stroke** is the outline around it. The **Stroke Weight** is the thickness of that **Stroke**.

A **Gradient** is a fill that is blended from one color to another.

Clicking the **Drop Shadow** option creates a shadow below your text or graphic. The characteristics of the gradient and the drop-shadow can be customized with the various settings.

- **Fill**, **Gradient** and **Drop Shadow** can be applied to any shapes drawn with the **Shape Tool**.

- **Fill**, **Gradient** and **Drop Shadow** can also be applied to any text. However, in order to apply a **Stroke** (outline) to the text, you *must* first apply to that text a **Text Style** that includes a **Stroke** outlining the text.

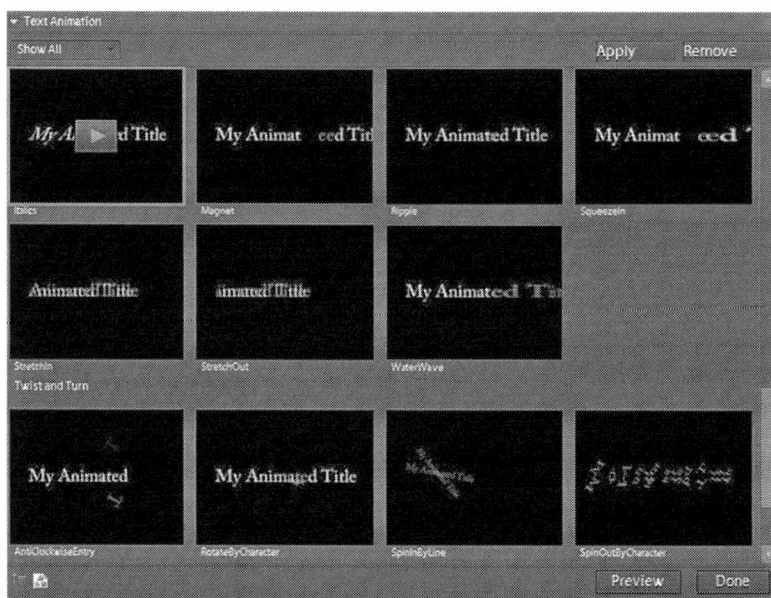

Premiere Elements Text Animation workspace includes nearly 40 ways to add life and excitement to your titles.

Text Animation is a pretty intensive function, and the performance of this feature, including previews, can be limited by your computer's RAM load and graphics card power.

In order to apply, or even *preview*, a **Text Animation** for your title:

- Your text or text block must be selected on the **Monitor** in the **Titles** workspace;
- Your text block must *not* be more than one line long; and
- A **Text Animation** must be selected.

To see a preview of **Text Animation** using your actual text or to apply a **Text Animation** to your text:

1. Select your text on the **Monitor** in the **Titles** workspace.
2. Click to select a **Text Animation.**
3. Click the **Apply** button.
4. Click the **Preview** button at the bottom right of the panel.
5. Before you apply a new **Text Animation** to your title, you must select the text again and click the **Remove** button.
6. Once you're satisfied with the **Text Animation** you have applied, click the **Done** button.

The program will return to the **Edit** workspace and your title, with any styles or animations you've applied, will appear on your timeline or sceneline at the position of the **CTI** (Current Time Indicator).

Roll/Crawl Options are launched from the button in the lower left corner of the Titles workspace panel

Roll/Crawl Options

Title Type
- Still
- Roll
- Crawl

Direction
- Crawl Left
- Crawl Right

Crawls move horizontally across the screen, Rolls move up from the bottom of the screen

Timing (Frames)
- Start Off Screen
- End Off Screen

Preroll	Ease-In	Ease-Out	Postroll
5000	0	5000	1

Options for starting or ending the title off the screen

Ease In and Ease Out slow the title at the beginning or end of the roll or crawl

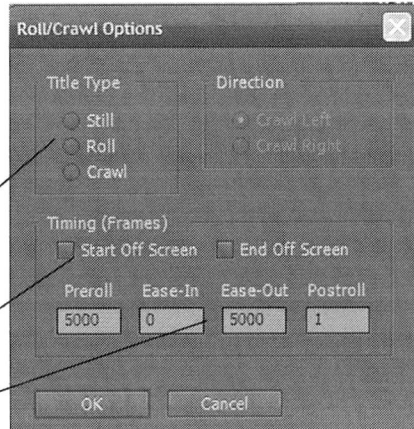

OK   Cancel

Create rolling or crawling titles

Any titles you create can automatically be made to **roll** (move up over a video frame) or **crawl** (move left to right, or right to left, across a video frame).

To access the **Roll/Crawl Options** screen, click on the **Roll/Crawl Options** icon in the lower left corner of the **Titles** panel – or select **Roll/Crawl Options** from the **>>** button on the upper right corner of the **Titles Monitor** panel. (If this button isn't visible, select **Show Docking Headers** from the **Window** drop-down menu.)

The options on this screen are fairly intuitive. If you select **Crawl**, for instance, you have the option of setting it to either **Crawl Left** or **Crawl Right** across the video frame.

The **Timing** options allow you to set the roll or crawl to start and/or end off screen.

- You have the options of setting your title to **Start Off Screen** or **End Off Screen**. Alternatively, you can manually set the **Preroll** or **Postroll** time for how long the title is off the screen before or after it rolls or crawls.

- The **Ease In** and **Ease Out** options allow you to change the rolling or crawling movement from a steady speed to one that begins slowly and then speeds up (**Ease In**), or vice versa (**Ease Out**).

The speed at which the title rolls or crawls is determined by how long the title is on your timeline. Extending (by dragging one end to lengthen) the title on your timeline will **increase its duration and thus slow the speed** of the roll or crawl; dragging in one end of the title to **decrease its duration will increase the speed** of the roll or crawl. (Note that changing the duration of a clip is a function of **Timeline** mode editing only.)

As an alternative to using these automatic roll and crawl options, you can manually keyframe the movement of your title so that it is revealed through any movement or effect you can imagine. To learn more about using keyframing, see **Chapter 27, Keyframing.**

Add a graphic to your title

To add a graphic to your title, click the Add Image icon on the Titles panel and browse to your custom graphic file.

To add a graphic or any image or photo from your computer to your title, click the **Add Image** icon on the lower left of the **Titles** panel and browse to the picture file.

Once you've added the graphic, use the **Selection Tool** to size and position it in your video frame. (See **The Titles Toolbar** on page 278.)

Save a title

If you like your title's layout and would like to save it for use in other Premiere Elements projects, you can do this by clicking to select the title either on your project's timeline or in your **Project media** panel and, from the **File** drop-down on the Menu Bar, select **Export**, then **Title**.

To import this title into another Premiere Elements project, just browse to it using the **PC Files and Folders** option for **Get Media**. (See **Get media from PC Files and Folders** in **Chapter 16, Get Media into Your Project**.)

Re-edit a title

If, after you've created a title, you need to re-edit it, you can re-open that title's workspace by double-clicking the title on your project's timeline.

In Sceneline mode, you can usually re-open a title by double-clicking it on the **Monitor** panel.

Duplicate a title

If you like how your title looks and you want to re-use the look and style for another title, you can duplicate it and then edit the duplicate.

To duplicate a title, **right-click** on it in the **Project** media panel (**Ctrl-click** on a Mac) and select **Duplicate**. You can then drag the duplicate title to your timeline and double-click on it to re-open its **Titles** workspace for editing.

It's important that you *duplicate* your title in the **Project** media panel rather than merely doing a copy-and-paste on the timeline.

If you create a *copy* of your title rather than a duplicate, you've merely created a "clone" – and any changes you make to *one* title will be made to *both*.

And that's likely not how you intend to use the title's copy.

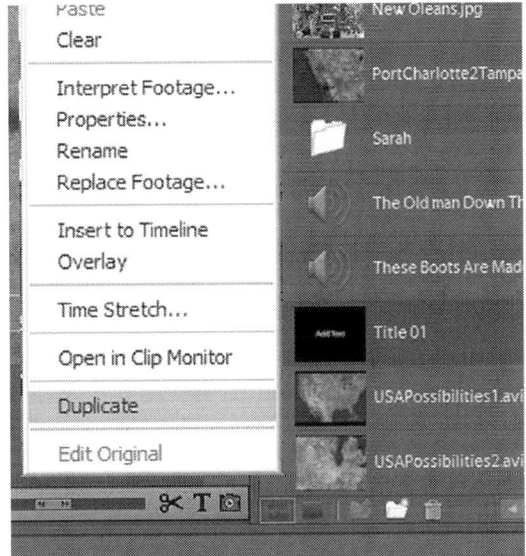

Duplicating a title creates a copy of it, which you can use as a template for a new title. Copying a title, on the other hand, creates a "clone" of your title, such that any changes you make to the original are made to both titles.

Duplicating creates an independent and editable copy of your title.

Render your title

Your title will likely look a bit rough when you first play it back from your timeline or sceneline. To get a better idea of what the segment will look like when you output your movie, press the **Enter** key (on a PC only) or select the option to **Render Work Area** from the **Timeline** drop-down menu to render your video or select the **Render Work Area** option from the **Timeline** drop-down on the program's Menu Bar. (For more information, see **Render your timeline** in **Chapter 19, Edit Your Video in Timeline Mode**.)

Chapter 24

Add Video and Audio Effects
Bringing excitement to your movie

There is an amazing number of effects available in Premiere Elements 9 – too many, in fact, to display in a single panel.

The program includes over 90 video and 17 audio effects as well as nearly 275 automatic, or "Preset" effects, that include applied effects as well as keyframed effects and motion paths – all of which are infinitely customizable.

The Effects panel in Video Effects mode

The Effects drop-down menu offers access to the other Effects sets

The categories filter drop-down gives you quick access to any category of effects

Quickly call up any effect by typing its name in the search box

>> Menu option to display only local or only downloadable content

Hover your mouse over any thumbnail to preview the effect

After effect is applied click Edit Effects to adjust it in the Properties panel

Click to apply effect to your selected clip or simply drag the effect onto a clip on your timeline or sceneline

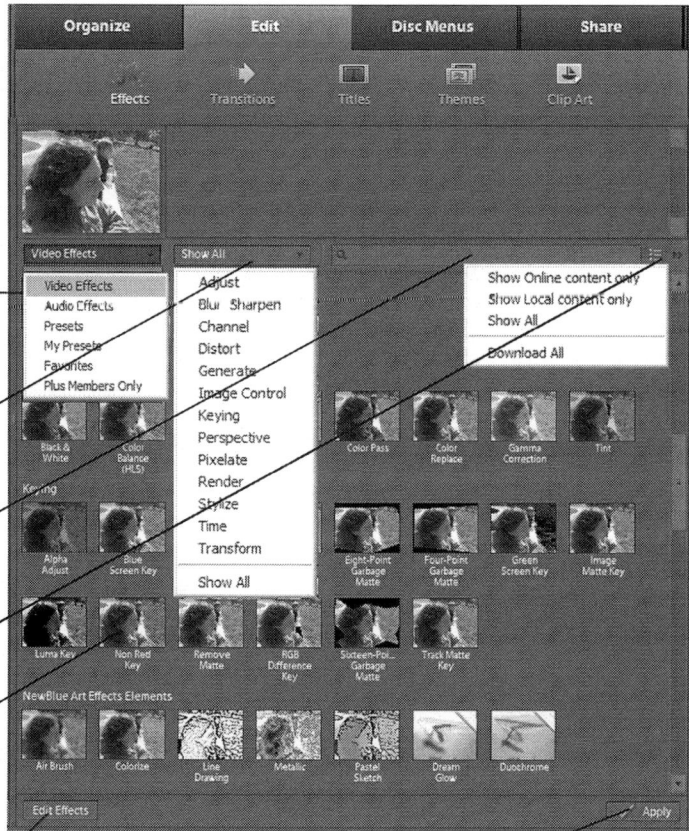

To open the **Effects** panel, click the **Effects** button under the **Edit** tab.

In addition to **Video Effects** and **Audio Effects**, the **Effects** panel includes categories in which you can store your own custom created effects and motion paths (**My Presets**) and your most-often used effects (**Favorites**), for easy access.

Presets and **Video Effects** will display in the panel as thumbnails demonstrating their effect. Animated effects can be previewed by clicking on the thumbnail image. And, if you have a clip selected on your timeline or sceneline when you open the various **Effects** panels, your clip will appear as the effect preview!

At the drop-down menu for each effect, you'll also find the option to access additional effects from Photoshop.com listed under **For Plus Members Only**. (See **Chapter 34, Photoshop.com**.)

If you have a **Plus** premium account at **Photoshop.com** and you are logged into the site at the Premiere Elements **Welcome Screen** (see **Chapter 15, Start a New Project**), you will regularly find additional effects automatically loaded into this panel category.

Apply an effect to several clips at once

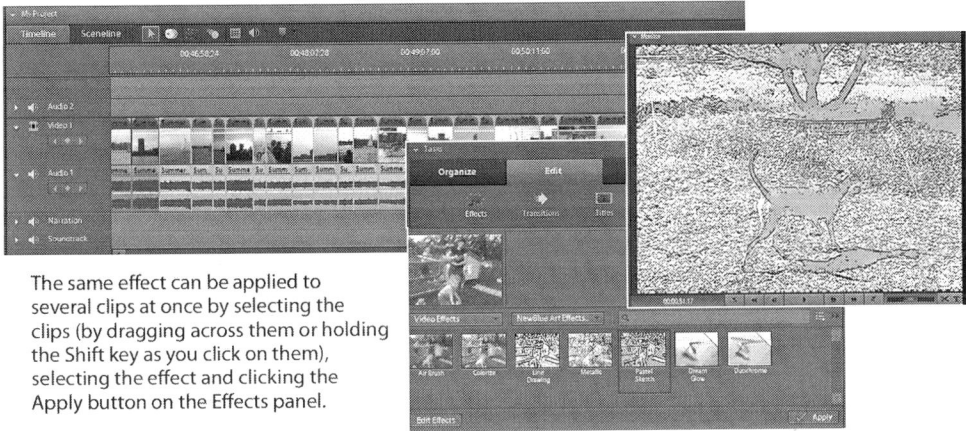

The same effect can be applied to several clips at once by selecting the clips (by dragging across them or holding the Shift key as you click on them), selecting the effect and clicking the Apply button on the Effects panel.

Premiere Elements 9 includes the ability to apply an effect to several clips at once.

To apply an effect to several clips in one move:

1. Select your clips, either by holding the **Shift** or **Ctrl** key as you click to select clips on your timeline or sceneline or by dragging across your timeline from beyond your clips to "lasso" the clips you'd like to apply the effect to. (You can also use **Ctrl+a** on a PC or ⌘+a on a Mac to select all of the clips on the timeline.)

2. Once the clips are selected, go to the **Effects** panel (by clicking on the **Effects** button under the **Edit** tab) and locate the effect you want to apply.

   Click the **Apply** button in the **Effects** panel.

The effect will be applied to all of your selected clips.

You can fine-tune the effects in the **Properties** panel by **right-clicking** each clip (one clip at a time) – **Ctrl-clicking** on a Mac –and selecting the option to **Show Properties**. (For more information on adjusting effects settings, see **Chapter 26, Customize Effects in the Properties Panel**.)

To create and customize an effect on one clip and then apply the same effect and settings to several other clips, use the **Paste Attributes** feature, as we also discuss in **Chapter 26, Customize Effects in the Properties Panel**.

You can apply any number of effects to a clip. In fact, you can even double-up the same effect on the same clip (such as **Volume** on an audio clip) to increase its intensity. Sometimes the way effects interact with each other on a clip can create a new effect all its own.

(For information on how to turn effects on a clip off and on, see **Disable or remove an effect** in **Chapter 26, Customize Effects in the Properties Panel**.)

Find and apply an effect

Effects are displayed as thumbnails representing the effect's effect. These effects are stored within categories, and you can filter the listing of any type of effect to display a specific category by selecting that category from a drop-down menu at the top of the panel (which, by default, is set to **Show All**).

You can also quickly call up an effect simply by typing its name in the **search box** to the right of the drop-down menus, as illustrated on page 286.

Applying an effect to a clip is as simple as selecting the clip on your timeline or sceneline, selecting the effect by clicking on it and then clicking the **Apply** button in the lower right corner of the panel. (You can also just drag the effect onto your clip.)

Some effects will cause an immediate change to your video. But nearly all effects can also be customized in the **Properties** panel and/or include settings which can or will need to be tweaked once the effect is applied to a clip in order to show any change.

Adjust an effect or property

To adjust the effect's settings, click to select the clip to which an effect has been applied on the timeline or sceneline and, on the lower left corner of the **Effects** panel, click **Edit Effects**. This will open the **Properties** panel for your clip.

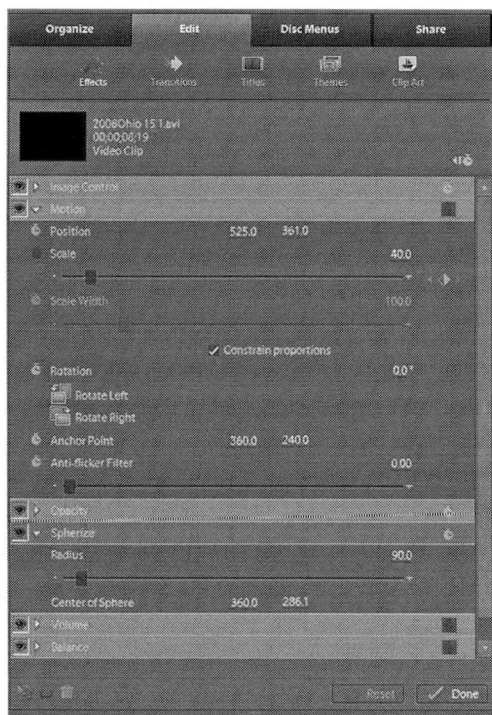

You can also open this panel by **right-clicking** on the selected clip on your timeline or sceneline (**Ctrl-clicking** on a Mac) and selecting **Show Properties** or by clicking on the **Properties** icon at the top left of the **Timeline**.

The **Properties** panel is a very useful and powerful workspace in Premiere Elements. With it you can not only customize your effect's settings (see **Adjust an effect or property** in **Chapter 26, Customize Effects in the Properties Panel**) but you can also create keyframed effects that change over the course of the clip or motion paths that move your entire clip around your video frame (as discussed in **Chapter 27, Keyframing**).

Effects that have been added to a clip appear in that clip's Properties panel, where they can be adusted and customized.

Video effects

By default, when you select **Effects** under the **Edit** tab, the **Video Effects** catalog will be displayed, as seen in the illustration at the beginning of this chapter.

Video effects are arranged in categories, and you can use the second drop-down menu on the panel to display only effects from one particular category.

Here are the various categories as well as brief descriptions of how some of the key effects in that category work.

Adjust. The **Adjust** effects work primarily with color. These are the effects you'll use if you want to change or correct color in your clip.

Additionally, **Lighting Effects** imposes a spotlight-like effect on your clip.

Posterize reduces the number of colors in your clip, making it appear more cartoon-like.

And the **Shadow/Highlight** effect is a great way to decrease contrast in a clip (e.g., the sky is too bright and the shade is too dark). Also available in Photoshop Elements, **Shadow/Highlight** is one of my personal favorite picture-saving effects!

Blur & Sharpen. These effects soften or sharpen your picture.

The **Ghosting** effects leaves a very cool trail behind objects that are moving in your clip.

Channel. Invert, the single **Channel** effect, turns your video's picture into its negative.

Distort. The **Distort** effects warp, twist and/or bend your video image.

Generate. The **Lens Flare** effect in this category adds a bright, white flare to a spot on your video picture, as if a light is being shone back at the camcorder.

GPU Effects. These effects do some higher-end bending of your video picture, such as making it look as if it is a turning page in a book. (Note that these effects will *only* appear in your effects listing if your graphics card supports GPU effects.)

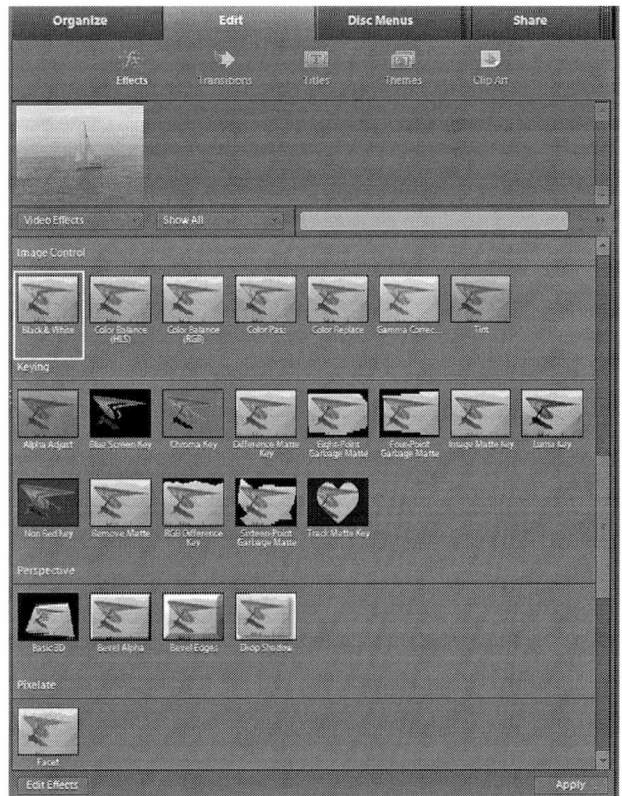

Image Control. These effects offer tools for color and light adjustments. For more information on **Image Control**, including the default **Image Control** properties, see **Default clip properties** in **Chapter 26, Customize Effects in the Properties Panel.**

Keying. Keying effects remove or make transparent a portion of your video's picture.

A powerful tool in this category is the **Chroma Key** effect, which we discuss in detail on page 294.

Other effects in this category are essentially the **Chroma Key** preset applied to certain colors (**Green Screen Key, Blue Screen Key**). The **Non Red Key** can be used to remove some of the "fringe" around the edge of a keyed area on a clip to which **Chroma Key** has been applied. (Yes, you can add more than one **Key** effect to a clip to fine tune the effect!)

Others, like the **Garbage Mattes**, create transparent areas in a clip that can be shaped with user-defined corner handles.

NewBlue Art Effects, NewBlue Film Look, NewBlue Motion Effects. These effects categories include high-level image effects created by NewBlue, one of the world's top video effects companies.

One of the most popular of these is the **Old Film** effect, a highly customizable effect which makes your video look like a damaged, worn, old movie.

And new to version 9 is **NewBlue Cartoonr Plus Elements**, an effect for making your videos look cartoon-like!

Perspective. These effects can be used to make your video image look as if it is floating or rotating into space.

Pixelate. The **Facet** effect in this category reduces your video picture to a group of large color blocks.

Render. The **Lightning** effect is great fun, although it takes a lot of computer power to create and customize it!

The very cool, new NewBlue Cartoonr effect.

The **Ramp** effect fades your video out across the screen in a gradiated pattern.

Stylize. The effects in this category, as the category name implies, can be used to create a highly stylized video.

Time. Effects in this category change how your video displays motion by reducing or affecting the look of the frame rate.

Note that this is *not* the place to go if you want to slow down or speed up a clip. That's the **Time Stretch** effect, available by clicking on the clock icon on the **Timeline/Sceneline** panel. (See the discussion of **Time Stretch** in **Chapter 19, Edit Your Video in Timeline Mode**.)

Transform. A real hodgepodge of effects, this category includes some stylized effects, some 3D transformations and, for some reason, **Clip** and **Crop**, two effects for trimming off the sides of your video picture.

(For the record, **Clip** trims away the sides of your video and replaces them with color while **Crop** trims away the sides and replaces them with transparency – a significant difference, if you're using your cropped clip on an upper video track with another clip on a track below it).

To learn more about using the **Crop** tool (or **Clip** tool, since you use the same method to adjust both) see **Types of effects settings** in **Chapter 26, Customize Effects in the Properties Panel**.

Video Stabilizer. The **Stabilize** effect can be used to take some of the shake out of a handheld camera shot.

Videomerge. This effect is essentially a more automatic version of the **Chroma Key** effect. When applied to a clip, it removes what it interprets to be the background in a single step. We show you how to use it on page 296.

For information on changing settings for effects, see **Adjust settings for effects and properties** in **Chapter 26, Customize Effects in the Properties Panel.** For information on keyframing effects to change over time, see **Chapter 27, Keyframing**.

Isolate an effect area with the Effects Mask

The **Effects Mask** enables you to isolate an area of your video and apply an effect to it without effecting the other areas of the clip. You can see an example of it how it works on the following page.

In other words, you can define an area – a square – in the center of your video frame and apply the **Black & White** effect to it. The area within the square will be black & white while everything in the video frame outside this square will remain in color.

The key to the way this effect works is that, when applied, it creates a duplicate of your selected clip and adds it to your timeline, directly above your selected clip. The area you define with the **Effects Mask** is actually the clip on the Video 2 track – with the area around your defined area "masked," or made transparent, revealing the clip on the Video 1 track below it, as illustrated on page 292.

(Because of the way it functions, the **Effects Mask** will only work in **Timeline** mode.)

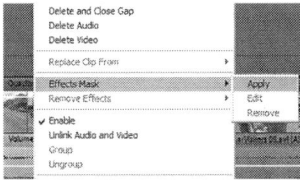

When the Effects Mask is applied (by right-clicking on a clip on the timeline), any effects are applied only to the area you define.

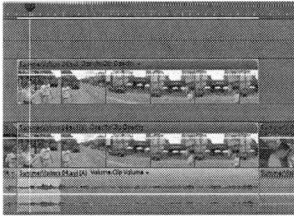

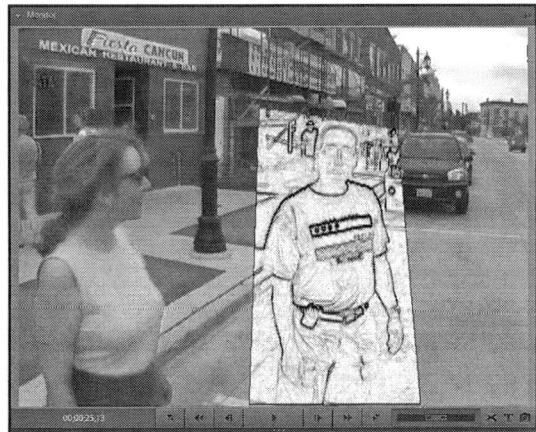

The tool actually creates a duplicate of the clip on a track directly above it, with any effects applied to the duplicate and seen through a mask you shape with corner handles.

To create an **Effects Mask**:

1. **Right-click** on a clip on your timeline (**Ctrl-click** on a Mac) and select **Effects Mask** and then **Apply** from the context menu.

   A duplicate of your clip will appear on the Video 2 track and a rectangle, with four active corner handles, will appear in your **Monitor**.

2. Click and drag the corner handles to define the mask area. This area can be moved and re-shaped later, if you'd like.

3. Select a **Video Effect** (from **Effects**, under the **Edit** tab) and click the **Effects** panel's **Apply** button. The effect will be applied only to the area defined by the rectangular mask only.

To fine tune the effect, select the clip(s) (they'll be grouped, and when you select one, you'll select both) and open the **Properties** panel by **right-clicking** on the clips (**Ctrl-clicking** on a Mac) and selecting **Show Properties**

Adjust your added effect as described in **Adjust an effect or property** in **Chapter 26, Customize Effects in the Properties Panel**.

- To re-edit the position and shape of the **Effects Mask**, **right-click** again on the clips and select **Effects Mask** then **Edit** from the context menu. The corner handles will again become active and you will be able to drag them or the mask box to any new position on the **Monitor** display.

- To remove the **Effects Mask**, **right-click** on the clip group on your timeline and select **Effects Mask** then **Remove**. The duplicate clip will be removed from the Video 2 track and any effects you've added will be applied to the entire original clip.

   The effect(s) can then be removed from the original clip by **right-clicking** on the clip and selecting the **Remove Effects** option.

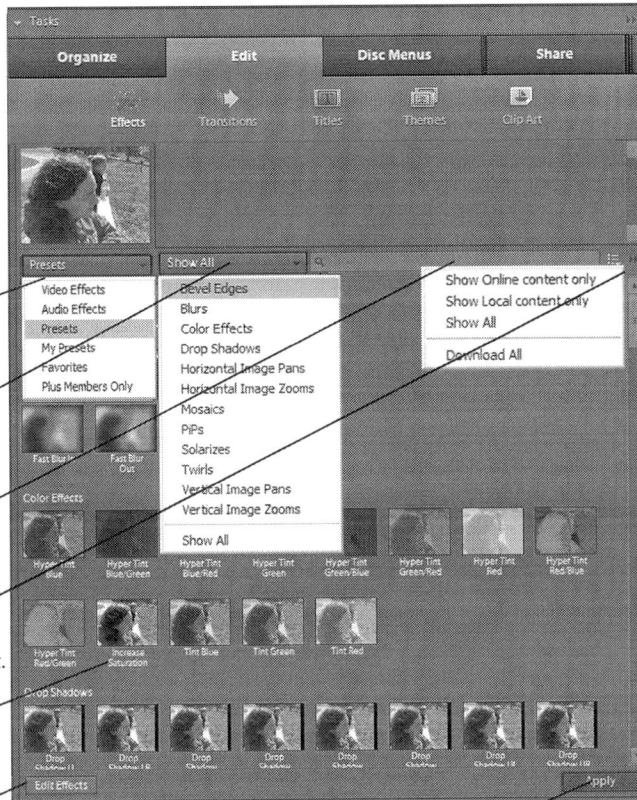

The Effects panel
in Presets mode

The Presets
drop-down menu
offers access to
the other Effects
sets.

The categories filter
drop-down gives
you quick access
to any category
of presets.

Quickly call up any
preset by typing its
name in the
search box.

>> Menu option
to display only
local or only
downloadable content.

Hover your mouse
over any thumbnail
to preview
the preset.

After preset is
applied, click Edit Effects to
adjust it in the Properties panel.

Click to apply effect to your selected clip, or simply drag
the effect onto a clip on your timeline or sceneline.

Preset Effects

To access Premiere Elements' **Preset Effects**, click the **Edit** tab, then click the
Effects button and chose **Presets** from the **Effects** drop-down menu.

Presets are represented as thumbnails in the panel and, if you hover your mouse
over those that are animated, a preview of the animation will play.

Presets are, essentially, effects to which settings have already been applied. Some
of these presets change the size or texture of your video clip or create a **Picture-
in-Picture** effect. Others include keyframed effects so that your video image
moves or changes scale or the setting for the effect changes over the course of
the clip. (For more information on motion paths and keyframed effects, see the
Chapter 27, Keyframing.)

In fact, once you apply a **Preset** to a clip, you can open the clip's **Properties** panel
and adjust the settings or keyframe positions to tweak it. (For information on
making these adjustments, see **Adjust settings for effects and properties** in
Chapter 26, Customize Effects in the Properties Panel.)

Chroma Key

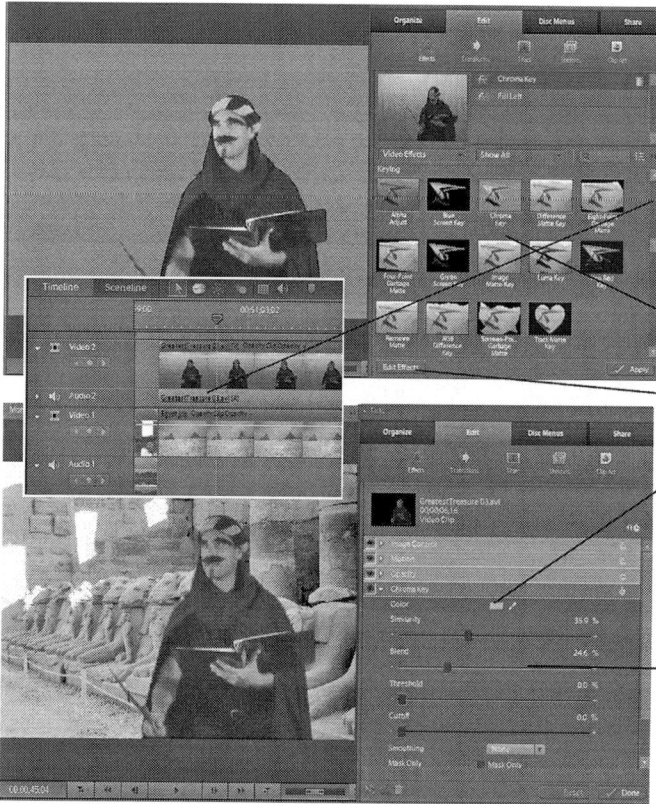

The Chroma Key Effect

Shoot your subject in front of an evenly-lit green or blue screen.

Place this clip on the Video 2 track and your new background on the Video 1 track.

Apply the Chroma Key effect to the clip on Video 2.

Click the Edit Effects button to open the Properties panel.

Click the eyedropper to activate the color sampler, then click on the green or blue background on your clip in the Monitor to set it as your "key" (transparency) color.

Fine tune the key color and range by adjusting the settings in the Properties panel.

The **Chroma Key** effect actually appears in a couple of forms in the **Key** category of **Effects**. Also known as the **Blue Screen Key**, the **Green Screen Key**, the function of the effect is essentially the same – a designated color, or range of colors, on a clip is made transparent. The **Green Screen** and **Blue Screen Keys** are merely preset to the two most commonly used "key" colors.

To create a **Chroma Key** effect you'll need two things: A video clip that has been shot with a subject standing in front of an evenly-colored, evenly-lit background (usually bright green or blue, because these colors don't show up in human skin tones) and a clip with a background you'd like to swap in.

You can only effectively do a **Chroma Key** effect in **Timeline** mode, because it requires two video tracks, as shown in the illustration on the following page.

1. Place the clip with the background you want to remove (we'll call it your **Key Clip**) on Video 2 and the background clip on Video 1, directly below it, as illustrated above.

Continued on facing page

To apply a preset effect to a clip, click to select the clip on your timeline or sceneline, then either drag the preset from the **Preset** panel or click the **Apply** button in the lower right corner of the panel.

The nearly 275 **Preset** Effects fall into a number of categories.

Bevel Edges. These presets create the illusion of a raised edge along the sides of your video clip.

Blurs. Animated **Blur** presets go from blurry to clear or clear to blurry, and can be applied to the beginning or end of a clip.

When using multi-track editing (See **Use L-Cuts, J-Cuts and multiple tracks** in **Chapter 19, Edit Your Video in Timeline Mode**), you can use these keyframed blurs as transitions between video tracks.

Color Effects. These presets can be used to tint your clip or to increase the color saturation.

Chroma Key (continued)

2. Apply the **Chroma Key** effect to your **Key Clip** and, with that clip selected, click **Edit Effects** or **right-click** on the clip (**Ctrl-click** on a Mac) and select **Show Properties**.

3. In the **Properties** panel, click on the little white triangle to the left of the **Chroma Key** effect listing in the panel to open its settings.

4. Click to select the little **eye dropper** icon next to the color swatch (Technically called the **Color Sampler**).

   The color swatch represents your key color, the color that will become transparent.

   Your cursor will become a little **eye dropper**. Use it to click on the colored background in your **Key Clip** in the **Monitor**.

5. Once you've selected your **key color**, most of the **Key Clip**'s background will become transparent, revealing your background clip, on Video 1.

You'll likely need to do some fine tuning with the sliders in the **Chroma Key** properties to remove the **Key Clip**'s background completely and smooth the edges between the keyed area and the subject in the foreground. But, if you've got a good, even-colored, well-lit background and an equally well-lit subject in the foreground, you should be able to make your key effect virtually seamless!

If you're having trouble "cleaning" your key, you can add an additional **Chroma Key** effect onto your existing key and double up on your effect.

Or apply and adjust the **Non-Red Key** to clean off some of the green 'fringing' around the edge of the transparent area.

For more details on using the **Chroma Key** effect, see my *Steve's Tips* article "Working with Chroma Key," available on the products page at Muvipix.com.

Videomerge

As with **Chroma Key**, **Videomerge** works by making areas on a clip transparent – though it tends to do so fairly automatically.

You'll find access to the **Videomerge** effect in several places throughout the program:

Videomerge can be applied by right-clicking on the clip on your timeline.

- **When you drag a potential "key" clip to your timeline** – If you drag to your timeline a clip which includes a flat, evenly-colored background, the program will launch a pop-up panel asking if you'd like **Videomerge** to be applied to the clip.

- **On the Effects panel** – Like **Chroma Key**, **Videomerge** can be applied to a clip by dragging the effect from the **Effects** panel onto a clip (or by selecting the clip and the effect and clicking the panel's **Apply** button).

- **Right-click on a clip** – Right-click (**Ctrl-click** on a Mac) on any clip on the timeline and you'll find the option to **Apply Videomerge** in the context menu.

- **On the Monitor** – If you drag a clip onto the Monitor while holding down the **Shift** key (as we discuss in **Add media options** in **Chapter 21, Edit with the Monitor Panel Tools**), the pop-up menu will offer you the option of adding the clip to the track directly above the currently-displayed video clip and applying **Videomerge** to it.

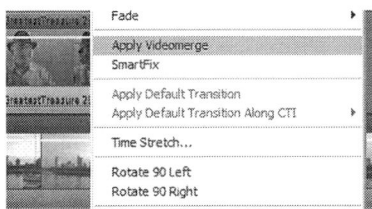

The Properties settings for Videomerge are much simpler than those for Chroma Key.

Once applied to a clip, the **Videomerge** effect has a greatly simplified "key" adjustment tool.

Open the **Properties** panel for the clip the effect has been applied to (by either **right-clicking** on it or **Ctrl-clicking** on a Mac) and selecting **Show Properties**, clicking the **Properties** button on the **Timeline** or by clicking the **Edit Effects** button on the **Effects** panel).

Click the white triangle to the left of the **Videomerge** listing to open its settings control panel.

The **Videomerge** effect's control panel includes only a few simple adjustments:

- An **eyedropper** for designating the color to be keyed. (Check the **Select Color** box to use the eyedropper to sample a color on the **Monitor's** display.)

- **A drop-down Preset list** for controlling how detailed the **Videomerge** key is.

- A **Tolerance** slider for setting the range of colors to be keyed.

- The option to **Invert Selection**, which makes the clip transparent *except for* the designated key area.

In our experience, **Videomerge** is easy to use and surprisingly effective. In many situations, it's a great alternative to the **Chroma Key, Blue Screen** and **Green Screen Key** effects.

Presets are pre-set Effects, often with keyframed motion.

Applying a Picture-In-Picture preset to a clip on Video 2 is a quick and easy way to create a PiP composite of the clips on Video 1 and Video 2

Presets, like all effects, can be further adjusted in the Properties panel by clicking the Edit Effects button.

Drop Shadows. These presets reduce your clip's scale and create a shadow effect so that your clip appears to be floating – an effect that's most effective when applied to a clip on Video 2 track, casting a shadow over a clip on Video 1 track.

Some of these presets use motion paths so that the shadow moves around over the course of your clip.

Horizontal Image Pans, Horizontal Image Zooms, Vertical Image Pans, Vertical Image Zooms. These presets are pre-programmed motion paths for panning and zooming around your photos – their names describe which size photo they are preset to pan or zoom across.

They'll do the job in a pinch, but you'll have much more control over the process if you use keyframing to create your own motion paths, as explained in **Chapter 27, Keyframing**.

The biggest challenge to using these preset pans and zooms is that they are designed for specific sizes of photos (as indicated in each preset's name). If the photo you are panning and zooming around is smaller than the effect, for instance, the effect may pan right off the edge of your photo!

With **keyframing**, you have the ability to control *precisely* how your motion path behaves.

Mosaics. These animated presets go to or from a mosaic pattern and can be applied to the beginning or end of your clip.

Picture-in-Picture (PiP). The **PiP** presets, when applied to a clip on the Video 2 track with another clip on the Video 1 track under it, automatically reduce the scale of the clip on the Video 2 track and reposition it in the video frame, so that both it and the clip under it are on screen at the same time (as illustrated above).

Create a custom preset

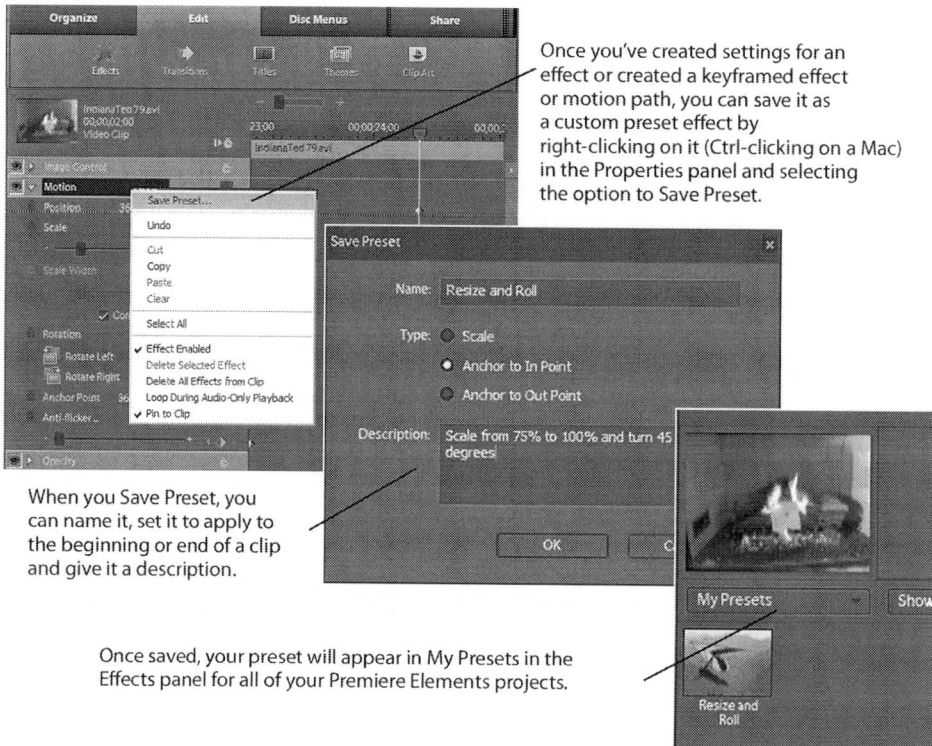

Once you've created settings for an effect or created a keyframed effect or motion path, you can save it as a custom preset effect by right-clicking on it (Ctrl-clicking on a Mac) in the Properties panel and selecting the option to Save Preset.

When you Save Preset, you can name it, set it to apply to the beginning or end of a clip and give it a description.

Once saved, your preset will appear in My Presets in the Effects panel for all of your Premiere Elements projects.

You can easily create your own presets, saving your custom effects settings or motion paths for future use.

To create a custom preset, **right-click** on the effect it represents in your clip's **Properties** panel (**Ctrl-click** on a Mac) and select the **Save Preset** option, as illustrated above.

Once you have saved the preset, it will be available under **My Presets** on the **Effects** panel.

Applying a custom preset to a clip is just like applying a default preset.

Click to select the clip on your timeline or sceneline and then either drag the preset from the **My Presets** panel or click the **Apply** button in the lower right corner of the panel.

Some **Picture-in-picture** presets will even add motion, changing the scale or position of **PiP** over the course of the clip – sometimes even incorporating an elaborate animation effect, such as spinning.

Solarizes. These animated presets go to or from a bright **Solarize** effect, and can be applied to the beginning or end of a clip.

Twirls. These animated twirling effects can be applied to the beginning or end of a clip.

Audio effects

To open the **Audio Effects** catalog, click the **Effects** button under the **Edit** tab and then select **Audio Effects** from the panel's drop-down menu.

Premiere Elements offers 23 audio effects which can be used to improve the sound quality in your project.

A number of these effects (**Bass**, **Treble**, **Volume** and **Channel Volume**) can easily be identified by their names. Others (**Denoiser**, **Highpass**, **Lowpass** and **Notch**) are filters for removing certain frequencies of sound. **Dynamics** and **Invert** are processors for "sweetening" your movie's sound.

New to version 9 are six audio enhancement effects from NewBlue – high-end, professional-style tools for reducing noise and sweetening your audio: **NewBlue Audio Polish**, **NewBlue Auto Mute**, **NewBlue Cleaner**, **NewBlue Hum Remover**, **NewBlue Noise Fader** and **NewBlue Noise Reducer**.

Four effects adjust the right and left channels of your stereo audio. **Balance** raises or lowers the volume of each stereo channel relative to the other. **Swap** switches the left and right channel's audio.

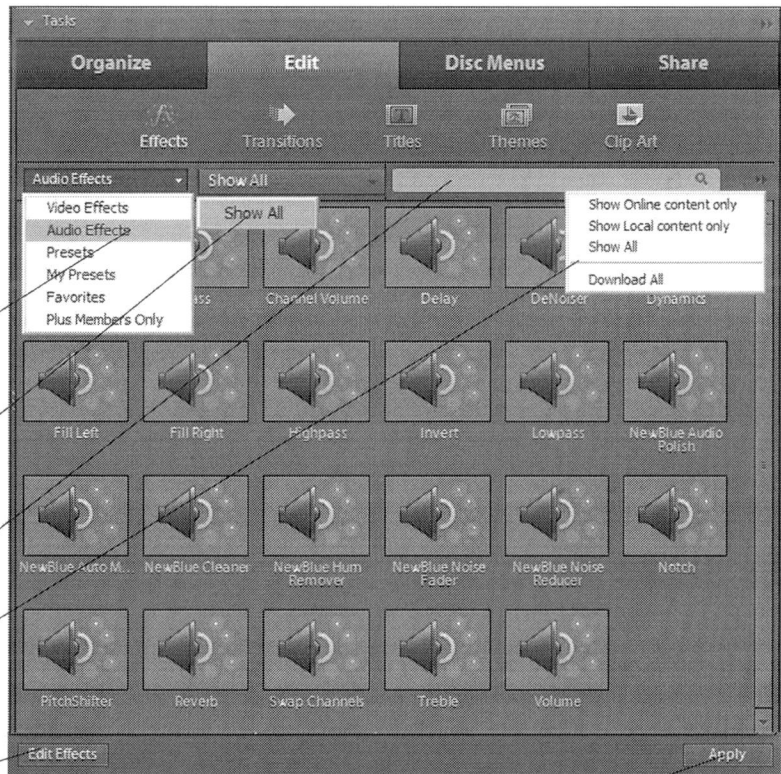

The Effects panel in Audio Effects mode

The Effects drop-down menu offers access to the other Effects sets.

Because there are only 23 audio effects, there are no categories of audio effects.

Quickly call up any effect by typing its name in the search box.

>> Menu option to display only local or only downloadable content.

After an effect is applied click Edit Effects to adjust it in the Properties panel.

Click to apply the effect to your selected clip or simply drag the effect onto a clip on your timeline or sceneline.

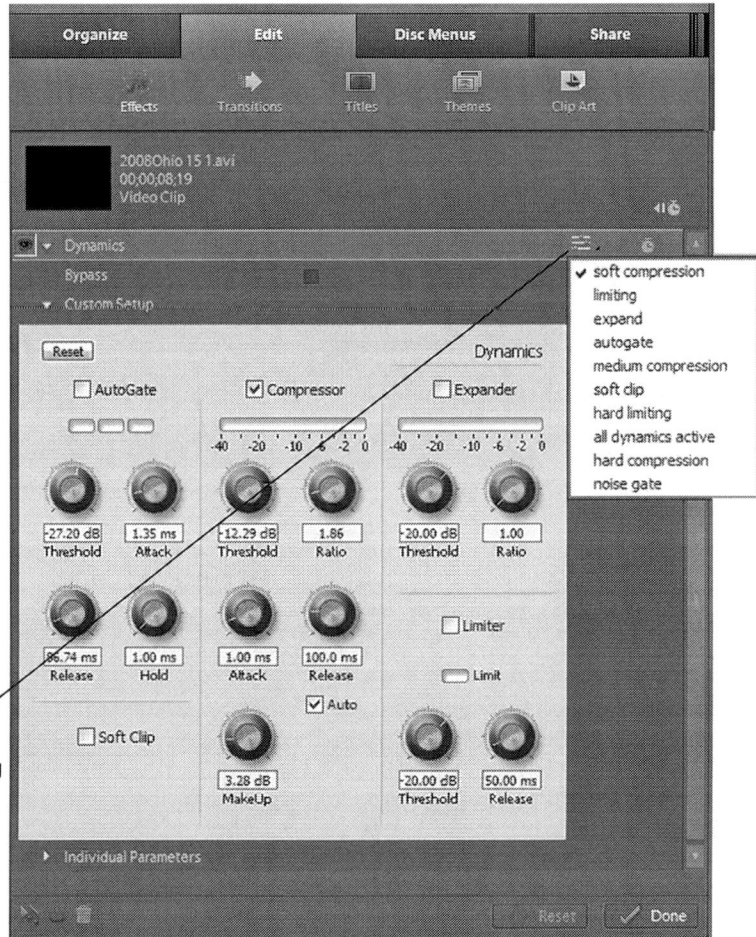

Some audio effects, like Dynamics, Reverb and Pitch Shifter, can be set using manual controls or by using presets from the drop-down list at the right end of the effect's listing in the Properties panel.

Fill Left and **Fill Right** are very helpful effects for those times when you have audio on only one of your stereo channels. Applying **Fill Left** or **Fill Right** takes the mono audio from one channel and uses it for both stereo channels.

Delay and **Reverb** create echo effects. The **Reverb** effect has a number of great presets among its properties for making your audio sound as though it's echoing through **a Small Room, a Large Church**, etc. These presets are available under the drop-down list to the right of the effect's listing in the **Properties** panel.

The **Dynamics** and **DeNoiser** effects likewise offer presets for affecting the sound of your audio clip (as seen in the illustration above). The **DeNoiser** is primarily designed to clean up tape noise that may have crept into your audio. **Dynamics** lets you "sweeten" the sound by removing some background noise, reducing distortion or otherwise balancing the dynamic range. Well tuned dynamics can give your video a richer, more professional, more big-screen movie-like sound.

And just for fun, there's the **PitchShifter**, which changes the pitch of an audio track, usually in very unnatural and often comic ways. The presets for this clip pretty much say it all: **Female Becomes Secret Agent, Cartoon Mouse, Boo!, Sore Throat, Breathless, Slightly Detuned**, etc.

As with video, there are a few basic adjustments that can be made using the **default properties** for any audio clip. Adjustable settings for **Balance** and **Volume** can be found in the **Properties** panel for any clip that includes audio by **right-clicking** on the clip on your timeline or sceneline (**Ctrl-clicking** on a Mac) and selecting **Show Properties**.

For more information on changing settings for effects, see **Adjust Settings for Effects and Properties** in **Chapter 26, Customize Effects in the Properties Panel.**

For information on keyframing effects, see **Chapter 27, Keyframing**.

As with video, there are a few basic adjustments that can be made using the **default properties** for any audio clip. Adjustable settings for **Balance** and **Volume** can be found in the **Properties** panel for any clip which includes audio by **right-clicking** on the clip on your timeline or sceneline (**Ctrl-clicking** on a Mac) and selecting **Show Properties**.

Additionally, audio levels can be controlled, and even raised and lowered at specific spots, right on your project's timeline. We explain how in **Adjust Audio Levels on the Timeline** in **Chapter 20, Edit Audio on the Timeline**.

Cool Tricks & Hot Tips for Adobe Premiere Elements

There is practically no limit to the special video and audio effects you can create with Premiere Elements.

If you'd like to learn some advanced tricks – like creating explosions in the sky or having a person confront his identical twin, making your photos look three-dimensional or creating amazing titling effects – check out my *Cool Tricks & Hot Tips for Adobe Premiere Elements*.

Full of bright, colorful illustrations and step-by-step instructions for creating 50 very cool special effects, with dozens of helpful "Hot Tips" thrown in for good measure, it's a book that will show you the amazing potential of this simple, inexpensive program.

The book is available through major book stores online as well as at the Muvipix.com store.

For more information as well as examples of some of the effects you'll learn to create, see Muvipix.com/CoolTricks.

Chapter 25
Add and Customize Transitions
Cool ways to get from one scene to the next

Transitions in Premiere Elements are very easy to use.

However, like most of Premiere Elements' tools, there is also a surprising amount you can do to customize them, if you know where to look.

The Transitions panel in Video Transitions mode

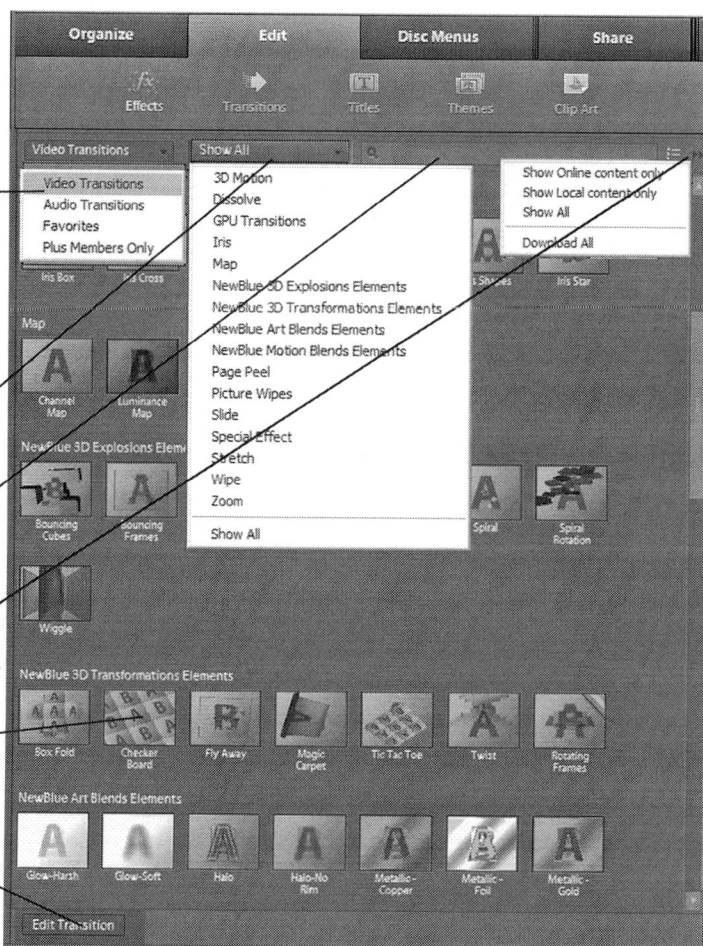

The Transitions drop-down menu offers access to the other Transitions sets.

The categories filter drop-down gives you quick access to any category of transitions.

Quickly call up any transition by typing its name in the search box.

>> Menu option to display only local or only downloadable content.

Hover your mouse over any thumbnail to preview the transition.

After a transition is applied, click Edit Transition to adjust it in the Properties panel.

To open the **Transitions** panel, select the **Edit** tab and click on the **Transitions** button.

You can access each of the **Transitions** categories from the left drop-down menu.

At this drop-down menu, you'll also find the option to access additional transitions from **Photoshop.com,** if you have a **Plus** premium account at **Photoshop.com** and you are logged into the site at the Premiere Elements **Welcome Screen** (see **Photoshop.com** in **Chapter 15, Start a New Project** and **Chapter 34, Photoshop.com**).

As with many of Premiere Elements' tools, **Video Transitions** are arranged in categories.

By default, the filter drop-down menu is set to **Show All**, displaying all 100 or so of the program's **Video Transitions**. By selecting a category from this drop-down menu, you can filter the list to display only the **Transitions** from a particular category.

Fade in or out of a clip

Fades, in and out of a clip, are most easily achieved by **right-clicking** on a clip on your timeline or sceneline (**Ctrl-clicking** on a Mac) and selecting a **Fade In** or **Fade Out** option.

This works for audio as well as video clips. By **right-clicking** on a clip which includes both audio and video, you'll find separate **Fade In** and **Fade Out** options for both the clip's audio and its video.

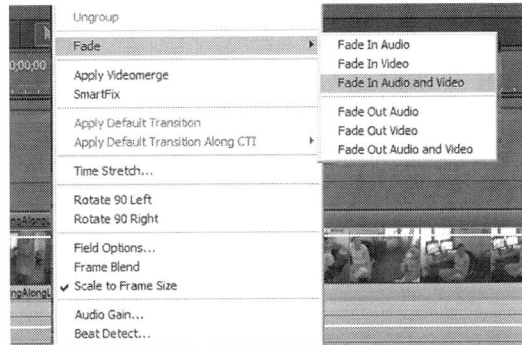

A fade in or fade out can be easily added to any video or audio clip by right-clicking (Ctrl clicking on a Mac) on on the clip and selecting the option from the pop-up menu.

For quick access to any transition, you can also type the name of a transition in the **search box** to the right of these drop-down menus (as seen in the illustration on the facing page), and the transition will be brought to the top as you type.

Video transitions

Video Transitions are displayed in the **Transitions** panel as thumbnails representing their effect. If you click or hover your mouse over any thumbnail, you will see an animated representation of the **Transition** in action.

The categories of **Video Transitions** are:

> **3-D Motion.** These transitions give the illusion that your video clips are transitioning by turning around or flipping over in three-dimensional space.

> **Dissolve. Cross-Dissolve** is the most basic transition, a dissolve from one clip to the next.

> The **Dip to Black** transition fades the first clip to black before fading the next clip in from black.

> **GPU Transitions.** These transitions include more advanced, three-dimensional, animated transitions, such as **Page Curl** and **Page Roll**. (You will only see these transitions listed in the panel, however, if your computer's graphics card supports GPU effects.)

> **Iris. Iris** transitions change from one clip to another through a shape.

Apply a transition to several clips at once

In Premiere Elements you can add a transition between several clips in one move.

The Default Transition can be applied to several clips at once by selecting the sequence and choosing the option from the right-click (Ctrl click) menu.

To apply the **Default Transition** to several clips at once:

1. Select your clips, either by holding the **Shift** or **Ctrl** key as you click to select clips on your timeline or sceneline, or by dragging across your timeline from beyond your clips to "lasso" the clips you would like to select. (You can also use **Ctrl+a** – ⌘**+a** on a Mac – to select all of the clips on the timeline.)

2. Once the clips are selected, **right-click** (**Ctrl-click** on a Mac) on the group and select **Apply Default Transition** from the context menu.

You may get a warning that your selected clips include "Insufficient media. This transition will contain repeated frames."

This means that one or more of your clips lacks enough "head" or "tail" material and that, if you proceed, some of your transitions will be composed of freeze frames. (For more information on why this happens and what you can do about it, see the discussion of **How transitions work** on page 310.) The only alternative to letting the program generate freeze frames is to trim back your clips so that at least one second of transitional material exists beyond the in and out points on each clip.

There is currently no way to add a transition other than the **Default Transition** to multiple clips in one move.

However, *any* transition can be designated as the **Default Transition**. To designate a transition as the default, locate the transition on the **Transitions** panel, **right-click** on it (**Ctrl-click** on a Mac) and select the option to **Set Selected as Default Transition**.

Map. These transitions map their transitional phase to your clip's luminance values.

NewBlue 3D Explosions, NewBlue 3D Transformations, NewBlue Art Blends, NewBlue Motion Blends. These categories contain very cool effects created by NewBlue, one of the world's top video effects companies.

Page Peel. These transitions give the illusion of a page peeling or rolling away between clips.

Slide. Slide transitions push one clip out of the way so that another is revealed or they transition between clips through sliding boxes or swirls.

Picture Wipes. These transitions use graphics (such as stars, travel signs or wedding dress lace) to transition from one clip to another.

Special Effects. A hodge podge of very showy transitions.

Stretch. These transitions seem to twist or stretch one clip away to reveal another.

Wipe. A variety of transitions that replace one clip with another with a clear line of movement. (See **Create custom transitions with the Gradient Wipe** on page 143 for information on the unique features of this transition.)

Zoom. High energy transitions that suddenly shrink or enlarge one clip to reveal another.

Audio transitions

To display the **Audio Transitions**, select **Audio Transitions** from the **Transitions** panel's drop-down menu.

There are only two **Audio Transitions** – **Constant Gain** and **Constant Power** – both variations of an audio cross-fade.

The difference between the two is minor, having to do with whether the effect transitions from one audio clip to another in a linear fashion or by varying the audio levels as they crossfade.

Of the two, **Constant Power** is generally considered to provide the smoother transitional sound– though, in reality, most people can't really tell the difference.

The Transitions panel in Audio Transitions mode

The Transitions drop-down menu offers access to the other Transitions sets.

There are only two audio transitions, subtly different audio crossfades.

After a transition is applied, click Edit Transition to adjust it in the Properties panel.

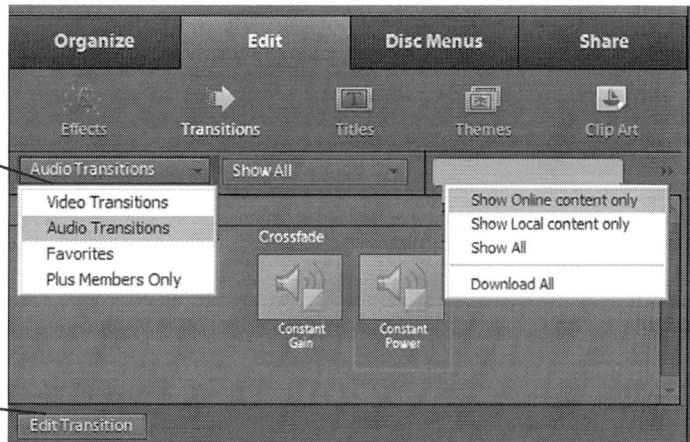

To apply a transition, drag it between two clips on your project's timeline or sceneline.

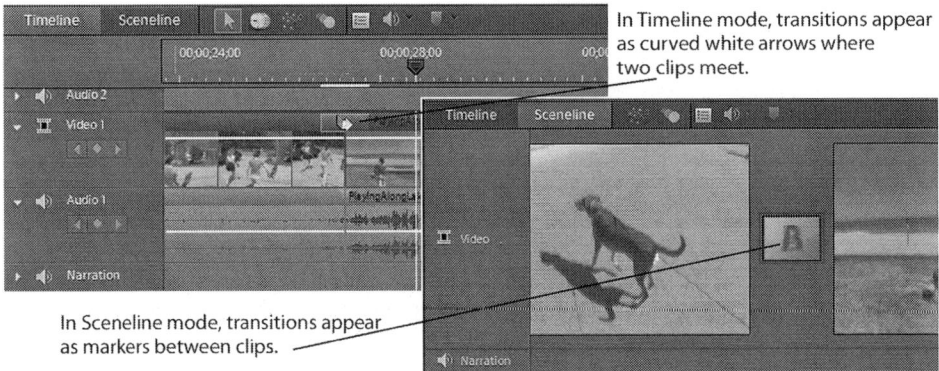

In Timeline mode, transitions appear as curved white arrows where two clips meet.

In Sceneline mode, transitions appear as markers between clips.

Add a transition to your movie

Adding a transition to your Premiere Elements project is as simple as dragging it from the **Transitions** panel to the point where two clips meet on your timeline or sceneline.

In **Sceneline** mode, there is even a placeholder in which to drag the transition between the clips.

In **Timeline** mode, you drag the transition onto a spot where two clips meet. The transition you've added between two clips is represented by a graphic overlapping one or both of the clips. (See **How transitions work**, on page 310, for information on why transitions position themselves where they do on your clips.)

Transitions, by default, are one second long. However, you can make them as long or as short as you'd like.

If you'd like to increase or decrease the speed of a transition on your timeline, you can do so by clicking on it and dragging it wider or narrower.

You can also customize virtually all of your transitions by changing their properties.

Customize your transition

Once you've placed a transition, you can also customize it in the **Transition Properties** panel. To open this panel, right-click on the transition on your timeline or sceneline and select **Show Properties** or simply double-click on it.

At the very least, you'll have a couple of basic customization options available in the **Properties** panel. Some transitions have several. You may need to scroll down in the panel to see all of the options available.

At **Alignment**, you can select whether the transition overlaps one or the other, or both, clips evenly.

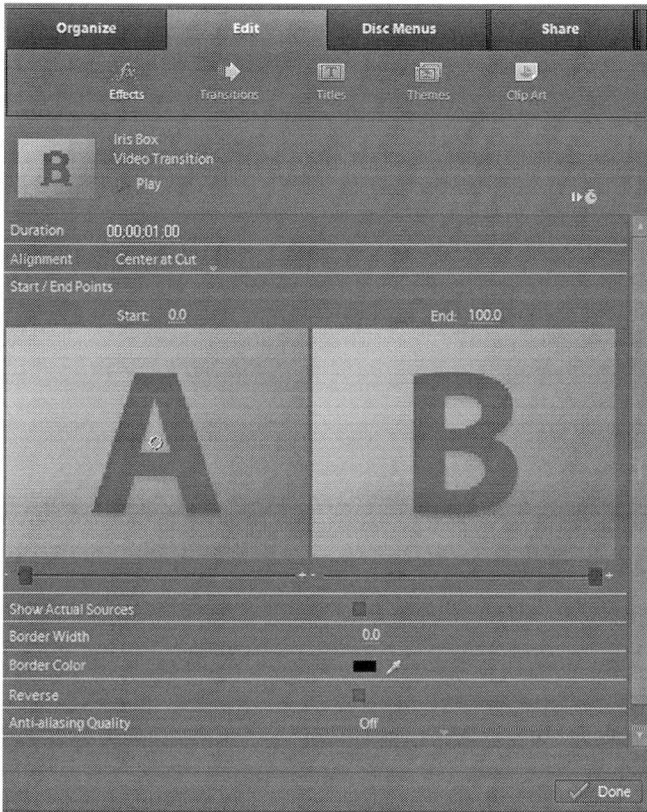

Customizing a transition in the Properties panel

To open a transition's properties, double-click on it in your project's timeline or sceneline, or click to select it, and click Edit Transition in the Transitions panel.

Each transition has its own set of customizable properties, but virtually all include the options to set where the transition centers and how long the transition lasts, as well as the option to reverse the transition's animation.

You can check the option to **reverse** the transition so that, for instance, it replaces the old clip with the new in a movement from left to right, rather than from right to left.

Many transitions include other options, and you can preview the transition, even with the actual source clips (check the **Show Actual Sources** box), right there in the **Properties** panel before you commit.

Create custom transitions with the Gradient Wipe

One of the most versatile **Video Transitions** available in Premiere Elements is the **Gradient Wipe**.

The **Gradient Wipe** will create a *custom* wipe from one clip to another based on any gradient (black to gray to white) pattern you provide!

Once you drag the **Gradient Wipe** onto a point between two clips, open the **Properties** panel by double-clicking on the transition on your timeline, or by selecting the transition on your sceneline, and clicking on the **Edit Transitions** button on the **Transitions** panel.

At the bottom of the options listing for the **Gradient Wipe** in the **Transition Properties** panel, you'll see a button labeled **Custom**.

How transitions work

To create the transitional sequence, the transition must "borrow" extra footage – from beyond the out point of clip 1 and from beyond the in point of clip 2, sometimes resulting in the transition showing frames you've trimmed away.

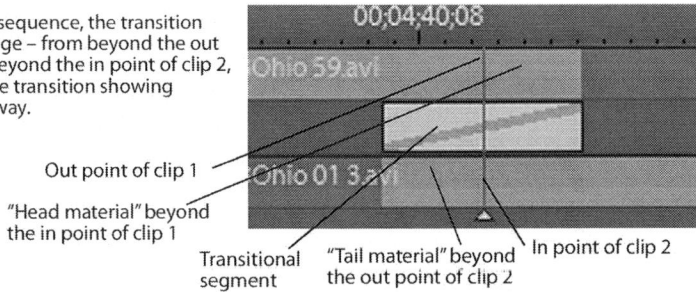

Out point of clip 1

"Head material" beyond the in point of clip 1

Transitional segment

"Tail material" beyond the out point of clip 2

In point of clip 2

Sometimes transitions seem to behave in mysterious ways. They may show frames of video you've trimmed away – or they may show a freeze frame of your video during the transition. However, once you understand what's actually going on, you may find it easier to work with the process to resolve these issues.

1. In order to create the transitional segment – the segment during which both clips are displayed – the transition that you've added needs *a few extra frames*, beyond one clip's end and the next clip's beginning, as illustrated above.

   Officially these extra frames are called "**head**" and "**tail**" material.

   Unfortunately, this sometimes means that frames you've trimmed away from the end or beginning of a clip will appear during this transitional segment!

   If this happens, you may need to trim a few more frames from the beginning or end of the clip so that, even amidst the transition, these unwanted frames are not displayed.

2. If there are no extra frames beyond the beginning or end of your clips for the program to use to create its transition, the program will create a **freeze frame** of the last available video frame for the clip and use that for the transitional material.

   This, too, can be a bit annoying if you're not aware of why it's happening. Once again, the solution is to trim back the clip so that the transition has at least a second of "head" or "tail" material to work with.

3. You may also find, sometimes, that the transition will not sit evenly between two clips on your timeline but, rather, seems to be entirely over one or the other clip.

   This is because the transition was not able to find the necessary head or tail material on at least one of the clips, and so it has positioned itself over the clip which offers the most available transitional footage.

   If this is not what you want, you can go to the **Transition Properties** panel, as described above, and set the transition's **Alignment** so that it sits evenly over both clips. However, you may find that this also creates an undesirable effect (such as a freeze frame in the head or tail material of one clip).

   So weigh your options carefully. The default point at which the transition lands is usually the best available position for it.

4. If you're using transitions between several photos (as in a slideshow) or even titles, you may find that the transition regularly rests over one or the other clip entirely. In this case, it's best not to bother to tweak its position since, with a still image, head, tail and freeze frames all look the same.

The Gradient Wipe transition creates a wipe in any shape you create, by following the pattern from black to white.

To load a custom pattern, click the Custom button in the Transition Properties panel, then click Select Image in the Gradient Wipe Settings and browse to your image.

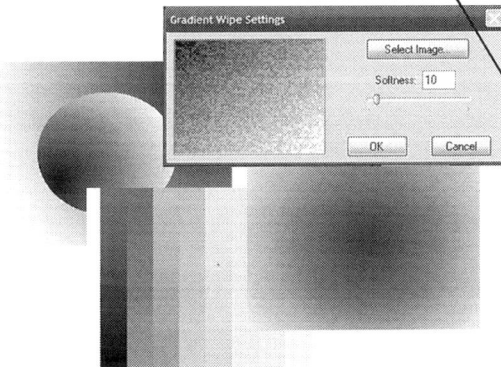

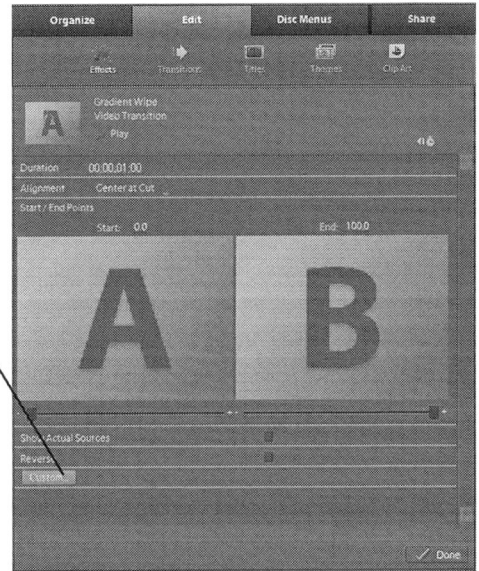

Click on the **Custom** button to open the **Gradient Wipe Settings** panel. This panel will display a default gradient pattern along with a slider to adjust its softness.

Click on **Select Image,** and you'll find the option to browse to any gradient image on your computer – or any photo or graphics file at all, in fact – and select it as a pattern for the wipe.

The **Gradient Wipe** will base its wipe pattern on a movement from the blackest to the whitest area in the graphics file or on a pattern you've provided.

In other words, by using a grayscale image you've created in Photoshop Elements, you can design virtually any transitional wipe pattern you can imagine!

For more information on the **Gradient Wipe** and how to use it – plus a free pack of several gradient patterns – see my *Steve's Tips* article "The Gradient Wipe" and the free "Gradient Wipe Pack" on the products page at Muvipix.com.

Set the Default Transition

If you ever use the **Create Slideshow** feature in Premiere Elements (see **Create Slideshow** in **Chapter 17, Explore the Project Media Panel**) you'll note that it offers you the option of applying the **Default Transition** between all of your slides.

By default, that transition is a **Cross-Dissolve**. However, you can designate any transition in the **Transition** panel as the **Default Transition**.

To designate a transition as your default, **right-click** on the selected transition in the **Transitions** panel (**Ctrl-click** on a Mac) and select the **Set Selected as Default Transition** option.

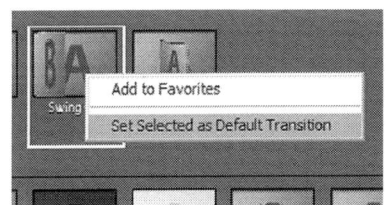

Chapter 26

Customize Effects in the Properties Panel
Adjusting your effects settings

The Properties panel is second only to the Timeline/Sceneline panel as the most powerful and important workspace in Premiere Elements.

The Timeline/Sceneline panel may be where you assemble, trim and order your clips, but the Properties panel is where you make the movie magic happen!

It's where the effects are added, adjusted and removed. It's where motion paths and many special effects are created.

Four ways to
open the
Properties panel

Select Properties
from the Window
drop-down menu.

Click Edit Effects
in the Effects
panel.

Click on the
Properties (list)
icon on the
timeline or
sceneline.

Right-click on a
clip (Ctrl-click on a Mac)
on your project's
timeline or sceneline
and select
Show Properties.

Open the Properties panel

When an effect is added to a clip, it is also added to that clip's list of
properties. The effect can then be adjusted, removed or keyframed in the
Properties panel.

You can launch the **Properties** panel workspace for any clip on your
timeline or sceneline in a number of ways:

- **Click on the Properties button** on the **Timeline/Sceneline** panel.
  You'll need to then click on a clip on your sceneline or timeline to see
  its properties and effects;

- **Right-click on a clip** on your timeline or sceneline (**Ctrl-click** on a
  Mac) and select **Show Properties**;

- Click to select a clip on your timeline or sceneline and, in the **Effects**
  panel, click the **Edit Effects button**; or

- Select **Properties** from the **Window** drop-down menu

Every clip has its own **Properties** panel, and when you select a clip and open
the panel, you'll see the properties for that particular clip.

Keyframing is the process of creating motion paths or effects that change
settings over time (such as a **Crop** effect with an animated cropping
movement or a **Ripple** effect that shows actual, moving ripples across
your clip). For a more detailed discussion of making magic by keyframing,
see **Chapter 27, Keyframing**.

The Properties panel

The Properties panel lists all effects applied to a clip, including certain default properties.

The default video properties are Motion and Opacity.

The default Audio properties are Volume and Balance.

Click triangle to open settings for your effects and properties.

Enable/disable effect or property.

Reset selected effect to default.

Loop audio playback for this clip.

Play audio for this clip.

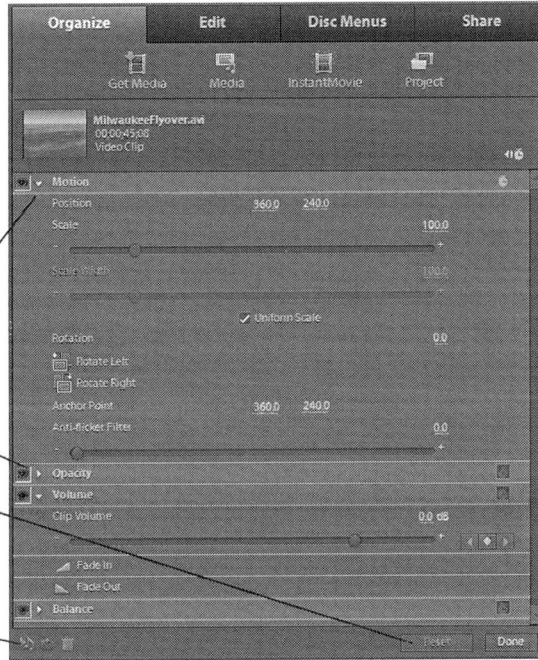

Default clip properties

There are some properties that are attached to every clip by default. Which of these appear in that clip's **Properties** panel depends on whether the clip is video only, audio only or both.

To see the individual settings for any effect or property, or to make an adjustment to a property or effect, click on the little, white triangle to the left of the property's listing. This will open the property and display its individual settings, as in the illustration above.

The default properties for every video or still clip are:

Motion. Includes the properties of **Position, Scale** and **Rotation** – the settings used to keyframe motion paths. (See **Chapter 27, Keyframing** for detailed information on how to create motion paths using these properties.)

Position is the position of the center of a clip in a video frame, measured in pixels.

Scale is the size or resizing measurement of your clip, listed as a percentage.

Rotation's setting is a measure of degrees of angle imposed on your video image.

The settings for the **Motion** properties can be changed numerically or, more intuitively, by clicking on the video image in the **Monitor** panel and dragging it or its corner angles to change its position, size or rotation.

Opacity. Opacity is the transparency level of a clip. (Well, technically opacity is the *non*-transparency level of a clip.)

The fading in or out of a clip (added to a video clip by right-clicking and selecting **Fade in** or **Fade Out**) is actually a function of **Opacity**, using keyframing to bring it from 0% opacity to 100% or vice versa.

The default properties for every audio clip are:

Volume. The sound level on an audio clip.

This effect is one of the most common to keyframe, so that levels can be set for specific points on a clip. The easiest way to keyframe the audio levels for a clip is right on the **Timeline** (as discussed in **Adjust the audio levels at specific points in your video** in **Chapter 20, Edit Audio on the Timeline**).

Balance. Balance affects the audio levels for left and right stereo audio channels relative to each other.

As effects are added to a clip, they are added to the list of effects and properties in that clip's **Properties** panel.

Many effects can be added to a single clip, and you can even add multiples of the *same* effect to increase its intensity.

To increase the audio level of a particularly quiet clip, for instance, you can add several **Volume** effects to it and adjust the slider in the **Properties** panel for each to its maximum setting (as in **Adjust an effect or property**, below) until the clip's audio is at an acceptable level.

(For more information on adding effects, see **Finding and applying an effect** in **Chapter 24, Add Video and Audio Effects.**)

Many effects, when first applied, may not show a significant change in your clip at their default settings. You may need to adjust the effect's settings in the **Properties** panel to see any real change.

Adjust an effect or property

Once you've opened the **Properties** panel for a clip, you'll see a list of all of the effects added to that clip as well as the default properties of **Image Control, Motion, Opacity, Volume** and **Balance,** as applicable.

Click the little white triangle to the left of any effect or property listing to display its settings controls.

Some effects (such as **Lightning**) offer dozens of settings for customizing the effect. Others (such as **Posterize**) may offer only a few – or even a single "intensity adjustment" slider.

Many effects (**Spherize**, for instance) will show almost no effect when applied to your clip *until* you adjust their settings.

Adjusting effects in the Properties panel

Open the effect's properties to adjust using numbers or the sliders.

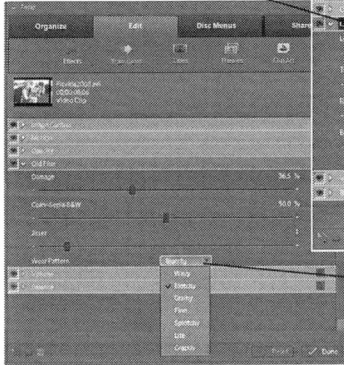

Many effects can be adjusted by selecting the effects listing for the clip in the Properties panel and dragging the corner handles in the Monitor display.

Settings vary with the specifics of an effect, and may even include a sub-menu of presets.

In nearly every case, once you've applied an effect to a clip, you'll need to change the settings to see any significant change to your audio or video. (A few effects, such as the **Black & White** effect, have no settings at all. They are either on or off.)

There are always several ways to adjust the settings for an effect.

Numerically – The numbers that represent an effect can, depending on the effect, represent the effect's **Position** (measured in pixels across the frame), percentage (as in **Opacity**) or intensity. To change a number, click on it and type in a new amount.

Alternatively, you can click and drag right and left over the number to increase or decrease its level.

Sliders – The intensity or percentage for a large number of effects settings can be increased or decreased by moving sliders back and forth in the **Properties** panel.

On the Monitor – The most intuitive way to adjust many effects is to click to highlight the effect in the **Properties** panel and then make your adjustments right on the video displayed in the **Monitor**.

When the effect listing is selected in the **Properties** panel, a position marker or corner handles for many effects will appear on the clip in the **Monitor**, as illustrated above. You can then click on this marker or corner handles and drag them into your desired positions.

For effects that involve motion (such as repositioning, rotating or resizing the video image) dragging the corner handles in the monitor will move, turn or resize the image.

Disable or remove an effect

Once you've adjusted the settings for an effect, you can do a before-and-after comparison by temporarily turning off – or disabling – the effect.

To temporarily turn off the effect, click on the eyeball icon to the left of the effect or property listing in the **Properties** panel.

Effect enabled

The eyeball will disappear and so will the effect's change on your video image.

Effect disabled

To turn the effect back on, click on the same spot. The eyeball icon will return and the effect will once again be enabled.

To remove an effect from a clip, **right-click** on the effect's listing in the **Properties** panel (**Ctrl-click** on a Mac) and select **Delete Selected Effect**. Alternatively, you can click to select the effect and click the trashcan icon at the bottom of the panel.

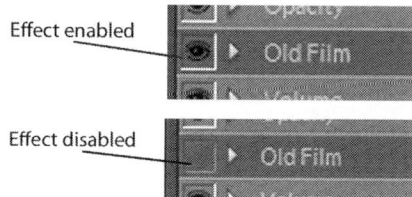

For effects that involve shaping or sizing (such as scaling, cropping or using one of the garbage mattes) dragging the corner handles will reshape the image or affected area.

Once you start adjusting the settings, the changes will be immediately displayed in your **Monitor** panel. (If they're not, it's because the **CTI** playhead isn't positioned over the clip you're adjusting on your timeline.) The exception is the **Lightning** effect, which is so intensive and erratic that you'll need to play back the clip to see how your adjusted settings have affected the clip.

Types of effects settings

Just as there is a wide variety of effects (some that shift colors, some that create transparency [see **Chroma Key** and **Videomerge** in **Chapter 24, Add Video and Audio Effects**], some that reshape or distort your video image), there is a wide variety of ways to change the *settings* for these effects.

Some settings increase the intensity of an effect. Some add optional elements to the effect. Other settings, depending on the effect, may shift color or define which areas on your video image are affected.

The **Crop** effect is an example. The settings for the crop effect define the percentage of the video image that will be cropped from each side. Dragging a slider representing any side's settings (or clicking to select the effect listing in the **Properties** panel and then dragging on the corner handles that become activated on the video image in the **Monitor**) crops away the clip's sides.

Additionally, any effect's settings can be set to change as the clip plays, creating an animated change, using **keyframes**.

- The **Basic 3D** effect, for instance, can be keyframed to create the illusion that your video image is tumbling back into space.
- The **Crop** effect can be animated using keyframes so that the amount of the video image that is cut away changes over the course of the clip.

For more information on how to create these types of motion paths and animated effects, see **Chapter 27, Keyframing** .

Save a custom Preset

Once you've adjusted, or even keyframed an effect or property (To learn more about keyframing and creating motion paths, see **Chapter 27, Keyframing**), you can save it as a **Preset** so that you can use it on another clip, even in another project.

To save your effect setting or keyframed effect as a **Preset**, **right-click** on the effect's listing in the **Properties** panel (**Ctrl-click** on a Mac) and select **Save Preset**.

The option screen will then prompt you to name your preset.

If your effect includes a keyframed motion, the screen will ask you if you'd like to set this animation to appear at the beginning or end of the clip it is applied to.

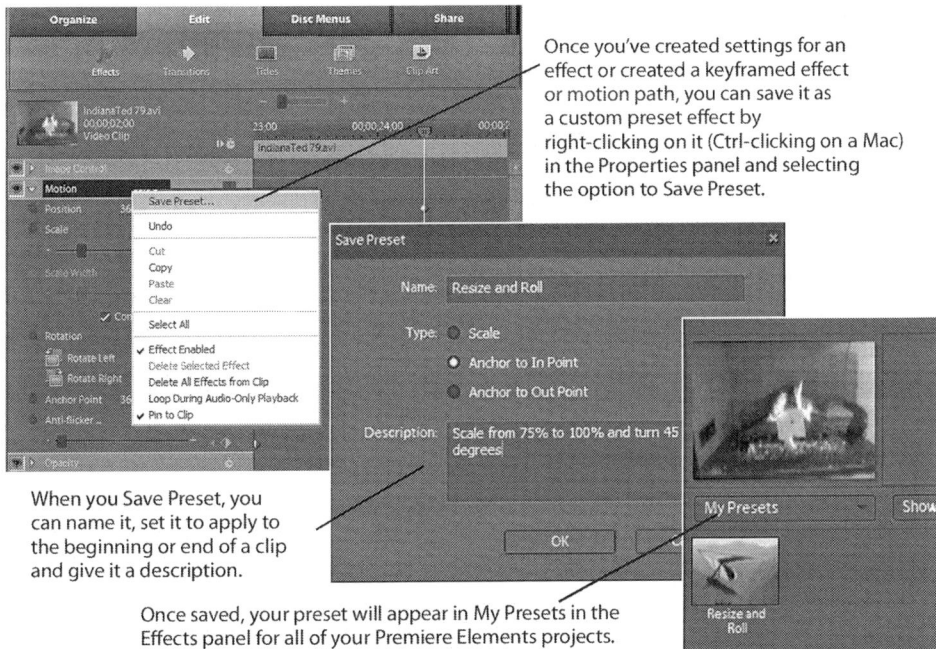

Once you've created settings for an effect or created a keyframed effect or motion path, you can save it as a custom preset effect by right-clicking on it (Ctrl-clicking on a Mac) in the Properties panel and selecting the option to Save Preset.

When you Save Preset, you can name it, set it to apply to the beginning or end of a clip and give it a description.

Once saved, your preset will appear in My Presets in the Effects panel for all of your Premiere Elements projects.

You can also include a description of the effect, if you'd like.

Click **OK** to save the **Preset**.

The new Preset will be available under **My Presets**, on the drop-down menu in the **Effects** panel. (See **Chapter 24, Add Video and Audio Effects** for more information.) You can apply this preset to any clip, just as you would apply any effect or any of the default presets, by dragging it onto a clip or by selecting the clip and clicking the **Effects** panel's **Apply** button.

Applying the preset to a clip automatically applies the motion path or effect, at the settings you initially customized, including any keyframed motion you've added to it.

Paste Attributes

If you've created an effect – even one that includes keyframed motion – for one clip, you can easily apply it several other clips in just a few clicks using **Paste Attributes**.

Right-click on a clip on your timeline to which you've added your effect or keyframes (**Ctrl-click** on a Mac) select **Copy** from the context menu.

Then select another clip – or even a group of clips – **right-click** (or **Ctrl-click**) and select **Paste Attributes**. All of the original clip's effects, adjustments and keyframed actions will automatically be applied to your selected clips!

Chapter 27

Keyframing
Animating effects and creating motion paths

Keyframing is the system that Premiere Elements uses to create motion paths, and to create and control effects that change their settings over time.

With keyframing, you can control the level of an effect or the scale and/or position of a clip at precise points throughout the duration of the clip.

You can raise and lower the audio level at precise points; you can create panning and zooming around a photo; you can even animate, at precise points in any clip, the intensity or movement of a video effect.

Keyframing is about creating animated effects or motion paths using points representing different position or effect settings.

Premiere Elements creates a smooth, animated transition between these "keyframes."

A motion path between Position and Scale settings on a photograph is called a motion path or a Pan & Zoom – or, commonly, a Ken Burns effect.

The principle is a simple one: You indicate which two or more points (**keyframes**) on your clip represent settings for a position, scale, effect or level of an effect and the program automatically generates the transitional frames between those points.

You can, for instance, using **Scale** and **Position** settings, set one keyframe point to display a close-up of one corner of a still photo in your video frame, and then set the **Scale** and **Position** of the next keyframe point to display the entire photo. Premiere Elements will then automatically create the smooth motion path between those two positions, seeming to zoom out from the corner to a view of the entire photo.

With Premiere Elements, you can add any number of keyframes to a clip, creating as much motion or as many variations in your effects' settings as you'd like.

But the real power of this tool is in how easy it is to revise and adjust those positions and settings, giving you, the user, the ability to fine tune your path or effect until it is precisely the effect you want to achieve.

Although there are other workspaces in which you can create and edit keyframes (See **Adjust the audio levels at specific points in your video**, in **Chapter 20, Edit Audio on the Timeline**), most of your keyframing work will likely be done on the **Properties** panel.

You can open the **Properties** panel for any clip by:

- **Clicking on the Properties button** on the **Timeline/Sceneline** panel. You'll need to then click on a clip on your sceneline or timeline to see its properties and effects;

- **Right-clicking on a clip** on timeline or sceneline (**Ctrl-clicking** on a Mac) and selecting **Show Properties**;

- Clicking to select a clip on your timeline or sceneline and, on the **Effects** panel, clicking the **Edit Effects button**; or

- Selecting **Properties** from the **Window** drop-down on the Menu Bar.

(For more information about opening the **Properties** panel for a clip and adjusting effects, see **Chapter 26, Customize Effect in the Properties Panel**.)

Keyframing vs. overall adjusting an effect

Until you begin a keyframing session (by clicking **Toggle Animation**, as described below), any positioning, scaling or settings you make for an effect or property in the **Properties** panel will apply to the *entire* clip.

In other words, if you change the **Scale** to 50%, your entire clip will appear at 50% of its size.

However, once you click **Toggle Animation** (the little stopwatch icon) and turn on keyframing, every change to the effect or property you make will generate a **keyframe point** at the position of the **CTI** (Current Time Indicator) on your timeline.

It becomes a sort of "waypoint" for your effect or motion path.

When you create another keyframe point later in the clip and apply new settings to the effect or property, the program will create a path of motion, animation or transition between the two points.

Open a keyframing session

When you first open the **Properties** panel for a clip, the keyframing workspace is hidden.

To reveal this workspace (the **Properties panel timeline**), click on the **Show Keyframes** button (the stopwatch icon with the arrow pointing left) in the upper right of the panel, as illustrated on the following page.

Accessing and understanding the Properties panel and the keyframing workspace

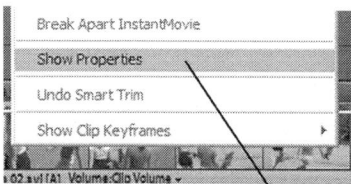

Easiest access to the Properties panel is by right-clicking on a clip on your timeline or sceneline (Ctrl-clicking on a Mac) and selecting Show Properties.

Click on the triangle to the left of the effect listing to open the effect detail settings. To create a motion path, open the Motion properties.

Click on the Show Keyframes button to open the Properties panel Timeline.

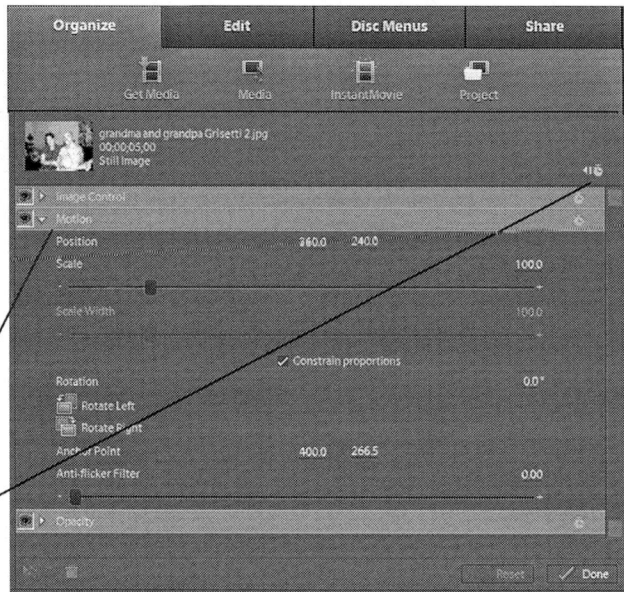

You can widen the display of this timeline by dragging on the edge between the timeline area and the effects and properties listings.

The **Properties panel timeline** (illustrated on the facing page) is your workspace for creating, adjusting and editing your keyframes.

The time positions on this timeline represent positions, in time, on the clip itself. In fact, if you're editing in timeline mode, you'll notice that, as you move the **CTI** on the **Properties panel timeline,** the **CTI** on your project's main timeline will move in sync with it.

Create a simple motion path using keyframes

To demonstrate how to use keyframes, we'll create a simple motion path – a pan and zoom from the middle of a photo.

1. With the **Properties** panel open and a still photo clip selected on your timeline or sceneline, click on the triangle to the left of the **Motion** property listing to reveal the settings for **Motion – Position, Scale** and **Rotation.**

2. Turn on keyframing for the **Motion** property by clicking on the **Toggle Animation** button (the stopwatch at the right end of the effect or property listing, as indicated at the top of the next page).

    When you click the **Toggle Animation** button, a keyframe point – or set of keyframe points – is automatically created at the position of the **CTI** representing the current settings for that effect.

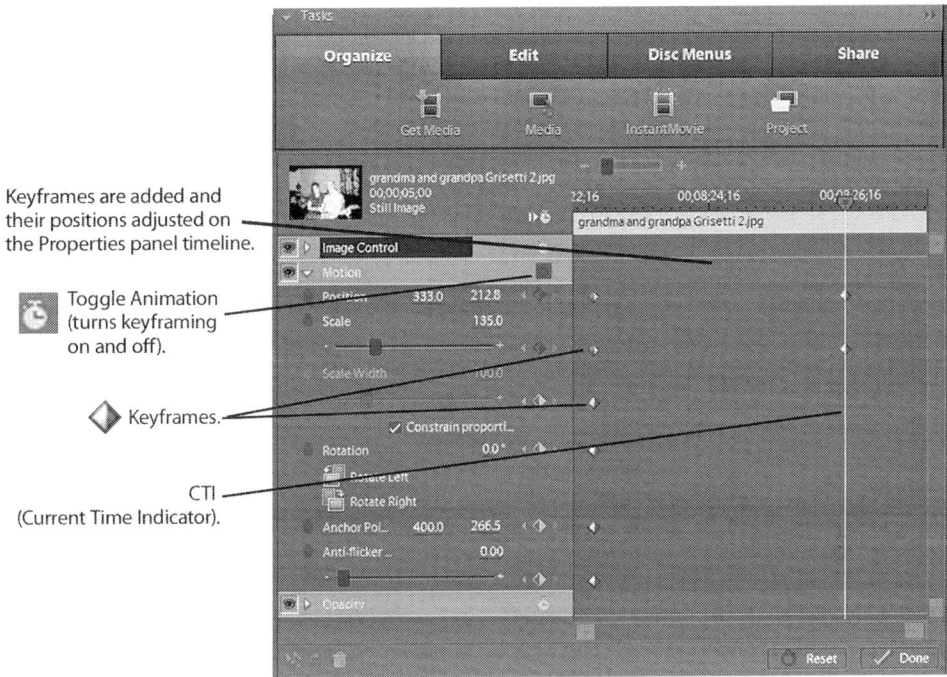

Keyframes are added and their positions adjusted on the Properties panel timeline.

Toggle Animation (turns keyframing on and off).

Keyframes.

CTI (Current Time Indicator).

3. Move the **CTI** to a new position, a few seconds to the right, on the clip's **Properties panel timeline.** Then change the **Position** and **Scale** settings, by changing the setting numbers or by clicking on the clip in the **Monitor** panel and either dragging the screen image to a new position or dragging on its corner handles, as in the illustration on the following page.

   As you change the settings at this new **CTI** position, new keyframe points will automatically be generated on the **Properties panel timeline**. (Note that you can also manually create new keyframes by clicking on the diamond-shaped **Make Keyframe** buttons to the right of each effect's setting.)

You have just created a simple motion path (as illustrated on the next page)!

If you play back the clip, you can see how the program creates the movement between your two sets of keyframe points, using your keyframed settings to define the path.

Edit your keyframes

The beauty of the keyframing tool is that any motion path or effects transition is infinitely adjustable.

By dragging the keyframe points closer together or further apart on the **Properties panel timeline**, you can control the speed at which the motion occurs. (The closer the keyframes are to each other, the faster the animation.)

317

A Simple Motion Path Created with Keyframes

CTI at the beginning of the clip.

Clicking Toggle Animation creates keyframe points for all settings for the effect or property.

When the CTI is in a new position, any changes to any setting automatically creates new keyframe points.

A line on the Monitor represents the path of motion in pan & zoom.

Details of Properties panel Motion settings.

Toggle Animation button.

Position is the location of the clip relative to the center of the frame, measured in pixels.

Scale is the percentage the clip has been increased or decreased in size.

Jump CTI to previous keyframe point on timeline.

Create new keyframe point at CTI's current position.

Jump to next keyframe point on timeline.

As with most effects, Motion's Position and Scale settings can be changed numerically here, or by clicking on the image in the Monitor and either dragging it to a new position or resizing it by dragging on the corner points.

You can add more keyframe points and/or delete the ones you don't want. And, if you really want to go deep, by **right-clicking** on any keyframe point (**Ctrl-clicking** on a Mac) you can select the option to use **Bezier** control handles to change the shape of the motion path or vary the speed throughout the motion.

Many applications for keyframing

Keyframing is used to control audio volume levels at precise points in your video project. (For more on controlling audio levels with keyframes, see **Adjust the audio levels at specific points in your video** in **Chapter 20, Edit Audio on Your Timeline**.)

Using Keyframes to create animated effects

Using Basic 3D effect with keyframes to animate screen image to spin in 3D.

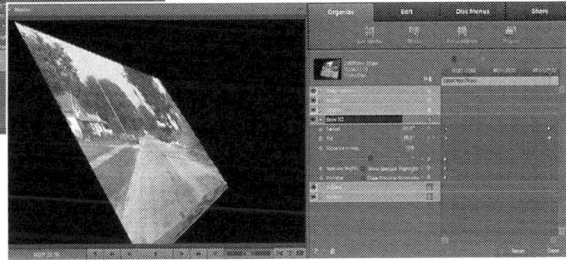

Using keyframes with Crop effect to animate and reposition trimmed sides of screen image.

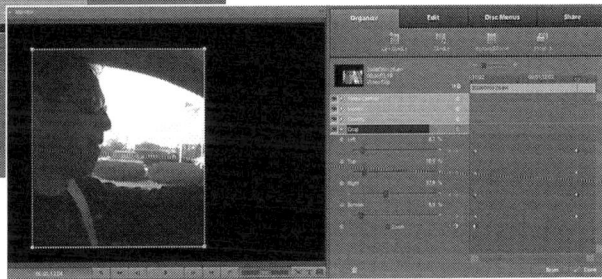

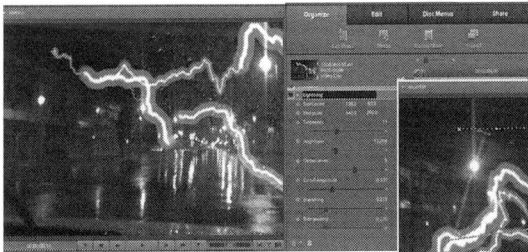

Using keyframes to change endpoints of Lightning over time so that the effect "follows" an image across the screen.

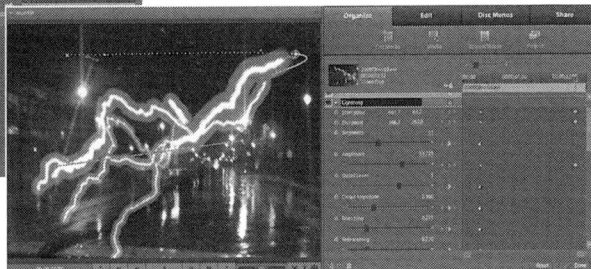

With keyframing, you can also control effects, such as **Crop**, so that the area of your image that's cropped widens, narrows or changes position as the clip plays, as illustrated above.

Or you can very precisely increase or decrease the intensity of an effect on a clip or animate a **Picture-in-Picture** effect. (See **Use L-cuts, J-cuts and multiple tracks** in **Chapter 19, Edit Your Video in Timeline Mode**.)

You can even use keyframes to create an animated 3D movement for your video image using the **Camera View** or **Basic 3D** effect so that your video images seems to tumble head over heels in space.

Indeed, mastering the keyframing tool is the key to getting to the deeper aspects of Premiere Elements. (It also plays a major role in Adobe After Effects and Apple's Final Cut programs.)

It may not seem intuitive at first. But, once you develop a feel for how it works, you'll soon find yourself able to see all kinds of applications for it in creating and refining all manner of visual and audio effects.

For more information on some of the deeper aspects of keyframing and their applications, see my *Steve's Tips* articles "Advanced Keyframing: Editing on the Properties Panel Timeline" and "Advanced Keyframing 2: Keyframing Effects," available on the products page at Muvipix.com.

There is practically no limit to the special video and audio effects you can create with Premiere Elements.

If you'd like to learn some advanced tricks with keyframing– like creating explosions in the sky or having a person confront his identical twin, making your photos look three-dimensional or creating amazing titling effects – check out my book *Cool Tricks & Hot Tips for Adobe Premiere Elements*.

Full of bright, colorful illustrations and step-by-step instructions for creating 50 very cool special effects – with dozens of helpful "Hot Tips" thrown in for good measure – it's a book that will show you the amazing potential of this simple, inexpensive program.

The book is available through major book stores online as well as at the Muvipix.com store.

For more information as well as examples of some of the effects you'll learn to create, see Muvipix.com/CoolTricks.

Add Menu Markers

Select a Menu Template

Customize Your Menu's Background and Music

Customize Your Menu's Text

Add Media to a Menu's "Drop Zone"

Chapter 28

Create DVD and BluRay Disc Menus
Authoring your DVDs and BluRay discs

Once you've finished your Premiere Elements video project, you'll want to share it in the most attractive package possible.

Premiere Elements includes over 100 templates for creating DVD and BluRay disc menus for your videos. And it includes tools for customizing them in a variety of ways!

Although the DVD and BluRay menu authoring system in Premiere Elements isn't as advanced as it is in many standalone disc menu authoring programs (like Adobe's Encore), you can do a surprising amount to personalize your disc menus just by using Premiere Elements' library of disc menu templates and basic menu customization features.

Once you've applied and customized your disc menus, you can then create a DVD or BluRay disc using the options under the **Share** tab, as described in **Output a DVD or BluRay Disc** in **Chapter 29, Share Your Movie.**

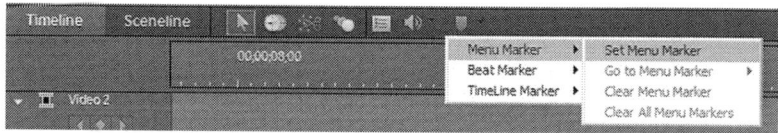

Add Menu Markers to your movie project

The **Set Menu Marker** tool is a very important part of the DVD and BluRay disc authoring process in Premiere Elements.

The **Menu Markers** you place on your timeline or sceneline will link to scene buttons on your disc's menu pages.

Selecting **Set Menu Marker** from the blue **Markers** drop-down menu (as in the illustration above) on the **Timeline/Sceneline** panel creates a **Menu Marker** on your timeline or sceneline at the position of the **CTI** (Current Time Indicator) playhead. You can later drag this marker to any other position on the timeline if you'd like.

When this **Menu Marker** is first created, a **Menu Marker** option screen will open. (You can reopen it at any time by double-clicking on the menu marker on your timeline or by **right-clicking** on your clip on the sceneline (**Ctrl+clicking** on a Mac) and selecting the **Set Menu Marker** option.) This screen includes a number of options for creating your marker.

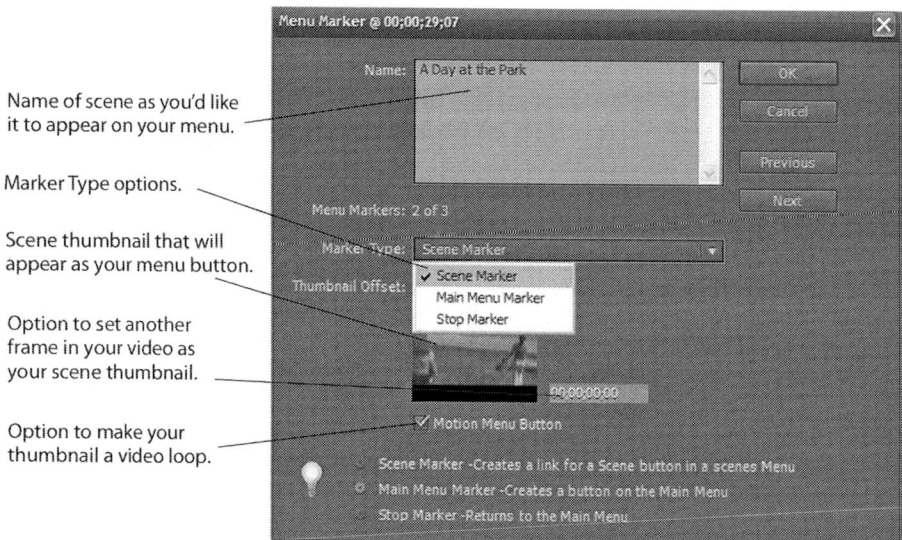

Name of scene as you'd like it to appear on your menu.

Marker Type options.

Scene thumbnail that will appear as your menu button.

Option to set another frame in your video as your scene thumbnail.

Option to make your thumbnail a video loop.

There are three different types of **Menu Markers** (as selected under the **Marker Type** drop-down), each with its own unique function.

Green Scene Menu Markers will be linked to buttons on your DVD or BluRay disc's scene menu page(s).

Blue Main Menu Markers will be linked to buttons on your DVD or BluRay disc's main menu page(s).

Red Stop Markers stop your movie's playback and return your viewer to your disc's main menu. By using these **Stop Markers**, you can create a disc with a number of short movies on it, your viewer returning to the main menu at the end of each.

Type a name for your marker in the space provided. This name will automatically appear as the name of the linked button on your disc's main or scene menu.

The image from your movie displayed in the **Thumbnail Offset** is what will appear as your menu button for this link on your menu page.

Changing the timecode that appears to the right of this thumbnail – either by typing in new numbers or by clicking and dragging across the numbers – will change which frame from your video is displayed as the button link. (Changing this thumbnail image will not affect the location of the marker itself on your project's timeline.)

Checking the **Motion Menu Button** checkbox will cause your button to appear as a short video loop rather than a freeze frame from your video.

For more information on how to create and use **Menu Markers**, see my *Steve's Tips* article "DVD Markers," available on the products page at Muvipix.com.

Add Menu Markers automatically

If you've not yet added menu markers to your project's timeline or sceneline, you will be prompted to create menu markers when you launch the **Templates** workspace. You can then opt to return to the **Edit** workspace and manually add menu markers – or you can select an option to automatically create markers.

- **If you choose to automatically create menu markers**, you'll be prompted with a number of options, including the option to set markers based on time, scene, etc.

- **If you choose not to include menu markers**, the program will generate a menu with a main menu page only and only a **Play** button linking to the beginning of your movie.

- **If you choose not to include menu markers at this time** and you later add a menu marker, a scene menu will automatically be generated for you at that time.

Premiere Elements offers dozens of high-quality, easily customizable menus for your DVDs and BluRay discs in a wide variety of categories.

The basics of adding a Disc Menu template

Premiere Elements comes bundled with well over 100 standard templates, in categories from Entertainment to Travel to Sports to Kids to Birthdays and Weddings – from playful to serious to silly to artistic.

Many of these templates come complete with audio and/or video loops that add life to your menus.

Also, many of these templates include a "drop zone," a designated area on the menu page into which you can place a video clip or still. (More about that on page 336.)

Apply a DVD or BluRay disc menu template

To apply a disc menu template to your project, select the **Disc Menus** tab and click on the **Templates** button.

Premiere Elements 9 includes a library of over 100 DVD and BluRay disc templates in 15 different categories.

If you have a **Plus** premium membership with **Photoshop.com** and an always-on Internet connection, you can find additional templates by selecting the **Plus Members Only** option from the drop-down menu in the **Templates** panel. (For more information on Photoshop.com, see **Chapter 34, Photoshop.com**.)

When you initially launch this workspace, the **Monitor** will be replaced by the **Disc Layout** panel, and the Tasks panel will display the library of disc menu templates.

You can filter this list by selecting a category of templates from the panel's category drop-down menu. You can then browse the templates in the panel or go directly to a specific template by selecting it from the second drop-down menu (which displays **Show All** by default).

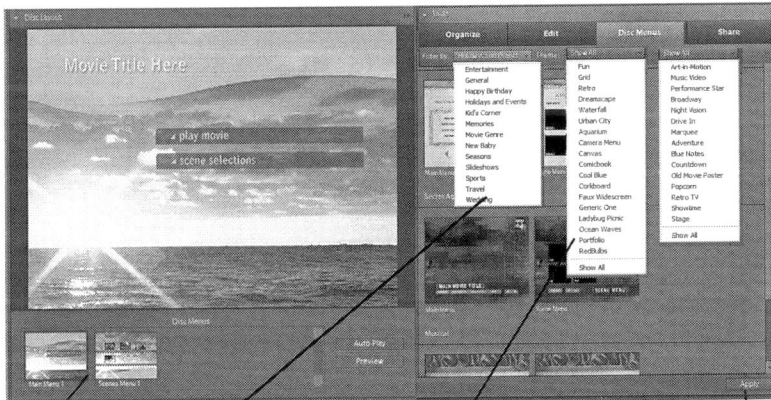

Select a Disc Menu category   View all or filter a specific template

Apply template

The Disc Layout panel will display your applied template
with links to your Menu Markers automatically generated

Once you've selected a template by clicking on it, click the **Apply** button in
the lower right of the panel.

Once you've applied a template, the **Disc Layout** panel will display your
entire menu set as thumbnails in the **Disc Menus** preview window at
the bottom of the panel. The program will add as many extra pages as
necessary to accommodate all of your scene and main menu markers.

The **Disc Layout** panel's main window will initially display your main menu,
as illustrated above. If you click on any of the menu page thumbnails in the
Disc Menus window, that menu page will appear in the big **Disc Layout**
window.

As mentioned in **Add Menu Markers**, earlier in this chapter, the names you
give to your main and scene menu markers will appear as the names of the
scene links and main menu links on your disc menus.

To see your menu system in action and test drive the links embedded in it,
click the **Preview** button.

An important note about this **Disc Layout Preview**: The purpose of the
preview is to allow you to see a *representation* of how your menu elements
will come together and to allow you to test the navigation buttons.

*It is not meant to be a representation of the **quality** of your final menu
template.* And, in fact, you'll probably be a bit disappointed with the
quality of the picture onscreen. **Preview** is merely an opportunity for you
test your navigation buttons.

So don't panic. Once your project is rendered and encoded as a disc, the
quality will be up to DVD or BluRay standards.

Click on background in Disc Layout panel to open background replacement options

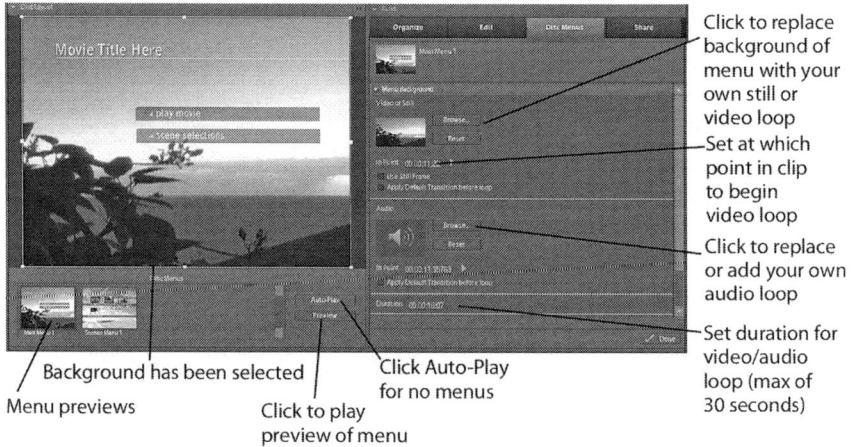

Click to replace background of menu with your own still or video loop

Set at which point in clip to begin video loop

Click to replace or add your own audio loop

Set duration for video/audio loop (max of 30 seconds)

Background has been selected

Menu previews

Click to play preview of menu

Click Auto-Play for no menus

Customize your menus

Adobe has made it very easy to customize your menu pages right in this **Disc Menus** workspace. As a matter of fact, once you've applied a template, as described above, in the **Disc Menus** workspace, the Tasks panel will change from a view of the templates library to the menu customization workspace.

Which customization options are available in this panel depends on which elements you have slicked to select on the **Disc Layout** panel.

- **If you have the menu background selected** in the **Disc Layout** panel, the Tasks panel will display options for replacing the menu background with a still, video and/or audio clip.

- **If you have a block of text selected** in the **Disc Layout** panel, the Tasks panel will display options for customizing the text's font, style and color.

- **If you have a menu button selected** that includes a thumbnail image selected in the **Disc Layout** panel, the Tasks panel will display options for replacing or customizing the thumbnail image as well as options for customizing the accompanying text's font, style and color.

Customize a menu background

When you have the menu page background selected in the **Disc Layout** panel, the Tasks panel will display options for replacing the background with a still or video, and/or replacing or adding a music or audio clip.

To add or replace any of these elements, click the **Browse** button and browse to a video clip, photo or audio clip on your computer.

(Note that some menu templates include foreground graphics that will remain, even if you swap out the background, and may partially obscure your new background. If you'd prefer not to include these graphics in your menus, you may want to start with one of the Generic templates, such as the one in the General set.)

Above, a new background clip has replaced the template background. When a text block is selected, the customization menu changes to a font, style and text color selection option screen. (Double-click on a text block to customize the content.)

If you're using a video clip as your menu background:

- You can use the **In Point** timecode (either by dragging your mouse across the numbers or by playing to a particular point) to set your video loop to begin at a specific point in the clip.

- You can set the **Duration** of the video loop for any length up to 30 seconds.

You can also add or swap out audio loops that play as your menus are displayed. And, likewise, you can set the **In Point** for your audio clip such that the audio loop begins playing at any point in the song or clip.

To revert back to your menu's default background, music or sound, click on the appropriate **Reset** button.

Customize your text and styles

When you click to select a text block in the **Disc Layout** panel, the text customization workspace will display in the Tasks panel.

Using this menu, you can change the font, font size and even color of the text.

The **Apply to All Text Items** button will apply your current font and text style to all of the text that appears on this menu page.

Once you've customized the look of your text, you can also customize its position on the menu page.

When a scene button or text block is selected, the Disc Menus panel will display options for customizing the text font, style and thumbnail with a still or video loop (motion menu).

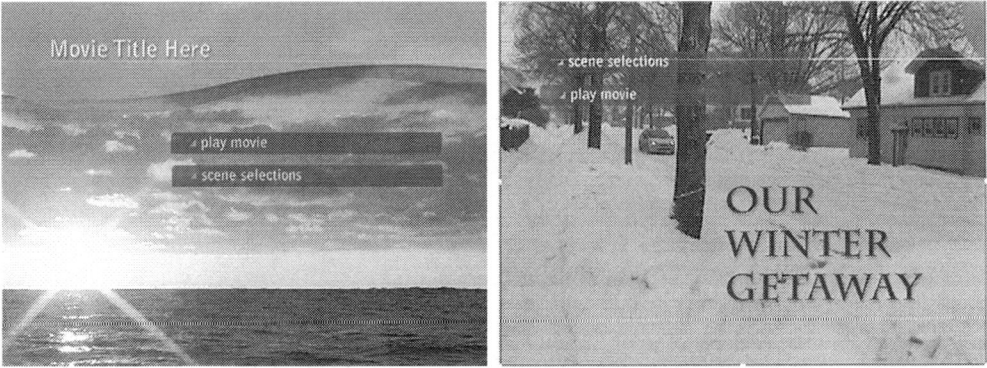

A before-and-after look at a customized Premiere Elements menu template.

Click on the text block or button on the **Disc Layout** monitor and drag it to where you'd like it to appear.

Double-click on a text block to edit or replace the content.

Add your media to a menu page "drop zone"

A number of disc menu templates include a "drop zone" – a designated area on the template into which you can drag your own pictures or videos.

You'll find examples of this in the Movie Genre/Fairytale template and the Wedding/Outdoor Wedding template.

To add a custom still or clip to one of these templates, click the **Organize** tab to open the Premiere Elements **Media** panel, then drag your clip or still from this panel onto the menu page in the **Disc Layout** panel, into the area labeled **"Add Your Media Here."**

(If the clip you want isn't displayed in the **Media** panel, click **Get Media** and browse to it first.)

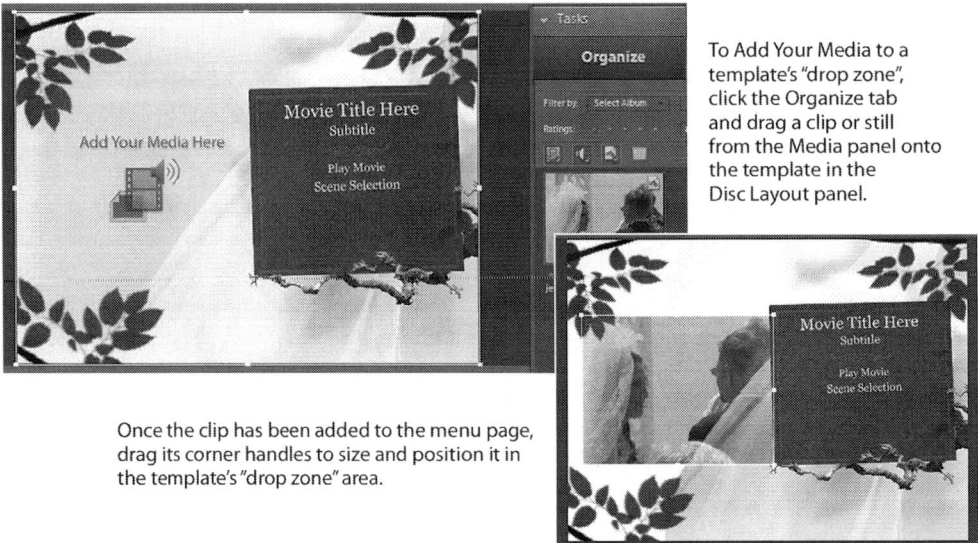

To Add Your Media to a template's "drop zone", click the Organize tab and drag a clip or still from the Media panel onto the template in the Disc Layout panel.

Once the clip has been added to the menu page, drag its corner handles to size and position it in the template's "drop zone" area.

Once you've placed your clip into the menu, drag the corner handles to resize and position it on the menu page.

The **"Add Your Media Here"** graphic is usually a guide for placement, based on the other graphics in the template. In most cases, you can size and place your new background clip wherever you'd like on the page.

An exception would be the General/Fun template, in which you'll need to size and position your clip pretty precisely in order for it to display in the template's provided picture box.

Share to a DVD or BluRay Disc

Share Your Movie Online

Share Your Movie as a Podcast

Share Your Movie as a Computer File

Share Your Movie to a Portable Device

Chapter 29

Share Your Movie
Outputting from Premiere Elements 9

Once you've finished your video masterpiece and – if you're planning to output it to disc – you have applied and customized your disc's menus, you're ready to output your video so that you can share it with the world.

There are a number of ways to output from Premiere Elements 9, and a surprisingly large number of formats you can output to.

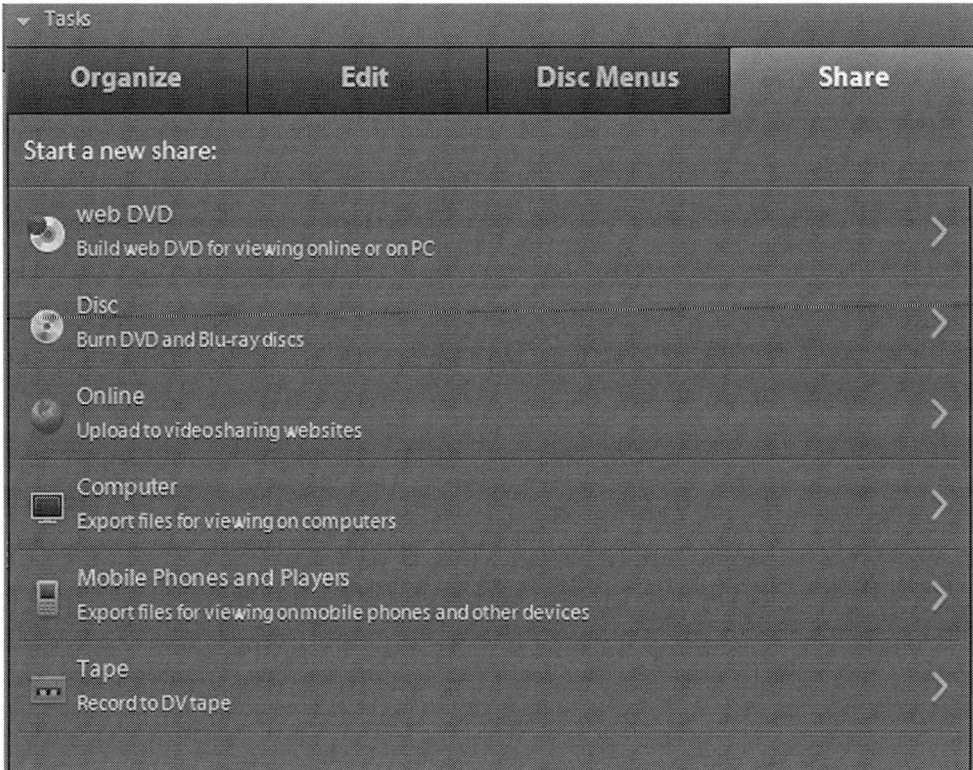

A click on the **Share** tab reveals a list of six output destinations for your video, each of which offers recommended formats and settings for your output as well as more advanced settings for more advanced users.

The **Share** destinations are:

WebDVD – Build a Web DVD for Viewing Online or on a PC

Disc – Burn DVD and BluRay Discs

Online – Upload to Video Sharing Websites

Computer – Export Files for Viewing on Computers

Mobile Phones and Players – Export Files for Viewing on Mobile Phones and Other Devices

Tape – Record to DV or HDV Tape

(If all six options don't show in this **Share** panel, you'll need to resize the panel by dragging on the boundaries between it and the adjoining panels.)

In most cases, these destination names do a pretty good job of leading you to the correct output settings. The exception is the **Computer** destination – which can create files that can be played on a computer, some portable devices and online and can be used to create video clips that can be used in other Premiere Elements projects.

The file-sharing interfaces

No matter which destination and format you choose, there are basically four ways to share your files:

- Burn to a disc.
- Upload to a Web site.
- Save to a file on your computer.
- Save for an external device, like a phone or portable media player.

All of the **Upload to a Web site** options use a similar interface:

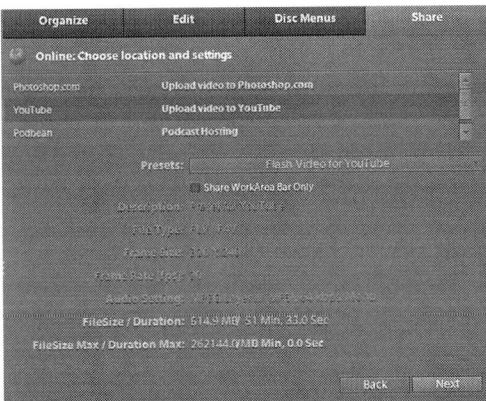

Select an online destination and preset. Click Next.

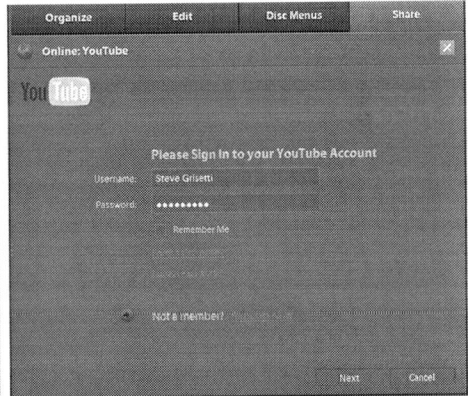

On the logon screen, sign in and the click Next.

Likewise, the options to **save a file to your Computer** and to **save for later uploading to another device** use a similar interface:

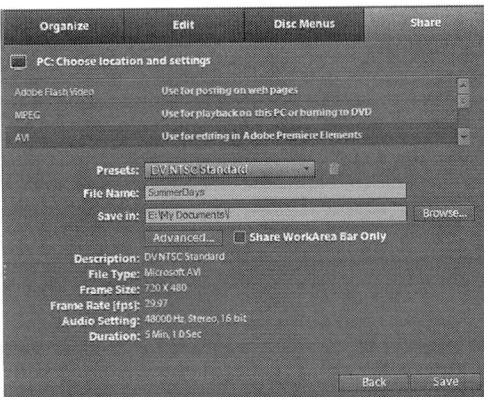

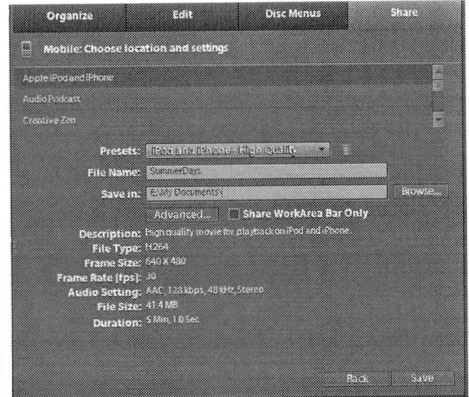

Select a preset, name your file and browse to a location. The saved files can then be moved to another device.

The methods for **burning to a disc** and to **sharing to tape** are detailed in their respective sub-chapters, later in this chapter.

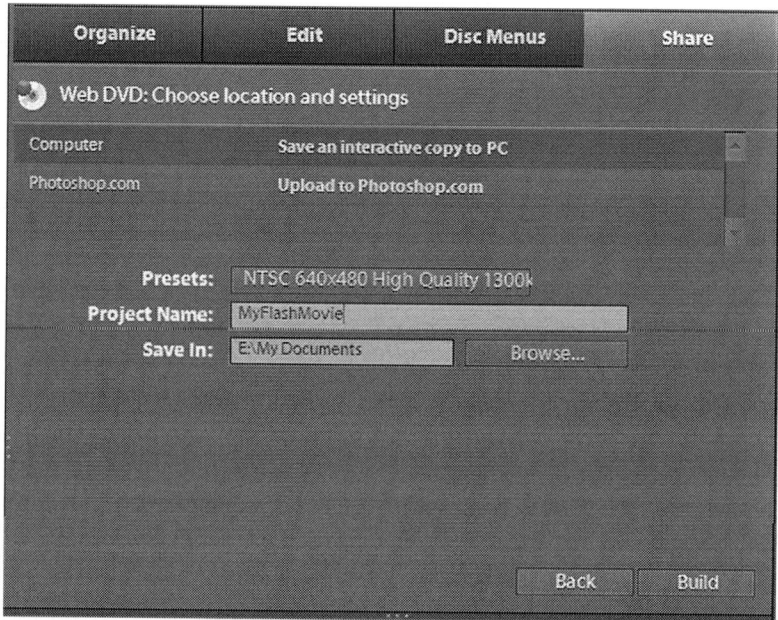

The WebDVD destination, under the Share tab, creates an interactive Web site that functions just like a DVD – complete with menus!

Output to a Web DVD

Web DVDs are interactive FLV and HTML files that can be posted to a Web site, but function like conventional DVDs – complete with main menus, scene menus and scene buttons.

Web DVD menus are created using **Menu Markers** and **Disc Menu** templates, as we describe in **Chapter 28, Create DVDs and BluRay Disc Menus**. However, because of the way they are produced, **Web DVD** files play on a Web browser (Internet Explorer, Safari, etc.) rather than on a traditional DVD or BluRay disc player.

To create a **Web DVD**:

1. Select the **Web DVD** destination under the **Share** tab.

2. On the **Web DVD** option page, select the **Computer** or the **Photoshop.com** option.

3. Name your file and browse to select a **Save In** location.

4. Click the **Make File** button.

A folder of files will be saved to the location you've selected.

Post this entire set of files to a Web site. The **Web DVD** is launched when a viewer goes to the site, connecting to the **Index.html** file.

Likewise, to play the **Web DVD** on a computer, launch the **Index.html** file with your Internet browser.

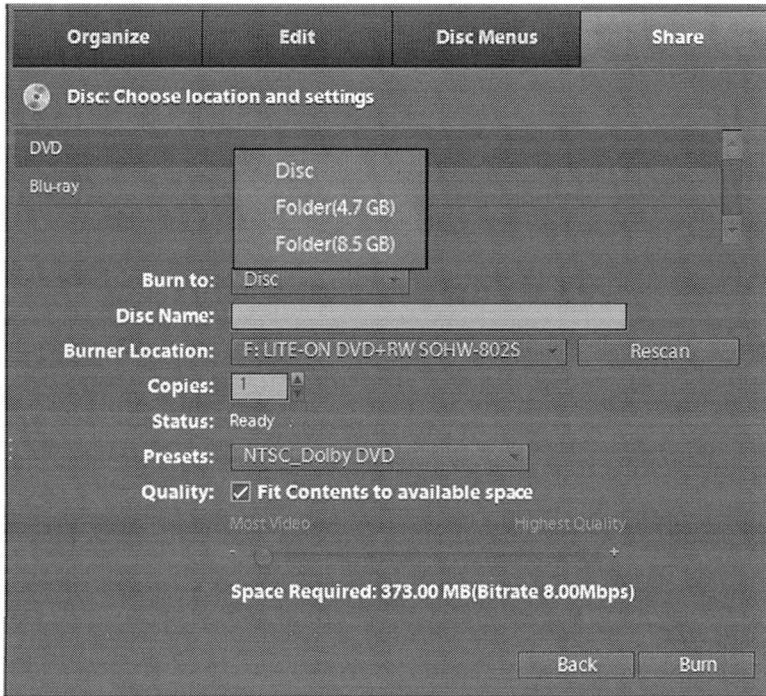

The Disc destination under the Share tab includes the options to burn directly to a disc or to save your DVD files to a folder on your hard drive.

Output to a DVD or BluRay Disc

Probably the most common way to output a movie from your Premiere Elements project is to burn a DVD or high-definition BluRay disc.

Premiere Elements will burn to both single-layer and dual-layer discs and to both standard DVD and BluRay formats. (The program automatically scans your system to see which disc burner hardware you have and if you have a disc in the drive.)

Click to select the disc type you want to create from the listing at the top of the panel.

1. If you are burning a DVD, the **Burn To** drop-down menu will allow you to select the option to burn directly to a disc or to burn your DVD files to a folder on your hard drive for either a single-layer or dual-layer disk.

2. Type the name for your project in the space provided. (This is more important if you plan to burn your disc files to a folder on your hard drive for later burning to a disc.)

3. Click the **Burn** button.

As a rule of thumb, you can fit about 70 minutes of video onto a standard (4.7 gigabyte) DVD at full video quality and about double that onto a dual layer disc.

A BluRay disc (which can store 25 gigabytes of data) can hold about two hours of hi-definition video, while a dual-layer BluRay disc can hold about twice that.

If you put more than these recommended capacities on a disc, Premiere Elements will automatically reduce the quality of the video as needed if you have the **Fit Contents** option checked. (This reduced quality may not be noticeable unless you try to squeeze considerably more content onto the disc than the optimal capacity.)

Increase the odds for disc creation success

In a perfect world, outputting a disc from Premiere Elements would be as simple as selecting the options at this screen and hitting the **Burn** button.

Unfortunately, your computer's operating system is something of a living, continually evolving environment, with programs constantly at war for control over your hardware. And failures to burn directly to a disc with this program are somewhat common – which can be quite frustrating if you've waited hours for the program to encode your disc files, only to have it suddenly throw up an error code at the last minute.

If this is a problem for you (and you'll know because the operation will fail in its very last stages), the simplest solution is to go to the **Burn To** drop-down menu and select the option to burn your files to a **Folder** on your hard drive rather than directly to a disc.

Once these DVD or BluRay files are created, you can then easily use your computer's disc burning software (Nero, RecordNow, etc.) to burn the VIDEO_TS folder that the program creates to a DVD or BluRay disk. This process is detailed in **The "Burn Disc" Workaround** in the **Chapter 30**.

This may seem like an unnecessary workaround at first, but there are a number advantages to using this two-step method for creating discs and very few liabilities. (It certainly doesn't take any more time, and it only adds a few clicks to the process.)

The challenge with home-burned DVDs

Although this is becoming less of an issue as home-burned DVDs and BluRay discs have grown in popularity, it's important to realize that not all DVD and BluRay players can play home-burned discs. This is because the process used to create commercial discs (pressing) is very different than the process you use to create discs on your computer (a chemical process).

Manufacturers have recognized the growing popularity of creating home-burned DVDs and BluRay discs and have been making their players more and more compatible with them. But be prepared for the occasional friend or client who simply can't play a disc you've created!

If nothing else, it makes outputting several copies of your disc easier, since creating each will be a simple matter of burning this same VIDEO_TS folder to another disc (a process which takes only a few minutes).

And, if for no other reason than because direct burns to disc can so commonly fail, we at Muvipix recommend regularly creating your DVDs with this two-step process. It really is worth the minimal extra effort to ensure the job gets done.

You can also increase the odds your disc burn will go smoothly and that your disc will be compatible with every possible DVD or BluRay player by using high-quality media.

Verbatim and Taiyo Yuden are two very reliable disc brands. Store brands, and even other popular name brands, can be a bit iffier. In our not-so-humble opinion, the little extra expense you'll incur by using one of these two quality brands will be more than offset by the knowledge that you'll get the best possible results and compatibility from them.

Also, *NEVER* stick a label onto your DVD or BluRay disc!

Labels can throw the spin and balance off when the discs are loaded into a player and the glue and label can damage the media itself. If you'd like to customize your discs, we recommend that you buy printable discs and use a good inkjet printer with disc printing capabilities. Epson and HP make very nice printers with this feature for under $100.

Upload to a Web site or create a podcast

The **Online** output option is designed to transcode your video to another file format and upload it directly to a web site (including YouTube) in just a few easy steps.

1. Select the **Online** destination.

2. On the **Online** option page, select your online destination: **Photoshop.com, YouTube** or **Podbean**.

   Podbean.com is a site for hosting podcasts – video or audio files that you post online on a regular basis and that your viewers can subscribe to and receive automatically.

   For more information on posting and subscribing to podcasts, see my *Steve's Tips* article "Podcasting with Premier Elements," on the products page of Muvipix.com.

3. Click the **Next** button.

4. **Photoshop.com's** output screen includes the option to automatically notify your friends that you've posted this video.

   Other site's output pages may require you to log on to your site.

5. Click **Next** to post your video.

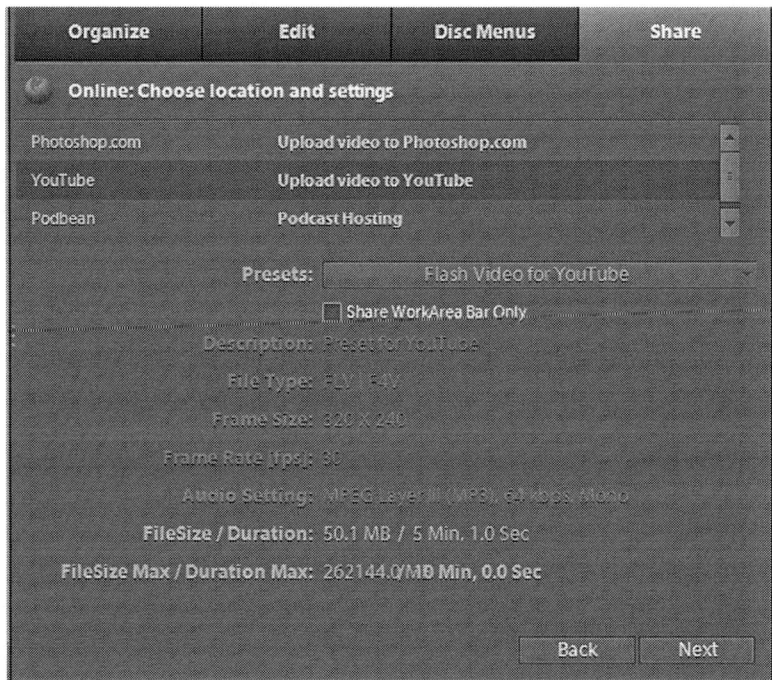

Online options let you load your video directly to a Web site, Photoshop.com, YouTube – or to output a podcast to Podbean!

The **Presets** drop-down menu, by default, will display the optimal file format for uploading. You can also drop-down this menu and select another preset, if you'd like.

To export only the segment of your project defined by the **Work Area Bar**, check the **Share Work Area Bar Only** option. (For more information, see **Output a segment of your video using the Work Area Bar** in **Chapter 19, Edit Your Video in Timeline Mode**.)

As with many automatic functions, this one may not always work as smoothly as it should. (This has less to do with Premiere Elements than with the fact that sites, like YouTube, are constantly changing the way they handle uploaded files.) And, if you have trouble getting your video directly to a site, you can click the **Back** button in the lower right corner of the panel and create your file using the **Computer** output option instead.

Once your video is created and saved to your hard drive (usually as a WMV or MOV file) you can manually upload it to your site using the site's upload interface or using FTP utility software, such as the excellent, free FileZilla or the equally easy-to-use Easy FTP (as we discuss in the **Chapter 30**).

Meantime, go the Premiere Elements's **Edit/Preferences/Web Sharing** and ensure that **Automatically Check for Services** is checked. This is one way of making sure that the Premiere Elements Web site interface is as up to date as possible.

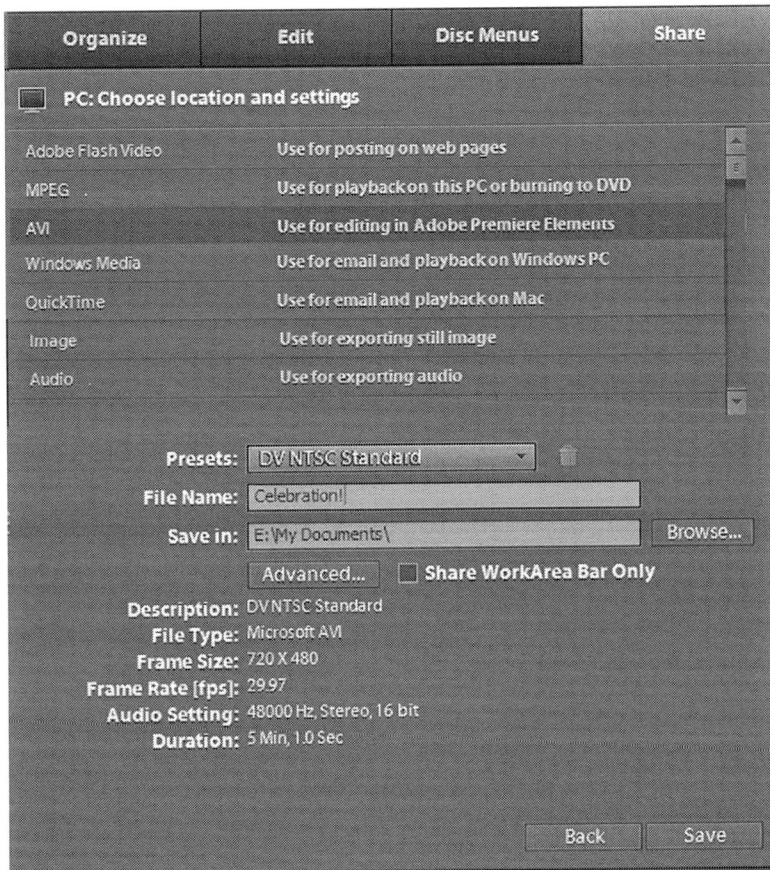

The most versatile output destination is Personal Computer, which allows you to save your video as a Flash, MPEG, DV-AVI, Windows Media, Quicktime (MOV) file, a still photo or an audio file.

Output a file to your computer

The description following the option to share to a **Computer** is a little misleading.

With this option you can not only create videos for viewing on a computer, but you can use it to save to any of the five major video output formats or to a still or audio only file.

In other words, you can not only output videos from this option for PC-based viewing, but you can also create videos that you can then post to web sites, send by e-mail, etc.

Also, this is where you'll find the option to output the all-important **DV-AVI** (full quality video) file (on Windows PCs only), as explained in **Output video for use in another editing project** on page 349.

Next to each file format listing in this **Share** output category is a descriptor explaining the best use for that particular file format. You'll find a detailed discussion of each file format in detail in **Video output formats** on page 353.

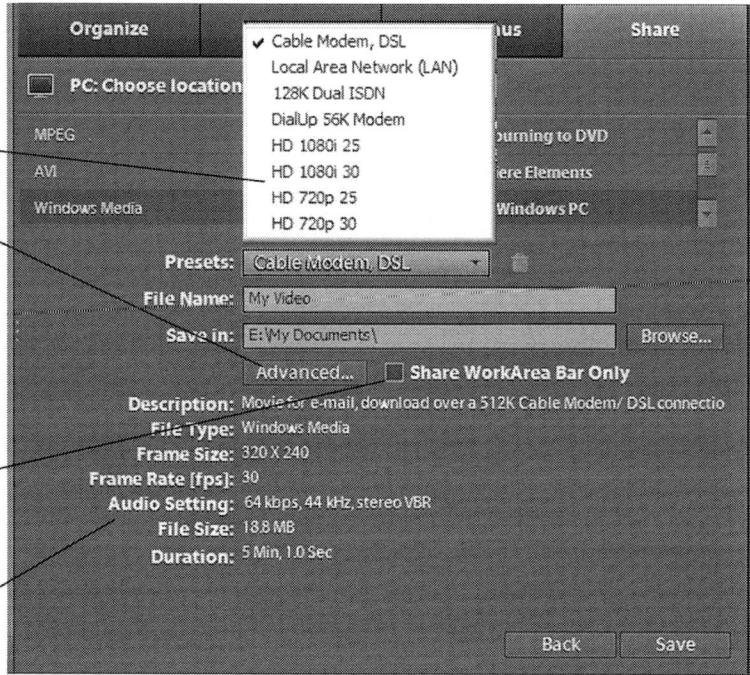

Most output options include a recommended preset and several alternative presets.

Many output options also include Advanced settings.

The Share Work Area Bar Only option allows you to output only a designated portion of your video project.

In half-tone text, the program will also provide you with information on the technical specs of your output file.

A number of these file formats are used for displaying your video on the Web – Flash, or **FLV** files; Windows Media, or **WMV** files (Windows PCs only); and Quicktime, or **MOV** files.

Once you've output any of these file types to your computer's hard drive, you can then use FTP software (such as the excellent FileZilla) or your Web site's upload software to post the video to a site.

This is an excellent workaround if, for some reason, the **Online** output option doesn't work, as discussed earlier in this chapter. (See our **Appendix** for more information on FTP utilities.)

Once you select a file format, the **Presets** drop-down list will display the recommended file compression setting for that output type. If you prefer another setting, you can drop down that list and select a different compression setting or click on the **Advanced** button to access deeper settings.

Once you've selected your output option, click the **Browse** button to select a location on your computer for your file to be saved.

To export only the segment of your project defined by the **Work Area Bar**, check the **Share Work Area Bar Only** option. (For more information, see **Output a segment of your video using the Work Area Bar** in **Chapter 19, Edit Your Video in Timeline Mode**.)

When you've selected all of the appropriate output options, click the **Save** button in the lower right corner of the panel.

Output video for use in another video project

For standard video

If you'd like to export your video project – or even a portion of your project – so that you can import it into another Premiere Elements standard video project on a Windows computer, your best **Share** format is the **DV-AVI**, available as a **Computer Share** output option.

The project you use this type of video file in should use the **DV project preset**, as we discuss in **Chapter 15, Start a New Project**.

The MacIntosh equivalent to the **DV-AVI** file is the **DV-MOV**. To output a **DV-MOV** file from your project, go to the **Share** tab and select the **Computer** destination. From the options listed, select **MOV** and, from the preset drop-down menu, select **DV**.

The file you output will have a **.mov** suffix.

For high-definition video

If you'd like to export your video project – or a portion of your project – from a high-definition project for use in another high-definition project, your best **Share** option is the **MPEG** using the **1440x1080i** preset, available as a **Computer Share** output option.

The project you use this type of video file in should use the **HDV project preset**, as we discuss in **Chapter 15, Start a New Project**.

Why these are the ideal Share options

The ideal source file for Premiere Elements and the universal language for PC-based video editors is the **DV-AVI**s. **DV-AVI**s maintain virtually all of the quality of your original source footage. Further, when used in a project using the **DV project preset**, your video will not need rendering until you apply an effect or transition to it.

For Premiere Elements, the ideal source format for high-definition video is the **HDV** format. When used in a project using the **HDV project preset**, this video will not need rendering until you apply an effect or transition to it.

Working on a long project in short pieces

You'll often find a longer project much easier to work on in shorter pieces. Doing this can minimize system lugging and maximize program responsiveness as well as reduce the likelihood that you'll run into problems when you try to export your video as a DVD or BluRay disc.

Once your segments are completed and output to the appropriate format, open a new project – using the appropriate project preset – and combine the segments into a final mix.

To export only the segment of your project defined by the **Work Area Bar**, check the **Share Work Area Bar Only** option. (For more information, see **Output a segment of your video using the Work Area Bar** in **Chapter 19, Edit Your Video in Timeline Mode**.)

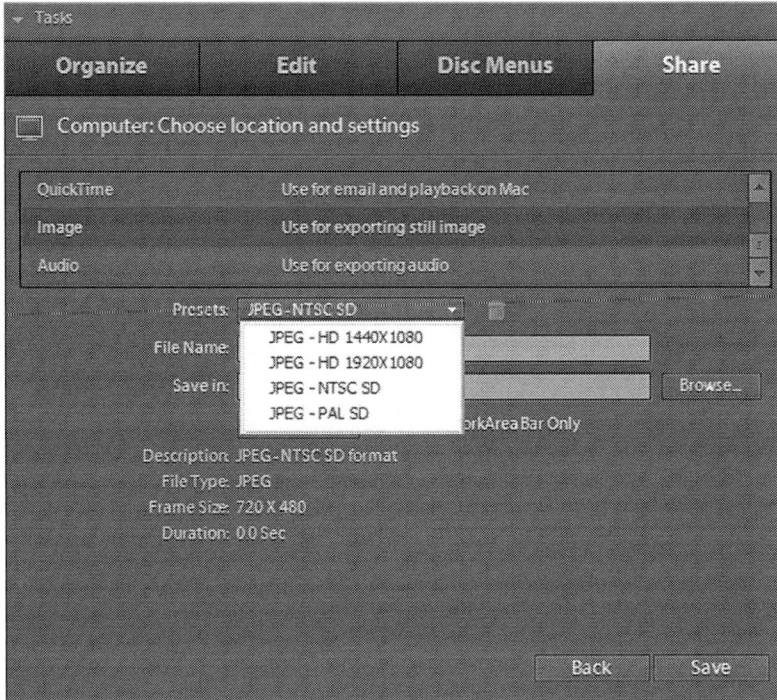

The option to Share an Image includes presets for a number of JPEGs stills.

Output a still of your current video frame

The **Computer** destination in Premiere Elements includes the option to **Share** your video as an **Image**. This **Image** option includes presets for saving the current frame of your video as a **JPEG** or a segment of your video as an **Animated GIF** (at a variety of frame sizes).

The **JPEG** output option here makes a great alternative to the **Freeze Frame** option available within the program's editing interface (discussed in **Chapter 8, Edit with Monitor Panel Tools**) since it includes more options for customizing the settings of your output, including the option to save it as a **JPEG** rather than a BMP file.

The one challenge with these presets is that they are all anamorphic. In other words, they all produce stills with non-square pixels. This is fine if you're outputting a still that you want to use in a video, since video frames are constructed of non-square pixels.

However, in many cases you'll want to output a still that can be printed out or used on a Web page. And, if you were to use one of these anamorphic presets, your printed photo would appear distorted or stretched unnaturally tall or wide.

The sidebar on the facing page shows you how to create your own preset for outputting an image that uses square rather than non-square pixels.

Create a custom JPEG output preset

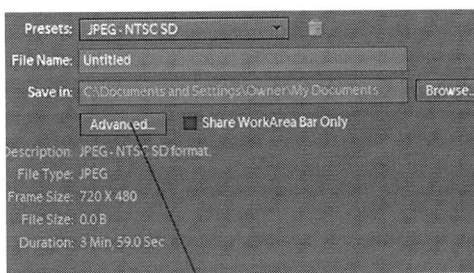

To create a custom square pixel preset, click the Advanced settings button on the Share option screen for outputting an Image.

Uncheck the Constrain Propertions link and change Width and Height to 640 and 480.

Set Aspect Ratio to Square Pixels.
Name the new preset on the pop-up screen.

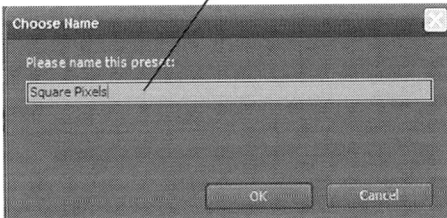

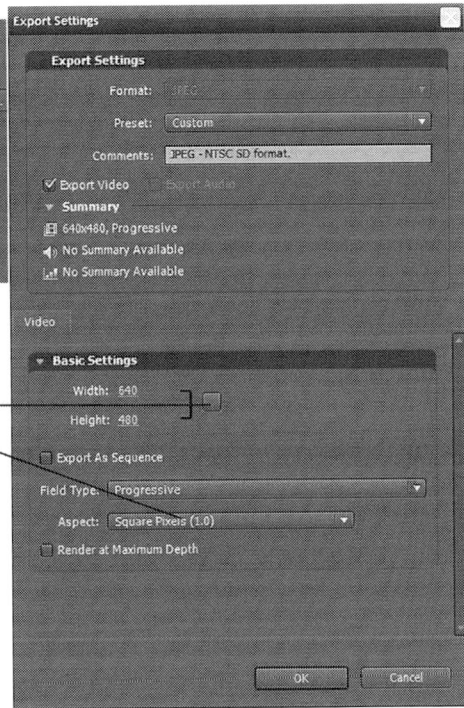

The **Image** output presets included with Premiere Elements are designed to produce a still photo that can be used in a video. Because of this, these options will produce a still that is composed of anamorphic – or *non-square*, video pixels. This means that, if you use one of these stills on a Web site or in a print project, it will produce an oddly distorted picture.

For this reason, we recommend that, in addition to the pre-loaded presets, you create an additional, *square pixel* output preset for your general-purpose JPEG frame grabs.

1. Go to the **Share** tab and select the **Computer** destination option.

   From the list of options that appear on the options page, select **Image**.

2. Set the **Preset** drop-down to **JPEG- NTSC SD**.

   Click the **Advanced** button.

3. In the **Export Settings** options panel, in the **Video** section, set the **Aspect** drop-down to **Square Pixels (1.0)**.

   Click the chain button to turn off **Constrain Proportions** and set the **Width** to 640 and the **Height** to 480.

   Click **Okay**.

3. In the **Choose Name** screen, type the name "**Square Pixels**," then click **Okay** to save it.

The **Square Pixels** option will now be available in the Presets drop-down whenever you use Share to create a JPEG still of your current video frame.

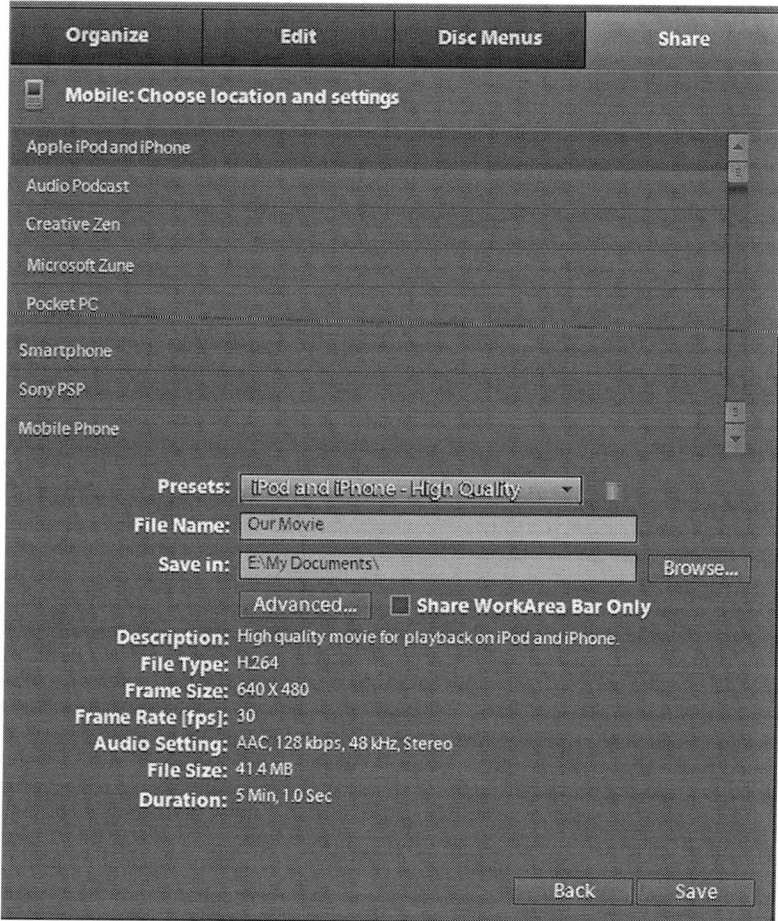

Output options to mobile devices include a variety of presets for many popular devices, including H.264/MPEG4s for both video and audio and WMVs for the Microsoft Zune.

Output to a mobile phone or video player

Selecting the option to share to **Mobile Phones and Players** takes you to a screen on which all of the major mobile devices for viewing video – from iPods, Zunes and Pocket PCs to Smartphones and even Sony PSPs. (You may need to scroll the list to see the entire listing.)

Whichever you choose, the program will recommend the optimal preset for that device.

You can, however, select other options from the **Preset** drop-down menu or click the **Advanced** button for deeper settings. You'll find a detailed discussion of each file option in **Video output options,** later in this chapter.

Type your file name in the space provided and click the **Browse** button to select the location on your computer in which you'd like to save your file.

You can also save directly to your device.

To export only the segment of your project defined by the **Work Area Bar**, check the **Share Work Area Bar Only** option. (For more information, see **Output a segment of your video using the Work Area Bar** in **Chapter 19, Edit Your Video in Timeline Mode**.)

When you've selected all of the appropriate output options, click the **Save** button in the lower right corner of the panel.

Output to tape

Now that DVDs and BluRay discs have become so universal and popular, it's much less common to send completed projects back to tape.

However, there's still no better way to archive your finished project in a high-quality, re-editable format than to send it back to the same device that created it in the first place.

Remember, miniDV and HDV camcorders and video editing programs speak the same language. This means that saving your finished project back to tape is a cheap and convenient way to store 13 gigabytes of high-quality, re-editable video data.

Video output formats

The main video output formats available under the various **Share** tab destinations are **DV-AVI**s (Windows only), **MPEG**s, **WMV**s (Windows Media Video – available on Windows computers only), **FLV**s (Flash video), **MOV**s (Quicktime video – including **DV-MOV** files) and **MP4**s. You'll find at least one of these options offered at each of the **Share** output destinations.

Here's what each file format is and what its main benefits and liabilities are:

DV-AVIs are the "purest" and highest quality video output format available on a Windows PC, though the files are considerably larger than the other options. (It's the file format that outputs from a miniDV camcorder and/or is created as part of the workflow within Premiere Elements.) This format is your best choice for creating an editable video output if, for example if you are outputting your project, or a segment of your project, for use as part of another video editing project. **DV-AVIs** are the universal language of PC-based video editors, the perfect balance of compression and file size for working with on a computer.

DV-MOVs are the MacIntosh equivalent of the **DV-AVIs**. A Quicktime-based file, this is the same format that is created when miniDV footage is captured to a MacIntosh computer. Like the **DV-AVI** on a Windows machine, the **DV-MOV** file will load into a standard-definition Premiere Elements project without needing to be rendered.

MPEGs are a high quality video delivery format. This means that they play at nearly the quality of your original footage. (A form of **MPEG**, called a VOB file, is the format used to store the video on DVDs.) However, because it is a much smaller video file, it is also highly compressed and can be challenging to re-edit later. As a general rule, you should think of **MPEGs**, then, as a delivery format rather than an editing or re-editing format.

WMVs, **MOVs** and **FLVs** are generally considered to be web formats, because they are highly compressed and often have reduced frame rates and frame sizes (most often 320x240 pixels – about one-fourth the size of your original video) in order to produce the smallest, most efficient file sizes.

Currently, **WMVs** (Windows Media Video) are considered the Internet standard for web-based video. This is because Microsoft's ubiquitous presence means that virtually every computer in the world has the necessary software to play them.

MOVs (Apple's Quicktime format) are also fairly ubiquitous (though PC users must load the Quicktime player manually the first time they play one). Apple's efforts to continually improve the format means that often they can produce a higher quality video than **WMVs**.

FLVs (Flash video files) are gaining tremendous popularity on the internet, thanks to video sharing sites, like YouTube, which appreciate the fact that **FLVs** produce excellent video quality while using minimal Internet bandwidth. The biggest challenge with **FLV** files is that they require a special player to view them – a player most people don't have on their computers. In order for **FLVs**, then, to be playable on your Web site, your Web page must have a Flash player embedded in it (as YouTube does).

If you select **Mobile Phones and Players** as your Share option, you'll have access to yet another file format output – the default output option for **iPods** and **iPhones, Audio Podcasts** and **Mobile Phones**. Using the **H.264** compression codec, this file format is also known as simply an **MP4**. (The **Mobile Phone** destination will also output an MP4, however, it uses the slightly less sophisticated H.263 codec.)

H.264 and **H.263** are advanced compression systems that can produce very high quality video and audio but can do so with remarkably small files.

The **H.263** option for Mobile Phones produces a file that, by default, is a mere 176x144 pixels – fine for a mobile phones but a rather small frame for, say, playback on a computer.

The **H.264** option for iPod and iPhone, however, produces video at a full 640x480 pixels and 30 fps, the same size and frame rate as an AVI, but at a reduced output file size.

True, with that kind of compression, the files do suffer a slight loss of picture quality. But, regardless, this is an ideal format for mobile devices that support it.

Chapter 30

A Premiere Elements Appendix
More things worth knowing

Recommended "Real World" computer specs

The rule of thumb for figuring out the minimum computer specs to run a program is to take the minimums recommended by the manufacturer and double them.

That's certainly true in the case of Premiere Elements, for which Adobe vastly understates the power needed to run this program effectively.

Virtually any computer made in the last couple of years should run Premiere Elements just fine – although laptops, which tend to be built for portability rather than power, often cost about 50% more for the same power as a desktop equivalent. They also tend to have limited hard drive space and smaller monitors than desktops. So, if you do decide to edit on a laptop, be ready and willing to put down the extra cash for the necessary power and hardware.

Here are our recommended *minimum* specs for running Premiere Elements as you edit standard DV and HDV footage.

- A dual-core processor running at at least 2.6 ghz
- 2-4 gigabytes of RAM
- 128 mb video card, ideally ATI or nVidia technology
- 100 gigabytes of free hard drive (This allows plenty of room for captured footage and scratch disk space)
- An ASIO (Audio Stream Input/Output) supported sound card
- DVD burner
- 19" monitor set to at least a 1280x1024 display (dual-monitors are even better)
- IEEE-1394/FireWire/iLink connection

Some of the new background functions (namely **Background Rendering** and the **Smart Tags Media Analyzer**) for Premiere Elements can pose a challenge for marginal or older computers (and many laptops, which are usually built for portability rather than power). If you find that these functions are challenging your system's performance, you may need to disable them, as we suggest in the section that follows.

AVCHD video editing specs

AVCHD, a highly compressed high-definition format, requires considerably more power to work with successfully.

For that reason, we recommend these minimums for AVCHD video editing.

- A fast quad-core or i7 processor
- 4 gigabytes of RAM
- 128 mb video card, ideally ATI or nVidia technology
- A DVD or, better, BluRay DVD burner
- 19" monitor set to at least a 1280x1024 display
  (a 22" widescreen or dual 19" monitors are even better)
- IEEE-1394/FireWire/iLink connection

The addition of a second hard drive (either internal or external) – one dedicated to your video projects and source files – can give your workflow a tremendous boost. Not only does it often make the process go more smoothly, since it keeps the video data flow and scratch disk files separate from your operating system's paging files, but it also reduces fragmentation of your video files.

If you install an internal second hard drive for video editing, make sure to set it up in your BIOS (the set-up that displays before the operating system launches, when you first start up your computer) as well as in your operating system.

And, whether you use an internal or external drive, make sure that the drive is formatted NTFS rather than FAT32 (which all drives are factory formatted as by default) in order to avoid FAT32's file size limitations.

Converting a drive from FAT32 to NTFS is easy and you won't lose any data already on the drive in the process. The instructions for doing so are available all over the Web, including on the Microsoft site.

Disabling Background Rendering and the Smart Tags Media Analyzer

Two new functions in Premiere Elements 9 are designed to work in the background, analyzing your video files and maintaining your timeline. However, unless your system is very powerful, they may interfere with your work and cause your computer to run slowly or bog down.

If this is the case, both can easily be disabled without a major impact on your editing workflow.

- **Background Rendering** is a great feature which renders the non-DV clips on your timeline automatically so that your computer is not constantly maintaining soft renders of your video. (More information can be found under **Enable or disable Background Rendering**, in **Chapter 19, Edit Your Video in Timeline Mode**.) It also can be such a resource hog that Adobe has it turned off by default.

To enable or disable it, go to Premiere Elements **Preferences** (under the **Edit** drop-down on the Menu Bar) and, on the **General** page, uncheck **Enable Background Rendering**.

- **Smart Tags** are metadata that the Organizer automatically adds to your clips, identifying characteristics such as blurriness, shakiness, motion, close-ups of faces, etc. Smart Tags are created by a feature of the Elements Organizer called the **Media Analyzer**.

  Having clips pre-analyzed can save some time when using tools like the **Motion Tracker** and, unless a clip is pre-**Smart Tagged,** you won't be able to use the **Smart Fix** feature to automatically adjust your video clips (as we discuss in **Smart Fix your clips** in **Chapter 19, Edit Your Video in Timeline Mode** and in **The Smart Tags Media Analyzer** in **Chapter 31, The Elements Organizer**).

  Ideally the Elements Organizer should run the **Media Analyzer** invisibly, when you're not doing other things. But, like **Background Rendering**, it does sometimes prove somewhat intrusive, especially on some slower systems.

  To disable or to enable this function, go to the Organizer's **Preferences** (under the **Edit** drop-down on the Organizer's Menu Bar) and, on the **Media Analyzer Options** page, uncheck **Analyze Media in the Catalog Automatically**.

Optimize XP for video editing

XP is a pretty efficient operating system, and you may have not problems running Premiere Elements on it without modification. However, to squeeze the most juice out of your XP machine:

1. Right-click **My Computer** and select **Properties** to bring up your **System Properties** panel.

   Under the **Advanced** tab, click the **Settings** button at **Performance**.

   Under the **Visual Effects** tab, uncheck all except (to keep the XP look) "Use visual styles on windows and buttons."

   Under the **Advanced** tab, make sure **Processor Scheduling** and **Memory Usage** are set to programs.

2. Click on **Virtual Memory**.

   For the most part, XP does a very good job of allocating Virtual Memory, so checking **System Managed** will work fine.

   Some people, however, recommend setting the VM manually. If you'd prefer, set both the **Minimum** and **Maximum** to 1½ times your RAM load. Then click **Set**.

3. Open **My Computer.**

   Right-click on each of your hard drive(s) and choose **Properties**.

   At the **Hard Drive Properties** window, uncheck both **Compress Drive to Save Space** and **Allow Indexing Service**.

   (The Indexing Service, which logs every new file added to your drive, frequently interrupts intensive processes such as captures.)

You will need to reboot your system for these settings to take effect.

Optimize Vista and Windows 7 for best performance

Most computers made in the past year can edit with Premiere Elements an up-to-date version of Vista or Windows 7 without modification. However, if you'd like to squeeze more juice out of your Vista or Windows 7 system, there are some mostly aesthetic features you can shut down:

1. From **Start**, go to your **Control Panel**, then select **Performance Information and Tools**.

   In the dialog box that opens, select **Indexing Options** in the left pane.

   Click the **Modify** button in the **Indexing Options** dialog box and click the **Show All Locations** button at the bottom of the Indexed Locations dialog box. For best performance, turn off **Indexing** on all of your drives.

2. Click **Start**, right-click on **Computer**, and click **Properties**.

   Click **Advanced System Settings**. Select the **Advanced** tab.

   Under **Performance**, click **Settings**.

   Uncheck these options:

   • Fade or slide menus into view

   • Fade or slide tooltips into view

   • Fade out menu items after clicking

   • Show shadows under menus

   • Slide open combo boxes

   • Slide taskbar buttons

   • Use a background image for each folder type

   Close the **Performance Options & System Properties** dialogs.

3. The **Windows Sidebar** provides instant access to gadgets. However, the **Sidebar** is one of Windows' top resource suckers. Turn it off and your computer will sigh in relief.

4. Turn off the **Aero** interface!

   Right-click on your desktop, select **Properties** and then **Appearance**. Select the **Basic Look**.

   It may not be quite as cool as Aero's semi-transparent windows, but it's well worth the trade-off in performance. And, in two days, you probably won't miss it anyway.

Maintain your Windows computer

Your computer doesn't just *seem* to run slower as it ages, it often *does* run slower. This is due to the accumulation of data 'sludge' on your hard drive – temp files and bits and pieces of programs you've installed and/or removed from your system. Additionally, any time spent on the Internet loads your hard drive with cache files, cookies and, often, spyware.

The regimen below will help keep your computer running like new. Think of it as cleaning the dust bunnies out of your system.

And, at the very least, keep Windows updated and check the Apple site regularly to **ensure you have the latest version of Quicktime!**

Quicktime plays an important role in Premiere Elements' functions, and a surprising number of problems (such as video not displaying in the monitor while capturing) can be cured simply by loading the newest version.

Do this weekly:

1. Go to **Microsoft Update** and make sure Windows is updated. In fact, don't just check for priority updates, click on the **Custom** button and look for other updates (like RealTek drivers and updated hardware drivers) that may not update automatically. (In Vista and Windows 7, select the option to **Restore Hidden Updates**.)

   You may not need everything offered, but it certainly doesn't hurt to have them.

2. Make sure your **virus software** is updated. (If your virus software isn't set to run in the middle of the night, waking your computer from sleep for a virus scan, you also may want to do a regular virus scan.)

   And, every once in a while, go to the Web site for your virus software and make sure you have the latest *VERSION* of the anti-virus software. You may have the latest virus definitions added automatically – but, if you're still using last year's version of the software, you could still be vulnerable.

3. Install the excellent (and free!) **Spybot Search & Destroy** and **Spyware Blaster** to clear off and block spyware. (Update them before you use them, and regularly check their Web sites to make sure you're using the latest versions before you run them.)

   You can pick both up from the links on this page:
   http://savemybutt.com/downloads.php

4. Run the free, excellent, easy-to-use tool **Advanced SystemCare Free** to tune up your registry and clear off temp and other files that are just taking up space. This program also is available at:

   http://www.iobit.com/advancedwindowscareper.html

5. Run the **Defragmenter** on all of your hard drives.

6. And don't forget to back up your files (at least the **My Documents** folder) regularly!

   The one piece of hardware on your computer that absolutely *WILL* eventually fail is your hard drive. If you're lucky, you'll have replaced your computer before then. But if not – *please* remember to back up your files regularly.

Do this monthly:

1. Check your graphic's card's manufacturer's site, your sound card's manufacturer's site and, if applicable, the **RealTek** site to make sure your drivers and firmware are up to date. Also, double-check the Apple site to ensure you have the latest version of **Quicktime**.

2. Secunia offers a free (for personal use) application that will automatically keep all of your computer's software updated. You can download it from:

   http://secunia.com/

   Click the **Software Inspectors** button.

   At the next screen, select and download **Secunia PSI for Personal Desktop**.

3. Go to your web browser and clear the cache.

    In Internet Explorer, you'll find the option for doing this right under the **Tools** drop-down.

    Older versions and other browsers (including Firefox) keep them under **Tools** and in **Internet Options**.

    You can leave the cookies – but do delete the **Temporary Internet Files**. Accumulate enough of them and they will slow down your entire computer system.

Valuable free or low cost tools and utilities
Windows video conversion tools

All video may look the same and sound the same, but it actually comes in many flavors, formats and compression systems (codecs).

Premiere Elements, on Windows computers, is built around a DV-AVI workflow. (DV-AVIs are AVI files that use the DV codec.) This means that DV-AVIs flow easily through it and place the least strain on the program and, ultimately, your system. Not all AVIs use the DV codec, and many AVI videos (such as video from still cameras) can cause real problems for Premiere Elements.

A good rule of thumb is that, whenever possible, use DV-AVIs as your video source files. (On Macs, the ideal format is the DV Quicktime file.)

A number of free or low-cost programs will convert your files. Here are some Muvipix favorites.

Additionally, we have included in this list software for converting AVCHD files to more conventional HDV.

AVCHD are highly compressed files and can prove to be pretty challenging to work with on even the more powerful personal computers.

Converting AVCHD to HDV can make for a much less intensive high-definition video editing experience.

Windows MovieMaker

If you've got a Windows-based computer, **Windows MovieMaker** is already on your system. Despite being a rather limited video editor, **MovieMaker** can handle a wider range of video formats than Premiere Elements (including, for instance, video from still cameras). It therefore makes an excellent tool for converting many video formats into more standardized DV-AVIs.

To convert a video into a DV-AVI with **MovieMaker**:

1. Import the video into a **MovieMaker** project and place it on the timeline.

2. From the **Main Menu** select **File/Save Movie File**.

    A dialog box will open.

3. Select the option to save to **My Computer** then click **Next**.

4. On the next option screen, name your new file and select/browse to a folder to put the file in.

    Click **Next**.

5. On the next option screen, click the link that says **Show More Choices**.

There will be three radio buttons to choose from.

6. Select **Other Settings** and, from the drop-down menu, select **DV-AVI**. Click **Make Movie**.

NOTE: **Windows Live MovieMaker**, the new, online version of **MovieMaker** included with Windows 7, will *not* output DV-AVIs.

To convert AVIs from a still cameras to DV-AVIs for use in Premiere Elements, the best free alternative solution is **MPEG Streamclip**, as discussed below.

For converting MOVs to DV-AVIs, use **Super** or *Quicktime Pro*.

MPEG Streamclip

A great tool for easily converting MPEGs and VOB files (DVD video files) to more Premiere Elements-friendly DV-AVIs.

1. Select the option to open your VOB or MPEG file(s) with **MPEG Streamclip** from its **File** menu.

2. Open the **AVI/DivX Exporter** window from **File/Export to AVI**.

3. Set **Compression** to the **Apple DV/DVPRO_NTSC** (or **DV PAL**, if appropriate) codec.

4. Set **Field Order** to **Lower Field First**.

5. Change the default sound settings from **MPEG Layer 3** to **Uncompressed**.

6. If you have widescreen footage click on **Options** at the top right.

    Leave the **Scan Mode** as is but change the **Aspect Ratio** from 4:3 to 16:9.

If you would like to save these settings, click on the **Presets** button at the bottom left of then panel, then click on the **New** button to name and save your preset. The next time you run **MPEG Streamclip**, you can go directly to the **Presets** button and load your saved settings.

7. Click on **Make AVI** and choose a folder and filename for your DV-AVI file.

MPEG Streamclip is free from http://www.squared5.com

Super Video Converter

Super can convert almost any video format to almost any other video format. The latest version of the program is capable of outputting both PAL and NTSC DV files.

To use **Super** to convert virtually any video to a Premiere Elements-compatible DV file:

1. Set the **Output Container** drop-down menu to DV.

    Leave everything else at its default setting.

2. To output a PAL video, ensure that *Video Scale Size* is set to 720:576
    To output an NTSC video, ensure that **Video Scale Size** is set to 720:480

3. Drag the video you want to convert from your Windows Explorer panel to the area indicated, just below the **Output** specs.

    Click **Encode**.

Your video will be created with a .dv suffix and should not require rendering in a standard Premiere Elements DV project.

Super is free – although finding the link to the download on its messy Web site can be very challenging.

It's available from www.erightsoft.com/SUPER.html

Quicktime Pro

Quicktime Pro is a great tool to own if your input sources tend to be MOVs (Quicktime) files. These files include video from still cameras and many MP4s.

Not only will it convert these files to DV-AVIs but the program also includes some basic video editing functions.

Quicktime Pro is available for $29 from www.apple.com.

Premiere Elements

Premiere Elements, especially current versions, can often do an excellent job of converting video. You can use the program to convert video from DVDs, hard drive camcorders and even HDV and AVCHD sources into more manageable DV-AVIs – a process that's particularly effective if you're mixing video from several sources.

Converting everything to DV-AVIs before mixing them into a final project will allow the program to work much more efficiently and with much less likelihood of problems.

To use Premiere Elements to convert your video, open a project (ensuring that the project presets match your source video), import your video into the project and place it on the timeline.

Click the **Share** tab, select click the **Personal Computer** destination and select the **AVI** output option as described in **Chapter 18, Share Your Movie**.

Virtual Dub

Virtual Dub is a terrific tool that should be on everyone's computer.

Less a conversion tool than a video processor, it will make many AVIs (including Type 1 DV-AVIs) compatible with Premiere Elements as well as converting many other file types to more standard, more editable video.

Converting your video into editable DV-AVIs with **VirtualDub** is as easy as opening your file in the program and then selecting the option to **Save As**.

Your newly saved AVI will be perfectly compatible with Premiere Elements!

VirtualDub is available from www.virtualdub.org.

Free Video Converter from KoyoteSoft

Free Video Converter will convert AVCHD video into more manageable HDV MPEG2 with virtually no loss of quality.

1. Open your AVCHD file in the **Free Video Convertor.**

2. Set the output bit rate to 25000kbs.

3. Output your file.

The output file will be 1920x1080 MPEG2.

One downside is that, when you install it, the program will automatically install a search tool to your browser toolbar – but this toolbar can easily be removed using Windows Add/Remove Programs.

The program is available from koyotesoft.com/indexEn.html

Other AVCHD converters

AVCHD UpShift, from NewBlue, will convert AVCHD video to more standard HDV (a hi-def MPEG .m2t).

AVCHD UpShift sells for $49.95 and is available from www.newbluefx.com/avchd-upshift.html

Another excellent AVCHD convertor is **VoltaicHD**. The program costs $34.99 and is available from www.shedworx.com/voltaichd

A great program for converting AVCHD to standard-definition DV-AVI, is **Corel VideoStudio Pro**, one of the best PC-based programs for working with AVCHD video.

The program sells for $59.99 and is available from www.corel.com.

Capture utilities

In the event Premiere Elements won't capture your video no matter what you do, these free or low-cost tools will capture miniDV and HDV as perfectly compatible video files.

WinDV (free from windv.mourek.cz/) – A great capture utility with a simple interface.

HDVSplit (free from strony.aster.pl/paviko/hdvsplit.htm) – A great capture utility for HDV video.

Scenalyzer ($30 from www.scenalyzer.com) – A low-cost capture utility with some great extra features.

Windows MovieMaker – Video captured from a miniDV camcorder into MovieMaker is perfectly compatible with Premiere Elements.

Nero – Sometimes Nero's presence on your computer is the *reason* you can't capture from Premiere Elements. However, if you've got it on your computer, you can use it to do your capture also.

If all else fails, you can use the software that came with your camcorder to capture your video. However, if this software will not capture your video as a DV-AVI (or MPEG2 for high-definition video) or convert to one of those formats, we recommend you convert your captured video using the software above before you bring it into a Premiere Elements project for best program performance.

Our favorite free audio utility

Audacity (audacity.sourceforge.net) is, hands down, the best *free* audio editing software you'll find anywhere. Easy to use, loaded with preset audio filters and yet extremely versatile.

Audacity can convert audio formats as well as adjust audio levels and "sweeten" your audio's sound. You can also record into it from a microphone or external audio device and edit audio with it. A real must-have freebie that you'll find yourself going to regularly!

FTP software

FTP software uploads files from your computer to a web site and downloads files from a site to your computer. There are many great applications out there.

Here are a couple of personal favorites.

FileZilla Client is the current favorite FTP utility of a number of Muvipixers. Efficient, dependable and easy-to-use, sending files to a Web site with **FileZilla** is as simple as dragging and dropping.

FileZilla Client is available free from filezilla-project.org.

Easy FTP (free from www.download.com and other sources) – Completely free and nearly as intuitive as **FileZilla**.

The "Burn Disc" workaround

In a perfect world, you could put together a project out of any media, click the **Share** tab and burn it to a disc.

Unfortunately, for a variety of reasons – some related to Premiere Elements, most related to operating system drivers or program conflicts, this sometimes doesn't go as smoothly as it should.

There are three main reasons for a problem burning a DVD or BluRay disc:

- Challenging source video (including photos that are larger than the recommended 1000x750 pixels in size);
- Interfacing issues with your disc burner (often the result of a program like Nero not sharing the burner with other programs);
- Lack of computer resources (namely lack of available scratch disk space on your hard drive). This workaround eliminates most Burn Disc problems. And when it doesn't eliminate them, it at least helps you isolate where the problems are occurring.

The simplest solution is to break the process down into its elements and then troubleshoot each element individually.

1. **Create a "pure" AVI project.** Click on the timeline panel and then go to **File/Export/Movie** to create an AVI of your entire project.

    If this works, do a **Save As** to save a copy of your project, delete all of the video except this newly created AVI, then place the AVI on the timeline in place of the deleted video (the DVD markers should still line up).

    If you find that you are unable to create an AVI from your project, it could be that your photos are too large or you lack the resources to render the files (as discussed in step 3, below).

Ensure that, whenever possible, your photos are no larger than 1000x750 pixels in size, as discussed in **Work with photos** in **Chapter 3, Get Media into Your Project.**

2. **Burn to a folder** rather than directly to a disc.

   Select the **Burn to Folder** option, as we discuss in **Output to a DVD or BluRay Disc** in **Chapter 29**.

   This eliminates the possibility that other disc burning software is interfering with communication with your computer's burner.

   Once the disc files are created, you can use your computer's burner software to burn the VIDEO_TS folder and its contents to a DVD or BluRay disc.

   If this doesn't work, it could be that your computer lacks the necessary resources, as discussed below.

3. **Clear space on and defragment your hard drive**. A one-hour video can require up to 50 gigabytes of free, defragmented space on your hard drive to render and process (depending on your source files).

   Even a "pure" AVI project can require 20-30 gigabytes of space.

   Clear off your computer and regularly defragment it, per **Maintain Your Computer**, earlier in this chapter, and you'll reduce the likelihood of this being an issue. Assuming you've got an adequately powered computer and an adequately large hard drive in the first place.

Chapter 30

Keyboard shortcuts for Premiere Elements

These key strokes and key combinations are great, quick ways to launch features or use the program's tools without having to poke around the interface.

In virtually every workspace the arrow keys (Down, Up, Left, Right) will move the selected object in that direction. Shift+Arrow will move it several steps in one nudge.

Many of these shortcuts are slightly different on a MacIntosh computer. Usually the **Command**(⌘) key is used in place of the **Ctrl** key – although a number of keyboard shortcuts may not work at all.

Program Controls

Ctrl O	Open project	Ctrl X	Cut
Ctrl W	Close project	Ctrl C	Copy
Ctrl S	Save project	Ctrl V	Paste
Ctrl Shift S	Save project as...	Tab	Close floating windows
Ctrl Alt S	Save a copy	Ctrl Q	Quit program
Ctrl Z	Undo	F1	Help
Ctrl Shift Z	Redo		

Import/Export

F5	Capture	Ctrl Shift M	Export Frame
Ctrl I	Add Media	Ctrl Alt Shift M	Export Audio
Ctrl M	Export Movie	Ctrl Shift H	Get properties for selection

Media and Trimming

I	Set in point	G	Clear all in/out points
O	Set out point	D	Clear selected in point
Q	Go to in point	F	Clear selected out point
Page Down	Go to next edit point	Ctrl E	Edit original
W	Go to out point	Ctrl H	Rename
Page Up	Go to previous edit point		

Play/Scrub Controls

Space bar	Play/stop	Shift Right	Step forward five frames
J	Shuttle left	Home	Go to beginning of timeline
L	Shuttle right	End	Go to end of timeline
Shift J	Slow shuttle left	Q	Go to in point
Shift L	Slow shuttle right	W	Go to out point
K	Shuttle stop	Page Down	Go to next edit point
Arrow Left	One frame back	Page Up	Go to previous edit point
Arrow Right	One frame forward	Ctrl Alt Space	Play in point to out point with preroll/postroll
Shift Left	Step back five frames		

Timeline Controls

Enter	Render work area
Ctrl K	Razor cut at CTI
+	Zoom in
-	Zoom out
\	Zoom to work area
Ctrl A	Select all
Ctrl Shift A	Deselect all
, (comma)	Insert
. (period)	Overlay
Ctrl Shift V	Insert Clip
Alt [video clip]	Unlink audio/video
Ctrl G	Group
Ctrl Shift G	Ungroup
X	Time stretch
Del	Clear clip (non-ripple)
Backspace	Ripple delete (fill gap)
S	Toggle snap
C	Razor tool
V	Selection tool
Alt [	Set Work Area Bar In Point
Alt]	Set Work Area Bar Out Point
Ctrl Alt C	Copy attributes
Ctrl Alt V	Paste Attributes
Ctrl Shift /	Duplicate
Shift * (Num pad)	Set next unnumbered marker
* (Num pad)	Set unnumbered marker
Ctrl Shift Right	Go to next clip marker
Ctrl Shift Left	Go to previous clip marker
Ctrl Shift 0	Clear current marker
Alt Shift 0	Clear all clip markers
Ctrl Right	Go to next timeline marker
Ctrl Left	Go to previous timeline marker
Ctrl 0	Clear current timeline marker
Alt 0	Clear all timeline markers

Title Window Controls

Ctrl Shift L	Title type align left
Ctrl Shift R	Title type align right
Ctrl Shift C	Title type align center
Ctrl Shift T	Set title type tab
Ctrl Shift D	Position object bottom safe margin
Ctrl Shift F	Position object left safe margin
Ctrl Shift O	Position object top safe margin
Ctrl Alt Shift C	Insert copyright symbol
Ctrl Alt Shift R	Insert registered symbol
Ctrl J	Open title templates
Ctrl Alt]	Select object above
Ctrl Alt [	Select object below
Ctrl Shift]	Bring object to front
Ctrl [	Bring object forward
Ctrl Shift [	Send object to back
Ctrl [	Send object backward
Alt Shift Left	Decrease kerning five units
Alt Shift Right	Increase kerning five units
Alt Left	Decrease kerning one unit
Alt Right	Increase kerning one unit
Alt Shift Up	Decrease leading five units
Alt Shift Down	Increase leading five units
Alt Up	Decrease leading one unit
Alt Down	Increase leading one unit
Ctrl Up	Decrease text size five points
Ctrl Down	Increase text size five points
Shift Up	Decrease text size one point
Shift Down	Increase text size one point

Media Window

Ctrl Delete	Delete selection with options	End	Move selection to last clip
Shift Down	Extend selection down	Page Down	Move selection page down
Shift Left	Extend selection left	Page Up	Move selection page up
Shift Up	Extend selection up	Right	Move selection right
Down	Move selection to next clip	Shift]	Thumbnail size next
Up	Move selection to previous clip	Shift [	Thumbnail size previous
Home	Move selection to first clip	Shift \	Toggle view

Capture Monitor Panel

F	Fast forward	Left	Step back
G	Get frame	Right	Step forward
R	Rewind	S	Stop

Properties Panel

Backspace	Delete selected effect

Narration Panel

Delete	Delete present narration clip	Space	Play present narration clip
		G	Start/Stop recording
Right Arrow	Go to next narration clip		
Left Arrow	Go to previous narration clip		

Note that Premiere Elements also allows you to modify any of these keyboard shortcuts and to create your own shortcuts for dozens of other tasks. You'll find the option to do so under the Edit drop-down menu.

Part 3

The
Elements Suite

File Management with the Organizer

The Photo Browser

Keyword Tags and Metadata

Smart Tags and the Media Analyzer

Albums

Stacks

Fix, Create and Share

Chapter 31
The Elements Organizer
Managing your media files

The Elements Organizer, which comes bundled with both Photoshop Elements and Premiere Elements, is Adobe's media file management tool.

It's a way to organize, to search and to create search criteria for your audio, video and photo files.

And it does this in some very imaginative ways!

Import files from your iPhoto catalog

If you're running the Elements programs on a Mac, you can easily import your catalog of photo files from iPhoto into the Elements Organizer catalog.

Just select, from the Elements Organizer's **File** menu, **Get Photos and Videos** and, from the sub-menu, **From iPhoto**.

The Photo Browser   Photoshop.com logon   Keyword Tags   Albums   Photo Browser Display Options

The Organizer is the "Elements" consumer version of Adobe's professional-level **Bridge** file management software (a standard feature in Adobe's Creative Suites).

It's not quite as powerful or as elegant as **Bridge**, of course. But the Elements Organizer offers some terrific tools for organizing, searching, cataloging and managing your media files.

Additionally, the Organizer includes a number of tools for working with your still pictures to create photo projects, like calendars and scrap books, and online or video slideshows.

The Elements Organizer links directly to both Premiere Elements and Photoshop Elements and it can be launched from both the Welcome Screens and from the editing workspaces of either program.

Think of your Elements Organizer as a giant search engine that can be programmed to store and retrieve the audio, video and still photo files on your computer, based on a wide variety of criteria – some of which you can assign and some of which are inherently a part of your photo, sound and video files when they're created.

These search criteria aren't limited to obvious details – such as the type of media or the date it was saved to your computer.

Search criteria can include **Keyword Tags** and metadata that you assign – or it can be minute technical details, such as what type of camera was used to shoot the photo or whether the photo was shot with a flash or natural light. And there are even some pretty innovative cataloging methods (such as the ability to catalog your photos and recall them based on the location where they were shot or the date when they were taken).

Furthermore, the Organizer includes features that support other tools and functions in both Premiere Elements and Photoshop Elements. (The **Smart Tags Media Analyzer**, discussed later in this chapter, for instance, preps your video files for use with a number of new tools in Premiere Elements.)

Your Elements Organizer's media files can also be stored in **Albums**, which have both a filtering function and play a role in the Organizer's online file back-up system (as we discuss in **Back your files up online** in **Chapter 34, Photoshop.com**).

The Photo Browser area

The large area in which your media files are displayed as thumbnails, and which dominates the Organizer workspace, is called the **Photo Browser**.

There are several types of media files, and they are each represented slightly differently in the **Photo Browser**. For instance:

Video files are represented as image thumbnails with a filmstrip icon on the upper right corner.

Photo files are represented by a plain thumbnail of the image file.

Audio files are represented by blue thumbnails with a speaker icon on them.

Under the **View** drop-down on the Organizer Menu Bar, in the **Media Types** sub-menu, you can filter which file types are displayed in the Photo Browser.

Update the Organizer and add files

Any video clips or photo files you edit with Premiere Elements or Photoshop Elements are automatically added to your Elements Organizer catalog.

By default, the **Photo Browser** displays your files according to dates they were saved, from most recent to oldest. However, you can change this workspace so that your media files are displayed in whatever view you find most intuitive – and sorted by date is by no means the only way to view your files.

Video file

Photo file

Audio file

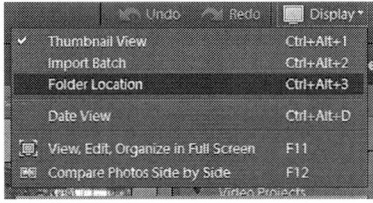

The **Display** button in the upper right corner of Elements' Organizer offers a variety of options for displaying your media files. Select the **Folder Location View** from the **Display** drop-down and the Organizer becomes a means of browsing the contents of your computer drive(s) by folder, with all the media files represented as previewable thumbnails.

An advantage of **Folder Location View** is that it is one of the ways you can use it to add files to your Organizer catalog.

To add a folder's files to the catalog, **right-click** on a folder displayed along the left side of the **Photo Browser** (**Ctrl-click** on a Mac), and select one of the following options:

An Unamanaged folder
(Files not included in catalog)

A Managed Folder
(Files added to catalog)

A Watched Folder
(Catalog auto-updates files)

Add to Watched Folders creates a dynamic link to the Organizer. Any media files you add to or remove from this folder will automatically be updated to the Organizer's catalog.

Add Unmanaged Files to Catalog immediately adds whatever media files are in the folder to the Organizer's catalog.

The changed status of the folder is reflected in the folder's icon, as illustrated on the left. (The **Managed Folder** icon indicates that the folder's files have been added to the Elements Organizer's catalog.)

What is metadata?

Metadata is the hidden information embedded in every file, including when the file was saved, who modified it last, what program created the file, etc.

By default, all of your media files carry certain metadata. When you first open the Organizer, for instance, in the default **Thumbnail View**, you'll immediately notice that the files are categorized according to the date they were saved to your computer's drive.

If you've poked around in the Organizer at all, you've probably noted that you can display these files from most recent to oldest or oldest to most recent.

You can isolate the files by type of media so that the **Photo Browser** (the area in which the thumbnails are displayed) displays only video, photo or audio files. Or, by using the **Timeline** (which is activated under the **Window** drop-down on the Organizer's Menu Bar), you can quickly browse to media for any specific date.

"**Date saved**" is the simplest display of metadata and the most basic way to search through your media files – but it's far from the only way to search your files.

In fact, you'd probably be surprised to learn how much metadata each file actually contains! **Right-click** on any photo file that you've downloaded from a digital camera in the **Photo Browser**, for instance, and select **Show Properties**. This opens the **Properties** palette. Now click on the **Metadata** button (the little "i" icon inside the blue circle) on the **Properties** panel.

Here you'll find a couple dozen lines of detailed information about your photo. Called **EXIF data**, this is information your digital camera writes to your photos, and it can include the date and time the photo was shot, the photo dimensions, the make and model of camera that was used to take the photo, the shutter speed, if a flash was used, what settings and F-stop setting was used, if it was shot with manual or automatic focus and so on. (Professional cameras that shoot in **Camera RAW** format contains about twice as much data, including such minutia as the serial number of the camera.)

All of this is metadata. And it can be used – along with any additional metadata you assign manually – as search criteria.

To search by metadata, go to the **Find** drop-down on the Organizer Menu Bar and select the option to **Find by Details (Metadata)**.

In the option screen that opens, you can set up a search to find, for instance, all photos shot on a specific date or at a specific time, at certain camera settings – in fact, you can search by pretty much any of the metadata attached to your photo or file!

Under this **Find** drop-down menu, you'll also find many more search methods for your files. One of the most amazing search functions, in my opinion, is the Organizer's ability to locate files that contain **Visual Similarity**.

That's right: If you have a picture of the beach or the mountains or even of an individual, the Organizer will find for you all of the other photos in your collection that have similar color schemes and visual details!

It's not magic, of course. I set it to search for photos similar to a bride in her gown and my hits included a photo of a hamburger, wrapped in waxed paper. But it's still pretty amazing that it does work to some extent.

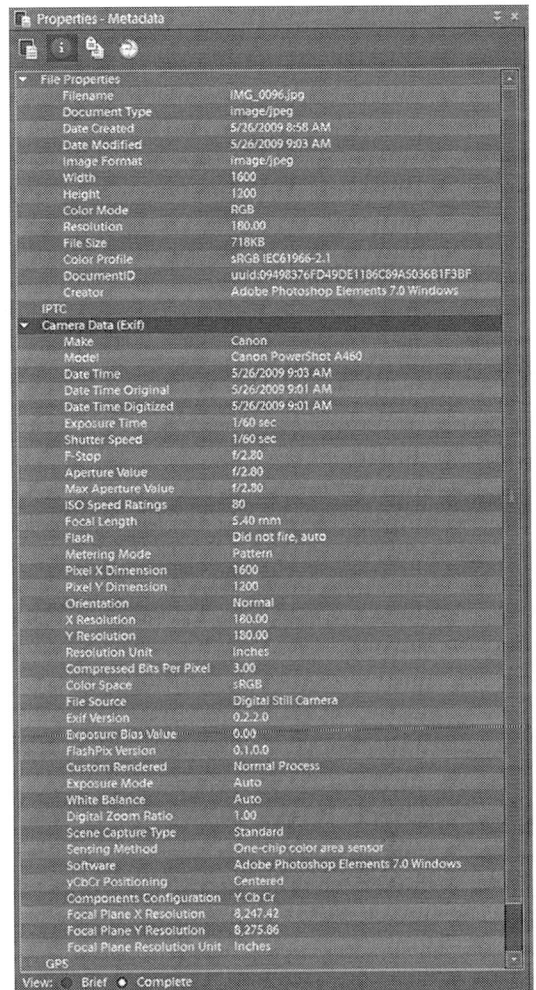

A sampling of the hidden Metadata that's a part of every digital photo's data

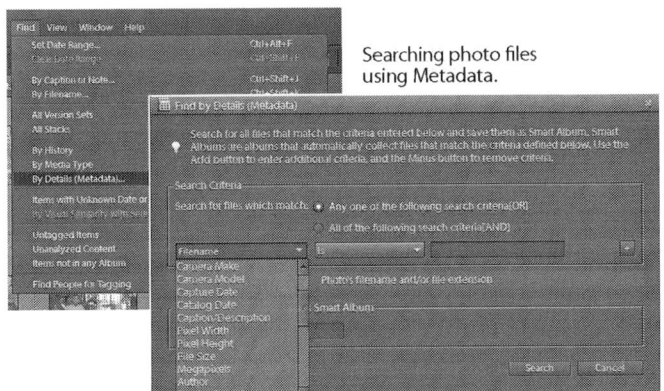

Searching photo files using Metadata.

The Smart Tags Media Analyzer

Smart Tags are **Keyword Tag** metadata that the Elements Organizer automatically adds to your media files.

As you are working on other things, the Organizer, by default, is **Media Analyzing** every video clip in its catalog and tagging each with metadata based on its audio, brightness and contrast, motion, shake, blur, face presence and object motion. The results are automatically added as **Smart Tags** in the **Keyword Tags** panel (as illustrated on the right) and can be used for filtering your **Photo Browser** view to include clips of similar traits.

The good news is that this is a *background* task and should not interfere with your other work.

The bad news is that, particularly on less powerful computers, it *does* sometimes interfere regardless.

If you find your computer's performance lagging a bit when you've got the Organizer open, you can turn off this feature and lose very little in the process. To turn off the feature, go to the Organizer's **Edit** drop-down on its Menu Bar and select **Preferences**. Under **Media Analysis Options**, uncheck the option to **Analyze Media Automatically**.

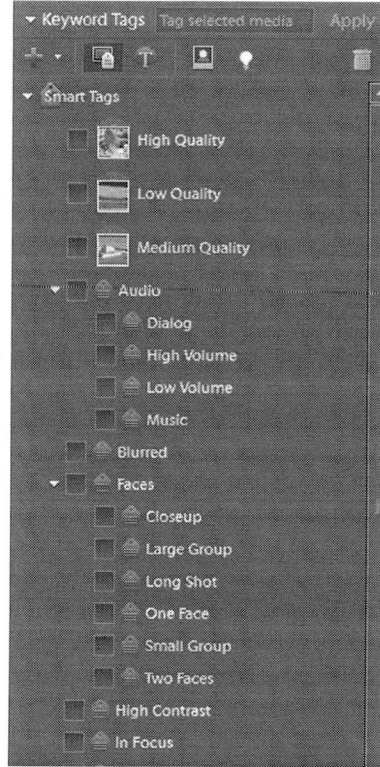

Smart Tags are Keyword metadata that the Organizer automatically generates based on its Auto Analysis of clips. These Smart Tags can not only be used to filter searches but also play a role in the function of several of Premiere Elements' tools.

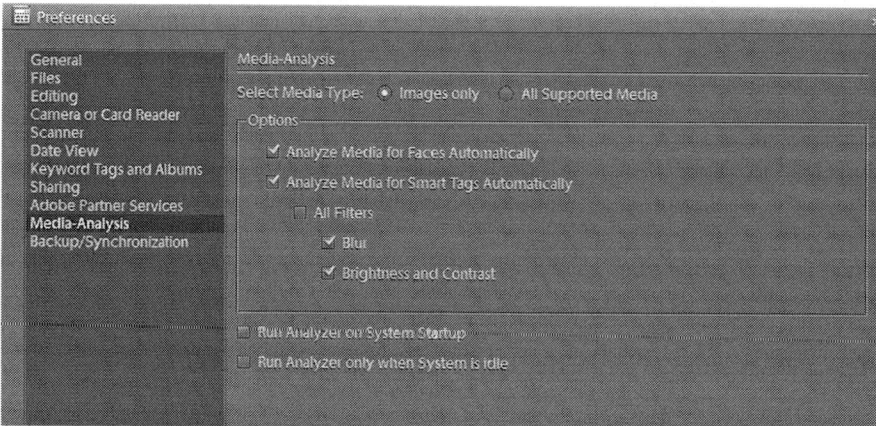

Media Analyzer settings in the Organizer's Preferences.

Continued on facing page

Metadata in different views

In the **Properties** palette, you can add captions or notes to your photos. Or, by dragging across the stars under each clip, you can assign a one- to five-star rating for the clip. Then you can, for instance, search for only five-star rated files or only files that include the caption text "Joey's birthday."

You can also add Metadata and catalog your media files in less literal ways. For instance, right-click on any photo (this one doesn't work with video or audio files) and you'll find the option to **Place on Map**. This opens up an option screen for adding an address. Click on the **Display** button in the upper right corner of the Organizer and select **Show Map**.

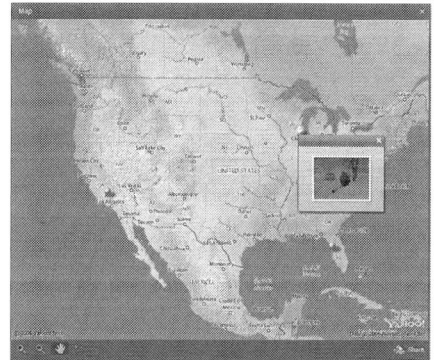

You can use Metadata to tag your photos with a location – so that you can retrieve them by clicking on pinpoints on a map!

Photos to which you have added **location** metadata – either by typing an address for or by simply dragging from the **Photo Browser** to the map – show up as pins on the map. In other words, you can catalog your photos according to where they were shot!

(Some new, higher-end digital cameras have GPS systems built into them and will automatically add location metadata to your pictures.)

Or, from the **Display** menu, you can also choose **Date View.** Instead of the Photo Browser, you'll be shown a calendar from which you can select your media files according to date.

Smart Tags Media Analyzer (continued)

Once you click **OK**, your computer should be much more responsive.

However, **Smart Tags** play a role in the functionality of a couple of tools in Premiere Elements. And disabling it can mean that these tools will perform more slowly or may not function at all. (Details on how these tools work can be found in **Chapter 19, Edit Your Video in Timeline Mode**):

- Both **Smart Trim** and **Motion Tracking** use information gathered by the **Media Analyzer** as part of their functionality. If you have not pre-analyzed a clip before you apply either of these tools to it, the program will offer to run the **Media Analyzer** on the clips before launching either of these tools.

- The **Smart Fix** tool in Premiere Elements (also discussed in **Chapter 19**) will *only* function with clips that have been **Media Analyzed** and **Smart Tagged** by the Organizer. In other words, if you have disabled the **Media Analyzer** and you have not generated **Smart Tags** for the clips that you are adding to your project, Premiere Elements will not offer to **Smart Fix** them and you will not be able to manually **Auto Enhance** them.

Even if you've disabled the automatic **Media-Analyzer,** you can *manually* run it on clips in the Elements Organizer. To do this, click or drag to select a clip or clips in the **Photo Browser**, **right-click** (**Ctrl-click** on the Mac) and select **Run Media Analyzer** from the context menu.

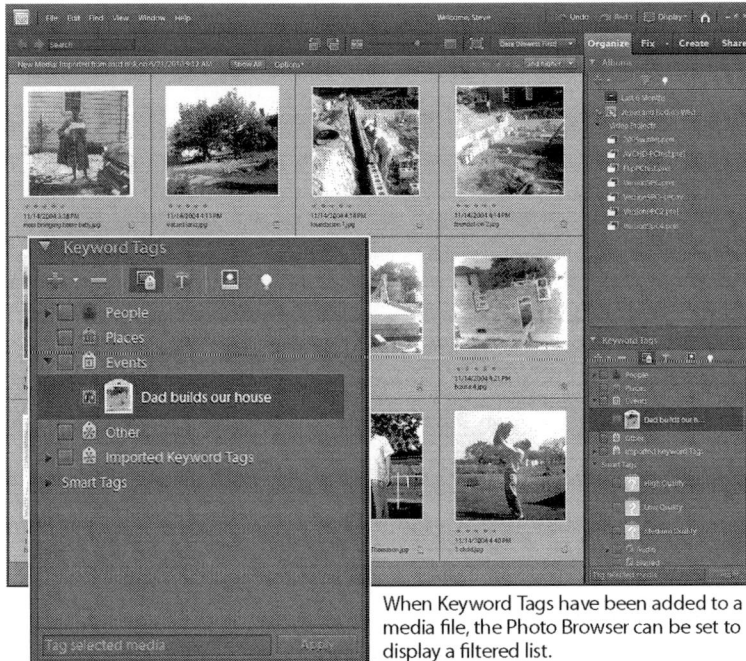

When Keyword Tags have been added to a media file, the Photo Browser can be set to display a filtered list.

Assign and filter with Keyword Tags

Tagging is another way of adding metadata to your media files.

In the **Keyword Tags** palette, you'll see a handful of basic **Categories** – People, Places, Events, Other.

Creating a new **Tag** is as simple as clicking on the **+** symbol on this palette. You can create as many **Tags** and as many **Categories** – and **Sub-Categories** under them – as you'd like. You can, for instance, create a **Sub-Category** under Places and name it France. And then, within that **Sub-Category**, create **Tags** for Cousin Pierre, Landmarks, The Louvre, etc. (You can even drag them in an out of sub-categories on the **Keyword Tags** panel!)

Assigning a **Tag** to a media file is as simple as dragging the **Tag** from the **Keyword Tags** palette onto the selected file(s) in the **Photo Browser**. (You'll notice that, once you do, a **Tag** icon will appear on the lower right of the file.)

You can assign as many **Tags** as you want to a file. And you can assign the same **Tag** to as many files as you'd like.

Adding **Keyword Tags** to your hundreds of accumulated digital photos may seem at first like a lot of housekeeping – but the payoff is great!

When you next want to locate the files for a particular **Tag**, you simply click on the **Tag** in the **Keyword Tags** palette to toggle it on. A little pair of binoculars will appear next to the selected **Tag**. Only media files that have been assigned to that **Tag** will appear in the Photo Browser area.

If you click on a major category, all of the files assigned to all of that category's sub-categories of **Tags** will appear. As you narrow your **Tag** search, only the files assigned to the **Tag** will be displayed.

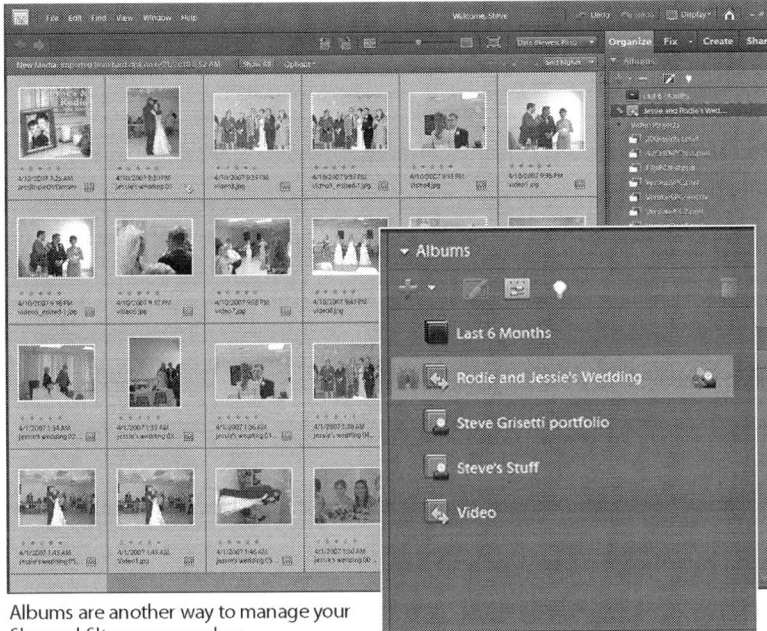

Albums are another way to manage your files and filter your searches.

Assign and filter with Albums

Just as you can add **Tags** to a file, you can catalog your media files into **Albums** for easier searching and filtering.

As with **Tags**, you click on the **+** icon in the **Album** panel to create an **Album**. And, as with **Tags**, to assign a file to an **Album**, you simply drag the **Album** from the **Albums** palette onto the media file or files in the **Photo Browser**. A little green icon will appear in the lower right of each file.

In addition, the Organizer automatically creates a new **Album** whenever you create a new Premiere Elements project and assigns all of the media for that project to it. These **Albums** will appear yellow in the panel rather than green, as the **Albums** you create manually.

To locate the media files assigned to a particular **Album**, click to select that **Album's** listing in the panel. A little pair of binoculars will appear next to the selected **Album** and only files assigned to that **Album** will appear in the Organizer's **Photo Browser**.

Create a Smart Album

An interesting feature of the **Album** palette is its ability to create **Smart Albums**. (You'll find the option under the **+** button in the **Albums** palette.)

When you create a **Smart Album**, you merely set up the criteria, based on metadata or **Tags**, and the Organizer will automatically assign your media files to an **Album** based on that criteria. You can, for instance, create a **Smart Album** that searches for files you've assigned five-star ratings to. As you rate and re-rate your media files, the **Smart Album** feature will automatically update its file collection for that **Album**.

Designate an Album for online back-up

Albums also play a role in **Photoshop.com's** online file back-up service. Once a media file has been assigned to an **Album**, it can be designated for online backup.

When you create a new **Album** (by clicking the green **+** button), the **Album** panel will display the option to **Backup/Synchronize** this **Album** online.

When you manually create a new Album in the Organizer, you'll have the option of setting it to backup online automatically.

On the **Backup/Synchronization** page of the Organizer's **Preferences** (located under **Edit** drop-down menu) you can see a list of all of the **Albums** that have been designated for online backup as well as an indicator of how much free space you have in your **Photoshop.com** account. For more information on using this service, see **Back your files up online** in **Chapter 34, Photoshop.com.**)

What are Stacks?

Another way to bring order to the many files in your **Photo Browser** is to store them in **Stacks**. **Stacks** are essentially groups of photos that you create – usually of similar photos, but that's up to you.

When you create a **Stack**, only one file in the stack is displayed in the **Photo Browser** (with a **Stack** icon on it). The rest of the files in the stack are hidden "behind" it – as if they were in a stack.

A Stack is a set of photo files stored under the same thumbnail in the Photo Browser.

The arrow link unstacks the set.

When Organizer Fixes are applied to a photo file, the changed and unchanged versions are saved as a Stack.

To create a **Stack**, select several files (by dragging across them, by holding the Shift key as you select the first and last in a series or by holding the Ctrl key and selecting one at a time) and then **right-click** (**Ctrl-click** on a Mac) and select the **Stack Selected Photos** option.

Stacks are also created automatically when you apply an Organizer **Quick Fix** to a photo. Within this **Stack** is both the cleaned-up and original photo.

To reveal all the files in a **Stack**, click on the unstack arrow button on the right side of the **Stack** thumbnail, as illustrated on the previous page.

To open all **Stacks**, go to the **View** drop-down on the Organizer menu bar and select the option to **Expand All Stacks**.

Manually update the Organizer

If you move, delete or change files using Windows Explorer or a program other than one of the Elements programs, you may find your Organizer **Photo Browser** will display thumbnails with broken or outdated links.

To update these connections manually or to remove the thumbnail of a deleted file from the Organizer catalog, go to the **File** drop-down on the Menu Bar and select the option to **Reconnect/All Missing Files**.

The Organizer will update your links and indicate for you all of the thumbnails in the **Photo Browser** that do not have files linked to them, offering you the option of deleting these dead thumbnails.

To avoid the program's losing track of these links, you can use the Organizer to move or remove files from your computer.

- To delete a file using the Organizer, **right-click (Ctrl-click** on a Mac) on the file(s) and select **Delete from Catalog**. You will then be given the option of merely removing the file from the Organizer's catalog or removing it completely from your hard drive.

- To move a file to a new location on your computer using the Organizer, click to select the file(s) and, from the **File** drop-down, select the option to **Move** and then browse to the new location.

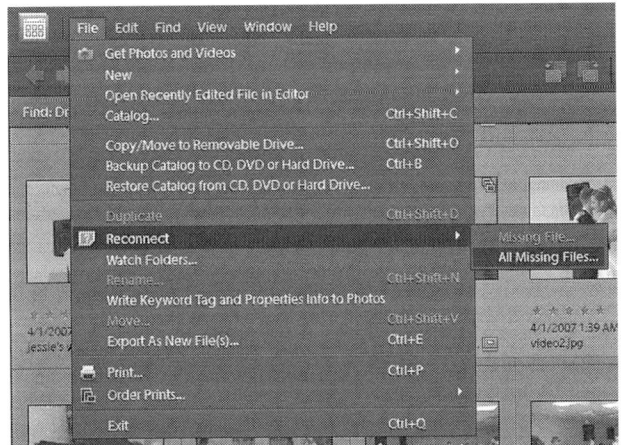

Reconnecting thumbnails to files – and deleting dead links.

You can also add files to your Organizer catalog manually.

- To add files and folders full of files to your Organizer's catalog, go to the **File** menu and select **Get Photos and Videos**. Then, from the sub-menu, select **From Files and Folders**. Browse to the file or folder of files you'd like to add click **Get Media**.

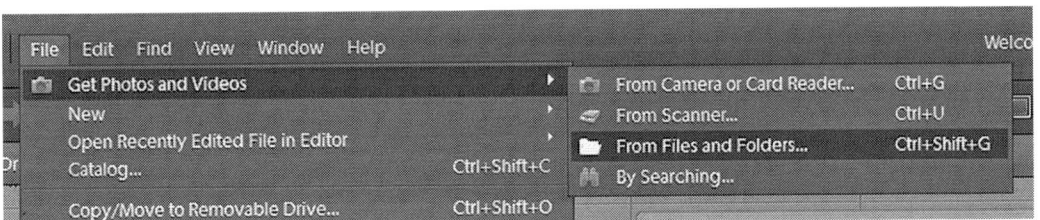

People Recognition

Adobe has given the Organizer's **People Recognition** feature a major reworking in version 9. The tool actually seems to learn as you use it – eventually getting to the point of recognizing faces on its own!

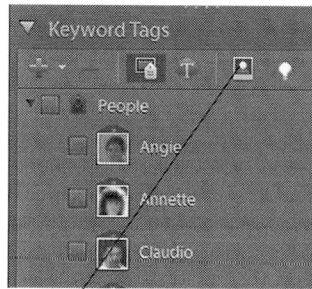

People Recognition Tool

1. Select one or more photos in the Organizer's **Photo Browser** workspace and click the **People Recognition** button on the **Keyword Tags** palette, as illustrated above. (**People Recognition** does not work with video clips.)

   The tool will display thumbnail images of the faces of the people in your selected photos with the words "**Who is this?**" below them.

2. Identify the person in the picture. Once you've typed in his or her name, it will appear as a **Keyword Tag** under the **People** category, linking to your photo.

3. As you continue to identify people, the program will build a database of features and will soon begin guessing at people's names. Sometimes this guess will appear as one of three possibilities. Other times it will ask simply, "**Is this –?**"

4. Occasionally the tool will try to identify something in your photo that's not a face at all. In that case, just click the **X** above the thumbnail. Other times it may not see a person in a scene. In that case you can ID the face manually.

   To manually add a **People Recognition** tag to a photo, double-click on the photo in the **Photo Browser**. The photo will zoom in to full-screen view.

Click the **Add a Missing Person** button (in the lower right of the photo space). An identification box will appear in the upper left corner of your photo. Position it over the person you want to ID and type in the person's name in the space provided.

The photo's identification tag will be added to the **People** category of **Keyword Tags**.

To locate all photos in which a given person appears, check the box next to his or her name in the **Keyword Tags** palette.

Chapter 32

Create Fun Photo Pieces
Make something of your photos

Photoshop Elements includes a number of tools for creating everything from a photo scrapbook to a greeting card, a calendar, a US postage stamp or a CD cover.

Using the templates and wizards in Photoshop Elements and the Organizer, creating these photo pieces is as simple as selecting your artwork and following the prompts.

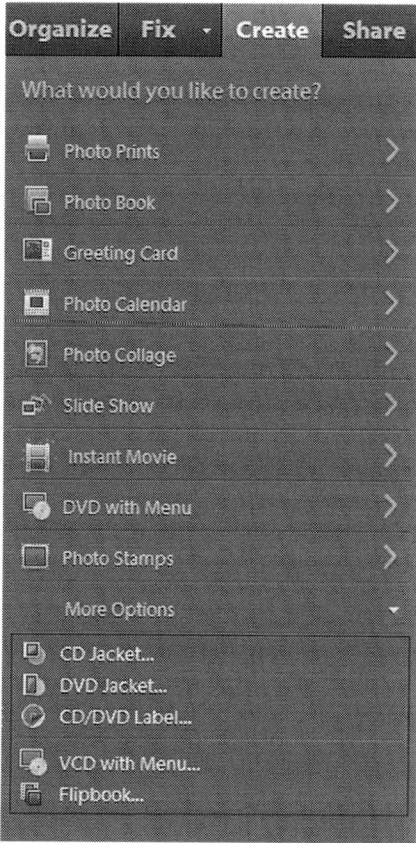

The **Create** tab on in the Elements Editor and the virtually identical tab in the Photoshop Elements' Editor serves as a portal to a number of tools for creating fun and attractive pieces from your photo files.

Whether you launch these tools from Editor or the Organizer, the tools behave exactly the same way. Launching from the Organizer simply allows you to select your photo assets in advance of launching the tool.

If you launch these tools from the Editor workspace, photos will automatically be added to your "Create" projects if they appear in the **Project Bin**. (The **Project Bin** can be set to display photo files from a number of sources, as we discuss in **Chapter 14, Get to Know Photoshop Elements**.)

If the "Create" tools are launched from the Organizer, the tools will automatically include any photos you've gathered in the Organizer's **Photo Browser**.

In most cases, however, these tools *will only work with photos or still graphics*. With few exceptions, you will not be able to use "Create" tools with video or audio files.

A few of the tools are only available on the Windows version of Photoshop Elements and the Elements Organizer. We've noted which will not work on a Mac in the detailed discussions of these particular tools.

Create Photo Prints

Photoshop Elements offers a number of options for producing print-outs of your photos.

Print Individual Prints on your local printer

It's no surprise that this option sends your selected photo(s) to your printer. But you may be surprised at the number of possible print layouts this option screen includes!

1. Click to select the **Photo Prints** option under the **Create** tab and then select **Print with Local Printer**.

    The photos selected in the Organizer's **Photo Browser** or open in Photoshop Elements Editor are sent to the **Print Photos** option panel. These photos are displayed as thumbnails along the left side of the panel, and you may add or remove photos from this list.

2. By default, your photos will print one per page, at their actual size. However, you have a number of options for changing the number and sizes of the photos on each page.

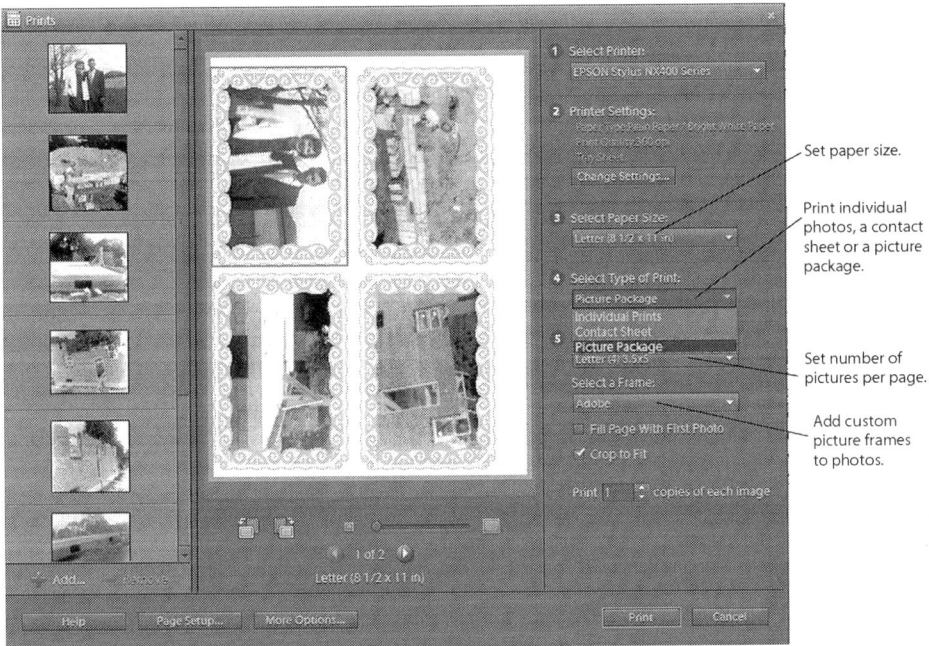

Set paper size.

Print individual photos, a contact sheet or a picture package.

Set number of pictures per page.

Add custom picture frames to photos.

The Print option includes settings for printing your photos in a variety of sizes and layouts as well as options for adding cool custom frames.

Under **Select Type of Print**:

Individual Prints prints photos to your printer at the size you designate.

Contact Sheet prints proof-style thumbnails of your photos, according to the layout settings you provide.

Picture Package prints a number of photos to your printer based on how many photos you designate per page. This option also allows you the option of printing these photos with a **Frame** around each.

Whenever you print any photo, it's important to consider the resolution of the image. Printing photos smaller than their actual size will usually not be a problem. However, if you set your photo to print at a size in which its final output resolution is less than 150-200 ppi, you will likely see reduced quality and fuzziness in your output. This could definitely be a problem if you selected the **Individual Print** option and set the photo to **Fit on Page** size.

Print a Picture Package or Contact Sheet on your local printer

The main difference between the **Picture Package** or **Contact Sheet** and **Individual Prints** print-out options is in how you set the size and number of photos that will appear on your print-out page. When **Type of Print** is set to **Individual Prints**, you will have the option of selecting the *size* your photos will print out at. When you set the **Type of Print** option to **Picture Package** or **Contact Sheet**, you have the option of selecting the *number* of photos you want to printed on each page.

379

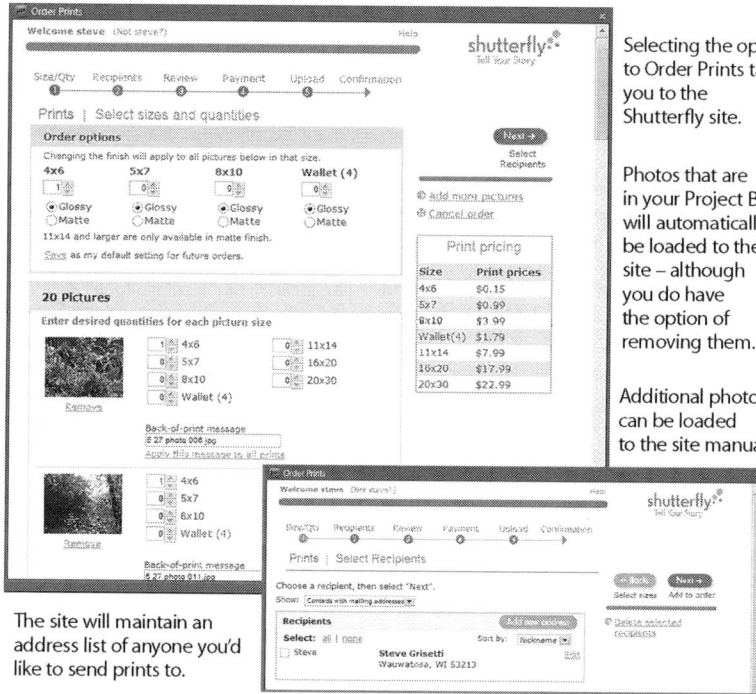

Selecting the option to Order Prints takes you to the Shutterfly site.

Photos that are in your Project Bin will automatically be loaded to the site – although you do have the option of removing them.

Additional photos can be loaded to the site manually.

The site will maintain an address list of anyone you'd like to send prints to.

Order prints through Shutterfly

When you select the **Shutterfly** option from under the **Create** tab's **Photo Prints** button, you can order high-quality prints of your photos from **Shutterfly**, an online photo service.

1. Sign on with or log on to **Shutterfly**.

2. Logging on opens an option screen at which you can add or remove photos and select the sizes of prints you would like.

    If you have photos open in your **Project Bin** when you launch this tool, they will be included in the order unless you **Remove** them.

    If you'd like to add additional photos, click on the **Add More Pictures** button on the upper right of the screen. Click **Next**.

3. In the screens that follow, you can list the names of anyone you would like prints shipped directly to (You'll need to include your own name and address, of course).

    Select your method of payment and upload your photos.

Once you've uploaded your photos and confirmed your information, the files will be sent to Shutterfly via the Internet. You should receive your prints by mail within a week.

Order prints through Kodak Gallery

Through Photoshop Elements, you can order high-quality prints of your photos from **Kodak Gallery**, an online photo service.

1. Under the **Create** tab, click the **Photo Prints** button and select the **Kodak Gallery** option. You'll be prompted to sign up with or log onto **KodakGallery.com**.

2. Logging on opens an option screen on which you can add or remove photos and select the sizes of prints you would like.

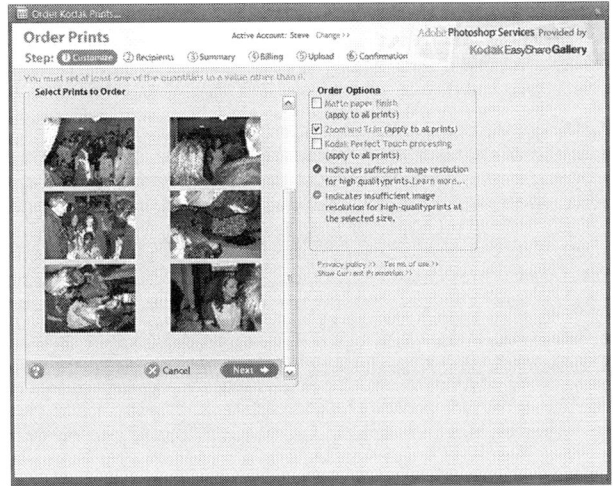

   If you have photos open in your **Project Bin** when you launch this tool, they will be included in the order, unless you **Remove** them.

   If you'd like to add additional photos, click on the **Upload** button along the top of the screen.

   Click **Next**.

3. In the screens that follow, you can list the names of anyone you would like prints shipped to. (You'll need to include your own name and address, of course.)

   Select your method of payment and upload your photos.

Once you've uploaded your photos and confirmed your information, the files will be sent to Kodak via the Internet. You should receive your prints by mail within a week.

Autofilling "Create" projects

When you've got **Autofill with Selected Images** checked on the option panel for your "Create" project, the program will automatically fill your project either with photos gathered in the Photoshop Elements **Project Bin** or selected in the Elements Organizer **Photo Browser**.

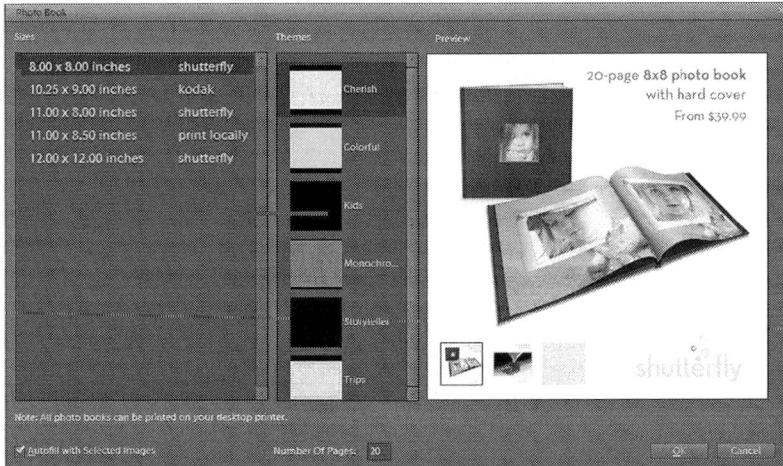

The Photo Book option panel.

Create a Photo Book

A **Photo Book** is a collection of photos laid out in from 20 to 80 custom-designed pages. The wizard takes you through the basic steps of setting up the book. Once the book is initially set up, you can add more photos to it and tweak the design and layout.

A **Photo Book** can be sent to **Shutterfly** or **Kodak** for professional printing and binding, or it can be printed out on your home printer.

1. Click the **Photo Book** button under the **Create** tab.

    Any photos you have in your **Project Bin** – whether because they are open in the **Editor** or selected in the **Organizer** – will automatically be loaded into your **Photo Book** in the order that they appear in the **Project Bin**. Photos may also be added or removed after the book is created.

    The first photo in the **Project Bin** will become your **Title Page Photo**. To designate another photo as your **Title Page Photo**, rearrange the order of the photos in the **Project Bin**.

2. Select a size and output options for your book from the **Photo Book** option screen (illustrated above). You can select to have the book professionally produced by **Shutterfly** or **Kodak** or you select the 11"x8½" version and print it out on your home printer.

3. On this same panel, select a **Theme** for your book and indicate the number of pages you'd like your book to have. (These features can be modified later. However, the minimum number of pages your **Photo Book** can have is 20).

    Click **OK**.

The program will generate your book with a minimum of 20 pages, filling as many as pages as possible with the photos in your **Project Bin**.

Click a block of text to customize it.

Click on photo to modify or replace it.

Select a page for editing from the Page bin.

Optional panels for modifying page layouts, theme artwork text and photo effects.

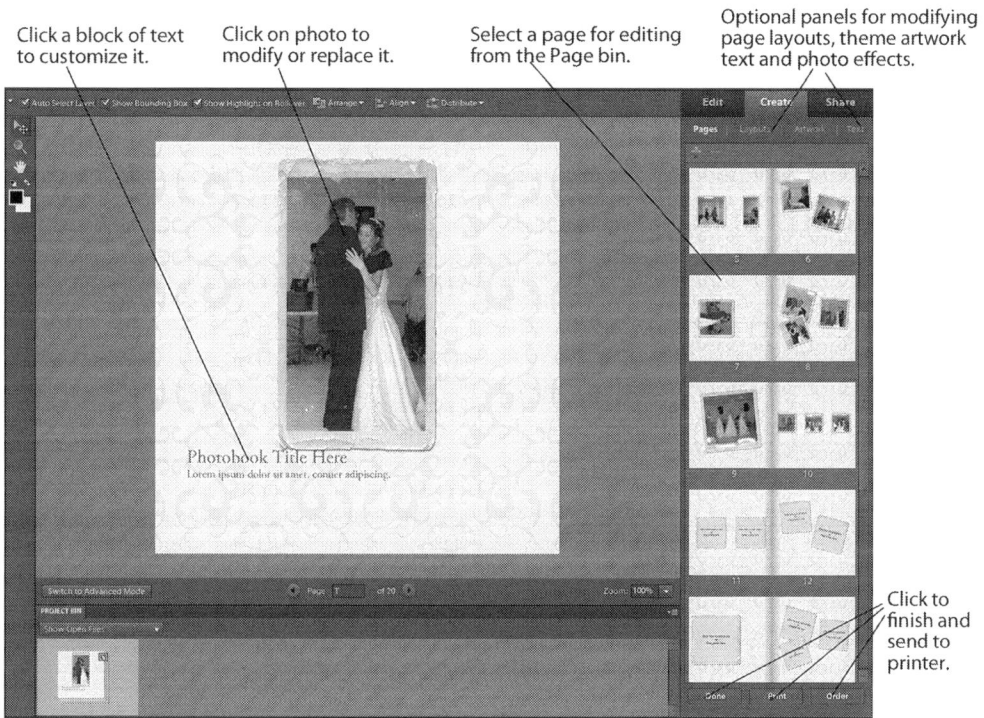

Photobook Title Here
Lorem ipsum dolor ut amet, conuer adipiscing.

Click to finish and send to printer.

You may add more pages to your book by clicking the green + sign along the bottom of the **Photo Book** panel and you may subtract pages by clicking the – button. (Your **Photo Book** must, however, include a minimum of 20 pages).

You may also change the theme and/or frames for the individual pages by selecting options under the **Artwork** button.

To add photos to unfilled frames – or to replace existing photos – click on the frame.

- If the frame is blank, you'll be prompted to browse for a photo on your hard drive.

- If a photo is already in the frame, options will be displayed to enlarge the photo within the frame, rotate it or replace it.

By dragging on their corner handles, photos and their frames can be resized and repositioned on the page.

Along the bottom of the **Photo Book** workspace panel, you will find the options to **Order** your book or to finish it and **Print** it on your home printer.

Double-clicking on a photo in your Photo Book displays tools for adjusting the size and position of the photo or even browsing for a replacement.

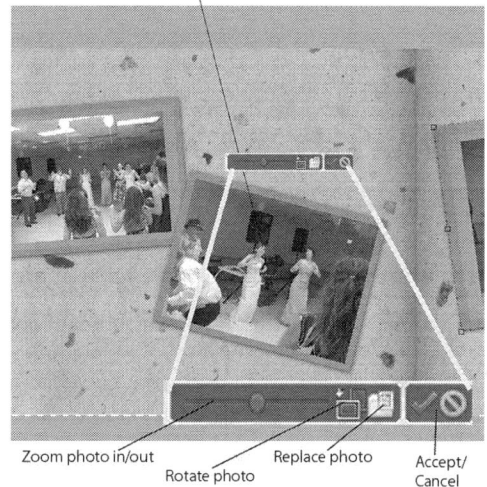

Zoom photo in/out

Rotate photo

Replace photo

Accept/Cancel

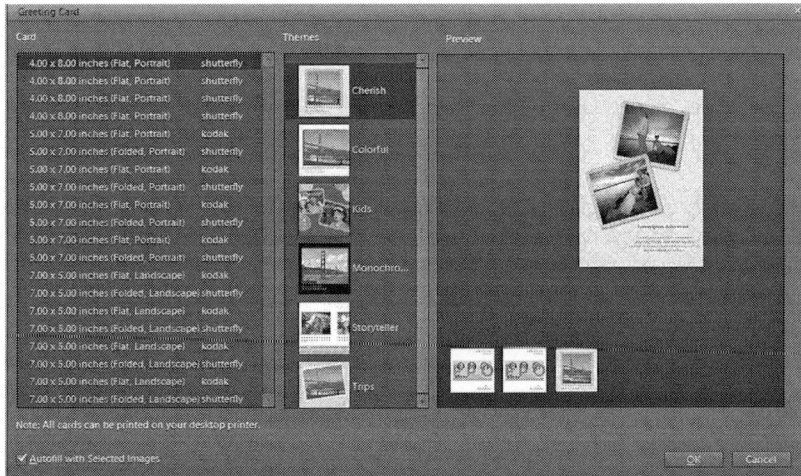

The Greeting Card option panel.

Create a Greeting Card

A **Greeting Card** can be sent to **Shutterfly** or **Kodak** for professional printing or it can be printed out on your home printer.

1. Click the **Greeting Card** button under the **Create** tab.

   The photos you have in your **Project Bin** – whether because they are open in the **Editor** or selected in the **Organizer** – will automatically be loaded into your **Greeting Card**. Photos may also be added or removed after the book is created.

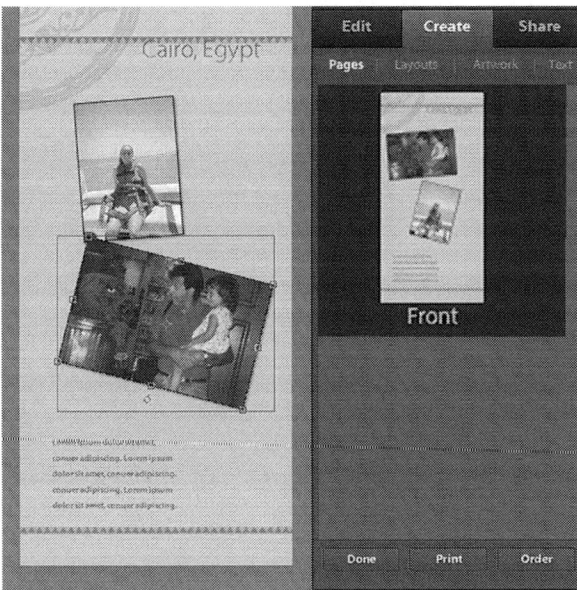

2. Select a size and output options for your book from the **Greeting Card** option screen (illustrated above). You can send your card to Shutterfly or Kodak for professional production or print it out on your home printer.

3. On this same panel, select a **Theme** for your card. (These features can be modified later.)

   Click **OK**.

   The program will generate your card.

   As with the **Photo Book**, you may swap out photos and modify your **Greeting Card's** theme, effects or text, as described on page 391.

After the program generates your card, you can modify its theme, text, photos and effects.

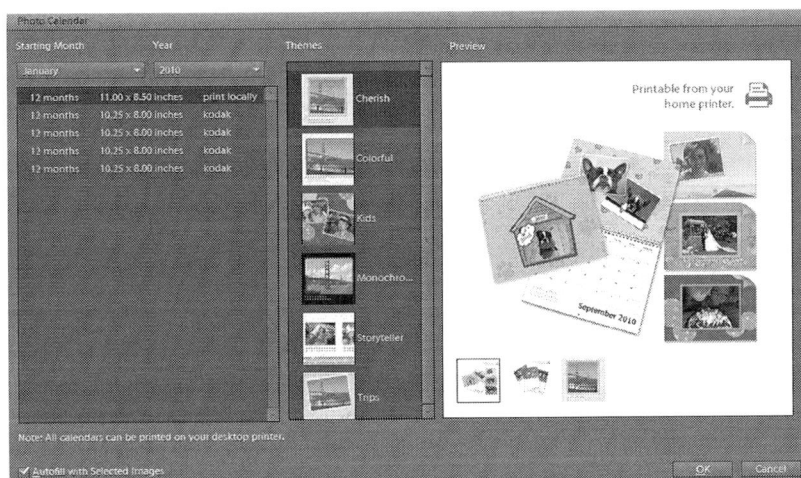

The Calendar option panel.

Create a Photo Calendar

A **Photo Calendar** can be sent to **Kodak** for professional printing or it can be printed out on your home printer.

1. Click the **Photo Calendar** button under the **Create** tab.

   The photos you have in your **Project Bin** – whether because they are open in the **Editor** or selected in the **Organizer** – will automatically be loaded into your **Photo Calendar.** Photos may also be added or removed after the book is created.

2. Select a size and output options for your book from the **Photo Calendar** option screen (illustrated above). You can send your card to Kodak for professional production or print it out on your home printer.

3. On this same panel, select a **Theme** for your card. (These features can be modified later.)

   Click **OK**.

The program will generate your card.

As with the **Photo Book**, you may swap out photos and modify your **Photo Calendar's** theme, effects or text, as described on page 391.

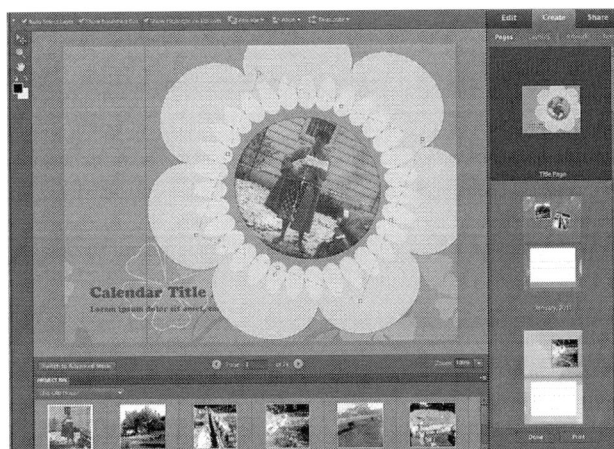

After the program generates your calendar, you can modify its theme, text, photos and effects.

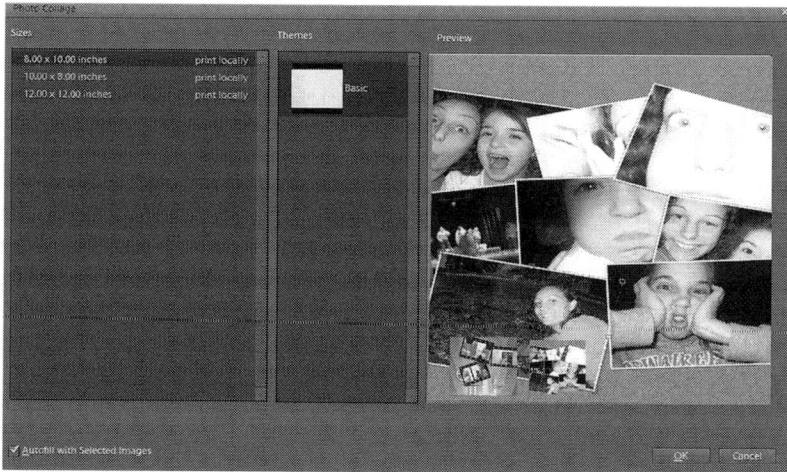

The Photo Collage option screen.

Create a Photo Collage

A **Photo Collage** is an arrangement of photos gathered together in an artful or playful way. Once you create your **Photo Collage**, you'll be able to print it out on your home printer.

1. Click the **Photo Collage** button under the **Create** tab.

   The photos you have in your **Project Bin** – whether because they are open in the **Editor** or selected in the **Organizer** – will automatically be loaded into your **Photo Collage.** Photos may also be added or removed after the book is created.

2. Select a size for your **Photo Collage** from the option screen (illustrated above).

3. On this same panel, select a **Theme** for your card. (These features can be modified later.)

   Click **OK**.

The program will generate your card.

As with the **Photo Book**, you may swap out photos and modify your **Photo Collage's** theme, effects or text, as described on page 391.

Create a Slideshow

Slideshows can be created in Photoshop Elements and then ported to Premiere Elements for output as a video or DVD. For more information see **Create a Slideshow** in **Chapter 35, Use the Elements Programs Together**.

(This feature, by the way, is not available on the MacIntosh version of the program.)

Create an InstantMovie

This option is available only under the Organizer's **Create** tab. Clicking the option to create an **InstantMovie** gathers the photos and video clips you've selected in the Organizer's **Photo Browser** and ports them to Premiere Elements, where an **InstantMovie Theme** is applied. For more information on **InstantMovies** and **Themes**, see **Chapter 22, Create InstantMovies and Use Movie Themes**.

Create a DVD with Menu

This option is also available only under the Organizer's **Create** tab. Clicking the option to create a **DVD With Menu** gathers the photos and video clips you've selected in the Organizer's **Photo Browser** and ports them to a Premiere Elements project for further editing.

For information on adding a menu to a video project, see **Chapter 28, Create DVD and BluRay Disc Menus**.

More Create projects

There are even more "**Create**" projects available under the **More Options** button.

These other photo projects are assembled similarly: You gather your assets (photos), either by opening them in the **Editor** or displaying them in the **Project Bin**; you select your template and generate your piece; you save your piece and then select the option of either printing it yourself or sending it to Adobe Photoshop Services, Kodak or Shutterfly for final production.

Other **Create** projects include:

PhotoStamps

This tool turns your photos into customized, perfectly legal US Postal stamps!

CD Jacket

Creates a 9¾" x 4¾" image that you can print out and fit into a CD or DVD "jewel case." (Note that disc jewel cases are 4¾" x 4¾", so this artwork is designed to wrap around the case and include a ¼" spine.)

Photoshop Elements even includes a tool for creating your own, custom, (and perfectly legal) US postage stamps!

DVD Jacket

Creates an 11" x 7½" label for a DVD case. This template is made to fit a 5¼" x 7½" case with a ½" wide spine.

CD/DVD Label

Creates 4¾", circular-shaped artwork for printing onto discs. It includes the necessary spindle hole through the center. (At Muvipix, we recommend never using glue-on labels for your DVDs and CDs. They can cause any number of problems. Use this template only for printable discs and inkjet printers designed to print them.)

VCD with Menu

Creates a CD of an existing slideshow, with a generic start menu, which can be played on a personal computer and many DVD players. (VCDs generally use a lower resolution video format and are considered of inferior quality to DVDs.)

(This feature is not available on the MacIntosh version of the program.)

Flipbook

A **Flipbook** is an animation created by combining several photo files, each photo acting as a frame in a WMV (Windows Media) movie. Your photos are displayed at speeds of between one and 30 frames per second. The final WMV output can be output at Web, VCD or DVD resolution and quality.

(This feature is not available on the MacIntosh version of the program.)

Share Your Photos as E-mail Attachments
Share Your Photos as Photo Mail
Share Your Photos and Videos Online
Share Your Photos to a CD or DVD
Share Your Photos to a PDF Slideshow
Send a Photo to a CEIVA Picture Frame

Chapter 33
Share Your Photos and Videos
Output and upload your files

Photoshop Elements includes a number
of tools for outputting your photos files
– from posting them online and e-mailing
them to creating a DVD or PDF slideshow.

You can even send your photos to an
online service that automatically loads
them, live, into a digital photo frame
almost anywhere in the world!

Organize	Fix ·	Create	Share

How would you like to share?

- 🖼 Online Album →
- 📎 E-mail Attachments →
- 💬 Photo Mail →
- 📀 Burn Video DVD / BluRay →
- 🌐 Online Video Sharing →
- 📱 Mobile Phones and Players →
- 📷 Share to Flickr →
- f Share to Facebook →
- 📷 Send to SmugMug Gallery →
- P Podcast with Podbean →

More Options ▾

- 📄 PDF Slide Show...
- 🖼 Send To CEIVA Photo Frame ...
- 🖼 Share with Kodak Easyshare Gallery ...

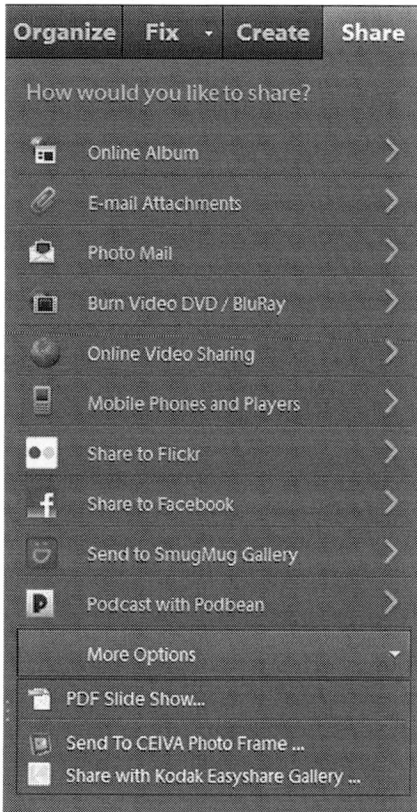

As with **Create** projects, most of the program's **Share** projects will automatically gather photo files you have open or that you have displayed in your **Project Bin** (along the bottom of the Editor workspace).

Your **Project Bin** can be set to display the photo files you have open in the **Editor**, photo files you have selected in the **Organizer** or photos that are stored in an **Album**. (For information on gathering photos into **Albums**, see **Chapter 31, The Organizer.**)

Share an Online Album

An **Online Album** is an attractive way to share your photos on a Web site, such as **Photoshop.com**, by displaying your pictures as a slideshow.

Photos in an **Online Album** can be viewed online, or your viewer can download them to his/her computer and print them out.

For information on how to create an **Online Album** and display it online, see **Create an Online Album with the Organizer** in **Chapter 34, Photoshop.com**.

Share E-mail Attachments

The **E-mail Attachment** option optimizes your selected photo files and then sends them off, with a brief note, to the person or group of people you designate as **Recipients**.

1. Click to select the **E-mail Attachment** option under the **Share** tab in the Organizer. (You can also launch this tool from the **Editor** workspace – however, the wizard itself launches in the Organizer.) The **E-mail Attachment** option panel will open (as illustrated on the facing page).

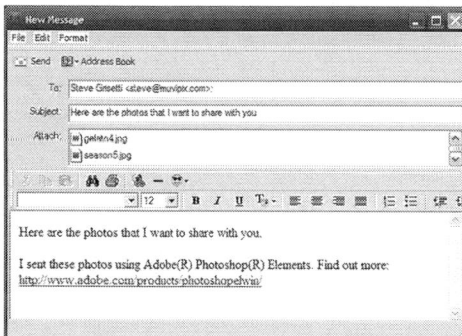

Your photos are optimized and then e-mailed from Adobe E-mail Services.

If there are photos open in your Photoshop Elements Editor workspace or selected in your Organizer's **Photo Browser,** they will automatically be added to your **E-mail Attachments Items** bin.

2. Drag any additional photo(s) you'd like converted into e-mail attachments from the Organizer's **Photo Browser** into the **E-mail Attachments Items** bin. To remove any you'd like removed from the bin by selecting them and clicking the **red minus** button on the panel.

You can add photos in any file format. The program will convert whatever you add to this bin into a JPEG for e-mailing.

Set the **Photo Size** and **Quality**. The **Estimated Size** indicator displays the approximate loading time for your e-mail over a 56 kbps modem.

In this age of high-speed Internet, that may not seem like a state-of-the-art measurement for load times.

However, the point is that you *do* want to keep any files you plan to e-mail small enough that they don't bog down your recipient's account.

When you are happy with your settings for this panel, click **Next**.

3. Create a message to accompany your photos and then **Select Recipients** from your list of contacts, as illustrated on the next page.

   (See the sidebar on page 401 – **Create an Elements Organizer Contact Book** – for information on creating your **Contacts** list.)

   When you are happy with your settings for this panel, click **Next**.

4. A preview of the outgoing e-mail – including your selected photo(s) – will display on your screen. This is one last chance to make any adjustments you'd like to the e-mail.

   When you are happy with your out-going e-mail, click the **Send** button.

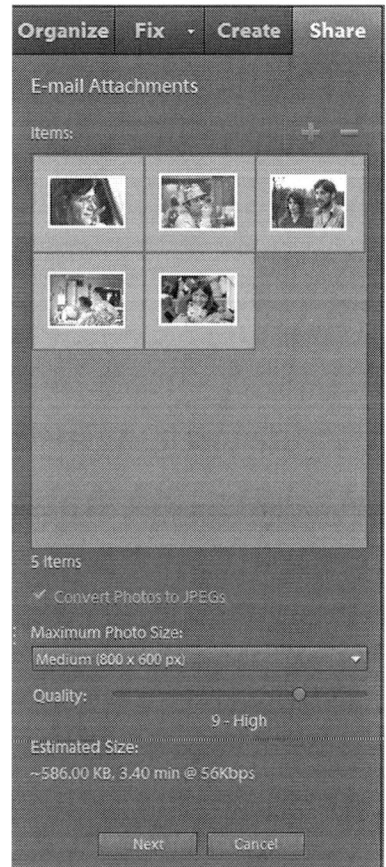

Photos are added to the Items bin from the Organizer Photo Browser. E-mail attachments will be converted to JPEGs and should be set to an optimized size and quality.

Set up e-mail sharing for the Elements Organizer

In order to use the Elements Organizer's e-mail **Share** options, you must have an active e-mail address listed on the **Sharing** page of the Organizer's **Preferences** (under the **Edit** drop-down on the Organizer Menu Bar).

The first time you use the **Share** options for either **E-mail Attachments** or **Photo Mail**, you will be prompted to enter a **Sender Verification Number.** This number will be sent, automatically, to you at the e-mail address you've listed in your **Preferences**.

Copy and paste that number into the Organizer's **HTML E-mail Sender Verification** screen to activate your account.

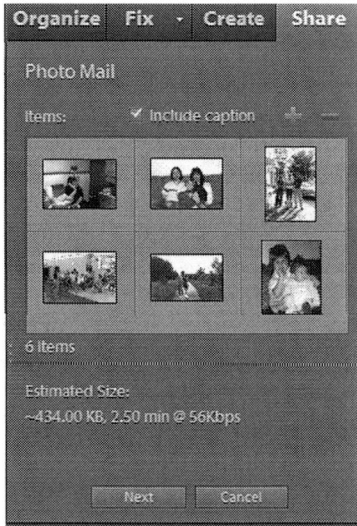

Collect the photos you'd like in your composition in the Photo Mail Items bin.

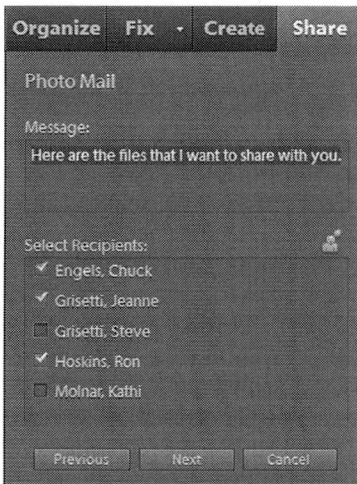

Your recipients are selected from your Photoshop Elements Contact Book, set up in the Organizer's preferences.

Using the Stationery & Layout Wizard, you can select a custom layout and background for your Photo Mail.

Share Photo Mail

Photo Mail creates an attractive HTML-based e-mail of your selected photo(s), on your choice of stationery backgrounds and in your preferred layout, as in the illustration at the bottom of this page.

1. Click to select the **Photo Mail** option under the **Share** tab in the Organizer. (You can also launch this tool from the **Editor** workspace – however, the wizard itself launches in the Organizer.) The **Photo Mail** option panel will open, displaying the thumbnails of the photos that will be included in your **Photo Mail** composition.

   If there are photos open in your Photoshop Elements Editor workspace or selected in your Organizer's **Photo Browser**, they will automatically be added to your **Photo Mail Items** bin.

2. Drag any additional photo(s) you'd like converted into e-mail attachments into the **Photo Mail Items** bin from the Organizer's **Photo Browser**. To remove any you'd like removed from the bin by selecting them and clicking the **red minus** button on the panel.

   When you are happy with your settings for this panel, click **Next**.

3. Create a message for your recipients and then **Select Recipients** from your list of contacts.

   (See the sidebar on the following page – **Creating an Elements Organizer Contact Book** – for information on creating your **Contacts** list.)

   When you are happy with your settings for this panel, click **Next**.

4. From the pop-up **Stationery & Layouts Wizard**, choose the background stationery you would like to display your photos on from the templates along the left of the panel.

   Click **Next Step**.

5. In the **Choose a Layout** screen, you can add captions to the photos and further customize the layout, if you'd like.

6. When you are happy with your settings for this panel, click **Next**.

   Your **Photo Mail** will be sent to the recipients you indicated.

Create an Elements Organizer Contact Book

In order to have the options to **Select Recipients** for your **E-mail Attachments** or **Photo Mail,** you will need to have these potential recipients listed in your Elements Organizer's **Contact Book**.

To create and add your contacts to this book, go to the **Edit** drop-down on the Organizer Menu Bar and select **Contact Book**.

Click **New Contacts** and type in your contacts' names and e-mail addresses.

Once they have been added to your **Contact Book, these names** will be listed under **Select Recipients** whenever your select the **E-mail Attachment** or **Photo Mail** option.

Burn Video DVD/BluRay Disc

When you click on the **Share** option to **Burn a DVD/BluRay disc**, the files you have selected in the Organizer's **Photo Browser** will be ported to a Premier Elements project. (This option is only available on the Organizer workspace.)

For information on creating menus for a DVD or BluRay disc in Premiere Elements, see **Chapter 28, Create DVD and BluRay Disc Menus**.

Share via Online Video Sharing

When you click on the **Online Video Share** option, the files you have selected in the Organizer's **Photo Browser** will be ported to a Premier Elements project. (This option is only available on the Organizer workspace.)

For information on sharing your photos and videos online from Premiere Elements, see **Upload to a Web site or create a podcast** in **Chapter 29, Share Your Movie**.

Share via Mobile Phones and Players

When you click on the **Mobile Phones and Players Share** option, the files you have selected in the Organizer's **Photo Browser** will be ported to a Premier Elements project. (This option is only available on the Organizer workspace.)

For information on sharing your photos and videos to a portable device from Premiere Elements, see **Output to a mobile phone or video player** in **Chapter 29, Share Your Movie**.

Share your photos to Flickr

Flickr is a photo sharing site hosted by Yahoo. If you haven't already got a Yahoo and Flickr account, you'll be prompted to set one up before you can proceed with this **Share** option. But, once you have your account set up, you will be able to use your Photoshop Elements Organizer to directly upload your photos to the site.

Your Flickr account, by the way, can also be linked in with your **Photoshop.com** library, as discussed in **Linking to other photo sites** in **Chapter 34, Photoshop.com**.

Share your photos and videos to Facebook

If you've got a Facebook account, you can upload your photos and videos directly from the Organizer's Photo Browser to Facebook.

Your Facebook account, by the way, can also be linked in with your **Photoshop.com** library, as discussed in **Linking to other photo sites** in **Chapter 34, Photoshop.com**.

Send your photos to a SmugMug Gallery

A higher-end gallery for displaying your photos as an online slideshow, SmugMug offers a wide variety of attractive and stylish templates for displaying your pictures. SmugMug offers their services at prices ranging from $39.95 to $149.95 per year, with a 20% discount for Photoshop Elements users.

Podcast with PodBean

When you click on the **Podcast with PodBean Share** option, the files you have selected in the Organizer's **Photo Browser** will be ported to a Premier Elements project.

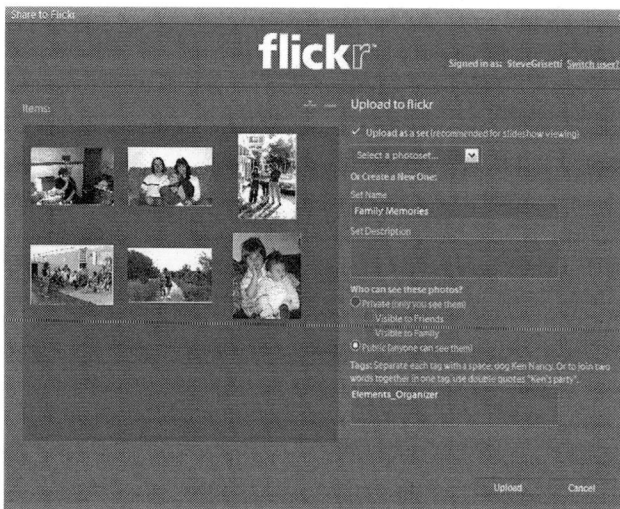

For information on posting podcasts from Premiere Elements, see **Upload to a Web site or create a podcast** in **Chapter 29, Share Your Movie**.

More Share Options

The **More Options** button under the **Share** tab offers some additional tools for sharing your photo files.

Share as a PDF Slide Show

Creates a dynamic slideshow of your selected photo files in PDF (Portable Document File) format and then e-mails the PDF to your selected recipients. The slideshow can be viewed using the free utility Acrobat Reader.

Send photos to a CEIVA Digital Photo Frame

The **CEIVA Picture Plan** is service that offers an online link to CEIVA digital photo frames all over the world. In other words, using this service, you can, for instance, upload a photo or photos directly from the Photoshop Elements Organizer in your home in Wisconsin to your mother's CEIVA digital picture frame in California!

CEIVA photo frames can be attached to the Internet via Ethernet or WiFi. In order to use this service, you or the recipient will need to purchase a **CEIVA PicturePlan**, at a cost of $9.95 per month.

Share with Kodak Easyshare Gallery

Like an **Online Album**, the **Kodak Easyshare Gallery** displays your selected photos as a very attractive online slideshow. An e-mail with a link to your Easyshare Gallery slideshow will be sent to the recipients you list.

Share via data CD/DVD

Available only under the Photoshop Elements **Share** tab, clicking the **CD/DVD** button under the **Share** tab burns your selected photo files to a CD or DVD. Note that this **Share** option creates a *data* disc rather than a *playable* disc. Its files can pretty much only be viewed on computer. To create a playable disc, add the photos to a Premiere Elements project and share your video slideshow as a DVD or BluRay disc.

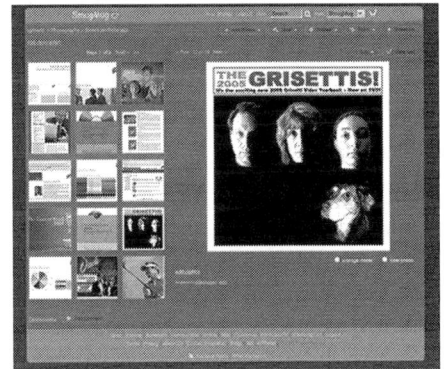

Kodak EasyShare and SmugMug Gallleries are attractive ways to display your work online.

Your Photoshop.com Account
Display Your Photos Online
Create an Online Album Slideshow
Back Up Your Media Files Online
Photoshop Express
The Inspiration Browser

Chapter 34

Photoshop.com
Your online connection

If you've used online photo-sharing sites like Flickr and Picasa, you'll likely feel right at home with many of the features on Photoshop.com.

But Photoshop.com adds a number of additional features – tools for editing and managing your photo files as well as tutorials, supplemental templates and tools for both Premiere Elements and Photoshop Elements.

In fact, it offers an awful lot for a free service. And even more for its premium package.

All your Photoshop.com media

Return to Welcome Screen

Browse others'
public Albums

Your Public Albums

Upload photos

Your Welcome
screen

Notifications
from Friends
and site
updates

Photo
Browser

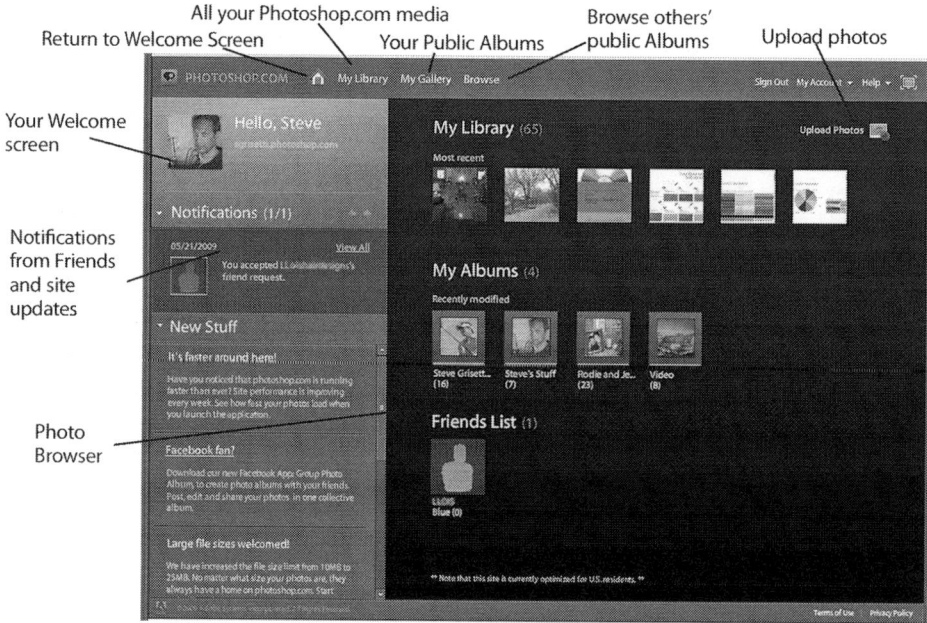

Photoshop.com is Adobe's online connection for Photoshop Elements and Premiere Elements.

Photoshop.com is an online service, included as a bonus feature with Premiere Elements and Photoshop Elements, which incorporates a number of tools for photo and video sharing and management. Although you don't need either of these programs to use the service, both Photoshop Elements and Premiere Elements include functions that take particular advantage of the features on the site.

Photoshop.com includes five categories of services:

1. **A photo sharing and display area**, which includes tools for managing and organizing your online files as well as accessing your other online galleries;

2. **A basic photo editing tool set** – online touch-up, fix and special effects tools for photos you've uploaded to the site;

3. **Online file back-up** and storage space;

4. **An Inspiration Browser**, including tutorials and other training materials for Adobe products;

5. **Additional templates and themes** for Premiere Elements and Photoshop Elements.

Like the Organizer, it's difficult to do the entire product justice with one short chapter. However, I'll try to give you a general overview of its key features.

At the writing of this book, this service is available only to US residents. However, Adobe does have plans to expand the service worldwide as it continues to grow.

Create an account and log in

Anyone can create an account on Photoshop.com. But, if you have Photoshop Elements or Premiere Elements, your logon gives you a live link-up to the site any time you're working in either program. This becomes a real bonus if you plan to take advantage of the free tutorials or the premium themes and templates, as we'll discuss later.

You can create your account by going to **www.photoshop.com** – or you can do it right from the Premiere Elements or Photoshop Elements start-up screens (or even from within either program's working interface).

When you create an account from Photoshop Elements or Premiere Elements, you'll be logged in automatically whenever you launch one of the programs.

Once you've created an account and logged in from within these programs, you'll be automatically logged in to the site any time you launch either program. (You must have an always-on Internet connection in order to have a live connection with **Photoshop.com**.)

Both programs send and receive data, to some extent, from **Photoshop.com** on a regular basis. Both also include features for sharing directly to the site.

In order to fully use **Photoshop.com's** services, you'll need to load the **Adobe Air Uploader**, a program for interfacing with the site and syncing its library with the media on your computer. You'll be prompted to load this program when you create a **Photoshop.com** account or when you access the content on the site.

Share and manage your photos

If you go to **Photoshop.com** through you Internet browser, you can access the photo management area by logging onto the site and clicking on the **Me** link at the bottom of the splash page.

The most visible area of **Photoshop.com** is its gallery for sharing your photos. Your photos are uploaded and stored in **Albums**. As with any photo sharing site, you can designate whether any **Album** is available for public viewing, for invitation only viewing or just for your own private use.

You can upload photos of any format and virtually any resolution to **Photoshop.com**. And, although the site will display a web-resolution version of the file in your gallery, the original file you've uploaded remains in its native state on the site, so that it can be downloaded later by you, your friends or your clients.

Your photos are managed in three areas:

The Library. The Library includes every photo or media file you have stored on the site, including those you are backing up from your computer. In addition, your Photoshop.com **Library** can include access to photos you've posted to Facebook, Flickr, Photobucket and Picasa, as described in **Link to other Sites**.

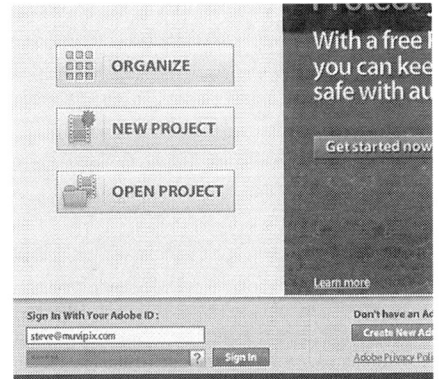

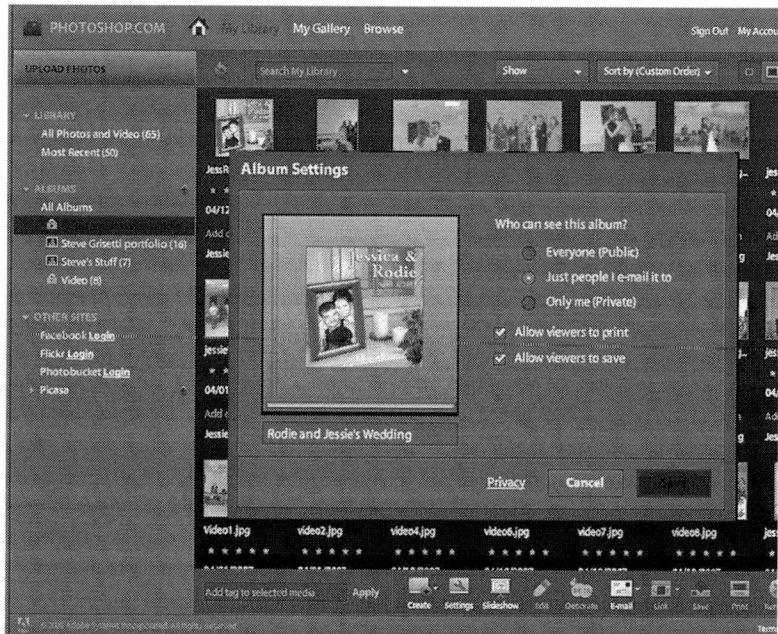

Your Albums can be left open for public viewing or can be locked so that only people you contact can view the contents.

Albums. Albums are packs of photos – electronic photo albums. You can elect to make any **Album** available for the public or you can keep it private or by invitation only.

The Gallery. The Gallery is where any **Albums** you've made public will appear. **Albums** you've placed in the **Gallery** are available for viewing by any other Photoshop.com user when he or she selects the option to **Browse**. (Likewise, you can **Browse** the **Galleries** of other **Photoshop.com** accounts.) Your **Friends** will be notified as you post new photos to your **Gallery**.

Upload photos to Photoshop.com

Once you've logged in to **Photoshop.com**, you'll be greeted with your personal **Welcome Screen**. This screen displays a list of notifications (such as any new friends you've invited, or who have invited you, to view their galleries) and notices of recent updates to the site.

The larger window to the right, called the **photo browser**, will display your **Library**, your **Albums** and your **Friends**.

As you browse around **Photoshop.com**, you can return to this page at any time by clicking the little house icon at the top of the screen.

Photos can be loaded from the interface on **Photoshop.com** or via the Elements Organizer program. To upload a photo from this **Welcome Screen**, click on the **Upload Photos** button on the upper right of your **Welcome Screen** or the big, green **Upload Photos** button on your **Library** page, as illustrated above.

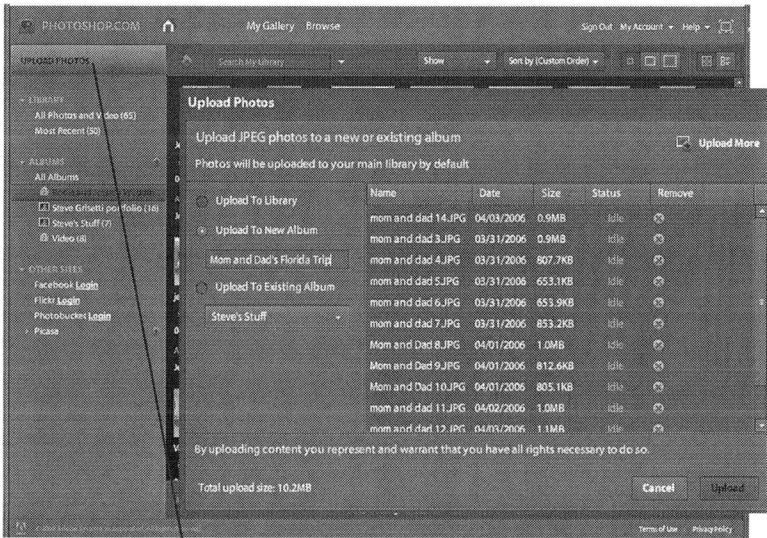

Clicking the Upload Photos link opens a browser to your computer's files. Once you've selected your photo or photo set, you'll be prompted to save the files to a new or existing Album.

After clicking this button, browse to the photos you'd like to upload. (By holding down the Shift or Ctrl key as you click to select your photos, you can choose several in one swoop.)

Once you've selected your photos and clicked **Okay**, the **Upload Photos option screen** will appear (as seen above). This screen gives you the option of adding your uploaded photo(s) to an existing **Album**, creating an **Album** or just loading them to the general **Library**.

Once you've set your preferences, click on the **Upload** button. The screen will let you know when your upload is complete.

Your uploads will be indicated with an updated tally number under the appropriate album.

Create an Online Album with the Elements Organizer

An **Online Album**, created in the Elements Organizer, can be a very cool way to display your photos.

I've used them to create some very attractive, professional-quality online portfolios of my design work.

To create and load an **Online Album** from the Organizer, select **Online Album** from the *What would you like to share?* options under the **Share** tab, as illustrated on the following page.

1. If you have photos selected in the Organizer's **Photo Browser** when you launch this wizard, these photos will appear in the **Items** bin on the **Album Details** screen.

You may add photos to this bin by dragging them in from the **Photo Browser**, and you may delete them from the list by selecting the photo(s) from the list and clicking the red − (minus) button.

When you're ready to create your slideshow, name your **Album** and click the **Share** button at the bottom of the screen.

2. A new screen will appear displaying a preview of your **Online Album** slideshow, using one of the program's very cool online templates. If you'd like to assign another template to your slideshow, you can browse through over two dozen options and even test drive each by clicking the **Apply** button.

(Included among these is a slideshow that builds your photos onto a road map, based on your photos' GPS metadata, if your camera supports it.)

When you're happy with the slideshow template you've applied, click the **Next** button at the bottom of the panel.

And, when you're satisfied with all of the **Album Details** and the online destination you've selected, click the **Next** button at the bottom of the panel.

3. The final screen will give you one last chance to rename your **Album** and to change your slideshow template.

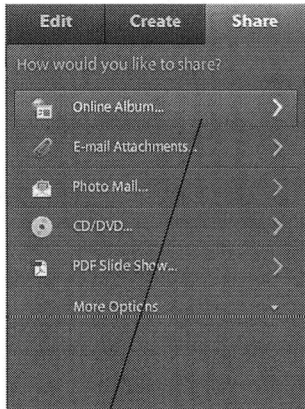

The Share Online Album button under the Organizer's Create tab launches a wizard for creating an online slideshow.

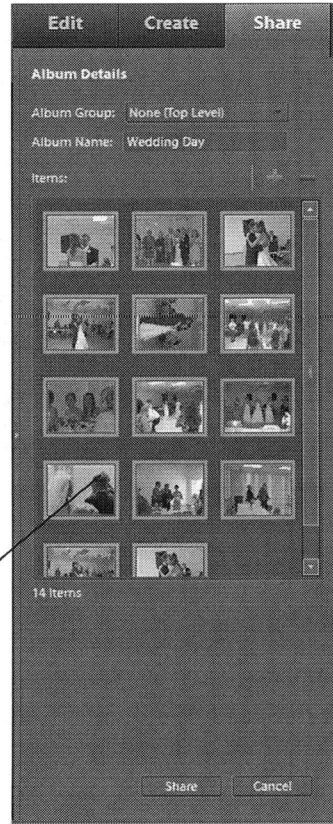

If photos are selected in the Organizer's Photo Browser, they will automatically be loaded into the slideshow Items bin. Photos can also be added, removed and arranged right on the panel.

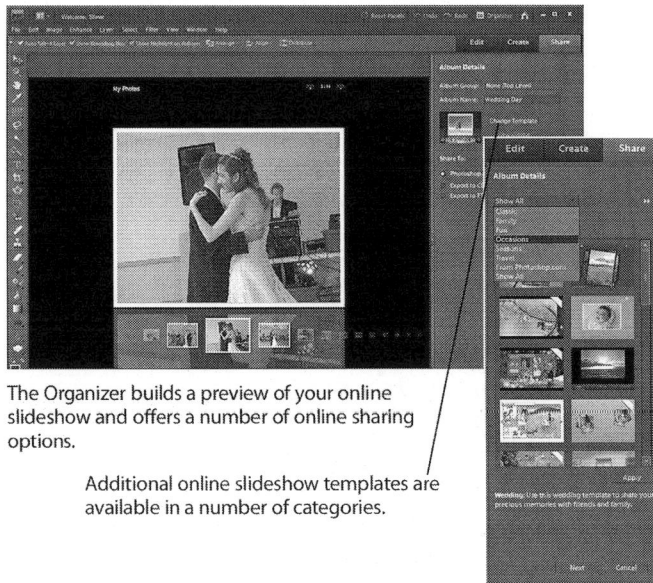

The Organizer builds a preview of your online slideshow and offers a number of online sharing options.

Additional online slideshow templates are available in a number of categories.

You will also be given the option of sharing the **Album** publicly or setting it up so that only those notified by e-mail will be able to see it.

4. When you're satisfied with all of your settings, click the **Share** button.

The slideshow and photos will be uploaded to Photoshop.com – a process that could take a few seconds or several minutes, depending on the sizes and number of your photos.

Remove photos and Albums

Albums and individual photos can be easily deleted from your Photoshop.com **Library**. To access these management tools, click on the words **My Library** or **My Album**s at the top of the interface.

Albums are displayed as books. To access the individual photos within an **Album**, double-click on the **Album**.

Whether you're managing **Albums** or individual photo files, this work area will display, along the bottom of the photo browser, a number of options. Included among them is an option button for removing the photo or **Album** you have selected in the photo browser space.

Removing an **Album**, however, does *not* remove the photo(s) that were in the **Album** from your online **Library**. Removing your photos is a separate process.

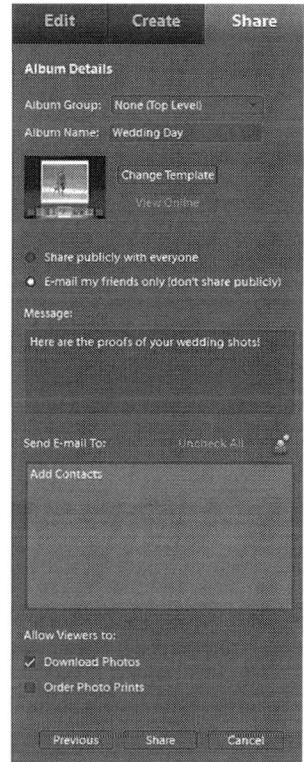

A final screen offers privacy and notification options.

Link to photos on other sites

A very cool feature on Photoshop.com is its ability to link its **Library** with other sites on which you have photo galleries.

To link to these other sites, click on the **My Library** link at the top of the Photoshop.com interface.

The **Other Sites** you can link to, listed along the bottom left of the interface, are **Facebook, Flickr, Photobucket** and **Picasa**.

Clicking the **Login** link for each of these sites, and agreeing to the required permissions, will make the photos you have posted to any of these sites visible in your **Photoshop.com** photo browser.

You can even use the **Photoshop Express** tools to touch up these photos.

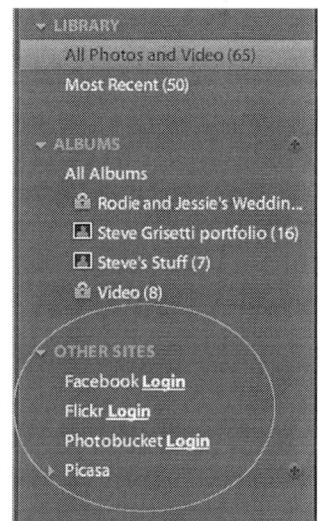

Your Photoshop.com Library can include photos ported in from your other gallery sites.

Automatic backup settings are under Edit/Preferences in the Elements Organizer.

Automatic synching,

Online space available,

Files to be backed up,

When a new Album is created (the + button), it can be added to the Backup/Sync list.

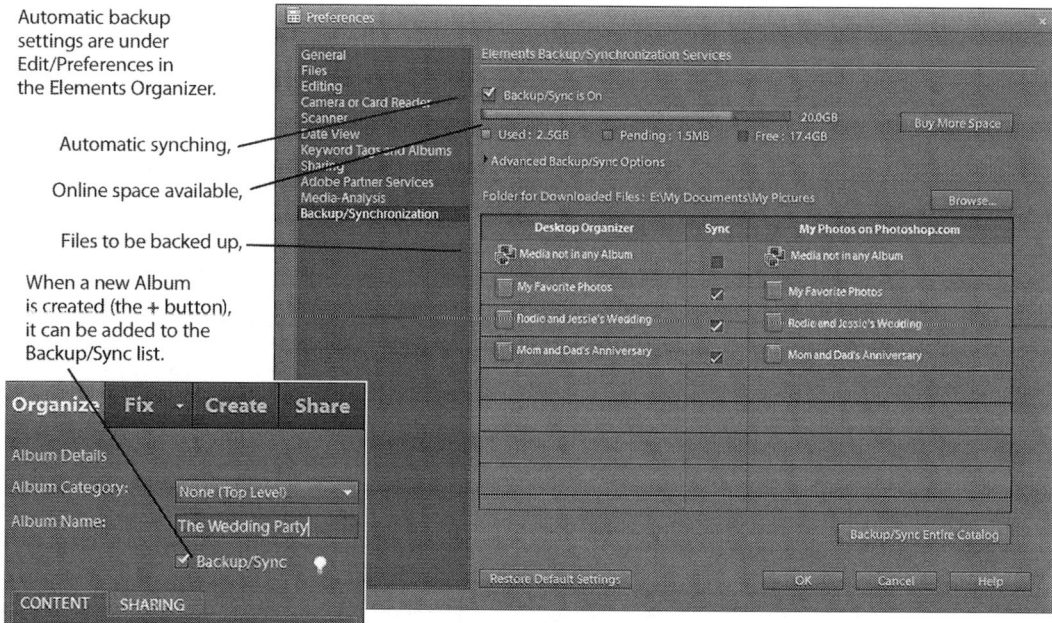

Back your files up online

A key function of the Organizer is its role in backing your files up to **Photoshop.com**. The options and settings for this back-up tool can be found in the Organizer's **Preferences**, under the **Edit** drop-down on the Menu Bar, under **Back-up/Synchronization**.

This **Back-up Synchronization** option screen will list the **Albums** you have designated for back-up as well as the option to back-up your media files not included in any **Albums**.

When the **Backup/Sync Is On** option is checked, at the top of the panel, the program will automatically store a copy of all of the media files you've indicated to your Photoshop.com account, usually backing up your files when your computer is idle.

Your free Photoshop.com account includes 2 gigabytes of storage space. A **Plus** account ($49.99 per year) increases your storage space to 20 gigabytes. Additional premium plans offer up to 500 gigabytes of online storage space. You can find the option to upgrade your account under the **My Account** link in the Elements programs and on the site page itself.

Whenever you create a new **Album** (by clicking the green **+** button at the top of the **Albums** panel), you will be given the option to set it to **Backup/Synchronize** to **Photoshop.com**, as in the illustration above. This **Album** will automatically be added to your Organizer's **Backup/Synchronization** list.

For more information on creating **Albums** and storing media in them, see **Albums** in **Chapter 31, The Elements Organizer**.

Touch up your photos with Photoshop Express

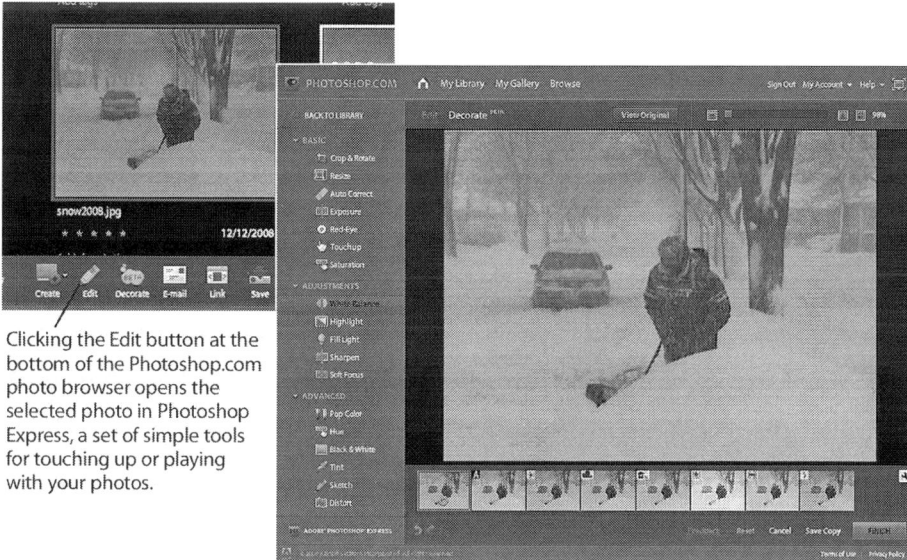

Clicking the Edit button at the bottom of the Photoshop.com photo browser opens the selected photo in Photoshop Express, a set of simple tools for touching up or playing with your photos.

Photoshop Express is an online set of basic tools built into Photoshop.com for cleaning up and touching up your photos.

To access this tool kit, click to select a photo in the Photoshop.com **Photo Browser** from either the **Library** or an **Album**.

Along the bottom of the **Photoshop.com** interface you'll see a listing of actions, as illustrated at the top left. Click on the **Edit** button to open Photoshop Express.

The photo you've selected will open in an editor workspace.

Along the left side of this workspace will be displayed a kit of basic touch-up tools – many of which you'll recognize from the similar tools in Photoshop Elements.

When you select any tool, its potential effects will be displayed as thumbnails along the bottom of the interface, as illustrated above.

To apply the effect, just select the thumbnail that best represents the change you're looking for

After editing your photo, you can then select, from the panel on the lower right of the interface, the option to **Reset** the photo, **Cancel** all changes and return to the **Photo Browser** or **Finish** and save the changes.

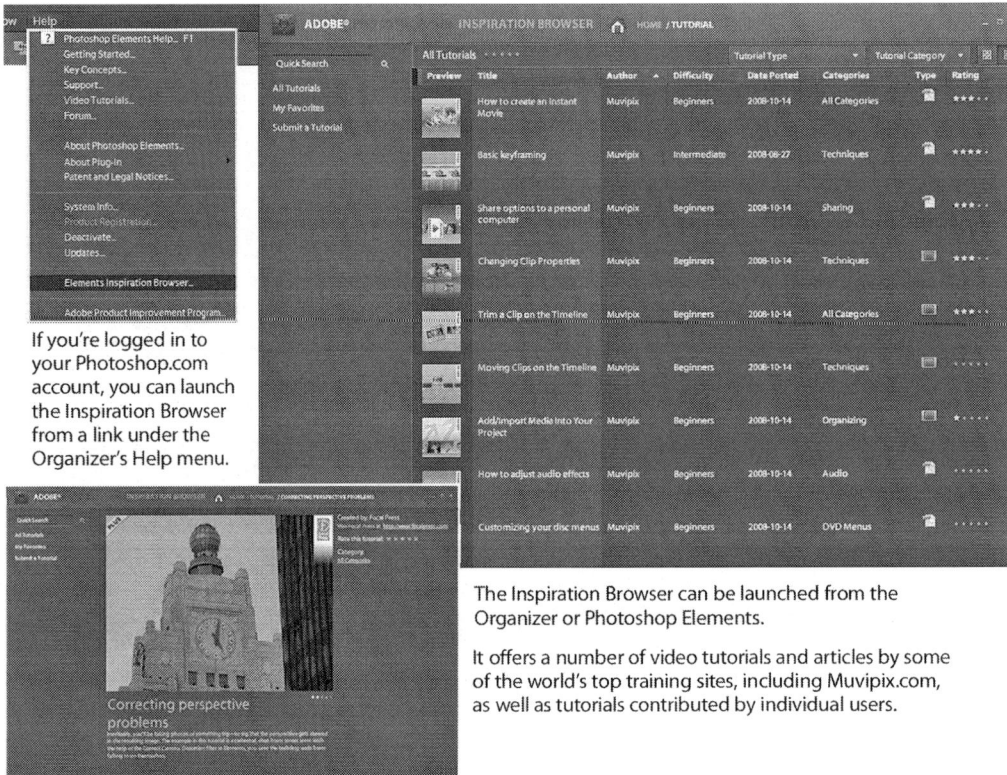

If you're logged in to your Photoshop.com account, you can launch the Inspiration Browser from a link under the Organizer's Help menu.

Correcting perspective problems

The Inspiration Browser can be launched from the Organizer or Photoshop Elements.

It offers a number of video tutorials and articles by some of the world's top training sites, including Muvipix.com, as well as tutorials contributed by individual users.

Access the Inspiration Browser

Your **Photoshop.com** account includes links to an ever-growing library of tutorials and articles for making the most of the site as well as for using Premiere Elements and Photoshop Elements.

These tutorials have been created by Adobe and by several of the world's top trainers, including **Muvipix.com**.

Basic tutorials for using the **Photoshop.com** site can be found by selecting the **Tutorials** link from under the **Help** button in the upper right of your **Photoshop.com** home page.

These video tutorials will show you how to create a **Photoshop.com** account, how to share your photos and how to use the photo touch-up tools available on the site.

A much larger library of tutorials for a number of Adobe products is available through the **Inspiration Browser**, an area of **Photoshop.com** that's only accessible from within Adobe's products.

You can reach the **Inspiration Browser** one of two ways from Photoshop Elements, Premiere Elements and/or the Elements Organizer:

1. From the **Welcome Screen for Photoshop Elements or Premiere Elements**, click on the **Tips & Tricks** link;

2. From within Photoshop Elements or the Elements Organizer programs, select the **Inspiration Browser** option from the **Help** menu.

Once you're in the **Inspiration Browser**, you can search or browse the entire library of tutorials for Adobe products, either by clicking the **All Tutorials** link or by typing a subject in the **Quick Search** window.

Clicking **All Tutorials** displays a listing of the entire library of animated tutorials and articles. The two drop-down menus on the upper right of the interface will filter the list by product and/or by subject.

By clicking on the appropriate column header, the tutorials can also be sorted by Rating, Difficulty, Author, etc.

If you feel so inspired, you can even contribute a tutorial of your own to this site (in either PDF or FLV format).

Adobe reserves the right to edit your submission, and you'll receive no monetary compensation for your contribution – but you will have the privilege of knowing you've contributed to a growing library of accumulated knowledge.

Access additional Plus Members Only content and templates

Finally, subscribing to **Photoshop.com** as a **Plus Member** gives you access to additional templates, themes and effects for both Photoshop Elements and Premiere Elements. (**Plus Memberships** start at $49 per year.)

This additional content is integrated into each program and loaded automatically. And, as long as you've got an always-on Internet connection and you're signed on to **Photoshop.com** when your program launches, this content will appear in programs automatically as you work. The templates and effects identified by a yellow or blue banner that appears over the upper right corner.

Links to this additional content can be found under **Themes**, **Transitions**, **Effects**, **Titles**, **Clip Art** and **Disc Templates**.

Similarly, under the **Share** tab on the Elements Organizer, if you select the option to create an **Online Album** (as described in **Create an Online Album with the Organizer**), you will find listed, among the **Album Template** categories, a link to **Photoshop.com Plus Members Only**.

The drop-down menus under Effects, Transitions, Titles, Themes, Clip Art and Disc Templates include links to additional online Photoshop.Com Plus Member content.

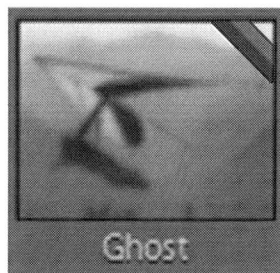

Plus Member Only templates, transitions and effects are indicated with a banner over the upper right corner.

In Photoshop Elements, this additional content can be found among some of the templates listed under the various tasks under the **Create** tab.

For instance, click on the **Create** tab in the **Editor** workspace and then select a **Project** (a **Photobook**, for instance). Click on the **Artwork** button.

Among the options in the drop-down menu on the **Content** palette, you'll find a listing for additional Photoshop.com artwork for **Plus Members Only**.

Once you apply a theme, template, effect or transition from **Photoshop.com**, you'll need to wait a few moments for it to download from the site to your computer. But, once it downloads, it should perform just as the themes, templates, effects and transitions that were included with the program.

Create an Organizer Slideshow

Edit Freeze Frames in Photoshop Elements

Edit DVD and BluRay Disc Menu Templates

Chapter 35

Use the Elements Programs Together
How the programs complement each other

One of the nicest things about using Photoshop Elements and Premiere Elements together is that the programs complement each other.

When you create a Freeze Frame photo from your video in Premiere Elements, it can be sent to Photoshop Elements for editing.

When you revise a Premiere Elements graphic or photo in Photoshop Elements, it will update in your Premiere Elements project automatically.

You can even use Photoshop Elements to edit Premiere Elements DVD menu templates!

Premiere Elements, Photoshop Elements and the Elements Organizer are designed to work together. They can pass files between each other, the Organizer serving as file manager between the other two. Media files that are updated in one program are updated in the whole program set.

But there are a couple of functions in which their relationship seems especially complementary.

In two of these functions, the relationship between the two programs is documented and obvious. But, as a bonus, we'll show you a third, undocumented way to use Photoshop Elements to improve your Premiere Elements experience – creating DVD and BluRay disc menu templates!

Create an Organizer Slideshow

Although **Slide Show** is actually a product of the Organizer's **Create** tools, we're discussing it in this chapter for a specific reason – this tool uses the best resources of Photoshop Elements, Premiere Elements and the Organizer all together. (Note that this tool is not available in the MacIntosh version of the Organizer.)

In fact, Premiere Elements has its own slideshow creator. But the more powerful and versatile method for creating slideshows involves using all of the programs – beginning the process in Photoshop Elements and finishing it in Premiere Elements.

1. For best performance and results, ensure that you've resized any photos you plan to use in a video project to no larger than 1000x750 pixels, as we discuss in **Use Photos in Premiere Elements** in **Chapter 16, Get Media into Your Project**.

    As we discuss in **Chapter 12, Utilize Advanced Photoshop Elements Tools**, Photoshop Elements includes a **Process Multiple Files** feature that will do batch resizing.

The Slide Show creator grabs the selected photos in the Organizer's Photo Browser.

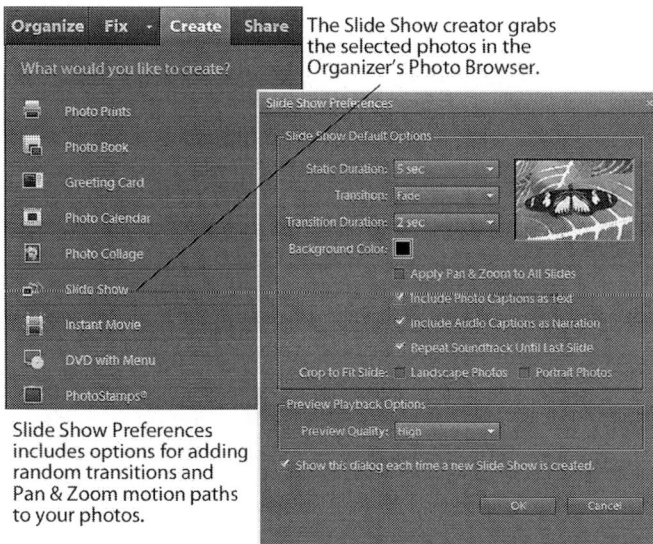

2. To create your slideshow in the Organizer, select the **Slide Show** option from under the **Create** tab.

This will launch the **Slide Show Preferences** window, as illustrated at the top of the following page. In this window you can set the preferences for many things, including the duration of each slide, the types of transitions (including Random) between them, settings for applying a **Pan & Zoom** over each slide as well as the options for adding an accompanying soundtrack.

Slide Show Preferences includes options for adding random transitions and Pan & Zoom motion paths to your photos.

Don't worry too much about committing to any decisions here. You can add to or revise any of your choices later.

When you've selected your options, click **OK**.

3. The program will launch the **Slide Show Editor**, the real heart of the slideshow creator (illustrated below).

    If you had photos selected in the Organizer when you launched the **Slide Show Creator**, these slides will already be added to your show.

    You can add more slides by clicking on the **＋ Add Media** button at the top of the **Editor**, and you can remove slides by right-clicking on them and selecting the **Remove** option.

4. If you'd like to **Add Audio** or music to your slideshow, you can do so by clicking on the link under the slides, along the bottom of the panel.

5. If you'd like to add **Titles** to your slides, click the "T" icon in the **Extras** panel.

    If you'd like to record narration, click on the **Microphone** icon.

6. In the **Properties** panel, you will find the option to create or adjust your **Pan & Zoom** motion path for each slide.

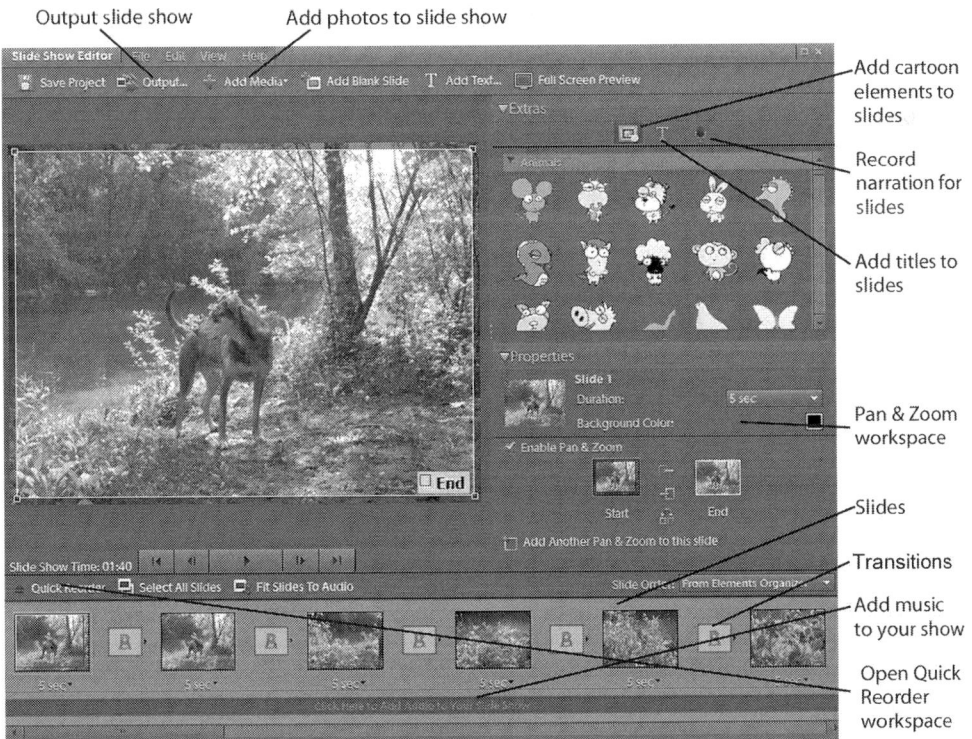

Output slide show

Add photos to slide show

Add cartoon elements to slides

Record narration for slides

Add titles to slides

Pan & Zoom workspace

Slides

Transitions

Add music to your show

Open Quick Reorder workspace

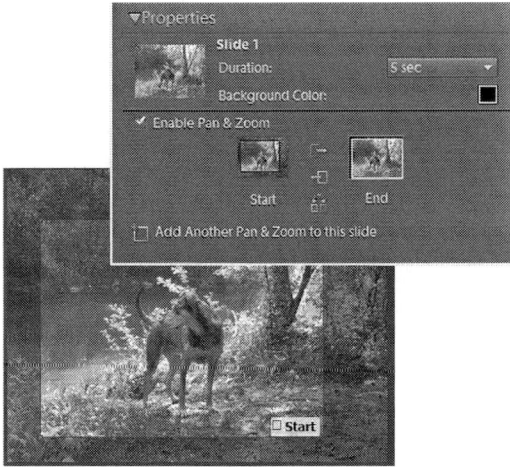

Setting starting and ending points for a Pan & Zoom effect.

Using this feature is very easy. Simply click to select the green-outlined **Start** thumbnail. This is your **Pan & Zoom** starting point – which you can define by dragging the outline's corner handles.

Then click the red-outlined **End** thumbnail and likewise define the **Pan & Zoom** ending point.

The program will automatically create a smooth motion path between those two settings – which you can preview by clicking the play button.

7. If you'd like to reorder your slides, click on the **Quick Reorder** button near the bottom left of the **Slide Show Editor** work space.

This opens a **Slide Sorter** window, in which you can drag each still into a new position or right-click and delete it.

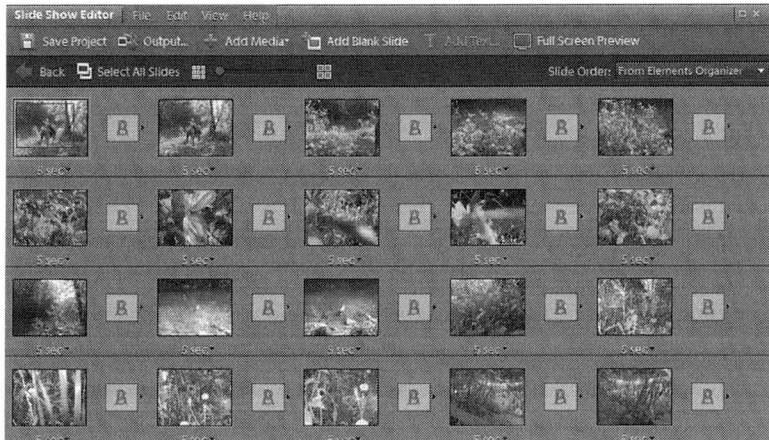

Changing the order of your slides in the Quick Reorder work space is as simple as dragging them to new positions.

You can also return to the **Slide Show Preferences** work space by selecting the option from the **Edit** drop-down on the Menu Bar.

Click the **Back** button to return to the **Slide Show Editor**.

8. When you're satisfied with your slideshow, click the **Output** button at the top of the window.

The **Output** window will give you a variety of file format options, including the option to save your slideshow as a **WMV** (Windows Media) file, a **PDF,** a **video CD** and even to output to your TV via Windows XP Media Center Edition.

To output your sideshow as a video or DVD, select the option to **Edit With Premiere Elements.** *If you want to create a quality video slideshow for burning to DVD, this is the option you want*!

9. If you've selected **Edit with Premiere Elements**, you'll be prompted to name and save the slideshow. Once you've done that, Premiere Elements will launch and your slideshow will be added to your video project's timeline, as a single file – in a slideshow interchange format– complete with the transitions and motion paths you added in the **Slide Show Editor**. The beauty of this slideshow interchange format is that it maintains all of the integrity and quality of your original photo files.

In fact, if you **right-click** on this slideshow on your timeline and select the option to **Break Apart Elements Organizer Slideshow**, the interchange format will break into your original photos (with the effects you've added intact). You can then continue to refine this slideshow in Premiere Elements.

In order to see your slideshow at full quality in Premiere Elements, you will need to render it. Press **Enter**.

Your slideshow needn't be sent to Premiere Elements for output. Particularly, if you are planning to show your slideshow on a computer, other output options can provide you with a much higher resolution output.

Save as File – WMV or PDF. The **File Settings** for a WMV's resolution can be set as high as 1024x768 pixels, which should fill a video monitor at full-screen with excellent results – though it can take a while for Photoshop Elements to create your output. PDF slideshows can be played by Acrobat Reader, but do not include pan & zoom animations.

Burn to Disc – VCD or DVD. A VCD is a low-resolution video file that can pretty easily fit on a CD. In fact, it's so low in quality you probably won't want to ever use it! If you select the option to save to a DVD from this screen, your file will be saved as a WMV file and then ported over to Premiere Elements for finishing.

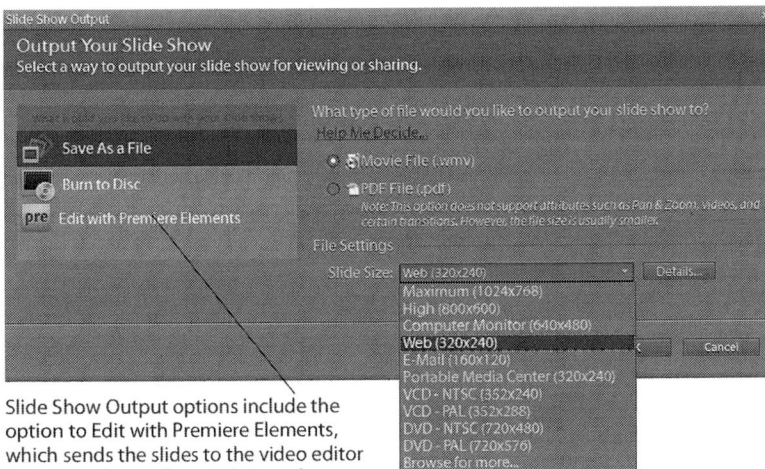

Slide Show Output options include the option to Edit with Premiere Elements, which sends the slides to the video editor in an interchange format that can be re-opened in Premiere Elements and edited further.

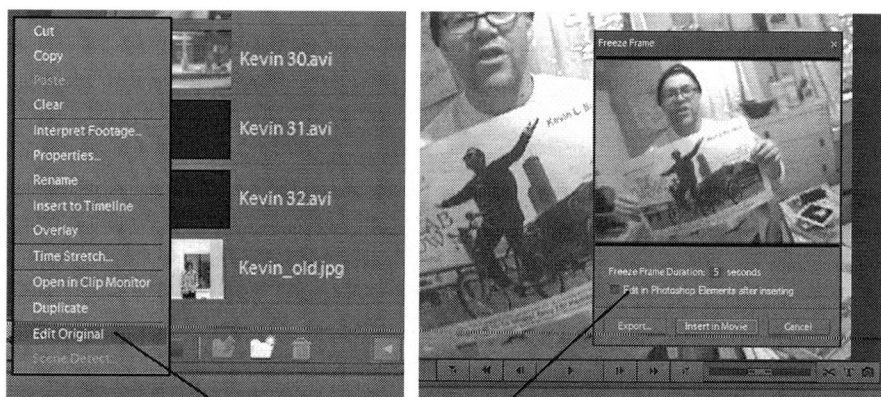

The Premiere Elements right-click option to Edit Original opens the photo file in Photoshop Elements, then updates changes.

A Freeze Frame created in Premiere Elements includes the option to edit the file in Photoshop Elements.

Edit Premiere Elements Freeze Frames in Photoshop Elements

Photoshop Elements serves as the default editor for the graphics and photos in your Premiere Elements video projects.

There are two situations in which a photo file in Premiere Elements will launch your Photoshop Elements editor.

1. If you right-click on any graphic or photo file in your Premiere Elements project and select the option to **Edit Original** from the context menu, the file will open in the Photoshop Elements Editor workspace;

2. When you create a **Freeze Frame** from a video in your Premiere Elements project (by clicking on the camera icon at the bottom of the **Monitor** panel), you will find, on the **Freeze Frame** panel, the option to **Edit in Photoshop Elements**, as illustrated above.

In both cases, your photo or graphic file will update automatically in Premiere Elements as soon as you save the file, reflecting any changes you've made in Photoshop Elements.

> ### Photos from video
>
> You can improve the clarity of any still photos you've grabbed from frames of your video by opening the photo in Photoshop Elements and selecting **Filter** from the Menu Bar, then **Video/De-Interlace**.

Edit DVD and BluRay disc templates in Photoshop Elements

You can do a lot of customizing of disc menus right in Premiere Elements (as discussed in **Chapter 28, Create DVD and BluRay Disc Menus**). You can customize the text on the buttons, change the fonts, change the locations of the buttons and titles on the menu pages and even swap out an existing template's background.

But, using Photoshop Elements, you can actually *create your own templates* virtually from the ground up! This template can include your own custom background, your custom graphics, your default fonts, your custom buttons and button frames – with each menu page's elements positioned right where you'd like them.

Menu templates are PSD files

Premiere Elements DVD and BluRay disc menu templates are really just PSD (Photoshop) files. They have a specific structure to them – but they are basically PSD files with layers and layer sets laid out in a specific hierarchy.

For a number of reasons, which we'll explain later, we recommend that, when you "create" any new menu template, you begin with an existing menu set.

Just copy and rename **Main Menu** and **Scene Menu** files from an existing template over to a new folder you've created in the DVD TEMPLATES directory.

This directory is located in:

C:/PROGRAM FILES/ADOBE/PREMIERE ELEMENTS X.0/DVD TEMPLATES

Create your template's folder in one of the sub-folders that represents the category you'd like your new template to appear under. (GENERAL, for instance. Or ENTERTAINMENT.) Studying how these files are named and stored in this folder will help guide you as you create your own.

The structure of the *names* of these files is nearly as important as the structure of the files themselves. Each segment of the template file's name has meaning.

In, for instance, **MyTemplate_pal_s_mm.psd**, the "**s**" means that the file is for standard video (as opposed to "**w**" for widescreen or "**hd**" for high-definition). The "**mm**" means it is a *main menu* template (as opposed, of course, to an "**sm**" *scene menu* template).

The "**pal**" designation used to mean that the template was designed for the PAL video system. However, since version 3 of Premiere Elements, both PAL and NTSC have used the same templates. The "**pal**" designation is just an artifact from the days when there were separate templates. *All* current disc templates are "**pal**" templates.

The illustration below shows how all of the PSD and media files combine to form a menu, based on their location and names.

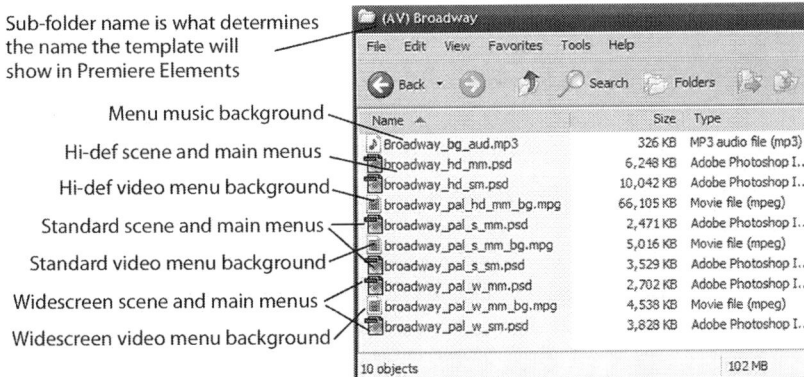

Sub-folder name is what determines the name the template will show in Premiere Elements

Menu music background

Hi-def scene and main menus

Hi-def video menu background

Standard scene and main menus

Standard video menu background

Widescreen scene and main menus

Widescreen video menu background

Naming and storing the files

Whenever you create a disc menu template, **you will need to create both a main menu and a scene menu template** – whether you actually intend to use both menu pages or not. This is because, in order for Premiere Elements to recognize your files as a template, two things are required:

- There must be both an **"mm"** (main menu) and an **"sm"** (scene menu) version of the template files. (The names of both menus must be identical, except for the "mm" or "sm" element, as we'll explain below.)

- Each menu set, as well as any accompanying media files (background music, motion background, etc.), must be in a *separate folder* on your hard drive, in the DVD TEMPLATES directory. The name you give this folder will become the name Premiere Elements uses for your template.

The basic template file structure

There are several good reasons for "creating" your new templates from an existing template set.

1. Unlike most graphic files you'll create or work with in Photoshop Elements, **disc templates use non-square video pixels**. And, when you work from an existing template, your working files will already be conformed to this video standard.

2. If you use an existing template, **all the necessary layer sets will already be included and named properly.** And it's much easier to discard what you don't want or need (or copy it if you need more) than it is to create a whole tree of layer set folders from scratch.

   And last but not least:

3. **Photoshop Elements can usually *edit* but it can not *create* layer sets!**

Layer sets are sub-folders (and sometimes sub-sub-folders) on the **Layers** palette which contain individual layers, as in the illustration above. How these

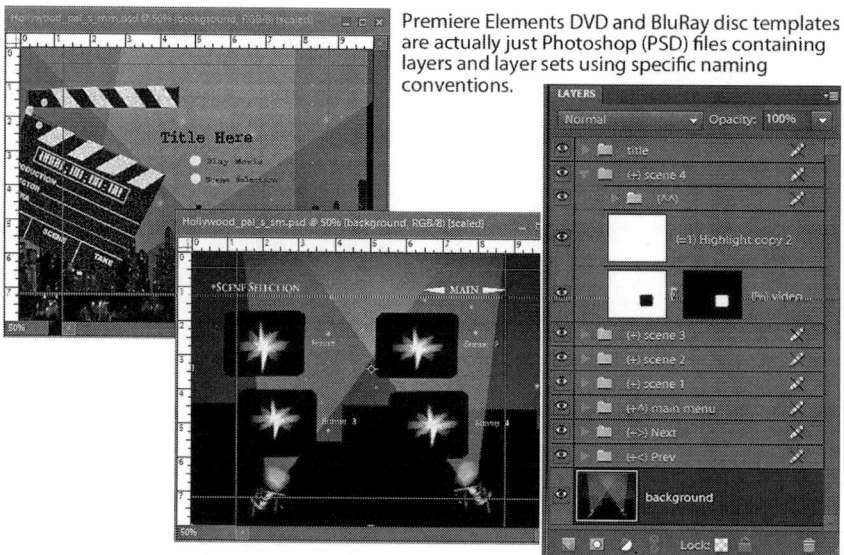

Premiere Elements DVD and BluRay disc templates are actually just Photoshop (PSD) files containing layers and layer sets using specific naming conventions.

Anatomy of a scene button layer set

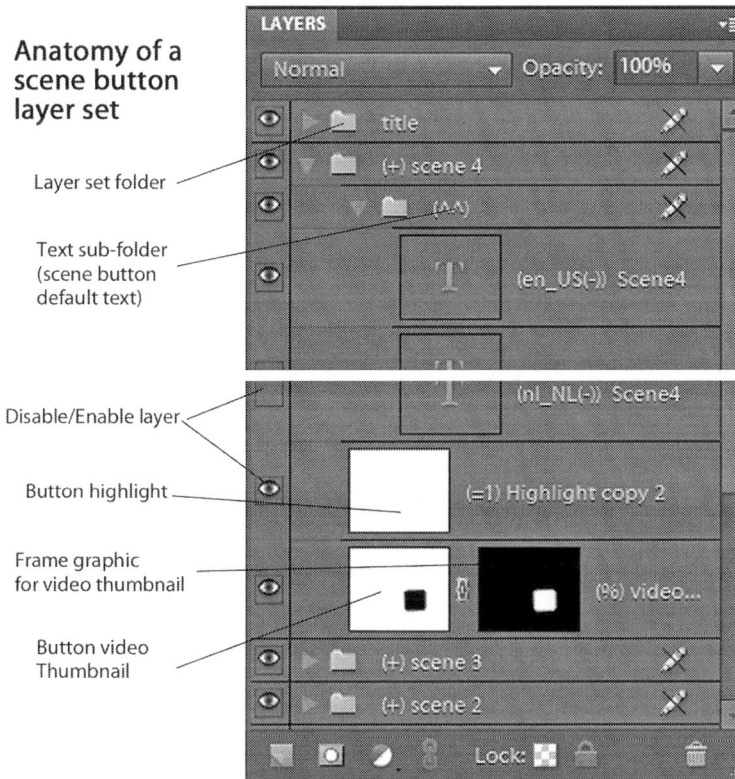

Layer set folder

Text sub-folder (scene button default text)

Disable/Enable layer

Button highlight

Frame graphic for video thumbnail

Button video Thumbnail

(Layers panel illustration showing: Normal, Opacity: 100%, title, (+) scene 4, (∧∧), (en_US(-)) Scene4, (nl_NL(-)) Scene4, (=1) Highlight copy 2, (%) video..., (+) scene 3, (+) scene 2, Lock)

sub-folders are set up and how the elements inside each are arranged plays an important role in how your template functions.

If the layer sets aren't set up right, your template won't work.

Trust us. You'll be way ahead of the game if you start with an existing template set, copied to a new folder.

Replace the background layer of a menu template

Replacing a background of an existing template is relatively easy.

To do this, have both the template you plan to revise and the photo you want to use for your replacement background open.

(If you can not display more than one photo file at once in your Photoshop Elements Editor because they appear as a tabbed set, go to the **Arrange** menu and set it to **Float All Windows**, as described in **The Full Edit Workspace** in **Chapter 2, Get to Know Photoshop Elements**.)

1. Size your new background photo to around 800x600 pixels. (1920x1080 for a high-definition template.)

    Drag this photo from its existing photo file onto the open menu template file that you want to revise, as illustrated on the next page. Your photo will automatically become a layer in your menu template file!

To replace a background in a menu template, drag a photo from its Layers palette onto an existing menu template.

The photo will appear as a new layer in the template's Layers palette. Rename it "Background" and drag the existing background layer to the trash can icon to delete it.

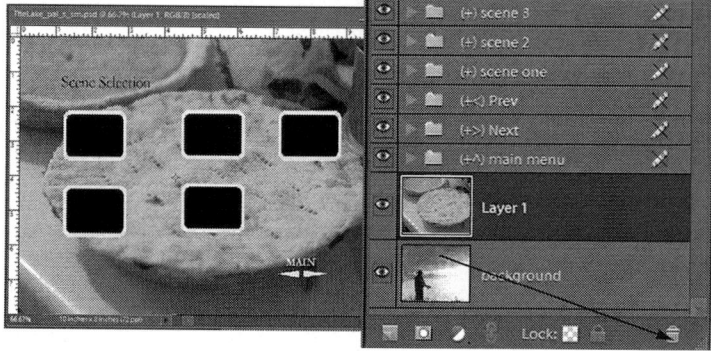

2. The photo will come in with corner handles, which you can drag to size and position the photo until it fits within the menu template.

Once it's all in place, press **Enter** to lock in the size.

3. To move this new layer into position as a background layer, grab the layer in the **Layers** palette and drag it down into position right above the layer currently named **Background** (the current background layer for your menu template), as in the illustration.

Now drag that current **Background** to the little trash can icon on the **Layers** palette to get rid of it.

Double-click on the name of the photo layer you have just added so that the name becomes editable and rename it "**Background**."

Naming this background layer "**Background**" isn't required in order for the template to work, but it is good housekeeping.

It also identifies the layer in the template as a background layer for Premiere Elements – necessary if you decide to replace the background for this template in the **Disc Menus** authoring workspace of Premiere Elements.

Now sit back and admire your work! Even if you do nothing else, you've essentially created your own custom disc menu template!

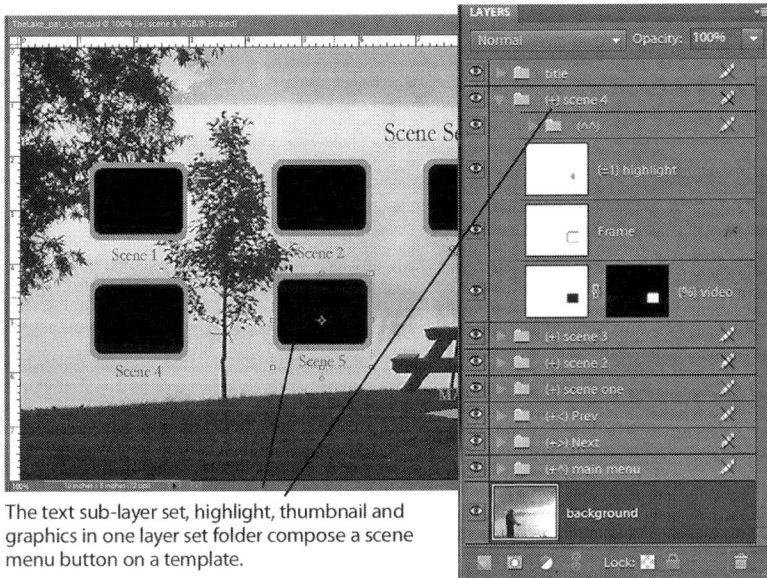

The text sub-layer set, highlight, thumbnail and graphics in one layer set folder compose a scene menu button on a template.

Scene layer sets

Each of the scene buttons in your disc template file is in a separate folder, or **layer set**, on the **Layers** palette, as illustrated above.

Inside each layer set, you'll find graphics for navigation (such as frames for the scene menu button thumbnails), a highlight graphic and a sub-folder layer set containing text and named (**^^**).

Along with the (**^^**) sub-layer set, each of these button layer sets also often contains a layer called (**%**) **video**. This layer includes a graphic (usually a black square but sometimes the Adobe logo) which serves as a placeholder for the disc navigation scene button, as designated by your **Menu Marker**. In other words, this layer indicates where the menu button's video thumbnail will display.

There is also a layer called (=) **highlight**. The graphic on this layer will serve as the highlight that appears over your scene menu button when someone watching your disc navigates over the scenes on your menu page.

You can customize these layers any way you want, as long as you keep them in their current layer sets and maintain their names – *as well as their accompanying symbols* – so that Premiere Elements can find them when it turns your template into disc menu pages.

1. Although you cannot create a layer set in Photoshop Elements, you can manipulate the individual layers within each layer set or sub-folder by holding down the **Ctrl** key as you click on the layer.

    With the **Ctrl** key held, you can edit, resize and reposition these sub-layers without affecting the other layers in that layer set.

2. You can also swap in any graphic you'd like as your menu highlight, replacing the current one in the layer set. You can even use a hand-drawn image or a photo. Just ensure that it is saved as a layer called (=) **highlight**.

   We do recommend, however, that you never use white as your highlight graphic's color. White often won't appear as a highlight on the final menu.

3. You can change the font, size, color or paragraph alignment for any (^^) text layer, as discussed below.

4. You can also add, remove or revise graphics used in these layer sets, such as the frames around the video thumbnail placeholders. And you can even remove the thumbnail placeholder itself, if you'd like your template to have text-only scene buttons.

Text layer sets

Within each layer set folder is a *sub*-layer set called (^^), which includes the text for that button or text block.

Open this layer set folder and you'll find the text for this button on eight layers, in eight different languages. Each language layer is named with an abbreviation identifying the language and the (-) symbol – as in (**en_US (-))** **Scene 5**.

You can change the font, font color, font size and paragraph alignment for any of these layers just by double-clicking on "**T**" icon on the layer.

If your text layer is disabled or turned off, click the eyeball icon to the left of the layer to turn it on. (Which layers are enabled and which are disabled has nothing to do with how the template ultimately functions.)

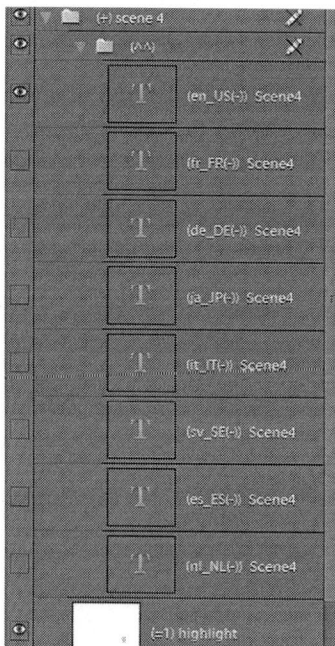

A text layer set includes support for 8 languages. The text can be edited for content or style by double-clicking on the "T" icon on the layer.

As with the graphics layers within the layer sets, you can move the individual layers or the entire (^^) text layer set to a new position on your menu page – independent of the rest of the layer set – by holding down the **Ctrl** key as you select it.

Layer sets are scene buttons

Each layer set – with its text, highlight and scene thumbnail – constitutes one menu button.

And, after you're finished customizing the individual elements for each scene button, you can position and scale each button as a single object. To do this, select the layer set in the **Layers** palette or click on the button on the

Additional graphics

Some menu templates also include a layer or two of graphics between the background and the scene layer set folders. The significance of these layers of graphics is that, if you replace the background (by including a media file background or by selecting a custom background in Premiere Elements' DVD workspace), these graphics layers will remain.

You can use this to your advantage, of course, if you'd like. You can include still images as a "foreground" layer to your animated background, for instance, or you can use them to create a frame graphic within which to play your background video.

PSD file in the Editor workspace, then drag it into position or drag the corner handles to resize it.

Adding scene menu buttons to a template

Perhaps you've come upon the perfect Premiere Elements template – only to find that it includes only four scene buttons on a menu page and you want six. Or you find a template that has no main menu scene buttons when you want three or four.

Fortunately, adding scene menu buttons to a template page is as easy as adding a photo or layer to a PSD file.

1. **To create additional scene buttons** on a menu page, drag an existing scene layer set folder from its position on the **Layers** palette to the **Add Layer** icon at the top of the **Layers** panel. This creates a duplicate of the entire layer set – and thus creates an additional menu button.

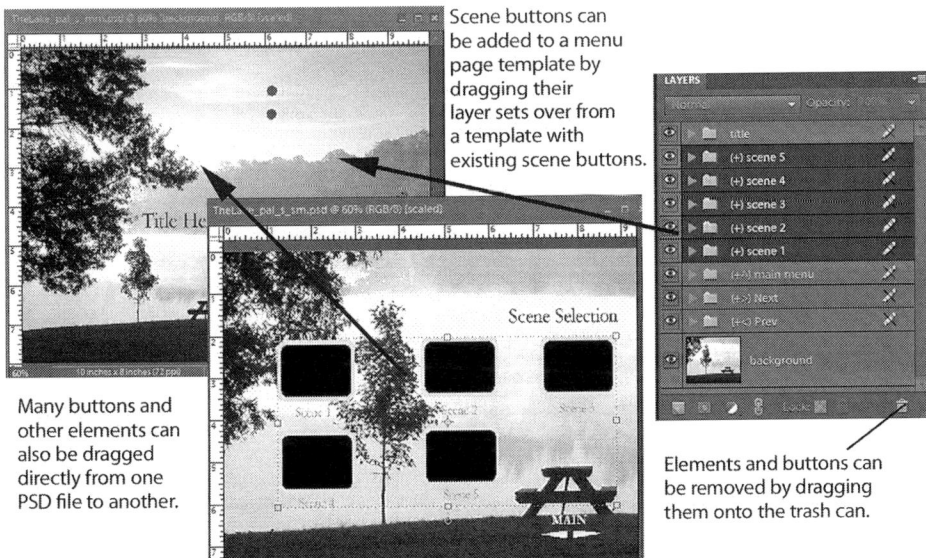

Scene buttons can be added to a menu page template by dragging their layer sets over from a template with existing scene buttons.

Many buttons and other elements can also be dragged directly from one PSD file to another.

Elements and buttons can be removed by dragging them onto the trash can.

The duplicate layer set and its contents will have the same names as the original set and its contents – except that the word "copy" will be added to its name. Double-click on the necessary layer names and rename them as appropriate.

2. **To add new scene buttons** to a main menu template that doesn't have any, drag one of the layer set folders from your scene menu template's **Layers** palette, or drag a scene button directly from the scene menu template, and place it onto the main menu template, as illustrated above.

   A copy of this layer set will appear in the main menu's **Layers** palette and the scene button will appear on your template file, to be customized and positioned as you'd like.

3. By holding down the **Shift** key, you can select several of these layer set folders at once and drag them all onto your main menu, if you'd like to add several scene buttons in one swoop.

   Once there, you can position them and/or their internal elements individually. (Scene Menu buttons link to green **Disc Scene Markers** on your Premiere Elements project timeline; Main Menu buttons link to blue **Disc Main Menu Markers**.)

4. Deleting a scene button from a menu template is as simple as dragging the layer set folder from its position on the **Layers** palette onto the little trashcan icon at the bottom right of the palette.

Menu buttons can not overlap!

Note that, as you hover your mouse over a scene button on a template file, Photoshop Elements will indicate the "live" area of your button by highlighting it with a blue box outline. This is a very important feature because *one thing Premiere Elements will not tolerate in a disc menu template is overlapping navigation.*

So, as a final test drive once you've finished revising your templates and positioning your buttons, be sure to hover your mouse over each of the buttons on your template page to make sure none of your navigation areas invades another's live space!

Sub-folder name is what determines the name the template will show in Premiere Elements

Menu music background

Hi-def scene and main menus

Hi-def video menu background

Standard scene and main menus

Standard video menu background

Widescreen scene and main menus

Widescreen video menu background

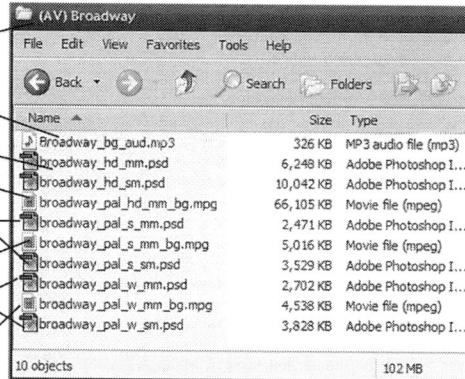

The order of the layers in a Disc Menu Template

It is important to note that the *order* of the layer sets in the **Layers** palette – not the *names* of the layer sets – determines the order that Premiere Elements uses them as scene markers. Your first scene, in other words, must be the *bottom*-most scene layer set in the **Layers** palette and the last scene, the top.

In other words, even if you call a layer set "Scene Five", if it is below the other layer sets in the **Layers** palette, it will be used for "Scene One" when Premiere Elements uses the template to create its DVD or BluRay disc menu.

Adding background video and audio

In addition to the PSD files that make up the basic DVD or BluRay disc template, Premiere Elements can use audio and video files in the template folder to add motion or music to the disc menu.

You can add any video and/or music to your menu template simply by including it in the same folder as your template files and then naming it appropriately.

Your background video and audio can be AVIs, MPEGs or SWFs. Your audio can be either MP3s or WAV files.

To include audio or video backgrounds as part of your templates, you need only *include them in the same directory folder as your disc menu templates* and then name them exactly the same as the template files except with the letters "**bg**" at the end.

In other words, a video loop background for the main menu

   TemplateName_s_pal_mm.psd

would be called

   TemplateName_s_pal_mm_bg.avi

A video background file for the scene menu

   TemplateName_s_pal_sm.psd

would be called

   Template_s_pal_sm_bg.avi

To apply the same AVI to both the main and scene menus, simply omit the "**mm**" or "**sm**" reference in the name as in

   TemplateName_s_pal_bg.avi

Any AVI or SWF video file you include in your template folder and name accordingly will automatically replace the background layer in your menu with video).

MP3s and WAV files will play audio or music behind your menu.

Each of these will, of course, be over-written if you choose to customize the background video or audio for the template in your Premiere Elements' **Create Disc** workspace.

Naming conventions

Finally, though Premiere Elements is surprisingly forgiving about the names used for its DVD and BluRay menu templates, I recommend you stick with the "traditional" names whenever possible.

More than once I've helped troubleshoot a custom menu for a client, only to find that the heart of the problem was in his naming one of the layer sets or template files incorrectly. Using standard names made all the difference.

Stick to these basic naming rules and you should be all set:

1. The template set *must* include both a main menu and a scene menu in order to be recognized by Premiere Elements, even if you ultimately plan to use only a main menu for your DVD or BluRay disc.

    This set of menu template files should be in its own folder in a category sub-directory of the DVD TEMPLATES folder. The name you give this folder is what Premiere Elements will use as the name of the menu template.

2. The main menu and scene menu template must have identical names, save for the "**mm**" and "**sm**" designation.

    "**s**" templates are for standard 4:3 video

    "**w**" templates are for widescreen 16:9

    "**hd**" templates are for high-definition BluRay discs

    Since version 3, all Premiere Elements disc menu templates, whether to be used in a PAL or NTSC video project, are PAL only. All, therefore, include the "**pal**" designation in their names.

That said, the following is the menu template naming convention we recommend you always use, just to stay safe.

TemplateName_s_pal_mm.psd
TemplateName_s_pal_sm.psd

TemplateName_w_pal_mm.psd
TemplateName_w_pal_sm.psd

TemplateName_hd_pal_mm.psd
TemplateName_hd_pal_sm.psd

For background video or audio, tag the letters "**_bg**" onto the ends of the files names.

If the name includes "**sm**" or "**mm**," the media file will function as background for only the scene menu or main menu page, as in:

TemplateName_s_pal_mm_bg.avi
TemplateName_s_pal_mm_bg.mp3

A media file without "**sm**" or "**mm**" in the name will function as background for *both* the main menu and scene menu.

TemplateName_s_pal_bg.avi

Index

Index

Index

Made in the USA
Lexington, KY
21 December 2010